ON MEANING AND MANTRAS
ESSAYS IN HONOR OF FRITS STAAL

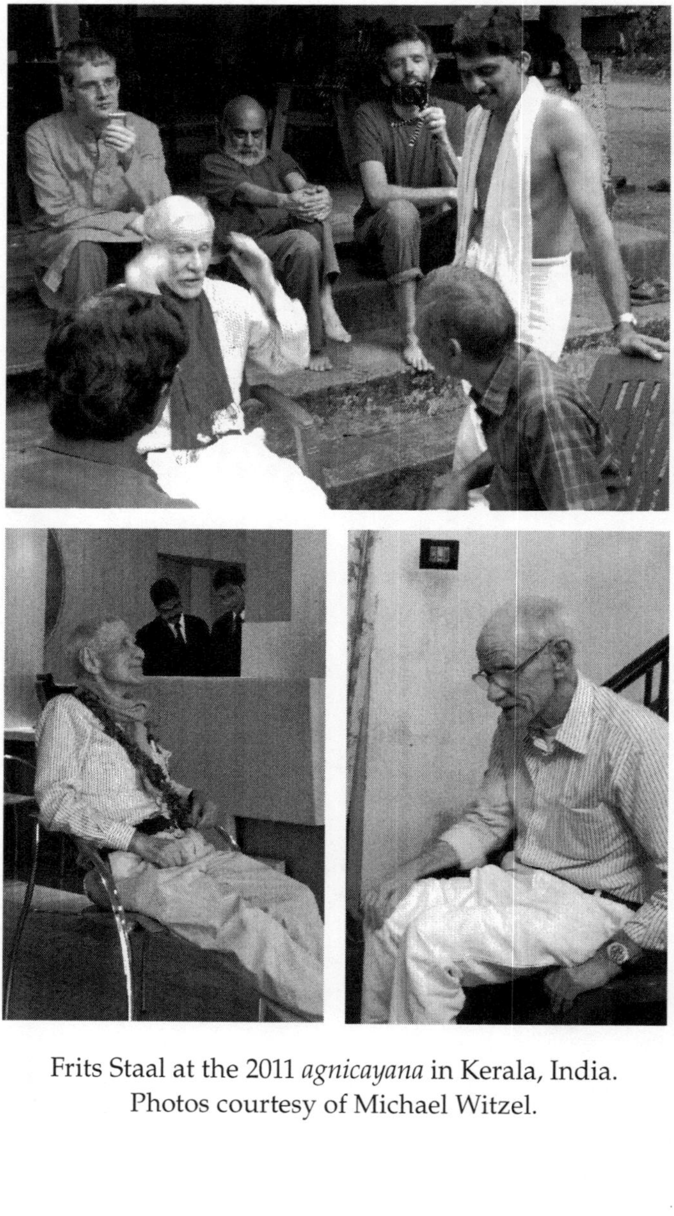

Frits Staal at the 2011 *agnicayana* in Kerala, India.
Photos courtesy of Michael Witzel.

On Meaning and Mantras
Essays in Honor of Frits Staal

Edited by

George Thompson
and
Richard K. Payne

Institute of Buddhist Studies and
BDK America, Inc.
2016

Contemporary Issues in Buddhist Studies

Series Editor, Richard K. Payne

First Printing, 2016
ISBN: 978-1-886439-64-1
Library of Congress Catalog Card Number: 2016962174

Published by
BDK America, Inc.
1673 School Street
Moraga, California 94553

Printed in the United States of America

Contents

Foreword *by Richard K. Payne* ix

Letter from HRH Princess Maha Chakri Sirindhorn of Thailand xi

Introduction *by George Thompson* xiii

On Meaning and Mantras: Essays in Honor of Frits Staal

Dharmarāja in the *Mahābhārata, Dhammarāja* in Early Buddhist Literature *by Greg Bailey* 3

AVŚ 19.68, 72::AVP.19.35.1–3: Using Oral Repositories of the Pre-redaction Veda *by Dipak Bhattacharya* 29

On a Textual Problem in Navya-nyāya *by Kamaleswar Bhattacharya* 51

Discovering Frits Staal *by Philo Bregstein* 59

Agniṣṭoma and the Nature of Sacrifice *by Johannes Bronkhorst* 79

Indian Mathematics in the Context of the Vedic Sacrifice (*Śulbasūtras*) *by Jean Michel Delire* 101

Predicament of the Maitrāyaṇīya Community in Maharashtra: Migration, Acculturation, and Identity Crisis *by Madhav M. Deshpande* 145

Vedic Poetry upon a Chariot: The "Last Journey" in the Light of *Ṛksaṃhitā* X 135, and of the *Veṅkaṭabhāṣya by Silvia D'Intino* 163

Melody, Mantra, and Meaninglessness: Toward a History of OM *by Finnian M. M. Gerety* 185

Poet as Seer, Poetry as Seen: Reflections on Visualization as a Critical Element in the Conceptualization of *Kāvya* *by Robert Goldman* 227

The Monstrous Feminine: *Rākṣasī*s and Other Others—The Archaic Mother of Bhāsa's *Madhyamavyāyoga* *by Sally J. Sutherland Goldman* 247

Philosophy as Drama: Amṛtacandra and Abhinavagupta
by Phyliss Granoff 275

The Divine Revolution of *Ṛgveda* X.124: A New Interpretation Beyond *Asura*s and *Deva*s *by Stephanie W. Jamison* 289

The Meaning of Ritual in the *Brāhmaṇa*s *by Joanna Jurewicz* 307

Eroticism in Hindu Texts and Modern Hindus
by P. Pratap Kumar 333

Universal Knowledge: Swami Vivekananda on the Vedas
by Jeffery D. Long 351

Vedic Turtles and Their Visiting Cards: Doing Vedas with Frits
by Thennilapuram Mahadevan 361

Notes sur les joutes védiques *by Boris Oguibénine* 385

The Shadow of Kālī Over the Goddess Kāmākṣī and Her City
by Carl Olson 407

For Frits Staal: On Mantras *by André Padoux* 433

On the Date of Bhavatrāta, the *Jaiminīya* Commentator
by Sudalaimuthu Palaniappan 439

Meetings with Frits Staal *by Asko Parpola* 451

Jesus Christ, Tantric Deity: Syntax and Semantics in Ritual Change *by Richard K. Payne* 455

The *Bhūtasaṃkhyā* Notation: Numbers, Culture, and Language in Sanskrit Mathematical Literature *by Alessandra Petrocchi* 477

Five Jewels in the University of Pennsylvania's Rare Book and Manuscript Library *by Peter M. Scharf* 503

What Did Arjuna Want to Know? *by Arvind Sharma* 517

Why Perform Vedic Sacrifice in the Twenty-first Century? Notes on Recent Vedic Ephemera *by Frederick M. Smith* 523

Remembering Frits Staal *by Romila Thapar* 549

A Brief Anthology of Hymns in the *Ṛgveda* Having to do With *Soma* (and Shamanism) *by George Thompson* 557

An Adventurous Mountaineer in the Lowlands: Frits Staal's Uncommon Presence in The Netherlands
by Laurens van Krevelen 579

Reminiscences of Frits Staal and the *Agnicayana*
by Michael Witzel 601

King Sūryavarman II and the Power of Subjugation
by Hiram Woodward 623

Foreword

Richard K. Payne
Institute of Buddhist Studies, Berkeley

This collection in honor of Johan Frederik Staal (1930–2012), who was almost universally known as Frits, includes essays and remembrances from his friends, colleagues, and students. The project was conceived and organized by George Thompson, whose contacts in the Sanskrit and Indian studies fields made it possible to bring together contributions by leading figures across a range of specializations. The essays included here reflect the range of Staal's own academic interests and pursuits.

Staal's early work in comparative philosophy culminated in the publication of his dissertation, *Advaita Vedanta and Neoplatonism.* Vedic studies, Sanskrit studies, and linguistics also drew his scholarly attention. This is reflected in his work on recovering the Indian grammatical tradition, which he found to be closely related to developments in grammatical studies in the second half of the twentieth century, and in his work on the syntax of birdsong. He also published an important study on mysticism and made significant contributions to ritual studies. In the latter field, the massive research project on the *agnicayana* ritual he initiated and led is still an unsurpassed example of the deeply interdisciplinary character of ritual studies. Similarly, Staal's interest in mathematics and science found expression in studies of artificial languages and the history of science in India.

Staal's role as a founding member of the Department of South and Southeast Asian Studies at the University of California, Berkeley was important for the Institute of Buddhist Studies (IBS). That department, along with the Department of East Asian Languages and Cultures, provided the institutional basis for the Group in Buddhist Studies at UC Berkeley, which has enriched the intellectual milieu for the study of Buddhism at IBS.

Frits, and his work, were often controversial. Many found his challenges to established orthodoxy misguided, while others welcomed them as thought-provoking and stimulating. The essays collected here reflect the various streams of thought and study his challenges provoked, and at the same time they offer insight into the personal character of his academic life.

I would like to thank George Thompson for his efforts to contact so many people who knew and worked with Frits, which resulted in the contributions included here, and for his assistance in compiling this collection. Thanks also to Marianne Dresser for copyediting and production, and to Kathleen Verani for the cover design.

Professor J. Frits Staal

I knew of Professor Staal, probably around 1984, first through my friend who was studying at the University of California at Berkeley where he worked as professor of Sanskrit and philosophy. Later I had an opportunity to meet him in person when he was in an exchange programme with another friend at Chulalongkorn University.

During his first long stay in Thailand he travelled the country far and wide, gathering data on Brahmanical and Buddhist rituals and ceremonies. I had a chance to be of his service by helping him gain permission to observe some royal ceremonies, especially the royal cremation of the Princess Mother. He was an example of scholars who never stopped searching for knowledge. Every time we met our conversation journeyed through different fields of study. Talking with him was always enlightening as well as amusing.

His love of Thailand was evident when, after his retirement in 1991, he chose Thailand to be his permanent home. He acquired a beautiful piece of land in the suburb of Chiang Mai and built a beautiful house. I was granted an honour of inaugurating his new house, and he was happily showing me his collection of books. In Chiang Mai he did not live a life of retirement but of activities: researching, giving lectures, forging through new fields of study such as Vedic mathematics and geometry as well as frequently travelling to places in and out of the country.

His passing away seemed sudden to me since to my regret I did not know of his illness at all. It is a great loss to the world of Sanskrit and Philosophy. Those who know him will agree with me that he was the best example of what Alexander Pope said, "The learned is happy, nature to explore."

HRH Princess Maha Chakri Sirindhorn

Introducing Frits Staal

When news of Frits Staal's death reached me in February 2012 from Michael Witzel, via the Indology email list, it was a great shock to me, even though by then I knew that Frits' health had been failing. I had known Frits for more than 30 years and he had always seemed to me to be quite robust and healthy. If I had been asked three decades ago how much longer I expected to have him here with us, I would have said that he was good for another 40 or more years. I am reminded now of the poet T. S. Eliot's memorable lines: "I grow old, I grow old / I shall wear the bottoms of my trousers rolled." I feel very old now. Even Frits—the seemingly ageless Frits of 30 years ago—had now succumbed to mortality!

Frits was both a most exhilarating Vedicist, and, at times, a quite exasperating one. The best-known example of this is, of course, his 1979 article "The Meaninglessness of Ritual," which at the time seemed to drive many if not all Vedicists crazy, myself included. Nevertheless, the point he made in that article has endured, and it seems to me that it has been very fruitful: rituals and mantras in general don't necessarily make much "sense," in the strictest semantic meaning of that word. Vedicists have been wrestling with this rather Heraclitean paradox ever since.

In 1997 a *Festschrift* edited by Dick van der Meij, *India and Beyond: Aspects of Literature, Meaning, Ritual an Thought: Essays in Honour of Frits Staal*, published by the International Institute of Asian Studies in Leiden and Amsterdam, included contributions from many of his colleagues and friends, including papers from both Richard K. Payne and myself, the co-editors of this memorial volume, *On Meaning and Mantras: Essays in Honor of Frits Staal*. Many of his other surviving friends and colleagues who contributed to that volume have contributed to this memorial volume as well.

The range of topics in the present volume is more limited than in *India and Beyond*. The focus here is more on Indological studies, since we felt we could not do justice to Frits' broad expertise in such fields as the history of science and logic, Pāṇinian grammar, Plotinus, ethology, and anthropology. I am a Vedicist whose primary interest is the interpretation and poetic translation of the *Ṛgveda*. My scholarly pursuits also include the identity of the Vedic *soma* plant and the nature of the juice (*sóma*) extracted from it, and the traces of archaic shamanism evident in the RV, as can be seen in my contribution to this volume, "A Brief Anthology of Hymns in the *Ṛgveda* Having to do With *Soma* (and Shamanism)" (pp. 555–575) Frits shared these interests. My co-editor, Dr. Richard Payne, is Dean and Professor of Japanese Buddhism and Religion at the Institute of Buddhist Studies and a member of the doctoral faculty of the Graduate Theological Union in Berkeley. While I am interested in the archaic features of the early Vedic, Richard's field of study is Tantric Buddhism in East Asia. The temporal gap between the early Vedic period that I study, 1500–1000 B.C.E., and the Tantric period that Richard focuses on is more than a millennium.

What connects our diverse fields of study with Frits' scholarly pursuits is our shared interest in a theoretical understanding of rituals and mantras in general. We have both participated in conferences and panel discussions devoted to the study of Frits' theories about rituals and mantras, one of which was organized by Dr. Payne. There have been many other panel discussions of Frits's theory of ritual studies that we have been unable to attend. This is to say that Frits's view of rituals and mantras has had an enormous influence on us both, and on many others as well.

This volume also includes contributions from younger scholars who have not been directly influenced by Frits Staal but who value his work as much as we do. In addition, we received essays from non-Indologists who offer insights into Frits before he was an Indologist, as a young man in the Netherlands.

While thinking about how to introduce this collection, I returned to Frits's last book, *Discovering the Vedas,* wanting to hear his voice once again. Frits always denied being one of us "book" Vedicists (though, of course, he was), but he was also a consummate "field" Vedicist. He frequently visited India to record and document Vedic rituals, as noted in the contributions of Finnian M. M. Gerety, Thennilapuram Mahadevan, and Michael Witzel. I remain only a book Vedicist, as I have never visited India. Unfortunately, I don't possess any recordings of Frits talking about Vedic matters, apart from his early recordings of the Four Vedas. But Frits was quite a good writer and when I read his books I hear his voice, as well as I could from an audio recording or film.

On a personal note, in the past year I lost my wife, Susan, to cancer and my son Nikolai is now struggling with cancer as well. My other son, Akira, is flourishing and he and his wife, Nicole, are expecting a child in 2017. Of course, as Indologists we are sensitive to the cycles of death and rebirth. I recently had a dream in which I was conversing with fellow Vedicists, not just living ones. Louis Renou was there, as were Paul Thieme and F. B. J. Kuiper; Jan Gonda and Alfred Hillebrandt were also there, along with Karl Friedrich Geldner, Hermann Oldenberg, and Abel Bergaigne. Tatanya J. Elizarenkova, Manfred Mayrhofer, and Calvert Watkins were there, as well as J. C. Heesterman. And Frits was there, too.

I was not able to visit Frits during his final years in Thailand. He often urged me to visit but my family obligations prevented it. Instead, I would send him writings—not just Vedic papers I had written but such works as a biography of Claude Lévi-Strauss that I knew he would like (and indeed he liked it very much). In return, Frits sent me news clippings about Lévi-Strauss's triumphal visit to UC Berkeley, sometime in the 1970s before I had arrived on campus. At the time I was playing the role of a poet in San Francisco.

In some ways, Frits was an iconoclast, of course. Yet as I got to know him better I realized that he was also a traditionalist as well. I was surprised to learn of his passion for Mozart and Beethoven, for example. His philately also always seemed to me to be rather "old school." On my first visit to his lovely home in the Berkeley hills I was deeply impressed by its elegance, and by the lovely garden he cultivated there with careful passion. This is a side of Frits that his many friends know very well. I mention it here because those who may not have had the good fortune to know Frits so intimately should also know that he was also a connoisseur of such pleasurable things. Though I myself have never seen his compound in Thailand, some friends of mine have. A couple here in New Hampshire, Tom and Bev, visit Thailand often (Bev is Thai). When I told them about Frits's beautiful compound in Chiang Mai they asked if they might be able to visit him there. Frits, always gregarious, immediately agreed, "Of course!" My friends returned from their visit with Frits with a series of photographs of his last home, a paradise filled with Asian art and books, surrounded by a lovely garden.

I would like to share a few anecdotes about Frits. I last saw him on his return to the U.S. in November 2009 to give presentations on his latest work on Vedic ritual. I was invited to a symposium at Yale University, where Frits gave a stimulating opening talk, accompanied by film of his recent visits to Vedic rituals in Kerala and elsewhere. During his talk he chanted some of the mantras used in these ceremonies. But the wintry weather in New Haven during the weekend was bitterly cold and wet, and Frits fell ill. We took him to my hotel room where he could rest and stay warm. After we made sure that Frits was comfortable, we returned to the symposium hall and a panel of four of us expressed our views of his work on Vedic materials. We had all wished to do this in his presence because we so greatly admired his work, but Frits was too weak to join us.

Because I didn't know the Yale campus well, I had arrived at the hall where the symposium was being held about an hour early. I found Frits talking with Phyllis Granoff, who had organized and sponsored the event. The three of us talked for a few minutes, and then Frits pulled me aside, as he wanted to speak to me in private. He turned to a table that held a large object wrapped in finely woven Thai cloth, picked it up, and handed it to me. Wrapped in the beautiful cloth was a deluxe leather-bound first edition of R. G. Wasson's book *Soma: The Divine Mushroom of Immortality.*

A year or two earlier Frits had given a talk at Harvard on, of course, Vedic ritual, to which he had invited me. His presentation went well, and afterward Michael Witzel invited Frits and me to his office for more conversation. At some point the topic of *soma* came up. What was the nature of the substance that was extracted from this famous plant? Michael was content to accept Harry Falk's popular view that *soma* juice was a stimulant, something like ephedra. Frits and I both believed that it was in fact an hallucinogen. Where Michael was diffident, Frits was adamant. They both turned to me, almost at once, and said, "You should work on this and figure it out." Frits asserted, "The only person I know who can solve this is you."

Encouraged by his confidence in me, I decided, based on all the evidence, that the *soma* drink was hallucinogenic and I published a paper on this topic in the *Electronic Journal of Vedic Studies.* Although Frits had given me Wasson's book in order to encourage me to work on "the *soma* problem," he also had another reason: he knew of my financial difficulties at the time and he thought that I might be tempted to sell this treasure to make ends meet. He concluded, "I hope that you don't sell it. But if you really need to, go ahead. Just don't tell me about it." I have not sold it. It sits here now in my study, right next to me.

I fondly recall one last image of Frits in Berkeley. He used to drive around town in a flashy sports car with a custom license plate that read:

> *idam agnaye, na mama*
> "This is for Agni, not for me."

This of course is a traditional Vedic mantra.

My mantra is:

> "This is for Frits, not for me."

ON MEANING AND MANTRAS
Essays in Honor of Frits Staal

Dharmarāja in the *Mahābhārata,* *Dharmarāja* in Early Buddhist Literature

Greg Bailey
La Trobe University, Melbourne

In searching for intertextual parallels between Buddhist literature and the *Mahābhārata* (MBh), little consideration seems to have been given to the occurrence of the compound *dhammarāja/dharmarāja* in both. Given the huge profile of Yudhiṣṭhira in the MBh and the unambiguous connection of this name with a seminal figure in whom the tensions within dharma are explored, other figures who carry this epithet may be considered worthy of study. Attention has been given to Aśoka as a king with a very specific and highly publicized relationship to dhamma, and while comparisons have been made between him and Yudhiṣṭhira[1] the use of the title *dhammarāja* for the Buddha seems to have gone unnoticed.

In this article I present some texts in which the Buddha is called *dhammarāja/dharmarāja* or refers to himself as such, and contrast these instances with a brief sketch of the kind of *dharmarāja* that Yudhiṣṭhira is depicted as in the MBh. I do not intend to argue that the latter is modeled on the former; nevertheless the parallels in name are worthy of exploration. Initially, of course, it must be borne in mind that we are dealing with two considerably different types of literature, composed with different intentions, though arguably both are multigeneric in their literary style and content. Yet in both cases two extremely prominent figures are presented who are intimately connected with dharma, in whatever way the content of this word might be understood, and these concepts are central to the texts in which they are enshrined. Additionally, the texts dealing with *dhammarāja/dharmarāja* in Buddhist literature also connect the *dhammarāja* directly with the idea of the *cakkavattin* so that there is a partial correlation of a religious figure with a king. This may not be only a consequence of the Buddha coming from a *kṣatriya* background but an effort to extend the Buddhist dhamma into the broader political sphere beyond the perhaps more limited sphere of the sangha and lay worshipers.

In attempting to analyze possible intertextual connections between Buddha and Yudhiṣṭhira as recipients of the title *dhammarāja/dharmarāja* the main problem is what either of the two components of the compound term mean. *Dharma* remains a problematic concept, despite the enormous amount of attention paid to it over the past twenty years. Rupert Gethin[2] identifies six complexes of meaning in the Pāli canon and James Fitzgerald[3] finds three similar complexes in the MBh. If the compound in question should be regarded as a genitive *tatpuruṣa,* it then begs the question of what exact or inexact content should be assigned to the first part of the compound. Equally, some of the Buddhist evidence is suggestive of reading it as an instrumental *tatpuruṣa,* making it "a king by dharma," "a king [who rules] in accord with dharma," but this still requires the content of dharma to be specified.

This becomes especially interesting in the contrasting attitudes the two bodies of texts take toward dharma writ large, and here there may be questions of differing historical circumstances. In the Pāli canon, although it is not always easy to pin down the exact meaning assigned to dhamma, this concept is never seemingly treated in a negative light. As the body of the Buddha's teachings and as right conduct, *dhamma* is an unambiguously positive concept. Contrast this with the MBh, in which dharma is a much more troubling concept where close adherence to dharmic behavior leads to unjust results[4] and even the figure of the *dharmarāja* is itself fractured as an exemplar of a life led in accord with dharma. This is exacerbated by an underlying subtext in the MBh that dharma is subtle, underscoring the interpretative problems in understanding it. Patrick Olivelle is almost certainly right in suggesting that dharma became a fundamentally important concept in late Vedic texts, which postdate the earliest Pāli texts, and that it was extended beyond a connection with kingship but still maintained this connection.[5] Even here the cracks in the interpretative possibilities pertaining to the term were becoming evident because of the varying sources of dharma that came to be accepted. The MBh faces these interpretative problems head on but never successfully resolves them, even in attempting to develop dharma as a governing brahmnical concept.

The Buddha as *Dhammarāja* in Some Pāli Sources

I have not found a reference in Pāli canonical texts or Buddhist Sanskrit texts that defines what the word *dhammarāja* means,[6] though some of the later commentaries attempt a paraphrase and there is a passage in the *Milindapañho* that attempts to explain what it means to call the Buddha a king. Absence of such definitions suggests that the composer(s) of the texts assumed that its meaning was so well known that no definition was required. Moreover, the difference between a buddha and a *cakkavattin* is clear to the extent that while both are *dhammarājas*, the former leaves the world while the latter immerses himself in it. Alternatively, might it have been the case that the various meanings attached to dhamma, and the possible predominance of the dhamma as the totality of the Buddha's teachings, made it unwise to attach too specific a meaning to the term?

Yet it must bespeak an intimate connection between dhamma and the person who is ascribed with the title *dhammarāja*, and a reasonably clear understanding of what their function might be. Why a buddha should be called *rāja* in this context is still a mystery, although he might be said "to rule" through his *sāsana*.[7] Here are some instances of the use of the compound in contexts that provide no enlightenment as to its meaning:

Majjhima Nikāya III, p. 262 (occurs twice) = *Saṃyutta Nikāya* 1, p. 34; p. 55:[8] "This is the Jeta forest, visited by groups of sages, inhabited by the King of Dhamma, bringing joy to me."

Or in the *Vimānavatthu*,

> With reverence for the illustrious Dhamma-king (*dhammarājino*) I have come to salute the Unrivalled One and to bow before the monks who inspire devotion and who delight in what is skilled, an auspicious meeting of recluses.[9]

Here *dhammarāja* is just one epithet among many in this series of verses. And still without explanatory discourse:

> 702. And remorse is mine [in that] I made a mistake and did wrong, sir; I would not hear Dhamma well taught by the King of Dhamma (*sudesitaṃ dhammarājena*).
>
> 703. Therefore I say to you, O blessed one, whoever there might be who is to be shown pity by me, him should you cause to take up Dhamma well taught by the King of Dhamma.[10]

This is the stated regret of a woman reborn as a *devatā* who did not hear the dhamma taught by the Buddha at a particular time before she died as a human.

And finally from the *Theragāthā*:

> 389. Who towards his fellow students
> Shows no reverence,

He stands far from nibbāna,
Within the doctrine (*sāsane*) of the King of the Law.[11]

Beyond these, the majority of other references occur in passages dealing with the *cakkavattin,* a title claimed by the Buddha himself in some cases, as well as applied to some other kings.[12] I will look at some of these in more detail later on. To begin with, however, one passage where the Buddha declares himself to be a *dhammarāja* is worthy of investigation, both for what it tells us and what it omits. It occurs in a dialogue between the Buddha and the brahman Sela,which is found three times in the canon itself and is alluded to a fourth time, with a useful piece of commentary, in the *Milindapañho.*

> Sela the highly educated and esteemed brahmin journeys to the hermitage of Keṇiya, accompanied by three hundred brahmin students. He is acquainted with the meaning of the thirty-two marks of the *mahāpurisa,* and learns from Keṇiya that the Buddha will be visiting for a meal on the morrow. This greatly arouses his interest and he thinks: "Even this word 'Buddha' is hard to obtain in the world. Thirty-two marks of a great man have, however, come down to us in our mantras. For a great man endowed with these marks two courses are open, and no other: If he inhabits a house he will become a king, a wheel-turning monarch, righteous, a king of righteousness (*dharmarāja*), a conqueror of the whole world, who has obtained stability in his country, a possessor of the seven jewels. . . . He will dwell conquering this sea-girt land without violence, without a sword, (but) by righteousness. But if he goes forth from the house to the houseless state, he will become an arahat, a fully enlightened one, of widespread fame in the world."[13]

Sela then decides to visit the Buddha in order to determine if he really does possess the thirty-two marks. That is, he wants proof. Immediately Sela recognizes thirty of the marks, but he does not see the unsheathed penis or the long tongue. Knowing this, the Buddha reveals both of these attributes, but this is still not enough for Sela and he thinks to himself that he had

> heard it said by brahmans who are venerable, aged, teachers and teachers of teachers (*brāhmaṇānaṃ vuddhānaṃ mahallakānaṃ ācariyapācariyānaṃ hāsamānānaṃ*): "Those who are arahats, fully enlightened ones, reveal themselves when their own praise is being spoken (*gāthāhi abhitthaveyyanti*)."[14]

Sela then attempts this strategy with a series of verses:

> 548. You have a perfect body, you are shining, you are well-born, strikingly handsome. Your complexion is golden, Blessed man. You have very white teeth, and you are powerful.

549. Whatever the marks of a well-born man, all those characteristics of a great man are in your body.

550. You have clear eyes, a nice face, you are lofty, upright, splendid. You shine like the sun in the midst of a collection of ascetics.

551. A *bhikkhu* with skin like a god is good to look at, but what is the point of a superb appearance if you live in the manner of an ascetic.

552. You ought to be a king, a wheel turning monarch, a bull of charioteers, a conqueror of the whole world, the Lord of Jambusaṇḍa.

553. *Kṣatriya*s and minor kings will be your attendants. You should be the king of kings, lord of men, ruling the kingdom, Gotama.

The Buddha then responds to this praise received from such an eminent brahman. Whether his response to Sela is in some sense ironic or is to gently upbraid him cannot easily be determined, yet the note of confidence is unmistakable.

554. "Sela, I am certainly a king!" said the unsurpassed king of the law.[15] "I set rolling the wheel by means of the law, that wheel which cannot be stopped rolling forwards."

555. "You profess to be fully enlightened, the unsurpassed king of the law, Gotama. You say I roll the wheel by means of the law," said Sela.

556. "But who is the revered one's general, the disciple who follows the teacher? Who keeps this wheel of the law rolling that was set rolling by you?"

557. "Sela," said the Blessed One, "Sāriputta, taking after the Tathāgata, keeps the unsurpassed doctrine-wheel rolling that has been set rolling by me."[16]

Here we have two figures, both of very high status, both possessing considerable acknowledged learning, who are implicitly in competition with one another. Of course, the Buddha cannot be seen to be in competition, as this could be considered a form of desire that he should have entirely eradicated from himself. As such, the emphasis is on Sela's side. He is clearly aware there exist those who have the thirty-two marks but for him this is not enough to establish definitively that they are buddhas. More likely is that they are kings, and usually this would mean *cakkavattins*. Even when the Buddha's possession of the thirty-two marks is proved to Sela empirically, his initial response is that the Buddha should be a king because of his body, which shines spectacularly and is handsome.

Qualities of shining and brightness are common to the Buddha as well as to all ascetics who perform *tapas.* But they are equally common to kings and prominent warriors who are required to exude *tejas.*

Why in his response does the Buddha not simply deny he is a king and declare that he is a buddha, as he does in verses 558–561, in language that sums up well his own career as a buddha? On the basis of these verses it appears that Gautama is both buddha and king but not a *cakkavattin,* which he had been in a previous life. In the verse "'Sela, I am certainly a king!' said the unsurpassed king of the law. 'I set rolling the wheel by means of the law, that wheel which cannot be stopped rolling forward,'" the wheel and the dhamma form correlative functions: dhamma is the means/instrument by which the wheel is turned. But dhamma is also, of course, what the Buddha teaches and embodies, and if the compound *dhammarāja* is taken as a third-case *tatpuruṣa,* the priority would be again accorded to dhamma as a functioning aspect of the Buddha.

This is an important passage that either glosses over the problem of the *cakkavattin*/buddha or places a new slant on it. Confronted with the Buddha's claim that he is *dhammarāja* and not questioning this, Sela pushes the Buddha, leading us to ask whether anyone would have ever questioned his status as *dhammarāja.* This may imply that the meaning of *dhamma* was already very well known and required no elaboration, but it still does not explain why the word *rāja* should be appended to the term when it is used of a buddha, as opposed to a *cakkavattin.* Sela is fully aware that when he declares the Buddha as saying, in two separate *pādas, sambuddho paṭijānāsi dhammarājā anuttaro,* that this is precisely the distinction between a buddha on the one hand and a *cakkavattin* on the other. I take this to mean that Sela is implying that according to traditionally transmitted knowledge the Buddha should be either a *dhammarājā* or a *cakkavattin,* yet the Buddha claims to be both.

As the verses proceed beyond this brief exchange the Buddha goes on to declare himself as a buddha in the traditional sense:

> 558. What is to be known is known by me; what is to be developed is developed by me; what is to be eliminated is eliminated by me; therefore I am a buddha, brahman. (*tasmā buddho 'smi brāhmaṇa*)
>
> 559. Dispel your doubt in me. Have faith, brahman. It is difficult to obtain a sight of the fully enlightened ones repeatedly.
>
> 560. I am a fully enlightened one, an unsurpassed barb-remover (*. . . saṃbuddho sallakatto anuttaro*), [one of those] whose appearance in the world is difficult for you to obtain repeatedly.

561. Having become Brahmā, unequaled crusher of Māra's armies, who would not have faith, even one who is base-born?

Though these may be clichéd phrases, I read them as the Buddha himself convincing Sela that he really is a buddha and not merely a king living in society, despite his regal appearance and title. Verse 560 has a variant on verse 555 in which *dhammarājo* is replaced by *sallakatto,* a compound definitely relating more to a buddha's religious function than to a *cakkavattin.* Surely this is because the Buddha felt compelled to distinguish between himself and a regal *dhammarāja,* even though he still retains the title. In most of the other texts where the clichéd formula about the *cakkavattin* is used, the Buddha is not called *dhammarāja.* And in these cases the text simply ends with the statement that he has left the household and become a fully enlightened buddha. It is in the use of dhamma as an instrument that unites and differentiates both the Buddha and the *cakkavattin* and allows them to actively fulfill their respective positions in an exemplary manner.[17] The king can rule without weapons because the people recognize his rule as being one defined by dhamma, whereas the Buddha turns the wheel by utilizing dhamma; in the latter case the wheel is somehow qualified by dhamma in both an adjectival and an instrumental manner. In this function the meaning of the epithet seems clear. The Buddha is king of dhamma because he "rolls the wheel through dhamma, that wheel that cannot be rolled back."

In the verses included after Buddha's declaration of himself as *dhammarāja,* Sela and his group achieve nirvana as a direct consequence of the Buddha's talk. So he is a *dhammarāja* because he proclaims the enlightening teaching,[18] leading the *brahmacariya* to replicate the Buddha's own lifestyle. All sorts of epithets are used here, making the passage highly devotional in its import, and at the end Sela responds with what is effectively a *stotra.*

If he "rules by" does he also rule over"? Is it dhamma or something else? One way to further unpack this is to look at its reworking in the *Milindapañho,*[19] where Nāgasena is asked to explain how the Buddha can be termed both a brahman and a *rāja* (*Bhante nāgasena bhāsitampetaṃ tathāgatena 'abhamasmi bhikkhave brāhmaṇo yācayogo'ti. Puna ca bhaṇitaṃ 'rājāhamasmi selā'ti*).[20] A description is given of a series of qualities, including the capacity to meditate, to stay in a mental condition beyond doubt, to live as a *deva,* to know his past lives, etc.— all qualities of a buddha known from elsewhere in the canon. Milinda wishes to know why the Buddha can be called both a *brāhmaṇa* and a *rāja,* and begins his definition of a king, which must apply also to a buddha:

> One who is called a king, great king, means someone who rules the kingdom and governs the people (*rājā nāma mahārāja yo koci rajjaṃ kāreti lokam anusāsati*). The illustrious man, great king, rules the kingdom in the ten thousand world system by dhamma (*dhammena rajjaṃ kāreti*), he rules the subjects including gods, the people, with the Māras, Brahmās, ascetics, and Brahmins. Just for that reason the Tathāgata is called a king.[21]

Three other similarities between a king and the Buddha are then given, before the text again returns to the subject of *dhamma:*

> By instructing the tradition of former law-abiding kings, by elucidating what is the law and what is not the law, and ruling the kingdom by the law, the king is desired, liked, sought after by the people of the nations. By the power of the quality of the law he sustains his royal lineage for a long time. By instructing the tradition of previous Self-born men, by elucidating what is the law and what is not the law, the Illustrious Buddha, great king, instructs the world in accord with the law (*dhammena lokam anusāsamāno*), and is desired, liked, sought after by gods and men. He makes his teaching proceed for a long time by the power of the quality of the law (*ciraṃ sāsanaṃ pavatteti dhammaguṇabalena*). For that reason too the Tathāgata is called "king."[22]

On each of the five occasions he is compared with a king (*rāja*) but his title of *dhammarāja* is not elucidated. Yet the tight link between the Buddha and the king in respect of their use of dhamma is maintained. There may also be some significance in the use of the prefix *anu* three times in the final description of the Buddha, because it has the sense of "following, after," confirming that he acts after/in accord with the dhamma.[23] Analogy with the king gives the Buddha a sense of universality and totality, and the idea that he commands by his teaching is consistent with the language of kingship.

This leads us briefly back to the subject of the *cakkavattin.* In the *Aṅguttara Nikāya* there is a brief *Dhammarājasutta* (AN III 5, 3, 4, 3), which again equates the Buddha and the *cakkavattin,* placing both under the aegis of dhamma.

> "*Bhikkhu*s, whoever is that righteous universal monarch, king of the law, he too does not turn the wheel without a king (*arājakam*)."
>
> When this was said, a certain *bhikkhu* said thus to the Blessed One: "Venerable sir, who is the king (*rājā*) of the righteous universal monarch who is king of the law?"
>
> The Blessed One said: "*Bhikkhu,* it is the Teaching (*dhammo*)."[24]

And just as the king protects through the law, so too does the Buddha:

> In the same manner, *bhikkhus*, the Tathāgata, worthy, fully enlightened, law-abiding, king of the law, relying on the law, honouring the law, venerating the law, respecting the law, whose banner is the law, whose standard is the law, who is sovereign by the law, organizes righteously the guard, protection and defence (*rakkhāvaraṇaguttiṃ*) of the monks. He says, "Bodily actions like these should be practiced and bodily actions like these should not be practiced. . . ."

And so,

> *Bhikkhus*, the Tathāgata is worthy, fully enlightened, law-abiding, king of the law, relying on the law, honouring the law, venerating the law, respecting the law, whose banner is the law, whose standard is the law, who is sovereign by the law, having organized righteously the guard, protection and defence of the monks, and having organized righteously the guard, protection and defence for the *bhikkhunis*, lay male disciples and lay female disciples, then causes to turn the unsurpassed wheel of the law by the law alone. That wheel cannot be stopped rolling by anyone in the world, not by a recluse, a Brahmin, a god, Māra, or even Brahma.[25]

Here the crossover with the king seems quite evident, especially in the use of the compound *rakkhāvaraṇaguttiṃ* in respect of the king's subjects and the protection of the monastic order by the Buddha. Both figures are of course identified totally by their encompassing of dhamma, but is the king's dhamma the same as the Buddha's? Which has priority? Or is it a question of civil[26] and religious forms of dhamma that is intended here, raising a bifurcation not unlike the *Milindapañho* passage in which the Buddha is entitled to be called both *brāhmaṇa* and *rāja*? Even in the absence of precise answers to these questions, it is safe to assume that the epithet *dhammarāja* when used of the Buddha implies regal qualities. Such vagueness, with matching precision in the regal context, may help us understand some of the tensions that continually fracture the persona of Yudhiṣṭhira.

The Buddha as *Dharmarāja* in the *Saddharmapuṇḍarīka* and the *Lalitavistara*

Much that is found in Buddhist Sanskrit literature in relation to the word *dharmarāja* replicates the dichotomy between the Buddha and the *cakravartin*. There are some passages in the *Saddharmapuṇḍarīka* (SP) and the *Lalitavistara* (LV), however, where some different usages occur. This reflects the probability that though both are strongly devotional texts, the first is a strong initial statement of the bodhisattva doctrine, while the second is a heavily mythologized biography of the Buddha.

In the LV instances of *dharmarāja* are very much like what occurs in the Pāli texts, where there is no context for elaboration of what the term *dharmarāja* might mean. In a long list of epithets included in Chapter 2 we find "the turner of the precious wheel of the excellent, preeminent teaching of the unimpeded king of the law."[27] This occurs at the beginning of the text, mirroring what will become a *sahasranāmastotra.* Later, as the bodhisattva makes the intention to leave his palace before becoming a buddha, he declares that he has no attachment to the senses and that his previous auspicious intention has now been fulfilled: "I will be Sarvābhibhu, Lord of all dharmas, king of the law, a sage."[28] Here Sarvabhibhū is the name of a former buddha, but what is surely interesting is the compound *sarvadharmeśvaro,* which is seemingly different from *dharmarāja.* This is also a first-person statement as well, so the future buddha sees himself as a *dharmarāja,* though not as a *cakravartin.*

A little further on in this same chapter he is described as a *dharmarāja* by a group of *apsaras* in deliberate comparison to prominent gods of the time:

> He is the refuge of the terrified, the lamp to the blind, sanctum of those assailed, the physician to those who have been ill for a long time; he is like a king, king of the law (*rājeva dharmarājo*), Indra with a thousand eyes, Brahmā the self-born, his body and mind tranquil.[29]

Again, this is very much in the *stotra* mode and establishes both the future buddha's functions and his status, no doubt above the Hindu gods. It is much of a devotional piece but provides no elaboration on why the Buddha is a *dharmarāja,* unless here the term is intended to distinguish him from the other deities by virtue of qualities they may lack. Brahmā would surely be associated with dharma through his connection with Vedic knowledge, and Indra is a king associated with physical force. Somehow the *dharmarāja* transcends both of these.

Similar is 23, 47, where the gods led by Śakra approach him for refuge: ". . . we approach you for refuge, O Foremost of the Śākyas, the king of the law in the world."[30]

Still later Brahmā approaches, requesting instruction from him:

> I am a seeker of instruction from you, King of the law, having made all the gods accompany me. By this merit I too will soon turn the excellent wheel of the law (*pravartayeyaṃ varadharmacakram*).[31]

This presumably means that he is the *dharmarāja* because he has successfully followed the path and is capable of teaching its underlying methods and doctrines.Other instances where the title occurs throw no more light on its meaning, except where Māra predicts that his army will not be weakened when all the arahants and *pratyekabuddhas* attain nirvana, "But that single conqueror will become king of the law, so that the incalculable line of the conqueror will not be broken."[32]

The *Saddharmapuṇḍarīka* is more interesting, yet even here the title *dharmarāja* is assumed rather than explained.

> [So wonderful] and far more wonderful is the law I proclaim. Anyone hearing a good exposition of it shall cheerfully accept it and [if they] recite but one word of it, [they] will have done honour to all Buddhas.
>
> Give up all doubt and uncertainty in this respect; I declare that I am the king of the law; I am urging others to enlightenment, but I am here without disciples.[33]

Is he a *dharmarāja* because he proclaims dharma and is the declaration of this status equivalent to a buddha having declared himself to have attained nirvana? A seemingly similar declaration is:

> I am the Dharmarāga (sic), born in the world as the destroyer of existence. I declare the law to all beings after discriminating their dispositions.[34]
>
> Superior men of wise understanding guard the word, guard the mystery, and do not reveal it to living beings.[35]

Here there may be a direct connection between being born into the world for a particular function and that function being the dissemination of dharma to those judged to be capable of receiving it. In such a case the Buddha is a *dharmarāja* because he knows the dharma and has the capacity to teach it. In the prose part that begins this chapter the Tathāgata's regal attributes are alluded to in a very prominent way:

> dharmasvāmī kāśyapa tathāgataḥ, sarvadharmāṇāṃ rājā prabhur vaśā
>
> The Tathāgata, Kāśyapa, is the master of the law, the king, lord and master of all laws.[36]

Apart from the regal titles, this sentence may confirm the supposition that the compound *dharmarājā* itself should be interpreted as a *ṣaṣṭhi-tatpuruṣa*. What follows gives further clarification to the Buddha's status in relation to dharma:

> And whatever law for any case has been instituted by the Tathāgata, remains just that. And all laws have been appropriately instituted by the Tathāgata, Kāśyapa. Using his knowledge as a Tathāgata, he has instituted those laws so that they go right to the stage of the omniscient. The Tathāgata also distinctly examines the course of the meaning of all the laws. The Tathāgata who is the arahat who is perfectly enlightened has obtained the status of being master of the meaning of all the laws, arrived at the control of meaning of all the laws, who has arrived at the highest perfection of knowledge, so that he is able to skillfully engage in philosophical disquisition of all laws, displays the knowledge of the all-knowing, imparts the knowledge of the all-knowing, and institutes the rules of the knowledge of the all knowing.[37]

The word *dharma* here could be translated as "teachings," or it may refer to all things that constitute the universe. However, the gist is that the Buddha is in possession of all the teachings, he controls and understands them in their entirety in the most fullest penetrating sense, and he can lay them down and exposit them exactly as they are. It is this sense of complete control he has acquired without teaching and without question that seems to allow him to be designated as having lordship over the teachings, because they are utterly in his grasp.

Finally, consider these two verses:

> And from what are they liberated, Śāriputra? They are liberated from false beliefs. Yet they are not wholly freed. The chief (*nāyaka*) declares that they have not reached final rest in this world.
>
> Why do I not pronounce the liberation of one before he has reached the highest supreme knowledge? Because such is my will. I am the King of the law, born in the world to lead people to happiness.[38]

Thus, because he is *dharmarāja* he has the ability and the right to declare certain fundamental truths, including the one just pronounced in verses 103–104. Similar is 7, 34:

> But now he has appeared, owing to our good works, who is [our] eye, refuge, resting-place, protection, father, and kinsman; he, the benign and bounteous one, the King of the Law.[39]

Later on in the text we find:

> I have a remembrance of past ages when I was law-abiding, the king of the law, and ruled the kingdom for the sake of the law, but not for the sake of desire, as for sake of the best law (*dharmahetoḥ kṛtaṃ tanna ca kāmahetor jyeṣṭhadharmahetoḥ*).[40]

This occurs in a chapter that details the discovery of the *Saddharmapuṇḍārikasūtra,* and it refers to the Buddha as a *cakravartin* in a previous life. It bears a close resemblance to a few passages where Yudhiṣṭhira indicates that his rulership is for the law and not for *artha* or *kāma*.[41]

Finally, the martial aspect of Buddha's role as *dharmarāja* emerges in a similar form as that found in the Pāli sources:

> In the same manner, Mañjuśrī, the Tathāgata . . . lord of the law, king of the law, rules the kingdom of the law in the triple world by the law he himself has conquered by the strength of his arms and conquered by the power of his good merit. His triple world is assailed by Māra the Evil One. Then the Āryas, the soldiers of the Tathāgata, fight with Māra. Then, Mañjuśrī, the lord of the law, the king of the law, expounds to the Āryas, his soldiers, whom he sees fighting, hundred thousands of Sūtras in order to encourage the four classes.[42]

> *tathaiva buddho ahu dharmarājā kṣāntībalaḥ prajñaprabhūtakośaḥ /*
> *dharmeṇa śāsāmimu sarvalokaṃ hitānukampī karūṇāyamānaḥ //*
> *sattvāṃśca dṛṣṭvātha vihanyamānān bhāṣāmi sūtrāntasahasrakoṭyaḥ /*
> *parākramaṃ jāniya teṣa prāṇināṃ ye śuddhasattvā iha kleśaghātinaḥ //*
> *atha dharmarājāpi mahābhiṣaṭkaḥ paryāyakoṭīśata bhāṣamāṇaḥ* / (13, 51–53ab)

> Likewise do I, the Buddha, the king of the law, I who have the force of patience and a large treasure of wisdom, govern the whole world by the law, benign, compassionate and pitiful. And then when I have see those living beings being damaged, I recite hundreds of kotis of Sūtrāntas, having recognized the courage of those living beings, those of pure mind who strike the painful inclinations. And the king of the law, the great physician, expounding hundreds of kotis of Sūtrāntas, when I perceive the heroism of those living beings who by pure-mindedness overcomes the sinful inclinations of the world.[43]

Obviously dharma is a weapon of restraint capable of regulating behavior without the use of material weapons that render physical injury. Yet the impression given is still the same: the Buddha is a king who gives commands (*śās*) that will influence both the religious and the nonreligious spheres of activity, though in this environment these two spheres cannot be separated. In the final analysis, the role of the *cakkavattin* and the Buddha as *dhammarāja* overlap but remain decisively different. Such a dichotomy is implied in regard to Yudhiṣṭhira, but the difference in commonality is never successfully achieved.

Yudhiṣṭhira

The Dharmarāja is said over and over to be *dharmātman,* "always mindful of Law," or "always mindful of what is Right," but as we noted earlier,

> Yudhiṣṭhira is more than once enmeshed in issues where truthfulness or identity is seriously compromised in one way or another. Yudhiṣṭhira's troubles reflect the profound dilemma of dharma that the *Mahābhārata* addresses from beginning to end. . . .[44]

With this conclusion to his article on Yudhiṣṭhira and violence in the MBh, James Fitzgerald points to one of the principal qualities of Yudhiṣṭhira as a living exemplar of dharma, which, because of its apparent conceptual fractures, places him constantly in a dilemma as regards practical behavior. Because no such dilemma exists for the Buddha when he is treated as *dhammarāja,* this quality of Yudhiṣṭhira seems to mark a fundamental difference between them as exemplars of what the term might mean.

Despite the hundreds of times Yudhiṣṭhira is called *dharmarāja,* it is much harder to trace the origin of this title in relation to him. Often also called *dharmātman* and *dharmaputra,* Yudhiṣṭhira is so strongly tied into dharma, its usages, contradictions, and weaknesses, as to cause us to overlook explanations for why he is called *dharmarāja.* The association of the title with Yama has been frequently alluded to, but I have not been able to find any clues in the MBh about the application of this compound as a privileged epithet of Yudhiṣṭhira (the term *adharmarāja* is never found).[45] Yet because it is so clichéd, and contextualized only in the many instances where dharma seems inadequate to guarantee human felicity, it seems to have been accepted that there was no need to explain the meaning of *dharmarājā,* suggesting that the term was already widely known, a tendency surmised earlier for the Buddhist texts.

Little is explained by examining a passage dealing with Paṇḍu's decision that Kuntī should invoke Dharma to give birth to a son:

> Lovely woman, call Dharma, for he among the Gods partakes of merit. For Dharma would in no way yoke with us if it were not lawful, elegant woman. And people will now think that this is the Law. And of a certainty this son shall become the standard of Law (*dhārmika*) for the Kurus; and having been given by Dharma, his mind will not rejoice in lawlessness.[46]

As soon as he is born a disembodied voice says:

> He shall of a certainty be the greatest of the upholders of the Law, Pāṇḍu's firstborn son, who shall be named Yudhiṣṭhira. He shall be a celebrated king, widely renowned in all three worlds, glorious, lustrous and of correct behaviour.[47]

Now that he has produced a son who is *dhārmika,* Pāṇḍu wants another son who is *kṣatraṃ balajyeṣṭhaṃ,* and so Bhīma is eventually born (1, 115, 8). None of this is especially enlightening except that it distinguishes Yudhiṣṭhira from the other sons by his anchoring in dharma.

The only place I have found where he describes himself as the *dharmarāja* is at 3, 12, 26ab: "I am Pāṇḍu's son, King Dharma. Perhaps you have heard of me."[48] But this tells us nothing of the content of the compound itself. Perhaps a more illuminating passage is 3, 180, 16–21, where Kṛṣṇa praises Yudhiṣṭhira:

> The Law is higher than a kingdom won, son of Pāṇḍu;
> They say that austerity leads to it, king.
> By living by your own Law, uprightly and truly,
> You have won this world and the world beyond.
> At first you studied, obeying vows,
> Then acquired entire all the lore of war,
> Obtained your wealth by baronial Law,
> And regained all ancient sacrifices.
> You found no joy in the Laws of the rustics,
> Nor, Indra of men, pursued your desires,
> Nor abandoned the law out of greed for Profit,
> And thus by nature (*svabhāvād asi*) you are King Dharma.
> Liberality, truth, austerities, sire,
> And faith and peace and endurance and patience
> Were always your greatest joy, O Pārtha,
> After winning kingdoms, riches and comforts.
> Who else but you could endure, son of Pāṇḍu,
> That spectacle robbed of all Law and manners,
> When the gathering folk of the Kuru jungles
> Saw Kṛṣṇā afraid and reduced to a slave?[49]

What does this really tell us? There are several kinds of law that Yudhiṣṭhira seems to have mastered or practiced (*car*): *svadharma* (16c), *kṣatreṇa dharmeṇa* (17c), *grāmyadharmeṣu*[50] (18a), and dharma (16a, 20c), with no qualifications. In addition, it is clear that the other two members (*artha* 16b, 18c, and *kāma* 18a) of the *trivarga* are present here, even if only implied by *śleṣa,* and although Yudhiṣṭhira is shown to subjugate them to dharma, nonetheless there is present the sense in ancient Indian political theory that the king must encompass all that is in the *trivarga.* The apparent lack of unity in the different dharmas, however, defines perfectly the dilemma Yudhiṣṭhira always faces between his duty—stated always by others—to remain as king in the world and his desire for the forest life of the renunciant. As king he must place a watching brief over all of these dharmas, as impossible as this may seem to be.

So it is his *svabhāva* to be *dharmarāja* because he has followed his class dharma, he has been honest and upright and acted solely from a concern for dharma, not from *artha* or *kāma* (a swipe at Duryodhana's avarice).[51] As a reward, he has obtained certain things: dharma is higher than gaining the kingdom (*rājyalābhāt* 16a); he attained (*avāpya*) complete knowledge of archery; he obtained (*labdhvā*) wealth; he gained (*avāptāḥ*) all the ancient sacrifices; and he obtained (*avāpya*) the kingdom with its wealth and enjoyments (19c). This is unlike the Buddha, who does not "acquire" nirvana, because it is a state he enters rather than something that can be attained.

The apprehension Yudhiṣṭhira experiences toward kingship after the great battle is brilliantly exposed in 12, 76, 15–17, where he laments:

> I have not sought the pleasures of kingship! I have not wanted kingship, not even for an instant! I acquiesced to kingship for the sake of Law, and yet there is no Law in it. So I have had enough of kingship where there is no Law. And I will just go to the forest in my desire to do Meritorious Lawful Deeds. There in the fresh, verdant wilds, having lain down the royal rod of force,[52] having conquered my senses, a sage eating only roots and fruit, I will worship the Good Law.[53]

These sentiments lead me to ask whether Yudhiṣṭhira could have been called *dharmarāja* if he had renounced his royal position and gone to live in the forest to practice the contemplative life. I assume not, because part of the king's dharma is to protect those who live in the social world within the kingdom, as well as ascetics who have turned their backs on the world in order to live in the forest. That is, the king's dharma would now be only a partial one, as reflected well in Fitzgerald's translation of the term *dharma* by several different words. He rejects the king's dharma—as ambiguous as this now seems to be—virtually without justification because it is not dharma, here possibly harking to the grievous bloodletting on the battlefield in the name of dharma, or to the Kauravas' behavior in which dharma was consistently violated. This critique is very strong; it is repeated twice and almost seems to be a contradiction of his title of *dharmarāja*.

The last two *śloka*s offer a quite different view of dharma, though it is never qualified separately except for delineation of the environment where it is to be practiced and the fact that a king is utterly different from a *muni.*[54] We might note here that Yudhiṣṭhira will throw down his *daṇḍa,* a powerful symbol of kingship, and superficially this might put him in the same category as the *cakkavattin* who is *adandya,* ruling entirely through dhamma. But the *dharmarāja* in the MBh is required to enforce dharma by using the *daṇḍa,* which was in fact the case for the kings to whom the Buddha served as an advisor, even when the ideal was not to use it.

In the MBh the perception of dharma is a much more fractured and ambiguous concept than the dhamma of the Pāli canon and early Buddhist Sanskrit texts, largely because so many of the agents in its narrative show no concern about whether or not it should be respected.[55] This applies even given the six different understandings of dhamma listed by Gethin. From this we learn, in my estimation, that the distinction between the *cakkavattin* and the Buddha, which makes it possible for both to be *dhammarāja,* does not apply in the case of Yudhiṣṭhira, who is attempting to fulfill both of these roles at the same time, and failing in this effort. The *cakkavattin* idea is played down in the MBh, in part because the *dharmarāja* or the *rāja* as such is required, in an ideal sense, to have adopted in his behavior some of the ascetic's attitudes, e.g., equanimity toward all things.

Conclusion

There is an immediate difference between the Buddha and Yudhiṣṭhira as recipients of the epithet *dharmarāja/dhammarāja.* Yudhiṣṭhira receives this title before he is finally consecrated as king, but throughout the MBh his persona is highly fissured from the perspective of both the understanding of and the ultimate validation of dharma. He is trapped within it in the short term, even if his entrapment may have positive long-term effects. No such fracturing occurs in the image of the Buddha, whose designation as *dhammarāja,* although constructed, is not entirely a literary creation.

What, we might ask, is the significance attached to the possession of this title? In the case of the Buddha there is no ambiguity at all, except whether the term is a third- or a sixth-case *tatpuruṣa.* If there is any room for interpretation, it is in the understanding of *rāja.* For Yudhiṣṭhira it is rather the understanding of dharma. His kingship is never really in doubt, only its acceptance by others (especially the Dhārtarāṣṭras). Nor is dharma especially misunderstood, it is just not adhered to by those who should adhere to it. The Buddha is the king of dharma, if it is a genitive *tatpuruṣa,* because he has such control over it, proven through his own execution of dharmic principles.

Let us be aware that both sets of texts where this compound occurs are entirely different. In the Buddhist context the meaning of dhamma in the compound *dhammarāja* is seemingly clear: it denotes the totality of the teachings. The only problem is that we cannot equate this easily with the sense of dhamma when the term *dhammarāja* is used of the *cakkavattin,* unless it is the same and meant to be vague. The commentators' explanation begs the question of the meaning of dhamma, suggesting that it is well understood already. In fact, the king ruling by dhamma, not by the *daṇḍa,* is centrally tied into the Buddhist myth of the *cakkavattin* (and could be read into the Aśokan inscriptions and the depiction of Aśoka in later Buddhist texts), but this does not occur in the MBh where the *daṇḍa* is glorified in such passages as 12, 16.

What is also significant are the many times Yudhiṣṭhira is called *dharmarāja* in the MBh, in comparison to the limited number of times the parallel term *dhammarāja* is used to describe the Buddha. The Buddha has developed and elaborated the dhamma and embodies it in his teachings. Being enlightened, he is beyond the self-doubts Yudhiṣṭhira constantly experiences in the MBh, especially in regard to the cost of violence, and the confidence exuded by the Buddha seems only to be matched by that of Aśoka in his inscriptions. Yudhiṣṭhira, as Alf Hiltebeitel has shown, is in a constant state of learning about dharma and subsequently being tested as to his adherence to it.[56] In the final summation, the compound *dharmarāja* in Buddhist texts operates as a description of two related but different roles, but when these are combined in the figure of Yudhiṣṭhira it leads to many unresolved tensions.

Notes

1 See especially Nick Sutton, "Aśoka and Yudhiṣṭhira: A Historical Setting for the Ideological Tensions of the Mahābhārata," *Religion* 27 (1997): 333–341; James Fitzgerald, *The Mahābhārata, Volume 7* (Chicago: University of Chicago Press, 2004), pp. 114–123. Cf. also Alf Hiltebeitel, *Dharma* (Honolulu: University of Hawai'i Press, 2010), pp. 162–163.

2 Rupert Gethin, "He Who Sees Dhamma Sees Dhammas: Dhamma In Early Buddhism," *Journal of Indian Philosophy* 32 (2004): 515–516.

3 James Fitzgerald, "Dharma and its Translation in the Mahābhārata," *Journal of Indian Philosophy* 32 (2004): pp.673–674.

4 See Emily T. Hudson, *Disorientating Dharma: Ethics and the Aesthetics of Suffering in the Mahābhārata* (New York: Oxford University Press, 2013).

5 Patrick Olivelle, "The Semantic History of Dharma: The Middle and Late Vedic Periods," *Journal of Indian Philosophy* 32 (2004): 504.

[6] But see also Isaline B. Horner, *The Collection of the Middle Length Sayings (Majjhima Nikāya)* (London: Luzac, 1957), vol. 2, p. 318, n. 4: "[In] MA. Iii. 365, he is a king delighting the world with the four wonderful aspects of protection (given at D. iii 232, A. 11 32)," and earlier, (p. 135): "having succeeded to the throne through *dhamma* (i.e., legitimately, rightly), he is the 'natural,' *jāta*, king. Or, he is *dhammika* because of his 'rightness,' *dhamma*, in regard to the good of others, just as he is *dhammarājā* because of his 'rightness' in regard to his own good, *attahita*."

[7] On which see Steven Collins, *Nirvana and other Buddhist Felicities* (Cambridge: Cambridge University Press, 1998), p. 472; Olivelle, "The Semantic History of Dharma," p. 504.

[8] All references are to the Pāli Text Society editions. References to the *Mahābhārata* are to the Critical Edition.

[9] *Sā vandituṃ anadhivaraṃ upāgamiṃ*
Pāsādike kusalarathe ca bhikkhavo
Namassituṃ samaṇasamāgamaṃ sivaṃ
Sagāravā sirimato dhammarājino. (PTS, p. 13)

Peter Masefield, trans., *Elucidation of the Intrinsic Meaning: So Named the Commentary on the Vimana Stories* (Oxford: Pali Text Society, 1989), p. 117.

[10] PTS, p. 13; Masefield, *Elucidation of the Intrinsic Meaning*, p. 276. Cf. *Mahāvastu* 1. 301.

[11] *yassa sabrahmacārīsu gāravo nūpalabbhati,*
ārako hoti nibbānā, dhammarājassa sāsane (392 is very similar).

Cf. Danièle Masset, trans., *Stances Des Theras (Theragāthā)* (Bristol, U.K.: Pali Text Society, 2011), p. 96 (see also n. 218): "se trouve en l'enseignement du Roi par la doctrine très éloigné de l'extinction."

[12] *Dīgha Nikāya* I, p. 85, II, p. 202, where Bimbisāra refers to Ajātasattu as a *dhammikaṃ dhammarājānam*. . . (–86); *Majjhima Nikāya* II, p. 74, Makhādeva; p. 79, King Nimi.

[13] Kenneth R. Norman, trans., *The Group of Discourses (Sutta-Nipāta)* (London: Pali Text Society, 1984), p. 96; Dines Andersen and Helmer Smith, *Sutta Nipāta* (London: Pali Text Society, 1965 , p. 106.

[14] Pali Text Society, p. 108; Norman, *The Group of Discourses (Sutta-Nipāta)*, p. 97.

[15] Norman, *The Group of Discourses (Sutta-Nipāta)*, p. 98, translates this as "[doctrine-king]."I. B. Horner and Walpola Rāhula, cited in Norman, *The Group of Discourses (Sutta-Nipāta)*, p. 100, render it as "king of Dhamma." In the *Middle Length Sayings*, vol. 2, p. 337, Horner gives "a matchless king under *dhamma*."

[16] *rājāham asmi selāti dhammarājā anuttaro /*
dhammena cakkaṃ vattemi cakkaṃ appativattiyaṃ //
sambuddho paṭijānāsi dhammarājā anuttaro /
dhammena cakkaṃ vattemi iti bhāsasi gotama //
konu senāpatī bhoto sāvako satthudanvayo /
ko te imaṃ anuvatteti dhammacakkaṃ pavattitaṃ //

mayā pavattitaṃ cakkaṃ dhammacakkam anuttaraṃ /
sariputto anuvatteti anujāto tathāgatam //

Very similar is *Theragāthā* 818–830 (Pali Text Society, pp. 78–79). Cf. Masset, *Stances Des Theras*, pp. 157–158.

17 Here Collin's warning is timely (*Nirvana and other Buddhist Felicities*, p. 472):

> Despite the similarities between a Buddha and a CV, it is easy to oversimplify and overemphasize the parallel between them. . . . Both a Buddha and a CV can be "kings of dhamma" *dhammarājā*, and the Buddha can be "a Wheel-turning King of the (excellent) Good Dhamma" but commentaries specify that the CV's Dhamma is the ten Paths of Good Action, while a Buddha's is the nine Transcendental Attainments (MP II, 178–80, on A 179–10).

But also compare Masset, *Stances Des Theras*, pp. 334–335, n. 399, where she offers insightful comments on the differences between the two on the basis of *Theragāthā* 818–830:

> [L]e terme dhammarāja (n), qui peut designer le "roi selon l'ordre"– c'est-a-dire le roi don't la conduit justes est en harmonie avec l'ordre du monde–prend ici le sens spécifiquement bouddhiste de "roi par la doctrine": un roi qui règne et gouverne les êtres par le biais de la doctrine don't il assure la transmission. L'idéal de souveraineté temporelle se trouve donc transposé dans le domaine spirituel. . . .

18 See also *Apadāna* 1230.

19 Vilhelm Trenckner, ed., *The Milindapañho: Being Dialogues between King Milinda and the Buddhist Sage Nāgasena* (London: Luzac, 1962).

20 For the passages, see Trenckner, *The Milindapañho*, pp. 225–227.

21 Isaline B. Horner, trans., *Milinda's Questions* (London: Luzac, 1964), vol. 2, p. 25. I have added the Pāli.

22 Horner, *Milinda's Questions*, p. 27 (Pali Text Society, p. 227, modified).

23 Just as for the *cakkavattin* who rules by dhamma as in the clichéd passage: *adaṇḍena asatthena dhammena abhivijiya ajjhāvasati*. Cf. MBh 12, 92, 45cd: *na hi śakyam adaṇḍena klībenābuddhināpi vā //*, where *adaṇḍena* is used in a strongly critical sense.

24 AN III (Pali Text Society), p. 149. Nyanaponika Thera and Bhikkhu Bodhi, trans., *Aṅguttara Nikāya: Discourses of the Buddha. An Anthology*, Part I (Kandy, Sri Lanka: Buddhist Publication Society, 1970), online edition, 2010, p. 14.

25 AN III, pp. 150–151; Thera and Bodhi, *Aṅguttara Nikāya*, pp. 14–15:

Sa kho bhikkhu tathāgato arahaṃ sammāsambuddho (Pali Text Society, p. 151) *dhammiko dhammarājā dhammaṃ yeva nissāya dhammaṃ sakkaronto dhammaṃ garukaronto dhammaṃ apacāyamāno dhammaddhajo dhammaketu dhammādhipateyyo dhammikaṃ rakkhāvaraṇaguttiṃ saṃvidahitvā bhikkhusu, dhammikaṃ rakkhāvaraṇaguttiṃ saṃvidahitvā bhikkhunīsu, dhammikaṃ rakkhāvaraṇaguttiṃ saṃvidahitvā upāsakesu, dhammikaṃ rakkhāvaraṇaguttiṃ saṃvidahitvā upāsikāsu, dhammeneva anuttaraṃ dhammacakkaṃ pavatteti. Taṃ hoti cakkaṃ appativattiyaṃ samaṇena vā brāhmaṇena vā devena vā mārena vā brahmunā vā kenaci vā lokasmin ti.*

26 Suggested by Hiltebeitel, *Dharma*, pp. 162–163.

27 See Paraśurama L. Vaidya, ed., *Lalita Vistara* (Darbhanga: Mithila Institute, 1958), p. 8: *apratihata-dharmarājāvarapravaradharmaratnacakrapravartakasya*. . . .

28 *bheṣyi sarvābhibhū sarvadharmeśvaro dharmarājo muniḥ* // 15.47

29 15, 97; Vaidya, *Lalita Vistara*, p. 163; Bijoya Goswami, trans., *Lalitavistara. English Translation with Notes* (Calcutta: The Asiatic Society, 2001), p. 211; modified.

30 Vaidya, *Lalita Vistara*, p. 265; Goswami, *Lalitavistara*, p. 332:

trimalakhilaprahīṇa śāntendriyā śāntacittā mune
śaraṇu tavamupema śākyarṣabhā dharmarājā jage // 23.47 //.

31 Vaidya, *Lalita Vistara*, p. 289; 32, 21, 9; Vaidya, *Lalita Vistara*, p. 220. Cf. 19, 27; Vaidya, *Lalita Vistara*, p. 204, where Suddhodhana is the *dharmarāja* who is *dharmeṇānuśāstā*.

adhyeṣako 'haṃ tava dharmarāja adhyācarākṛtvana sarvadevān /
anena puṇyena ahaṃ pi kṣipraṃ pravartayeyaṃ varadharmacakram // 25.16.

33 Paraśurama L Vaidya, ed., *Saddharmapuṇḍarīkasūtram* (Darbhanga: Milithila Institute, 1960), p. 42; Hendrik Kern, trans., *Saddharma-Puṇḍārika or Lotus of the True Law* (New York: Dover, 1963), p. 58.

ataś ca āścaryataraṃ vadāmi śrutvāna yo dharmam imaṃ subhāṣitam /
anumodi ekaṃ pi bhaṇeya vācaṃ kṛta sarvabuddhāna bhaveya pūjā //
vyapanehi kāṅkṣām iha saṃśayaṃ ca ārocayāmi ahu dharmarājā /
samādapemi aham agrabodhau na śrāvakāḥ kecid ihāsti mahyam // SP 2, 138–139.

34 Kern, *Saddharma-Puṇḍārika*, p. 122, n. 1: "It is known from the Kaṭha Upanishad that the Dharmarāga, Death, knows all about death and the next world, and is questioned about it by Nakiketas." To my knowledge, however, while Yama is mentioned there, it is not as *dharmarāja*. However, the real parallel might be with Yama in the MBh, where as the god of death he truly is the destroyer of existence, though Yudhiṣṭhira, the other *dharmarāja*, is reluctant to do this.

35 Vaidya, *Saddharmapuṇḍarīkasūtram*, p. 85; Kern, *Saddharma-Puṇḍārika*, p. 122:

dharmarājā ahaṃ loke utpanno bhavamardanaḥ /
dharmaṃ bhāṣāmi sattvānām adhimuktiṃ vijāniya //
dhīrabuddhī mahāvīrā ciraṃ rakṣanti bhāṣitam /
rahasyaṃ cāpi dhārenti na ca bhāṣanti prāṇinām // SP 5.1–2

36 Vaidya, *Saddharmapuṇḍarīkasūtram*, p. 84; Kern, *Saddharma-Puṇḍārika*, p. 118.

37 Vaidya, *Saddharmapuṇḍarīkasūtram*, p. 84; Kern, *Saddharma-Puṇḍārika*, pp. 118–119, modified.

yaṃ ca kāśyapa tathāgato dharmaṃ yatropanikṣipati, sa tathaiva bhavati / sarvadharmāś-ca kāśyapa tathāgato yuktyopanikṣipati / tathāgatajñānenopanikṣipati / yathā te dharmāḥ sarvajñabhūmimeva gacchanti / sarvadharmārthagatiṃ ca tathāgato vyava-lokayati / sarvadharmārthavaśitāprāptaḥ sarvadharmādhyāśayaprāptaḥ sarvadharmaviniś-cayakauśalyajñānaparamapāramitāprāptaḥ sarvajña-jñānasaṃdarśakaḥ sarvajñajñānā-vatārakaḥ sarvajñajñānopanikṣepakaḥ kāśyapa tathāgato 'rhan samyaksaṃbuddhaḥ //

38 Vaidya, *Saddharmapuṇḍarīkasūtram*, p. 64; Kern, *Saddharma-Puṇḍārika*, pp. 90–91, modified.

kutaśca te śārisutā vimuktā asantagrāhātu vimukta bhonti /
na ca tāva te sarvata mukta bhonti anirvṛtāṃs tān vadatīha nāyakaḥ //
kikāraṇaṃ nāsya vadāmi mokṣam aprāpy imām uttamam agrabodhim /
mamaiṣa chando ahu dharmarājā sukhāpanārthāyiha loki jātaḥ //; SP 3, 103–104

39 Vaidya, *Saddharmapuṇḍarīkasūtram*, p. 111; Kern, *Saddharma-Puṇḍārika*, p. 166.
so dāni cakṣuśca gatiśca leṇaṃ trāṇaṃ pitā co tatha bandhubhūtaḥ /
utpannu lokasmi hitānukampī asmāka puṇyairiha dharmarājā //

40 SP 11, 42. Vaidya, *Saddharmapuṇḍarīkasūtram*, p. 158; Kern, *Saddharma-Puṇḍārika*, p. 245, modified.

41 Kern, *Saddharma-Puṇḍārika*, p. 245. Cf. MBh 12, 91, 3: *dharmāya rājā bhavati na kāmakaraṇāya tu / māndhātar evaṃ jānīhi rājā lokasya rakṣitā //.*

42 Vaidya, *Saddharmapuṇḍarīkasūtram*, p. 174; Kern, *Saddharma-Puṇḍārika*, p. 275, modified.

evameva mañjuśrīstathāgato 'pyarhan samyaksaṃbuddho dharmasvāmī dharmarājā svena bāhubalanirjitena puṇyabalanirjitena traidhātuke dharmeṇa dharmarājyaṃ kārayati / tasya māraḥ pāpīyāṃs traidhātukam ākrāmati / atha khalu tathāgatasyāpi āryā yodhā māreṇa sārdhaṃ yudhyante / atha khalu mañjuśrīstathāgato 'pyarhan samyaksaṃbuddho dharmasvāmī dharmarājā teṣāmāryāṇāṃ yodhānāṃ yudhyatāṃ dṛṣṭvā vividhāni sūtraśatasahasrāṇi bhāṣate sma catasṛṇāṃ parṣadāṃ saṃharṣaṇārtham /.

43 Vaidya, *Saddharmapuṇḍarīkasūtram*, pp. 175–176; Kern, *Saddharma-Puṇḍārika*, p. 277, modified.

44 James L. Fitzgerald, "Making Yudhiṣṭhira the King: the Dialectics of Violence in the Mahābhārata," *Rocznik Orientalistyczny* LIV/1 (2001): 89–90. Cf. Madeleine Biardeau, *Études de mythologie hindoue, T. II: Bhakti et avatāra* (Pondichéry: Publications De L'École Française D'Extrême-Orient, 1994), p. 156: "Yudhiṣṭhira in himself does not incarnate the reign of dharma, but the collection of forces which will preside over the crisis of the world and lead it to a result desired by the gods and all the friends of dharma."

45 It is also used of Janamejaya (1, 50, 11) and Janaka (12, 312, 19), and, of course, of Yama.

46 Johannes A. B. van Buitenen, trans., *The Mahābhārata, Volume 1: The Book of the Beginning* (Chicago: University of Chicago Press, 1973), p. 255, modified.
dharmam āvāhaya śubhe sa hi deveṣu puṇyabhāk //
adharmeṇa na no dharmaḥ saṃyujyeta kathaṃ cana /
lokaś cāyaṃ varārohe dharmo 'yam iti maṃsyate //
dhārmikaś ca kurūṇāṃ sa bhaviṣyati na saṃśayaḥ /
dattasyāpi ca dharmeṇa nādharme raṃsyate manaḥ // (1, 113, 39c–41).

47 van Buitenen, *The Mahābhārata, Volume 1*, p. 255.
eṣa dharmabhṛtāṃ śreṣṭho bhaviṣyati na saṃśayaḥ /
yudhiṣṭhira iti khyātaḥ pāṇḍoḥ prathamajaḥ sutaḥ //
bhavitā prathito rājā triṣu lokeṣu viśrutaḥ /
yaśasā tejasā caiva vṛttena ca samanvitaḥ // (1, 114, 6–7).

48 *paṇḍavo dharmarājo 'haṃ yadi te śrotram āgataḥ /.*

49 Johannes A. B. van Buitenen, *The Mahābhārata, Volume 2: The Book of the Assembly Hall, 3. The Book of the Forest* (Chicago: University of Chicago Press, 1975), pp. 571–572, modified.

dharmaḥ paraḥ pāṇḍava rājyalābhāt; tasyārtham āhus tapa eva rājan /
satyārjavābhyāṃ caratā svadharmaṃ; jitas tavāyaṃ ca paraś ca lokaḥ //
adhītam agre caratā vratāni; samyag dhanurvedam avāpya kṛtsnam /
kṣātreṇa dharmeṇa vasūni labdhvā; sarve hy avāptāḥ kratavaḥ purāṇāḥ // 17
na grāmyadharmeṣu ratis tavāsti; kāmān na kiṃ cit kuruṣe narendra /
na cārthalobhāt prajahāsi dharmaṃ; tasmāt svabhāvād asi dharmarājaḥ // 18
dānaṃ ca satyaṃ ca tapaś ca rājañ; śraddhā ca śāntiś ca dhṛtiḥ kṣamā ca /
avāpya rāṣṭrāṇi vasūni bhogān; eṣā parā pārtha sadā ratis te // 19.

50 van Buitenen, *The Mahābhārata, Volume 2,* in a note on p. 831, describes this as sex, a reading backed up by the other instances where it occurs: 3, 266, 5; 13, 117, 7; 131, 38.

51 Cf. SP 11, 42, cited above.

52 On which see Biardeau, *Études de mythologie hindoue,* p. 216, discussing the scene where the four *lokapālas* appear before Arjuna, to whom the *daṇḍa* is given by Yama: "This scene must therefore be a fine confirmation of the particular character of Yudhiṣṭhira's royalty, who does not himself wield the *daṇḍa* (he only knows how to pardon!) and entrusts it all to Arjuna." Whether the constant affirmation that the *cakkavattin* rules by *dhammena* and so by *adaṇḍena* anticipates this, I cannot say.

53 Fitzgerald, *The Mahābhārata,* Vol. 7, p. 359.

yudhiṣṭhira uvāca
nāhaṃ rājyasukhānveṣī rājyam icchāmy api kṣaṇam /
dharmārthaṃ rocaye rājyaṃ dharmaś cātra na vidyate // 15
tad alaṃ mama rājyena yatra dharmo na vidyate /
vanam eva gamiṣyāmi tasmād dharmacikīrṣayā // 16
tatra medhyeṣv araṇyeṣu nyastadaṇḍo jitendriyaḥ /
dharmam ārādhayiṣyāmi munir mūlaphalāśanaḥ // 17.

Cf. Madeleine Biardeau, *Mahābhārata: Un récit fondateur du brahmanisme et son interpretation* (Paris: Seuil, 2002), vol. 1, p. 404: "Quoique certains ārya se sentient enclins à faire confiance à la vertu et pensent que le respect du dharma entraîne le réussite, le Bonheur, d'autres au contraire constatent—Yudhiṣṭhira en serait un bon example—qu'il vaut mieux observer le dharma pour lui-même et non pour ce qu'on en retire de bienfaits."

54 Cf. Fitzgerald, *The Mahābhārata,* Vol. 7, p. 104: "The newer concept of dharma often replaces personal self-interest with a devaluation of one's particular being affiliated with a sense of connectedness to others and a concomitant sense of kindness toward others. . . . The highest good of the old dharma is its power to yield benefits on the other side of death. . . ."

55 But it is still more complex than this because of the two fundamentally different understandings of dharma. See Fitzgerald, *The Mahābhārata,* Vol. 7, pp. 127–128:

"Yudhiṣṭhira is more than once enmeshed in issues where truthfulness or identity is seriously compromised in one way or another. Yudhiṣṭhira's troubles reflect the profound dilemma of dharma that the Mahābhārata addresses from beginning to end. . . . The basic ambivalence of dharma is, in part, behind the character of Yudhiṣṭhira and the anguish with which he wages war and weighs the ethical burden of kingship afterwards." This is not addressed in Buddhism, though the possibility is that there are multiple dharmas associated with other religious groups. See also, more generally, Alf Hiltebeitel, *Dharma: Its Early History in Law, Religion, and Narrative* (New York: Oxford University Press, 2011), Chapter 9; Braj M. Sinha, "*Arthaśāstra* Categories in the *Mahābhārata*," in Arvind Sharma, ed., *Essays on the Mahābhārata* (Leiden: E. J. Brill, 1991), pp. 380–383.

56 Alf Hiltebeitel, *Rethinking the Mahābhārata: A Reader's Guide to the Education of the Dharma King* (Chicago: University of Chicago Press, 2001), pp. 208–209: "Yudhiṣṭhira is never said to know the highest dharma or to recognize it so easily in a brother. If Rāma would seem to incarnate it, Yudhiṣṭhira must learn it."

References

Andersen, Dines, and Helmer Smith. *Sutta Nipāta.* London: Pali Text Society, 1965.

Basak, Radhagovinda, ed. *Mahāvastu Avadāna.* Calcutta: Sanskrit College, 1963-1965.

Biardeau, Madeleine. *Études de mythologie hindoue, T. II: Bhakti et avatāra.* Pondichéry: Publications De L'École Française D'Extrême-Orient, 1994.

—. *Mahābhārata. Un récit fondateur du brahmanisme et son interpretation,* vol. 1. Paris: Seuil, 2002.

Buitenen, Johannes A. B. van, trans. *The Mahābhārata, Volume 1: 1. The Book of the Beginning.* Chicago: University of Chicago Press, 1973.

—. *The Mahābhārata, Volume 2: The Book of the Assembly Hall, 3. The Book of the Forest.* Chicago: University of Chicago Press, 1975.

Collins, Steven. *Nirvana and other Buddhist Felicities.* Cambridge: Cambridge University Press, 1998.

Feer, Leon and Rhys-Davids, Caroline, eds., *The Saṃyutta-nikāya.* London: Pali Text Society, 1973-1989.

Fitzgerald, James. "Dharma and its Translation in the Mahābhārata," *Journal of Indian Philosophy* 32 (2004): 671–685.

—. "Making Yudhiṣṭhira the King: the Dialectics of Violence in the Mahābhārata," *Rocznik Orientalistyczny* LIV/1 (2001): 63–92.

—. *The Mahābhārata, Volume 7.* Chicago: University of Chicago Press, 2004.

Gethin, Rupert. "He Who Sees Dhamma Sees Dhammas: Dhamma In Early Buddhism," *Journal of Indian Philosophy* 32 (2004): 513–542.

Goswami, Bijoya, trans. *Lalitavistara. English Translation with Notes.* Calcutta: The Asiatic Society, 2001.

Hiltebeitel, Alf. *Dharma.* Honolulu: University of Hawai'i Press, 2010.

— *Dharma: Its Early History in Law, Religion, and Narrative.* New York: Oxford University Press, 2011.

—. *Rethinking the Mahābhārata: A Reader's Guide to the Education of the Dharma King.* Chicago: University of Chicago Press, 2001.

Horner, Isaline B., trans. *Milinda's Questions.* London: Luzac, 1964.

—. *The Collection of the Middle Length Sayings (Majjhima Nikāya),* Vol. 2. London: Luzac, 1957.

Hudson, Emily T. *Disorientating Dharma: Ethics and the Aesthetics of Suffering in the Mahābhārata.* New York: Oxford University Press, 2013.

Kern, Hendrik, trans. *Saddharma-Puṇḍārika or Lotus of the True Law.* New York: Dover, 1963, reprint. Original edition Oxford, 1884.

Masefield, Peter, trans. *Elucidation of the Intrinsic Meaning: So Named the Commentary on the Vimana Stories.* Oxford: Pali Text Society, 1989.

Masset, Danièle, trans. *Stances Des Theras (Theragāthā).* Bristol, UK: Pali Text Society, 2011.

Morris, R, Warder, A. K, and Hardy, E, eds. *The Aṅguttaranikāya.* London: Pali Text Society, 1955–1961.

Norman, Kenneth R., trans. *The Group of Discourses (Sutta-Nipāta).* London: Pali Text Society, 1984.

Olivelle, Patrick. "The Semantic History of Dharma: The Middle and Late Vedic Periods," *Journal of Indian Philosophy* 32 (2004): 491–511.

Sinha, Braj M. "*Arthaśāstra* Categories in the *Mahābhārata,*" in Arvind Sharma, ed., *Essays on the Mahābhārata,* pp. 380–383. Leiden: E. J. Brill, 1991.

Sukthankar, V. S., et al., eds. *The Mahābhārata.* Poona: Bhandarkar Oriental Research Institute, 1933-1969.

Sutton, Nick. "Aśoka and Yudhiṣṭhira: A Historical Setting for the Ideological Tensions of the Mahābhārata," *Religion* 27 (1997): 333–341.

Thera, Nyanaponika, and Bhikkhu Bodhi, trans. *Aṅguttara Nikāya: Discourses of the Buddha. An Anthology,* Part I. Kandy, Sri Lanka: Buddhist Publication Society, 1970; online edition, 2010.

Trenckner, Vilhelm, ed. *Majjhimanikāya.* London: Pali Text Society, 1974-79.

—, ed. *The Milindapañho: Being Dialogues between King Milinda and the Buddhist Sage Nāgasena.* London: Luzac, 1962.

Vaidya, Paraśurama L., ed. *Lalita Vistara.* Darbhanga: Mithila Institute, 1958.

—, ed. *Saddarmapundarikasūtraṃ.* Darbhanga: Mithila Institute, 1960.

AVŚ 19.68, 72::AVP.19.35.1–3: Using Oral Repositories of the Pre-redaction Veda

Dipak Bhattacharya
Visva Bharati University, Santiniketan, India

Introduction

AVŚ 19.68 and 19.72, parallel to AVP 19.35.2–3, defied an intelligible interpretation and translation from Sāyaṇa and William D. Whitney. Two unknown words, *vyácas* and *ávyas,* are the apparent source of the trouble. The second verse also speaks of *māyā́,* "extraordinary power," used in utilizing the two. The verses speak of using an orally current "unredacted" mass of Atharvan mantras and a primitive oral ritual manual. The considerable intellectual power required for the exercise has been called "extraordinary power." The *Śaunakīya* version shows structural deficiency when compared with its parallel in AVP 19.35.1–3, the original *tṛca* to which the verses belonged.

The verse-hymns under discussion in this paper, including three intervening hymns, run as follows in the VVRI edition of the *Atharvaveda Śaunakīya* (AVŚ):

AVŚ 19.68 = *Atharvaveda Paippalāda* (AVP) 19.35.2:
ávyasaś ca vyácasaś ca bílaṃ ví ṣyāmi māyáyā /
tā́bhyām uddhṛ́tya védaṃ átha kármāṇi kṛṇmahe //

AVŚ 19.69.1–4 = AVP 19.55.12–15 (Kashmir MS 19.54.11–14):
1. *jīvā́ stha jīvyā́saṃ sárvam ā́yur jīvyāsam /*
2. *upajīvā́ sthópa jīvyāsaṃ sárvam ā́yur jīvyāsam /*
3. *saṃjīvā́ stha sáṃ jīvyāsaṃ sárvam ā́yur jīvyāsam /*
4. *jīvalā́ stha jīvyā́saṃ sárvam ā́yur jīvyāsam /*

AVŚ 19.70.1 (AVP 20.43.1):
índra jī́va sū́rya jī́va dévā jī́vā jīvyā́sam ahám/ sárvam ā́yur jīvyāsam //

AVŚ 19.71.1:
stutā́ máyā varadā́ vedamātā́ prá codayantāṃ pāvamānī́ dvijā́nām /

ā́yuḥ prāṇám̐ prajā́m̐ paśúm̐ kīrtím̐ drávinam̐ brahmavarcasám /
máhyam̐ dattvā́ vrajata brahmalokám //

AVŚ 19.72.1 (AVP 19.35.3):

yásmāt kóśād udábharāma védam̐ tásminn antár áva dadhma enam /
kṛtám iṣṭám̐ bráhmaṇo vīryèṇa téna mā devās tápasā 'vatehá // [1]

Existing Interpretations

William D. Whitney considered AVŚ 19.68 an "obscure verse."[2] The obscurity persists in Ralph T. Griffith's translation.[3] Maurice Bloomfield did not include these in his translation[4] and Sāyaṇa's explanation, invoking tantric ideas, is partly anachronic.[5] All these have resulted in the verses remaining largely enigmatic.

Some new developments have opened the possibility of interpreting the verses anew. The earlier exegetes could not avail of a reliable version of the *Paippalāda-Saṃhitā* for comparison. Since then it has been reedited with help from new Oriya script manuscripts.[5] A comparison of the two recensions brings to light some structural peculiarities of Atharvavedic hymns, leading to the possibility of a new understanding of the verses and their textual history.

AVŚ 19.72 speaks of putting the Veda down in a receptacle. From this, Bloomfield concludes that at some point in time the AVŚ ended at 19.72. He adds that even before this, the book ends with its eighteenth *kāṇḍa.*[6] Charles R. Lanman has the same opinion.[7] This is mentioned to point to the importance the verses might have gained sometime in the history of the redaction of the AVŚ. As we shall see, however, the matter stands differently with the AVP.

The available English translations do not tally. Griffith's popular rendering is hardly a guide, and is cited only for the first verse under discussion, AVŚ 19.68. After that the citations are from Whitney and Lanman, and Sāyaṇa, for self-evident reasons.

AVŚ 19.68:

> Both of broad and narrow I with magic power unclose the mouth. With these when we have raised the bunch of grass we pay the holy rites.[8]

Védam does not mean "the bunch of grass," as understood by Griffith. This is because the raising of the *véda* from the *ávyas* and the *vyácas* is followed by *kármāṇi,* which Griffith correctly translates as "holy rites." It is only reasonable to conclude, then, that the meaning of "holy scripture," not a "bunch of grass," better suits the context.

Whitney's translation of this verse differs:

> Of non-expansion and expansion do I untie the aperture with magic; by those two having taken up the Veda, we then perform acts.[9]

Keeping *vedam* as such is correct, but Whitney emends the first word of the verse to *ávyacasaś* (*ca*) from the *ávyasaś* (*ca*) of the manuscripts.[10] Whitney follows Sāyaṇa in this, and also in translating his *avyacasas* as "of non-expansion." Sāyaṇa bases his interpretation on √*vyac* Cl, 3, "to extend": *vyacatir vyāptikarmā.*[11]

Word-by-word Analysis

Ávyasas and *Vyácasas*

The two key words of the verse are *ávyasaś* (*ca*) and *vyacasaś* (*ca*) from the stems *á-vy-as-* and *vyácas-*. AVP has the same reading. This forces us to disagree with Sāyaṇa and Whitney, and stick to the reading uniformly transmitted in both recensions. Also, it does not seem to me that there is a necessity to emend the received text.

The first word is not attested outside this verse but an etymological explanation will suit the context. The verb *vy* as (*vi-as*), "to separate, to divide," when compared with *vi-ny-āsa*, "arrangement," vyāsa "redactor," would seem quite appropriate here, provided that the context (discussed below) is taken into consideration. Vyāsa was later personified as the mythical redactor of the Vedas, the *Mahābhārata*, and the *Purāṇas. Ávyasas,* from the unattested radical noun *a-vy-as,* meaning "of the nonredaction (mantras)," though unattested, is not inappropriate or impossible.

So far as the proposed meaning is concerned, the onetime existence of unredacted mantras is a reality known in the Śāstric tradition. Cf. *Nirukta* 1.21:

> *sākṣātkṛtadharmāṇo ṛṣayo babhūvus, te 'varebhyo 'sākṣātkṛtadharmabhya upadeśena mantrān samprādur, upadeśāya glāyanto 'vare bilmagrahaṇāyemaṃ granthaṃ samāmnāsiṣur vedaṃ ca vedāṅgāni ca*
>
> The sages perceived dharma directly; they delivered the mantras by way of sermon to juniors who had not perceived dharma directly; growing averse to sermons the juniors recited this redaction called Veda and Vedāṅga in order to learn [dharma] part by part.

See also:

> *maṇḍalāny ṛṣayo dṛṣṭvā sarva eva samāgatāḥ /*
> *vinyāsaṃ dadṛśuḥ paścād iti vṛddhebhya āgamaḥ //*[12]

> Having seen (= composed) the *maṇḍala*s, the seers subsequently saw to the arrangement as they all came together—such is the tradition handed down from the elders.

In view of the reality of the existence of unredacted mantras prior to their oral redaction, it will not be surprising that the word *ávyasas* should mean "of the nonredaction (mantras)," meaning the floating mass of *ātharvaṇa* mantras before they were orally redacted into twenty *kāṇḍa saṃhitā*. Naturally, this should mean the entire mass of floating *ātharvaṇa* mantras, unwieldy and unemployable without aid (i.e., without notes), as far as possible and appropriate in an oral tradition.

The idea of a nonredaction should be preceded by the knowledge of redaction. Most probably the poet knew of the ten-*maṇḍala* redaction of the *Ṛgveda*. This came into being before the twenty-*kāṇḍa Atharvaveda*. The *Nirukta* (7.8, 7.20, 11.16, 12.40) uses the term *daśatayī* to mean the *Ṛgveda* in ten *maṇḍala*s, but it does not speak of a twenty-*kāṇḍa* redaction. The word *viṃśin* occurs in the sense of the twenty-*kāṇḍa Atharvaveda* in the phrase *viṃśino 'ṅgirasaḥ*[13] in *Mahābhāṣya* on P 5.2.37, and also in *Gopatha-Brāhmaṇa* 1.1.8.1. Our verse is certainly later than the *Ṛgveda* and older than the *Mahābhāṣya* and the *Gopatha-Brāhmaṇa*. Hence, there is nothing wrong in assuming the Atharvavedic poet's knowledge of the existence of the Ṛgvedic redaction and his mentioning the floating mass of Atharvan mantras as "nonredaction."

As to the etymology of the word, a stem ending in the verb √*as* is unattested. But radical nouns from –*s*-ending roots, e.g., *visrásaḥ*< *visrá*(*ṃ*)*s*- (RV 2.39.4), are not unknown. So, theoretically, the formation of a noun from √*as* is not impossible as *Augenblicksbildung*. The word *viśrás*, unlike our proposed *vy-as*, is, however, in the weak grade. Nominal formation from √*as* and its weakening, found in *-sti*, are, however, both rare. Also it is not impossible that the weak grade has not occurred by way of avoiding homonymy in the resultant form that would have been **viṣ*.

As for *vyácasaś ca*, it might first appear that since the natural contrast to the "unredacted" is the redaction, the same should be the meaning of *vyácas;* however, it is difficult to accept this meaning. In that sense, the root √*vic* cl. 7, "to sift," would have been suitable, and not √*vyac* cl. 3, "to extend." The former is not known to have the normal-grade vowel between the last two radicals generating –*ya*- in Sanskrit; cf. AVŚ 6.61.2: *viveca;* RV 7.3.4: *vivekṣi;* etc. Unless we admit an erroneously conceived and unattested *schwebeablaut*, a derivation from √*vic* is unacceptable.

There is also difficulty with an etymology based on √*vyac* cl. 3, "to extend." The literal meaning of *vyacas*, "the extended one" or "expanse," which none of the previous interpreters could avoid, hardly suits a "redaction." Second, the context indicates ritual connection. The untying of the two apertures is followed by ritual acts. That means there are two repositories from which the material for ritual is collected. If one of them is, as we guessed, a floating mass of Atharvan mantras, then the other should not be a redaction of the compositional units of prayers, like the mantras of the *Ṛgveda* and the *Paippalāda-Saṃhitā,* which as such do not contain rules for ritual; instead it should be a manual for ritual, a forerunner of the *Brāhmaṇa*s. Some discussion on the possible nature of such a hypothetical manual is called for before enquiring into the etymology of *vyácas.*

If *vyácas* is a ritual book of the AV it should have been in its rudimentary form at that time—a collection not of mantras but of *pratīka*s, or other hints as per the evidence of the ancient manuals (as distinct from the later *paddhati*s and digests) handed down to us in the form of *Brāhmaṇa*s. Some idea of its actual earliest form during such rudimentary existence, when the *Saṃhitā* literature was still being composed, can be inferred partly from Dārila's description of contemporary use of various types of *Saṃhitā*s in the introductory lines to the commentary on the *Kauśika-Sūtra.*[14] But, as we shall see below, in order to fill up certain gaps one may also have to correlate that to the current practice adopted by priests.

Oral Repositories, Redaction, and the Book

Dārila speaks of three varieties of *Saṃhitā*s in use: *ārṣīsaṃhitā,* "the seer's book," *ācāryasaṃhitā,* "the teacher's book," and *vidhiprayogasaṃhitā,* "the book for rules and application." As explained by Dārila himself, the *ārṣīsaṃhitā* is the complete ideal text that was revealed to the *ṛṣi.* The second book is the one with which the *ācārya* teaches the student. Here the repetitions are avoided. That means the manuscripts with understood verses that are used by modern scholars for editions consist of *ācāryasaṃhitā*s. The *vidhiprayogasaṃhitā* is for the priest's use. He adds suitable indications to parts of the mantras to be employed by him.

Since the *vidhiprayogasaṃhitā* is for the priest's use for practice, it could perhaps vary from priest to priest, as the priest would keep in memory mostly those mantras that are usually necessary. We have to assume a few things not said by Dārila. Thus, a situation may arise in which the priest requires a new mantra for an uncommon rite that has become necessary for some event or for any reason. Naturally, the priest will collect that from the redaction, as the Paippalādas of Orissa do to this day.

According to my knowledge of Vaidika reciters, most of them have only memorized parts of the Veda. The Orissa Paippalādas keep in memory only a few clusters of mantras that are most often necessary. So also do the Āpastambins of South India whom I have met.

Among the Paippalādas, the commonly used mantras (*vivāha, upanayana,* very popular *kāmya* rites) are memorized or at least recorded in a modern school exercise-type notebook that is placed conveniently nearby, so that it is easily available when the necessity to consult it arises. The rest of the book remains in palm leaf folios, the carefully preserved written repertory called *Biśkāṇḍi,* "the twenty-*kāṇḍa* (*Atharvaveda*)." If the *Biśkāṇḍi* has to be consulted for some rarely used mantra or for any other reason, the book is brought down from the loft where it is usually kept, the necessary part is photocopied, and the palm-leaf folio is returned to safekeeping in storage.

The picture in the post-redaction oral age could not have been much different, except for the fact that one had to use oral records instead of written books, which became common only in the middle ages. One had the living Vaidika, as described, among others, in the *Ṛkprātiśākhya,* Ch. 15, and hinted at in Dārila's *Bhāṣya* on the *Kauśika-Sūtra,* who would act for the book. The priests who regularly perform the village service would know the essential parts necessary for the most common rituals. If more would be necessary they would go to the living oral repository, a Vaidika who could recite the entire *Saṃhitā* and thus functioned like a latter-day written manuscript.

It should be clear that for an ancient priest this redaction would be human and oral. The period we are dealing with, however, has not yet seen the oral redaction. In the pre-redaction stage the floating mass of mantras preserved among many served as the big repository—our *ávyas.* The *vyácas,* if it had been the source of the ritual rules as we have posited, could have been a one-man affair and easier to handle. It is not difficult to surmise that the bigger floating repositories would not be easy to rummage through. I shall return to this topic below.

Let us try to comprehend the contemporary condition of the Vedas, as distinct from that in the age of post-redaction oral or written Vedas. There are floating unredacted mantras memorized by different poets. The mass of mantras in the memory of various composers would, naturally, vary in quantity, arrangement, and detail from poet to poet at first. Until the final redaction they might further change during the process of being handed down from generation to generation. The floating mass at this stage, preserved by families or the community as a whole, is the ávyas, a mass of unwieldy mantras that exist in the memories of several people.

Apart from this, I propose that there exist the *vyácas,* the collection of ritual specific mantras, or rather of their *pratīka*s, the primitive version of both the *vidhiprayogasaṃhitā,* mentioned by Dārila, and of the *Brāhmaṇa* texts—the edited, official, and common *vidhiprayogasaṃhitā* of the late Vedic period that has been handed down to us.

The abovementioned matter is emphasized to point to the compelling situation that should be kept in mind in determining the meaning of *ávyas* and *vyácas* and their relation. We have to keep in mind that if *ávyas* are regarded as unredacted floating mantras, then *vyácas* cannot be regarded as the redacted *Saṃhitā.* The floating mass and the redaction belong to two mutually exclusive stages of evolution of the mantra material. Hence, the *vyácas* could not be the redaction. It would rather be the first ritual-based collection of mantras or *pratīka*s, most probably with hints of the ritual context, a fact strongly indicated by the sentence *átha kármāṇi kṛṇmahe* and the mention of *bílam* (see below). Second, the employment of mantras under these conditions must have involved a complex and difficult process, requiring mastery of mnemonic techniques. Even then, either two or more men would have to have been involved in the rummaging process, or there were prodigies who kept the ritual rules and order and the employable mantras separately in memory.

Another fact should be mentioned in passing. We know from the *Saṃhitā*s of the *Yajurveda* that a ritual-based collection can also be a mantra-*saṃhitā*. But since the overall arrangements of the received *saṃhitā*s of AV (also of RV) are not according to rituals, as with the *Yajurveda saṃhitā*s, then the ritual-based collection, if such a thing is really meant by *vyácas,* could not have been the first redaction of the AV *Saṃhitā.* However, the matter requires more in-depth treatment, which I will take up in the section on "Ritual and Compositional Hymn Structures in the Two *Atharvaveda*s," below.

The above, partly hypothetical, explanatory account of *vyácas* is proposed on the ground of circumstantial evidence. It calls also for some Vedic internal comparison apart from etymological consideration for support.

Karl Hoffmann[15] has shown that an accusative *vyac-viañc* means *schöpfen,* "to draw (from)" in, e.g., AVŚ 4.27.2: *útsam ákṣitaṃ vyácanti yé sádā yá āsiñcánti rásam óṣaadhīṣu,* "Who always draw from[16] the source, who water the plants with the sap,"[17] or *imáṃ sāhasráṃ śatádhāraṃ útsaṃ vyacyámānaṃ sarirásya mádhye* (VS 13.49, etc.): "This thousandfold, hundred-streamed source, which is drawn upon, i.e., from which one draws in the midst of the ocean."[18] Accordingly, when *vyácas* is conceived of as a source from which ritual material can be drawn, its etymology may be justified, after Hoffmann's plausible explanation, as from *vi+√añc.*

On this ground, the unattested *-as* ending noun *vyácas* may be understood. It is not from the radical √*vyac* but from *vi+√añc,* "to draw from a source," in its weak grade that the noun *vyácas,* meaning "the source to be drawn upon," has been formed.

As to the historical propriety of the formation of an *-as*–ending noun from *vi√añc/ac,* there are quite a few *-as*–ending nouns derived from verbal roots, many of them inherited,[19] such as *ávas, śrávas, édhas,* etc. The weak grade too is found in inherited words with Indo-European cognates, such as *uṣás* <√*vas, upás* <√*vap,* and *bhiyás* < √*bhī.* So there cannot be much objection against the proposed derivation of *vy-ac-as* from *vi√añc.*

From the meaning and relevance of *ávyasaś ca vyácasaś ca:* "Of the unredacted and the source (of the holy act)," I now turn to the meaning of the next part of the verse.

***Bílaṃ ví ṣyāmi māyáyā:* "I unbind the orifice by special power."**

It was pointed to above that if our inference about *ávyas* and *vyácas* is correct, that is to say, if they are two oral repertories, then it could not have been easy to know where and how to seek hints about a ritual from the *vyácas* and then find the relevant full mantra or mantras in the unwieldy mass of á*vyas.*

Let us try again to comprehend the process. A ritual is to be performed. Its necessary mantras are indicated in the *vyácas.* The Atharvan priest has to find the hint first from the *vyácas,* then he has to find the entire set of mantras in the *ávyas.* In short, he is compelled to go from the arranged to the unarranged. Some of this must have been a common affair, but not every ritual and its mantras were commonplace. For these, aside from depending on human help as far as available, mastering a mnemonic technique would have been required. It is not difficult to comprehend that the Atharvan priest could not proceed without having memorized many things—complexes of procedures and mantras.

The process is figuratively described in our verse. *Ávyas* and *vyácas* are imagined as two big jars, and finding the necessary material from within them is imagined as opening an orifice. Mastery of the technique of finding the necessary material, with or without brotherly help (about which we cannot know) is understood as an extraordinary power (*māyā́*). This is not unnatural. The whole phenomenon takes place on the intellectual plane—the act, its objects, and its instruments. Since all in it appear as shadows of physical dealings, the driving power seems extraordinary.

We can infer the actual nature of the technique. Memorization was the prime instrument, but it had to be aided too. From the existing texts we at least know that they are arranged according to some principles. The *Yajurvedas*, for example, have a visible order. There is an order in the *Āśvalāyana Śrautasūtra* and the *Aitareya-Brāhmaṇa* as well. The *vyácas* too must have had some system of order. Mastery of these materials is the *māyā́* of the poet-priest, the key with which one can rummage through the oral mass of mantras or *pratīkas* and hints. This is the act that is meant by the phrase *bílaṃ ví ṣyāmi māyáyā*, "I open the orifice by special power," i.e., gaining access to the necessary material through superior knowledge of the two collections.

Now the poet extracts the *veda* from the two. This *veda* cannot be the Veda, i.e., the "canonical redaction," as we understand it. Without doubt it is holy but it is a redaction, the making of which only a primitive oral collection of *pratīkas* with ritual hint has been formed as a primitive *Brāhmaṇa*. The *Saṃhitā* is still not available. The term *veda*, however, is already in use. Perhaps this had something to do with the emergence of the ritual manual. At this stage the floating mantras, together with this, were understood as the Veda.

According to the proposed explanation we may thus translate AVŚ 19.68:

> Of the unredacted [mass of Atharvan verses] and of the source [book of ritual], I untie [the covering of] the orifice by [my] extraordinary power. [Then,] having extracted the Veda [of the necessary rules and mantras] from them, subsequently we perform the [ritual] works.

AVŚ 19.72: 19.69–19.71 and AVP 19.35

The six verses of AVŚ 19.69.1–4, 70.1, 71.1 that follow the verse-hymn 19.68 appear to be later insertions. This means that, as in AVP, it is the last verse, 19.72 (AVP 19.35.3), that stood after 19.68 (AVP 19.35.2). I will show its relevancy in that position before taking up the extraneous elements of AVŚ.

It will be clear from the location indicated in the citation given at the beginning of the paper that the two verse-hymns AVŚ 19.68 and 19.72 occur as two consecutive verses, 19.35.2–3 in the AVP. They are preceded by 19.35.1, which, together with the two verses under discussion, forms a compositional unit known as a tṛca, which gives the nineteenth *kāṇḍa* (AVŚ 6) its name. The three verses, AVP 19.35.1–3, form a compositional unit and its aforementioned context indicates that they are also meant for a specific ritual. This is dealt with below.

AVP hymn 19.35 runs as follows:

1. *viśve devā idaṃ havir ādityāsaḥ saparyata(ḥ)*[20] /
   asmin yajñe mā vyathiṣyam ṛtāya haviṣ kṛtam //
2. *avyasaś ca vyacasaś ca bilaṃ viṣyāmi māyayā* /
   tābhyām uddhṛtya vedam atha karmāṇi kṛṇmahe //
3. *yasmāt kośād udabharāma vedaṃ tasminn antar ava dadhma enam/*
   kṛtam iṣṭaṃ brahmaṇo vīriyeṇa tena mā devā tapasā 'vateha //

1. O All Gods, O Ādityas, this offering is the worshiper's! May I not falter in this sacrifice, the offering is made for the truth.

(For this, the translation of AVŚ 19.68 given above is repeated:)

2. Of the unredacted [mass of Atharvan verses] and of the source [book of ritual], I untie [the covering of] the orifice by [my] special power. [Then] having extracted the Veda [with necessary rules and mantras] from them, subsequently we perform the [ritual] works.
3. The repository from which we dug up the Veda, within that do we set it down. The sacrifice has been performed with the might of the prayer, with that fervor, O gods, do you favor me here!

In terms of composition, the three-verse hymn constitutes an integral unit. The All-gods and the Ādityas are meant to be celebrated without faltering, according to the rules. The poet speaks of actually performing the ritual according to rules laid down in the manual, and then "puts down" the utilized rule and mantra to where they belong.

The verses are related also in ritual procedures described in the much later *Kauśika-Sūtra* (Kauś). Among other verses, Kauś. 139.10 prescribes AVŚ 19.68 in the ceremony of introduction to Vedic study. AVŚ 19.72 is prescribed by Kauś. 139.25 at the end of the *svādhyāya.* In contrast, while AVŚ 19.69 is mentioned in Kauś. 3.4 in connection with a different ceremony, AVŚ 19.70–71 are not noted in it.

The intervening verses do not fit into the compositional structure. When one compares the consecutive verses of the AVP *tṛca* with the six intervening verses in three hymns in AVŚ, it appears that the thematic unity in an account of ritually utilizing pre-redaction Vedic entities has been disturbed by the insertion of mantras meant as general prayers.

The English translation of the intervening verses of AVŚ (text at the beginning) is given below.

AVŚ 19.69:

1. You are living, may I live. May I live the whole span of life.
2. You are subsisting on, may I subsist on. May I live the whole span of life.
3. You are living together, may I live together. May I live the whole span of life.
4. You are lively, may I live. May I live the whole span of life.

AVŚ 19.70:

Live, O Indra; live, O Sūrya; live, ye, O gods; may I live; may I live my whole life-time.

These verses are not in praise of the Veda or related to any relevant theme. Even if these five verses are somehow understood as the matter the poet means to extract from and put back into the repositories, 19.71 is not relevant to the context. At first 19.71 may look a bit different from 19.69 and 19.70 and as apparently related to the Veda theme, but on close examination it appears to be an insertion.

Whitney, admitting that the rendering hardly gave any sense,[21] translates 19.71:

> Praised by me [is] the boon-giving Veda-mother. Let them urge on the soma-hymn of the twice-born. Having given to me life-time, breath, progeny, cattle, fame, property, Vedic splendor, go ye to the brahma-world.

The concept of the "boon-giving Veda-mother" is new and post-Vedic. Outside AVŚ 19.71 the word varadā occurs in Vedic literature in *Taittirīyāraṇyaka* 10.26 and *Nārāyaṇopaniṣad* 34a, in a verse beginning with *ā yātu varadā devī,* etc., as an adjective of Gāyatrī. The phrase *varadā vedamātā* is found in its only Vedic occurrence outside AVŚ in a corrupt, partially accented version of the AVŚ verse in the same *Nārāyaṇopaniṣad* (36b),[22] which is an appendix to the *Taittirīyāraṇyaka.* The word occurs also in some minor *Upaniṣad*s that can be ignored as non-Vedic occurrence. Even the *Taittirīyāraṇyaka* itself is late, while the *Nārāyaṇopaniṣad* is almost Puranic. In view of this, it reasonable to suspect that the addition of this verse to AVŚ took place during its revision and re-edition, as suggested by Bloomfield.[23] The re-editors chose the particular location in AVŚ in view of the occurrence of the concept of Veda found in it. However, as I have proposed, the Veda and, consequently, its concept, were still in a nebulous stage. To conceive the Veda as a Puranic, or at least late Vedic, wish-fulfilling mother at such a stage is absurd.

Ritual and Compositional Hymn Structures in the Two *Atharvaveda*s

The question was raised above that the *vyácas,* as we conceive of them—as a collection of mantras arranged in some ritual order with hints—could have been the original AV *Saṃhitā.* My answer to this question is in the negative, and coming to this decision was not difficult. We know that ritually arranged *Saṃhitā*s do exist but they are limited to the *Yajurveda.* The oldest Vedic Saṃhitā, the *Ṛgveda,* is mainly compositionally structured. There is, of course, a deity-wise arrangement, but there too the size of the hymn counts also as the composer's family. This chronological precedence of the compositional structure speaks against a ritually arranged AV emerging first as its *Saṃhitā.*

The matter is verifiable. A comparison of the hymn structures of the *tṛca* and *ekarca kāṇḍa*s of the two *Atharvaveda*s points to the same conclusion. The position of AVŚ looks interesting. AVP 19 and 20, as well as their parallels, AVŚ 6 and 7, are called *tṛca* and *ekarca-kāṇḍa,*[24] respectively. Apparently, however, the name is more valid with AVŚ than with AVP. The apparent validity is due to the fact that most of the hymns in the AVŚ *tṛca kāṇḍa,* 122 out of 142, consist of three verses; thus, they are actually *tṛca* hymns. Similarly, many of its *ekarca-kāṇḍa* hymns (60 out of 123 or 56 out of 118)[25] also consist of one verse only. On the other hand, in the AVP's *tṛca-kāṇḍa,* i.e., in AVP 19, the hymns consist of five or more *tṛca*s, and in AVP 20 there are usually ten *ekarca*s in a hymn. This difference brings out important distinguishing features of the AVŚ, as shown below.

The *tṛca*s of AVŚ form ritual units. That means each unit is wholly applicable to a single ritual. There is nothing peculiar in this; many *tṛca*s extracted from Ṛgvedic hymns have been enjoined for rituals in the *Āśvalāyana-Śrautasūtra.* There is a technical rule for this: *adhike tṛcaṃ sarvatra* (Āśv.Ś.S. 1.1.19), "When more than a *pāda* of a verse occurs in the rule for employment, a unit of three consecutive verses is to be understood." While this is not difficult to understand, the formation of a whole hymn with a triad of verses is peculiar to AVŚ. Moreover, when one compares them with the AVP version it appears that the *tṛca* units have been extracted out of bigger units whose structures have not been disturbed in AVP.

This means that the AVP *tṛca-kāṇḍa* hymns have been handed down in their original form as single hymns. Unfortunately, until now no attempt has been made to examine the unity, if any, of the *tṛca-kāṇḍa* hymns of AVP. As a result, their compositional unity has never come to notice. The following examination may show that such a unity does exist, at least in the examined hymns of the AVP *tṛca-* and *ekarca-kāṇḍa*.

AVP 19.1. This hymn consists of 15 verses; that is, theoretically, of five *tṛca*s. Of these, only nine verses, 19.1.1–6 and 13–15, occur in the AVŚ *tṛca-kāṇḍa* as 6.1.1–3, 6.2.1, 3, 2, and 6.3.1–3. Verses 7–8 occur in AVŚ outside its *tṛca-kāṇḍa* as 1.26.1–2, and verses 9–12 are not found in AVŚ.

In AVP to the end of 6b the prayer is mainly an altruistic extolment of Savitṛ and Indra. In one instance (verse 3) it praises Savitṛ for producing riches without any desire to hurt others. This is followed by a half verse (6cd) of *āṅgirasa,* a violent witchcraft character desiring the death of enemies, and one full verse (7) for warding off missiles, which is a continuation of the charm against enemies in the preceding half-verse. It is noteworthy that this seventh verse, and also the eighth, occurs in AVŚ 1, which means not in its *tṛca-kāṇḍa.* This will be seen below. In AVP 19.1.8–9 the friendship and protection of the gods and their wives are requested. This theme—prayer for protection—continues to the end. Even evil beings are praised for this in verse 10, though after verse 10 only the common gods are invoked for protection.

In AVP the *āṅgirasa* verse 19.1.6 ends a *tṛca,* but in the AVŚ *tṛca-kāṇḍa* it comes in the middle of a *tṛca,* the second hymn of AVŚ 6, where the sequence is 1, 3, 2 with reference to the AVP order. As noted above, the seventh and eighth verses of the AVP hymn do not occur after AVŚ 6.2 but in AVŚ 1.26. It may be noted that a meaningful sequence visible in AVP is thereby disturbed in AVŚ. When we take the AVP hymn as a whole, the *āṅgirasa* theme of verses 6cd and 7 may be regarded as occurring in the mid-part of the hymn. Now the initial five and a half verses can be regarded as preparatory to the intended prayer of the hymn—to kill the enemy and ward off evil. This petition desiring harm to others is followed by seven verses of nonviolent type. One can interpret the mid-hymn *āṅgirasa* prayer of 19.1.6cd and 7, flanked by two series of peaceful prayers, as the climax of the whole prayer. This mid-hymn climax is not an unnoticed feature of Vedic prayers and, sometimes, of discourses.[26]

If the above observations are correct, this means that there is a unified theme in the AVP hymn that has been disturbed, purposefully it appears, in various ways in AVŚ. The latter changes the order of AVP 19.1.4, 5, 6 to 1, 3, 2 in AVŚ 6.2, thereby breaking the chain of the witchcraft theme it had formed with AVP 19.1.7. It does not stop there. Shifting verse 7 to *kāṇḍa* 1 undermines its *āṅgirasa* character and thereby any such perception of a unified prayer. A detached desire that missiles should remain away is a harmless appeal for protection; only the association of desire with the previous invocation for killing infused the hymn with an *āṅgirasa* air. That is done away with in AVŚ by setting two consecutive verses apart in two different *kāṇḍa*s and by regarding each *tṛca* of the AVP hymn as separate hymns.

However, this mid-climax, parabolic structure is not universal, nor is it that the same type of unity will be found in every hymn. But the AVP *tṛca-kāṇḍa* hymns appear to be compositionally integrated. Since the matter has been treated elsewhere,[27] I refrain from further discussion of the hymn structures found in the other hymns of the nineteenth *kāṇḍa*. I end this section with brief observations on the first hymn of AVP 20 and its AVŚ parallels.

AVP 20.1 consists of ten verses. Their parallels are dispersed without any visible order in six hymns of the AVŚ, as shown below.

> P. 20.1.1–2 = Ś. 7.1.1–2; 1.3 = 7.2.1; 1.4 = 7.43.1; 1.5, 7, 8, 9 = 7.6.1, 4, 2, 3; 1.6 = 7.7.1; 1.10 = 7.4.1

The disjointed presentation and the absence of any order hinder perceiving any thematic unity in the AVŚ verses, but the AVP hymn is rituo-cosmogonic. The Atharvavedic character of the first hymn somehow eluded Whitney, who commented upon the initial verses of the AVŚ.7 in dismissive language: "The book like some of those preceding, begins with mystic, obscure and un-Atharvanic material."[28] The adjective "un-Atharvanic" contradicts Whitney's own observation that some preceding *kāṇḍa*s begin with similar material. AVŚ 2 (AVP 2.6), 4 (AVP 5.2), and 5 (AVP 6.2) also begin similarly. RV 4.58 is similar, and also, in part, RV 1.164. These are records of attempts, begun in the late Ṛgvedic period and continued in the *Atharvaveda*, at a cosmogonic conceptualization of the ritual fire.[29] The hymn under discussion, while exhibiting some similarity, is more advanced than these, in that it has more abstract qualities, such as "deep thought," "mind," "third brahman"—counterpart of the third quarter of *vāk*—and the fourth name of the cow, i.e., human speech.

The first four verses deal with divine and human speech; verse 5 extols the infinite (*aditi*) as everything; verse 6 extols the sons of both Diti and Aditi and the "great powerful" gods; verses 7, 8, and 10 refer to the production of strength (food?), to the keepers of good vow, and to good offerings, respectively, and verse 9 refers to the divine boat; these are all praises of the offering in cryptic language.

The translation given below is, for all practical purposes, the one done by Whitney of the parallel AVŚ verses.[30] Some stylistic changes replacing archaic forms have been made and the verses are arranged in the order of the AVP hymn. Since this is a translation of the AVŚ verses made in the order found in AVP, it should be decisive in determining if a thematic unity really existed in an integral hymn that any AVŚ rearrangement disturbed.

7.1.1: *dhītī́ vā yé ánayan vācó ágraṃ mánasā vā yé 'vadann ṛtā́ni/ tṛtī́yena bráhmaṇā vāvṛdhānā́s turī́yeṇāmanvata nā́ma dhenóḥ* // = AVP

Either they who by meditation led the beginning of speech, or who by mind spoke righteous things—increasing with the third prayer, with the fourth [they] perceived the name of the cow.

7.1.2: *sá veda putráḥ pitáraṃ sá mātáraṃ sá sūnúr bhuvat sá bhuvat púnarmaghaḥ / sá dyā́m aurṇod antárikṣaṃ suvàr sá idáṃ víśvam abhavat sá ā́bhavat* // = AVP

He the son knows the father, he the mother; he has been the son, he has been one of generous returns; he enveloped the sky, the atmosphere, he the heaven; he became this all; he came to be here.

7.2 (AVP 3) (verse-hymn): *átharvāṇaṃ pitáraṃ devábandhuṃ* (AVP *viśvadevaṃ*) *mātúr gárbhaṃ pitúr ásuṃ yúvānam / yá imáṃ yajñáṃ mánasā cikéta prá ṇo vocas tám ihéhá bravaḥ* // cd AVP *ya īṃ ciketā amṛtasya dhāman nityasya rāyaḥ paridhīṃr apaśyat*

Father Atharvan, god-relative, mother's fetus, father's life-breath, young, who understands with the mind this sacrifice—him may you proclaim to us here, here may you speak! (AVP cd: "who has known the abode of immortality, he saw the line encompassing the permanent treasure.")

7.43 (AVP 4) (verse-hymn): *śivā́s ta ékā áśivās ta ékāḥ sárvā bibharṣi sumanasyámānaḥ / tisró vā́co níhitā antár ásmin tā́sām ékā ví papātā́nu ghóṣam* //

AVP . . . *ahṛṇīyamānaḥ/guhā vāco nihitās tisra etā eked idaṃ vi babhūvānu sarvam* / Propitious to thee are some, unpropitious to thee are some; all you bear without malice. Three speeches are laid within him (it?); of these one flew away (*vi papāta;* Whitney, "fell asunder," i.e., became the varied human speech? Cf. the AVP version)[31] following sound.

7.6.1 (AVP 5): *áditir dyáur áditir antárikṣam áditir mātā́ sá pitā́ sá putráḥ / víśve devā́ áditiḥ páñca jánā áditir jātám áditir jánitvam* // = AVP

Aditi is heaven, Aditi the mid-region, Aditi mother, she father, she son; all the gods are Aditi, the five races; Aditi is what is born, Aditi what is to be born.

7.7 (AVP 6) (verse-hymn): *díteḥ putrā́ṇām áditer akāriṣam áva devā́nāṃ bṛhatā́m anarmáṇām/*
té ṣāṃ hí dhā́ma gabhiṣák samudríyaṃ náinān námasā paró asti káś caná //

b Read *ávo * * anarváṇām* = RV 10.36.11b; AVP . . . *akārṣaṁ mahāśarna-ṇāṃ mahatām anṛmṇām / * * * * naiṣāṃ ye 'pasaḥ * * kiṃ cana //* (The AV readings are emendable.)

Of Diti's sons, of Aditi's, I have commemorated the aid, of the great inviolable gods; for their domain is deep in the sea; no one whosoever has surpassed them by homage. (AVP d: "nothing is beyond those who are active.")

7.6.4 (AVP 7): *vā́jasya nú prasavé mātáraṃ mahī́m áditiṃ nā́ma vácasā karāmahe /*
yásyā upástha urùv àntárikṣaṃ sā́ naḥ śárma trivárūthaṃ ní yachāt //

cd AVP *yasyām idaṃ viśvaṃ bhuvanam āviveśa sā no devī suhavā śarma yacchatu //*

Now, in the impulse of might, will we commemorate with utterance the great mother, Aditi by name, whose lap is the broad atmosphere; may she confirm to us thrice-defending protection. (AVP: "into whom all this becoming entered, she the radiant, easy to call, give us protection.")

7.6.2 (AVP 8): *mahī́m ū ṣú mātáraṃ suvratā́nām ṛtásya pátnīm ávase havāmahe /*
tuvikṣatrā́m ajárantīm urūcī́ṃ suśármāṇam áditiṃ supráṇītim //

We call for aid verily on the great mother of those of good courses, the spouse of righteousness, on her of mighty authority, not growing old, wide-spreading, on the well-sheltering, well-conducting Aditi.

7.6.3 (AVP 9): *sutrā́māṇaṃ pṛthivī́ṃ dyā́m anehásaṃ suśármāṇam áditiṃ supráṇītim /*
dáivīṃ nā́vaṃ suvaritrā́m ánāgaso ásravantīm ā́ ruhemā suvastáye / /

The well-preserving earth, the unenvious sky, the well-sheltering, well-conducting Aditi, the well-oared ship of the gods, unleaking, may we guiltless, embark on for well-being.

7.4 (AVP 10) (verse-hymn): *ekáyā ca daśábhiś cā suhū(u-ed)te dvā́bhyām iṣṭáye viṃśatyā́ ca /*
tisŕ̥bhiś ca váhase triṃśátā ca viyúgbhir vāya ihá tā́ ví muñca //

Both with one and with ten, O easily invoked one (fem.); with two and with twenty, for [our] wish; both with three and with thirty separately yoked ones drive you, O Vāyu—those do thou here release.

The key ideas of the hymn appeared to me as follows: (1) The first designers (= the forefathers) of fourfold speech (2) are magnified as one and all-pervasive, (3) and as the all-god father Atharvan, the womb of the mother, new born, the knower of immortality and of the circumference of the permanent treasure, (4ab) and the sustainer of both good and evil; (4cd) the three secret quarters of speech and the open one that became "all-this." (5) Aditi (infinite) as all-pervasive deity, most probably as divine speech and the female counterpart of Atharvan. (6) Aditi's counterpart Diti's (finite's) sons are praised, perhaps as the human quarter of speech or what it signifies. (7, 8) praise of Aditi's as mother continues; (9) sheltering and well-conducting Aditi as the protecting earth, the well-disposed heaven, and the well-oared faultless divine ship leading to welfare.

The last verse (Ś 7.4 = P 20.1.10) is a riddle. It seems to speak of one and 10 oblations or sacrifices, then of two and 20, and of three and 30. Most of the numbers involved—one, two, three, 10, 11, and 33 in particular—are holy numbers of completion. The holy numbers and also the riddle structure, like etymology,[32] seem to have been employed, aiming at enhancing the wish-fulfilling power of the prayer. Since the hymn can be understood without the last verse I will not go into further details here.

One may note the close stylistic and mythological similarity of the hymn with AVŚ 2.1 (AVP 2.6) and AVŚ 4.1 (AVP 5.1). The ritual fire is extolled as a cosmogonic element there. The world-generating couple, the sovereign "This" (*iyam*) and Vena/Bṛhaspati/father Atharvan, are magnified in the noted AV hymns as well.[33] The similarity shows that it is a single hymn dissected into several parts in AVŚ for ritual convenience.

It should be additionally stated here that in the AVP hymn there is something common with another comparable but more ancient Agni hymn, RV 4.1. The last quarter of the third AVP verse, *nityasya rāyaḥ paridhīṃr apaśyat,* "he saw the bordering line of the permanent treasure," is reminiscent of a sentence occurring in the aforementioned Ṛgvedic hymn glorifying the ritual Agni's speech related cosmic aspect: RV.4.1.10ab: *sá tū no agnír nayatu prajānánn áchā rátnaṃ devábhaktaṃ yád asya,* "May that Agni who knows lead us toward the treasure that is his divine share."

The foregoing discussion should have made clear my position regarding the occurrence of the long hymns of AVP *tṛca-* and *ekarca-kāṇḍa*s as divided into *tṛca-* and *ekarca* hymns in AVŚ. The purpose served by the operation was to create a convenient method of remembering the *tṛca*s for employing them separately in rituals.

As to the relative chronology of the two hymn arrangements, it is not difficult to conclude that the compositional structure came into being with the hymn. Rituals went on being invented, while the norm of employing *tṛca*s remained. The urge toward ritual and after-thought made the ritualist envisage an AVŚ 6 made of *tṛca* hymns and an AVŚ 7 of *ekarca* hymns, while AVP retained the original compositional structure/order.

At the beginning of this section I noted that the oldest Vedic *Saṃhitā,* the *Ṛgveda,* is mainly compositionally structured. The order of the Ṛgvedic *maṇḍala*s shows more concern with compositional structure or division than with any ritual order. The *soma* hymns have been collected at one place, the family books, too, begin according to the order of deities, but the order is a historically developed one and is not dictated by ritual necessity.

These considerations dissuade one from assuming that a ritually oriented repository of mantras should have been the first redacted *Saṃhitā* of the *Atharvaveda*. Formally, AVP is more akin to the *Ṛgveda* than is AVŚ.

AVŚ 19.72 as the Final Hymn of Some Nineteen-*kāṇḍa* Redaction

Bloomfield thought that the theme of putting the Veda back to its repository in AVŚ 19.72 indicated that AVŚ once ended at that verse.[34] Perhaps he was correct. Even then, Bloomfield did not note that 19.72 could have been conceived as the concluding verse of a redaction only on a wrong notion that missed the meaning of the original verse. The *tṛca* AVP 19.35 1–3, as I have shown, means to conclude a ritual and a *tṛca* but not a *Saṃhitā*. When an AVŚ redactor[35] puts the same verse at the end of a book he surely misses the meaning and spirit of the verse.

Still, Bloomfield was most probably correct. Ritualists were not concerned with any original context. There are well-known guiding maxims, such as *liṅgoktā devatā* or *liṅgokto viniyogaḥ,* "Know the deity/ritual employment from some sign." Such rules ask one to ignore the original context, if necessary. For a late Vedic (early medieval?) redactor, this must also have worked in arrangement. Something has been said about putting the Veda into something. Even though that does not mean redaction, the very occurrence of the idea of "putting something in" induced the late redactor to end his book there.

The rearrangement, discussed in the section "Ritual and Compositional Hymn Structures in the Two *Atharvavedas*," was also done under the impulse of a later developed notion of priority, and in negligence of the original context. The ritual had become the main focus of arrangement—its order in the *Yajurveda,* its employed mantra-units in the *Śaunakīya Atharvaveda.* So, other parameters of structural unity were deliberately obliterated. What had been ritually integrated was cut off from the original prayer-context in which it had been created, and was set apart as an independent unit.

Notes

1 The last two *kāṇḍa*s are in press.

2 William D. Whitney and Charles R. Lanman, *Atharva-veda-Saṁhitā* (Cambridge, MA: Harvard University, 1905), p. 1006.

3 Ralph T. H. Griffith, *The Hymns of the Atharva-Veda Translated with a Popular Commentary* (Benares: E. J. Lazarus, 1916–1917, second ed.).

4 Maurice Bloomfield, trans., *Hymns of the Atharvaveda: Together with Extracts from Ritual Books and Commentaries* (Delhi: Motilal Banarsidas, 2006, reprint).

5 Visva Bandhu, ed., *Atharveda (Śaunaka) with the Padapāṭha and Sāyaṇācāryaa's Commentary,* 5 vols. (Hosiarpur: VVRI, 1960–1964).

6 Maurice Bloomfield, *The Atharva-veda and the Gopatha-brāhmaṇa* (Strassburg: K. J. Trübner, 1899), pp. 34–35.

7 Whitney translated the nineteenth *kāṇḍa* into English but not the twentieth. Whitney and Lanman, *Atharva-veda-Saṁhitā,* 7, p. cxli; 8, pp. 895–898.

8 Griffith, *The Hymns of the Atharva-Veda,* vol. 2, pp. 319, 320.

9 Whitney and Lanman, *Atharva-veda-Saṁhitā,* p. 1006.

10 The manuscript reading of the first word, i.e., *ávyasaś,* is not given in the Berlin edition. Whitney reports the manuscript reading only in the notes to his translation; *Atharva-veda-Saṁhitā,* p. 1007. Lanman has a curious thing to report: "If I understand the Collation Book, W's P. actually begins with *avyacásaś cá vyácasáś cá. . .*"; *Atharva-veda-Saṁhitā,* p. 1007. That such a reading existed in the Paris manuscript is unlikely. In the Berlin edition by Rudolf von Roth and William D. Whitney, *Atharva-veda Saṁhitā,* vol. 1 (Berlin: Ferd. Dümmler's Verlagsbuchhandlung, 1856); reprinted with a foreword and correction of readings by M. Lindenau, edited *ávyacasaś ca* without mentioning the manuscript reading. But if *ávyacasaś ca* was actually a manuscript reading, Whitney would have reported that in his notes, where he clearly states: "All the mss have at the beginning *ávyasas*"; *Atharva-veda-Saṁhitā,* p. 1007. The long argument in defense of his emendation would not have been necessary if Lanman's guess was correct. Moreover, the report on manuscripts used by Whitney mentions

that M and P are identical; *Atharva-veda-Saṁhitā,* p. cxii. Since there is no report of such a reading in M we may be sure that such a reading did not exist in any manuscript. Perhaps Whitney meant something other than P's manuscript reading in his "Collation Book" reported by Lanman.

Visva Bandhu adds to the confusion by reporting that the Roth-Whitney edition read *ávyacaś ca; Atharveda (Śaunaka) with the Padapāṭha and Sāyaṇācāryaa's Commentary,* vol. 4, p. 2001. I do not know why Bandhu made this report when he had access to the Roth-Whitney edition. Moreover, Lindenau, in his article "Vorwart zur zweiten Auflage" (reprinted in Roth and Whitney, eds., *Atharva-veda Saṁhitā*) clearly reports that *ávyacasaśca vyacásaśca* is Roth and Whitney's own reading. The confusion is generated by the fact that the Berlin edition was never endowed with a scientific critical apparatus in a single volume. As I have already urged elsewhere, the manuscripts used by Roth and Whitney for the Berlin edition should be consulted again toward the preparation of a scientific critical apparatus of the AVŚ.

11 Sāyaṇa, in Visva Bandhu, trans., *Atharveda (Śaunaka) with the Padapāṭha and Sāyaṇācāryaa's Commentary.*

12 *Veṅkaṭa-Mādhava, Ṛgarthadīpikā, Aṣṭaka* 5, *Adhyāya* 8, verse 22 in the introductory part. See Dipak Bhattacharya, *The Paippalāda-Saṃhitā of the Atharvaveda* (Kolkata: The Asiatic Society, 2011), vol. 3, Introduction, p. lxix

13 The *Gopatha-Brāhmaṇa* has a different sense. See Bhattacharya, *The Paippalāda-Saṃhitā of the Atharvaveda,* Introduction, p. l.

14 H. R. Diwekar, et al., eds., *Kauśikasūtra-Dārilabhāṣya* (Poona: Tilak Maharashtra Vidyapitha, 1972), pp. 1–2.

15 Karl Hoffman, "Materialen zum altindischen Verbum," A*ufsätze zur Indo-Iranistik* 1 (1975): 162–165.

16 Whitney and Lanman, "who open"; see *Atharva-veda-Saṁhitā.*

17 Hoffmann, "Welche allezeit die unverziegliche Quelle schöpfen, die den Saft auf die Pflanzen gießen," in "Materialen zum altindischen verbum."

18 Hoffmann, "diese tausendfache, hundertströmige Quelle, die geschöpft wird (d.h. auf der geschöpft wird)," in "Materialen zum altindischen verbum"; Whitney and Lanman, "expanded," *Atharva-veda-Saṁhitā.* See Hoffmann, "Materialen zum altindischen Verbum," for references.

19 Jacob Wackernagel and Albert Debrunner, *Altindische Grammatik* (Göttingen: Vandenhoeck und Ruprícht, 1954), vol. 2, part 2, p. 229.

20 The Orissa manuscripts read *saparyata;* the Śāradā manuscript has *paryataḥ.*

21 Whitney and Lanham, "The translation given above makes no pretense to being an intelligent one"; *Atharva-veda-Saṁhitā,* p. 1008n.

22 See also Whitney and Lanham, *Atharva-veda-Saṁhitā,* 8, p. 1008n.

23 Bloomfield, *The Atharva-veda and the Gopatha-brāhmaṇa,* p. 34. See Bhattacharya, *The Paippalāda-Saṃhitā of the Atharvaveda,* vol. 3, p. li (= §3.4).

24 *Pañcapaṭalikā* 2.3 and 4; *Bṛhatsarvānukramaṇikā* 4.1 and 5.1 for AVŚ. The names of the AVP *kāṇḍa*s are mentioned in its manuscripts. See Bhattacharya, *The Paippalāda-Saṃhitā of the Atharvaveda,* vol. 3, pp. xlviii, xlix.

[25] Whitney and Lanham, *Atharva-veda-Saṁhitā*, 7, p. 388, counts 56 out of 118. The VVRI edition follows S. P. Pandit in counting the total number of verses and hymns differently. Pandit had followed the division of the *Bṛhat-Sarvānu-kramaṇikā*. See Pandit's Critical Notice, pp. 16–18.

[26] Stephanie W. Jamison,"Poetry and Purpose in the Ṛgveda: Structuring Enigmas," in Arlo Griffiths and Jan E. M. Houben, eds., *The Vedas: Texts, Language and Ritual: Proceedings of the Third Annual Vedic Workshop* (Leiden: Groningen, 2004), pp. 237–249; Bhattacharya, "The Vedic *dṛti* as Skin Float: AVP 2.19," p. 311; see remarks on "the maximum prayer" in AVP 2.19.4. Also relevant is Jean-Marie Verpoorten, "Unité et distinction dans les speculations rituelles védiques," *Archiv für Begriiffsgeschichte* 21/1 (1977): 63 (= AVP 2.3) on the unity and symmetry of a discourse. The last one deals with *Brāhmaṇa* prose.

[27] It comes up in the Introduction to AVP, vol. 4, AS edition (not yet published).

[28] Whitney and Lanham, *Atharva-veda-Saṁhitā*.

[29] Dipak Bhattacharya, *Mythological and Ritual Symbolism: A Study with Reference to the Vedic and Tantric Ani* (Calcutta: Sanskrit Pustak Bhandar, Calcutta, 1984), pp. 100–124, deals extensively with AVŚ 2.1 = AVP 2.6 and AVŚ 4.1 = AVP 5.2. M. Lindenau, *Zeitschrift für Indologie und Iranistik*, vol. 1 (1920), p. 43 ff, made the first attempt to treat AVŚ 2.1 extensively.

[30] Whitney and Lanham, *Atharva-veda-Saṁhitā*.

[31] See TS 7.5.6.2 for *vipapāta* = "fell asunder." See also Bhattacharya, "The Vedic *dṛti* as Skin Float: AVP 2.19," p. 319.

[32] Dipak Bhattacharya, *Indian Etymologists and Their Etymologies* (Kolkata: School of Vedic Studies, Rabindra Bharati University, 2002), pp. 49–50.

[33] Discussed, along with AVŚ 2.1 (AVP 2.6) in Bhattacharya, *Mythological and Ritual Symbolism*, pp. 101–124.

[34] Bloomfield, *The Atharva-veda and the Gopatha-brāhmaṇa*, p. 34.

[35] He must have been the second redactor. As Bloomfield shows in *The Atharva-veda and the Gopatha-brāhmaṇa*, the first one, Śaunaka by all probability, redacted an eighteen-*kāṇḍa* AVŚ. The second one extended the same to nineteen *kāṇḍa*s. The third redactor added the twentieth!

References

Bloomfield, Maurice, trans. *Hymns of the Atharvaveda: Together with Extracts from Ritual Books and Commentaries* (1897). Sacred Books of the East, vol. 42. F. Max Müller, general ed. Delhi: Motilal Banarsidas, 2006, reprint.

—. *The Atharva-veda and the Gopatha-brāhmaṇa*. Strassburg: K. J. Trübner, 1899.

Bhattacharya, Dipak. *Indian Etymologists and Their Etymologies.* Kolkata: School of Vedic Studies, Rabindra Bharati University, 2002.

—. *Mythological and Ritual Symbolism: A Study with Reference to the Vedic and Tantric Ani*. Calcutta: Sanskrit Pustak Bhandar, Calcutta, 1984.

—. *The Paippalāda-Saṃhitā of the Atharvaveda*, vol. 3. Kolkata: The Asiatic Society, 2011.

—. "The Vedic *dṛti* as Skin Float: AVP 2.19," *Journal of the Royal Asiatic Society*, Series 3, 18/3 (2008): 311–326.

Diwekar, H. R., et al., ed. *Kauśikasūtra-Dārilabhāṣya*. Poona: Tilak Maharashtra Vidyapitha, 1972.

Griffith, Ralph T. H. *The Hymns of the Atharva-Veda Translated with a Popular Commentary* (1895–1896). Benares: E. J. Lazarus, 1916–1917, second ed.

Hoffmann, Karl. "Materialen zum altindischen verbum," *Aufsätze zur Indo-Iranistik* 1 (1975): 162–182.

Jamison, Stephanie W. "Poetry and Purpose in the Ṛgveda: Structuring Enigmas," in Arlo Griffiths and Jan E. M. Houben, eds., *The Vedas: Texts, Language and Ritual: Proceedings of the Third Annual Vedic Workshop*, pp. 237–249. Leiden: Groningen, 2004.

Lindenau, M. "Vorwart zur zweiten Auflage" (1924): XIX. Reprinted in Roth and Whitney, eds., *Atharva-veda-Saṁhitā* (Berlin: Ferd. Dümmlers Verlagsbuchhandlung, 1856).

Verpoorten, Jean-Marie. "Unité et distinction dans les speculations rituelles védiques," *Archiv für Begriiffsgeschichte* 21/1 (1977): 59–85.

Wackernagel, Jacob, and Albert Debrunner. *Altindische Grammatik,* 3 vols. Göttingen: Vandenhoeck und Rupricht, 1954.

Whitney, William D., and Charles R. Lanman. *Atharva-veda Saṁhitā.* Harvard Oriental Series 7–8. Cambridge, MA: Harvard University, 1905.

On a Textual Problem in Navya-nyāya

Kamaleswar Bhattacharya

My last meeting with Frits Staal was at the logic conference in Hangzhou, China, mentioned by Staal in *Discovering the Vedas.*[1] Of course, for our Chinese colleagues there was no other system of logic in India than that of the Buddhists. But what was most striking was that for most participants their study of Buddhist logic had stopped with Theodore Stcherbatsky (c. 1930). While climbing the Flying Mountain of Hangzhou with Frits, we talked about logic, including the "New Logic" (Navya-nyāya), a subject that was dear to him. I therefore offer, in his memory, a somewhat revised and enlarged version of a paper I wrote on the subject in 1979.[2]

Jagadīśa Tarkālaṃkāra, the famous seventeenth-century Navya-naiyāyika of Navadvīpa (Bengal), in his commentary on the *Siddhānta-lakṣaṇa-Dīdhiti* of Raghunātha Śiromaṇi, explains the *Dīdhiti* passage *yo yadīyayāvadviśeṣābhāvavān sa tatsāmānyābhāvavān,* "that which possesses the totality of the particular absences of a certain thing possesses the generic absence of that thing," as follows:

> *yo yajjātisamānādhikaraṇobhayāvṛttidharmāvacchinayatsaṃbandhāvacchinna-pratiyogitāka-yāvadabhāvavān sa tajjātyavacchinnatatsaṃbandhāvac-chinnaprati-yogitākābhāvavān.*
>
> That which possesses the totality of the absences the counterpositivenesses to which are delimited, on the one hand, by properties which share a locus with a certain generic property and do not occur in two things taken together, and, on the other hand, by a certain relation, possesses the absence the counterpositiveness to which is delimited by that property and by that relation.

This is a fine example of the specific language that Navya-nyāya built up.[3] To explain: If the determination "which does not occur in two things taken together" (*ubhayāvṛtti*)[4] is omitted, then it would be possible to take, as properties sharing a locus with contact-ness (*saṃyogatva*), which is a generic property (*jāti*), the property of being a quality (*guṇatva*) or existence (*sattva, sattā*); and the absences the counterpositivenesses to which are delimited by these properties, being included in the totality of the absences, would be the "reason" (*hetu*). However, these absences do not exist in the subject (*pakṣa*), namely a substance (*dravya*) like a tree, where an attempt is made to prove the generic absence of contact (*saṃyoga-sāmānyābhāva*): there is in a substance neither absence of quality (*guṇa*) nor absence of something that has existence (*sattāvat*). In other words, the "reason" here would only be a "semblance of reason" (*hetvābhāsa*), being vitiated by the defect of "not being established according to its own nature" (*svarūpāsiddhi*). Thanks to the determination *ubhayāvṛtti*, however, one can take, as a property sharing a locus with contact-ness (*saṃyogatva*), only the "property of being such and such contact" (*tat-tatsaṃyogatva*), which is a property that occurs in only one thing and, consequently, does not co-occur in two things taken together; and the totality of the absences the counterpositivenesses to which are delimited by this property exists, indeed, in a substance like a tree.

The following objection may be raised: the determination *ubhayāvṛtti*, preventing only "non-establishment according to its own nature" (*svarūpāsiddhi*), is superfluous (*vyartha*). It is generally admitted that when a "reason" (*hetu*) is accompanied by a determination, this determination is significant (*sārthaka*) only insofar as it prevents the defect of "deviation" (*vyabhicāra*), which consists in the fact that the "reason" is present where the object to be established (*sādhya*) is absent. In fact, the apprehension of the deviation constitutes an obstacle to the apprehension of the Invariable Concomitance (*vyāptigraha*) that is the ground of all inferential knowledge (*anumiti*). A determination that prevents only the defect of "nonestablishment according to its own nature" is superfluous: the apprehension of this defect constitutes an obstacle only to the Consideration (*parāmarśa*), and, consequently, only to the inferential knowledge in a given subject.

According to Gaṅgeśa, however, every determination without which it is impossible to apprehend the Invariable Concomitance (*yena viśeṣaṇena vinā vyāptir grahītuṃ na śakyate*) is significant and, for that reason, a determination that prevents "nonestablishment" is also significant in certain cases.[5] "Where there is apprehension of the Invariable Concomitance even without the determination, there (the reason) has a superfluous determination."[6] Be that as it may, the determination *ubhayāvṛtti* here is superfluous: it only prevents the defect of "nonestablishment according to its own-nature." True, without this determination, it would be possible to take, as properties sharing a locus with contact-ness (*saṃyogatva*), the property of being a quality (*guṇatva*) or existence (*sattva*); but the absences, the counterpositivenesses to which are delimited by these properties, i.e., the absence of a quality or the absence of something that has existence, exist in all the categories of Nyāya-Vaiśeṣika except substance (*dravya*); and there is also, in the same categories, a generic absence of contact. Thus, there is apprehension of the Invariable Concomitance. But there cannot be any inferential knowledge if one takes as subject a substance.

However, Jagadīśa justifies the use of this determination by citing the authority of the well-known pre-Raghunātha commentator on the *Tattvacintāmaṇi*, Pakṣadhara (Jayadeva) Miśra:

> *vyabhicāravārakasyevāsiddhivārakasyāpi viśeṣaṇasya sārthakatāyāḥ Pakṣadharamiśrādisaṃmatatvāt.*
>
> Pakṣadhara Miśra and others admit that a determination that prevents "nonestablishment" is as significant as one that prevents "deviation."

He then refers to a passage in Pakṣadhara's commentary *Āloka* on the *Śabdakhaṇḍa* of the *Tattvacintāmaṇi*. This passage of the *Jāgadīśī*, as we usually have it, runs as follows:

> *ata eva śabdo 'nityaḥ sāmānyavattve sati viśeṣaguṇāntarāsamānādhikaraṇabahirindriyagrāhyatvād iti hetāv asiddhivārakasya śabdetarārthakasya viśeṣaguṇāntarapadasya Śabdamaṇyāloke taiḥ sārthakatvaṃ samarthitam.*[7]

Modern commentators are aware that the reading *śabdo nityaḥ* is also found, and efforts are made to justify logically both readings in the context. This is, of course, the procedure usually followed today by traditional learning in Navya-nyāya. We may nevertheless raise the question: which is the correct reading? It should not be particularly difficult to answer this question. The first step, evidently, would be to see whether a similar passage is found in the relevant section of the *Śabdakhaṇḍa* of the *Tattvacintāmaṇi* in connection with the siddhānta of the Naiyāyikas (who hold that sound is noneternal: *śabdo 'nityaḥ*), or in the *pūrvapakṣa* of the Prābhākara-Mīmāṃsakas (who hold that sound is eternal: *śabdo nityaḥ*). Both hold in common that sound is a quality—the "specific quality" (*viśeṣaguṇa*) of space (*ākāśa*)—and thus they are differentiated from the Bhāṭṭa-Mīmāṃsakas, who hold that sound is a substance (*dravya*). The next step would be to consult Pakṣadhara's commentary. This is a bit more difficult, since this part of the *Āloka* has not yet been edited. Manuscripts of this important text are available, however, and one is preserved in the Bibliothèque Nationale in Paris.

After some investigation, I am able to say that all that has been written on the subject is useless. The allusion is clearly to one of the inferences used by the Prābhākara-Mīmāṃsakas to prove the eternity of sound:

> *śabdo nityaḥ, viśeṣaguṇāntarāsamānādhikaraṇaikavṛttiguṇatvāt.*
>
> Sound is eternal, because it is a quality which resides in a single locus and which does not share a locus with another specific quality.[8]

In his commentary Pakṣadhara states that the expression *viśeṣaguṇāntarāsamānādhikaraṇa* means here "which does not share a locus with a specific quality other than sound" (*śabdetaraviśeṣaguṇāsamānādhikaraṇety arthaḥ*), and he observes:

> Although (the determination) *śabdetara* ("other than sound") is superfluous, this should be considered in accordance with the point of view of the others for whom a determination which prevents non-establishment is also significant (*yady api śabdetareti vyartham, tathāpi pareṣām asiddhivārakaviśeṣaṇasyāpi sārthakatayedaṃ draṣṭavyam*).[9]

In the light of all this, it is now easy to restore the correct reading of the passage under consideration. Basically, it is the same as the reading given in the Chowkhamba edition of the Jāgadīśī:[10]

> *ata eva nityatvasādhyakānumāne viśeṣaguṇāntarāsamānādhikaraṇaikavṛttiguṇatvahetau*
> *śabdetarārthakasyāntarapadasya Śabdamaṇyāloke sārthakatvaṃ taiḥ samarthitam.*
>
> (The determination *samānyavattve sati*, which in this edition precedes *viśeṣaguṇāntarāsamānādhikaraṇa*, is incongruous in the context of the Prābhākara doctrine.) Thus, in the *Śabdamaṇyāloka*, he (Pakṣadhara Miśra) has established the significance of the word *antara*, "other," meaning "other than sound," in the reason "property of being a quality which resides in a single locus and which does not share a locus with another specific quality," in connection with the inference where the object to be established is eternity.

It was not evident to me how without the determination *śabdetara* there would ensue the defect of "nonestablishment" (*asiddhi*) in the inference in question. Pakṣadhara does not explain this. But the explanation is found in the *Prakāśa* commentary by his pupil Rucidatta, who, commenting on the same passage of the *Tattvacintāmaṇi*, observes: "Because the same thing shares a locus with itself" (*svasyāpi svasamānādhikaraṇatvāt*).[11] Mathurānātha Tarkavāgīśa also states in his commentary on this passage: "Because sound also shares a locus with the specific quality consisting in sound" (*śabdasyāpi śabdātmakaviśeṣaguṇasamānādhikaraṇatvāt*).[12]

Thus, without this determination, the "reason" (*hetu*)—which would be "property of being a quality which occurs in a single locus and which does not share a locus with a specific quality" (*viśeṣaguṇāsamānādhikaraṇaikavṛttiguṇatva*)—would not exist in the subject, sound (*śabda*). It would only be a "semblance of reason" (*hetvābhāsa*), being vitiated by the defect of "not being established according to its own nature" (*svarūpāsiddhi*). The determination *śabdetara* prevents this defect and therefore it is significant.

Now it is also manifest that the theory under consideration is not Pakṣadhara's own but the theory "of the others" (*pareṣām*), i.e., of the Prābhākara-Mīmāṃsakas; Pakṣadhara only mentions it without approving it. The Prābhākaras hold that a determination that prevents the defect of "nonestablishment," without being at the same time indispensable for the apprehension of the Invariable Concomitance, is also significant—obviously because it leads to an inferential knowledge (which, for this reason, would be considered suspect by the Naiyāyikas).[13]

It is hardly conceivable that Jagadīśa thus misread the *Āloka* by ascribing this theory to Pakṣadhara. The passage seems to be an interpolation.

In any case, the idea that such a theory was held by Pakṣadhara Miśra should now be discarded. The "thought" of Miśra, as cited, for instance, by Vāmācaraṇa Bhaṭṭācārya,[14] seems to exist only in the imagination of modern exegetes.

The late Professor Erich Frauwallner insisted on the importance of the pre-Raghunātha commentaries on the *Tattvacintāmaṇi* for the understanding of Raghunātha's *Dīdhiti*.[15] We have now seen that they can help us understand the commentaries on the *Dīdhiti* as well. Unfortunately, only a small portion of these commentaries has been properly edited so far.[16] As Staal noted, "The study of Navya-nyāya logic is still in its infancy. Of the huge mass of manuscript material only a fragment has been published. . . ."[17]

Notes

1 Frits Staal, *Discovering the Vedas: Origins, Mantras, Rituals, Insights* (New Delhi: Penguin Books India, 2008), p. 344.

2 Kamaleswar Bhattacharya, "On a Passage of the *Siddhāntalakṣaṇa-Jāgadīśī*," *Ludwik Sternbach Felicitation Volume* (Lucknow: Akhila Bharatiya Sanskrit Parishad, 1979), pp. 479–483.

[3] See Kamaleswar Bhattacharya, "On the Language of Navya-nyāya: An Experiment with Precision through a Natural Language," *Journal of Indian Philosophy* 34 (2006): 5–13.

[4] On the other elements of this formulation, see Kamaleswar Bhattacharya, "Le *Siddhāntalakṣaṇaprakaraṇa* du *Tattvacintāmaṇi* de Gaṅgeśa, avec la *Dīdhiti* de Raghunātha Śiromaṇi et la *Ṭīkā* de Jagadīśa Tarkālaṃkāra (suite)," *Journal Asiatique* CCLXVIII (1980): 290–291, nn. 32–33.

[5] *Tattvacintāmaṇi* (Bibliotheca Indica edition 1888–1901), I (*Pratyakṣakhaṇḍa*), *Nirvikalpavāda*, pp. 820–821.

[6] *viśeṣaṇaṃ vināpi yatra vyāptigrahas tatra vyarthaviśeṣaṇatvam; Tattvacintāmaṇi* I (*Pratyakṣakhaṇḍa*), *Nirvikalpavāda*, p. 821.

[7] Guruprasāda Sāstrī, ed., *Siddhāntalakṣaṇa-Jāgadīśī*, with commentaries of Vāmācaraṇa Bhaṭṭācārya, Guruprāsada Sāstrī, and Kālīśaṅkara Bhaṭṭācārya (Benares: Chowkhamba Sanskrit Series Office, 1933), pp. 51–53.

[8] *Tattvacintāmaṇi* IV (*Śabdakhaṇḍa*), I, pp. 424–425.

[9] Paris: Bibliothèque Nationale, Sanskrit 903, fol. 54a.

[10] Somanāthopādhyāya, ed., text of *Dīdhiti* with the *Jāgadīśī* Chowkhamba Sanskrit Series (Benares: Chowkhamba Sanskrit Series Office, 1908), vol. I, p. 216. See also Bhattacharya, "Le Siddhāntalakṣaṇaprakaraṇa," pp. 321–322.

[11] Rucidatta, "Prakāśa on the Śabdakhaṇḍa of the Tattvacintāmaṇi," *The Paṇḍit* VI (1872): 287.

[12] *Tattvacintāmaṇi* IV, 1, p. 425.

[13] Cf. also Rucidatta, *Prakāśa* 286b: *paramate vā svarūpāsiddhivārakasyāpy anumitiprayojakatvena sārthakatvāc ca;* 287: *paramate asiddhivārakasyāpi sārthakatvān na śabdabhinnapadaṃ vyartham.*

[14] Bhaṭṭācārya, *Siddhāntalakṣaṇa-Jāgadīśī*, 51; cf. 53. See also Dharmadatta (Baccā) Jha, *Siddhāntalakṣaṇatattvālokaḥ* (Benares, Chowkhamba Sanskrit Series Office, 1925), pp. 104–105. Jha was a foremost authority on Navya-nyāya in the nineteenth-twentieth centuries.

[15] Erich Frauwallner, "Raghunātha Śiromaṇi," *Wiener Zeitschrift für die Kunde Süd- und Ostasiens* [*Südasiens*] *und Archiv für indische Philosophie* X (1966): 86–207; XI (1967): 140–208; XIV (1970): 161–208.

[16] See, in the last instance, Kamaleswar Bhattacharya, Review of Saccidānanda Miśra's edition of Yajñapati Upādhyāya s *Tattvacintāmaṇiprabhā* (*Anumānakhaṇa*), *Saṃbhāṣā, Nagoya Studies in Indian Culture and Buddhism* 30 (2013): 101–102.

[17] Frits Staal, "Formal Structures in Indian Logic," in *Universals: Studies in Indian Logic and Linguistics* (Chicago: University of Chicago Press, 1988), p. 79.

References

Bhaṭṭācārya, Vāmācaraṇa. *Siddhāntalakṣaṇa-Jāgadīśī.* Guruprasāda Sāstrī, ed., with commentaries of Vāmācaraṇa Bhaṭṭācārya, Guruprāsada Sāstrī, and Kālīśaṅkara Bhaṭṭācārya. Benares: Chowkhamba Sanskrit Series Office, 1933.

Bhattacharya, Kamaleswar. "Le *Siddhāntalakṣaṇaprakaraṇa* du *Tattvacintāmaṇi* de Gaṅgeśa, avec la *Dīdhiti* de Raghunātha Śiromaṇi et la *Ṭīkā* de Jagadīśa Tarkālaṃkāra (suite)," *Journal Asiatique* CCLXVIII (1980): 290–291, nn. 32–33.

—. "On a Passage of the *Siddhāntalakṣaṇa-Jāgadīśī*," *Ludwik Sternbach Felicitation Volume*, pp. 479–483. Lucknow: Akhila Bharatiya Sanskrit Parishad,, 1979.

—. "On the Language of Navya-nyāya: An Experiment with Precision through a Natural Language," *Journal of Indian Philosophy* 34 (2006): 5–13.

—. Review of Saccidānanda Miśra's edition of Yajñapati Upādhyāya's *Tattvacintāmaṇiprabhā (Anumānakhaṇa), Saṃbhāṣā, Nagoya Studies in Indian Culture and Buddhism* 30 (2013): 101–102.

Frauwallner, Erich "Raghunātha Śiromaṇi," *Wiener Zeitschrift für die Kunde Süd- und Ostasiens* [*Südasiens*] *und Archiv für indische Philosophie* X (1966): 86–207; XI (1967): 140–208; XIV (1970): 161–208.

Jha, Dharmadatta (Baccā). *Siddhāntalakṣaṇatattvālokaḥ*. Benares, 1925.

Rucidatta. "*Prakāśa* on the *Śabdakhaṇḍa* of the *Tattvacintāmaṇi*," *The Paṇḍit* VI (1872).

Somanāthopādhyāya, ed. Text of *Dīdhiti* with the *Jāgadīśī*. Chowkhamba Sanskrit Series. Benares: Chowkhamba Sanskrit Series Office, 1908.

Staal, Frits. *Discovering the Vedas: Origins, Mantras, Rituals, Insights*. New Delhi: Penguin Books India, 2008.

— *Universals: Studies in Indian Logic and Linguistics*. Chicago: University of Chicago Press, 1988.

Tattvacintāmaṇi. Calcutta: Bibliotheca Indica, 1888–1901.

Discovering Frits Staal[1]

Philo Bregstein

Frits Staal's *Discovering the Vedas,*[2] a sturdy Penguin pocket edition, has been praised all but unanimously by critics in both the U.S. and India as a high point in an oeuvre already studded with high points. The statement "First published by Penguin Books India" is very telling: after fifty years of discoveries of Indian culture, Staal is now at home as an author, too, in his promised land of India.

Since the book opens with an autobiographical introduction, I also want to begin with a few autobiographical notes. My association with Frits Staal began sixty years ago, when, as an upcoming student at the University of Amsterdam, I found my way into a fraternity with the revealing name of Homer, whose secretary was Staal. I already knew him from high school, the Barlaeus Gymnasium, where he had been a class ahead of me. He had taken the beta finals but had always been interested in Greek, so at the university he studied it as his minor. For him, this was a natural progression that anticipated his further education, where the customary division between the language-oriented alpha program and the math- and science-oriented beta program constantly broke down. In a recent essay,[3] Staal demonstrated the random origins and relative senselessness of this division, which developed only in the nineteenth century in Europe and which does not occur in Indian culture, for instance.

According to a ritual tradition in the fraternity, Staal bestowed upon me a new name: Philo, which has been the name I have gone by ever since, instead of Rudolf, the name given me by my assimilated Jewish father and my Dutch-Reformed, non-Jewish mother. I suspect that, at the time, my parents preferred to give me an Aryan-sounding name. After forty years of delving into the recent past, I no longer blame them for doing so.

Regarding the names given in the Homer fraternity, it was striking that Frits gave me the stamp of the Jewish philosopher Philo of Alexandria, who tried to reconcile Greek and Jewish philosophy. Raised without any Jewish traditions, I only later became interested in Judaism and Jewish history, motivated, of course, by the fact that I survived World

War II because I was "half-Jewish." Nazi racist rules considered children with one Jewish parent and one Gentile parent to be half-Jewish.

Frits himself had been given the name Daniel, which never caught on outside the fraternity. Only decades later did he tell me that he, too, was "half-Jewish," according to the Nazi rules. According to the Orthodox Jewish "Halacha" rules, however, children with a Jewish mother are fully Jewish. Since in Frits's case it was his mother who was Jewish and in my case my father, he was considered to be Jewish according to Halacha law. I did not have that honor.

An interesting aspect of that naming is that in *Discovering the Vedas* Staal demonstrates that it is a misconception to have language start with naming, as is written in the Old Testament, but also accepted in China and ancient Greece, and even in a particular text in the Indian Vedas. He explains that the Vedas developed linguistics for the first time and this reveals that language does not start with naming but with grammatical rules and, particularly, with thoughts. Still, the ritual effect of the naming in our fraternity was a bit like when, as Staal also describes, one enters a Buddhist monastery as a monastic: it constitutes a second birth, in which one receives a new name.[4]

We were at university together in the early 1950s. Frits/Daniel was studying math and logic, both beta subjects, as well as the alpha subject of philosophy, reading Heidegger and Bergson, thinkers who were difficult for me to access. As a law student, I was primarily interested in novelists like Dostoevsky, Faulkner, Kafka, and Proust, and wanted to write novels myself.

Frits/Daniel's refined features, framed by jet-black, wavy hair, made an impression on me. I saw a novelistic Proustian, Dostoevskian character in him. In those days, homosexuality was, of course, taboo in the student world, even though in retrospect it is clear that several fraternity members had been secretly gay. Frits/Daniel, too, came out only later, in California in the 1970s. I suspect, looking back, that there was a latent, homosexual, Proustian bond between us. I had great admiration for him, and he always listened attentively to my stories about contemporary literature and modern music, subjects of which he knew little. His critical questions stimulated me in a Socratic sense to try to formulate my thoughts more clearly. What also bonded us was a mutual love of classical music, such as Beethoven's *Diabelli Variations* or Bach's partitas. Frits played violin and was in the student orchestra and also in a quartet. If I remember correctly, I accompanied him a few times on the piano for a Mozart violin sonata. Later he sacrificed his violin when he immersed himself in Brahman sacrificial rituals in India.

I remember very clearly a lecture he presented to our fraternity on the cyclical and linear concepts of time. It is one of the first essays published in his 1986 collection (in Dutch),[5] although in the introduction he finds the article to be "just as romantic as Eliade's work." The lecture has always stayed with me. He placed the Western, Christian linear concept of time, with its notion of progress, in opposition to the Eastern cyclical concept of time, displaying an obvious preference for the latter. His lecture opened unexpected perspectives for me.

This was before Frits received a scholarship to India, which took his life and work in a radically new direction. Dutch author Harry Mulisch once wrote about Staal's "somnambulistic certainty": "It's as if from the very beginning he went for his great discovery with great certainty."[6]

I still recall how the alarm sounded in our fraternity when he had to be admitted to the hospital with severe bleeding in his lungs, after which he had to spend a long time recovering from tuberculosis at the student sanatorium in the affluent Gooi area of woodland and heath in North Holland. I visited him there, and from his hospital bed he questioned me, interested in all kinds of things, cheerful as always, in the respectable tradition of Thomas Mann's *The Magic Mountain.*

The second piece of alarming news was that no sooner had he been released from the sanatorium than he decided to leave for India on a study grant. This was seen as a reckless, life-threatening venture. However, to my knowledge, Frits never again had serious problems with his lungs, and we in the fraternity received beautiful pictures accompanying his travelogues about his motorcycle trips across India. We had no idea, of course, that at that time Staal was making the discovery of his life, recording Vedic recitations on a tape recorder. After his return to Amsterdam in 1957, he played the recordings during an unforgettable, hours-long presentation to our fraternity. What stayed with me as a key concept was that those who faithfully transmitted the Vedic recitations in Sanskrit by way of oral tradition had no understanding of the material themselves. This was the exact opposite of the rule taught to me in high school that "You should understand what you say." The key to the exact transmission of the oral tradition of the Vedas was precisely that you did *not* understand what you were saying!

While Staal was discovering India, I left university life after receiving a Master's degree in law and started working on my first novel. I went to a film school in Rome just as he became a professor of philosophy in Amsterdam. We lost track of each other, both absorbed in our own fields.

In 1956, from India, he sent me a reprint of an article about existentialism and Martin Heidegger,[7] which held little appeal for me. The interesting thing today is how that article shows that at that time he himself was far from being done with Heidegger, the father of hermeneutics. His other publications, on Plotinus, Augustine, Advaita, and Euclid,[8] also lay far beyond my horizons. Although I found the Indian Vedic recitations he had played for us intriguing, they were in my opinion at the time also very religious.

The next news I had about Frits was that at the end of the 1960s, under the pressure of intrigues at the University of Amsterdam, he had given up his position as a professor of philosophy and moved to the U.S. There, he was first invited to the Massachusetts Institute of Technology (M.I.T.) in Boston by the linguist Noam Chomsky, and after that he built up the Department of Philosophy and South and Southeast Asian Studies at the University of California, Berkeley. Frits had clearly found his way.

In my mind, at that time, California was part of "the West," and further removed from me than the Far East. I had not been in touch with Staal for over twenty years when, while serving as a writer-in-residence at the University of Michigan at Ann Arbor, I went to San Francisco in spring 1983 to give film presentations and lectures. I was excited about seeing him again, and I called him to suggest that I show him a couple of my films. His surprising response was, "Excellent! I'll take a projector home from the department and I'll show you my film, too!" This was the last thing I expected to hear from a professor of Sanskrit and Indian philosophy.

It turned out to be a lively get-together, as if we had not aged twenty years, with an equal number of years' worth of interruption in our friendship. Frits appeared rejuvenated. He had lost his wavy, jet-black hair, but he was effervescent with passion and energy. He had been married to an Indian anthropologist and had fathered two children, but had since divorced. I, likewise divorced, arrived at his place with my new girlfriend. He in turn introduced us to his gorgeous Filipino and other Asian boyfriends who filled his new life as a gay man. He remarked that it was "more important for me to find someone beautiful than if it's a man or a woman," an echo of Plato's dialogues about Socrates and his young friends.

I showed him my film first: *The Past That Lives* (*Dingen die niet voorbijgaan*), about Jacob (Jacques) Presser, the author of *Ashes in the Wind: The Persecution and Destruction of Dutch Jewry*.[9] Frits became reflective and related that he had been acquainted with Presser, a colleague at the

University of Amsterdam. He then disclosed that his mother was a Jew and had been murdered in the Sobibor concentration camp. His non-Jewish father, the architect J. F. Staal, was representative of the well-known Amsterdam School and had designed such buildings as "The Skyscraper" and "The Jewish Invalid" in Amsterdam. His father passed away before the war and his Jewish mother had been left unprotected and was unable to escape deportation. Frits had been adopted as a war orphan by friends of his parents, and, like me, as a "half-Jew" he did not have to go into hiding. However, unlike me, he did not want to immerse himself in the wartime past and felt no connection to his Jewish identity or to Judaism. He was also against Freud ("According to Buddha, you have multiple lives") and a proponent of psychological repression. He clearly felt at home in California, far from Europe, with a view of the Pacific, to which he gestured with the remark that here the Far East had become the West: Japan, China, and India lay beyond the horizon; these were the countries he traveled to regularly.

I then got to see his film, *Altar of Fire,* which had been made together with the anthropological filmmaker Robert Gardner, about a three thousand-year-old Vedic fire ritual to Agni.[10] The ritual was performed by Nambudiri Brahmans for the first time in 1975 in South India, after an extended hiatus, thanks to Frits' support; he had spent years gathering the funds to finance the performance. After that he spent more years working out the filmed and recorded material in a monolithic two-volume orange-clad tome entitled *Agni: The Vedic Ritual of the Fire Altar,*[11] the page proofs of which he had just received. The film that he and Robert Gardner made was an impressive documentary that entailed possession of a great deal of knowledge regarding the ritual; Frits had studied it for decades and could therefore guide Gardner well. Instead of meeting a professor of Sanskrit, as I had expected, to my surprise I met a fellow filmmaker.

Frits told me that years before he had gone to study Indian philosophy in Madras (now Chennai). His first important decision was to learn Sanskrit because he understood that he could not study any Indian philosophy in English. He found a *paṇḍita* who taught young children Sanskrit and in this way discovered the famous fifth-century B.C.E. Sanskrit grammar of Pāṇini, a predecessor to modern linguistics. Aside from this, he had become interested in Vedic recitation: "I'm very geared to the ear and the Indian tradition is an oral tradition." He had then set out with a tape recorder to collect the various styles of Vedic recitation in different parts of India, sparking an interest in the orthodox Brahmans who chanted the Vedas. A student at the University of Madras, who belonged to an inaccessible community of Brahmans in South India, the Nambudiri, invited him to stay with them. He reported:

> They also chanted the Vedas. Recitation wasn't supposed to be heard by non-Brahmans. But then I played a recording of a particular hymn for them that I had made in Madras, and they said, "That's not the way it's supposed to go!" So that's how I managed to get them to recite. Those recitations belonged to rituals that all the academics in Europe thought had died out long ago. And it was only then that I heard what the Nambudiris had never told me—namely that they also recited the hymns I was recording while they performed rituals. That's how I finally succeeded in gaining access.

That is how what began as a sideline for Staal developed into his life's work.

His Californian life also had another connection to his fascination for Vedic rituals. The *soma* plant that priests press into juice and drink has an obvious hallucinogenic effect. In California there was a cult around psychoactive substances, such as marijuana and LSD, and it was obvious that Frits was actively interested.

He gave me one of his recent publications, *Exploring Mysticism.*[12] Suddenly it was as if the door to the Far East that had always been closed to me opened up. I had identified Asia with irrationality, mysticism, and religion, which I strongly resisted, having been shaped by antireligious thinkers such as Friedrich Nietzsche. However, Staal demonstrated that mysticism can be studied rationally and that as a rationalist one can find a lot of interest in religion regarding earlier forms of human consciousness.

Staal himself had also undergone a Nietzschean revaluation of values. In the narration in *Altar of Fire,* he explains the ritual in traditional fashion as based on Vedic myths that allegedly formed the groundwork. He had made a radical turnaround since then. Rituals did not interpret mythology. The mythology grafted itself onto rituals that were meaningless in and of themselves. If you ask priests what something in a ritual means, they will tell you anything, usually what you want to hear. It does not matter to them what a ritual "means" because it is only important to perform the rite as well as possible. Orthodoxy is secondary; it is all about orthopraxy. With this understanding, Staal swept the prevailing anthropological and sociological interpretations of ritual out of the picture.

In 1979 he wrote his first article on this topic, "The Meaninglessness of Ritual."[13] He demonstrates that ritual has more to do with beta subjects than with religion.

The essence of rituals lies in their structure and in the actions with which humans have developed themselves as organizing "language animals." Human rituals, according to Staal, are more akin to animal rituals. According to Staal, the incomprehensible mantras, often overloaded with profound interpretations, recited during Vedic rituals are not magical formulae but meaningless sounds, more akin to the croaking of frogs or the singing of birds. According to him, mantras existed long before humans developed religions and myths, and, just like rituals, they lie at the base of human language. The science of ritual that is laid down in the Vedas led to Pāṇini's Sanskrit grammar and to modern linguistics. It was due to this discovery that linguist Noam Chomsky had invited Staal to M.I.T.

However, Staal shows great respect for the Brahmans who perform the rituals and for the superlative human feat of preserving their oral tradition and ritual practices for thousands of years: "What a victory of the human spirit over the limitations of matter and of the body!" This runs parallel to what he has written about other techniques developed in Asia, such as yoga, meditation, and acupuncture. Practice is often very effective and for this a student might well study with a guru. However, he maintained that one shouldn't listen to what that guru says, particularly not to any mystical, profound interpretations, because "they're just saying whatever."

In the mid-1980s, Staal made a comeback in the Netherlands when *Altar of Fire* was broadcast on television, and I made a brief TV profile of him in which I included a fragment of his controversial lecture at the Balie in Amsterdam in 1984, "Just Saying Whatever or Abracadabra for Intellectuals" (Maar-wat-zeggen of abracadabra voor intellectuelen). In his talk, Staal denounced the West's religious projection onto Asian cultures, and ridiculed the famous cult-figure Bhagwan, who was all the rage at that time, and the veneration of gurus. But he also settled his score with the irrationalism and obscurantism of the current Western philosophy in the wake of Heidegger's and Gadamer's hermeneutics, which were then in fashion.

Major recognition in the Netherlands came to him in 1986 with his collection of essays in Dutch, *Over zin en onzin in filosofie, religie en wetenschap* ("On Sense and Nonsense in Philosophy, Religion, and Science").[14] Harry Mulisch wrote in his foreword to the book:

> The birth of language from the spirit of ritual! This suddenly opens new vistas, as is always the case with a revolutionary hypothesis. . . . The time has come for the Netherlands to call this prodigal son back from the diaspora. This is an obligation.

Staal became the talk of the town for a while and a lot of interviews with him appeared in the media, even though the attention was clearly more about his radical attitude than his ideas about Indian culture and the Vedas. He received prestigious assignments in the Netherlands, including being tapped to help set up the International Institute of Asian Studies (IIAS) in Leiden. He was also permitted to work out a plan for the Dutch government to regroup "small language" studies. He was also one of the founders of the Islam Institute (not incidentally, now defunct). Despite his resistance to the monotheistic religions, Staal had a positive view of particular aspects of Islam, a stance that today once again obviously runs against the grain of prevailing opinion. He emphasized that Islam had been an enlightened culture for centuries, and science was highly developed in Islamic cultures at a time when Christian Europe was submerged in religious fanaticism and obscurantism. Thanks to Islam, many achievements of Greek and Arabic culture and scholarship, such as algebra, ended up in Europe, from which the Renaissance and later the Enlightenment would emerge.

Staal nevertheless continued to encounter a lot of resistance. He challenged the criminologist and writer Andreas Burnier, who had many supporters in her vision of the irrational East supposedly being superior to our rational West. He also attacked the Palestinian-American philosopher Edward Said, popular in left-wing circles, whom he dismissed as "utterly incompetent." According to Staal, Said had not understood anything about the great contribution to the knowledge of Indian culture, for instance, that European scholars had made in the nineteenth century, which Said dismissed as Western imperialism in disguise. It seemed as if Staal only became more defiant and radical in response to the resistance he provoked. He also challenged the internationally famous anthropologist Jack Goody, who had characterized the written word as the essential stage in our civilization. Staal refuted this by referring to the oral tradition of the Vedas, in which the most advanced ideas were developed.

Staal did not succeed in breaking through with his cultural critiques and incurred the hostility of many, which apparently gave him some pleasure. He recently wrote, "I even became notorious for it." There was something arrogant about him, as if he thought he could cause a revolution in prevailing beliefs, which didn't happen. His attack on the basic ideas of both Claude Lévi-Strauss and Jean-Paul Sartre—in fact, on all of French philosophy—was received in the Parisian scholarly world as blasphemous. Staal characterized the philosopher Jacques Derrida, who was then in vogue, as "an abomination." Only Foucault, with whose "archeology of knowledge" he clearly had an affinity, found mercy in his eyes, although Staal also showed respect for Lévi-Strauss for working out the lessons of the linguist Roman Jakobson, whom Staal admired. However, he radically rejected Lévi-Strauss's main idea that myth was the basis of rituals, holy ground for most French anthropologists.

His last collection of essays, *Drie Bergen en zeven rivieren* ("Three Mountains and Seven Rivers")[15] received various negative reviews. Michel Leezenberg, despite his appreciation for the fact that Staal focused on Asiatic, non-Western traditions that had been neglected in Holland, wrote in the popular Dutch weekly magazine *Vrij Nederland,* "Today, Staal's work in the academic field is at most a curiosity." Staal's bibliography reveals that he simply continued to publish in American, international, often Indian journals, as well as in the Netherlands. For the Amsterdam in-crowd, though, he was out and drifted into the background.

A small group of fans in the Dutch academic world published a commemorative book in his honor, offered to him in 1997 by the International Institute for Asian Studies (IIAS) for his sixty-fifth birthday.[16] The collection includes contributions by Dutch icons such as the linguist Henk Verkuyl, the Daoist Kristopher Schipper, and J. C. Heesterman, professor of Indian culture at Leiden University. Several of his nonacademic friends were asked to contribute to a small supplement, including the poet Cees Nooteboom, new classical composer Peter Schat, parliamentary leader and European Commissioner Frits Bolkestein, and the honor even fell to me. This gave me the opportunity to confront his ideas, and in an open letter[17] I tried to ascertain where his arguments convinced me and where they didn't.

It was obvious that his controversial basic ideas about rituals and mantras belonged to his inspired ideas. I did, however, criticize him for making an overly dogmatic and puritanical distinction between the "sensible" and "nonsense." Staal himself had determined that Isaac Newton, whom he esteemed, had been interested in esoteric traditions and alchemy. Pāṇini, too, had believed in the eternality of the Vedas. Nevertheless, both had made precise and important discoveries. My question was: If incorrect hypotheses can go together with good, concrete discoveries, why would there be the need to reject out of hand every "wrong" hypothesis as "nonsense"? Wouldn't the thought processes toward finding solutions be paralyzed that way?

I also thought that reducing rituals solely to their academic, linguistic aspects is too one-sided. To my mind, neglecting their "nonsense" aspects cuts off other important aspects of rituals that are located at the origin of dramatic art, theater, and dance. Mantras, no matter how meaningless, clearly form the basis for the later development of song and poetry.

Another criticism concerned the parallels Staal drew between rituals and classical music. Until recently, Vedic rituals took place without an audience. Classical music is always played for an audience and the interpretation and response of the listeners are an essential factor. If musicians are admired as great interpreters, is that because they give something extra besides merely playing the notes, something that doesn't apply to performing rituals because they only have to be performed "as well as possible"?

My strongest criticism concerned Staal's negative opinion of monotheism, particularly of Judaism and Christianity. Nowhere does he mention that the orthopraxy he so admired on the part of the Brahmans has a direct parallel in Judaism.

I thought that Staal's rejection of practically all of Western contemporary philosophy, particularly French philosophy, was tendentious and one-sided. Why wouldn't a scholar such as Staal, in spite of pointing out "nonsense," also be able to find inspired, usable ideas from philosophers he condemned as irrational? Gilles Deleuze's concept of the multiple "rhizome" structure fits well, in my mind, with the Vedic view of the plural origin of the world, about which Staal asserts that it conforms better to current scientific knowledge of the universe than the monotheistic creation story. Yet Staal found Deleuze to be "too Luddite." This pinpoints what I criticized him for: a too-rigid, puritanical, "beta"-subject opinion of the dividing line between what makes "sense" and what is "nonsense," and a narrow-minded rejection of the "Luddite" subjectivity in science and philosophy—"The Gay Science," as Nietzsche called it.[18] To my surprise, one of Staal's later publications, *Een wijsgeer in het Oosten. Op reis door Java en Kalimantan* ("A Philosopher in the East: Traveling through Java and Kalimantan"),[19] is a Luddite, subjective report of his visit to the Borobudur temple in Java. I finished my letter with the hope that he would continue further down that path.

In 2009, following once again a period of more than ten years in which we spoke to each other only sporadically, I received a copy of his latest book, *Discovering the Vedas,* in which he had obviously nuanced his view and developed it further. Had I accurately foreseen the direction he would continue to develop? Of course I had not been the only one from whom Staal had received criticism. More so than in the past, he was able to draw me along into a lively, often exciting story, in which I flew like a bird, traveling with him over Central Asia, India, and the Himalayan region. I suspect that an important factor contributed to this renewal: his decision to move from California to Thailand when he became professor emeritus. He was clearly more at home in Asia than in the U.S. or in his native country, the Netherlands. The fact that he is showered with praise for his contributions to the knowledge of Indian culture in the Indian press offers an even more significant homecoming. In India, the oral tradition of the Vedas is the subject of as much interest as is the Bible for us in Europe, in the tradition of "The Book."

After many academic, often complex books and articles, the compact Penguin edition of *Discovering the Vedas* is easy to read. The book jacket states that the book "is for both the scholar and the interested lay reader." In fact, at first glance one might think of it as a *Reader's Digest*–like compendium, in which much of Staal's important highly specialized research is presented in an airy, easily readable style for nonspecialists.

When read closely, however, *Discovering the Vedas* contains much more. There are surprising updates in every area Staal wrote about in earlier publications. The title, which appears casual, turns out to have multiple meanings. Staal himself compares his research to peeling an onion, which seems to progress, but without the certainty of finding anything. He has fewer pretensions to possessing the truth than in the past. His report on looking into puzzles that concern life thousands of years ago sometimes reads like an exciting detective story. At other times, he plays the guide and takes the reader on an adventurous expedition of discovery. Staal claims that this book is no more than an introduction. But for the first time he provides a coherent picture of the Vedas, their history and development—which is like reaching the top of a Himalayan peak and finally getting a view of the whole landscape.

Staal now usually introduces himself as a researcher, and he has clearly lost his distaste for introducing subjectivity. Even his style has a new, Luddite element, with amusing "I will be pleased" interruptions. I finally recognized Nietzsche's *The Gay Science* and Johan Huizinga's *Homo Ludens*[20] in it, to which Staal himself often refers in his work.

Another interesting aspect of *Discovering the Vedas* is the form. Staal usually begins a new topic by posing a question, like a teacher addressing students, and then he often comes up with a series of hypotheses from colleagues from East and West as well as his own, which he then weighs one against the other, without passing judgment in the curt "off with your head!" way he used to.

With the "imaginary dialogue" between himself and the reader, Staal is clearly referring to the Upanishads—highly esteemed by Staal—which originated from the Vedas and are often written in the form of teacher-student dialogues. This lends a Socratic element to *Discovering the Vedas,* as in Plato's dialogues. While Staal remains true to his pursuit of knowledge and insight as the highest goal worth striving for, he says remarkably often in this book that much is unknown to us, and he thereby places himself in the context of generations of researchers through the ages who have collectively sought knowledge of and insight into the Vedas.

I will select a few highlights from this book, a few pearls from among the many. In the introduction Staal immediately presents a couple of fundamental assertions. The Vedas are not "holy books," as is often claimed. It is also wrong to consider them to be "of nonhuman (i.e., divine) origin." They are not the "revelations" of the monotheistic Bible and Koran. Instead, the Vedas are cycles of oral transmissions, originally composed by nomadic peoples and transferred from father to son, teacher to student, for generations, over thousands of years, and only slowly codified. They also do not contain religious doctrine, as we know it in Europe, but are depositories for knowledge—in fact, the very meaning of the word "Veda." Above all, the Vedas embody a civilization.

The first part of *Discovering the Vedas,* "Origins and Backgrounds," is the precipitate from Staal's research over the past twenty years. It concludes that the Vedas, contrary to the general, nationalistic opinion in India, did not originate in India but in Central Asia, a region that nowadays usually surfaces in the news only because of Al Qaeda and Islamic terrorism in Pakistan and Afghanistan. The Vedas are of Indo-European origin, which has been confirmed by linguistic studies of a number of languages, in which traces of encounters between various peoples can be found through words that come from different languages.

Staal concludes that new developments in the civilization of humanity always come about in the exchanges between peoples. Greek civilization, too, arose in this way, and there is an obvious affinity between the Indian Vedas and Greek culture, such as the geometry that came from building altars. Both likely took this from the Babylonians, who had developed geometry long before. On the basis of this information, Staal believes that the history of science should be placed in a Euro-Asiatic whole.

He then takes us along on his investigation. Small clans of Asiatic nomads who spoke Indo-European and who recited the Vedas probably migrated south under the duress of external pressures, by way of river valleys and some of the most accessible mountain passes across the Himalayas, to settle in the Indus Valley. There, they turned to agriculture and mixed with the local population. The Vedas developed further over the ages in India until the present, codified form was attained. Through reconstruction, the beginning of this process can be dated to about 3,000 or 4,000 years ago. Staal challenges the much-touted opinion that a major invasion by Asiatic hordes took place in India, and his thoughts have been confirmed by recent DNA research, linguistic research, and also by archeological research. In the 1950s, north of Afghanistan in the Central Asian Republics, the remains of large, walled cities called the Bactria-Margiana Archeological Complex (BMAC) were discovered. This was a highly developed culture that dated to about 2,000 B.C.E. In addition, Chinese archeologists in the 1970s in Xinjiang, a desert area that was being developed for oil drilling, by chance found the so-called Tarim mummies, which were in excellent condition and date to 2,000 B.C.E. DNA testing of the mummies confirms Staal's hypothesis that the site involved an Indo-European population. He then poses the disarming question, "What then was the language of these mummies before they were mummies?"[21] This remains an unanswered question to the present day, even though a combination of linguistic and archeological discoveries helped to reconstruct the journey of the Vedic nomads in Central Asia on their way to India.

Another exciting investigation concerns the origin of the soma plant used in Vedic rituals, of which the best quality probably comes from high in the Himalayas. In the Vedas, this is the mythical Mount Mujavat, never specifically localized, but which, according to Harvard Sanskritist Michael Witzel, must lie in the Himalaya.[22] This reinforces Staal's hypothesis about the Vedic nomads from Central Asia who took along with them the soma plant found in the Himalayas on their way to India; substitutes were later used in Vedic rituals.

The history of the multispoked wheel, which plays a key role in the Vedas, is fascinating. Staal demonstrates that this type of wheel originally comes from Central Asia and did not exist in India at the time. He links this to the conclusion that the nomads who brought the Vedas across the high Himalayan passes did not take wagons and horses, which was practically impossible. However, they had been very familiar with spoked wheels in Asia and introduced their imagery into the Vedas. Spoked wheels therefore crossed the Himalayas only by way of recitation. This became the beginning of an interiorized image of the spoked wheel that would increasingly characterize the Vedas and lead to meditation, where mantras and rituals were no longer spoken out loud or performed but silently intoned to oneself, and subsequently only in the imagination. The image of the spoked wheel was later adopted in

Buddhism, where the eight-spoked wheel became a key symbol for the cyclical course of life (*bhavacakra*), as well as for the eightfold teaching itself (*dharmacakra*). The reason for the success of the Vedas, imported to India, remains uncertain. Staal offers as a hypothesis that it was due to the "power of mantras" and the "power of soma rituals," subjects to which he devotes many pages without arriving at a definitive answer.

It is interesting that in his subsequent presentation of the four Vedas, Staal alternates it with often poetic Veda texts, which he cites apparently not just to support his argument but because he thinks they are so beautiful, like the long, riveting, repetitive "Yes" hymn: "Yes! Have I drunk of the Soma? Yes!"[23] This made me think of Molly Bloom's orgasmic monologue in James Joyce's *Ulysses.*

In Staal's analysis of the Vedas, the amusing although, from a writer's perspective, cruel, story appears of Kautsa, a scholar from the fifth century B.C.E. whose work survived only through quotations from his opponents. Kautsa had at that time already asserted that rituals and mantras have no meaning. His most convincing argument, "There is a tradition for mantras to be learnt by heart, but no corresponding tradition to teach and thereby preserve their meaning," is quoted by Staal four times, almost like a mantra itself![24]

Two of Kautsa's arguments for the meaninglessness of mantras are, in my opinion, "nonsense," however:

> In the Veda, the order of words may not be changed . . . the *sound* of the mantras may not be changed: words may not be replaced by synonyms . . . as is common in ordinary language.[25]

This observation also applies to all poetry from Homer to Dante, which does not necessarily make poetry meaningless.

Staal is critical of the obscurities in the fourth Veda, the *Atharvaveda,* and particularly of the commentaries that have been added to those Vedas, like the *Brāhmana*s and *Āranyaka*s, in which a lot of magic can be found, defined by Staal as pure superstition.

"[S]hould we not be charitable? We should be, but there is a limit." He offers a nice example of a patent "nonsense" statement he came up with himself: "[B]lue is green because everything is green and cheese is everything." He continues, "If a mother says [that] to her child, in any language . . . the child asks: 'What do you mean, Mama?'"[26]

In connection with his rejection of irrationalism and esotericism, Staal writes, "Some people say: we cannot know, and stop there. I say: we must explore the unknown." He cites a great Indian mathematician,

Aryabhata, who described one of his discoveries as "a precious sunken jewel from the ocean of true and false knowledge." It is clear that Staal has a changed attitude here, with respect to his previously held views, as far as "sense" and "nonsense" are concerned. "[T]he lotus is born from mud . . . should we expect the bulky Brāhmanas to be excluded? They are not and it is time for us to look for gold pellets."[27] By this he demonstrates that even in the irrational *Brāhmana*s important information can be found.

After analyzing recently developed theories about Vedic rituals, Staal comes to the conclusion that none of the modern academic fields has succeeded in giving a satisfying interpretation. He even rejects John L. Austin's performative theory, where "saying is doing,"[28] with convincing arguments, once again counter to the prevailing opinion in scholarly circles.

In reliving Vedic rituals since the Agni ritual of 1975, Staal, together with the Indian ritual expert T. P. Mahadevan, investigated the meanings assigned to the newly performed rituals. They found that the explanations were always based on myths and interpretations dating from after the rituals came about and so could never lie at their root.

In the chapter "What Can We Learn from the Vedas?" Staal shows as one of the most important aspects of Veda ritual expertise the development of metarules and other orderly rules that turn out to be important for modern logic, math, and computer science. He finds that the Vedic idea of the infinity of language and the use of infinite numbers—with which neither the Greeks nor European academics wanted much to do—are more up to date than many recent philosophical and scientific developments.

The greatest contribution of Vedic linguistics is synchronic linguistics, which was developed in India two millennia before Ferdinand de Saussure initiated it in nineteenth-century Europe. Staal emphasizes:

> As far as I know, the Vedic discovery of the sound pattern of language was made only once in human history. Modern linguistics uses distinctive features, but they would not exist if the sound pattern of language had not been discovered two-and-a-half millennia earlier.[29]

The rules and metarules in the Vedas are the beginning of the metalinguistic study of language. Vedic linguists thus laid the foundation for the concept and the formation of artificial languages, which today are very real.

In a final chapter, Staal shows how the Vedas inspired Buddhism. In contrast to the Vedas, though, he asserts that Buddhism is a religion that did not want anything to do with rituals. Buddhism transformed rituals into meditation. One of the new traditions developed in Buddhism is entering into the monastic order, which is seen as a second birth, a tradition where Buddhism is close to Catholicism.

Staal finishes with a fascinating report on the first university in the world, in Nālandā, not far from Buddha's birthplace, founded by Buddhist monks around 500 C.E., to which students from all over Asia came. This was the beginning of a great Asian university tradition. By way of conclusion, Staal makes a bold prediction, backed by comparative statistics regarding students at universities in the U.S. and in Asia: "[C]ivilization [will] return to Asia under the intellectual guidance of India and China."[30]

After engaging with this brief collection, most of the objections to Staal's radicalism I stated in my "open letter" of 1997 have dropped away. I remain critical on one point, however. Staal discusses the human sacrifice that is mentioned in the "Hymn of Purusha" and asserts that sacrifice had already been sublimated into symbolic acts early on, as is more often the case with Vedic rituals. However, he refers erroneously to the monotheistic traditions, which, according to him, started with Abraham's willingness to sacrifice his own son to God. Human sacrifice was practiced all around the world in many cultures: not only among the Incas and Mesopotamians, but also in an early stage among the Greeks and Romans, as well as among the Celts. Why is Judaism presented as the only example of human sacrifice? According to the prevailing view among historians,[31] the parable about Abraham and Isaac means just the opposite. With this parable, the Jews aim to explicitly forbid human sacrifice, parallel to the myth of Iphigenia in Aulis, putting an end to human sacrifice in Greece.

This is connected with a criticism in my "open letter," which I still maintain, even after reading *Discovering the Vedas.* Contrary to his thorough presentation of the Vedas and Indian culture, in my view Staal again presents Western monotheistic religion in a simplistic and exaggeratedly negative manner. While he writes most respectfully of the Vedic tradition, "Revere memory!" he seems to forget that a similar injunction is one of the pillars of Judaism. His criticism of monotheism, in my view, reveals more about his personal attitude than that it offers an objective viewpoint. This does not take away from the fact that I consider *Discovering the Vedas* to be an unprecedented high point in Staal's body of work. It is the precipitate of his universal mindset that he so admires in the development of the tradition of Vedic ritual: In the end, the priests utter their mantras and pour their soma, "looking in all directions," and in this he recognizes the striving for universality.

An important aspect of this book for the Netherlands is that it provides a counterweight to the tortured pettiness of perspective that has occurred here over the past decades, where problems of immigration and the question of whether or not Islam is a threat are the main topics of the day. Staal's comments apply both to so-called Islamophobia as well as to fundamentalist Islam: "A narrowing religious outlook and intolerance are two sides of the same coin."[32] In today's climate, Staal's *Discovering the Vedas* could help open us up to the world and to others. The book should in the foreseeable future find its way into French, German, and other translations, and hopefully also into a Dutch edition, even if only to pay tribute to one of our most important contemporary thinkers. His ideas are more relevant today than ever before, even where the "nonsense" that is often churned out in the name of rationalism is concerned—which would make Staal, with his love of tolerance and universality, shudder. He represents a rare phenomenon today: the return of the Renaissance man or woman who cuts a path straight through all the specialisms to universality.

Staal's book on the Vedas points the way to a global civilization. We blind ourselves when we shut ourselves off in autochtone preconceptions of identity. We should try to grasp to what extent major human achievements have been attained elsewhere in the world, including the Far East, achievements from which we can learn so much.

Notes

1 Translated from the Dutch by Wanda Boeke.

2 Frits Staal, *Discovering the Vedas: Origins, Mantras, Rituals, Insights* (London: Penguin Global, 2008.

3 Frits Staal, "Alfa, Bèta en verder," in *Drie bergen en zeven rivieren* ("Three Mountains and Seven Rivers") (Amsterdam: Meulenhoff, 2004) pp. 115–145.

4 Staal, *Discovering the Vedas,* Part V. Vedas and Buddhism, "Entering the Order, Women and Sexuality", p. 321, and on "The Gayatri Mantra," p. 213 ff.

5 Frits Staal, "Over het cyclische en het rechtlijnige tijdsbegrip" ("On the Cyclical and the Linear Concepts of Time"), in *Over zin en onzin in filosofie, religie en wetenschap* ("On Sense and Nonsense in Philosophy, Religion, and Science") (Amsterdam: Meulenhoff, 1986), p. 12.

6 Harry Mulisch, foreword to *Over zin en onzin,* pp. 7–8.

7 Frits Staal, *Rules without Meaning: Ritual, Mantras and the Human Sciences* (New York-Bern-Frankfurt am Main-Pairs: Peter Lang Publishing, 1989) p. 26 ff.

[8] Frits Staal, *Advaita and Neoplatonism: A Critical Study in Comparative Philosophy* (Madras: University of Madras, 1961); *Exploring Mysticism: A Methodological Essay* (Berkeley and Los Angeles: University of California Press, 1975, reprint); *Universals: Studies in Indian Logic and Linguistics* (Chicago and London: University of Chicago, 1988).

[9] Jacques Presser, *Ashes in the Wind: The Persecution and Destruction of Dutch Jewry* (1965) (London: Souvenir Press, 2010, reprint).

[10] *Altar of Fire,* a film by Robert Gardner and J. F. Staal, Film Study Institute at Harvard University, 1976, 58 min.

[11] Frits Staal, *Agni: The Vedic Ritual of the Fire Altar,* 2 vols. (Berkeley: Asian Humanities Press, 1983).

[12] Staal, *Exploring Mysticism: A Methodological Essay* (originally published in Dutch in 1978).

[13] Frits Staal, "The Meaninglessness of Ritual," *Numen* 26/1 (1979): 2–22.

[14] Harry Mulisch, foreword in Frits Staal, *Over zin en onzin in filosofie, religie en wetenschap* (*About Sense and Nonsense in Philosophy, Religion, and Science*) (Amsterdam: Meulenhoff, 1986), p. 9.

[15] Frits Staal, *Drie Bergen en zeven rivieren* ("Three Mountains and Seven Rivers") (Amsterdam: Meulenhoff, 2004).

[16] Dick van der Meij, ed., *Liber Amicorum Frits Staal* (Leiden and Amsterdam: International Institute for Asian Studies [IIAS], 1997).

[17] Philo Bregstein, "Beste Frits" ("Dear Frits") in Dick van der Meij, ed., *Liber Amicorum Frits Staal* (Leiden and Amsterdam: International Institute for Asian Studies [IIAS], 1997), pp. 7–25.

[18] Friedrich Nietzsche, *The Gay Science: With a Prelude in Rhymes and an Appendix of Songs,* translated with commentary by Walter Kaufmann (New York: Vintage Books, 1974). Originally published in German: *Die fröhliche Wissenschaft* (1882).

[19] Frits Staal, *Een wijsgeer in het Oosten. Op reis door Java en Kalimantan* ("A Philosopher in the East: Traveling through Java and Kalimantan") (Amsterdam: Meulenhoff, 1988).

[20] Johan Huizinga, *Homo Ludens: A Study of the Play-Element in Culture* (London, Boston and Henley: Routledge & Kegan Paul, 1949; 1980, reprint).

[21] Staal, *Discovering the Vedas,* p. 27.

[22] Staal, *Discovering the Vedas,* p. 28.

[23] Staal, *Discovering the Vedas,* pp. 96–97; he makes use of George Thompson's translation of "Soma, Hymn of the Tenth Circle (10.119)" from George Thompson, "Rgveda 10.119," *Electronic Journal of Vedic Studies* (EJVS) 9/1 (2003).

[24] Staal, *Discovering the Vedas,* pp. 144, 215, 216, 221.

[25] Staal, *Discovering the Vedas,* p. 143.

[26] Staal, *Discovering the Vedas,* pp. 151–153.

[27] Staal, *Discovering the Vedas*, pp. 154–156.

[28] Staal, *Discovering the Vedas*, pp. 206-207

[29] Staal, *Discovering the Vedas*, p. 281.

[30] Staal, *Discovering the Vedas*, pp. xxvi, 344.

[31] I cite Léon Poliakov, an authority in this area, "Introduction par Léon Poliakov," *Histoire de l'antisémitisme: 1945–1993* (Paris: Editions du Seuil, 1994) pp. 15–16, although many theologians and rabbis say the same thing; Gunnar Heinsohn, "The Israelite Origins of Monotheism and the Prohibition of Killing," *Catastrophism and Ancient History* 4/1 (1982): 31–40.

[32] Staal, *Discovering the Vedas*, p. 289.

References

Bregstein, Philo. "Beste Frits," ("Dear Frits") in Dick van der Meij, ed., *Liber Amicorum Frits Staal*, pp. 7–25. Leiden and Amsterdam: International Institute for Asian Studies (IIAS), 1997.

der Meij, Dick, van, ed. *Liber Amicorum Frits Staal*. Leiden and Amsterdam: International Institute for Asian Studies (IIAS), 1997.

Gardner, Robert, and J. F. Staal. *Altar of Fire*. Film Study Institute at Harvard University, 1976, 58 min.

Huizinga, Johan. *Homo Ludens: A Study of the Play-Element in Culture*. London, Boston and Henley: Routledge & Kegan Paul, 1949; 1980, reprint.

Nietzsche, Friedrich. *The Gay Science: With a Prelude in Rhymes and an Appendix of Songs*. Translated with commentary by Walter Kaufmann. New York: Vintage Books, 1974.

Presser, Jacques. *Ashes in the Wind: The Persecution and Destruction of Dutch Jewry*. London: Souvenir Press, 2010, reprint.

Staal, Frits. *Advaita and Neoplatonism: A Critical Study in Comparative Philosophy*. Madras: University of Madras, 1961.

—. *Agni: The Vedic Ritual of the Fire Altar*, 2 vols. Berkeley: Asian Humanities Press, 1983.

—. *Discovering the Vedas: Origins, Mantras, Rituals, Insights*. London: Penguin Global, 2009.

—. *Drie bergen en zeven rivieren* ("Three Mountains and Seven Rivers"). Amsterdam: Meulenhoff, 2004.

—. *Een wijsgeer in het Oosten. Op reis door Java en Kalimantan* ("A Philosopher in the East: Traveling through Java and Kalimantan"). Amsterdam: Meulenhoff, 1988.

—. *Exploring Mysticism: A Methodological Essay*. Berkeley and Los Angeles: University of California Press, 1975, reprint.

—. *Over zin en onzin in filosofie, religie en wetenschap* ("On Sense and Nonsense in Philosophy, Religion, and Science"). Amsterdam: Meulenhoff, 1986.

—. *Rules without Meaning: Ritual, Mantras and the Human Sciences*. Toronto Studies in Religion. New York-Bern-Frankfurt am Main-Pairs: Peter Lang Publishing, 1989.

—. "The Meaninglessness of Ritual," *Numen* 26/1 (1979): 2–22.

—. *Universals: Studies in Indian Logic and Linguistics.* Chicago and London: University of Chicago, 1988.

—. Thompson, George, trans. "Soma, Hymn of the Tenth Circle (10.119)," in "Rgveda 10.119," *Electronic Journal of Vedic Studies* (EJVS) 9/1 (2003).

Agniṣṭoma and the Nature of Sacrifice

Johannes Bronkhorst
University of Lausanne

Ever since the studies of Sylvain Lévi in 1898[1] and Henri Hubert and Marcel Mauss in 1899,[2] it has been taken for granted that the victim in a Vedic sacrifice is a substitute for the sacrificer.[3] In this paper I argue that while this may often be true, it is not always the case. In certain sacrifices the victim does not represent the sacrificer but his enemy. The *Agniṣṭoma* will serve as example.

The outline of this sacrifice is well known.[4] The soma plant (or rather its stalks) are "bought" from a "*soma* merchant," who is in reality either a brahman or a *śūdra* who plays that role. The purchase follows on a prescribed process of barter, and the payment is a one-year-old brown cow. At this point the "*soma* merchant" is beaten. The *soma* itself is henceforth treated not as a plant but is personified as a king: It is placed on a throne and hospitality is offered to "him." The pressing of the *soma* stalks to extract the liquid at the end is referred to as "killing."[5]

The victim in this sacrifice is thus clearly the *soma* itself. Is it plausible to maintain that "King Soma" is a substitute for the sacrificer? Nothing in the texts suggests anything of the kind, as far as I know. Quite the contrary, the strange way in which King Soma is obtained suggests something altogether different. It suggests that the king of a neighboring and therefore inimical territory is obtained by unfriendly means. Once in the possession of the sacrificer, "he" is well treated but yet does not escape death as a sacrificial victim.

This reading of the *Agniṣṭoma* does not require advanced skills of symbolic interpretation. The texts are suggestive enough. Moreover, we know that similar types of sacrifices were practiced in other parts of the world, with real human victims. We know that the Aztecs, for example, obtained their human victims by unfriendly means (i.e., warfare with other groups), that they preferred victims of high rank, that they treated their captured enemies well until the day of their inevitable sacrificial death.[6]

It is not even necessary to leave India in order to find sacrificial practices with a human victim. Vedic literature itself mentions the *puruṣamedha,* "human sacrifice." Here, as in the *Agniṣṭoma,* the victim (a male human being) is bought from his family for a price of a thousand cows and a hundred horses. The victim must belong to one of the two highest classes, brahman or warrior (*kṣatriya*). Before being finally put to death, he is relatively free for a year and can pursue most of his wishes (with some exceptions, such as engaging in sexual intercourse).[7] It is relatively unimportant for our present purposes to determine whether the *puruṣamedha* was ever actually performed in ancient India; many scholars think it was not.[8] It gives expression, once again, to the idea that a high-ranking person from a presumably inimical community is obtained to be sacrificed.

If this is, in outline, the (or a) correct way of interpreting the *Agniṣṭoma,* the view that the victim is always a substitute for the sacrificer needs adjustment. I propose that in certain sacrifices the victim is a substitute for the sacrificer, while in others he may be regarded as a substitute for his enemy.

It may be objected that in most modern interpretations of sacrifice there is no place for enemies. In answer to this objection, it must be pointed out that there is plenty of space for enemies in Vedic sacrificial literature. The notion of killing enemies, or rivals, is frequent even in connection with Vedic sacrifices that do not carry out or hint at inimical actions. Instead, the sacrifice that on first glance seems "innocuous" turns out to be *a means to kill the enemy.* H. W. Bodewitz writes about this:

> It is remarkable that killing persons who hate the sacrificer or his priest plays an important role in the Vedic ritualistic texts. . . . The one who will be killed is called a (hating) rival (*bhrātṛvya*) and there is no mentioning of an official war. In a rather old prose text like the [*Taittirīya Saṃhitā*] we often read about someone "who hates us and whom we hate." A later text like the [*Jaiminīya Brāhmaṇa*], in which such a killing is frequently mentioned, the stereotyped expression is "he who knows thus kills his hating rival." In the [*Taittirīya Saṃhitā*] often gods are invoked to kill the one who is hated and hates the sacrificer or his priest. . . . In the [*Jaiminīya Brāhmaṇa*] the killing is mostly caused by, or based on, an incantation. By (or with the help of) sacrifice the rival becomes killed. Often one also tries to obtain his cattle in this way. A particular arrangement or way of singing the Sāmans in this Sāmavedic text guarantees the death of the rival. This ritualistic magic is also current in the Yajurvedic [*Śatapatha Brāhmaṇa*]. Whether this killing is only realized by magic or should be supported by this ritualistic magic in a fight is not clearly indicated in the texts.[9]

It must be admitted that there may be no Vedic text that explicitly identifies the sacrificial victim with the enemy. Moreover, there are sacrifices whose confrontational nature is beyond doubt, but that culminate nonetheless in the slaughter of a victim who is a substitute for the sacrificer. An example is the horse sacrifice (*aśvamedha*), which establishes the sacrificer's superiority over his neighbors; the victim is not one of these neighbors but a horse. The chief queen performs sexual intercourse with the horse, thus identifying it as a substitute for the sacrificing king.

If there is no explicit evidence in the Vedic texts and their auxiliary literature that the victim in certain sacrifices is a substitute for the enemy (or even the enemy himself), does this mean that this notion is mistaken? Must we retract this theory altogether and return to the earlier one in which the sacrificial victim is always a substitute for the sacrificer?

I think we must not do so until we have heard the testimony of some other brahmans from approximately the same period, the authors of the *Mahābhārata*.[10] The main story of this epic was told during a snake sacrifice (*sarpasattra*) with the goal of destroying all snakes. The fact that the sacrifice did not succeed is irrelevant for our present purpose. Christopher Minkowski sums up how this sacrifice came about:

> The story of Janamejaya's sattra belongs to the Āstīka parvan of the Mahābhārata's first book (1.45–53). The events of the Āstīka parvan, the curse of Kadrū (1.18), the death of Parikṣit (1.36–40), and the birth of Āstīka (1.33–44), culminate in the story of the snake *sattra,* which begins with Janamejaya learning that his father Parikṣit was killed by the serpent Takṣaka. Seeking revenge, Janamejaya asks his priests whether they know a rite that would enable him to propel Takṣaka and his relations into blazing fire (1.47.4). The priests reply that there is a rite that will accomplish such a task, created by the gods especially for Janamejaya (*tvadartham devanirmitam*), known as the sarpasattra, and described in the Purāṇic lore (*purāṇe kathyate*) (1.47.6). Janamejaya is the only man eligible to sponsor this rite, and the priests have the training to perform it (1.47.7). Janamejaya agrees and orders the priests to prepare (1.47.8–9).[11]

This sacrifice may not fit into any of the traditional Vedic categories, least of all the *sattra,* yet it is clear that it is nonetheless a sacrifice in which the victims are also the enemies of the sacrificer. This is not the only such example from the *Mahābhārata.* Two famous passages compare the epic war in the *Mahābhārata* itself with sacrifice. Duryodhana, addressing his father, Dhṛtarāṣṭra, says the following:

> I am not putting the burden of war on you, or on Droṇa, or on Aśvatthāman, or on Saṃjaya, or on Vikarṇa, or on Kāmboja, or on Bāhlīka, Satyavrata, Purumitra, Bhūriśravas, or any others of your party, when I make this challenge! I and Karṇa, father, have laid out the sacrifice of war (*raṇayajña*) and here we stand consecrated *with Yudhiṣṭhira as the victim*, bull of the Bharatas. This chariot is the altar, this sword the spoon, this club the ladle, this armor the *sadas*. My steeds are the four sacrificial priests, my arrows the *darbha* grass, my fame the oblation! Having offered up ourselves in war to Vaivasvata, O king, we shall triumphantly return, covered with glory, our enemies slain. I, Karṇa, and my brother Duḥśāsana, we three, father, will kill Pāṇḍavas in battle. I shall kill the Pāṇḍavas and rule the earth. I should rather surrender my life, wealth, and realm, steadfast king, than ever dwell together with the Pāṇḍavas! We shall not cede to the Pāṇḍavas as much land as you can prick with the point of a sharp needle, father![12]

In this comparison, Duryodhana is the sacrificer and Yudhiṣṭhira the victim. Clearly Yudhiṣṭhira is Duryodhana's enemy, but this appears to be no obstacle to his role also as the sacrificial victim. Yudhiṣṭhira's role in this imaginary sacrifice is parallel to that of the snakes in Janamejaya's *sattra* and of King Soma in the *Agniṣṭoma.*

We know from the remainder of the *Mahābhārata* story that Duryodhana's imagined sacrifice never took place. Yudhiṣṭhira was not killed in battle, while Duryodhana himself (along with Karṇa) were vanquished. It is interesting, that Duryodhana figures as sacrificial victim in another comparison, this one made by Karṇa, who also compared the approaching battle with a sacrifice but one in which sacrificer and victim were identical:

> Vārṣṇeya, the Dhārtarāṣṭra will hold a grand sacrifice of war (*śastrayajña*). Of this sacrifice you shall be the Witness, Janārdana, and you shall be the Adhvaryu priest at the ritual. The Terrifier with the monkey standard stands girt as the Hotar; Gāṇḍīva will be the ladle; the bravery of men the sacrificial butter. The *aindra, pāśupata, brāhma,* and *sthūṇākarṇa* missiles will be the spells employed by the Left-handed Archer. Saubhadra, taking after his father, if not overtaking him, in prowess, will act perfectly as the Grāvastut priest. Mighty Bhīma will be the Udgātar and Prastotar, that tiger-like man who with his roars on the battlefield finishes off an army of elephants. The eternal king, law-spirited Yudhiṣṭhira, well-versed in recitations and oblations, will act as the Brahmán. The sounds of the conches, the drums, the kettle drums, and the piercing lion roars will be the Subrahmaṇā invocation. Mādrī's two glorious sons Nakula and Sahadeva of great valor will fill the office of the Śamitar priest. The clean chariot spears with their spotted staffs will serve as the sacrificial poles at this sacrifice, Janārdana.

The eared arrows, hollow reeds, iron shafts and calf-tooth piles, and the javelins will be the Soma jars, and the bows the strainers. Swords will be the potsherds, skulls the Puroḍāśa cakes, and blood will be the oblation at this sacrifice, Kṛṣṇa. The spears and bright clubs will be the kindling and enclosing sticks; the pupils of Droṇa and Kṛpa Śāradvata the Sadasyas. The arrows shot by the Gāṇḍīva bowman, the great warriors, and Droṇa and his son will be the pillows. Sātyaki shall act as Pratiprasthātar, *the Dhārtarāṣṭra as the Sacrificer* (*dīkṣita*), his great army as the Wife. Mighty Ghaṭotkaca will be the Śamitar when this Overnight (*atirātra*) Sacrifice is spun out, strong-armed hero. Majestic Dhṛṣṭadyumna shall be the sacrificial fee when the fire rite takes place, he who was born from the fire.

The insults I heaped on the Pāṇḍavas, to please Duryodhana, those I regret. When you see me cut down by the Left-handed Archer, it will be the Re-piling of the Fire of this[13] sacrifice. When the Pāṇḍava drinks the blood of Duḥśāsana, bellowing his roar, it will be the Soma draught. When the two Pāñcālyas fell Droṇa and Bhīṣma, that will be the Conclusion of the sacrifice, Janārdana. *When the mighty Bhīmasena kills Duryodhana, then the great sacrifice of the Dhārtarāṣṭra will end.* The weeping of the gathered daughters-in-law and granddaughters-in-law, whose masters, sons, and protectors have been slain, with the mourning of Gāndhārī at the sacrificial site now teeming with dogs, vultures, and ospreys, will be the Final Bath of this sacrifice, Janārdana.[14]

Many of the detailed comparisons here are quite fanciful. However, one identification in particular is significant: the sacrificer, Duryodhana, is also the victim. Here, then, the authors of the *Mahābhārata* give the identification we would expect to find on the basis of our reading of Lévi and Hubert and Mauss. But why did they not do so in the earlier comparison, the one spoken by Duryodhana himself?

The answer I propose is straightforward. This identification does not figure in the earlier comparison because sacrificer and victim are not always identical, either in the imagination of the authors of the *Mahābhārata* or in Vedic sacrifice itself. To be precise, in some sacrifices the victim is or stands in for the sacrificer, while in other sacrifices the victim is or stands in for the enemy of the sacrificer. King Soma stands for the enemy (or an enemy) of the sacrificer. Only this way can we make sense of the strange treatment of the material substance of the *soma*.

I have assumed in the preceding that the *Mahābhārata*'s authors may or may not have had detailed knowledge of all the specifics of Vedic sacrifice; but they did have an understanding of what sacrifice is all about. This understanding implied that in certain sacrifices the victim is or represents the enemy of the sacrificer. This vision finds expression in the story of the snake sacrifice, as we have seen. It also finds expression in other stories; for instance, in what the *Mahābhārata* tells us about King Jarāsandha of Magadha:

> After he had defeated them all, [Jarāsandha] imprisoned the kings in his mountain corral, Girivraja, as a lion imprisons great elephants in a cave of the Himālaya. King Jarāsandha wants to sacrifice the lords of the earth, for it was after he had worshiped the Great God that he defeated the kings on the battlefield. Whenever he defeated kings in battle, he took them in fetters to his own city and built a corral for men![15]

About these imprisoned kings we read:

> What joy of life is left to the kings who are sprinkled and cleansed in the house of Paśupati as sacrificial animals. . . ?[16]

It is true that Kṛṣṇa criticizes King Jarāsandha for wishing to perform a human sacrifice, claiming that human sacrifice has never taken place in the past.[17] It hardly matters whether or not Kṛṣṇa's claim is correct. He does not accuse Jarāsandha for failing to understand what sacrifice is all about, and indeed, it appears that Jarāsandha understood sacrifice very well.

We may conclude that there are two types of sacrifice distinguished from each other in that in one type the victim is or stands in for the *sacrificer,* while in the other type the victim is or stands in for the *enemy of the sacrificer.* I propose to look upon these two types as applicable not only in India but wherever sacrifices are performed. We have already seen that a particularly good example of the type of sacrifice in which the victim is or stands in for the enemy of the sacrificer is provided by the Aztecs, but there are more examples from outside India. I have collected some of this evidence in a recent article.[18] I drew attention to the social aspect of the need to sacrifice: sacrifices sanctify, in the sense of anchoring in a higher reality, relations of superiority and inferiority. Where the victim is or stands in for the sacrificer, the sacrificer solemnly sanctifies his inferior position, normally with respect to a higher, non-human being. Where the victim is or stands in for the enemy, the sacrificer sanctifies his superiority with respect to that enemy.[19]

Here I wish to concentrate on a consequence of this position with which I have only superficially dealt so far. It concerns the kinds of victims that are actually sacrificed, most notably animals. If the victim stands for the sacrificer, one may expect that the sacrificed entity is something or someone of value to him, something he owns or that is dear to him. If the sacrificial victim is an animal, it should be an animal that the sacrificer owns, in other words, a domestic animal.

If, on the other hand, the victim stands for the enemy of the sacrificer or is itself his enemy, the situation is rather different. In principle, anything that is dear to the enemy may do as substitute, at least in theory. This might conceivably be an animal that belongs to the enemy, which then again, by its nature, would be a domesticated animal. The whole procedure might be executed on such a level of abstraction that no real enemy is left. The *Agniṣṭoma* shows that in such cases an imaginary enemy—in this case, King Soma—will do, and the imaginary enemy is ceremoniously put to death.

There is no obvious place in this understanding for the sacrifice of wild animals. And indeed, the question whether wild animals can ever be sacrificed is contested. Jonathan Z. Smith, for example, writes:

> I know of no unambiguous instance of animal sacrifice performed by hunters. *Animal sacrifice appears to be, universally, the ritual killing of a domesticated animal by agrarian or pastoralist societies.*[20]

Beattie and Hénaff express themselves similarly.[21] Smith dedicates the end of his article to a discussion of the putative evidence for the use of wild animals in sacrifice. He writes, "the only contemporary putative evidence for a wild animal being used in sacrifice is the circum-polar bear festival."[22] In discussing this claim, Smith makes a number of observations that are worth repeating:

> In fact, the bear festival does not fit, although it was used as the hermeneutic key to interpret the Paleolithic remains. (a) The peoples who practice the bear festivals are pastoralists, not hunters. . . . (b) In the circum-polar bear ritual, the animal is domesticated for a period of years before being slain. (c) In the case of the Ainu (for whom there is the best ethnographic documentation), both the most distinguished native Ainu anthropologist, K. Kindaichi. . . , and the bear festival's most distinguished recent interpreter, J. M. Kitagawa. . . , vigorously deny that the ritual should be classified as a sacrifice. . . .
>
> On the issue of Paleolithic sacrifices, the evaluation of the evidence has been one of steady retreat from confidence to uncertainty. For example, J. Maringer, who confidently declared in 1952 that "the practice of sacrificing the head, skull and long bones of animals survived from earliest times right up to the Upper Paleolithic". . . , retreated by 1968 to declaring that sacrifice is not evident in Lower and Middle Paleolithic deposits, and that it is possible to speak "with relatively great certainty" (*"mit mehr oder minder grosser Sicherheit"*) of animal sacrifices only in the Upper Paleolithic. . . . Yet even

> here, strong alternative hypotheses that account for the "evidence" as non-sacrificial have been proposed. . . .
>
> The fact that sacrifices are invariably of domesticated animals in contrast to wild ones (and hence from a different "sphere" than religious practices associated with hunters or Paleolithic man) was already quite properly insisted upon by L. Franz [in 1937]. Several months of checking in a variety of ethnographic monographs have turned up no exceptions. Here, I distinguish between killing an animal in sacrifice and the postmortem offering of some portion of an animal routinely killed for food. The latter is certainly present among some hunters and gatherers.[23]

We will study these observations in more detail below. First I must point out that despite these assertions, a few more recent scholars continue to assume that there were animal sacrifices—i.e., sacrifices of wild animals—in the remote past. An example is Michael Witzel's recent book, *The Origins of the World's Mythologies*, a *tour de force* that presents a sustained argument that human mythologies can be traced back to a time before our ancestors left Africa.[24] Mythology is not, however, our concern at present. We are rather concerned with Witzel's discussion of the origins and development of sacrifice. He writes:

> The origins and development of sacrifice are related to forms of shamanism by a series of progressions, from the Stone Age hunt to recent and current practices. . . .
>
> The shamanistic aspect of the religion of the Stone Age hunter societies presupposes, in its Laurasian version, the dismemberment and/or sacrifice of a primordial deity. Examples include that of the giant, such as the southern "Chinese" (Miao) Pangu, the Vedic Indian Puruṣa, the Old Norse Ymir, the Roman Remus, the Egyptian Osiris, and the Mesopotamian Kingu (and Tiamat).[25] The giant has a human correspondent, man. In many if not most societies, however, human sacrifice is substituted by that of other animals: dog, goat, bull, boar, reindeer, bear, and more recently, horse. Or in the classical Vedic Indian order of "the five domestic animals": man, horse, cow, sheep, and goat, while the wild animals are not considered; this is justified in a myth reported in a late Vedic text.[26]

So far this agrees by and large with what I have said about sacrifice above, and most particularly with the first type of sacrifice in which a sacrificer (human or divine) puts himself or a substitute for himself to death. One detail, however, is disturbing: the presence of nondomesticated animals, most notably the bear, in Witzel's discussion. Is there such a thing as a bear sacrifice? Smith remarked that "the only contemporary putative evidence for a wild animal being used in sacrifice is the circumpolar bear festival," and stated his reservations about this.

Like Smith before him, Witzel refers to the Ainu bear sacrifice. It is time for us to refine our theoretical reflections and, armed with these, turn to an inspection of this sacrifice.

It is clear from Smith's passage, cited above, that at least part of the problem connected with the use of wild animals in sacrifice has to do with what exactly we understand by "sacrifice." The preceding reflections can be of use here. If we think of sacrifice as the "ritualized," i.e., holistic and ceremonial[27] destruction either of the sacrificer or his substitute, or of the enemy or his substitute, how might wild animals fit in? One possible answer is that they might become sacrificial victims after being caught. They might then be considered the property of the person(s) who caught them, the sacrificer, and become his/their substitute. Alternatively, the wild animal, once caught, might be treated as is the soma plant in the *Agniṣṭoma:* as a vanquished enemy who will be ceremoniously put to death. Being killed in the hunt, on the other hand, does *not* turn wild animals into sacrificial victims, because at the time of their capture they belong to no one, least of all the sacrificer. High-ranking warriors of a neighboring king were caught and sacrificed by the Aztecs and others, but the Aztecs did not just kill warriors on the battlefield, rather they (like King Jarāsandha) caught them and held them as prisoners until the time they were ritually put to death. Slaughtering enemy soldiers in battle would not count as sacrifice. Similarly, killing a wild animal during a hunt is not sacrifice. For it to be sacrifice, the animal has to be captured alive and put to death ritually, after some interval of time. The case of King Soma is similar: the *soma* is obtained, kept, and finally "killed" in ritually prescribed manner. To say it once again, merely killing a wild animal on a hunt cannot be seen as animal sacrifice.

Let us push the analysis somewhat further. Theoretically, one can imagine several scenarios. Wild animals might play a role as victims in the first type of sacrifice (in which the sacrificer parts with something that is dear to him or that he owns) only if the wild animals have become, one way or another, dead or alive, the property of the sacrificer. In that case, the sacrificer would be parting with something that belongs to him, something that can for that reason be considered a substitute for himself. There are two ways in which one can become the owner of a wild animal. The animal is captured when young and is then domesticated it to the extent possible, before it is killed in a sacrifice. Or an animal is killed in the hunt, and the hunter thus becomes the owner of its flesh, part of which can then be offered in sacrifice. The second possibility is less interesting for us at present, and less contested. Smith himself, as we have seen, admits that "the postmortem offering of some portion of an animal routinely killed for food . . . is certainly present among some hunters and gatherers."[28]

In order to find a place for wild animals in the second type of sacrifice, the wild animal has to somehow be regarded as or represent an enemy. The *Agniṣṭoma* sacrifice shows that this can happen on an abstract level, so that no real enemy is involved: King Soma is the enemy, but he is not a real enemy. A wild animal may similarly *be* or *represent* an enemy, without itself actually being a real enemy. As in the cases of King Soma or the warriors caught by the Aztecs, the wild animal as enemy must have first been caught and kept as prisoner before its sacrificial execution. This would fit the second sacrifice scenario. Modern human societies also know a variant of this: headhunting.[29] In the case of headhunting, the enemy or its representative is first killed and the sacrificial ritual is subsequently carried out on a significant part of the dead body (normally, the head). We could regard this as a variant of the second type of sacrifice. Similarly, a wild animal is killed during the hunt and an important part of it or an organ is subsequently used in sacrifice.[30] These latter two types (or a mixture thereof) is well attested among at least some present-day hunter/gatherer cultures. As stated above, these two options are less interesting for the present discussion because they cannot be considered to be the sacrificial killing of a wild animal.

The first type of wild animal sacrifice may exist, or may have existed until recently, among the Ainu of Hokkaido, Japan, in which a bear cub is captured, then raised in the village, and finally killed. Joseph Campbell describes this:

> When a very young black bear cub has been brought alive into the village, he is adopted by one of the families and treated as one of the children, suckled by the mother, and affectionately pampered. When it becomes big enough to hurt the others when playing, however, it is put into a strong wooden cage, fed on fish and millet porridge, and kept for about two years, until time is thought to have arrived for it to be released from its body and returned to its parents in their mountain.[31]

It is possible to understand this passage as describing a rudimentary attempt to "domesticate" the bear, so that, in the end, it is a "domesticated" animal that is sacrificed. It is equally possible to interpret it in terms of the type of sacrifice in which an "enemy" is caught, kept, and subsequently sacrificed. The situation is ambiguous, because the bear receives both affectionate and cruel treatment.

> The bear, secured with ropes, then is taken from the cage and made to walk around in the circle of the people. Blunt little bamboo arrows, bearing a black and white geometrical design and a compact clump of shavings at the tip . . . are let fly at the animal and he is teased until he becomes furious.[32]

The Ainu are not the only ones who practiced this kind of bear sacrifice. There are convincing traces to show that something quite similar took place in different regions in Europe in recent times. For example:

> Là, c'est-à-dire en Béarn, en Navarre, en Catalogne, en Roussillon et dans une bonne partie du Languedoc méridional, l'ours est souvent la seule vedette du carnaval: une fête spécifique lui est consacrée, qui ne diffère d'un village à l'autre que par quelques variantes. Elle se déroule le plus souvent le jour de la Chandeleur (2 février) ou bien le dimanche suivant, quelquefois le jeudi gras. La trame en est à peu près toujours la même: un homme déguisé en ours descend de la montagne ou sort de la forêt; il enlève une jeune fille qui dansait avec des garçons—en général la plus jolie—et l'emmène dans son repaire; on le poursuit, on le cherche, on l'appelle, on le trouve; il est alors capturé, ligoté, conduit au centre du village selon un parcours bien précis; mais le fauve s'échappe en chemin, terrorise la foule, simule un second enlèvement; pris de nouveau, il est cette fois enchaîné, humilié, rasé puis mis à mort.[33]

> Concernant les Balkans et les Carpates, les travaux des ethnologues ont surtout porté sur les rituels ursin du coeur de l'hiver et de la période du carnival . . . un ours est mené en procession, décoré de pailles, de branches ou de feuilles; on lui offre des graines et des fruits, on le cajole, on le fait tourner et danser, on monte sur son dos. Le plus souvent, il ne s'agit pas d'un ours véritable mais d'un homme déguisé en ours, qui s'amuse à faire peur aux femmes et aux enfants. Parfois, notamment lorsqu'il s'agit d'un mannequin de paille, on en fait un souffre-douleur, on le met à mort symboliquement puis on le brûle.[34]

It seems reasonable to assume that testimonies like these count as evidence that bear sacrifices did exist until quite recently. This would then count as proof that wild animals *can* occasionally be sacrificial victims, but there is no denying that these animals have in some sense been "domesticated." Indeed, our theoretical reflections oblige us to think that a live wild animal can only be sacrificed after some degree of domestication, even if that domestication consists only of keeping the wild animal for some period before it is sacrificed.

It is possible that there are other examples of wild animal sacrifice but if so, it would seem that they follow the same pattern. Mark E. Lewis, for example, writes that in early China warfare and hunting were identified with sacrifice, adding that prey was taken in the hunt to be used as sacrificial victims, and of

> the old Zhou identification of hunting as a form of warfare and in the equation, as potential sacrifices, of prey taken in the hunt with prisoners captured in combat. . . . [T]he Zhou had emphasized hunts as . . . a practical means of securing sacrificial victims. . . .[35]

This appears to confirm that wild animals, in order to become sacrificial victims, must first be caught and "domesticated" (in the sense of being held captive for some period of time).

Some scholars claim that the sacrifice with domesticated animals evolved out of prehistoric hunting and killing for food that was somehow thought of in religious terms. Walter Burkert is the most important representative of this position.[36] The problem with this position is that sacrifice (and ritual in general) tends to be "a stately and solemn ceremony,"[37] so that whatever the historical relation between hunt and animal sacrifice, the hunt itself cannot be looked upon as ritualized animal sacrifice.

Witzel nonetheless maintains that animals depicted in prehistoric paintings—he mentions large animals such as lion, wild bull, or antelope—were sacrificial animals.[38] If my reflections so far are correct, this would imply that such animals were caught alive by members of the tribes to which the prehistoric artists belonged. Is this conceivable? Did these remote ancestors have the means and materials to keep such wild animals captive? And if so, are there reasons to think that Stone Age hunters would have gone to so much trouble?

Witzel himself knows that there is no certain evidence to support all this:

> We do not yet have actual proof of animal sacrifice during the Stone Age period—perhaps with the exception of the Lascaux and nearby scenes of the bison bull and the "shaman"—but the same attitude toward the offering and sacrifice of bears is seen in the Stone Age plastic art of France. In the case of Montespan, the body of a bear had roughly been fashioned out of clay. It was found draped with a bear's pelt, with a bear's head still attached, which another bear's skull was found in front of this image. Some sort of bear cult is also seen in the Paleolithic enshrinements of bear skulls at Drachenloch in Switzerland, where the long bones of a bear were inserted into his mouth; and we can see its continuation in the [pre]modern circumpolar bear cult.[39]

What is problematic in this passage is that "bear cult" and "bear sacrifice," and perhaps more generally "animal cult" and "animal sacrifice," are identified and therefore confused. Indeed, the following note accompanies the remark about Montespan:[40]

> This is controversially discussed by Bahn (1991), who does not reject Paleolithic hunting magic but denies that it had a dominant role and calls for much more caution in the interpretation of Paleolithic art. But note the recent find of a bear skull on an "altar" in the undisturbed Chauvet Cave, 32,000 BP.[41]

In this note what was meant to be evidence for animal sacrifice in Montespan becomes evidence for hunting magic. But these two, whatever their link, cannot be identified.

What does all this mean? Both the theoretical considerations and the evidence at hand seem to confirm that only "domesticated" animals can be sacrificial victims. Domestication must be understood here in a broad sense: beside ordinary domestic animals, captured wild animals can be included. Animal sacrifice should not be identified with animal cults or animal magic; even if the presence of an animal *cult* or animal *magic* in a certain population can be proven, this does not yet prove the presence of animal *sacrifice.*

What does this imply for pre-agricultural and pre-pastoral times? Self-sacrifice (whether in actual or mythological terms) is conceivable, and does indeed figure in Laurasian mythology, if Witzel's reconstructions are accepted. The sacrifice of a substitute for oneself presupposes a (perhaps rudimentary) notion of ownership:[42] the most obvious substitute for oneself in a largely possessionless society may well be a member of one's family, e.g., one's child. But it is difficult to imagine that such societies had the means or the infrastructure to catch and keep wild animals for any length of time. The same difficulty applies to the sacrifice of a wild animal that represents (or "is") the enemy. Stone Age animal sacrifice seems therefore unlikely.

However, sacrificial offering of (at least part of) the flesh and meat obtained through hunting (the first type of wild animal sacrifice, or even the animal equivalent of headhunting, a variant of the second type) seems possible or even likely. This is not animal sacrifice of domesticated stock but sacrifice in which the newly acquired flesh of the killed animal is offered as a substitute for the sacrificer or for the enemy. This custom may be as old as the myths that mention self-sacrifice, or even older.

Notes

1 Sylvain Lévi, *La doctrine du sacrifice dans les Brāhmaṇas* (1898) (Turnhout: Brepols, 2003, reprint), p. 132.

2 Henri Hubert and Marcel Mauss, "Essai sur la nature et la fonction sociale du sacrifice," *Année sociologique* 2 (1899): 45; English translation in W. D. Halls, Henri Hubert, and Marcel Mauss, *Sacrifice: Its Nature and Function* (London: Cohen & West, 1964), p. 32.

3 See, e.g., Madeleine Biardeau, "Le sacrifice dans l'hindouisme," in Madeleine Biardeau and Charles Malamoud, eds., *Le sacrifice dans l'Inde ancienne* (Paris: Presses Universitaires de France, 1976), p. 19; Ganesh U. Thite, *Sacrifice in the Brāhmaṇa-Texts* (Poona: University of Poona, 1975), pp. 143–144.

4 Willem Caland and Victor Henry, *L'agniṣṭoma. Description complète de la forme normale du sacrifice de soma dans le culte védique* (Paris: Ernest Leroux, 1906–1907).

5 *Śatapatha Brāhmaṇa* (Mādhyandina recension) (ŚPaBr) 3.9.4.17. See B. Schlerath, "The Slaying of the God Soma," *Annals of the Bhandarkar Oriental Research Institute* 68 (1987): 345–348; Georges-Jean Pinault, "About the Slaying of Soma: Uncovering the Rigvedic Witness," in L. Kulikov and M. Rusanov, eds., *Indologica. T. Ya. Elizarenkova Memorial Volume*, Book 1 (Moscow: Russian State University for the Humanities, 2008), pp. 353–388.

6 For details, see Johannes Bronkhorst, "Rites Without Symbols," *Method and Theory in the Study of Religion* 24 (2012): 236–266.

7 Alfred Hillebrandt, *Ritual-Litteratur: Vedische Opfer und Zauber* (Strassburg: K. J. Trübner, 1897), p. 153; Willibald Kirfel, "Der Aśvamedha und der Puruṣamedha," *Beiträge zur indischen Philologie und Altertumskunde. Walter Schubring zum 70. Geburtstag dargebracht* (Hamburg: Cram, DeGruyter, 1951), pp. 39–50; James L. Sauvé, "The Divine Victim: Aspects of Human Sacrifice in Viking Scandinavia and Vedic India," in Jaan Puhvel, ed., *Myth and Law among Indo-Europeans* (Berkeley: University of California Press, 1970), p. 184 f.; Charles Malamoud, "Modèle et réplique: Remarques sur le paradigme du sacrifice humain dans l'Inde védique," *Archiv für Religionsgeschichte* 1/1 (1999): 27–40.

8 See, however, Hans Bakker, "Puruṣamedha, Manasarapuruṣa, Vāstupuruṣa: The Image of Man in the Sacrificial Context," *Journal of Indological Studies* 20–21 (2008–2009): 1–23. It is appropriate to note here what Bruce Lincoln wrote in "Debreasting, Disarming, Beheading: Some Sacrificial Practices of the Scyths and Amazons," in *Death, War and Sacrifice: Studies in Ideology and Practice* (Chicago: University of Chicago Press, 1991), p. 198:

> I should note the possibility that some of these practices, like some of these peoples (particularly the Amazons), were more imaginary than actual, although . . . this in no way diminishes their interest or importance, for one can learn much from the imaginary practices of an imaginary people, particularly regarding the thoughts and values of those whose imaginations they inhabit.

9 H. W. Bodewitz, "Sins and Vices: Their Enumerations and Specifications in the Veda," *Indo-Iranian Journal* 50/4 (2007): 329–330.

[10] See also Johannes Bronkhorst, "Sacrifice in the *Mahābhārata* and Beyond, Or: Did the Author(s) of the *Mahābhārata* Understand Vedic Sacrifice Better Than We Do?", forthcoming.

[11] Christopher Minkowski, "Snakes, Sattras, and the Mahābhārata," in Arvind Sharma, ed., *Essays on the Mahābhārata* (Leiden: E. J. Brill, 1991), p. 385.

[12] *Mahābhārata* (Mhbh) 5.57.10–18: *nāhaṃ bhavati na droṇe nāśvatthāmni na saṃjaye/ na vikarṇe na kāmboje na kṛpe na ca bāhlike // 10 // satyavrate purumitre bhūriśravasi vā punaḥ/ anyeṣu vā tāvakeṣu bhāraṃ kṛtvā samāhvaye // 11 // ahaṃ ca tāta karṇaś ca raṇayajñaṃ vitatya vai / yudhiṣṭhiraṃ paśuṃ kṛtvā dīkṣitau bharatarṣabha // 12 // ratho vedī sruvaḥ khaḍgo gadā sruk kavacaṃ sadaḥ/ cāturhotraṃ ca dhuryā me śarā darbhā havir yaśaḥ // 13 // ātmayajñena nṛpate iṣṭvā vaivasvataṃ raṇe / vijitya svayam eṣyāvo hatāmitrau śriyā vṛtau // 14 // ahaṃ ca tāta karṇaś ca bhrātā duḥśāsanaś ca me / ete vayaṃ haniṣyāmaḥ pāṇḍavān samare trayaḥ // 15 // ahaṃ hi pāṇḍavān hatvā praśāstā pṛthivīm imām / māṃ vā hatvā pāṇḍuputrā bhoktāraḥ pṛthivīm imām // 16 // tyaktaṃ me jīvitaṃ rājan dhanaṃ rājyaṃ ca pārthiva/ na jātu pāṇḍavaiḥ sārdhaṃ vaseyam aham acyuta// 17 // yāvad dhi sūcyās tīkṣṇāyā vidhyed agreṇa māriṣa/ tāvad apy aparityājyaṃ bhūmer naḥ pāṇḍavān prati// 18 //.* J. A. B. van Buitenen, trans., *The Mahābhārata* (University of Chicago Press, 1978), vol. 2, p. 325.

[13] van Buitenen, *The Mahābhārata*, vol. 3 p. 447, has "their" instead of "this" here.

[14] Mhbh 5.139.29–51: *dhārtarāṣṭrasya vārṣṇeya śastrayajño bhaviṣyati / asya yajñasya vettā tvaṃ bhaviṣyasi janārdana / ādhvaryavaṃ ca te kṛṣṇa kratāv asmin bhaviṣyati // 29 // hotā caivātra bībhatsuḥ saṃnaddhaḥ sa kapidhvajaḥ / gāṇḍīvaṃ sruk tathājyaṃ ca vīryaṃ puṃsāṃ bhaviṣyati // 30 // aindraṃ pāśupataṃ brāhmaṃ sthūṇākarṇaṃ ca mādhava / mantrās tatra bhaviṣyanti prayuktāḥ savyasācinā // 31 // anuyātaś ca pitaram adhiko vā parākrame / grāvastotraṃ sa saubhadraḥ samyak tatra kariṣyati // 32 // udgātātra punar bhīmaḥ prastotā sumahābalaḥ / vinadan sa naravyāghro nāgānīkāntakṛd raṇe // 33 // sa caiva tatra dharmātmā śaśvad rājā yudhiṣṭhiraḥ / japair homaiś ca saṃyukto brahmatvaṃ kārayiṣyati // 34 // śaṅkhaśabdāḥ samurajā bheryaś ca madhusūdana / utkṛṣṭasiṃhanādāś ca subrahmaṇyo bhaviṣyati // 35 // nakulaḥ sahadevaś ca mādrīputrau yaśasvinau / śāmitraṃ tau mahāvīryau samyak tatra kariṣyataḥ // 36 // kalmāṣadaṇḍā govinda vimalā rathaśaktayaḥ/ yūpāḥ samupakalpantām asmin yajñe janārdana // 37 // karṇinālīkanārācā vatsadantopabṛṃhaṇāḥ/ tomarāḥ somakalaśāḥ pavitrāṇi dhanūṃṣi ca // 38 // asayo 'tra kapālāni puroḍāśāḥ śirāṃsi ca/ havis tu rudhiraṃ kṛṣṇa asmin yajñe bhaviṣyati // 39 // idhmāḥ paridhayaś caiva śaktyo 'tha vimalā gadāḥ / sadasyā droṇaśiṣyāś ca kṛpasya ca śaradvataḥ // 40 // iṣavo 'tra paristomā muktā gāṇḍīvadhanvanā / mahārathaprayuktāś ca droṇadrauṇipracoditāḥ // 41 // prātiprasthānikaṃ karma sātyakiḥ sa kariṣyati/ dīkṣito dhārtarāṣṭro 'tra patnī cāsya mahācamūḥ // 42 // ghaṭotkaco 'tra śāmitraṃ kariṣyati mahābalaḥ / atirātre mahābāho vitate yajñakarmaṇi // 43 // dakṣiṇā tv asya yajñasya dhṛṣṭadyumnaḥ pratāpavān / vaitāne karmaṇi tate jāto yaḥ kṛṣṇa pāvakāt // 44 // yad abruvam ahaṃ kṛṣṇa kaṭukāni sma pāṇḍavān / priyārthaṃ dhārtarāṣṭrasya tena tapye 'dya karmaṇā // 45 // yadā drakṣyasi māṃ kṛṣṇa nihataṃ savyasācinā / punaś citis tadā cāsya yajñasyātha bhaviṣyati // 46 // duḥśāsanasya rudhiraṃ yadā pāsyati pāṇḍavaḥ / ānardaṃ nardataḥ samyak tadā sutyaṃ bhaviṣyati // 47 // yadā droṇaṃ ca bhīṣmaṃ ca pāñcālyau pātayiṣyataḥ/ tadā*

yajñāvasānaṃ tad bhaviṣyati janārdana // 48 // duryodhanaṃ yadā hantā bhīmaseno mahābalaḥ / tadā samāpsyate yajño dhārtarāṣṭrasya mādhava // 49 // snuṣāś ca prasnuṣāś caiva dhṛtarāṣṭrasya saṃgatāḥ / hateśvarā hatasutā hatanāthāś ca keśava // 50 // gāndhāryā saha rodantyaḥ śvagṛdhrakurarākule / sa yajñe 'sminn avabhṛtho bhaviṣyati janārdana // 52 //. van Buitenen, *The Mahābhārata*, vol. 3, pp. 446–447.

15 Mhbh 2.13.62–64: *tena ruddhā hi rājānaḥ sarve jitvā girivraje / kandarāyāṃ girīndrasya siṃheneva mahādvipāḥ // 62 // so 'pi rājā jarāsaṃdho yiyakṣur vasudhādhipaiḥ / ārādhya hi mahādevaṃ nirjitās tena pārthivāḥ // 63 // sa hi nirjitya nirjitya pārthivān pṛtanāgatān / puram ānīya baddhvā ca cakāra puruṣavrajam / 64 //*. van Buitenen, *The Mahābhārata*, vol. 2, p. 60.

16 Mhbh 2.13.17: *prokṣitānāṃ pramṛṣṭānāṃ rājñāṃ paśupater gṛhe / paśūnāṃ iva kā prītir jīvite bharatarṣabha // 17 //*. van Buitenen, *The Mahābhārata*, vol. 2, p. 61.

17 Mhbh 2.20.10: *manuṣyāṇāṃ samālambho na ca dṛṣṭaḥ kadācana / sa kathaṃ mānuṣair devaṃ yaṣṭum icchasi śaṃkaram //*.

18 Bronkhorst, "Rites without Symbols."

19 *Hertha Krick, "Nārāyaṇabali und Opfertod," Wiener Zeitschrift für die Kunde Südasiens* 21 (1977): 101–102, paints the following picture of Vedic sacrifice:

> Dem klassischen Ritual ist . . . der freiwillige Opfertod an sich fremd, da es ganz auf den Yajamāna als Sieger ausgerichtet ist. Dagegen ergibt sich aus der Sicht des Besiegten die Notwendigkeit, den eigenen Tod, die Niederlage als sinnvoll zu interpretieren und dazu bietet sich die alte Opfermythologie vom geopferten Gott an: Der Tod wird nicht als Niederlage, als Verlust des Lebens, sondern als Opfer zum Gewinn neuen Lebens für sich selbst gesehen, als Überwindung des Todes, und so wird der Tod als Selbstopferung sogar primär als einzige Erlösungsmöglichkeit angestrebt. Es kommt auch im Ritual und in der Dharmaliteratur die Idee des Opfertodes wieder zum Vorschein, teils in der Sannyāsa-Struktur und im Krieger-Dharma, teils in der Rechtsprechung als Sühnetod und in der Höchtstbewertung der Opferwilligkeit. . . , die bis zur Selbstaufopferung reicht und besonders stark im ātmadānam des Mahāyāna-Buddhismus sowie in der Praxis des religiösen Selbstmord überhaupt ausgeprägt ist.

I find this kind of reasoning unconvincing. As I wrote in "Buddhism and Sacrifice," *Asiatische Studien/Études Asiatiques* 66/1 (2012): 10, "[W]hy should [Buddhists] wish to mutilate themselves and give up their lives under [Vedic] influence, where even Vedic sacrificers did no such thing?" More than ideas and interpretations are needed to drive people to such extreme behavior.

20 Jonathan Z. Smith, "The Domestication of Sacrifice," in Robert G. Hamerton-Kelley, ed., *Violent Origins: Walter Burkert, René Girard, and Jonathan Z. Smith on Ritual Killing and Cultural Formation* (Palo Alto, CA: Stanford University Press, 1987), pp. 203–204.

21 J. H. M. Beattie, "On Understanding Sacrifice," in M. F. C Bourdillon and Meyer Fortes, eds., *Sacrifice* (London: Academic Press, 1980), p. 30; Marcel Hénaff, *Le prix de la vérité: Le don, l'argent, la philosophie* (Paris: Éditions du Seuil, 2002), p. 223.

22 Smith, "The Domestication of Sacrifice," p. 202.

23 Smith, "The Domestication of Sacrifice," pp. 203–204.

[24] Michael Witzel, *The Origins of the World's Mythologies* (London: Oxford University Press, 2012).

[25] In this connection see Witzel, *The Origins of the World's Mythologies*, p. 120:

> While the Germanic and Vedic myths of Puruṣa and Ymir may thus go back to Indo-European mythology, the southern Chinese (Austric), Austronesian, Polynesian, and Hittite versions represent other traditions. However, in all these cases they were no longer told by ancient hunters and gatherers but by food-producing societies; in sum, they were reminiscences of an earlier stage of culture—and presumably, of mythology.

[26] Witzel, *The Origins of the World's Mythologies*, pp. 394–395.

[27] I discuss the reason why rituals are, and must be, holistic, i.e., following set patterns from which no deviations are allowed, in *Absorption: Human Nature and Buddhist Liberation* (Paris: UniversityMedia, 2012), p. 31 ff.

[28] Smith, "The Domestication of Sacrifice," p. 204; see above. Cf. Ina Wunn, *Die Religionen in vorgeschichtlicher Zeit* (Stuttgart: W. Kohlhammer, 2005), pp. 158–159:

> Auch die völkerkundlichen Parallelen, die bei Rust ebenso wie bei Maringer und Eliade die Hypothese eines frühen Primitialopfers zu stützen scheinen, erweisen sich bei näherer Betrachtung als nicht überzeugend. So pflegen traditionell lebende Wildbeuter wie die Pygmäen des Kongo oder die Buschmannvölker der Kalahari keineswegs einen grossen Anteil der Jagdbeute zu opfern, noch kennen sie eine kultische Verehrung von Gottheiten, die mit Opferhandlungen einherginge. Als einzige bedeutende Ritualhandlung ist das Primitialopfer im Zusammenhang mit Jagden üblich. Nach erfolgreichem Beutezug wird ein Stück von Herz und Lunge auf den Waldboden gelegt oder vernichtet, während der grösste Teil der Beute ins Lager geschafft und verzehrt wird. Auch solche Jägervölker, die elaborierte Jagdrituale kennen, pflegen keineswegs das erlegte Wild vollständig zu opfern. . . . Damit belegt ein korrekt angewendeter ethnographischer Vergleich, dass bei traditionell lebenden Wildbeutern das Primitialopfer durchaus zu den gebräuchlichen religiösen Handlungen gehört, ebenso wie Jagdrituale, in deren Verlauf mit dem erbeuteten Tier nach bestimmten religiös motivierten Vorschriften verfahren wird. In keinem Fall werden jedoch komplette Tiere geopfert. . . .

[29] See Bronkhorst, "Rites without Symbols," pp. 244–245.

[30] This part could conceivably be the head of the hunted animal, in which case the term "headhunting" would be appropriate. According to one interpretation, this happened in the cave of Montespan, where a headless statue of a bear was found, along with a real bear skull: "La statue était sans doute recouverte d'une peau d'ours fraîchement dépecée et à laquelle adhérait encore la tête; elle servait à des simulacres de capture et de mise à mort: dans l'argile se voit encore la trace des coups reçus par l'animal au cours de ces cérémonies"; Michel Pastoureux, *L'Ours: Histoire d'un roi déchu* (Paris: Seuil, 2007), p. 41, with reference to Michel-Allan Garcia and Philippe Morel, "Restes et reliefs: présence de l'homme et de l'ours des cavernes dans la grotte de Montespan-Ganties, Haute-Garonne," *Anthropozoologica* 21 (1995): 73–77.

[31] Joseph Campbell, *Historical Atlas of World Mythology. Volume I: The Way of the Animal Powers, Part 2: Mythologies of the Great Hunt* (New York: Harper and Row, 1988), pp. 152–154. Cf. Mariko Namba Walter and Eva Jane Neumann

Fridman, eds., *Shamanism: An Encyclopedia of World Beliefs, Practices, and Culture* (Santa Barbara, CA: ABC Clio, 2004).

32 Campbell, *Historical Atlas of World Mythology,* p. 154. See also Walter and Neumann Fridman, *Shamanism,* p. 661.

33 Pastoureau, *L'Ours: Histoire d'un roi déchu,* pp. 318–319.

34 Pastoureau, *L'Ours: Histoire d'un roi déchu,* p. 318.

35 Mark E. Lewis, *Sanctioned Violence in Early China* (Albany, NY: State University of New York Press, 1990), pp. 18 f; 150.

36 See, e.g., Walter Burkert, *Structure and History in Greek Mythology and Ritual* (Berkeley: University of California Press, 1979), p. 54 ff. Witzel, *The Origins of the World's Mythologies,* p. 264, follows this position in part (emphasis added):

> Typically, deities and rituals connected with food production are calqued on the earlier offering of the primordial giant *or a large hunted animal,* and they still stand out in the mythologies of societies that did not predominantly have agriculture but relied on pastoralism.

37 See Johannes Bronkhorst, *Absorption: Human Nature and Buddhist Liberation,* p. 31 ff.

38 Witzel, *The Origins of the World's Mythologies,* p. 396 ff.

39 Witzel, *The Origins of the World's Mythologies,* pp. 398–399.

40 Witzel, *The Origins of the World's Mythologies,* p. 570, n. 211.

41 Cf. Pastoureau, *L'Ours: Histoire d'un roi déchu:* "la grotte Chauvet, en Ardèche, . . . de toutes les images pariétales d'ours connues à ce jour, abrite à la fois les plus anciennes (vers – 32000 à – 30000) et les plus nombreuses (au moins douze exemples repérés). En raison des étranges crânes d'ours qui y ont été disposés—peut-être rituellement—, c'est également cette même grotte qui, plus que toute autre, invite à supposer l'existence d'un culte de l'ours" (p. 26). In spite of the fact that "[a]ujourd'hui, les adversaires du culte de l'ours semblent être majoritaires" (p. 34), Pastoureau himself seems inclined to consider the finds in this cave evidence for a bear cult: "[La grotte Chauvet] met [l'ours] en scène et semble en faire, plus que nulle part ailleurs, un animal digne de vénération: au centre d'une salle en rotonde, soigneusement débarrassée de tout mobilier et de tous les os et fragments d'os ayant traîné sur les sols, un grand crâne a été installé sur un bloc rocheux à surface plane, semblable à un autel; autour de lui, par terre, plusieurs dizaines d'autres crânes ont été disposés en cercle. Il y a manifestement là une mise en scène, qui est non pas le fait des ours ni la conséquence des accidents géologiques ou climatiques, mais bien due à la volonté des hommes. . . . Quelles que soient les découvertes à venir, la grotte Chauvet oblige à revoir bien des opinions. Ainsi le refus a priori de toute forme de pratiques cultuelles liées à l'ours chez les hommes du Paléolithique, ou bien l'existence possible d'un culte de l'ours chez l'homme de Neanderthal mais disparu avec ce dernier" (pp. 38–39). Here, too, bear cult is not identical with bear sacrifice.

For images from Chauvet and other caves, see Jean Clottes, *L'art des cavernes préhistoriques* (Paris: Phaidon, 2008).

[42] The notion of individual ownership is not unproblematic for the early period, during which societies may have been essentially egalitarian; see Christopher Boehm, *Moral Origins: The Evolution of Virtue, Altruism, and Shame* (New York: Basic Books, 2012).

References

Bahn, Paul G. "Where is the Beef? The Myth of Hunting Magic in Paleolithic Art," in Paul Bahn and Andrée Rosenfeld, eds., *Rock Art and Prehistory,* pp. 1–13. Oxford: Oxbow Monograph, 1991.

Bakker, Hans. "Puruṣamedha, Manasarapuruṣa, Vāstupuruṣa: The Image of Man in the Sacrificial Context," *Journal of Indological Studies* 20–21 (2008–2009): 1–23.

Beattie, J. H. M. "On Understanding Sacrifice," in M. F. C. Bourdillon and Meyer Fortes, eds., *Sacrifice,* pp. 29–44. London: Academic Press, 1980.

Biardeau, Madeleine. "Le sacrifice dans l'hindouisme," in Madeleine Biardeau and Charles Malamoud, eds., *Le sacrifice dans l'Inde ancienne,* pp. 7–154. Paris: Presses Universitaires de France, 1976.

Biardeau, Madeleine, and Charles Malamoud, eds. *Le sacrifice dans l'Inde ancienne.* Bibliothèque de l'École des Hautes Études, Section des Sciences Religieuses 79. Paris: Presses Universitaires de France, 1976.

Bodewitz, H. W. "Sins and Vices: Their Enumerations and Specifications in the Veda," *Indo-Iranian Journal* 50/4 (2007): 317–339.

Boehm, Christopher. *Moral Origins: The Evolution of Virtue, Altruism, and Shame.* New York: Basic Books, 2012.

Bourdillon, M. F. C., and Meyer Fortes, eds. *Sacrifice.* London: Academic Press, 1980.

Bronkhorst, Johannes. *Absorption: Human Nature and Buddhist Liberation.* Paris: UniversityMedia, 2012.

—."Buddhism and Sacrifice," *Asiatische Studien/Études Asiatiques* 66/1 (2012): 7–17.

—."Rites Without Symbols," *Method and Theory in the Study of Religion* 24 (2012): 236–266.

—."Sacrifice in the *Mahābhārata* and Beyond, Or: Did the Author(s) of the *Mahābhārata* understand Vedic Sacrifice Better Than We Do?", in *Proceedings of DICSEP 6: The Sixth Dubrovnik Conference on the Sanskrit Epics and Purāṇas,* August 15–20, 2011.

Buitenen, J. A. B. van, trans. *The Mahābhārata,* 3 vols. Chicago: University of Chicago Press, 1973, 1975, 1978.

Burkert, Walter. *Structure and History in Greek Mythology and Ritual.* Berkeley: University of California Press, 1979.

Caland, Willem, and Victor Henry. *L'agniṣṭoma. Description complète de la forme normale du sacrifice de soma dans le culte védique,* 2 vols. Paris: Ernest Leroux, 1906–1907.

Campbell, Joseph. *Historical Atlas of World Mythology. Volume I: The Way of the Animal Powers, Part 2: Mythologies of the Great Hunt.* New York: Harper and Row, 1988.

Carter, Jeffrey, ed. *Understanding Religious Sacrifice: A Reader (Controversies in the Study of Religion).* London and New York: Continuum, 2003.

Clottes, Jean. *L'art des cavernes préhistoriques.* Paris: Phaidon, 2008.

Garcia, Michel-Alain, and Philippe Morel. "Restes et reliefs: présence de l'homme et de l'ours des cavernes dans la grotte de Montespan-Ganties, Haute-Garonne," *Anthropozoologica* 21 (1995): 73–77.

Hamerton-Kelley, Robert G., ed. *Violent Origins: Walter Burkert, René Girard, and Jonathan Z. Smith on Ritual Killing and Cultural Formation.* Palo Alto, CA: Stanford University Press, 1987.

Hénaff, Marcel. *Le prix de la vérité: Le don, l'argent, la philosophie.* Paris: Éditions du Seuil, 2002.

Hillebrandt, Alfred. *Ritual-Litteratur: Vedische Opfer und Zauber.* Grundriss der Indo-arischen Philologie und Altertumskunde III.2. Strassburg: K. J. Trübner, 1897.

Hubert, Henri, and Marcel Mauss. "Essai sur la nature et la fonction sociale du sacrifice," *Année sociologique* 2 (1899): 29–138. Reprinted in Henri Hubert and Marcel Mauss, *Mélanges d'histoire des religions,* see below.

—. *Mélanges d'histoire des religions.* Paris: Félix Alcan, 1929, deuxième édition.

—. *Sacrifice: Its Nature and Function.* W. D. Halls, trans. London: Cohen & West, 1964. English translation of Hubert and Mauss, "Essai sur la nature et la fonction sociale du sacrifice," see above.

Kirfel, Willibald. "Der Aśvamedha und der Puruṣamedha," in *Beiträge zur indischen Philologie und Altertumskunde. Walter Schubring zum 70. Geburtstag dargebracht,* pp. 39–50. Alt- und Neu-Indische Studien 7. Hamburg: Cram, DeGruyter, 1951. Reprinted in Willibald Kirfel, Kleine Schriften, pp. 179–190. Wiesbaden: Steiner, 1976.

—. *Kleine Schriften.* Wiesbaden: Steiner, 1976.

Krick, Hertha. "Nārāyaṇabali und Opfertod," *Wiener Zeitschrift für die Kunde Südasiens* 21 (1977): 71–142.

Lévi, Sylvain. *La doctrine du sacrifice dans les Brāhmaṇas* (1898). Bibliothèque de l'École des Hautes Études, Sciences Religieuses 118. Tournhout: Brepols, 2003, reprint.

Lewis, Mark E. *Sanctioned Violence in Early China.* Albany, NY: State University of New York Press, 1990.

Lincoln, Bruce. *Death, War and Sacrifice: Studies in Ideology and Practice.* Chicago and London: University of Chicago Press, 1991.

—. "Debreasting, Disarming, Beheading: Some Sacrificial Practices of the Scyths and Amazons," in Bruce Lincoln, ed., *Death, War and Sacrifice: Studies in Ideology and Practice,* Chapter 16, pp. 198–208. Chicago and London: University of Chicago Press, 1991. Reprinted in Jeffrey Carter, ed., *Understanding*

Religious Sacrifice: A Reader (Controversies in the Study of Religion), (London and New York: Continuum, 2003), pp. 359–369.

Malamoud, Charles. "Modèle et réplique: Remarques sur le paradigme du sacrifice humain dans l'Inde védique," *Archiv für Religionsgeschichte* 1/1 (1999): 27–40.

Minkowski, Christopher. "Snakes, Sattras, and the Mahābhārata," in Arvind Sharma, ed., *Essays on the Mahābhārata*, pp. 384–400. Leiden: E. J. Brill, 1991.

Pastoureau, Michel. *L'Ours: Histoire d'un roi déchu.* Paris: Seuil, 2007.

Pinault, Georges-Jean. "About the Slaying of Soma: Uncovering the Rigvedic Witness," in L. Kulikov and M. Rusanov, eds., *Indologica. T. Ya. Elizarenkova Memorial Volume*, Book 1, pp. 353–388. Orientalia et Classica: Papers of the Institute of Oriental and Classical Studies 20. Moscow: Russian State University for the Humanities, 2008.

Sauvé, James L. "The Divine Victim: Aspects of Human Sacrifice in Viking Scandinavia and Vedic India," in Jaan Puhvel, ed., *Myth and Law among Indo-Europeans*, pp. 173–191. Berkeley: University of California Press, 1970.

Schlerath, B. "The Slaying of the God Soma," *Annals of the Bhandarkar Oriental Research Institute* 68 (1987): 345–348.

Smith, Jonathan Z. "The Domestication of Sacrifice," in Robert G. Hamerton-Kelley, ed., *Violent Origins: Walter Burkert, René Girard, and Jonathan Z. Smith on Ritual Killing and Cultural Formation*, pp. 191–205. Palo Alto, CA: Stanford University Press, 1987. Reprinted in Jeffrey Carter, ed., *Understanding Religious Sacrifice: A Reader (Controversies in the Study of Religion)* (London and New York: Continuum, 2003), pp. 328–341.

Sukthankar, V. S., ed. *Mahābhārata*, critical edition. Poona: Bhandarkar Oriental Research Institute, 1933–1966.

Thite, Ganesh Umakant. *Sacrifice in the Brāhmaṇa-Texts.* Poona: University of Poona, 1975.

Walter, Mariko Namba, and Eva Jane Neumann Fridman, eds. *Shamanism: An Encyclopedia of World Beliefs, Practices, and Culture.* Santa Barbara: ABC Clio, 2004.

Witzel, Michael. *The Origins of the World's Mythologies.* London: Oxford University Press, 2012.

Wunn, Ina. *Die Religionen in vorgeschichtlicher Zeit.* Stuttgart: W. Kohlhammer, 2005.

Indian Mathematics in the Context of the Vedic Sacrifice (*Śulbasūtras*)

Jean Michel Delire
University of Brussels, Belgium

Introduction

The Vedas and the *Brāhmaṇas*

The Indo-Aryans first entered India[1] around the beginning of the second millennium B.C.E. They were one of the Indo-European tribes[2] coming from the steppes of Eurasia and they brought with them horses, which were still unknown in that part of the world, and some new technologies, such as the spoked wheel and the horse-drawn chariot. In India they probably encountered the Harappan civilization, which flourished around the Indus during the third millennium but had at that time shifted to the east into what is today India.[3] The influx of Indo-Aryans was somewhat continuous during the first half of the second millennium, and they also moved further east and encountered the heirs of the Harappans or a mixed culture resulting from the previous meeting of the autochtonous people of north India with the Harappans. During these centuries the Indo-Aryans developed an important literature, first represented by religious hymns that were later collected between 1500 and 1300 B.C.E., in *saṁhitās* ("collections"). These *saṁhitās* were named after the different schools of ritual thinking to which they belonged (e.g., *Taittirīya Saṁhitā*), but also after the specific part of the ritual with which they were concerned:

The *Ṛg-Veda*, "*veda* of praise" (ca. 1000), consist of versified praises addressed to the various gods, "a kind of anthology made of the texts preserved by ancient priestly families."[4]

The *Sāma-Veda*, "*veda* of chants," composed with the hymns of the *Ṛg-Veda* (except 75) "rearranged for the performance of the sacred chant (for the sacrifice) with musical notations."[5]

The *Yajur-Veda*, "sacrificial *veda*," which comprises also nonversified formulae, contrary to the other two. It includes the *kṛṣṇa-yajur-veda*, "black sacrificial *veda*," in which the formulas are mixed with explanations (as in the *Taittirīya Saṁhitā*, for example), and the *śukla-yajur-veda*, "white sacrificial *veda*," which distinguishes the formulae from the explanations, compiled separately in the *Śatapatha Brāhmaṇa*.

The word *veda* means "knowledge," "science," but also refers to the entire literature of ancient India until the approximate beginning of the Christian era. This literature is divided into *śruti*, "revelation," which was allegedly received by the ancient *ṛṣi*s, "inspired poets or holy men," and *smṛti*, "tradition," the origin and transmission of which are human (as opposed to divine).

The most ancient mathematics of India are expounded in the *Śulba-sūtra*s, a class of works that aim to explain in detail the necessary construction of ritual spaces for the Vedic sacrifices. Since these works are intimately related to the most ancient literature of India and to the sacrifice, it would be useful to first further explain this literature and the role sacrifice played in Vedic and Brahmanic society.

The *Śatapatha Brāhmaṇa* belongs to the second level of the Vedic literature, the *Brāhmaṇa*s, which is still embodied in the *śruti*. These are "prose anthologies which intend to give justifications of the religious observances, to illustrate them with legends and sometimes to interpret literally their formulas."[6]

The very aim of the compilers (of the *Brāhmaṇa*s) is not to describe, but to explain the origin, meaning, and *raison d'être* of the ritual acts to be performed and to prove their validity and the significance and suitability of the mantras ("prayers") and chants used as the mutual relations of the acts and their connections with the phenomenal reality.[7]

Every Veda, except, of course, the *kṛṣṇa-yajur-veda*, possesses several *Brāhmaṇa*s, according to its schools.

The Sacrifice

The Indo-Aryan sacrifice was comparable to other Indo-European sacrificial practices (for example, the Greek), consisting of gifts of the first products of livestock, farming, or agriculture to the gods. These products were arranged on an altar (agricultural products) or poured into an hearth (meat from livestock).

The fire was considered the vehicle by which humans communicated with the gods. As such, the fire is personified as the god Agni, priest of the gods and god of the priests. Agni is supposed to invite the other gods to the sacrifice and transport them to its location. The protection he gives to the people against every kind of enemy and his ability to provide space to his followers by consuming expanses of unwanted forest are other characteristics inherited from prehistorical times. Of course, the sun is considered to be one of Agni's emanations.

The most important god of the Vedic pantheon is Indra, portrayed as a mighty warrior but also as a god of creation. His destruction of the demon Vṛtra, which symbolizes the primordial chaos, is unquestionably a creation myth (or rather, a myth explaining the ordering of the world), but it also reflects some historical aspects taken from the Indo-Iranian raids. Georges Dumézil[8] considers the Maruts, Indra's companions during the fight against Vṛtra, to represent the young warriors who fronted the Aryan expansion into India. Indra and the Maruts are heavy drinkers of *soma,* a juice extracted from an unknown plant, usually described as the elixir of the gods that gives life and vigor to the drinker. Personified as a god, Soma is a representation of the water element in life and nature and also of their cyclical aspects.

The preparation and offering of *soma* is the central part of many Vedic sacrifices, and it is believed to feed and reinforce the gods and all the powers that enable the world to be maintained. The sacrifice of *soma* provides fresh supplies of water in the ascending steam, which then is redistributed to the earth, where it is so necessary. The moon, following its nightly path approaching the zenith (when viewed at low latitudes) is compared to a bowl filling up with *soma* during the first half of the lunar month and then emptied by the gods during the second half.

The sacrifice was very important in Vedic India:

> Its purpose was to ensure the fertility and well-being of the individual, his family and domestic animals, and ultimately the whole community. The sacrifice was an offering to the gods to sustain them in their task of maintaining the world and directing its manifold generative activities.[9]

The sacrifice functions simultaneously for those who cause it to be performed, the *yajamāna,* by ensuring the welfare of both themselves and their kind, as well as for the world in maintaining or reactivating its arrangement.

The *agnihotra,* "oblation to the fire," for example, is "the shortest rite. It is a simple milk offering to Agni, performed in the morning and in the evening."[10] It is supposed to secure the longevity and fecundity of the *yajamāna*'s family but its primary function is to maintain the daily sunrise and the sun's revolution through the sky: "But, assuredly, [the sun] would not rise, were he not to make that offering."[11] This kind of sacrifice is called *nitya*, "usual, fixed, necessary," as are the full and new moon sacrifices (*darśapaurṇamāsa*) or the seasonal sacrifices (*caturmāsya*).

Usually, the sacrifice rituals are extremely complicated; every detail, from the recitation of a formula or a physical action such as kindling a fire, building the hearth, or clearing the sacrificial area, must be accomplished in the strictly prescribed time, place, and manner. Any error or failure must be repaired by an atonement sacrifice; otherwise the consequences of the sacrifice might be opposite of the *yajamāna*'s wishes.

The priests who accomplish the sacrifice belong to several classes. The brahman, physician of the sacrifice, verifies that everything follows the rules and executes the atonements if necessary. The *hotṛ*, "offerer" of the oblation, selects the *Ṛg-Veda* hymns to be recited. The *udgātṛ* is the "singer" of the *sāman* (*Sāma-Veda*) in the soma sacrifices. The *adhvaryu* pronounces the *yajus* (*Yajur-Veda*) and his role in the manual part of the sacrifice is essential: he measures the ground, builds the hearths, places the bricks, etc. Following Martin Haugh,[12] the *adhvaryu* was originally the assistant of the *hotṛ* for all of the material acts (preparation of oblations, implements) and gradually assumed parts of the *hotṛ*'s tasks, even singing mantras when pouring oblations or placing the bricks of the hearth. In the *agnicayana* (discussed below) each priest has three assistants, for a total of sixteen priests that take part in the sacrifice.[13]

Besides the *nitya* sacrifices there also appeared *kāmya*, "votive," sacrifices performed for the attainment of a particular wish. For these rites a grand altar made of bricks was built. In this aspect, the Indian sacrifice had already diverged from the general Indo-European pattern. The Vedas never mention the use of bricks,[14] so the use of bricks for the altar has been imputed to Harappan influence.[15] Bearing the name *caya, cit,* or *citi* (√*CI; cinoti,* "pile up"[16]), the altar's shape is related to the pursued aim.

Text 1. The Different Shapes of Altars[17]

> . . . The one desiring heaven, he should pile up an altar in the shape of a bird of prey (*śyena-cit*), for the bird of prey is the best of birds for flying, and so he becomes a bird of prey and flies to heaven. . . . The one desiring a stable position, he should pile up an altar in the shape of an *alaja* bird[18] (*alaja-cit*) with four furrows and so he stands firmly oriented in the four directions. The one having enemies, he should pile up an altar in the shape of a triangle (*praüga-cit*) and so he repels his enemies before him. The one desiring: "that I repel my enemies born before and still to come," he should

pile up an altar in the shape of a double triangle (*ubhayataḥ-praüga-cit*) and so he repels his enemies born before and still to come. The one having enemies, he should pile up an altar in the shape of a chariot wheel (*ratha-cakra-cit*), for the chariot is the thunder[19] and so he throws the thunder on his enemies. The one desiring food, he should pile up an altar in the shape of a dish (*droṇa-cit*) and so he confines food in his belly. The one desiring cattle, he should pile up an altar in the shape of a heap (*samuhya-cit*) and so he becomes the owner of cattle. The one desiring a village, he should pile up an altar in the shape of a circle (*pariccāya-cit*) and so he becomes the owner of a village. The one desiring: "that I prosper in the ancestor world," he should pile up an altar in the shape of a grave (for the bones of burned corpses, *śmaśāna-cit*) and so he prospers in the ancestor world. (*Taittirīya Saṁhitā* 5.4.11.1–3)

The Cosmic Function of the *Agnicayana*

The building of these altars by piling up bricks occurred in a complex rite called *agnicayana*, "piling up of the fire (altar)." Aside from its precise aim to satisfy the *yajamāna*'s wish, it had also a cosmological function. In the case of the *śyena-cit*, this function is the reconstitution of Prajāpati, "Lord of Creatures," identified with the cosmic person, the puruṣa of the *Ṛg-Veda*, whose dismemberment created the universe.

Text 2. Creation of the Universe

When they divided the Puruṣa, how many parts was he made?
What was his mouth, his arms? What [were] called his thighs and his feet?
His mouth was the brahman (*brāhmaṇa*), his arms the man of royal descent (*kṣatrīya*).
His thighs were the *vaiśya*, from his feet the *śūdra* was born.
From his mind the moon was born, from his eye the sun.
From his mouth Indra and Agni, Wind (Vāyu) from his breath.
(*Ṛg-Veda* X.90)[20]

It is noteworthy that this part of the hymn already institutes the hierarchical division of Vedic society in the four traditional classes (*varṇa*s) of brahmans, *kṣatrīya*s, *vaiśya*s, and *śūdra*s with their typical occupations: study of the Veda and performance of the rites for brahmans[21] (belonging to priestly families), defense and warriorship for *kṣatrīya*s (belonging to the ruling families), and production and craft industry for *vaiśya*s, who made up the part of Vedic society that was allowed to attend the sacrifices. The lowest class, the *śūdra*s, was excluded from the cult. They are usually considered servants, drawn from the autochtonous population conquered by the Aryans. We have already seen, however, that some autochtonous practical knowledge was incorporated into the construction of the altar, and even some religious conceptions of the autochtons have been added to the Vedic conceptions (discussed further below), so it is untenable to maintain that no autochton was ever admitted to the Vedic sacrifices.

Text 3. Significance of the *Agnicayana*

> This same vital air in the midst doubtless is Indra. He, by his power (*indriya*), kindled those [other] vital airs from the midst; and inasmuch as he kindled (*indh*), he is the kindler (*indha*): the kindler indeed, him they call "Indra" mystically (esoterically), for the gods love the mystic. They (the vital airs), being kindled, created seven separate persons (*puruṣa*).
>
> They said: "Surely, being thus, we shall not be able to generate: let us make these seven persons one Person!" They made those seven persons one Person (*puruṣa*): they compressed two of them [into] what is above the navel, and two of them [into] what is below the navel; [one] person was [one] wing (or side), [one] person was [the other] wing, and one person was the base (i.e., the feet). . . . That same Person became Prajāpati ("Lord of Generation"). And that Person which became Prajāpati is this very Agni (fire altar), who is now [to be] built. (*Śatapatha Brāhmaṇa* 6.1.1.2–5)[22]

Figure 1 illustrates the *agnicayana* as the (re)construction of the cosmic Puruṣa described by Text 3, but it is also an example of a more primitive form of the *śyena-cit*, called *caturaśra-śyena-cit*, "square bird of prey altar."

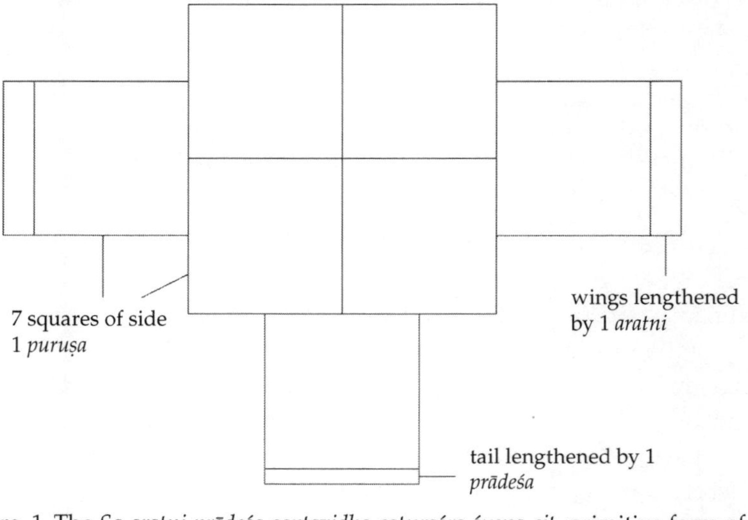

Figure. 1. The *Sa-aratni-prādeśa-saptavidha-caturaśra-śyena-cit*, primitive form of the *śyena-cit*.

The *agnicayana* rite is also intended to ensure that the *yajamāna* could obtain the "heaven" he desires. This "heaven" is understood to be a good earthly life, in conformity with the original ideology of the Indo-Aryans, and also as the goal of transcending this material life. The reconstitution of Prajāpati's body is carried out along with some other aspects of the rite, such as burying a golden human figurine under the layers of the altar, which is intended to give the *yajamāna* a body that enables him to go beyond the tribulations of human life. This second aspect has been appended to the original goal of the rite, though it was originally in contradiction with it. This seems to reflect the mixture of the two traditions, the Indo-Aryan and the autochtonous.[23] This mixture reveals some agreement between different people and cultures, but such a synthesis occurred only after centuries of fierce fighting and opposition to each other's tradition.

These battles are testified by the *Ṛg-Veda* itself, where the Dāsa people are very often in conflict with the Indo-Aryans led by Indra. Though generally antagonistic toward one another, the Dāsa and the Indo-Aryans are also sometimes associated, as in the solar (Vedic) dynasty, whose ancestors are called Divodāsa and Sudās(a).[24] On the other hand, opposition to non–Indo-Aryan tradition is testified in different texts, such as *Śatapatha Brāhmaṇa* 6.6.2.7,[25] in which opposition to a particular method of firing the *ūkhā*, an earthenware jar used during the *agnicayana* ritual, is expressed; or *Śatapatha Brāhmaṇa* 2.3.3.17–8, which shows opposition to the *agnicayana* itself.[26]

The developed shape of the *śyena-cit*, called *vakra-pakṣa-śyena-cit*, "altar [in the shape of a] bird of prey with curved wings," is shown in Figure 2 and described in the following text.[27]

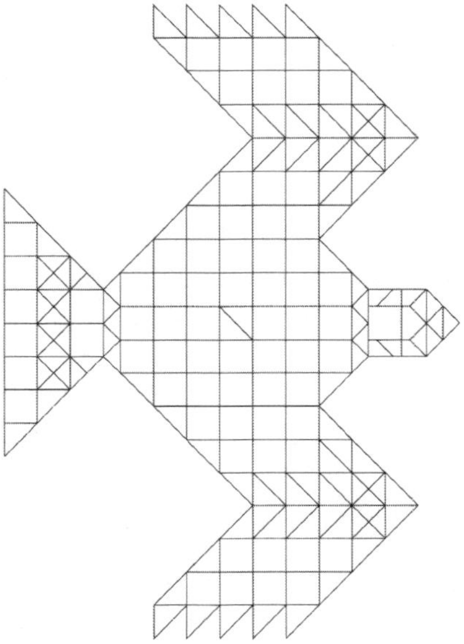

Figure 2. The developed form of the *śyena-cit*.

Text 4. The Bird's Shadow

And also: "what is piled up in the shape of birds, that really is the sacrificial fire,"[28] the meaning is "in the shape of the birds taking their flight." (*Baudhāyana Śulbasūtra* III.8–9)

The Auxiliaries of the Veda and the *Sūtra* Style

The following literary works concerned with Vedic ritual are usually described as belonging to the Vedāṅgas, "members, auxiliaries of the Veda." They are the first realizations of *smṛti*, "memorized tradition."

There are six auxiliaries: (1) *śikṣā*, "phonetics"; (2) *chandas*, "metric," the aim of which is the correct pronunciation of the Vedic hymns to be recited during the ritual; (3) *vyākaraṇa*, "grammar"; (4) *nirukta*, "etymology," which is intended to ensure correct comprehension of the hymns. These first four auxiliaries are concerned with speech, while the last two, (5) *jyotiṣa*, "astronomy," and (6) *kalpa*, "ritual," enable the ritualists to establish the calendar of the sacrifice and the material details of the ritual itself.

The Vedāṅgas are represented by numerous *sūtra*s, "treatises" (*sūtra* also means "rule expressed as a proposition, final element of the treaty") that give a survey, as short and systematic as possible, of the innumerable procedural details preserved in the *Brāhmaṇa*s. The term *sūtra*, meaning originally "thread," "clue," but translated usually as "aphorism," recalls the principal characteristic of these treatises, their extreme concision, which prevents us from understanding them without their detailed commentaries.[29]

The *kalpasūtra*s are distributed among the *śrautasūtra*s, devoted to the grand, solemn sacrifices; the *gṛhyasūtra*s, describing the rites and sacraments that every individual must celebrate and receive in his own house; and the *dharmasūtra*s, which concern the law from a religious point of view. We are most interested here in the last chapters (generally where they are placed in the texts) of the *śrautasūtra*s, the *śulbasūtra*s.

These are practical manuals giving the measures necessary for the construction of the *vedi*, of the altars, and so forth. They show quite an advanced knowledge of geometry, and constitute the oldest Indian mathematical works.[30]

For the following description of the mathematics of Vedic India, I have used the four principal *śulbasūtra*s: the *Baudhāyana Śulbasūtra*, the *Āpastamba Śulbasūtra*, and the *Mānava Śulbasūtra*, which all go back to the black *Yajurveda* (the *Baudhāyana* more specifically to the *Taittirīya Saṁhitā*); and the *Kātyāyana Śulbasūtra*, which belongs to the white *Yajurveda*. Since I have undertaken a complete translation of the *Baudhāyana Śulbasūtra* and its commentaries I will refer more frequently to this work. It is generally accepted that the *Śulbasūtra*s were composed between the eighth and fourth centuries B.C.E. and that the *Baudhāyana Śulbasūtra* is the oldest text among them.

The Sacrificial Ground

Units of Measure

Everything is measured in the Vedic sacrifice, as we shall see. The first chapter of the *Baudhāyana Śulbasūtra* is devoted to the definition of the principal units of measure.

Text 5. Principal Units

> Then, the measure of an *aṅgula* ("finger's breadth") is fourteen *aṇus* ("seed of *sesamum indicum*") or thirty-four *tilas* ("seed of *panicum miliaceum*") joined in breadth, following another [doctrine].
>
> A *kṣudra-pada* ("little foot") is ten *aṅgulas* long, a *prādeśa* ("short span") twelve, . . . a *pada* ("foot") fifteen, . . . a *prakrama* ("step") is two *padas* long, an *aratni* ("cubit") contains two *prādeśas*, . . . the *puruṣa* ("person") is five *aratnis* long. (*Baudhāyana Śulbasūtra*, I.3–7, 9, 15–16, 19)

All of these measures are anthropometric, as the sacrifice is based on the proportions of the *yajamāna* ("the one who causes the sacrifice to be performed"): his height, with arms uplifted, defines the basic measure of the *puruṣa*. However, they are not completely anthropometric, since the relations between them are fixed: 1 *puruṣa* = 5 *aratnis* = 10 *prādeśas* = 120 *aṅgulas*, and 1 *prakrama* = 2 *padas* = 30 *aṅgulas* = 3 *kṣudra-padas*. The relationships between these measurements may be imposed by a sort of harmony convention, as we find in art, but there are some variations in the coefficients. For example, *Āpastamba Śulbasūtra* VI, 2 defines a *prakrama* as 2 or 3 *padas*, *Kātyāyana Śulbasūtra* 5.9 defines a *pada* as 12 *aṅgulas*, and *Mānava Śulbasūtra* 10.1.4.4 defines a *prādeśa* as 10 *aṅgulas*.

These inconsistencies explain *sūtras* such as *Baudhāyana Śulbasūtra* I.18: "In the *padas*, *yugas*, *prakramas*, in the *aratnis* of the same scale and in the *śamyā* ("pin of a yoke"), as units of measure, one acts according to one's own way." The case of a *yajamāna* being too short is even taken into consideration by *Mānava Śulbasūtra* 10.1.4.1: "If the *yajamāna* is short from an infirmity or by birth, how in that case are the measures to be used by the priests?" *Āpastamba Śulbasūtra* VI, 2 seems to give an answer:

> A *prakrama* is two or three *padas* long; for the *prakrama*, one acts according to its own way because of the uncertainty of the sense of the word; it is the

> measure of the *yajamāna* or the *adhvaryu* for he is the author of the acts in the sacrifice.

In other words, a more proportionally pleasing *adhvaryu* can replace the *yajamāna* in such embarrassing cases.

Another answer could be suggested by the part of text 5 not yet analyzed (which is actually the way also followed by *Mānava Śulbasūtra*, 10.1.4.2–5), which seems to seek the stability of the (originally) anthropometric measure by deriving it from natural measures, as the size of a *tila* or an *aṇu*. One can note that the great (but peculiar) number (34 and 14, respectively) of such grains given by the *Baudhāyana Śulbasūtra* ensures that even individual variations in the sizes of the components won't alter the size of the composite measure, here the *aṅgula*.

The principle of this explanation is quite satisfactory for us who are familiar with the difficulty of defining a sufficiently stable standard of measure, but is it not an anachronism here?[31] And how can we explain the use of the strange factors 34 and 14 instead of the usual 2, 3, 5, and their multiples? An explanation of this choice appears below in the section on "The Quadrature of the Circle and the Approximations of the Diagonal of the Square."

Besides these anthropometrical measures, we find units related to the chariot, an important element of Vedic culture.

Text 6. Units Related to the Chariot

> The *īṣā* ("shaft") is a hundred and eighty-eight [*aṅgulas*] long, the *akṣa* ("axle") a hundred and four, the *yuga* ("yoke") eighty-six, . . . the *śamyā* and the *bahu* ("arm") thirty-six. (*Baudhāyana Śulbasūtra* I.10–14).

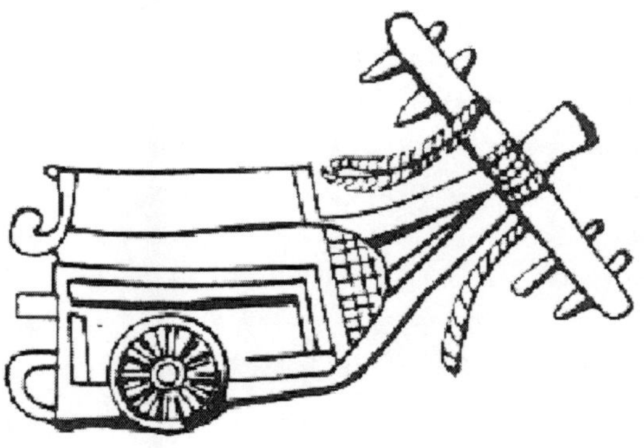

Figure 3. The Parts of the Chariot.[32]

The *īṣā* is the shaft, the *akṣa* the axle, the *yuga* the yoke. The element called *śamyā/bahu* is not easily determined. It could be the front part of the shaft or the part of the yoke between the two sticks to impede lateral movements of the oxen.

The Three Fires

The Vedic cult didn't use temples. The ceremonies took place in the house of the *yajamāna* or a nearby field, where three fires (*agnis*) were maintained and an offering table (*vedi*) constructed between them.

Figure 4: The Three Fires and the *Vedi*.[33]

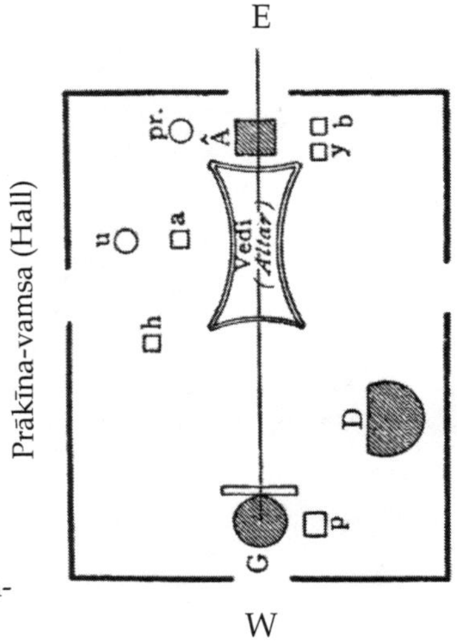

Explanations
A = Āhavanīya fire
G = Gārhapatya fire
D = Dakṣiṇāgni
C = Seat of Brahman
y = Seat of Yagamāna (sacrificer)
p = Seat of Patni (sacrificer's wife)
h = Seat of Hotri
a = Seat of Āgnidhra
pr = Place for pranitāh
u = Utkara (heap of rubbish)

Text 7. The Three Fires

> Agni, priest of the family, the man kindled it in a triple seat. (*Ṛg-Veda* V, 11.2)[34]

The first fire, placed to the west, is the Gārhapatya, "fire of the master (*pati*) of the house (*gṛha*)," which he received from his father and will transmit to his son, and from which the other fires must be kindled. The second, placed to the east, is the Āhavanīya, which "receives the oblations" cooked beforehand in the Gārhapatya (though *Śatapatha Brāhmaṇa* 1.7.3.27, seems to indicate that the Āhavanīya exclusively is used for the cooking and oblation). It is compared to the world of gods, as the Gārhapatya is compared to the human world (*Śatapatha Brāhmaṇa* 7.3.1.10) and must be perfectly square, while the Gārhapatya is circular (though certain schools have it square also), with the same area, as we will see below.

Text 8. The Relative Position of the Gārhapatya and Āhavanīya

> Now, about the disposition of the fires that are to be placed on the sacrificial ground, the Āhavanīya from the Gārhapatya: it is prescribed "that the *brāhmaṇa* placed the fire at eight *prakramas*, the *rajanya* (*kṣatrīya*) at eleven, and the *vaiśya* at twelve.[35] (*Baudhāyana Śulbasūtra* I.63)

The distance, measured between the centers[36] of the two fires, depends on the stature of the *yajamāna:* if he is a brahman, the distance is the shortest;[37] if he belongs to the *kṣatrīya*s, the distance is medium. It is the longest for the third class, the *vaiśya*s.

The third fire, called Dakṣiṇāgni, is placed in the south (*dakṣiṇa*), the region of the ancestors, where it is supposed to repel the evil powers and spirits and receive the offerings intended for the ancestors. It also serves for cooking the food for the priests.

This fire must stand precisely southeast of the Gārhapatya at a distance from it equal to half of its distance from the Āhavanīya.

Text 9. The Relative Position of the Dakṣiṇāgni

> The place of the Dakṣiṇāgni is closest to the Gārhapatya, on [its] southeast, at the third (of a cord fixed to the two first fires). (*Āpastamba Śrautasūtra* V.4.5 and *Āpastamba Śulbasūtra* IV.3)[38]

There are thus seemingly two conditions to be satisfied by the Dakṣiṇāgni, of direction (D, the Dakṣiṇāgni, must be placed southeast of G, the Gārhapatya) and of ratio (the distance between A, the Āhavanīya, and D, the Dakṣiṇāgni, must be twice the distance between the Gārhapatya and the Dakṣiṇāgni, that is, DA = 2DG). The exact place of the Dakṣiṇāgni could be precisely determined as the intersection of the southeast line drawn from the Gārhapatya (direction condition) and a circle (traditionally called Apollonius' circle) locus of all the points that satisfy the ratio condition. One point (P) of this circle is naturally placed on the segment GA at a distance from G equal to GA/3, and the Apollonius' circle has its center at the symmetrical point of P with respect to G. Its diameter is thus equal to 4GA/3. Since the Indians didn't know the Apollonius' circle, they developed approximate methods to find the spot to place the Dakṣiṇāgni. One method requires the construction of a square and, since the Āhavanīya itself is a square, we will first see how Baudhāyana proceeds to construct a square.

Text 10. Construction of a Square

> Desiring to construct a square of which side is as long as the cord, one has to put a mark in the middle [of the cord], after having made a loop at its two extremities.

Having marked the ground at the middle [of the planned square], one fixes a pole (A) and, having fixed there the two loops [of the cord], draws a circle around with the help of the mark. One fixes two poles at the extremities (B, C) of the [east-west] diameter.

After having fixed a loop to the east [pole], one draws a circle with the help of the [other] loop.

The same at the west and, by [the points] where those two circles meet, one draws a second [north-south] diameter. Poles are fixed at the two extremities (D, E) of this diameter.

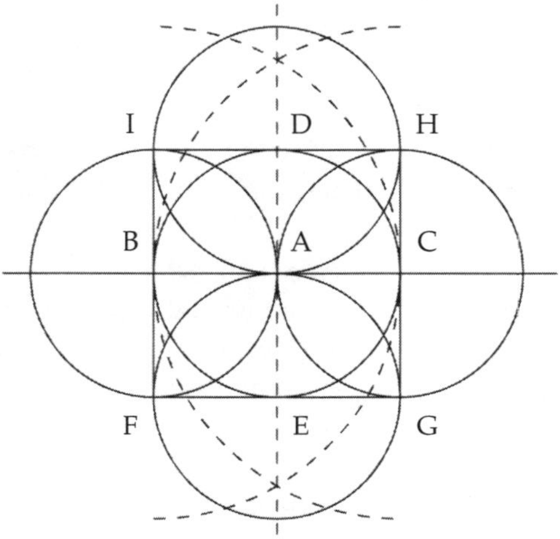

Figure 5. Construction of a square.

After having fixed the two loops at the east [pole], one draws a circle with the help of the mark, same at the south, same at the west, same at the north, and the square is the meeting of the last points (F, G, H, I) of contact. (*Baudhāyana Śulbasūtra* I.22–28)

Text 11. Approximate Constructions of the Place of the Dakṣiṇāgni

With the third of the distance, one should construct three adjacent squares. The Gārhapatya is on the northern hip of the west square, the Anvāhārya-pacana[39] at the southern shoulder of the same square (D1), and the Āhavanīya at the northern shoulder of the east square.

Or else, after the division in five or six equal parts of the interval between the Gārhapatya and the Āhavanīya and the adjoining of a sixth or seventh such part to a cord of which length is the interval, after the division of the new cord in three equal parts, one marks the two parts (= two thirds) counted from the east extremity. Having attached both extremities of the cord to the Gārhapatya and Āhavanīya and gone with the mark to the south, one fixes a pole at the spot where the mark falls. It is the place of the Dakṣiṇāgni (D2a and D2b).

Or else, one should lengthen a cord equal to the interval with its fifth part. After the division of the new cord in five equal parts, one marks it at the two parts (= two fifths) counted from the west extremity. After having attached the two loops to the two extremities of the *pṛṣṭhyā* and gone to the south, one fixes a pole at the spot where the mark falls. It is the place of the Dakṣiṇāgni (D3). (*Baudhāyana Śulbasūtra* I.67–69)

The way the Indians used a cord to construct a square is very much like the use of a compass. In the determinations of the place for the Dakṣiṇāgni, however, we see for the first time how they proceeded to improve this simple "compass-like" construction. They used a cord of a precise length, marked it at a determined spot, fixed its two extremities by two loops at two poles (generally marking the extremities of the west-east axis, called the *pṛṣṭhyā* or prācī), and stretched it (to the south in this text, but also to the north elsewhere) by holding the cord at the mark. Finally, they note the spot where the mark falls. Since the sacrifice is for the gods who are supposed to dwell in the east, this direction catches the eye of humans and animals, thus the terms "hip" and "shoulder" for the west and east parts of every geometrical object (generally associated with humans or animals).

Let us now see how these four constructions satisfy the two conditions imposed on the Dakṣiṇāgni. D1 satisfies the direction condition, the D2s satisfy the ratio condition, and D3 satisfies none of them. But, in modern terms of relative error, D2b is definitely much nearer to the exact position: it stands within 0.0072d (d is the exact distance between the Gārhapatya and the Dakṣiṇāgni) from the exact position D; that is, within a relative error of 0.72%, with an angular error of 0°22′54″ (to the west). D2a makes an error of 0.085d in distance (8.5%) and an angular error of 4°27′30″ (to the west), D3 an error of 0.2439d in distance (24.39%) and an angular error of 2°52′25″ (to the east), and D1 an error of 0.2153d in distance (21.53%) with no angular error.

Coming back to the first two fires, there seems to be a rule in the Śatapatha Brāhmaṇa that they should have the same area, so the Indians could have been interested in finding how to transform a disk (the Gārhapatya fire) to a square having the same area (the Āhavanīya fire) and conversely: the famous quadrature (or circulature) problem. Actually, the Śulbasūtras contain sūtras describing how to approximately resolve these problems, as we will see below.

Text 12. Surfaces of the Two Principal Fires

It (the Gārhapatya hearth) measures a fathom (= *puruṣa* squared), for man is a fathom high, and man is Prajāpati, and Prajāpati is Agni: he thus makes the womb of equal size to his body. It is circular, for the womb is circular; and moreover the Gārhapatya is this (terrestrial) world, and this world doubtless is circular. . . . From the raised [site] of the Gārhapatya he strides seven steps eastward. From there he measures off a fathom toward the east and, having in the middle thereof thrown up [the ground] for the Āhavanīya, he sprinkles it with water. (*Śatapatha Brāhmaṇa* VII.1.1.37 and X.2.3.1)[40]

It is not clear whether this text and others of the same kind (*Mānava Śulbasūtra* 10.3.4.6, *Baudhāyana Śulbasūtra* II.61–63, *Āpastamba Śulbasūtra* VII.5–11), which state that the Gārhapatya could be square or circular following the different schools, require that their respective areas should be the same. R. C. Gupta[41] showed that *Mānava Śulbasūtra* 10.3.4.6, for example, gives a rule to obtain a square and a circular Gārhapatya having the same perimeter. He also cites a text, given by a commentator of the *Baudhāyana*, stating that the square and the circular Gārhapatya should have the same breadth (side or diameter). However, it seems[42] that the transformation of a square into a disk of the same area was very common in the construction of circular altars like the *parimaṇḍala śmaśāna-cit* ("altar in the shape of a circular burial place"), the *ratha-cakra-cit* ("altar in the shape of a chariot wheel"), *parimaṇḍala droṇa-cit* ("altar in the shape of a dish"), etc. On the other hand, it should not be too surprising that the Indians had tried to express in a geometrical form (by the equality in area of the Gārhapatya, "terrestrial world," and the Āhavanīya, "world of the gods") an equivalence promoted by the ritual itself, whose aim is to permit the accession of the profane to the sacred world.

Text 13. The Circulature of the Square

If one wishes to transform a square into a disk, he should stretch the half of the diagonal cord along the west-east line from the center [of the square]. Together with the third part of what is left outside of the square, he should draw (through A) a circle. (*Baudhāyana Śulbasūtra* I.58; also *Kātyāyana Śulbasūtra* 3.13, *Mānava Śulbasūtra* 10.3.2.10 and 10.1.1.8; and *Āpastamba Śulbasūtra* III.2)

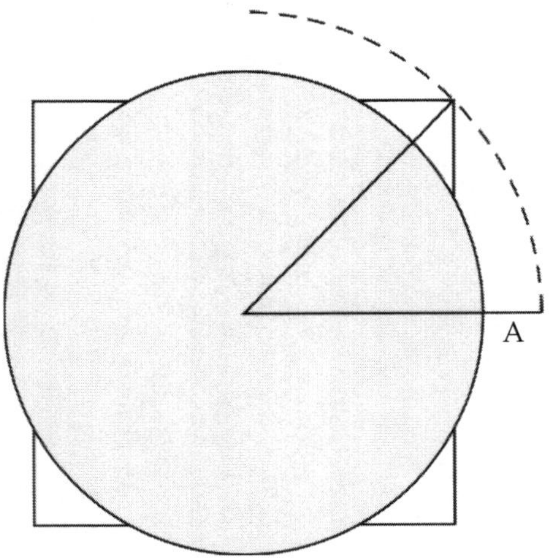

Figure 6.

This construction assigns to the diameter of the circle the length $s(2+\sqrt{2})/3$, where s is the length of the side of the square. It is equivalent to giving to π the approximate value 3.088.[43]

We will see below the inverse transformation, i.e., the quadrature of the circle, obtained with the help of this circulature and a good approximate value of the diagonal of the square known to Baudhāyana. Note that it is the circulature, not the quadrature, that was primary to the *Śulbasūtra*s.

> Let us now consider the last element of the first sacrificial area, the *vedi.*
>
> It is a part of the sacrificial field, slightly excavated and covered with sacrificial herbs (*barhi*), on which were placed the offerings and [to which were] invited the gods; sitting on this "bed" while eating them. It is a rectangle, placed between the fires, having its sides cut into segments in order to receive the offerings.[44]

More precisely (for the new and full moon sacrifices), it is a trapezium whose sides are curved (see Figure 6, below), as the *Baudhāyana Śulbasūtra* explains, and the dimensions and shape of which are consistently interpreted by the *Śatapatha Brāhmaṇa* with the cosmic function of creation (pro-creation here, rather than re-creation) of the sacrifice. Other shapes exist, as we will see below with the *paitṛkī vedi*, "altar for the ancestors."

Text 14. Dimensions and Construction of the *Vedi*

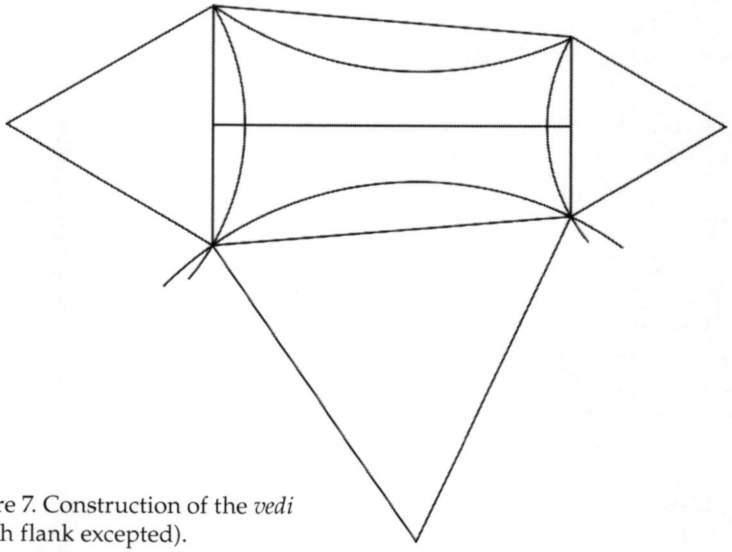

Figure 7. Construction of the *vedi* (north flank excepted).

It is prescribed for the *vedi darśapaurṇamāsikā* (new and full moon sacrifices): "to the west of the Āhavanīya, it has the size of the *yajamāna*." The breadth to the west is equal to two-thirds of this, the breadth to the east exactly to the half of this. After having so built a rectangle smaller at one side (a trapezium), let one fix poles at the corners.

Having made loops at the two extremities of a cord as long as [the length] doubled, one marks the middle. Having fixed the two loops to the two south sides and gone to the south with the mark, let one fix a pole at the spot where the mark falls.

Having fixed the two loops there, let one draw around the south flank with the mark. So is explained the north flank. With the help of the [cord] doubled, let one draw around the east flank and, so, the west. (*Baudhāyana Śulbasūtra* I.71–75)

Text 15. "Explanation" of the Form and Position of the *Vedi*

The two shoulders [of the *vedi*] he carries along both sides of the [Āhavanīya] fire. For the *vedi* (fem.) is female and the fire (*agni*, masc.) is male; and the woman lies embracing the man: thereby a copulation productive of offspring is obtained. For this reason he carries the two shoulders [of the *vedi*] along both sides of the fire.

It should be broader on the west side, contracted in the middle, and broad again on the east side; for thus shaped they praise a woman: "broad about the hips, somewhat narrower between the shoulders, and contracted in the middle (or, about the waist)." Thereby he makes it [the *vedi*] pleasing to the gods. (*Śatapatha Brāhmaṇa* I.2.5.15–16)[45]

The Extension of the Sacrificial Ground and "Pythagorean" Theorem

Other rites, like those involving animal sacrifices, require a purely trapezoidal *vedi* whose dimensions are too large for it to be placed between the three fires. This new *vedi*, called *mahāvedi*, "grand *vedi*," or *saumikī vedi*, "*soma vedi*," in the *soma* sacrifices, is placed east of the Āhavanīya fire. This fire will then be moved to the extreme east of the new vedi and set on the *uttarā vedi*, "upper *vedi*," for it is a *vedi* on the *mahāvedi*.

The *Mahāvedi*

Its dimensions are 36 *prakrama*s for the length, 30 *prakrama*s for the west breadth, and 24 *prakrama*s for the east breadth. It is already mentioned in *Taittirīya Saṁhitā* 6.2.4.5 and *Śatapatha Brāhmaṇa* X.2.3.4. Let us look at its construction (see also Figure 8), as described by the *Āpastamba Śulbasūtra*.

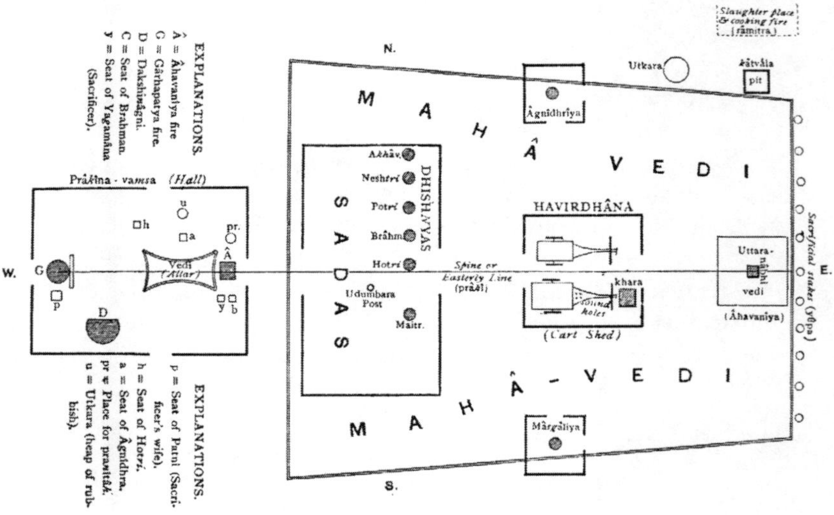

Figure 8. Plan of the extended sacrificial ground.[46]

Text 16. Construction of the *Mahāvedi*

Add to a [cord of] length thirty-six eighteen and make two marks on the cord, one at twelve, the other at fifteen, beginning from the western end; tie the ends of the cord to the ends of the west-east line . . . and taking it by the sign at fifteen, draw it toward the south; at the place reached by the mark, after the cord has been well stretched, fix a pole. Do the same on the northern side. . . . By this process, the two hips, the southwest corner and the northwest corner of the *vedi,* are fixed. After that, exchange the ends of the cord and fix the two shoulders, the southeast corner and the northeast corner. This is done by stretching the cord toward the south having taken it by the mark at fifteen and by fixing a pole on the spot reached by the mark at twelve; and by repeating the same operation on the northern side. The result is the two shoulders. This is the measurement of the vedi by means of one cord. (*Āpastamba Śulbasūtra* V.2)[47]

Another construction needs two cords (Figure 9).

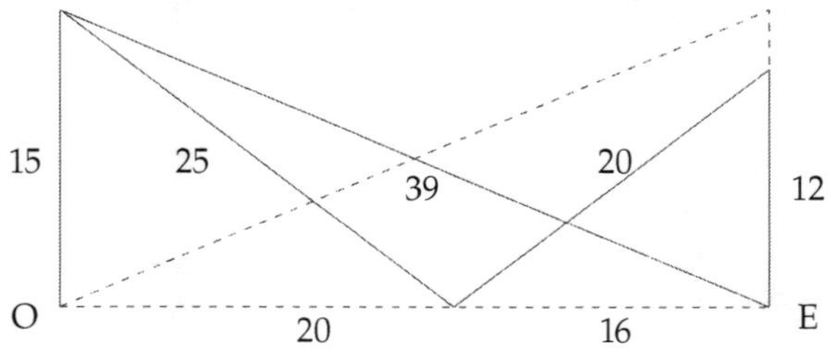

Figure 9. Construction of the *mahāvedi* with one and two cords.

Text 17. A Second Construction of the *Mahāvedi*

> The diagonal cord of an oblong, the side cords of which are three and four, is five. With these cords increased three times by itself, the two eastern corners of the *vedi* are fixed. With the same cords increased four times, the two western corners of the *vedi* are found. (*Āpastamba Śulbasūtra* V.3)[48]

Knowledge and Use of "Pythagorean Triples"

Those two constructions are based on the knowledge of triples of integers (x, y, z) satisfying the so-called "Pythagorean" relation $x^2 + y^2 = z^2$, where x, y, and z represent the sides and hypotenuse of a right-angled triangle. It is already clear in the above text that the Indians knew this property, or, rather, that x, y, and z satisfying $x^2 + y^2 = z^2$ represent the sides and diagonal of a rectangle (instead of a right-angled triangle). This property is stated in the general case by Baudhāyana:

Text 18. The Property of the Diagonal of a Rectangle

> What the length and breadth produce separately, the diagonal of a rectangle produces both. The observation is made in the following: of breadth and length consisting of 3 and 4, 12 and 5, 15 and 8, 7 and 24, 12 and 35, 15 and 36 units. (*Baudhāyana Śulbasūtra* I.48–49)

"Produces" translates here the term *karoti* (root *KṚ*,"to do, to produce), meaning the production of a square from its side, just as the Greek δύναται (from δύναμαι, "to be capable") in enunciations of the Pythagorean relation earlier than Euclid's Elements. The parallelism between the Sanskrit term *karaṇī* (same root *KṚ*), meaning the cord on which one constructs a square (for example the *dvi-karaṇī* is the side of a square of area double of a given square), and the Greek δύναμις, meaning (as in Plato's *Theaetetus* 147d–148b) the side of a square whose surface is not the square of an integer, is also to be noted.

So, having taken a cord of length 36 + 18, with a mark at distance 15 from its extremity, Āpastamba was confident that he was building a right angle when he stretched the cord by the mark to draw a triangle of sides 36, 15, and 39, since these numbers are multiples of 12, 5, and 13, the sides and diagonal of an authenticated integer rectangle. In the second construction, he clearly announced that he used multiples of 3, 4, and 5, the sides and diagonal of another authenticated integer rectangle.

For the construction of the *mahāvedi, Baudhāyana Śulbasūtra* I.29–35 and I.42–44 proceeds as does Āpastamba, but generalizes somewhat the procedure by taking, for the construction of any right angle, a cord to which is added half its length marked at its sixth part, which yields multiples of 5, 12, 13, or its entire length marked at its fourth part, which yields multiples of 3, 4, 5. More generally, it can be shown that the procedure consisting of augmenting a cord of length L by its nth part marked at its first 2n(n+1)th part and stretching it by the mark, when its extremities are attached to two poles at distance L, always yields a right-angled triangle with sides proportional to (2n+1, 2n(n+1), 2n(n+1)+1). Moreover, this triple represents all the primitive[49] right-angled triangles with integer sides whose hypotenuse exceeds the longest side by 1 unit.

In text 18, Baudhāyana cites only three such triples (omitting the hypotenuse, which we may readily calculate): 3, 4, 5; 12, 5, 13; and 7, 24, 25, which seems to indicate that he didn't generalize the procedure in this case. On the other hand, he cites other triples, such as 15, 8, 17 and 12, 35, 37, where the difference between the hypotenuse and the longest side is 2 (the triple 15, 36, 39 is a multiple of 5, 12, 13, as already observed). We will see in the next section how these numbers have probably been obtained, but it is clear that the Indians knew the property corresponding to the Pythagorean relation for the diagonal of the square.

Text 19. The Property of the Diagonal of the Square

> The cord taken on the diagonal of the square produces a surface twice as big. (*Baudhāyana Śulbasūtra* I.45)

This diagonal, which is used as the side of a new square having a surface twice as big as the original square, is called *dvi-karaṇī,* "producer of two," and also serves as the length of a rectangle, the breadth of which is the side of the original square, to build the *tri-karaṇī,* "producer of three," and the *tṛtīya-karaṇī,* "producer of one third," with the help of the property of the diagonal of the rectangle.

Text 20. Construction of the *Tri-karaṇī*

> If the side of the square is the breadth of a rectangle, the *dvi-karaṇī* the length, the diagonal of this rectangle is the *tri-karaṇī.* By this is also explained the *tṛtīya-karaṇī;* the ninth part of the surface is thus used. (*Baudhāyana Śulbasūtra* I.46–47)

The *tṛtīya-karaṇī* produces a square whose area is the ninth part of the area of the square produced by the *tri-karaṇī,* its length is equal to a third of the *tri-karaṇī.*

The question now is why there is a difference between the enunciations of the properties of the diagonal of the rectangle, on the one hand, and of the square, on the other hand. Both are geometrically expressed, but while the first one is corroborated, if not "proved,"[50] by numerical examples, the second is not. We know today that it could not be and perhaps the Indians also knew this, or at least guessed that it would be very difficult, as will be explained below. However, I rather think that they didn't need any explanation because of the obviousness of the property, which was possibly manifested, if required, by the geometric argument given in the following figure.

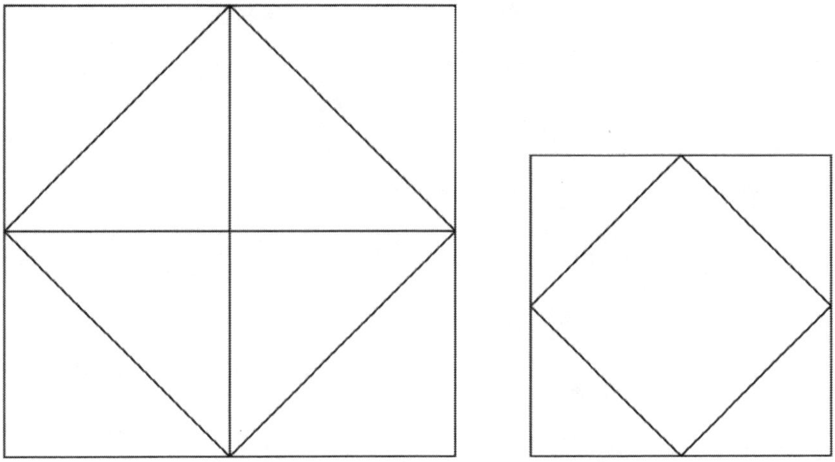

Figure 10. "Proof" of the theorem of the diagonal of the square.

This figurative demonstration conforms to Indian knowledge of how to construct a square whose corners (not sides) are pointed at the four cardinal points, as is required for the *paitṛkī vedi* needed for the ancestor's cult.[51]

Text 21. Construction of the *Paitṛkī Vedi*

> In the case of the *paitṛkī vedi,* one should construct a square having an area of two square puruṣas. Drive pegs at the midpoints of the four sides [of this square]. The lines joining these pegs form a square. This is the construction. (*Kātyāyana Śulbasūtra* 2.6)[52]

This context for the discovery of the "proof" may be preferable to the one using the four external (not passing through the center) diagonals of the four squares composing the body of the *caturaśra-śyena-cit* (see Figure 10, above). Indeed, this last one could have been suggested to historians of science by Socrate's demonstration in Plato's Meno (82b–85b), in which the description looks very much like this figure and could have inspired it. However, there is another figure (see Figure 17, below) suggested by Baudhāyana to transform a square into a rectangle, which gives more weight to the previous construction.[53] Notable is a geometrical pattern, present on many vases of the Indus civilization, that recalls these figures.

Figure 11. Geometrical pattern on Indus pottery.

Finally, the answer to the question of the different enunciations could be that the Indians probably felt a difference between the two types of "proof"[54] and possibly knew that the property of the diagonal of the square could not be "proved numerically," as could the other property.[55]

The Gnomon

We know that the Indians used "Pythagorean" triples (integer numbers x, y, z satisfying the relation $x^2 + y^2 = z^2$) to construct right angles, but how did they discover these triples? Five primitive (x, y, and z have no common divisors) triples were known: 3, 4, 5; 12, 5, 13; 7, 24, 25; 15, 8, 17; and 12, 35, 37; and they could have been discovered by using small pebbles, for example, as Thibaut suggests,[56] to recompose two squares from one bigger square. But then why is the triple 20, 21, 29 missing? In this case, the bigger square is $29^2 = 841$, which is less than $37^2 = 1{,}369$, and should have been discovered if the search had been systematically made with every integer square up to 37^2.

This suggests another research procedure, less exhaustive but more clever, in which a new square is constructed from an existing one by adding a structure called a gnomon (a set square-shaped structure, see Figure 12, below) so that it is transformed into a square. For example, add to the square of side 4 a gnomon of width 1, that is, of surface 9 = 4

+ 1 + 4, and a new square $5^2 = 25 = 16 + 9$ is obtained. To a square of side 15, add a gnomon of width 2, that is, of surface 15 + 1 + 15 + 16 + 1 + 16 = 64, and a new square $17^2 = 289 = 225 + 64$ is obtained. This hypothesis[57] not only explains why we have triples having a difference of 1 or 2 (the widths of the gnomon) between the diagonal and the longest side of the rectangle, but also why the triple 20, 21, 29 is missing. It has a difference of 8 and would have necessitated too many steps to be undertaken. Moreover, as we will see below, the gnomon was known to the *Śulbasūtras*, and especially the way its area could be decomposed (and probably computed) was described.

Text 22. Area of the Gnomon

> Now, a rule about what is exceeding [the square]: as much, each time, as what one draws about [the square] with the excess, one places it on the two sides of the square, and the square produced by the [excess is] on the top. (*Āpastamba Śulbasūtra* III.9)

Figure 12. Decomposition of the gnomon.

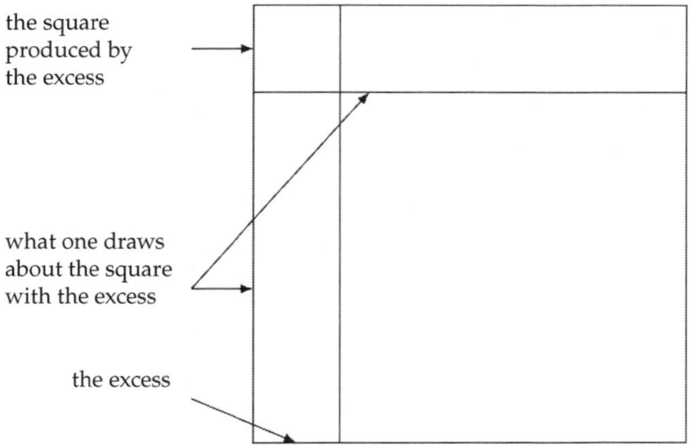

Mathematical Rules Useful for Building the Grand Altar

On the east of the *mahāvedi* was built the grand altar, facing east; the different shapes have already been described in the introduction. It is made of several (usually five) layers of bricks, and the forms and disposition of the bricks are precisely set out in the texts. I won't describe all the bricks or the different shapes the altar can take, but rather focus on the plan of the *caturaśra-śyena-cit,* the altar in the shape of a "square bird of prey." This permits us to place in context the mathematical tools the *Baudhāyana Śulbasūtra* presents.

As mentioned, the *caturaśra-śyena-cit* is composed of four squares of which side is the *puruṣa,* constituting the body (*ātman*) of the bird, to which two squares for the wings and one square for the tail were added. Each wing and the tail are lengthened by a rectangle of breadth 1 *aratni* (1/5 *puruṣa*) and 1 *prādeśa* (1/10 *puruṣa*) respectively, which give the altar an area of 7½ square *puruṣa*s and explain its other name, *sa-aratni-prādeśa-sapta-vidha,* "having seven divisions with *aratni* and *prādeśa.*"

These dimensions are valid for the first construction of this altar. But if the same *yajamāna* wishes to build it a second time (for example, if he didn't succeed in obtaining what he wanted by the rite), the area of the altar must be increased by 1 square *puruṣa.*

Text 23. Dimensions of the Successive Altars

> The first fire altar has seven and half square puruṣas, the second eight and half, the third nine and half. (*Baudhāyana Śulbasūtra* II.1–3)

Moreover, the shape shouldn't be altered and this homothetic requirement explains the need for the following geometrical constructions. How did Baudhāyana propose to increase the area of the *sa-aratni-prādeśa-sapta-vidha*?

Text 24. Proportional Increase of the Areas of the Different Parts of the Altar

> And now, in which manner must one increase a part? What is different from the original form, after having divided it into fifteen parts, let each pair of parts be assembled with each part of the altar. Let the fire altar be constructed with the help of the seven and half. (*Baudhāyana Śulbasūtra* II. 11–13)

Increasing the Seven Squares of the *Caturaśra-śyena-cit*

For the first increase, we thus understand here that the supplementary square of one square *puruṣa* should be divided into fifteen strips and each pair of the fourteen first strips adjoined to the seven squares of the altar (see Figure 13, below). This yields a rectangle of sides 1 and 1 + 2/15 *puruṣa*s that must be transformed into a square, an operation the *Śulbasūtra*s easily describe.

Text 25. Transformation of a Rectangle into a Square

If one wishes to square a rectangle, after having made of the breadth the side of a square one should place the rest, divided into two equal parts, on the two sides of the square. One should fill the void by inserting a square. The subtraction of it has been explained. (*Baudhāyana Śulbasūtra* I.54)

Figure 13. Enlargement of one square of the *caturaśra-śyena-cit*.

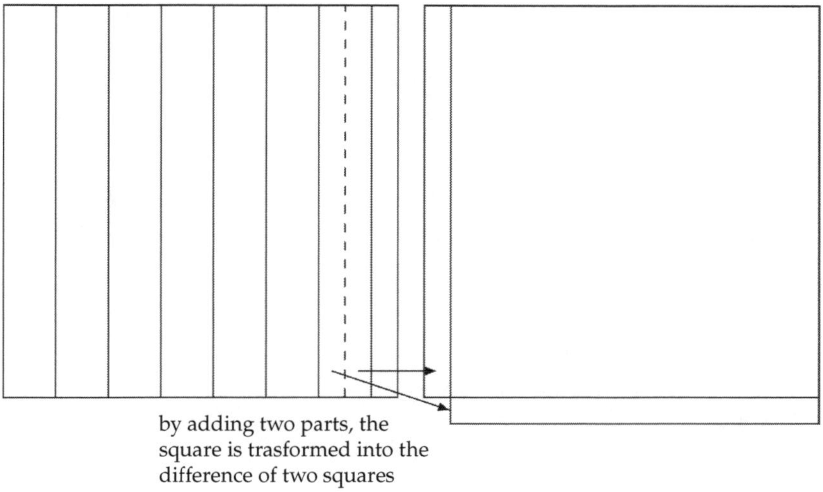

The rectangle is thus transformed into a gnomon, a difference of two squares. In the case of the first increase of the altar, a gnomon is readily obtained by adding the two strips on two adjacent sides of the original square. This gnomon must then be transformed into a square by a rule Baudhāyana has already given.

Text 26. Transformation of a Difference of Two Squares into a Square

If one wishes to subtract a square from a square, one must cut from the bigger a strip having as breadth the side of the square one wishes to subtract; then one should bring diagonally into contact the length of the strip with the other side of it and, where it falls, should take away the rest of the side. (*Baudhāyana Śulbasūtra* I.51)

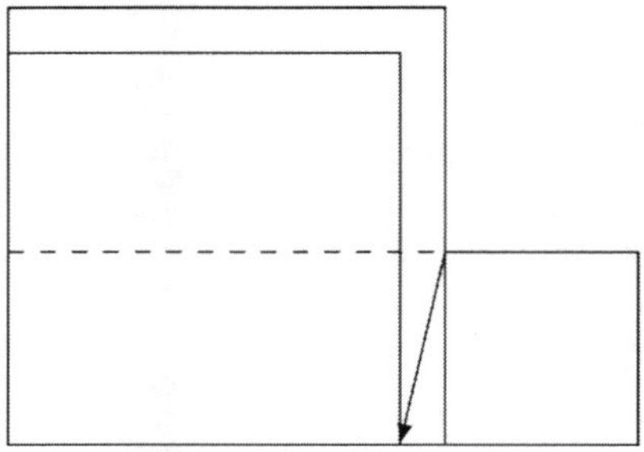

Figure 14a. Construction of the square equal to the difference of two squares.

Another way, especially useful when the altar is not a *sapta-vidha* or when it should be increased by more than one square *puruṣa,* is to square the rectangle (the breadth of which is 2/15 *puruṣa,* for example) by *Baudhāyana Śulbasūtra* I.54 and then add it to the other square. The final step is to transform the two squares into one.

Text 27. Transformation of a Sum of Two Squares into a Square

> To unite two different squares, one should cut a strip from the bigger with the side of the shorter; the diagonal of the strip is the side of the two united squares. (*Baudhāyana Śulbasūtra* I.50)

Increasing the Wings and Tail of the *Caturaśra-śyena-cit*

So far, so good: we know how to increase the seven squares, forming the essential part of the altar. But how can the squares that represent the wings and tail of the altar be proportionally enlarged? This is not an easy problem, because after having added to each wing and to the tail the part of the last strip (see Figure 13, above, and Figure 15, below, for two possible methods) proportional to its size, it must be adapted to the size of the new square wing (resp. tail). This requires the transformation of a rectangle, or a square, into another rectangle of a specified length (or breadth).

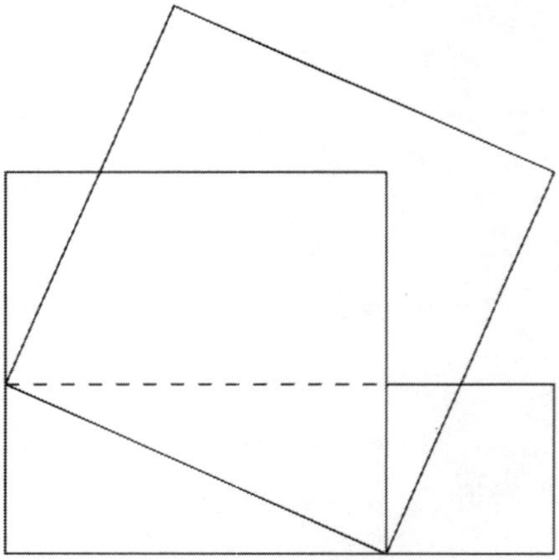

Figure 14a. Construction of the square equal to the sum of two squares.

The *Śulbasūtras* give no method to transform a rectangle into another, but Baudhāyana gives two rules to transform a square into a rectangle (see Figures 15 and 16).

Figure 15. Different methods to increase the extension of the wing.

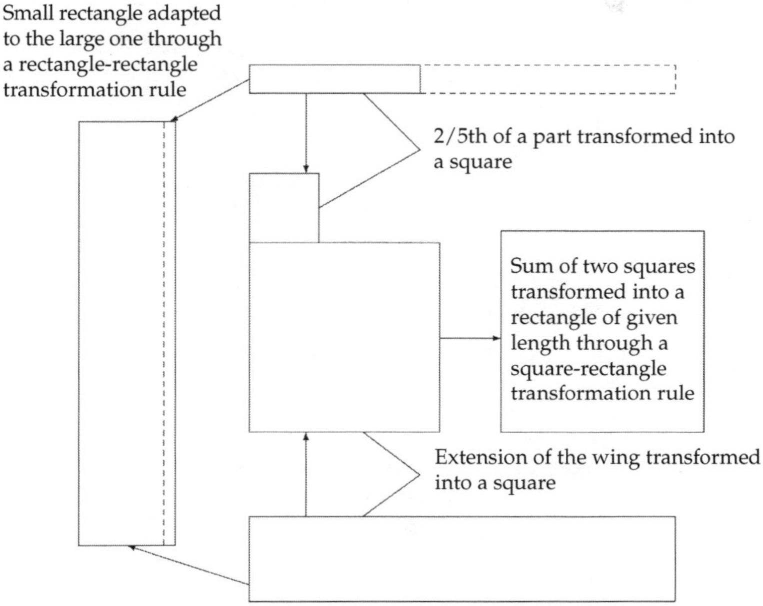

Text 28. Transformation of a Square into a Rectangle

If one wishes to transform a square into a rectangle, after having cut it by the diagonal and divided in two-fourths a part, one should place them properly on the two sides of the squares. In that case also, after having cut the square with this same rectangle, let one place the rest elsewhere. (*Baudhāyana Śulbasūtra* I.52–3)

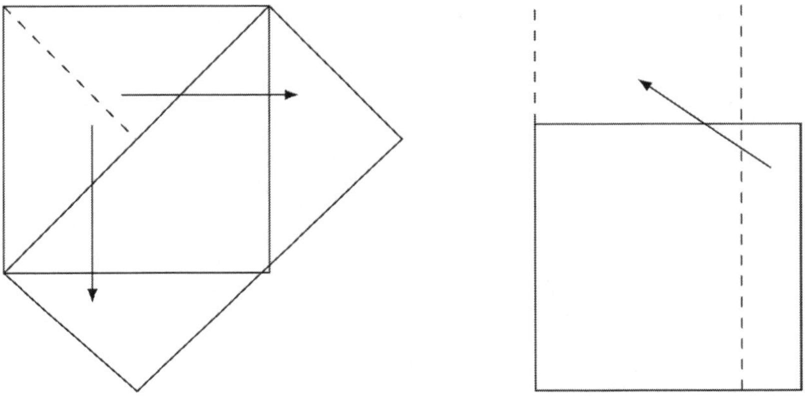

Figure 16. Transformation of a square into a rectangle (Baudhāyana).

It is clear that these sūtras don't give the general method. The first one transforms the square into a rectangle whose length is the diagonal of the square, and it was surely inspired by (or inspired) the graphical demonstration of the property of the diagonal (see Figure 10). The second one is incomplete, since it doesn't explain how to arrange the rest of the square into a rectangle.

Dvārakānātha, a commentator of the *Baudhāyana Śulbasūtra*, gives the exact rule to transform a square into a rectangle[58] (see also Figure 17, below).

Text 29. The Exact Transformation of a Square into a Rectangle

> And another method: after having extended the two sides of the square to the east up to ~~the desired~~ desired length, one should stretch a diagonal cord to the northeast. Placed on the rectangle, where it falls on the "breadth" of the square; there, after having removed the north, one should make with the southern part the breadth of the rectangle. This is the rectangle. (Dvārakānātha's commentary to the preceding *sūtra*.)

Figure 17. Transformation of a square into a rectangle (Dvārakānātha).

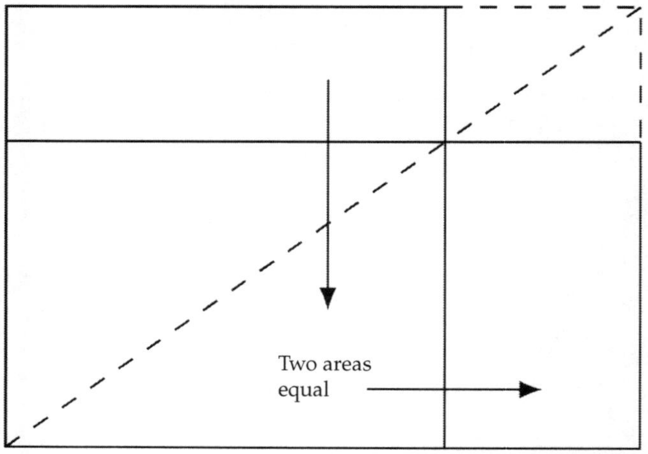

In practice, the *adhvaryu* would have proceeded like Āpastamba, who proposed to divide the supplementary square *puruṣa* into fourteen equal strips, instead of fifteen, in order to increase only the seven squares; the wings and tails, would simply be adapted in length to the new sides of these squares, their breadth remaining one *aratni* and one *prādeśa* respectively.[59] The new altar, however, would not have an area of 8½ square puruṣas exactly. Or they could have defined a new unit *puruṣa* equal to the side of one of the seven new squares and, from this derived the new *aratni* and *prādeśa* for the wings and tail. This method is inspired[60] by the way the *Kātyāyana Śulbasūtra* (2.19) proposed to construct a vedi for the new and full moon sacrifices, which would have the same shape as the *mahāvedi* but an area equal to a third of its area. Kātyāyana replaces the original *prakrama* used to construct the *mahāvedi* by the *tṛtīya-karaṇī* (see Text 19) of a square of side 1 *prakrama*, thus defining a new *prakrama* unit. This method, at least applied to the *caturaśra-śyena-cit*, would yield an altar that is 8½ square (original) *puruṣa*s and of the same shape as the altar of 7½ square *puruṣa*s.

The Quadrature of the Circle and the Approximations of the Diagonal of the Square

The *Śulbasūtra*s knew how to transform a square into a circle of (approximately) the same area, a problem usually called "circulature of the square" (see Text 13 and Figure 6, above). The inverse problem, to transform a circle into a square of the same area, the famous "quadrature of the circle," was also studied[61] by the Indians, who simply described how to construct the side of the square as a fraction of the diameter of the circle.

Text 30. The Quadratures of the Circle

> If one wishes to make square a disk, after having divided the diameter of the disk into eight equal parts and such a part into twenty-nine, let one remove from the diameter twenty-eight such parts and the sixth of such a part minus its own eighth part. (*Baudhāyana Śulbasūtra* I.59)
>
> Or else, after having made fifteen equal parts, let one remove two; this is the usual[62] side of the square. (*Baudhāyana Śulbasūtra* I.60; also *Kātyāyana Śulbasūtra* 3.14 and *Āpastamba Śulbasūtra* III, 3)[63]

The first sūtra equates the side of a square to the $(1 - \frac{28}{8 \times 29} - \frac{1}{8 \times 29 \times 6} + \frac{1}{8 \times 29 \times 6 \times 8})$th of the diameter of the "equivalent" circle, while the second sūtra evaluates it to the $(1 - \frac{2}{15})$th.

The first sūtra yields a value of 3.088 for π, while the second sūtra gives 3.004.

Baudhāyana's Approximation of the Diagonal of the Square

These fractions have been obtained by inversing the process of circulature with the help of an approximation of the diagonal of the square. The best approximation has been given by Baudhāyana (and also in *Āpastamba Śulbasūtra* I.6).

Text 31. Approximation of the Diagonal of the Square

> Let the side of the square be increased by a third, and this by the fourth diminished by the thirty-fourth part of itself. . . . (*Baudhāyana Śulbasūtra* I.61)

We have here a diagonal/side ratio evaluated to $1 + \frac{1}{3} + \frac{1}{3 \times 4} - \frac{1}{3 \times 4 \times 34}$ approximately 1.414215686 and equal to $\sqrt{2}$ (~1.414213562) to the fifth decimal. We will see how Baudhāyana could have obtained this fraction with the help of the gnomon, but let us first explain the relation between the circulature of the square and the quadrature of the circle, through the following approximation.

Expressed in *tila*s, the diagonal of a square of which side is one *prakrama* (12 *aṅgula*s or 12 x 34 *tila*s) measures $(1 + \frac{1}{3} + \frac{1}{3 \times 4} - \frac{1}{3 \times 4 \times 34}) \times 34 \times 12 =$ 577 *tila*s. If we apply to this approximation of the diagonal the process of circulature, that is, divide by 3 what exceeds the side, we obtain $\frac{169}{3}$ or $56\frac{1}{3}$ for the excess and $464\frac{1}{3}$ for the diameter of the circle having (approximately) an area of 1 square *prakrama*. Inverting the process means to express the ratio between the side (408) and the diameter ($464\frac{1}{3}$) as a sum or difference of unit or complementary fractions. A first approximation, without the inconvenient third, yields $\frac{408}{464} = \frac{7}{8} + \frac{1}{8 \times 29} = 1 - \frac{28}{8 \times 29}$, but this can be ameliorated: following Thibaut,[64] 408 and 464 were multiplied by 3 in order to avoid the fractions, yielding 1,224 and 1,393. Taking $\frac{7}{8}$ of 1,393 (or 7 x 174), we obtained $1{,}218\frac{7}{8}$, which is $5\frac{1}{8}$ less than 1,224; the difference can be expressed as $(6 - 1) + \frac{1}{8}$. These numbers were then converted into parts of 174, considered now as the exact 8th of 1,393,[65] which yields $\frac{1}{29} - \frac{1}{6 \times 29} + \frac{1}{8 \times 6 \times 29}$. As 174 is considered the 8th of 1,393, and adding $\frac{7}{8}$, we have finally the fractional expression described by the sūtra, where $\frac{7}{8} + \frac{1}{8 \times 29}$ has been replaced by $1 - \frac{28}{8 \times 29}$.

The Origin of Baudhāyana's Approximation of the Diagonal of the Square

The beginning of this explanation was made easier by the fact that thirty-four *tila*s are equal to one *aṅgula*. The factor 34 was chosen on purpose, of course, and is related to the approximation of the diagonal of the square, as we will now see.

Probably in order to give to the property of the diagonal of the square some numerical evidence, the Indians investigated the integer numbers, the squares of which could be expressed as the sum of two equal squares. We know that due to the irrationality of $\sqrt{2}$ there are no such numbers, but only some approximate ones, such as 7 ($7^2 = 2\times5^2 - 1$), 17 ($17^2 = 2\times12^2 + 1$), and infinite others.[66] The value given by Baudhāyana Śulbasūtra I.61 proves that he knew the approximation 17 for a square of side 12, if the following derivation is correct (see Figure 18, below).

A first approximation for the diagonal of a square of side 12 aṅgulas is 17, since $17^2 = 2\times12^2 + 1$, so that it suffices to subtract from the square of side 17 a gnomon of an area 1 square aṅgula to obtain the exact area. Since the side of the gnomon would be 17, its width is evaluated to 1/34 and should be subtracted to yield the diagonal. However, this value of the diagonal is only approximate since we have subtracted a gnomon of area $2\times(17\times1/34)-(1/34)^2$, which is less than 1. The value of the diagonal is still too large but a much better approximation than 17. See Figure 18, below.

In order to express the result (17 *aṅgula*s, 1 *tila*[67] for a square of side 12 *aṅgula*s) in terms of fractions, independently of the side of the original square (12), Baudhāyana has probably decomposed 17 *aṅgula*s, 1 *tila* into 12 + 4 + 1 (*aṅgula*s) + 1 *tila*[68] and divided each term by 12, which yields the fraction given in the sūtra at I.61, when the *tila* is expressed in *aṅgula*s.

Mānava's (and Others') Approximation of the Diagonal of the Square

The fact that the definition of the *tila* could be explained with the help of the derivation of a better approximation than 17 for the diagonal of a square of side 12 makes us suspect that the definition of the *aṇu* as 1/14th of an *aṅgula* could be related to the approximation 7 for the diagonal of a square of side 5. A derivation of the type used for *Baudhāyana Śulbasūtra* I.61 would lead us to a diagonal of 7 *aṅgula*s 1/14 or 7 *aṅgula*s, 1 *aṇu* for a side of 5 *aṅgula*s and, more generally, to the fraction 1 + 2/5 + 1/14

Figure 18. Derivation of the approximation to the diagonal of the square of side 12.

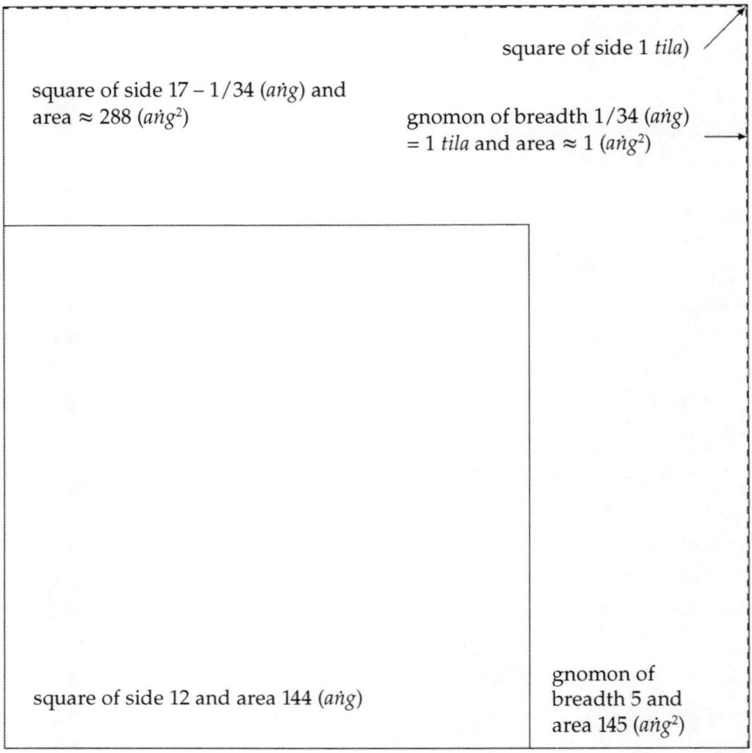

for the ratio of the diagonal of a square to its side. Once again, this value is too large, since we have added a gnomon of which area is $1 + 1/14^2$ square *aṅgula*s.

But there exists also a more direct attestation of the approximation 7, which could be derived from Mānava's construction of the *paitṛkī vedi.*

Text 32. The Construction of the *Paitṛkī Vedi* by Mānava

> The whole cord is ten *aratni*s, in its middle is the *nirāñchana;* he shall make the west-east line at seven *aratni*s; this is the *vedi* with its angles turned toward the four quarters, prescribed for the fathers. The whole cord is seven aratnis, in its middle is the *nirāñchana;* he shall make the west-east line at five *aratnis*; this is the *vedi* with its angles turned toward the four quarters, prescribed for the fathers. (*Mānava Śulbasūtra* 10.1.2.6–7)[69]

The *nirāñchana* is the mark on the cord by which one has to stretch it when attached to two poles placed at the two extremities of the west-east line.

Figure 19. Construction of the northern part of the *paitṛkī vedi* by Mānava.

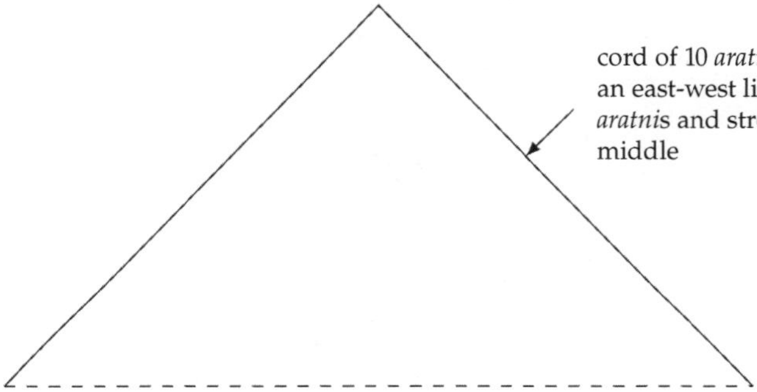

Figure 19 reveals how easily the second construction of the *paitṛkī vedi* could have been deduced from the first one. Thus, *Mānava Śulbasūtra* 10.1.2.7 attests the knowledge by the *Śulbasūtrakaras* that 7 is an approximation of the diagonal of a square of side 5.[70]

Still other evidence exists of the Indians' knowledge of this approximation, by instance the second rule of quadrature (see Text 30). Suppose the circulature process is applied to a square whose side is 5 and the diagonal is supposed to be 7. The diameter of the corresponding circle would be then 5 + 2/3 and the ratio of the diameter to the side 1 + 2/15 = 17/15. Now, attempting to deduce from this arithmetical circulature rule a quadrature rule, the Indians could have simply replaced the addition of 2/15 by a subtraction of 2/15,[72] which yields the rule given in *Baudhāyana Śulbasūtra* I.60 and elsewhere.

Conclusion

We thus see that Baudhāyana, and the *Śulbasūtrakaras* in general, knew several approximations of the diagonal of certain squares with integral sides (7 for 5, 17 for 12) and also had built a procedure, via the gnomon, to improve these approximations (7+1/14 for 5, 17-1/34 for 12). If Baudhāyana noted, as we did, that the area of the gnomon is not exactly 1 in each case and, consequently, that the value of the diagonal could still be improved by removing another gnomon,[72] and this ad infinitum, he may have also realized that it would never be possible to find by this procedure the exact diagonal of a square of integral side.[73] This is of course not a discovery, a fortiori not a proof, of the irrationality of the diagonal of a square of integral side, but it is at least an intuition that something "goes wrong" with the square, something that differentiates it from the rectangle and justifies another treatment for it and the property of its diagonal.

Notes

1 By this, I mean the large territory called India before the 1947 partition between Pakistan and present-day India. It comprised a region including the Indus River and its tributaries.

2 The term "Indo-European tribes" does not refer to people having some specific physical or racial characteristics but to those populations that spoke languages belonging to the Indo-European family, which today contains all the nonautochtonous languages of America and Australia, almost all the European languages (except Hungarian, Finnish, and some dialects) and all the Asiatic languages belonging to the countries from Iran to north and central India. Indo-European languages are also spoken in some countries of Africa.

3 The Indo-Aryans would have found in the Indus region only the remnants of the Harappans, who probably migrated from the area due to some natural disaster, such as floods and rivers altering their courses.

4 Louis Renou, *L'hindouisme* (Paris: Presses Universitaires de France, Paris, 1991), p. 7.

5 Renou, *L'hindouisme,* p. 7.

6 Renou, *L'hindouisme,* p. 13.

7 Jan Gonda, *A History of Indian Literature: Vedic Literature (Saṁhitās and Brāhmaṇas)* (Wiesbaden: Otto Harrassowitz, 1975), p. 339.

8 George Dumézil, *Les dieux des Indo-Européens* (Paris: Presses Universitaires de France, 1952), p. 23.

9 Margaret and James Stutley, *A Dictionary of Hinduism: Its Mythology, Folklore, and Development* (London: Routledge and Kegan Paul, 1977), p. 343.

10 Renou, *L'hindouisme,* p. 15.

11 *Śatapatha Brāhmaṇa* 2.3.1.5.

12 *Aitareya Brāhmaṇa* 1, 31.

13 Frits Staal, ed., *Agni: The Vedic Ritual of the Fire Altar* (Berkeley: Asian Humanities Press, 1983), vol. 1, p. 189.

14 Hyla Stuntz Converse, "The *Agnicaya* Rite: Indigenous Origin?", *History of Religions* 14/2 (1974): 83–84.

15 In Mohenjo-Daro, Harappa (present-day Pakistan), and some other places, such as Kalibangan (India), archaeologists have found remnants of large cities, originally laid out in squares with a regular orientation, with straight large avenues running from north to south and narrower ones, sometimes

staggered, running from east to west. The width of the large passages is always an integer (2, 3, or 4) multiple of the width of the smaller ones, and the fired or sundried clay bricks used for the buildings have integer proportions such as 4:2:1; Bridget Allchin and Raymond Allchin, *The Rise of Civilization in India and Pakistan* (Cambridge: Cambridge University Press, 1988), pp. 171–177.

16 In Sanskrit dictionaries the verbs are generally mentioned by their root (here *ci*), supplemented by the first-person singular of the indicative present (here *cinoti*), in order to specify its class (there are ten classes of verbs).

17 Except where explicitly mentioned, all the translations are mine. They are as close to the Sanskrit text as permitted given my concern that the translated passages are clear and understandable to the reader.

18 *Alaja* refers to a kind of bird, but there is no further information about it.

19 According to Monier Monier-Williams, *A Sankrit-English Dictionary* (Delhi: Motilal Banarsidass, 1995), *vajra* refers also to Indra's weapon, usually represented as a disk.

20 Translation in Gonda, *A History of Indian Literature,* p. 138.

21 Not to be confused with the brahman, the physician of the sacrifice, for all the other priests performing the sacrifices (see above) are also brahmans.

22 Translation in Julius Eggeling, *Sacred Books of the East* (Delhi: Motilal Banarsidass, 1978, reprint), vol. 40, pp. 143–144.

23 It must be remembered that before the Indo-Aryans reached the easternmost part of India, such "heresies" to brahmanical ideology as Buddhism and Jainism developed in these regions. They share a common characteristic in that they underestimated the value of this life and this world, which is certainly not the case of the materialistic ideology of the Indo-Aryans. It seems that the Indian belief in the transmigration of the soul derives ultimately from these new ideologies.

24 Allchin and Allchin, *The Rise of Civilization in India and Pakistan,* p. 308.

25 Converse, "The *Agnicaya* Rite: Indigenous Origin?", pp. 85–86.

26 Other cultural traits seem to divide the two groups, such as the shape of their burial mounds: square for the Indo-Aryans, round for the others. This is perhaps the origin of the equivalence square-disk that is so often seen in the altar constructions (see below).

27 The texts from the *Śulbasūtra*s have been extracted from the following editions: for Baudhāyana, George Thibaut, *The Pandit,* Old Series, vol. 9 (1874); for Āpastamba, Albert Bürk, *Zeitschrift der deutschen morgenländischen Gesellschaft* 15 (1901): 543–591; *Zeitschrift der deutschen morgenländischen Gesellschaft* 16 (1902): 327–391; for Mānava and Khadilkar, Jeannette M. van Gelder, ed., *Mānava Śrautasūtra, belonging to the Maitrāyaṇī Saṁhitā,* Śata-Piṭaka Series, vol. 27 (New Delhi: Indo-Asian Literatures, 1963); for Kātyāyana, Jeannette M. van Gelder, *Mānava Śrautasūtra, belonging to the Maitrāyaṇī Saṁhitā.* This explains why the reference numbers of the sūtras may differ from those found in the edition by S. N. Sen and A. K. Bag, *Śulbasūtras of Baudhāyana, Āpastamba, Kātyāyana, and Mānava* (New Delhi: Indian National Science Academy, 1983).

For a more recent critical edition of the *Baudhāyana Śulbasūtra*, with its commentary *Śulbadīpikā*, see Jean Michel Delire, *Les mathématiques de l'autel védique*, forthcoming.

28 The quotation marks in a translation indicate that the text itself quotes a previous text, as, for instance, when a portion of a *Brāhmaṇa* is included as authoritative in a sūtra.

29 According to Louis Renou, "Sur le genre du Sūtra dans la littérature sanskrite," *Journal Asiatique* 251 (1963): 166.

30 Arthur A. Macdonell, *A History of Sanskrit Literature* (Delhi: Motilal Banarsidass, 1971), pp. 222–223.

31 The excerpts of the *Mānava Śulbasūtra* and the *Āpastamba Śulbasūtra* quoted above show that the size of the *yajamāna* (or the *adhvaryu*) is actually used as a standard for the units of the sacrificial ground. It could then have come into conflict with the "stable" units derived from the *tila* or the *aṇu*.

32 Diagram from a medallion of Bārhut (second century B.C.E.), Jean Deloche, *Contributions à l'histoire de la voiture en Inde* (Paris: Ecole Française d'Extrême Orient Publications, 1983), vol. 138, fig. IX.h.

33 From Eggeling, *Sacred Books of the East*, vol. 26, p. 475.

34 For the Sanskrit text see http://www.sacred-texts.com/hin/rvsan rv05011.htm.

35 *Śatapatha Brāhmaṇa* 1.7.3.23–25.

36 This is not specified in the text itself, but in the commentaries.

37 This relative proximity should perhaps be compared to the brahmin-Agni association. As already mentioned, Agni, the fire god, is called "priest of the gods and god of the priests" (*Ṛg-Veda* III.20.3).

38 The two citations are identical except for the last word: *dakṣiṇāgnerāyatanam*, "the position of the Dakṣiṇāgni," is replaced in the *Śulbasūtra* by *dakṣiṇāgnervijñāyate*, "is taught about the Dakṣiṇāgni."

39 This name designates the Dakṣiṇāgni as the hearth on which one cooks (*pacati*, from the root PAC), the rice remaining after cooking the sacrificial cakes. This rice is called *anvāhārya* (*anv-ā-harati*, √HṚ), "what is to be added as a supplement."

40 Translated in Eggeling, *Sacred Books of the East*, vol. 41, p. 309; vol. 43, p. 307.

41 R. C. Gupta, "New Indian Values of π from the *Mānava Śulbasūtra*," *Centaurus* 31/2 (1988): 116.

42 Following N. K. Majumder, "Sacrificial Altars: Vedis and Agnis," *Journal of the Indian Society of Oriental Art* 7 (1939): 39–60; *Journal of the Indian Society of Oriental Art* 8 (1940): 21–40.

43 This canonical way of evaluating the precision of such a construction is of course completely anachronistic, since the *Śulbasūtra*s contain no clues to the Indians' knowledge of the constancy of the ratio of a circle's area to the square of its radius, still less a direct approximation of this ratio. However, *Baudhāyana Śulbasūtra* I.112–3 has for the ratio of the circumference of a circle

to its diameter the usual approximation 3: "The sacrificial posts have one *pada* as diameter, the bases of the sacrificial posts have three *padas* as circumference." This does not necessarily mean that they were aware of the constancy of this ratio. Finally, it should be noted that the equality of these two different ratios (generally distinguished as π2, quadratic, and π1, linear) was not evident for the ancients, even when they knew good approximations of each.

44 Gonda, *A History of Indian Literature*, pp. 172, 176.

45 Translated in Eggeling, *Sacred Books of the East*, vol. 7, p. 63.

46 From Eggeling, *Sacred Books of the East*, vol. 26, p. 475.

47 Translated in Thibaut, *The Pandit*, Old Series, vol. 10 (1875): 235.

48 Translated in Thibaut, *The Pandit*, Old Series, vol. 10, p. 236.

49 That is of which lengths of sides have no common factors. This results from the fact that two integer numbers (≥ 4 since $n \geq 1$) whose difference is one cannot have common factors.

50 Geoffrey E. R. Lloyd, in *Demystifying Mentalities* (Cambridge: Cambridge University Press, 1990), pp. 74–75; 98–104, considers that it is extremely unlikely the Indians had the use of a concept of proof. I agree with this assertion, as it means that they did not use "an exact procedure of general validity, establishing by way of a general, deductive justification the truth of the theorem or proposition concerned" (p. 74). But they probably had another sort of "proof" (also considered by Lloyd, p. 74), rather, verification or a visual evidence that explains my use of the quotation marks. Furthermore, Lloyd maintains that the Indians made "no distinction . . . between exact procedures and approximate ones" (p. 75) or "between exact and approximate results" (p. 104). Against this last assertion, I can testify that nowhere in the *Baudhāyana Śulbasūtra* is found a construction for which at least two procedures of different nature (exact and approximate) are given. For example, let us recall the four different constructions of the place of the Dakṣiṇāgni (*Baudhāyana Śulbasūtra* I, 67–9), which prove that Baudhāyana at least was concerned with the approximate nature of some constructions and tried to improve them. I will show below that Baudhāyana extended his concern to other matters, including the search for a more exact value for the diagonal of the square or a more appropriate quadrature of the circle. But, of course, in such a conservative field as the Indian ritual tradition, it is still possible to put forward that Baudhāyana simply collected different traditional procedures, without any concern for their improvement.

51 B. Datta, *The Science of the Śulba: A Study in Early Hindu Geometry* (Calcutta: University of Calcutta, 1932), p. 113; T. A. Sarasvati Amma, *Geometry in Ancient and Medieval India* (Delhi: Motilal Banarsidass, 1979), p. 20.

52 Translated in S. D. Khadilkar, ed., *Kātyāyana Śulbasūtra, with English translation, explanatory notes, diagrams, and articles* (Pune: Vaidika Saṁśodhana Maṇḍala, 1974), p. 10.

53 Proposed by Bürk, *Zeitschrift der deutschen morgenländischen Gesellschaft* 15 (1901): 557; Thibaut, *The Pandit*, Old Series, vol. 10, p. 234.

[54] Geoffrey E. R. Lloyd, *Demystifying Mentalities* (Cambridge: Cambridge University Press, 1990), p. 101, quoting Thibaut, *The Pandit*, Old Series, vol. 10, p. 232, rather thinks that the difference between the two enunciations was done for practical reasons. In fact, he considers that all the *Śulbasūtra* mathematics were done for practical use.

[55] It is surprising that the Indians went on with their numerical investigations (research of integer values for the diagonal and side of a square; see below) while they had at their disposal a geometric "proof." This perhaps had its origin in their building procedures based on marked ropes (see below this type of construction for the *paitṛkī vedi*, a square altar). However, the fact that they separated the two properties, even though they had (approximate) values for the square, shows that they distinguished between exact and approximate constructions, contrary to Lloyd's interpretation.

[56] Thibaut, *The Pandit*, Old Series, vol. 10, p. 238.

[57] Already proposed by Bürk, *Zeitschrift der deutschen morgenländischen Gesellschaft* 15 (1901): 566–571.

[58] It is not known where and when this commentator lived, but he is surely later than Āryabhaṭa, as he quotes Āryabhaṭa's text about the quadrature of the circle. Like many other commentators of Śulbasūtras, he lived several centuries after the author of the commented text. This is due to the Indian oral tradition, which permitted the teacher to comment on a sūtra text that he is asking his pupils to learn by rote, but only the formal transmission of the sūtra text is allowed. Only after the use of palm leaves or paper became widespread could the commentaries and the sūtra texts been written. For instance, the other commentator of the *Baudhāyana Śulbasūtra*, Veṅkaṭeśvara, lived in the sixteenth century in the region of Thañjāvūr. This could also be the case for Dvārakānātha; for more details, see Jean Michel Delire, "Chronological Inferences from a Comparison between Commentaries on Different *Śulbasūtras*," *Papers of the 12th World Sanskrit Conference* (Helsinki, July 13–18, 2003), vol. 7, Dominik Wujastyk, ed., *Mathematics and Medicine in Sanskrit* (Delhi: Motilal Banarsidass, 2007), pp. 37–62.

[59] *Āpastamba Śulbasūtra* VIII.6, confirmed by his commentator Sundararāja; Bürk, *Zeitschrift der deutschen morgenländischen Gesellschaft* 15 (1901): 549; *Zeitschrift der deutschen morgenländischen Gesellschaft* 16 (1902): 354–357.

[60] Following Datta, *The Science of the Śulba*, pp. 153–158.

[61] This shows that Baudhāyana, at least, was interested in inverting mathematical procedures. This interest could have arisen in the context of an imaginary construction of the 8½ square–*puruṣa*s altar, like the one I proposed above, or simply from the intellectual need to be able to do and un-do procedures.

[62] The Sanskrit text is ambiguous: *eṣānityā* can be translated "this [one is] inexact" (*eṣā anityā*) or "this [one is] usual" (*eṣā nityā*). Due to the *saṁdhi* phenomenon, which doesn't distinguish a written *ā* + *a* from a simple *ā*, it is impossible to come to a decision. Lloyd, *Demystifying Mentalities*, p. 103, chooses the second reading *eṣā nityā* and proposes to translate it as "this [one is] regular," i.e., "accepted by the very builders of the altars." I agree all the more with this

translation since Baudhāyana seems here to oppose the "regular," simpler, construction to another one that is impracticable but more exact. Once again, Baudhāyana's concern is to improve others' results and to invert procedures with the greatest accuracy.

63 van Gelder, editor of the *Mānava Śulbasūtra,* gives the same rule as the interpretation of sūtra 10.3.2.13. But Gupta, "New Indian Values of π from the *Mānava Śulbasūtra,*" p. 116, has shown that this sūtra enunciates a rule relating the perimeter of a circle to its diameter, giving to π the value 3.2, and not a quadrature rule. The rule 10.3.4.6, quoted above in text 12, corresponds to the same value of π.

64 Thibaut, *The Pandit,* Old Series, vol. 10, pp. 253–254.

65 The missing third is the only term neglected by Baudháyana in the inversion itself. It implies an error of approximately 0.00368 over 1,224; that is, a relative error of only three-millionths. Taking into account that the value of the diagonal is also an approximation, we can understand why there is a slight difference between the values of π yielded by the circulature (3.08831175. . .) and the quadrature (3.08832649. . .).

66 They are solutions of the Pell equation $y^2 - 2x^2 = \pm 1$ and they could be obtained by using the recurrence relations $x_n = x_{n-1} + y_{n-1}$, $y_n = 2x_{n-1} + y_{n-1}$, with $x_0 = 0$, $y_0 = 1$. The solutions providing +1 and –1 in the Pell equation occur respectively for *n* even and *n* odd.

67 The definition of the tila as 1/34 of an *aṅgula* may have already been decided here, to avoid fractions in the practical expression of the diagonal of a square of side 12 *aṅgula*s.

68 The reason of this decomposition, leading to a sum of unitary fractions instead of a composite (17/12) plus a unitary one (1/34 × 12), is probably to be found in a linguistic reluctance to designate more than one nth, due to the fact that the expression for the *n*th fraction and the *n*th ordinal have the same origin in the concept of *pūraṇa* ("completive"). However, we find sometimes in the *Baudhāyana Śulbasūtra* expressions like "two parts" for 2/3 (I.68), the complement of a unitary fraction, and even for 2/5 (I.69), or "two fifteenth parts" for 2/15 (I.60). For more details, see P. S. Y Filliozat and G. Mazars, "La terminologie et l'écriture des fractions dans la littérature mathématique sanskrite," *Bulletin d'études indiennes* 5 (1987): 67–96; and Delire, "Les fractions dans le *Baudhāyana Śulbasūtra.*"

69 Translated in van Gelder, ed., *Mānava Śrautasūtra,* p. 289.

70 Gupta, "New Indian Values of π from the *Mānava Śulbasūtra,*" p. 121, studied a circulature method (*Mānava Śulbasūtra* 10.3.2.15), which states that a circle of which diameter is the 4/5th of the diameter of the circle circumscribed to a given square has the same area as the square. Just before this, *Mānava Śulbasūtra* 10.3.2.14 gives the side of the inscribed square as the 7/10th of the diameter of the circle, from which Gupta derived the knowledge of the approximation 10/7 for √2 and even of 7/5, from the fact that "1/√2 is the same as √2/2." I suggest the explanation given above of the derivation of the couple 7, 5 from the couple 10, 7 to replace Gupta's too-modern justification.

71 This is a very rough inversion but, since the rule appears in different *Śulbasūtras* (not in Mānava, as we have seen), the 15 could not be interpreted as a copy mistake for 17. Moreover, the rule must be rather old and practical, since keeping up the division by 15 instead of 17 makes it much easier to apply.

72 The next step would have yielded $7+1/14-1/(14^2\times 2(7+1/14)) = 7+1/14-1/(14\times 198)$ and $17-1/34-1/(34^2\times 2(17-1/34)) = 17-1/34-1/(34\times 1154)$ for the diagonal of the squares of sides 5 and 12 respectively. Even if Baudhāyana had computed them, the complexity of their expression as fractions of the side of the square would have prevented him from incorporating them in his *Śulbasūtra,* which was orally composed and transmitted. But it is not necessary to compute anything to realize that the process would never end.

73 In fact, the procedure, when applied to any integer solution xn, yn of the Pell equation, leads to the solution x_{2n}, y_{2n}. It is not clear whether Baudhāyana was aware that his reasoning produced new integer couples of approximate diagonal and side, i.e. 308, 577 or 70, 99, but it is probable since they can be obtained simply by multiplying an intermediate result by the width of the added or removed thin gnomon. The fact that Baudhāyana never mentions explicitely the couples 5, 7 or 12, 17 reinforces this probability. Surprisingly, when applied to 7, 10, which is a solution of the "Pell equation" with 2 in the second member (and thus, not a x_n, y_n), the procedure also yields 70, 99 as it does with 5, 7.

References

Primary Sources

Āpastamba Śulbasūtra:

Bürk, Albert, ed., trans., and comenmtary. *Āpastamba Śulbasūtra,* in *Zeitschrift der deutschen morgenländischen Gesellschaft* 15 (1901): 543–591; *Zeitschrift der deutschen morgenländischen Gesellschaft* 16 (1902): 327–391.

Sen, S. N., and A. K. Bag. *Śulbasūtras of Baudhāyana, Āpastamba, Kātyāyana, and Mānava, with Text, English Translation, and Commentary.* New Delhi: Indian National Science Academy, 1983.

Garbe, Richard, ed. *Āpastamba Śrautasūtra, belonging to the Taittirīya Saṁhitā, with the Commentary of Rudradatta.* Bibliotheca Indica, 3 vols. Calcutta: Asiatic Society, 1882, 1885, 1902.

Baudhāyana Śulbasūtra:

Delire, Jean Michel. *Baudhāyana Śulbasūtra et son commentaire Śulbadīpikā,* in *Les mathématiques de l'autel védique,* forthcoming.

Sen, S. N., and A. K. Bag. *Śulbasūtras of Baudhāyana, Āpastamba, Kātyāyana, and Mānava, with Text, English Translation, and Commentary.* New Delhi: Indian National Science Academy, 1983.

Thibaut, George, ed. and trans. *Śulbasūtra of Baudhāyana, with commentary by Dvārakānāthayajvan,* in *The Pandit,* Old Series, vol. 9 (1874), vol. 10 (1875); New Series, vol. 1 (1876–1877).

Kātyāyana Śulbasūtra:

Khadilkar, S. D., ed. *Kātyāyana Śulbasūtra, with English translation, explanatory notes, diagrams, and articles.* Pune: Vaidika Saṁśodhana Maṇḍala, 1974.

Sen, S. D., and A. K. Bag. *Śulbasūtras of Baudhāyana, Āpastamba, Kātyāyana, and Mānava, with Text, English Translation, and Commentary.* New Delhi: Indian National Science Academy, 1983.

Maitrāyaṇī Saṁhitā:

Schroeder, Leopold von, ed. *Maitrāyaṇī Saṁhitā.* Wiesbaden: Franz Steiner, 1970–1972, reprint. Originally published by Verlag der Deutschen Morgenländischen Gesellschaft, 1881–1886.

Mānava Śrautasūtra:

Gelder, Jeannette M. van, trans. *Mānava Śrautasūtra, Belonging to the Maitrāyaṇī Saṁhitā.* Śata-Piṭaka Series, vol. 27. New Delhi: Indo-Asian Literatures, 1963.

Mānava Śulbasūtra:

Sen, S. N., and A. K. Bag. *Śulbasūtras of Baudhāyana, Āpastamba, Kātyāyana, and Mānava, with Text, English Translation, and Commentary.* New Delhi: Indian National Science Academy, 1983.

Śatapatha Brāhmaṇa:

Eggeling, Julius, trans. *Śatapatha Brāhmaṇa.* M. Müller, ed., Sacred Books of the East, vols. 12, 26, 41, 42, and 44. Delhi: Motilal Banarsidass, 1978, reprint. Originally published by Clarendon Press, 1885.

Taittirīya Saṁhitā:

Weber, Albrecht, ed. *Die Taittirīya Saṁhitā.* Hildesheim: Georg Olsen Verlag, 1973, reprint. Originally published by Indische Studien, vols. 11, 12, 1871–1872.

Secondary Sources

Allchin, Bridget, and Raymond Allchin. *The Rise of Civilization in India and Pakistan.* Cambridge: Cambridge University Press, 1988.

Converse, Hyla Stuntz."The Agnicaya Rite: Indigenous Origin?", *History of Religions* 14/2 (1974): 81–95.

Datta, B. *The Science of the Śulba: A Study in Early Hindu Geometry.* Calcutta: University of Calcutta, 1932.

Delire, Jean Michel."Chronological inferences from a comparison between commentaries on different Śulbasūtras," in Dominik Wujastyk, ed., *Papers of the 12th World Sanskrit Conference (Helsinki, July 13–18, 2003), Vol. 7: Mathematics and Medicine in Sanskrit*, pp. 37–62. New Delhi: Motilal Banarsidass, 2007.

— "Les fractions dans le Baudhāyana Śulbasūtra: la fonction complétive des ordinaux en grec et en sanskrit et ses implications dans le domaine du calcul des fractions, in Robert Halleux et Anne-Catherine Bernès, eds., *Proceedings of the National Conference "Nouvelles tendances en histoire et philosophie des sciences" (October 15–16, 1992)*, pp. 95–102. Bruxelles: Palais des Académies, 1993.

—. *Les mathématiques de l'autel védique: le Baudhāyana Śulbasūtra et son commentaire Śulbadīpikā, Texte édité, traduit et commenté, avec une introduction sur l'histoire des mathématiques indiennes,* forthcoming

Deloche, Jean. *Contributions à l'histoire de la voiture en Inde.* Paris: Ecole Française d'Extrême Orient Publications, 1983, vol. 138.

Dumézil, George. *Les dieux des Indo-Européens.* Paris: Presses Universitaires de France, 1952.

Filliozat, Pierre-Sylvain, and Guy Mazars. "La terminologie et l'écriture des fractions dans la littérature mathématique sanskrite," *Bulletin d'études indiennes* 5 (1987): 67–96.

Gonda, Jan. *A History of Indian Literature: Vedic Literature (Saṁhitās and Brāhmaṇas).* Wiesbaden: Otto Harrassowitz, 1975.

—. *Les religions de l'Inde (I-Védisme et hindouisme ancien).* Paris: Payot, 1962.

Gupta, Radhan C. "New Indian Values of π from the Mānava Śulbasūtra," *Centaurus* 31/2 (1988): 114–126.

Lloyd, Geoffrey E. R. *Demystifying Mentalities.* Cambridge: Cambridge University Press, 1990.

Macdonell, Arthur A. *A History of Sanskrit Literature.* Delhi: Motilal Banarsidass, 1971.

Majumder, N. K. "Sacrificial Altars: Vedis and Agnis," *Journal of the Indian Society of Oriental Art* 7 (1939): 39–60; *Journal of the Indian Society of Oriental Art* 8 (1940): 21–40.

Malamoud, Charles. *Cuire le monde.* Paris: Éditions La Découverte, 1989.

Michaels, *Axel. Beweisverfahren in der vedischen Sakralgeometrie (thèse).* Wiesbaden: Franz Steiner Verlag, 1978.

Monier-Williams, Monier. *A Sankrit-English Dictionary.* Delhi: Motilal Banarsidass, 1995.

Renou, Louis. *L'hindouisme.* Paris: Presses Universitaires de France, Paris, 1991, reprint.

—. "Sur le genre du Sūtra dans la littérature sanskrite," *Journal Asiatique* 251 (1963): 165–216.

Sarasvati Amma, T. A. *Geometry in Ancient and Medieval India.* Delhi: Motilal Banarsidass, 1979.

Seidenberg, Abraham "The Geometry of the Vedic Ritual," in Frits Staal, ed., *Agni: The Vedic Ritual of the Fire Altar,* vol. 2, pp. 95–126. Berkeley: Asian Humanities Press, 1983.

Staal, Frits, ed. *Agni: The Vedic Ritual of the Fire Altar,* 2 vols. Berkeley: Asian Humanities Press, 1983.

Stutley, Margaret, and James Stutley. *A Dictionary of Hinduism: Its Mythology, Folklore, and Development.* London: Routledge and Kegan Paul, 1977.

Thibaut, George. "On the Śulvasūtras," *Journal of the Asiatic Society of Bengal* 44 (1875): 227–275.

Varenne, Jean. *Le Veda, premier livre sacré de l'Inde,* 2 vols. Paris: Marabout Université, 1967.

—.*Mythes et légendes extraits des Brāhmaṇas.* Gallimard: UNESCO, 1967.

The Predicament of the Maitrāyaṇīya Community in Maharashtra: Migration, Acculturation, and Identity Crisis

Madhav M. Deshpande
University of Michigan, Ann Arbor

In this paper I outline the history of a long-standing dispute on the status of the Maitrāyaṇīya brahmin community in the region of Nasik in Maharashtra; this affair is referred to as *Maitrāyaṇī-Prakaraṇa* in the Marathi sources.[1] I will briefly summarize the previous research relating to the history of the Maitrāyaṇīya community before discussing the details of the specific *Maitrāyaṇī-Prakaraṇa.* Michael Witzel has traced the original home of the Maitrāyaṇīyas in the region of Pañcāla and their subsequent migration from that region to Gujarat.[2] C. G. Kashikar has given further historical details of the Maitrāyaṇīya community in the regions of Gujarat and northern Maharashtra. Discussing the history of the Mānava Maitrāyaṇīya school, Kashikar informs us that, as seen from epigraphical records, grants were made to the Maitrāyaṇīya pandits by royal families in different regions such as Sambalpur (Orissa), Saurashtra, Surparaka, etc.[3] Kashikar further points out that manuscripts procured for preparing the editions of the *Maitrāyaṇīya Saṃhitā,* the *Mānava Śrauta,* and the *Gṛhya Sūtra*s belonged to the region known as Baglan (present-day Gujarat and northern Maharashtra). This means that in historical times Maitrāyaṇīyas lived only in this region.

The migration of the Maitrāyaṇīya community from the northern regions of Punjab or Pañcāla to the southerly regions of Gujarat and northern Maharashtra seems to be well established from Witzel's and Kashikar's research. However, how this community perceived its own status and how it was perceived by others in these regions is not entirely clear from their work. Kashikar writes that from the fact that the royal family of the Baguls brought with them the Maitrāyaṇīya families from Kanauj to Baglan, it is evident that the Maitrāyaṇīyas were originally included among the five Gauḍa sects. He further points out that a verse from the *Sahyādri-khaṇḍa* of the *Skandapurāṇa* supports this fact.[4] According to Kashikar, after settling in Baglan the Maitrāyaṇīyas were enumerated among the five Drāviḍa sects. But he also shows that the Gujarat and the Maharashtra branches of the Maitrāyaṇīyas underwent different developments. The generations of Maitrāyaṇīyas living in Baglan were divided into two branches because of their different spoken languages, Gujarati and Marathi. Naturally the Maitrāyaṇīya traditions also developed along rather different lines. In recent times, even a *Padapāṭha* was newly devised for priestly purposes. While the *Padapāṭha* in the Gujarat tradition was based in the mantra portions only, that in the Maharashtra tradition was based on the *Saṃhitā* text, including mantra and *brāhmaṇa* portions. Kāshikar shows that while selecting only the mantra portions for the *Padapāṭha,* the Gujarat tradition followed the *Śukla Yajurveda* tradition.[5] The Maharashtra tradition, on the other hand, followed the *Kṛṣṇa Yajurveda Taittirīya* tradition in which the *Saṃhitā* consisting of both the mantras and the brāhmaṇa is provided with a *Padapāṭha.*

Kashikar refers to the categories of Gauḍa and Drāviḍa brahmans in his discussion. While it seems appropriate to assume that the Maitrāyaṇīyas, migrating north to south, were earlier counted among the Gauḍas, they eventually settled in northern Maharashtra where they were counted among the Drāviḍas. This account, however, does not deal with the excruciating complexities involved in the transition from Gauḍa to Drāviḍa status. In this paper I will deal with this aspect of the history of the Maitrāyaṇīyas. I have elsewhere discussed the history and ramifications of this very important classification of the brahmins of India into these two broad groups, Gauḍa and Drāviḍa. The northern group, consisting of five subgroups, is included in the title Gauḍa, while the southern group, consisting of five subgroups, is included in the title Drāviḍa.[6] The five subgroups that normally fall under the term Gauḍa are the Sārasvata, the Kānyakubja, the Gauḍa, the Maithila, and the Utkala. The five subgroups under the term Drāviḍa are the Gurjara, the Mahārāṣṭra, the Tailanga, the Karnāṭaka, and the Drāviḍa.

The eighteenth-century text *Vedavicāra,* ascribed to Draviḍa Śāmaśāstrī,[7] provides some further interesting traditional linkages between the Gauḍa/Drāviḍa classification and the different branches of the four Vedas. Besides the regional distinctions among the Pañca Gauḍa/Draviḍa brahmans, Śāmaśāstrī adds specific configurations of Vedic branches to Gauḍa and Drāviḍa groups, but in so doing he makes an exception for the Gurjaras. Though they are normally included among the Drāviḍas in the lists of Drāviḍa brahmins, Śāmaśāstrī includes the Gurjaras with the Gauḍas in terms of their Veda Śākhā affiliation and ritual practices.

Veda / śākhā	Gauḍa and Gurjara	Drāviḍa (except Gurjara)
RV	Sāṃkhyāyana	Śākalya
YV	Vājasaneyi	Taittirīya
SV	Kauthuma	Rāṇāyanīya
AV	Śaunakīya	Paippalāda

Given this basic structure of the Vedic configurations for the Gauḍas and Drāviḍas, Śāmaśāstrī writes that the Gauḍas can participate in ritual and marriage with other Gauḍas, and the Drāviḍas can participate in ritual and marriage with other Drāviḍas (*yajñakanyāvibhāginaḥ*).[8] Śāmaśāstrī, however, recognizes that the widespread migrations of brahmans in every direction complicates these issues. Conceiving of a steady-state ancient period when the Gauḍas and Drāviḍas happily lived under righteous kings in their own Gauḍa and Drāviḍa regions, he points out that things are different nowadays. Due to the decline in dharma, with the destruction of good kings and the expansion of the Mlecchas, brahmins have migrated to different regions seeking a livelihood, so there are Drāviḍas in Gauḍa regions and Gauḍas in Drāviḍa regions. This has created chaotic conditions as far as the study of the Veda is concerned. There are Gauḍas learning from Drāviḍas, and vice versa. Śāmaśāstrī writes that such crossover in learning the Veda is acceptable and one should not find fault with it, especially under difficult circumstances. However, he does not approve of ritual participation and intermarriage across the Gauḍa / Drāviḍa divide, and asserts that intermarriage across this divide is not observed, though crossover in sacrificial rites is occasionally seen.[9]

Śāmaśāstrī offers a detailed analysis of the situation of the Gurjaras in this scheme.[10] Having found the Gurjaras in the list of Pañca Drāviḍas, he is puzzled to find that they follow the *Vedaśākhā*s of the Gauḍas. Instead of the *Śākala Ṛgveda* of the Drāviḍas the Gurjaras follow the *Śāṃkhyāyana Ṛgveda* of the Gauḍas. Instead of the *Taittirīya Yajurveda* of the Drāviḍas they follow the *Vājasaneyi Yajurveda* of the Gauḍas. Instead of the *Paippalāda Atharvaveda* of the Drāviḍas they follow the *Śaunakīya Atharvaveda* of the Gauḍas. Finally, instead of the *Rāṇāyanīya Sāmaveda* of the Drāviḍas they follow the *Kauthuma Sāmaveda* of the Gauḍas. Śāmaśāstrī faults them for abandoning their Drāviḍa heritage and adopting the Gauḍa heritage. Historically speaking, there is no reason to believe that there was any such abandonment of Drāviḍa heritage by the Gurjaras. Their inclusion among the Drāviḍas took place purely on the basis of geography[11] and had no connection to the distribution of the *Vedaśākhā*s. It is the conflation of two originally unrelated concepts that has created a problem for Śāmaśāstrī. However, he is relentless in his criticism of the Gurjaras. There is no sharing of food between the Gurjaras and the rest of the Drāviḍa brahmans, nor do they share in the study of the Veda. Sāmaśāstrī, a defender of the purity of the Drāviḍa brahman group, says that like the unrighteous behavior in the Gauḍa regions, the Gurjara region is also filled with unrighteousness, and hence it was cursed by the Ācārya (?), and, for this reason, Drāviḍa brahmans are not supposed to have any dealings with Gurjara brahmans.[12]

This brings me back to the main topic of this paper, the vicissitudes of the Maitrāyaṇīya community in northern Maharashtra as reflected in the *Maitrāyaṇī-Prakaraṇa.* There are a large number of documents that serve as the main sources of information regarding the nonacceptance of the Maitrāyaṇīya brahmans by the other brahman communities in and around Nasik, and the former's vigorous efforts in seeking acceptance by the others. Some of these documents were collected and published in V. P. Arakadi's *Maitrāyaṇīya Śākhā Prakaraṇa.*[13] As the title page proudly declares, this collection includes decisions, verdicts (*nirṇaya*), and injunctions (*ājñāpatra*) issued by the Śaṃkarācāryas of Dvārakā and Śṛṅgerī stating that this Vedic *śākhā* of the Maitrāyaṇīyas should be counted among the Drāviḍas (*draviḍāntaḥpātī*) and considered ritually pure to be included in a shared meal (*paṅktigrāhya,* lit., "acceptable for sitting in the same row for dinner").

A second source of information regarding this *Maitrāyaṇī Prakaraṇa* is an 1890 booklet published by D. L. Upasani, the *Maitrāyaṇīya śākhetīl brāhmaṇāṃśī paṅkī-vyavahārācā śāstrārtha,* "The Śāstric determination regarding the meal shared with the brahmans belonging to the Maitrāyaṇīya branch," reprinting articles from a local journal called *Āryāvartta* that was published by various legal authorities (*śāstrajña*).

The last source of information comes from a collection of original documents regarding this affair preserved in the library of the Vaidika Saṃśodhana Maṇḍaḷa (VSM) of Pune. This set of documents entitled *Maitrāyaṇī śākhesambandhī kāhī kāgad-patre,* "Some documents regarding the *Maitrāyaṇī Śākhā,*" is in no. 14521 of the Janorkar Saṃgraha (Janorkar

Collection) of the VSM library. Most of these documents are copies of correspondence, appeals, and verdicts dating to around 1906. Some of these documents are in Sanskrit but most are in Marathi, written both in Devanagari and Modi scripts.

While these sources give a picture of this dispute as it raged from the late nineteenth into the early twentieth centuries, it probably goes back many decades, as indicated by a reference to the "Maitrāṇī Prakarṇa" in the papers of the Peshwa court, though there are no clear details.[14] In an account found in the Peshwa court papers from the mid-eighteenth century regarding a dispute among the brahmans from Nasik about the order in which the various Vedas should be recited at a ceremonial recitation of the Vedas (*mantrajāgara*), it appears that the main contestant branches of Yajurveda were Taittirīya and Vājasaneyī, and the dispute makes no reference to the recitation of the *Maitrāyaṇī Saṃhitā* during such occasions.[15] The order of recitation, determined by the assembly of learned pandits at the court of the Peshwa and backed by an executive order issued by the Peshwa court, is as follows: (1) *Ṛgveda,* (2) *Taittirīya Yajurveda,* (3) *Vājasaneyi Yajurveda,* (4) *Sāmaveda,* and (5) *Atharvaveda.* This suggests that the Maitrāyaṇīyas were excluded from such occasions by the other brahmans, though these other brahmans also disputed among themselves about the order of presentation of their *Śākhā*s. Thus the exclusion of the Maitrāyaṇīya brahmans by the other brahmans in the region of Nasik is an old phenomenon, though there is no surviving documentation from earlier periods.

The available documentary evidence is fairly extensive and goes into minute detail of specific families and towns as well as of specific incidents, so it is not possible to present it here except by way of a few illustrations. The first document is an article in the nineteenth issue of the journal Āryāvartta (December 6, 1890) from Dhule:

A Mess in Dhule

> There is no restraining in Dhule. It seems that everyone is free to do what he wants. It seems to have happened like "The king speaks and his beard moves." Mr. Kṣīre Dharmādhikārī of this town has passed a resolution that since Mr. Bāḷaśāstrī Ghāṇekar went [to dinner] at the home of a brahman belonging to the Mānavasūtra of the Maitrāyaṇī branch, no one should go to dinner at his home, nor should anyone go where he goes to dinner or where he receives sandal-paste and unbroken rice grain (i.e., respectful reception). Some brahmans seem to be inclined to follow him. However, after Mr. Ghāṇekar went to dinner at the home of a Maitrāyaṇīya brahman around the 7th or 8th of the dark fortnight of the Adhika month, there was a Veda

> recitation (*mantrākṣatā*) and a reception (with sandal paste and unbroken rice grain, *gandhākṣatā*) on the 11th of that fortnight at the home of honorable (*rāv bahādūr*) Govindarāv Garuḍ. Then there was a dinner for brahmans on the 14th of the same fortnight at the home of honorable Kāśināth Dādā Úakale and a Veda recitation the same night at the home of Deputy Collector Mr. Nānāsāheb Somaṇ. On all these occasions, along with other brahmans, Mr. Kṣīre, the person who passed the above mentioned resolution, shared a meal and the reception with Mr. Bāḷaśāstrī Ghāṇekar. However, when an invitation for an ancestral rite (*pakṣa*) arrived around the 9th or 10th in the Śukla fortnight of Bhādrapada from the Assistant Engineer Mr. Āpaṭe, [Mr. Kṣīre] passed the above mentioned resolution the day before and sent a message to Mr. Āpaṭe: "If Mr. Gopāḷabhaṭ from the Ghāṇekar family is going to be the priest at your home, then we will not attend the ancestral rite." Upon [receiving this message,] Mr. Āpaṭe responded by saying that it would not be proper to cancel the invitation sent to the priest (i.e., Mr. Ghāṇekar), and that everybody (including Mr. Kṣīre) should attend the occasion the next day. . . . After informing everyone this way, [Mr. Āpaṭe] next day carried out the rite with those brahmans who did attend. Previously, you all had shared food with Mr. Ghāṇekar without qualms, and it would not have been too difficult to pass your resolution after the ritual function at Mr. Āpaṭe's home was over.[16]

In the next article, *Āryāvartta* 20 (December 13, 1890),[17] the writer provides a list of fifty names of brahmans who regularly had meals at the home of Maitrāyaṇīya brahmans, and points out that Mr. Kṣīre had on many occasions shared meals with these brahmans. The documents give us a sense of the widespread complexity and confusion of prescribed and proscribed norms of association with Maitrāyaṇīya brahmans by other brahmans of the region, and the consternation it produced for the Maitrāyaṇīya community.

The next document I want to present is a testimony sent on February 11, 1908, from the village of Umreth by Mr. Amṛt L. Deshpande to a query from the Śaṅkarācārya of Dvārakā regarding the local customs dealing with the Maitrāyaṇīya community. Mr. Deshpande testifies:

> There is no sharing of food with [members of] the Maitrāyaṇī branch. I do not know myself why the Maitrāyaṇī branch is ineligible for a common dinner. I also do not know why this custom came into being. Members of families like Bhide, Bhagwat, Paranjpe, Kannadkar, and Mhaiskar do not go for dinner at the homes of Maitrāyaṇīyas. I don't know if the Maitrāyaṇīyas are included among the Pañca Gauḍas or Pañca Drāviḍas. Like the Hiraṇyakeśī and Āpastamba brahmans, the Maitrāyaṇīyas do have the right to all six Brahmanical duties (= *adhyayana, adhyāpana, yajana, yājana, dāna, pratigraha*).

[But] I have no idea of how the Maitrāyaṇīyas behave or think.

Question: What do you do with people who join for meals with the Maitrāyaṇīyas?

Reply: We do not join for meals with those who join for meals with the Maitrāyaṇīyas. There are five or seven households who currently join for meals with the Maitrāyaṇīyas in the town of Ammalner.

Question: Do you know the names of households who join the Maitrāyaṇīyas for meals?

Reply: Mr. Bhide, the advocate, Mr. Bhagwat, Mr. Paranjpe, Mr. Lakshmanrao Bhagwat, Mr. Mhaiskar, and Mr. Mahadeo Mishal. Until recently no one used to join the Maitrāyaṇīyas for meals. Some started doing it since a month and a half, and since then there have been two separate camps. That is why I do not go to their home for a meal.

They (i.e., the Maitrāyaṇīyas) have been excommunicated by the members of our Śākhā. There are about 25 or 30 households of the Āśvalāyanīyas. I am a manager at the temple run by Sakhārām Bowa. Members of the Maitrāyaṇī śākhā do not come for meals to Sakhārām Bowa. Members of that śākhā are not allowed even to serve food at these meals. My job is to distribute *Dakṣiṇā* at these meals. When a Maitrāyaṇīya brahman, Mr. Eknāth Muṭhe, went there to offer *Dakṣiṇā,* we took away the container from his hand, and pushed him out. The people who have eaten at the homes of Maitrāyaṇīyas are different from us. We will accept them back only after we make them undergo an expiation rite (*prāyaścitta*).

My father has told me that since two or three hundred years there is no tradition of joining the Maitrāyaṇīyas for a meal, and my report is based on what I have heard from him.

I know that an expiation rite was prescribed for those who joined the Maitrāyaṇīyas for a meal. I knew who these people were, but I am unable to tell their names.

The religious rites of the Maitrāyaṇīyas do not take place in association with other brahmans, and this is the traditional custom.[18]

In his review of the received testimony, the Śaṅkarācārya of Dvārakā found Mr. Amṛt Deshpande to be the most determined opponent of the Maitrāyaṇīyas and he refused to trust his testimony, especially since it was contradicted by others' testimony.19 When the Maitrāyaṇīyas filed appeals with various authorities, including the Śaṅkarācāryas of Dvārakā and Śṛṅgerī, the documents show that these authorities in turn sent questionnaires to hundreds of locations asking for reports about local practices, opinions, and the śāstric support, if any, used at different locations for either joining with the Maitrāyaṇīyas or keeping them away. The questionnaire included the following questions:

1. How many households of the Maitrāyaṇīyas are there in your town?
2. How many households of other brahmans are there in your town?
3. Is there currently uncontested association of other brahmans with the Maitrāyaṇīya brahmans in joining for meals?
4. If such association was broken, since when was it broken?
5. Is mutual hatred the reason, or is this just a common custom?
6. Are there households in your town that have been excommunicated for associating with the Maitrāyaṇīyas?
7. How many such households are there? Please provide a list with names and their addresses.
8. Besides the Āśvalāyanīyas, do other branches associate with the Maitrāyaṇīyas for meals?
9. Do the Āśvalāyanīyas associate with those in meals who associate with the Maitrāyaṇīyas in meals?
10. In your town, in the temple of Sakhārām Buwa and in ceremonies in other places, did the Maitrāyaṇīyas join for meals in earlier times?
11. If brahmans of other śākhās join with the Maitrāyaṇīyas for meals, is their a reason for this to result in a sin?
12. Do the Maitrāyaṇīya brahmans have a right for the six Brahmanical duties?
13. Is there any difference in their conduct and thinking?
14. Do you have a view against associating with the Maitrāyaṇīyas in meals?
15. Do the śāstras proscribe association with the Maitrāyaṇīya brahmans?
16. Is there a custom of offering an expiation rite to those who associate with the Maitrāyaṇīyas?[20]

The documents collected and published by V. P. Arakadi include hundreds of detailed responses to such questionnaires sent out by the various authorities such as the Śaṅkarācāryas of Dvārakā and Śṛṅgerī.

Some documents seem to point to specific local reasons for the treatment of the Maitrāyaṇīyas, at least in certain places. In a 1906 letter to Vedaśāstra-sampanna Mr. Puruṣottam Tryambak Shastri Dashputre, of Tryambakeśvar, near Nasik, the Maitrāyaṇīya brahmans Yajñeśvar Gopāḷ Purāṇik, Lakṣmaṇ Viṭṭhal Purāṇik, and Dinkar Ganeś Muṭhe of Nasik responded with some specific localized information:

> Question: It is learned that your community is split from other śākhās in the town of Bhadgaon for a long time. What might be the reason for this dispute?
>
> Reply: Forty years ago, there was no dispute between our śākhā and other *śākhā*s. However, around that time, a member of our śākhā divorced his wife. This act resulted in a local dispute and this person was excommunicated by members of our śākhā as well by those of other śākhās. However, our śākhā ritually cleaned him (*punīt kele*), without consulting other śākhās. That is why other śākhās got together and decided to break association with

> the Maitrāyaṇīyas in meals. This is the reason for the split between the communities. This is what we have heard, and some people from those days are still alive in Bhadgaon. (no. 14251, Janorkar Saṃgraha, VSM Library, Pune)

This document indicates that it is possible that there were very localized causes for specific responses of various communities. It is possible that the dispute originated in one locality such as Bhadgaon and then spread to other localities. However, other documents indicate that the dispute was argued out by using various grounds, customary as well as textual.

Many opponents of the Maitrāyaṇīya brahmans claimed that there was a document from the Peshwa court during the time of court judge Rāmaśāstrī Prabhuṇe in the late eighteenth century that banned other brahmans from associating with the Maitrāyaṇīyas, but there was no one actually in possession of such a document, or who was willing to bring it to public meetings for various reasons.[21] The Maitrāyaṇīyas, in repeated appeals to various authorities, insisted: "We are Drāviḍas, and our conduct and thinking is like other Drāviḍa (brahmans of the region), and there is no difference. We are willing to prove this fact."[22] A Sanskrit pandit, Mr. Hari Vishnu Palnitkar of Panwel, near Mumbai, was brought in to argue the case that the Maitrāyaṇīyas were Drāviḍas and not Gauḍas, and he evidently argued his case on the basis of Śāmaśāstrī's *Vedavicāra*.[23] Palnitkar argued that the conduct of the Maitrāyaṇīyas was different from that of the Gauḍas and was identical with that of the Drāviḍa brahmans. Their Vedic recitation was similar to that of the Taittirīyas, and like the Taittirīyas, the Maitrāyaṇīyas must also be counted among the Drāviḍa brahmans.[24] Palnitkar further states:

> The behavior of the Maitrāyaṇīyas is very different from the Gurjara brahmans and very similar to that of the four other Drāviḍas. . . . Last year on the Kojāgirī Paurṇimā I had the occasion to listen to the recitation of the Maitrāyaṇī śākhā. At that time, when I was engrossed in that auspicious recitation of the mantras, I almost felt like I was listening to the recitation of the Taitttirīyas. The pronunciation of the *anusvāra* as a *guṃkāra* seen in passages like *haṃsaḥ* as heard in the Taittirīya recitation is very similar to that found in the Maitrāyaṇī recitation. Like the *Taittirīya Saṃhitā,* one also finds a mixture of the mantra and brāhmaṇa portions in the *Maitrāyaṇī Saṃhitā.* Therefore, like the Taittirīyas, the Maitrāyaṇīyas must also be included among the Drāviḍas.[25]

Many other scholars were brought in to assert the "Drāviḍa-ness" of the Maitrāyaṇīyas.[26] Many of these observations regarding the "Draviḍa-ness" of the Maitrāyaṇīyas seem to be indications of their linguistic and cultural naturalization in the region of northern Maharashtra and show how the Maharashtra branch of the Maitrāyaṇīyas gradually developed a different cultural, social, and linguistic identity from their counterparts in Gujarat. They also indicate that in the region of northern Maharashtra the Taittirīyas were in a more dominant position in relation to the Maitrāyaṇīyas. They had probably migrated and became linguistically and culturally naturalized in this region earlier. The Taittirīyas thus provided the dominant template for the Maitrāyaṇīyas to follow in their own process of naturalization in this region.[27]

As the discussion above indicates, the objective history of migration from the northern regions to the south, assuming that such a history was known to the community, was more of a hurdle for the Maitrāyaṇīya community, and they preferred to highlight the synchronic fact of their known residence in the region of northern Maharashtra. To this end, they often cited verses from Mahārṇava that are quoted in the commentary on the Caraṇavyūha. The highlighted verse reads:

> *mayūrādriṃ samārabhya yāvat gurjaradeśataḥ /*
> *vyāptā vāyavyadeśe tu maitrāyaṇī pratiṣṭhitā //*
>
> The Maitrāyaṇī tradition is established in the northwesterly direction from the Mayūra mountain up to the Gurjara region.

The Sanskrit name Mayūra refers to the region of Mulher in northern Maharashtra. The term *samārabhya*, "beginning from," in the verse seems to suggest a local perception that the Maitrāyaṇī tradition was original to the region of Mulher and that it spread to the Gurjara region. This verse, often cited in the debate, already seems to presume that the Maitrāyaṇīyas were native to the region of Maharashtra. One of the documents contained in the VSM library collection (Janorkar Saṃgraha, no. 14251) clearly states the views of a Maitrāyaṇīya responder to questions put by the Śaṅkarācārya:

> The original residence of our Vedic branch (*āmace śākhece mūḷa vasatisthāna*) is from the Mayūra mountain (= Mulher) up to the border of Gujarat (*mayūraparvatāpāsūn gujarāthasarahaddīpāveto āhe*).

This particular Maitrāyaṇīya respondent, in his Marathi nativism, denies the Gujarat branch of the Maitrāyaṇīyas the status of residents of the "original home" of the Maitrāyaṇī Śākhā. In his opinion, the Gujarati Maitrāyaṇīyas migrated to the region of Gujarat from their original home in Maharashtra.[28] This self-image of the community of the Maitrāyaṇīyas in northern Maharashtra is clearly at variance with the conclusions of modern research, not only as far as the question of the "original home" of the Maitrāyaṇī tradition is concerned (cf. Witzel, "Tracing the Vedic Dialects"), but it is also at variance with the relative strength of the Gujarat and Maharashtra branches of the Maitrāyaṇīya community. Kashikar, in the context of the condition of preserved texts of this Vedic school, notes that

> It seems the tradition in northern Maharashtra suffered more than in Gujarat. . . . Since the Maitrāyaṇīya tradition was restricted to the Baglāṇ (i.e., Gujarat and northern Maharashtra), and since the Gujarat tradition seems to be better preserved . . . the Gujarat tradition may reasonably be preferred.[29]

Currently we do not have sufficient evidence for reconstructing historical movements of this tradition within the region of Baglan, but it is evident from Kashikar's research that the Gujarat tradition of the Maitrāyaṇīyas is better preserved as compared to the tradition in northern Maharashtra.

The textual evidence from the *Sahyādrikhaṇḍa* was somewhat more problematic. The following verses from the *Sahyādrikhaṇḍa* of the *Skandapurāṇa* are discussed and disputed in this debate:

> *sārasvatāḥ kānyakubjā gauḍamaithilakotkalāḥ /*
> *pañcagauḍā bhavanty ete vindhyāduttaravāsinaḥ //*[30]
>
> *trihotrāś cāgniveśyāś ca karṇakubjāḥ kanojakāḥ /*
> *maitrāyaṇāḥ pañcavidhāḥ pañcagauḍā itīritāḥ //*

While the first verse lists the Five Gauḍas as consisting of the Sārasvata, Kānyakubja, Gauḍa, Maithila, and Utkala brahmans, the subsequent verse lists the Five Gauḍas as consisting of the Trihotra, Āgniveśya, Karṇakubja, Kanojaka, and Maitrāyaṇa brahmans. The second verse was often cited by the opponents of the Maitrāyaṇīyas to "prove" that they were Gauḍa brahmans, and not Drāviḍas. On the other hand, the Maitrāyaṇīya argument, ultimately accepted by the Śaṅkarācārya of Dvārakā in 1908, was that these verses are inconsistent and should not be relied upon as authoritative. The Śaṅkarācārya says that this second verse is very strange and any learned scholar would laugh at it.[31] The first verse lists the Kānyakubjas among the Gauḍas, while the second verse seems to include the Karṇakubjas along with the Kanojakas. The Śaṅkarācārya says that no one knows the meaning of the term "Karṇakubja." Does it refer to humans or animals? "We have not heard anywhere in the world a species of animals called Karṇakubja." Since this term is senseless, this leaves only four names in the second verse, and thus its claim that there are Five Gauḍas makes no sense. With this argument, the Śaṅkarācārya of Dvārakā rejects this "evidence." The Maitrāyaṇīya argument is further strengthened by textual citations. The first verse given above says that the Gauḍas live to the north of the Vindhya mountains (*vindhyād uttaravāsinaḥ*). On the other hand, the Sahyādrikhaṇḍa defines the Drāviḍas as residing to the south of the Vindhyas:

> *drāviḍāś cāndhrakarnāṭamahārāṣṭrāś ca gurjarāḥ /*
> *pañcaite drāviḍāḥ proktā vindhyadakṣiṇavāsinaḥ //*

> The five communities of Drāviḍas, Āndhras, Karnāṭas, Mahārāṣṭras, and Gurjaras, living to the south of the Vindhyas are called Drāviḍas.[32]

The Maitrāyaṇīyas point to the Mahārṇava verse "proving" their residence in the region of Mayūra (Mulher in Marathi) mountain in northern Maharashtra, and argue that since this region is south of the Vindhyas and in Maharashtra, they are bona fide Drāviḍa brahmans. What is most interesting is that the verdict from the Śaṅkarācārya of Dvārakā cites as an "authority" H. H. Wilson's *A Sketch of the Religious Sects of the Hindus*,[33] a Marathi translation of which had been given to him in by an advocate, Mr. Paranjpe, of the town of Ammalner.[34] From this Marathi translation of Wilson's work, the Śaṅkarācārya quotes:

> There are at this time very few brahmans of the Maitrāyaṇīya branch in Nasik, but they are also found in a few other places along the banks of Godāvarī. . . . These brahmans do share meals with brahmans of other Vedic affiliations (*anna va paṅktivyavahāra*), but they do not intermarry with them.

On the basis of Wilson's authority, the Śaṅkarācārya concludes that it is "established" (*siddha*) that at least until 1877 the Maitrāyaṇīyas shared food with brahmans of other Vedic affiliations.[35]

Arakadi's 1927 book concludes with the verdict rendered by the Śaṅkarācārya Abhinava Nṛsiṃhabhāratī of Śṛṅgeri[36] that came out on March 31, 1911:

> The Maitrāyaṇīya śākhā with its *Mānavasūtra* is part of the original *Yajurveda* (*ādyayajurvedāntargata*) and is part of the Pañca Drāviḍas. It is being ordered (*ājñā*) that there is no impropriety in brahmans of other Śākhās associating with the brahmans of this Śākhā in meals and assembly. Those who will not accept this order will be subject to the fault of having insulted brahmins.[37]

The discussion above indicates how notions like "Drāviḍa community" were constructed and authenticated through the verification of a long list of customs and behaviors. Otherwise known only from late Dharmaśāstric works, categories such as Gauḍa and Drāviḍa were constructed with complicated perceptions and behaviors, and impinged very directly on the daily lives of the various Vedic śākhā communities and their ability to carry out their religious and social activities in specific localities. The theme of alleged migration to the region leading to an extended "outsider" status, and a vigorous rejection of the notion of migration in order to legitimate a claim to being an "insider" are evident in this premodern dispute, long before they become manifest in the modern Hindu nationalist disputes over the Aryan migration theory.

Notes

1 The Sanskrit word *prakaraṇa* has acquired the meaning of "affair" in Marathi, as in the expression *prem-prakaraṇ*, "love affair."

2 Michael Witzel, "Tracing the Vedic Dialects," in Colette Caillât, ed., *Dialectes dans les littératures Indo-Aryennes* (Paris: L'Institut de Civilisation indienne, Collège de France, 1989), p. 113.

3 C. G. Kashikar, "(A Sample of) *Mānavaśrautasūtra*," in T. N. Dharmadhikari, R. S. Shastri, N. P. Jain, and S. S. Bahulkar, eds., *Vedic Texts: A Revision* (Delhi: Motilal Banarsidass, 1990), p. 105.

4 Kashikar, "(A Sample of) *Mānavaśrautasūtra*," p. 106.

5 Kashikar, "(A Sample of) *Mānavaśrautasūtra*," p. 107.

6 For a detailed historical analysis, see Madhav M. Deshpande, "Pañca-Gauḍa und Pañca-Drāviḍa. Umstrittene Grenzen einer traditionellen Klassifikation," in Michael Bergunder and Rahul Peter Das, eds., *Arier und Draviden* (Halle: Verlag der Franckeschen Stiftungen, 2002), pp. 57–78.

7 I am currently preparing a critical edition and a translation of this text. Page references in this article refer to an earlier edition of this text, Kāśīnātha Vāmana Lele, ed., *Vedavicāra* (Vai: Śrīkṛṣṇa Mudraṇālaya, 1912).

8 Lele, ed., *Vedavicāra*, p. 165. The same idea is expressed in verse 97 of the *Kānyakubjavaṃśāvalī* (p. 35):

> *drāviḍair drāviḍeṣv eva gauḍair gauḍeṣu caiva hi /*
> *tathā svajñātimadhye tu yatra ṣaṭkarmaśuddhitā // 97 //*

9 Lele, ed., *Vedavicāra*, p. 166; the text goes on to say (p. 167) that due to regional differences and differences in local languages there is generally no intermarriage among the Drāviḍa (= Tamil), Āndhra, Karnataka, and Maharashtra brahmans, but there is no prohibition on such intermarriage, since they are all Drāviḍa brahmans. See also C. G. Kashikar, *Śrauta Dharmācī Svarūpacikitsā* (*Analysis of the Nature of the Śrauta Religion*) (Pune: University of Pune Publications, 1977), p. 142 ff.

10 Lele, ed., *Vedavicāra*, pp. 174–175.

11 Certain communities in Kathiawar seem to allow the cross-cousin marriage typical of the Dravidians, and Gujarat falls in a sort of frontier zone between the north and south on this issue; cf. Thomas Trautmann, "The Study of Dravidian Kinship," in Madhav M. Deshpande and Peter Edwin Hook, eds., *Aryan and Non-Aryan in India* (Ann Arbor: University of Michigan Press, 1979), pp. 160–163. Dharmaśāstra writers have noted a shared lack of certain rites among the Gurjaras and Dākṣiṇātyas, cf. *dākṣiṇātyānāṃ gurjarāṇāṃ ca vistṛtavṛddhiśrāddhābhāvat. . .*, Gadādhara's commentary on the *Pāraskara-gṛhyasūtra*, p. 32.

12 The notion that the Pañca Drāviḍas, with the exception of the Gurjaras, can intermarry is found in Siddheshwar Shastri Chitrao, *Vivāhasaṃskāra* (Pune: Kāḷa Prakashan, 1927), Introduction, p. 19, though he gives no explanation for the exclusion of the Gurjaras. He notes that intermarriage among the Pañca Drāviḍas is confirmed by the practice of the Deśastha brahmans.

13 Vaman Purushottam Arakadi, *Yajurvedāntargata Mānavasūtrī Maitrāyaṇīya Śākhā-Prakaraṇa* (in Marathi, *The Maitrāyaṇīya Śākhā Affair)* (Nasik: Dinkar Ganesh Muthe, 1927).

14 An undated letter from Sakharam Sadashiv to Vitthalpant Mama, in G. S. Sardesai, ed., *The Social and Religious Matters under the Peshwas (1727–1797)* (Mumbai: Govt. Central Press, 1934), selections from the *Peshwa Daftar,* vol. 43, pp. 98–99, says that the Maitrāyaṇī affair took place during the judicial term of Rāmaśāstrī Prabhuṇe and people were excommunicated. At that time, expiatory rites were prescribed for those who had shared food with the Maitrāyaṇīyas. The letter also states that there are documents relating to this affair, copies of which could be sent if required.

15 Document no. 62, dated 1751. Sardesai, ed., *The Social and Religious Matters under the Peshwas* (1727–1797), *Peshwa Daftar,* vol. 43, p. 62.

16 Included in Damodar Lakshman Upasani, *Maitrāyaṇīya Śākhetīl brāhmaṇāṃśī paṅktī-vyavahārācā śāstrārtha* (in Marathi, *Śāstric Verdict Relating to Sharing Food with Brahmans of the Maitrāyaṇīya Śākhā*) (Dhule: Aryavarta Chapkhana, 1890), pp. 22–24.

17 Upasani, *Maitrāyaṇīya Śākhetīl*, pp. 26–27.

18 Arakadi, *Yajurvedāntargata Mānavasūtrī,* p. 37 ff.

19 Arakadi, *Yajurvedāntargata Mānavasūtrī,* pp. 350–351.

20 Arakadi, *Yajurvedāntargata Mānavasūtrī,* pp. 362–363.

21 Arakadi, *Yajurvedāntargata Mānavasūtrī,* pp. 33, p. 129.

22 Appeal from Mr. Sakhārām Bāpuji Joshi to the Śaṅkarācārya of Dvārakā, in Arakadi, *Yajurvedāntargata Mānavasūtrī,* p. 2.

23 Arakadi, *Yajurvedāntargata Mānavasūtrī,* p. 133.

24 Arakadi, *Yajurvedāntargata Mānavasūtrī,* p. 292.

25 Arakadi, *Yajurvedāntargata Mānavasūtrī,* p. 329 ff.

26 Arakadi, *Yajurvedāntargata Mānavasūtrī,* pp. 144, 187, 191, 191.

[27] Mahadeva Shastri Divekar, *Brāhmaṇātīl poṭ-jātīṃce ekīkaraṇa* (in Marathi, *Unification of Subcastes among Brahmans*) (Pune: Samartha Bhārat Chāpkhānā, 1928), part II, section 1, p. 98, points out that the Maitrāyaṇīyas had no desire to merge with the Mādhyandina Yajurvedīs of the region. The Maitrāyaṇīyas ridiculed the Mādhyandina pronunciation of *ṇ* as *n*. Divekar also indicates (p. 96) other aspects of naturalization of the Maitrāyaṇīyas by pointing out that they worshiped many specifically Marathi divinities, such as Viṭṭhala of Pandharpur, Khaṇḍobā of Jejurī, and Ambābai of Kolhapur.

[28] The politics of nativism involved in such statements by the Maitrāyaṇīyas is reminiscent of the nationalist claims raised by Marathi authors such as N. B. Pavgee. Compare his views in *Āryāṃce Mūḷa Vasatisthāna,* where he argues, interestingly, against Bāl Gangādhar Tilak's *The Arctic Home in the Vedas* (Poona City: Tilak Bros., Gaikwar Wada, 1903) and tries to establish India as the original home of the Aryans, from where they migrated all over the world. For a detailed discussion of Pavgee's views, see Madhav M. Deshpande, "Aryan Origins: Arguments from the Nineteenth-century Maharashtra," in Edwin F. Bryant and Laurie L. Patton, eds., *The Indo-Aryan Controversy: Evidence and Inference in Indian History* (New York: Routledge, 2005), pp. 407–433. In the Maitrāyaṇīya argument, not just India but Maharashtra becomes part of the original home of the Vedic Aryans. See also Madhav M. Deshpande, "The Arctic Home in the Vedas: Religion, Politics, and the Colonial Context," forthcoming.

[29] Kashikar, "(A Sample of) *Mānavaśrautasūtra,*" p. 106.

[30] Arakadi, *Yajurvedāntargata Mānavasūtrī,* pp. 354–355.

[31] Arakadi, *Yajurvedāntargata Mānavasūtrī,* p. 355.

[32] Cited in Arakadi, *Yajurvedāntargata Mānavasūtrī,* p. 354.

[33] H. H. Wilson, *A Sketch of the Religious Sects of the Hindus* (Berlin: Trübner, 1862).

[34] Arakadi, *Yajurvedāntargata Mānavasūtrī,* p. 361.

[35] I should note that I belong to the Deśastha Ṛgvedī subgroup of Marathi brahmans, and one of my cousin's daughters is married to a Maitrāyaṇīya from Nasik. The Maitrāyaṇīyas are also locally considered to be Deśastha brahmans, though of a different Vedic affiliation from that of my family. Such intermarriage was not common until recently.

[36] The Maitrāyaṇīyas and their opponents were simultaneously taking their appeals and counter-appeals to the Śaṅkarācāryas of Dvārakā, Śṛṅgerī, and Kañcī, in addition to such institutions as the Sanātana Dharma Mahāsabhā of Prayag. The Śaṅkarācārya of Dvārakā, in his 1908 verdict, exhibits irritation at the behavior of both parties in their spirited agitation to resolve this *kṣullak bhāṇḍaṇ,* "minor squabble"; Arakadi, *Yajurvedāntargata Mānavasūtrī,* p. 369.

[37] Arakadi, *Yajurvedāntargata Mānavasūtrī,* p. 376 ff.

Bibliography

Arakadi, Vaman Purushottam. *Yajurvedāntargata Mānavasūtrī Maitrāyaṇīya Śākhā-Prakaraṇa* (in Marathi; *The Maitrāyaṇīya Śākhā Affair*). Nasik: Dinkar Ganesh Muthe, 1927.

Bakre, Mahadev Gangadhar, ed. *Pāraskaragṛhyasūtra,* with 5 commentaries. Mumbai: The Gujarati Printing Press, 1917.

Chitrao, Siddheshwar Shastri. *Vivāhasaṃskāra,* with a Marathi translation and Introduction. Pune: Kāḷa Prakashan, 1927.

Deshpande, Madhav M. "Aryan Origins: Arguments from the Nineteenth-century Maharashtra," in Edwin F. Bryant and Laurie L. Patton, eds., *The Indo-Aryan Controversy: Evidence and Inference in Indian History,* pp. 407–433. New York: Routledge. 2005.

—."Pañca-Gauḍa und Pañca-Drāviḍa. Umstrittene Grenzen einer traditionellen Klassifikation," in Michael Bergunder and Rahul Peter Das, eds., *Arier und Draviden,* pp. 57–78. Neue Hallesche Berichte-2. Halle: Verlag der Franckeschen Stiftungen, 2002.

—."The Arctic Home in the Vedas: Religion, Politics, and the Colonial Context," in dited by Vinay Lal, ed., *Political Hinduism: The Religious Imagination in Public Spheres,* pp. 33–57. Delhi: Oxford University Press. 2009.

—."Vedic Branches: Conflicted Relationships," in *Professor Pierre Filliozat Festschrift.*

__."Vedas and Their Śākhās: Contested Relationships," in François Voegeli, et al., eds., *Devadattīyam: Johannes Bronkhorst Felicitation Volume,* pp. 341–362. Bern: Peter Lang. 2012.

Divekar, Mahadeva Shastri. (śake 1849). *Brāhmaṇātīl poṭ-jātīṃce ekīkaraṇa* (in Marathi; *Unification of Subcastes among Brahmans*), Part II, section 1. Pune: Samartha Bhārat Chāpkhānā, 1928.

Kashikar, C. G. "(A Sample of) *Mānavaśrautasūtra,*" edited with an introduction, in T. N. Dharmadhikari, R. S. Shastri, N. P. Jain, and S. S. Bahulkar, eds., *Vedic Texts: A Revision. Professor C. G. Kashikar Felicitation Volume,* pp. 98–114. Delhi: Motilal Banarsidass, 1990.

—.*Śrauta Dharmācī Svarūpacikitsā* (in Marathi; *Analysis of the Nature of the Śrauta Religion*). Pune: University of Pune Publications, 1977.

Misra, Narayan Prasad. *Kānyakubjavaṃśāvalī, arthāt Kānyakubjaprabodhinī.* Mumbai: Shri Venkateshwar Press, 1987.

Sardesai, G. S., ed. The Social and Religious Matters under the Peshwas (1727–1797), selections from the *Peshwa Daftar,* vol. 43. Mumbai: Government Central Press, 1934.

Shastri, Anantarama Dogara, ed. *Caraṇavyūhasūtra.* By Śaunaka, with the *Bhāṣya* by Mahīdāsa. Kashi Sanskrit Series, no. 132. Banaras: Chaukhambha Sanskrit Sansthan, 1980, second ed.

Tilak, Lokamanya Bāl Gangādhar. *The Arctic Home in the Vedas: Being Also a New Key to the Interpretation of Many Vedic Texts and Legends.* Poona City: Tilak Bros. and Gaikwar Wada, 1903.

Trautmann, Thomas. "The Study of Dravidian Kinship," in Madhav M. Deshpande and Peter Edwin Hook, eds., *Aryan and Non-Aryan in India,* pp. 153–173. Ann Arbor: University of Michigan Press, 1979.

Upasani, Damodar Lakshman. *Maitrāyaṇīya Śākhetīl brāhmaṇāṃśī paṅktī-vyavahārācā śāstrārtha* (in Marathi; *Śāstric Verdict Relating to Sharing food with Brahmans of the Maitrāyaṇīya Śākhā*). Dhule: Aryavarta Chapkhana, 1890.

Lele, Kāśīnātha Vāmana, ed. *Vedavicāra*. By Śāmaśāstrī Dravida Dvivedī. Vai: Śrīkṛṣṇa Mudraṇālaya, 1912.

Wilson, Horace Hayman. *A Sketch of the Religious Sects of the Hindus*. Berlin: Trübner, 1862. Originally published in *Asiatick Researches* XVI (1828): 1–136; *Asiatick Researches* XVII (1832): 169–314.

Witzel, Michael. "Tracing the Vedic Dialects," in Colette Caillât, ed., *Dialectes dans les littératures Indo-Aryennes*, pp. 97–266. Paris: L'Institut de Civilisation indienne, Collège de France, 1989.

Vedic Poetry upon a Chariot: The "Last Journey" in the Light of *Ṛksaṃhitā* X 135, and of the *Veṅkaṭabhāṣya*

Silvia D'Intino
National Center for Scientific Research, Paris

Abstract

Among the numerous chariots mentioned in the *Ṛksaṃhitā* (ṚS), the mental *ratha* a boy rides for an uncertain journey in ṚS X 135 offers an argument to penetrate into Vedic poetics. Generally considered as a funeral hymn, the ritual implications of this composition provide a (contextual) frame for its understanding; they are part of the reflection on death and life it contains, and on their relation with poetry (and speech). A sort of paradise is sketched out in the first and last stanzas, and for a while the text invites us to see life from that other world. A *brahmodya*-like questioning stays at the center of the composition: as in ritual discourse and practice, it expresses a tension. Dealing with death requires a *mise à distance,* which is also at work in the hymn. With the help of Veṅkaṭamādhava's twelfth-century commentary, we attempt to shed light on this mysterious hymn in which one of the first images of the *manoratha* takes shape.[1]

Infancy and Childhood in the *Ṛksaṃhitā*

Looking at the *Ṛksaṃhitā* as a whole, themes of infancy and childhood are granted little space in the hymns. Young boys and girls are practically never explicit subjects, and they appear only rarely as an ideal or metaphor for a state of mind. Yet the rare evocations of childhood found in the *Ṛksaṃhitā* make a strong impression. In the fifth *maṇḍala* one comes across the well-known yet mysterious story of the rescue of Atri (ṚS V 78), described as a boy (*kumārá*) freed by the Aśvins from a sort of pit. The poet compares this story to the birth of a child, delivered from the mother's womb, and in the last stanzas of the hymn the Aśvins are invoked for a safe birth (ṚS V 78, 7–9):[2]

yáthā vā́taḥ puṣkaríṇīṃ samiṅgáyati sarvátaḥ / evā́ te gárbha ejatu niraítu dáśa-māsyaḥ //

As the wind stirs up a lotus pond on all sides, so let the child (*gárbha*) in your womb stir and come out when it is ten months old.

yáthā vā́to yáthā vánaṃ yáthā samudrá éjati / evā́ tváṃ daśamāsya sahā́vehi jarā́-yuṇā //

As the wind and the wood and the ocean stir, so let the ten-month-old child come down together with the afterbirth.

dáśa mā́sāñ chaśayānáḥ kumāró ádhi mātári / niraítu jīvó ákṣato jīvó jī́vantyā ádhi //

When the boy (*kumāró*) has lain for ten months in the mother, let him come out alive and unharmed, alive from the living woman.

Whatever this hymn refers to—a true episode of Atri's life, the ritual rebirth the poet goes through, or both—the term *kumārá,* which in classical Sanskrit clearly indicates the stage of life following infancy, designates in this passage, as most often in the *Ṛksaṃhitā,* the newborn, or even the fetus (*garbha*) and the baby that is not yet born. It is noteworthy that the term *bāla,* largely used in classical Sanskrit to indicate childhood, is completely absent in the hymns. The close term *kumārá* is partially superposed to the well attested term *śíśu,* mainly used in reference to Soma—the "prodigious little one," *śíśuṃ pánipnatam* (ṚS IX 85, 11; IX 86, 31), who cries as a newborn while flowing into the wooden pot (ṚS IX 74, 1). This term is also largely comparable to *vatsá,* the calf that depends on its mother, which comes to designate the offspring of any animal. In fact, all of the terms for the first stage of life in the *Ṛksaṃhitā* point to very earliest infancy, and even more so to the time of birth and prenatal life.

The term *kumārá* (m.) does not have a clear etymology; its primary meaning of "tender, weak" is uncertain. It generally indicates the life stages that follow early infancy up to adolescence;[3] yet it has a wider application in Ṛgvedic hymns, where it is used as an epithet for Agni (ṚS V 2, 1 sq.; X 79, 3)[4] and other little ones, e.g., the Maruts, playing as little boys (ṚS VII 56, 16).[5] One is also reminded of the *kitavasūkta* (ṚS X 34), where the die are compared to *kumārádeśna,* "presents given by a child," who takes back what he has just given,[6] a clear allusion to early infancy. At the beginning of ṚS V 2 the term *kumārá* again designates a newborn or yet to be born infant, in two stanzas that bring into play a complex imagery about the double birth, ritual and cosmic, of Agni,[7] whose entire mythology turns around its latent nature (ṚS V 2, 1–2):[8]

kumārám mātā́ yuvatíḥ sámubdhaṃ gúhā bibhárti ná dadāti pitré / ánīkam asya ná mináj jánāsaḥ puráḥ paśyanti níhitam arataú //

The young mother secretly keeps the boy tightly swathed and does not give him to the father. The people no longer see before them his altered face, hidden by the charioteer.

kám etáṃ tváṃ yuvate kumārám péṣī bibharṣi máhiṣī jajāna / pūrvír hí gárbhaḥ śarádo vávardhā́paśyaṃ jātáṃ yád ásūtā mātā́ //

"Who is the boy that you are carrying, young woman? The chief queen, not the stepmother, gave him birth, for the embryo grows for many autumns. I saw him born when his mother bore him."

The *kumārá* mentioned in this *sūkta* is once more the baby in the mother's womb, and the birth is regarded as a dangerous journey. Concealed in the waters, as the embryo concealed by the two *aráṇis*, the fire sticks (ṚS III 29, 2),[9] encircled by the fingers, his "ten sisters" (ṚS III 29, 13), concealed here by a stepmother (*péṣī?*), Agni is a hidden god, difficult to find, always hiding himself far away. He has been found by the thoughtful mortal (**XXX**, ṚS I 72, 4), by the inspired seers, the ones who know its tracks (*náro dhiyaṃdhā́,* ṚS I 67, 2; *padavyò dhiyaṃdhā́ḥ,* ṚS I 72, 2). One time he is discovered by Yama (ṚS X 51, 3), the king of death, who is thus portrayed as the first human (and officiant). There is an intimate alliance, a mutual involvement between the two gods: being "not-born" (*ajá*),[10] Agni has always been there; he has the characteristics of eternity and immortality of a founder god. Like Agni, Yama is "(always) born and what is (always) to be born," *yamó ha jātó yamó jánitvam* (ṚS I 66, 8),[11] and yet their respective immortality is marked by their different births: in Yama's legend it is the result of his mortal birth and of the endless progress of human generation, a sort of continued life.

In the *Ṛksaṃhitā* there is only one *kumārá* directly addressed in the vocative case: the main character of the hymn ṚS X 135, labeled by modern interpreters "The Boy and the Chariot."[12] The image of childhood that emerges from this text is far from the solar lightheartedness, curiosity, audacity, and levity of infancy and childhood; the youngest age rather seems to be a field of anxiety and nostalgia.

Dying and Being Born

The *sūkta* ṚS X 135 is dedicated to Yama,[13] and it is generally listed among the funeral hymns. A few elements that relate to a funeral ritual can indeed be traced back in the images used in the hymn. In the last stanza, for instance, the chants intoned for Yama, and rejoicing him, reconstitute the general atmosphere of a funerary ceremony;[14] in the fourth stanza, the image of a chariot that is led onto a boat by the songs may recall the ritual release of the burned body to the waters (of a river). This is human imagery of death. We know that Yama, who is explicitly named at the beginning and end of the *sūkta,* and seems to be there just as "framing an allegory of the secret of death,"[15] is also actually the first being born of the human race, the god who renounces his divine immortality and goes through the experience of death, thus opening the path of human generations (ṚS X 14, 2):[16]

> *yamó no gātúm prathamó viveda naíṣā́ gávyūtir ápabhartavā́ u / yátrā naḥ pū́rve pitáraḥ pareyúr enā́ jajñānā́ḥ pathyā̀ ánu svā́ḥ //*
>
> Yama was the first to find the way for us, this pasture that shall not be taken away. Where our ancient fathers passed beyond, there everyone who is born follows, each on his own path.

Yama's intricate personality and legend—a god who dies, and was indeed humanly born, thus initiating the adventure of human life[17]—appear to be more than a contextual feature in ṚS X 135; when closely considered, they allow a fresh interpretation of the hymn. I have to emphasize here that the proposed reading is not a personal one. It derives mainly from an ancient commentary by Veṅkaṭa, also named Mādhava or Veṅkaṭamādhava,[18] whose gloss—an "essential" if not a short one on the whole of the *Saṃhitā*—dates to the twelfth century.

Traditionally this *sūkta* is considered to be the recounting of the singular story of a boy who, missing his recently deceased father, undertakes a visionary journey to reach him among the ancestors. This is a curious interpretation, which Sāyaṇa tries to justify by looking at this story as anticipating one recorded in the *Taittirīya-brāhmaṇa* (3.11.8.1–6) and in the *Kāṭha-upaniṣad,* the legend of Naciketas, whose travel in the afterworld is a sort of *mise à l'épreuve* or apprenticeship.

It is difficult, however, to retrace a first draft of this legend in the hymn; too many details deviate too far from the story, and among them the curious vehicle evoked in the *sūkta.* For his journey the boy has built a chariot in his mind (*manasā́*), and embarks on it without knowing (it)—literally, "without seeing (it)"—for a difficult quest. Does the boy also die? Is it a dead boy who goes looking for his deceased father, traveling himself to reach the ancestors? Such a *mise en abyme* is tremendously poetic, at least for contemporary sensibilities. Yet is the boy of this hymn really looking for his dead father? What precisely is going on in this scenario, and which is the *scène* of the hymn?

Enigmas

The hymn converges, so to say, toward its center. In the middle stanzas (3–5), a series of questions are either addressed directly to the boy or they concern him. These verses reveal the true content of the hymn, which takes the shape of a *brahmodya,* a dialogue about ritual and/or cosmic mysteries (*bráhman*). This is why Louis Renou considered the hymn to be a cosmogonic one.[19] As in any *brahmodya,* there are questions without answers, unsolved enigmas: questions echoing other questions—always built on the mystery of life—about cosmic life, human life, and ritual. They often point to a paradox, and while they may have a particular answer, it does not solve all aspects of the question.[20] The essence of the *brahmodya* presented in ṚS X 135 lies in the words *rátha, kumārá,* and in the verbal roots *jan-* and *bhū-,* "to be born," "to be," "to become."

The questions concern first the mystery of the chariot: how could it proceed, how could this *rátha*—the first *manoratha* we come across in the *Ṛgveda,* the term appearing here in its early analytical form—move without wheels, with a single shaft, and turn in all directions? And second, the passenger: who gave birth to him, who can say how it was that "the following one" (*anudéyī*) came into being? Karl Friedrich Geldner, and Renou after him, remark that we are still in the dark about the meaning of the *sūkta* mainly because we don't know exactly to what the term *anudéyī* refers. Geldner translates it as "die Amme," Arthur A. Macdonnell as "the equipment," Renou as "le chargement," and Wendy Doniger as "the gift for the journey."[21] These scholars also note that the word is used only once more in the *Ṛksaṃhitā,* in the wedding hymn (X 85, 6), where it is associated with the term *nyócanī,* and seems to mean "stepmother" or "nanny."

Indeed, this last one was already Sāyaṇa's interpretation. However, as we have seen, in Sāyaṇa's time the global meaning of the hymn was probably already lost, perhaps as early as two centuries earlier, when Veṅkaṭa composed his commentary. This process began very soon, along with the completion of the Vedic canon, and is already attested in Kautsa's argument, as Frits Staal observes in his memorable study on the emergence of metalanguage in India.[22] Still, the *Veṅkaṭabhāṣya* (VeṅkBh.) gives another interpretation of the hymn, which culminates in the in the enigma of Yama's birth alluded to in the central stanza (ṚS X 135, 5):

> *káḥ kumārám ajanayad ráthaṃ kó nír avartayat / káḥ svit tád adyá no brūyād anudéyī yáthā́bhavat //*
>
> Who gave birth to the boy? Who made the chariot roll further? Who could tell us today how was the accompanying one?

Commenting on the second half of this stanza, Veṅkaṭa observes:[23]

kaḥ svit tat adya asmākam bruyāt yathā asya svasā anudeyī / yamī abhavat iti

Who may say now to us how [it was that came into being] his sister, the *anudeyī*, that is Yamī? (VeṅkBh. ad loc.)

According to Veṅkaṭa, the term *anudéyī* refers here to a crucial feminine figure in the legend of Yama, his twin sister. Who would know better than Yamī about Yama's birth? In recognizing Yama's sister as the figure alluded to in ṚS X 135, 5, Veṅkaṭa solves in an unexpected way the strange equation formulated in the following stanza of the hymn, dealing with the respective birth of the twins:

yáthā́bhavad anudéyī táto ágram ajāyata /
purástād budhná ā́tataḥ paścā́n niráyaṇaṃ kṛtám //

As was the *anudéyī* (the sister), so was [he] born in the beginning. First the foundation was fashioned, then was made the opening.

On this point, in his commentary Veṅkaṭa observes that first came Yama, then Yamī (VeṅkBh. ad ṚS X 135, 6):

yáthā abhavat anudeyī yamasya svasā tathā tasmāt eva sthitāt agram ajāyata iti yamam āha / purastāt budhnaḥ yamaḥ ātataḥ paścāt anudeyā nirayaṇam kṛtam iti / prathamam yamo jātaḥ tataḥ smṛtā yamīti nūnam arthaḥ //*

As came into being the *anudeyī,* [that is,] Yama's sister, so, it is because at the beginning [he] was born—this refers to Yama. First the *budhna* (i.e., Yama) was fashioned, then through the *anudeyī* the opening was done: "First Yama was born, then, according to the tradition, Yamī"—that is the meaning [of the stanza].

The enigma of Yama's birth is thus doubled by the enigma of the twins. It would be tempting to see the terms *budhná* and *niráyaṇa* as alluding to male and female elements, though they cannot be considered to form a regular pair in a ritual coupling.[24] Doniger remarks that one may see in this stanza "simultaneously a literal description of the chariot and the figurative reference to the chant, with its opening and closing phrases."[25] I will return to this point below. The temporal gap in the twins' respective births is mentioned also in the *Bṛhaddevatā.*[26] What is remarkable in Veṅkaṭa's interpretation is that Yama appears to be at the same time the *kumārá* mentioned in the central stanzas, the main character of the hymn, and the hero of the "last journey" described in the *sūkta.*

Paradise?

Charles Malamoud observes that, as the one who goes beyond death "Yama is himself at the same time death and the one who allows for another place to stay after this end."[27] This post-death place seems to be the same place described in the last stanza of the hymn, Yama's proper realm (*idáṃ yamásya sā́danam*), where the god is "adorned with song" (*gīrbhíḥ páriṣkṛtaḥ*). Regarded as the "god's abode" (*devamānám*), it is not exactly, or not yet, the *svargaloka*. Veṅkata says that the place here mentioned is precisely the *antarīkṣa*, while Sāyaṇa says more generally that it is the divine abode of the Ādityas, which is alluded to in ṚS X 135, 7:

> *idáṃ yamásya sā́danaṃ devamānáṃ yád ucyáte / iyám asya dhamyate nāḷīr ayáṃ gīrbhíḥ páriṣkṛtaḥ //*
>
> This is the dwelling-place of Yama that is called the home of the gods. This is his reed pipe that is blown, and he is the one adorned with songs.

In the opening stanza of the hymn, quoted below, in a paradisiacal landscape similar to the divine abode just evoked, Yama is portrayed drinking with the other gods. A lengthy misunderstanding surrounds the second part of the stanza (1cd), where Sāyaṇa does not recognize the mentioned "master and father of our people" (*no viśpátiḥ pitā́*) as being Yama himself; he sees in the genitive *no* a *pluralis pro singulari*, and, as we have seen, he thinks of the whole hymn as a dialogue between Naciketas and his father—an identification already rejected by Geldner[28] as anachronistic. Let us come back to this stanza (ṚS X 135, 1):

> *yásmin vṛkṣé supalāśé devaíḥ sampíbate yamáḥ / átrā no viśpátiḥ pitā́ purāṇā́n ánu venati //*
>
> Beneath a tree with beautiful leaves where Yama drinks with the gods, there our father, the head of the family, turns with longing to the ancient ones.

According to Veṅkaṭa, in this stanza too a unique figure stands at the center of the whole scene: Yama as the father of all men (*asmakam viśāṃ patiḥ janakaḥ*)—the same who is called "assembler of men" (*saṃgámanaṃ jánānām*) and "king" (*rā́jānam*), as in ṚS X 14, 1:[29]

> *pareyivā́ṃsam praváto mahī́r ánu bahúbhyaḥ pánthām anupaspaśavam / vaivasvatáṃ saṃgámanaṃ jánānāṃ yamáṃ rājanáṃ havíṣā duvasya//*
>
> The one who has passed beyond along the great, steep straits, spying out the path for many, the son of Vivasvan, the gatherer of men, King Yama—honor him with the oblation.

Yama, who is drinking in the company of the Ādityas, is suddenly full of longing for the old *deva*s. Veṅkaṭa glosses this as follows (VeṅkBh. ad X 135, 1):

> *yasmin vṛkṣe supalāśe devaiḥ saha yamaḥ ādityaḥ pārthivaṃ rasaṃ pibati iti saṃvatsaraṃ vṛkṣam āha / atra asmākam viśāṃ patiḥ janakaḥ vaivaśvato yamaḥ purāṇān devān anu kāmayate / niruktaṃ draṣṭavyam* (12, 29) *iti //*
>
> Beneath a tree with beautiful leaves, Yama drinks with the gods the earthly juice; the tree is called *saṃvatsara* (the year); there the head of all our people, [that is,] Yama, son of Vivasvan, desires [to see] again the ancient gods, as it is said in the *Nirukta* (12, 29).

In fact, his death is a way for Yama to reconnect with his own mortal origins,[30] and this could explain the *leitmotiv* of nostalgia for the ancient ones (the fathers, or the ancient *deva*s he wishes to see again) that motivates Yama's journey. The tree, which is a holy tree (*pippal* or *aśvattha*) according to Sāyaṇa's gloss, is here an image of the year and also a symbol of human time. This suggests that we are here in an earthly paradise, where the *deva*s drink the earthly juice (*pārthivaṃ rasam*). Does Yama belong to an earlier generation of *deva*s, of the Ādityas' time, and is he thus nostalgic for a previous lifetime? It is as if the choice for his mortal life was not in front of Yama, but already behind him, which casts the entire hymn as a sort of reverie. Be that as it may, Yama's nostalgia is increased by a voice, speaking in the first-person singular, remembering that moment; this is someone who is trying to detain him on the difficult journey he has already begun (ṚS X 135, 2):

> *purāṇā́n anuvénantaṃ cárantaṃ pāpáyāmuyā́ / asūyánn abhy àcākaśaṃ tásmā aspṛhayam púnaḥ //*
>
> Reluctantly I looked upon him as he turned with longing to the ancient ones, as he moved on that evil way. I longed to have him back again.

The "evil" way that Yama is engaged in, as suggested by all the commentators, is the path of death. Veṅkaṭa says that the destiny of all living beings (*prāṇinaḥ*) is that Yama brings death to them. But who is speaking here? Something seems to be missing in Veṅkaṭa's gloss. If Yama is the same boy who started out on the mortal journey, who may thus be longing for him, hoping to reach him, to be in touch with him again (*tásmā aspṛhayam púnaḥ*)? Should we look for another character outside Yama's legend? I don't think so. The first person who comes naturally to mind here is not a father speaking from the afterlife, but Yama's mother. Yet a similar dialogue with Yama's mother is not found elsewhere in the hymns, nor in Vedic prose.

The other possible interlocutor is Yama's twin sister, Yamī, who is more directly involved in the myth of Yama's mortal journey. Yamī is the one who fondly misses him, who always emphasizes their intimate kinship, as in the dialogue Yama-Yamī (ṚS X 10), the natural counterpoint of ṚS X 135. She is inconsolable after the death of her brother, to the point that the gods decide to create the night in order to alleviate her pain (*Kāṭhaka-saṃhitā* VII 10; *Maitrāyaṇī-saṃhitā* I 5, 12).[31]

Yamī is not alien to the story of Yama's death. As Charles Malamoud reminds us, according to *Pañcaviṃśa-brāhmaṇa* 10, 20–22, she is the one who first recites the *sāman* of Yama, which enables his twin brother to reach the heavenly world. Here the heavenly world and the realm of death merge[32]—is this the unique paradise evoked in ṚS X 135? Malamoud also notes that Sāyaṇa, commenting on this passage, says that in ancient times Yamī had been Yama's wife, which may suggest that she is acting as a wife in accomplishing the funerary rites for her brother.[33] Some other passages where the presence of Yamī is similarly required are evoked by Malamoud, and he also remarks that in the *Anukramaṇī* the funerary hymn ṚS X 154 is ascribed to Yamī as if it were a song addressed to a dead brother.

The hymn we are trying to interpret belongs to the X *maṇḍala,* where description gives way to allusion and suggestion, and some new stylistic features, particularly, direct speech and dialogue, emerge:

> Le discours direct au livre X vient, en nombre de passages, affleurer sous l'expression usuelle: on passe de l'un à l'autre registre sans préparation, sans transition. *L'éloge de forme ancienne est abandonné peu à peu au profit d'une sorte de mise en scène:* qu'on observe à cet égard les éléments de discours enchâssés dans le récit de Śuṣṇa (22), les monologues du Chantre (33), du Joueur (34), de l'Homme ivre (119), l'*ātmastuti* d'Indra (27–28) *où le monologue sort insensiblement du dialogue.* C'est cette vitalisation, cette animation, qui donne son accent nouveau au Livre X.[34]

We cannot reopen the debate on the status of the dialogue hymns in the *Ṛgveda* in this essay. Let us just add that the hymn of the boy and the chariot perfectly fits in the list presented by Louis Renou above, and could be regarded as one of those monologues that are "imperceptibly coming out of a dialogue."

Chariots, Poetry

From a formal and stylistic point of view, the hymn X 135 is strongly structured: not only are there opening and closing stanzas that recall each other, but each stanza is strongly interconnected with the following one, thus creating a unique scene and a sort of drama, where the only thing that does eventually really move is the chariot. The three central stanzas present an anaphoric structure, with the constant repetition of the vocative *kumāra* in the second position; the general structure of the hymn thus adopts the scheme described by Stephanie Jamison as "the 'omphalos' shape, a formal pattern found primarily in 'mystical,' 'enigmatic,' and self-consciously poetic hymns."[35] ṚS X 135, 3 reads:

> *yáṃ kumāra návaṃ rátham acakrám mánasā́kṛṇoḥ/ ékeṣaṃ viśvátaḥ prā́ñcam ápaśyann ádhi tiṣṭhasi //*
>
> In your mind, o boy, you made a new chariot without wheels, which had only one shaft but can travel in all directions. And unseeing, you climbed into it.

According to Veṅkaṭa, as in the later *Sāyaṇabhāṣya*, the mental chariot the boy has built for his journey is a chariot made of time, *kālātmakam*,[36] a sort of time machine: the multiple directions toward which it turns are the divisions of time. It resembles the *ráthas tricakráh* of the *Ṛbhu* (ṚS IV 36 1), which introduces the main divisions of space, the triple world, and makes life prosperous and fruitful in the heavens and on earth. Similarly, Yama's death inaugurates the order of time, establishing a yesterday (and a tomorrow) out of the unique (present) day of the gods.

In his monograph on Vedic chariots, Max Sparreboom observes that particularly in Vedic prose, chariots become the symbol of heavenly conquests, thus prolonging the metaphor of the strides of Viṣṇu.[37] Yet, along with being a world-conquering *rátha*, the chariot is also a fragile vehicle in a more philosophic context, where it appears "suitable to express the idea of a journey to the 'ultimate' place or the place of no-return."[38] Sparreboom recalls the allegory in *Kāṭha-upaniṣad* III 3.9, where the image of a chariot is used to teach the essence of the *ātman*.[39] This is the same source Sāyaṇa has in mind when he identifies the chariot with the mortal body, though the mental *rátha* appears to be a much more elaborate image, discussion of which is more appropriate for a doctrinal discourse. However, we must seek another framework to better understand this metaphor in ṚS X 135, where the poet inserts a reflection about poetic art.

There is a familiarity between Yama's journey toward the ancient ones and the tension felt by the Vedic poet toward the distant past and the oldest poets.[40] Yama is in fact the hero of a poetic exploit, as Malamoud has shown:

> Entre Yama qui a vu et fait le chemin et les poètes qui ont vu, élaboré et énoncé les poèmes du Veda, il n'y a pas seulement une analogie: le chemin vers l'au-delà est aussi œuvre de langage; il est fait des paroles que les survivants doivent prononcer pour que le défunt accomplisse sa transformation en Père et parvienne à sa destination. Ces paroles rituelles, de même que les paroles védiques qui font connaître ce processus, relevant de la création poétique de Yama.[41]

A few more remarkable similarities between the poetic work and the making of the chariot in ṚS X 135 can be found in the expression of the hymn. As the *kumārá* in ṚS X 135 has fashioned a new chariot (*návaṃ rátham,* st. 2), the Vedic poet seeks and is requested to create a new song (*návyam stómam*), a new vision (*návyā́ dhī́, návyam mánma*), a new enigma (*návyam bráhman*). For a while, the two figures reflect into each other. This implicit discourse on poetry becomes more explicit in the fourth stanza of the *sūkta,* where the chariot is said to have rolled in front of the poets and a melody emanated from it, thus leading the chariot onto a boat (ṚS X 135, 4):

> *yáṃ kumāra prī́vartayo ráthaṃ víprebhyas pári / táṃ sā́mā́nu prā́vartata sám itó nāvy ā́hitam //*
>
> O boy, when you made the chariot roll forth in front of the inspired-poets, a melody rolled after it, from where it got upon a boat.

The chariot and the boat are well-established metaphors of the sacrifice, and the sacrificial scene tends to coalesce with the vehicle (chariot, boat, a chariot on a boat) that leads to it.[42] These are also images in the poem,[43] and it is a very charged symbolism. Among all the chariots one encounters in the *Rgveda,* the *manoratha* is really a peculiar vehicle, the vehicle of the poet, whose vision is conceived of as a mental journey through time and space.[44] The poet often evokes this experience as a journey to reach the assembly of the gods and, at the same time, the very sources of the word. "Make the boats" (ṚS X 101, 2), says the poet to his companions (other poets); "I have fashioned this hymn of praise . . . as the skilled artist fashions a chariot," *etā́ṃ te stómaṃ ráthaṃ ná dhī́raḥ svápā atakṣam* (ṚS V 2, 11).[45] What counts most, for the poet, is to engage in the journey of poetic creation.

In the *Ṛgveda* the term *rátha* designates the chariot of the Aśvins;[46] but also of Sūrya, Vāyu, Soma (ṚS IX 62, 17), Savitṛ (ṚS I 35, 2), Uṣas (ṚS I 4, 10; 113, 14), Indra (ṚS V 31, 1), Agni (ṚS I 13, 4; 14, 12; X 142, 5), Tvaṣṭṛ (488, 19), the Maruts (ṚS V 56, 6; VI 47, 11), and so on. Whereas many gods travel on their own chariots through the celestial realm, Yama does not have a chariot for himself. However, the *manorátha* found in ṚS X 135 resembles the Aśvins' *rátha* depicted in ṚS VI 49, 5, "yoked through the *manas*" (*yó rátho . . . mánasā yujānáḥ*), which appears to be both a sacrificial and a poetic vehicle in one, led by a "wide inspired-thought" (*bṛhatī́ manīṣā́*).[47] As the emblematic image for the work, Frits Staal observes that in the Vedas chariots represent more than a material vehicle:

> I counted 792 occurrences [in the ṚV] of the word *aśva* in various forms. The word for chariot, *ratha*, is equally common; but there was no need for chariot to be carried across mountains. It was the idea of the chariot and the precise knowledge of how to construct one that were transmitted across the mountains by a handful of experts. That knowledge was enough. . . . What may set the Indus Valley apart from these others areas [Near East and South Asia, but also southern Europe and other parts of Eurasia] is that such chariots were imported there by a small number of people through their minds.[48]

As an immaterial legacy, the chariot is more than a single savoir faire. Poetry and poetic art may certainly be included as a branch of that knowledge.

Not (Yet) Seeing

Commenting on ṚS X 135, Staal follows the traditional, i.e., Sāyaṇa's, interpretation. However, he imagines the boy having assembled a sort of chariot toy (like the models excavated at Harappa!), and points to a strange detail of the scene: the boy has embarked on the journey, yet he cannot see anything:

> RV 10. 135 is a dialogue between a son and his dead father. The son says: "I did not like him looking back at his ancestors and take the evil path. I want him back." The father responds: "The new chariot without wheels, which you, boy, has made, which has one drought pole and goes in all directions, standing on it you are seeing nothing." The father's sarcasm has been interpreted as making little of the boy's play, though it is, in fact, concerned with imagination and reality both.[49]

Following the clues given in Veṅkaṭa's gloss, the interpretation of the hymn we propose here is far from a father's sarcasm, and still quite close to power of imagination and poetry. If this interpretation is correct, then in what temporal frame does the scene evoked in the hymn truly happen? I will try to answer this question, and to better set the scene the poet presents in the *sūkta*. Yamī expresses her sorrow during Yama's last journey: it is an ideal dialogue about love, separation, and nostalgia between a mortal man and an immortal woman[50]—a sister that speaks as a wife, as a mother, as a lover. Yamī's lament on the death of the brother thus gives him the words (a song) to cross over. The allusion to the common birth of the twins adds to the dramatic tenor of the hymn. Yama's prenatal life thus comes to the heart of his poetic *gesta*, with its paradoxes and mystery. This point of view helps explain why the poet says the boy is *ápaśyan* in embarking on the chariot. The ancient commentators say that, since he is dead, he is not conscious of the journey he has undertaken. Yet if the boy is Yama himself, he does not see also because he has not yet been born and his senses are not yet active. So deeply connected are the mysteries of death and life in the legend of Yama.

In closing, I return to the entire hymn in light of the new elements gathered in this study.

The Boy and the Chariot, or the Lament of Yamī

1. *yásmin vṛkṣé supālāśé devaíḥ sampíbate yamáḥ / átrā no viśpátiḥ pitā́ purāṇā́n ánu venati //*

[The poet:] Beneath a tree with beautiful leaves where Yama drinks with the gods, there our father, the head of the family, turns with longing to the ancient ones.

2. *purāṇā́n anuvénantaṃ cárantaṃ pāpáyāmuyā́ / asūyánn abhy àcākaśaṃ tásmā aspṛhayam púnaḥ //*

[Yamī:] Reluctantly I looked upon him as he turned with longing to the ancient ones, as he moved on that uncertain way. I longed to have him back again.

3. *yáṃ kumāra návaṃ rátham acakrám mánasā́kṛṇoḥ / ékeṣaṃ viśvátaḥ prā́ñcam ápaśyann ádhi tiṣṭhasi //*

"In your mind, o boy, you made a new chariot without wheels, which had only one shaft but can travel in all directions. Unseeing, you climbed into it.

4. *yáṃ kumāra prā́vartayo ráthaṃ víprebhyas pári / táṃ sā́mānu prā́vartata sám itó nāvy ā́hitam //*

O boy, when you made the chariot roll forth in front of the inspired-poets, a melody rolled after it, from where it got upon a boat.

5. *káḥ kumārám ajanayad rátham kó nír avartayat / káḥ svit tád adyá no brūyād anudéyī yáthābhavat //*

Who gave birth to the boy? Who made the chariot roll further? Who could tell us today how was the accompanying one, [your sister]?

6. *yáthābhavad anudéyī táto ágram ajāyata / purástād budhná ātataḥ paścā́n niráyaṇaṃ kṛtám //*

As was the sister, so was [he] born in the beginning. First the foundation was fashioned, then was made the opening."

7. *idáṃ yamásya sā́danaṃ devamānáṃ yád ucyáte / iyám asya dhamyate nāḷīr ayáṃ gīrbhíḥ páriṣkṛtaḥ //*

[The poet:] This is the dwelling-place of Yama that is called the home of the gods. This is his reed pipe that is blown, he is the one adorned with songs.

Notes

1 The present study was already in press when an article by Stephanie Jamison on the same *sūkta* was published, "The Earliest Evidence for the Inborn Debts of a Brahmin: A New Interpretation of Ṛgveda X.135," *Journal Asiatique* 302/2 (2014): 245–257. Jamison's remarkable interpretation is recommended.

2 Translation in Wendy Doniger, *The Rig Veda: An Anthology. One Hundred and Eight Hymns, Selected, Translated and Annotated* (London: Penguin Books, 1981), p. 187.

3 See George-Jean Pinault, "Regard comparatif sur les âges de la vie dans le monde Gréco- romain et indien," in Christine Chojnacki, *Les âges de la vie dans le monde indien. Actes des journées d'études de Lyon (juin 2000)* (Lyon: De Boccard [diff.], 2000), pp. 26–27: "Ce mot ne réfère pas seulement à l'adolescence, mais peut couvrir toute la période suivant la petite enfance, avant la puberté."

4 However, how to understand the negative *ákumāra* and Agni's double epithet *yuvā́kumāraḥ* in ṚS I 155, 6? Karl Friedrich Geldner translates it as "der Jugendliche, der kein Knabe ist," *Der Rig-Veda aus dem Sanskrit ins Deutsche übersetzt und mit einem laufenden Kommentar versehen* (Cambridge, MA: Harvard University Press, 1951), vol. 1, p. 214; Louis Renou has "le (dieu) jeune, (quoique) non un enfant," *Études védiques et pāṇinéennes* (Paris: De Boccard, 1955–1969), vol. 15, pp. 37–38. On this point Renou refers to Abel Bergaigne, *La religion védique d'après les hymnes du Ṛg-Veda* (Paris: F. Vieweg, 1878–1883), vol. 2, p. 418, who translates it as "jeune . . . et non jeune, vieux," and assimilates this image to the expression *palitó yuvā́* in RS 144, 4, rendered as "jeune homme chenu." Personally, I would suggest "young, not (yet) a boy."

5 The diminutive, *śiśū́la* (hapax) is also employed to describe the Maruts in ṚS X 78, 6, where they are compared to the ritual pressing stones, and who play like little boys (*śiśū́lā ná krīḷáyaḥ*) under the benevolent gaze of their mothers.

6 ṚS X 34, 7: *akṣā́sa íd aṅkuśíno nitodíno nikṛtvānas tápanās tāpayiṣṇávaḥ / kumārádeṣṇā jáyataḥ punarháṇo. . .* ; "The dice goad like hooks and prick like whips;

they enslave, deceive, and torment. They give presents as children do, striking back at the winners. . . ."; Doniger, *The Rig Veda: An Anthology,* p. 240.

7 Thus already Bergaigne, *La religion védique d'après les hymnes du Ṛg-Veda,* vol. 1, pp. 71–90 et passim. Agni is called *dvimātṛ́* in ṚS I 31, 2; Bergaigne, *La religion védique,* vol. 3, pp. 55, 6–7. On this subject, see Charles Malamoud, "Parole, mère plurielle. Observation sur le nombre de mères dans l'Inde ancienne," in *Féminité de la parole: Études sur l'Inde ancienne* (Paris: Albin Michel, 2005), p. 133 sq.

8 Doniger, *The Rig Veda: An Anthology,* p. 102.

9 The fire sticks are regarded as the two mothers of Agni. See Malamoud, "Parole, mère plurielle," pp. 136–137.

10 ṚS I 67, 5. This epithet characterizes Agni as a god "without a unique birth" or/and "born without gestation"; Malamoud, "Parole, mère plurielle," p. 136.

11 In fact, in this passage Yama is assimilated to Agni, the *devatā* of the hymn. See Charles Malamoud, "Yama, Yamī et les diverses manières de former une paire," in Samra Azarnouche and Céline Redard, eds., *Yama/Yima: Variations indo-iraniennes sur la geste mythique* (Paris: De Boccard, 2012), p. 97, n. 8.

12 Doniger, *The Rig Veda: An Anthology,* p. 55. Thus already Geldner, *Der Rig-Veda,* vol. 3, p. 367, has "Der Knabe und der Wagen"; Louis Renou, "La composition du dixième maṇḍala," in *Études védiques et pāṇinéennes* (Paris: De Boccard, 1956), vol. 2, p. 129, has "L'enfant à la voiture."

13 The *Anukramaṇī* indicates Yama as the *devatā* and a certain Kumāra as the *ṛṣi* of the hymn. As it is often the case for uncertain attributions, this authorship is merely conventional—a name appearing in the first lines of the text is regarded as a mark of authorship. Veṅkaṭa attributes the *sūkta* to a Kumāra of the Yāmāyana family. See VeṅkBh. ad X 135 1.

14 Jan Gonda, *The Vedic Ritual: The Non-solemn Rites* (Leiden-Köln: Brill, 1980), p. 74: "Laughing and (or) dancing etc., while incompatible with the dignified demeanour of a *snātaka* who should not even look at dancing people . . . are, through rarely mentioned, prescribed auspiciously to enliven a wedding party (KG [*Kāṭhaka-Gṛhyasūtra*] 22, 1), and expected or hoped for by those who have performed a funeral ceremony (ĀgnG [*Āgniveśya-Gṛhyasūtra*] 3, 7, 1) or return from a journey (HG [*Hiraṇyakeśi-Gṛhyasūtra*] 1, 29, 1)."

15 Doniger, *The Rig Veda: An Anthology,* p. 55.

16 Doniger, *The Rig Veda: An Anthology,* p. 43.

17 Though nothing is known about the story of Yama's birth; the texts remain silent about it except for few glimpses of it that can be recognized in ṚS X 135, as will be discussed below.

18 Not to be confused with another commentator called Mādhava or Mādhavabhaṭṭa, the son of Veṅkaṭārya and author of a *Ṛgvedānukramaṇī,* as well as of a *Ṛgarthadīpikā* mentioned in SāyBh (ad ṚS X 86, 1). Cf. C. Kunhan Rāja, *The Ṛgvedānukramaṇī of Mādhavabhatta (son of Veṅkaṭārya)* (Madras: University of Madras, 1932).

19 Renou, "La composition du dixième *maṇḍala*," p. 255: "Ce poème si sobre, aux courtes phrases, est d'intention cosmogonique, comme tant d'autres du RV 'récent.'"

20 Renou first uses the term "enigma" to translate Skt. *bráhman*. See Louis Renou in collaboration with Lilian Silburn, "Sur la notion de bráhman," in Louis Renou, *L'Inde fondamentale: Études d'indianisme réunies et présentées par Charles Malamoud* (Paris: La Découverte, 1978), pp. 7–46. On the use of enigmas in the *Ṛgveda*, see Joel P. Brereton, "Edifying Puzzlement: Ṛgveda 10.129 and the Uses of Enigma," *Journal of the American Oriental Society* 119/2 (1999): 248–260.

21 Doniger, *The Rig Veda: An Anthology*, p. 57. Arthur A. Macdonnell, *A Vedic Reader for Students* (London: Oxford University Press, 1917), p. 215: "It is a f. of *anudéya*, which occurs in the sense of to be handed over; the exact sense is nevertheless uncertain. It not improbably means that which the deceased was supplied for the journey to Yama's abode." Renou remarks in a note in "La composition du dixième *maṇḍala*," p. 256: "mot incertain: l'autre attestation (RV. X. 85) inclinerait vers le sens, mal admissible ici, de 'dame accompagnant (la fiancée),'" and makes a similar remark in *Études védiques et pāṇinéennes*, vol. 16, p. 170: "*anudéyī* 'viatique' est concevable, mais mal ajustable à 85, 6. . . ."; and, in an earlier version of this hymn, in *Anthologie sanskrite* (Paris: Payot, 1947), p. 19, he translates it as "l'approvisionnement."

22 Frits Staal, "The Concept of Metalanguage and its Indian Background," *Journal of Indian Philosophy* 3 (1975): 369: "Kautsa's thesis that the mantras are meaningless was not merely an expression of a ritualistic and metalinguistic outlook; it also reflects the fact that the meaning of the Vedic mantras was at the time beginning to get lost."

23 I follow Doniger's translation for the whole of the hymn, except for a few details. See Doniger, *The Rig Veda: An Anthology*, pp. 55–56.

24 Because of the respective gender of the two terms (masculine and neuter). On the notion of *mithuna*, the different ways to form a pair, and their morphological implications, see Charles Malamoud, *Féminité de la parole*, pp. 36–59, and *La danse des pierres* (Paris: Seuil, 2005), pp. 59–81.

25 Doniger, *The Rig Veda: An Anthology*, p. 57, n. 9.

26 Cf. *Bṛhaddevatā* VI 163.

27 Malamoud, "Yama, Yamī et les diverses manières de former une paire," p. 97: "Yama est donc simultanément la mort et celui qui fait qu'il y a, après cette fin, un autre séjour." He comments here on *Atharvaveda-saṃhitā* (AS) XVIII 3, 63. On the legend of Yama and its different aspects, see Charles Malamoud, *Le jumeau solaire* (Paris: Seuil, 2002), a work to which I owe all the ideas about the relation between Yama and poetic art in Vedic texts developed in this paper.

28 Geldner, *Der Rig-Veda*, vol. 3, p. 367. Yet Renou notes in *Études védiques et pāṇinéennes*, vol. 2, p. 33, "l'hymne X 135 est répertorié parmi les hy. où apparaît la mort « les allusions à la mort dans le dialogue de Purūravas . . . , de l'Enfant au char—esquisse ṛgvédique du Nāciketa—. . . ."

[29] Doniger, *The Rig Veda: An Anthology*, 43. See also AS XVIII 3, 13 (which reproduces part of ṚS X 14, 1): *yó mamā́ra prathamó mártyānāṃ yáḥ preyā́ya prathamó lokáṃ etám/ vaivasatáṃ saṃgámanaṃ jánānām yamā́ṃ rā́jānaṃ havíṣā saparyata //*; "Him who died first of mortals, who went forth first to that world, Vivasvant's son, assembler of people, king Yama honor ye with oblation." William Dwight Whitney, trans., *Atharva-Veda Saṃhitā* (Delhi: Motilal Banarsidass, 1962), vol. 2, p. 852.

[30] Malamoud observes that in choosing death for himself, Yama comes back to his own origins; "Yama, Yamī et les diverses manières de former une paire," p. 96: "Pour être le guide et le maître des morts ainsi rassemblés et aussi des mortels promis à cette forme de survie, Yama choisit lui-même de mourir. Ce faisant, il renoue avec ses origines. Il faut noter en effet que le lien entre mortalité et humanité préexiste à la décision de Yama: le père de Yama, Vivasvant, le dieu soleil, immortel, est la transformation de Mārtāṇḍa, l' «Oeuf mort», ou «qui résulte d'un œuf mort» . . . ." ("In order to be the guide and the master of the dead men thus gathered and also of the mortals promised to this form of survival, Yama himself chooses to die. In doing that, he links back with his own origins. In fact, one must remark that the link between mortality and humanity preexists to Yama's decision: Yama's father, Vivasvant, the sun god, immortal, is the transformation of Mārtāṇḍa, the 'Dead Egg' or 'what comes out of a dead egg.'")

On this point, Malamoud recalls not only the passages of the Vedic prose where the story of Vivasvant's is narrated in detail (*Maitrāyaṇī-saṃhitā* I 6, 2; *Taittirīya-saṃhitā* VI 5, 6, 1; *Śatapatha-brāhmaṇa* III 1, 3, 3–4), but also ṚS X 72, 8 sq about Mārtāṇḍa's birth, and AS XVIII 3, 62–63, where a prayer is addressed to Vivasvant in order to ward off death, and immediately after Yama is invoked to prolong life beyond death (*sá no yamaḥ pratarā́ṃ jīvā́se dhāt*). Cf. Malamoud, "Yama, Yamī et les diverses manières de former une paire," p. 97.

[31] Cf. Malamoud, "La nuit du temps," pp. 55–65 (60); "Yama, Yamī et les diverses manières de former une paire," pp. 98–99. The latter, more recent article is the most advanced analysis of the dialogue hymn ṚS X 10, a text presenting a long interpretative history. For a discussion on the interpretation of the Ṛgvedic dialogue hymns, and particularly on the *ākhyāna* theory, see H. D. Velankar, "The Ṛgvedic Origin of the Story of Naciketas (ṚV X 135)," in *Mélanges d'indianisme à la mémoire de Louis Renou* (Paris: De Boccard, 1968), pp. 763–772; Robert Goldman, "Mortal Man and Immortal Woman: An Interpretation of Three *Ākhyāna* Hymns of the Ṛgveda," *Journal of the Oriental Institute of Baroda* 18/4 (1969): 274–303; Henk W. Bodewitz, "The Dialogue of Yama and Yamī (ṚV. 10, 10)," *Indo-Iranian Journal* 52 (2009): 351–286.

[32] Malamoud, "Yama, Yamī et les diverses manières de former une paire," p. 99: "Notons que le monde céleste, tel du moins qu'il est accessible aux mortels conduits par Yama et le monde de Yama sont ici confondus."

[33] Thus already Caland. See Malamoud, "Yama, Yamī et les diverses manières de former une paire," p. 99.

[34] Louis Renou, "La composition du dixième *maṇḍala*," in *Études védiques et pāṇinéennes* (Paris: De Boccard, 1956), vol. 2, p. 19; emphasis added.

[35] Stephanie Jamison, *Le Ṛgveda entre deux mondes (The Ṛgveda between Two Worlds)* (Paris: De Boccard, 2007), p. 80 sq. The ideal model for this scheme is ṚS X 129.

[36] VeṅkBh. ad ṚS X 135, 5.

[37] Max Sparreboom, *Chariots in the Veda* (Leiden: Brill, 1985), p. 17.

[38] Sparreboom, *Chariots in the Veda*, p. 17.

[39] Sparreboom, *Chariots in the Veda*, p. 19.

[40] See, e.g., ṚS I 72, 1.

[41] Malamoud, *Le jumeau solaire*, p. 24.

[42] On the notion of the "sacrificial scene," and its implications, I refer of course to Malamoud, *La danse des pierres*. See namely the Introduction to the volume.

[43] Cf. e.g. ṚS II 16, 7a: *prá te nā́vaṃ ná sámane vacasyúvam bráhmaṇā yāmi sávaneṣu dā́dhṛṣiḥ*. Geldner, *Der Rig-Veda*, vol. 1, p. 297: "Ich (rudere) dir gleichsam das Schiff der Beredsamkeit in dem Wettbewerb zu; kühn fahre ich mit der hohen Rede während der Somaspenden"; Renou, *Études védiques et pāṇinéennes*, vol. 17, p. 62: "J'(envoie) vers toi en avant, tel un navire, (un chant) éloquent pour la compétition, je pars avec la formule pour les pressurages, moi hardi."

[44] Jan Gonda, *The Vision of the Vedic Poets* (Leiden: Brill, 1965). Yet, should we think for ṚS X 135 of an ecstatic journey? See Geldner, *Der Rig-Veda*, vol. 3, p. 367, n. 1.

[45] Doniger, *The Rig Veda: An Anthology*, p. 103. The metaphor can be much more complicated, as in ṚS II 18, 1: *prātā́ rátho návo yoji sásniś cáturyugas trikaśā́ḥ saptáraśmiḥ / dáśāritro manuṣyàḥ svarṣā́ḥ sá iṣṭibhir matíbhī ráṅhyo bhūt //*. Geldner, *Der Rig-Veda*, vol. 1, p. 298: "Am Morgen wird der neue Wagen geschirrt, der gewinnreiche mit vier Jochen, drei Peitschen, sieben Zügeln, mit zehn Rudern, von Menschen gemacht, das Himmelslicht erringend. Er soll mit unseren Wünschen, mit unseren (frommen) Gedanken in Lauf gesetzt werden"; Renou, *Études védiques et pāṇinéennes*, vol. 17, p. 64: "Au matin le nouveau char a été attelé, qui gagne (les prix), à quatre jougs, trois fouets, sept rênes, / dix rames, fait pour les hommes, conquérant le soleil: il est propre a être mis en rapide–marche par nos quêtes, nos pensées-poétiques."

Even more complicated is the association of the chariot with the boat, as the hymn of the present study. The poetic implications of this double vehicle are undeniable, e.g., ṚS I 140, 12: *ráthāya nā́vam utá no gṛhā́ya nítyāritrām padvátīṃ rāsy agne / asmā́kaṃ vīrā́ṅ utá no maghóno jánāñś ca yā́ pāráyāc chárma yā́ ca //*. Geldner, *Der Rig-Veda*, vol. 1, p. 197: "Gewähre, Agni, unserem Wagen und Haus ein Schiff mit eigenen Rudern und mit Füssen, das unsere Mannen und unsere Lohnherren und die Leute hinübertrage und das eine Zuflucht sei"; Renou, *Études védiques et pāṇinéennes*, vol. 12, p. 33: "À (notre) char et à notre maison, donne, ô Agni, un bateau qui ait ses rames propres, qui ait (pour ainsi dire) des pieds, / (tel) qu'il fasse traverser (comme on traverse un fleuve) nos hommes-d'élite ainsi que nos (patrons) généreux et les gens (en général) et qui (soit) une protection!".

[46] Among the numerous images of the Aśvins' *rátha*, the incipit of ṚS X 40 (Ghoṣā's song) describes it as moved by the poetic vision and the sacrificial work (*rátham . . . váhamānaṃ dhiyā́ śámi*).

[47] It is worth mentioning here a stanza addressed to the Maruts, where *mánas* refers at the same time to the poet's interiority and to the organ of gods' delight (ṚS I 171, 2): *eṣá va stómo maruto nā́masvān hṛdā́ taṣṭó mánasā dhāyi devāḥ / úpem ā́ yāta mánasā juṣaṇá yūyáṃ hí ṣṭhā́ námasa íd vṛdhā́saḥ //*; "This praise and homage fashioned in the heart and in the mind was made for you, Maruts, for you are gods. Come and enjoy with your mind, for you are the ones who make homage grow"; Doniger, *The Rig Veda: An Anthology*, p. 171.

[48] Frits Staal, *Discovering the Vedas: Origins, Mantras, Rituals, Insights* (New Delhi: Penguin Books, 2008), p. 17; italics in original.

[49] Staal, *Discovering the Vedas*, pp. 36–37.

[50] I refer to Robert Goldman's enlightening article, "Mortal Man and Immortal Woman: An Interpretation of Three *Ākhyāna* Hymns of the Ṛgveda."

References

Aufrecht, Theodor. *Die Hymnen des Rigveda*, 2 vols. (1877). Wiesbaden: Harrassowitz, 1968, reprint.

Bergaigne, Abel. *La religion védique d'après les hymnes du Ṛg-Veda*, 3 vols. Bibliothèque de l'École des hautes études, Sciences philologiques et historiques 36, 53, 54. Paris: F. Vieweg, 1878–1883.

Brereton, Joel P. "Edifying Puzzlement: Ṛgveda 10.129 and the Uses of Enigma," *Journal of the American Oriental Society* 119/2 (1999): 248–260.

Bodewitz, Henk W. 2009. "The Dialogue of Yama and Yamī (ṚV. 10, 10)," *Indo-Iranian Journal* 52 (2009): 351–286.

Doniger, Wendy. *The Rig Veda: An Anthology. One Hundred and Eight Hymns, Selected, Translated and Annotated.* London: Penguin Books, 1981.

Geldner, Karl Friedrich. *Der Rig-Veda aus dem Sanskrit ins Deutsche übersetzt und mit einem laufenden Kommentar versehen*, 3 vols. Harvard Oriental Series 33, 34, 35. Cambridge, MA: Harvard University Press, 1951.

Goldman, Robert. "Mortal Man and Immortal Woman: An Interpretation of Three *Ākhyāna* Hymns of the Ṛgveda," *Journal of the Oriental Institute of Baroda* 18/4 (1969): 274–303.

Gonda, Jan. *The Vedic Ritual: The Non-solemn Rites.* Leiden-Köln: Brill, 1980.

—. *The Vision of the Vedic Poets.* Leiden: Brill, 1965.

Grassmann, Hermann. *Wörterbuch zum Rig-Veda.* Leipzig: F. A. Brockhaus, 1872–1875.

Jamison, Stephanie. *Le Ṛgveda entre deux mondes* (*The Ṛgveda between Two Worlds*). Publications de l'Institut de civilisation indienne 74. Paris: De Boccard, 2007.

—. "The Earliest Evidence for the Inborn Debts of a Brahmin: A New Interpretation of Ṛgveda X.135," *Journal Asiatique* 302/2 (2014): 245–257.

Kunhan Rāja, C. *The Ṛgvedānukramaṇī of Mādhavabhaṭṭa (Son of Veṅkaṭārya).* Madras University Sanskrit Series 2. Madras: University of Madras, 1932.

Lubotsky, Alexander. *A Ṛgvedic Word Concordance*, 2 vols. American Oriental Series 82, 83. New Haven, CT: American Oriental Society, 1997.

Macdonell, Arthur A. *The Bṛhaddevatā Attributed to Śunaka: A Summary of the Deities and Myths of the Ṛg-veda.* Harvard Oriental Series 5, 6. Cambridge, MA: Harvard University Press, 1904–1906.

—. *A Vedic Reader for Students.* London: Oxford University Press, 1917.

Malamoud, Charles. *Féminité de la parole: Études sur l'Inde ancienne.* Paris: Albin Michel, 2005.

—. *La danse des pierres.* Paris: Seuil, 2005.

—. "La nuit du temps: Le passage des jours d'après un rite et un mythe de l'Inde ancienne," *L'inactuel* 3 (1995): 45–53. Reprinted in Charles Malamoud, *Le jumeau solaire* (Paris: Seuil, 2002), pp. 55–65.

—. *Le jumeau solaire.* Paris: Seuil, 2002.

—. "Parole, mère plurielle. Observation sur le nombre de mères dans l'Inde ancienne," *Nouvelle Revue de Psychanalyse* 45 (1992): 199–216. Reprinted in Charles Malamoud, *Féminité de la parole: Études sur l'Inde ancienne* (Paris: Albin Michel, 2005), pp. 121–147.

—. "Yama, Yamī et les diverses manières de former une paire," in Samra Azarnouche and Céline Redard, eds., *Yama/Yima: Variations indo-iraniennes sur la geste mythique,* pp. 95–110. Paris: De Boccard, 2012.

Max-Müller, Friedrich. *Rig-Veda-Sanhita. The Sacred Hymns of the Brahmans together with the Commentary of Sāyaṇācharya.* London: Wim H. Hallen, 1849–1874.

Pinault, George-Jean. "Regard comparatif sur les âges de la vie dans le monde Gréco-romain et indien," in Christine Chojnacki, *Les âges de la vie dans le monde indien. Actes des journées d'études de Lyon (juin 2000),* pp. 15–30. Lyon: De Boccard (diff.), 2000.

Rāja, C. Kunhan. *The Ṛgvedānukramaṇī of Mādhavabhatta (son of Veṅkaṭārya).* Madras University Sanskrit Series, 2. Madras: University of Madras, 1932.

Renou, Louis. *Katha Upaniṣad.* Paris: A. Maisonneuve, 1943.

—. *Anthologie sanskrite.* Paris: Payot, 1947.

—. *Études védiques et pāṇinéennes,* 17 vols. Publications de l'Institut de civilisation indienne du Collège de France. Paris: De Boccard, 1955–1969.

—. *Hymnes spéculatifs du Véda. Traduits du sanskrit et annotés.* Paris: Gallimard/ UNESCO, 1956.

—. "La composition du dixième maṇḍala," in *Études védiques et pāṇinéennes,* vol. II, pp. 1–29. Paris: De Boccard, 1956.

—. *L'Inde fondamentale. Études d'indianisme réunies et présentées par Charles Malamoud.* Paris: La Découverte, 1978.

Renou, Louis, in collaboration with Lilian Silburn. "Sur la notion de bráhman," *Journal Asiatique* 237 (1949). Reprinted in Louis Renou, *L'Inde fondamentale: Études d'indianisme réunies et présentées par Charles Malamoud* (Paris: La Découverte, 1978), pp. 7–46.

Sarup, Laxman. *The Nighaṇṭu and the Nirukta: The Oldest Indian Treatise on Etymology, Philology, and Semantics* (1920–1926). Delhi: Motilal Banarsidass, 1967, reprint.

Sastri, A. M., ed. *The Taittirīya Brahmana, with the Commentary of Bhattabhaskaramisra,* 3 vols. Mysore Sanskrit Series 36, 57, 38. Mysore: Government Branch Press, 1908–1938.

Sparreboom, Max. *Chariots in the Veda.* Leiden: Brill, 1985.

Staal, Frits. *Discovering the Vedas: Origins, Mantras, Rituals, Insights.* New Delhi: Penguin Books, 2008.

—. "The Concept of Metalanguage and its Indian Background," *Journal of Indian Philosophy* 3 (1975): 315–354.

Velankar, H. D. "The Ṛgvedic Origin of the Story of Naciketas (ṚV X 135)," in *Mélanges d'indianisme à la mémoire de Louis Renou,* pp. 763–772. Publications de l'Institut de civilisation indienne 28. Paris: De Boccard, 1968.

Vishva Bandhu. *Ṛgveda: With the Padapāṭha and the Available Portions of the Bhāṣyas by Skandasvāmin and Udgītha, the Vyākhyā by Venkata-Mādhava, and Mudgala's Vṛtti based on Sāyaṇa-bhāṣya,* 7 vols. Vishveshvaranand Indological Series. Hoshiarpur: Vishveshvaranand Research Institute, 1963–1966.

Whitney, William Dwight, trans. *Atharva-Veda Saṃhitā,* 2 vols. Delhi: Motilal Banarsidass, 1962.

Melody, Mantra, and Meaninglessness: Toward a History of OM

Finnian M. M. Gerety
Department of Religious Studies,
Brown University

Perhaps no sound evokes the religions of South Asia as succinctly as the "sacred syllable" OM. For Hindu traditions, OM is a central and defining mantra that embodies in its single syllable the entire corpus of revealed texts, the Vedas, as well as the transcendent holism that undergirds all reality, *brahman*. The preeminence of the term OM was established quite early; already in the *Upaniṣad*s OM is central to Brahmanical theology and metaphysics, well on its way to becoming the epitome of mantra, yoga, and meditation in Classical Hinduism. But OM has an earlier history in Vedic texts and rituals, one that scholars have rarely addressed: Upaniṣadic OM is the crystallization of more than five centuries of ritual, recitation, and reflection. In the most ancient textual strata OM is one liturgical syllable among others, unindividuated and unremarkable, yet it emerges in later strata as the preeminent syllable of the Vedas, Classical Hinduism, and South Asian religions. How did this happen? How old is OM? When and where is it first attested? Why OM from among the thousands of other sounds in the Vedic liturgies?

Surprisingly, such questions about the world's most famous syllable have never been resolved—the complete story of OM remains to be written. This study explores a neglected but significant chapter of the history of the sacred syllable OM. Inspired by the work of Frits Staal, I argue that the Vedic tradition of liturgical song, *sāmaveda,* was integral to OM's early development. There is music in OM: the syllable emerges from melody and song.[1]

This study is divided into five sections. The first considers what Staal had to say about OM, from his ideas about the syllable's prehistory to his arguments about its place in Vedic ritual. The second section emphasizes the heuristic value of attending to *liturgical* OM, that is, OM as attested in mantras, recitation, and ritual, as opposed to its treatment in interpretive discourses. This approach is rooted in indigenous Vedic categories of text, which tend to separate liturgy from discourse, as well as in Staal's idea that ritual and meaning are distinct categories. The third and fourth sections are the heart of this study, presenting a comprehensive survey of OM in Sāmavedic traditions. These sections trace the oldest OMs in the Vedas and show how the syllable is put to use in the songs of the *soma* sacrifice. Finally, I conclude by reflecting on what my findings tell us about OM's history.

Frits Staal on OM

It comes as no surprise that Staal, who knew Vedic ritual traditions better than most, and who devoted considerable energy to theorizing the categories of mantra and ritual in a number of influential publications, gave some thought to the question of OM's significance, history, and place in the Vedic ritual system. He approached the syllable from two perspectives: first, as the signal instance of a prehistoric and universal pattern of human vocalization; second, as a ritual utterance historically connected with the Vedic tradition of liturgical song, *sāmaveda*.

Staal's ideas about OM's prehistory and universality are rooted in observations about the syllable's phonology.[2] He argues that OM is closely akin to breathing, the vocalization of breath passing from the back to the front of the mouth, followed by either the closure of the lips (*om*), the nasalization of the vowel (*oṃ, oṁ*), or a trailing off without closure (*o*). OM may therefore qualify as a "universal mantra," a vocalization occurring naturally before an infant acquires language. In the prelinguistic babbling stage the cries of an infant for food and affection bear a phonological resemblance to OM. In the famous formulation of the linguist Roman Jakobson, "the most natural order of sound production is an opening of the mouth followed by its closure."[3] Calling this "a very apt description of the mantra *oṃ*," Staal presses Jakobson's argument into service:

> The importance of *oṃ* and its priority to language is inherent in this scenario, which depicts how *oṃ* comes before *mama*, and *mama* before *papa* who introduces language.[4]

Staal argues for the priority of OM (and similar sounds) not only in the sense of preceding the acquisition of language by individual infants but also in the wider sense of preceding the origins of language in the human species. From this perspective OM is not only universal, it is also an "original mantra" and a signal instance of Staal's theory that mantras anticipate language in human evolution. In Staal's scheme of the prehistoric development of language, OM belongs to the earliest phase, which consists of meaningless monosyllabic "sounds subject to phonological constraints," and precedes the later phases when syntactic, and finally, semantic constraints are introduced.

> Let us assume that *oṃ* was an "original" mantra; that is, we assume it existed before language was born. Suppose that Pithecanthropus, for example, was humming *oṃ* but could not talk. Let us further assume that this *oṃ* reappeared in Sanskrit where it is now used in the manner mantras are used, e.g., preceding, following, or interspersed between chants and recitations, accompanying rites, meditation, etc. This *oṃ* is not used in the manner in which other words are used. . . .[5]

As such, OM exemplifies the phenomenon of "mantras-couched-in-language," whereby a primordial utterance from an earlier phase of human development persists or "reappears" and is integrated into verbal exchanges. For Staal, this explains how OM, like other mantras—which he considered as a category to be fundamentally nonlinguistic—comes to be enmeshed with verbal material. Thus we have *oṃ namo śivāya,* the combination of prelinguistic OM with a linguistic expression in a single Hindu mantra: "OM, homage to Śiva."[6] (Note that OM here also precedes the linguistic expression in syntactic terms.) According to Staal, OM is not the only original, universal mantra that survives atavistically in human utterances, it is just the most famous example of a broad group of nonlexical monosyllables that preceded language—*hi, ha, hay, o, ma, la,* and the like[7]—but remain embedded in archaic contexts, especially song and ritual. For India, he points to the Sāmavedic *stobha*s and Tantric *bīja*s as examples.

Another universal mantra according to Staal is the syllable *hiṃ* (with its variants *hiṅ, hṃ, hum*). This sound matches Jakobson's phonological criteria, while the aspiration can be explained as "an onomatopoeic representation of breathing" or of the wind.[8] Indeed, "the sound *hiṃ*" (*hiṃkāra*) is the earliest attested nonlexical monosyllable in the Vedic corpus: it appears in the "Riddle Hymn" of the *Ṛgveda Saṃhitā* (ṚV 1.164.41) to evoke the sound of a mother cow lowing as she suckles her calf. She is no ordinary cow, but rather the bovine embodiment of the goddess Vāc ("Voice"), whose streams of milk are the source of mantras and currents on which a primordial syllable floats.[9] *Akṣara,* the word for "syllable" in Vedic, simultaneously conveys a sense of "not flowing out" (*a* + *kṣar-*);

this syllable is inexhaustible, limitless, or "imperishable," as it is often translated. This primordial *akṣara* is integral to a tradition that ascribes infinite potency to ritual utterance and regards sound as the first principle of creation itself.[10] Staal insists that such passages are "not merely a matter of phenomenological, religious or spiritual metaphor" but rather literal assertions "that mantras are the predecessor of language in the process of human evolution."[11] While some have argued that the *akṣara* in this hymn must be an esoteric allusion to OM[12]—notwithstanding the fact that OM is not attested anywhere in the ṚV—the allusion may rather be to the sound *hiṃ*, which appears several times in the "Riddle Hymn." *Hiṃ* may be OM's precursor as "sacred syllable," an early embodiment of the same primordial themes that OM will come to represent.

While Staal's theory of the priority of mantras to language has not been accepted by Indologists and scholars of religion,[13] it has lately found support from an unexpected quarter. Steven Mithen, a prominent scholar on the origins of language, has popularized a scenario similar to Staal's, theorizing that a system of musical humming preceded linguistic utterance in Neanderthals and humans. Strikingly, the sound Mithen chooses as a rubric for his theory is *hmmmm.* Aside from being a nifty acronym for "holistic, multi-modal, manipulative, and musical,"[14] *hmmmm* is also phonetically very close to *hiṃ, hum,* and *oṃ,* Staal's "universal mantras." Mithen duly notes the parallels between his ideas on the origins of language and Staal's work on mantras.[15]

Moving away from OM's unattested prehistory, let's now consider how Staal addressed the syllable's attested history in the Vedas. The texts of the Vedic corpus, also known as *śruti*, "auditory revelation," codify an elaborate system of rituals known by the derivative term *śrauta.* In the preeminent *śrauta* ritual, the *soma* sacrifice, OM has more than 20 applications in distinct contexts, spanning the three liturgical Vedas: the *Ṛgveda,* the *Sāmaveda,* and the *Yajurveda.* OM is a way to say "yes" in priestly exchanges; it is an exclamation that marks the end of an utterance; it is an independent syllable that introduces mantras; and above all it is a "recitational modification" of existing mantras.[16] It takes on a range of forms, such as *om, oṃ, oṁ,* and *o,* that can be further modified depending on context. In short, as I argue elsewhere, OM in *śrauta* ritual performance does not correspond to a single form, liturgical context, or Veda; the chief characteristic of the syllable is its multiformity.[17]

And yet, rather than emphasize OM's multifariousness, Staal connects the syllable to Sāmavedic ritual performance in particular:

> The Yajur- and Samavedas are filled with ritual. Verse, phrases, bits, and pieces from the Rigveda, recur as *mantras*, formulas recited in the course of ritual performance in which form is more important than meaning. . . . The Samaveda turns verse into chants that are listed in their ritual sequence and introduce a great variety of meaningless sounds, especially long *o*'s, sometimes ending in *-m. One result is the famous mantra OM.*[18]

Sāmavedic singing weaves together lexical verses with a melody and nonlexical syllables (*stobhas*). The songs of the *Sāmaveda* do indeed contain a preponderance of long "*o*"s as *stobhas*, some of which end in *-m*. Staal suggests here that the mantra OM emerges as a "result" of this integrative praxis: OM is the recitational outcome of integrating meaningful language with meaningless sounds and melody.

The striking suggestion that OM in Vedic ritual emerges from the performance of liturgical song tracks with Staal's abiding interest in *stobhas*, the *Sāmaveda,* and nonlexical utterance. It seems apt that he would choose this Sāmavedic context, from among many others in Vedic ritual where OM figures prominently, as a window onto the syllable's history. Regrettably, however, he did not elaborate. As a gesture of my admiration for Staal's life's work, I now pick up the thread of his argument. What is the relation between OM and the *Sāmaveda*? Are there grounds for considering these musical uses of OM in the songs of the *Sāmaveda* as primary, or somehow more important than the others in the Ṛgvedic and Yajurvedic liturgies? And how might a consideration of OM within the parameters of the Sāmavedic liturgy inform a comprehensive "history of OM"?

Liturgical OM

In the following discussion I build on Staal's ideas about OM in the *Sāmaveda* with the aim of shedding light on OM's emergence in the Vedic corpus. In Vedic texts OM comes down to us in two currents, as a sound to be recited in ritual and as the topic of hermeneutic discourses about ritual. Accordingly, I conceive of OM's history in terms of *liturgical* OM, the syllable as it is attested in mantras and codified for ritual performance; and *discursive* OM, the syllable as it is interpreted and integrated into theological discussions. By maintaining this indigenous separation between liturgy and discourse we can better understand the contributions of each to OM's emergence. Ultimately, the ascendance of OM as a "sacred syllable" results from the constant interplay of both currents.[19]

This twofold division into liturgy and discourse does not apply only to the case of OM; rather, it stems from the arrangement of the Vedic corpus, which has liturgical sections and discursive ones, as a whole. Certain texts (*saṃhitās*, *śrauta sūtras*) isolate mantras, recitation, and praxis so as to accurately convey their intricacies, while other texts (*brāhmaṇas*, *āraṇyakas*, *upaniṣads*) take on the task of constructing meanings for the rites and their elements. Staal argues that the deliberate arrangement of the Vedic corpus in this fashion constitutes a veritable "theory of ritual" on the part of its composers: they understood liturgy and discourse as separate, albeit intertwined, categories. This reflects what he views as a fundamental disjuncture between the categories of ritual and meaning. Indeed, he credits the composers of one genre in particular, the *Śrauta Sūtras*, concise manuals of ritual, shorn of interpretation, as the inspiration for his own theory that ritual is "pure activity, without meaning or goal,"[20] and that mantras, as an element of ritual, also have no meaning.

Reading Staal against such a background is helpful, for it brings welcome nuance to his ideas about meaninglessness. Inspired by the Vedic texts he knew so well, Staal isolates ritual as a category unto itself, thereby revealing structures, syntax, and patterns of activity ignored by other scholars preoccupied with the rich tapestry of meanings that ritual evokes. Staal's method proved a boon for the study of Sāmavedic mantras in particular, which consist above all of "meaningless" elements: nonlexical vocables, melody, rhythm, tone, and patterns of alternation, repetition, substitution, and interpolation. The academy has tended to take Staal's invocation of "meaninglessness" as a reproach, but the Vedic treatment of ritual as an analytic category separate from meaning would teach us otherwise. In this frame, setting aside meaning is an efficacious division of labor and an invitation to deeper critical inquiry.

In the rest of this study I will follow Staal's lead, attending to liturgical OM exclusive of meaning. While the hermeneutic discourses that construct OM's meanings, found largely in the *Brāhmaṇas*, *Āraṇyakas*, and *Upaniṣads*, are tremendously important for understanding the religious development of the syllable, these discourses all take the ritual facts about OM as their point of departure. It is difficult to explain what OM means in the Vedas, whether etymologically or theologically, without taking stock of the ritual contexts in which it is employed.[21] To put it bluntly: *we cannot fully understand discursive OM without first taking the measure of liturgical OM.* This method in no way denies the syllable's meaningfulness; quite the opposite: by first attending to the structures and patterns of ritual and mantra on their own terms we are in a better position to understand OM's many meanings as constructed across a range of historical contexts.

What constitutes liturgical OM in the Vedic period, before it has been established as the "sacred syllable" of the *Upaniṣads*? What does it sound like? How can we locate it in the texts that have come down to us? A rich tradition of transmission and reception stands between us and the answers to these questions. OM has been made globally famous by post-Vedic religions in South Asia, especially Hinduism. In Hindu contexts the syllable has its own special sign (ॐ) that represents the sound *oṁ*. Since the Vedas were composed and transmitted orally and aurally there was no need for such a written sign in the Vedic period; however, later manuscripts and printed editions of Vedic texts, especially those that use *devanāgarī* script, do make use of this sign.[22] Other printed texts and translations into Western languages may represent OM in Roman script, using *om, oṃ,* or *oṁ* (the latter two represent the nasal sounds *anusvāra* and *anunāsika*).

Whatever the manner of representation, a key difficulty facing the historian of OM is to judge whether the syllable is an original part of the text from the time it was composed, or a post-Vedic insertion. When OM is given within the text as part of a mantra, such instances often represent authentically Vedic attestations of the syllable. In other cases OM may be a later insertion at the head of a work or chapter, influenced by the persistent, post-Vedic convention of beginning every sacred recitation with the syllable. Though sanctioned by tradition, such insertions are clearly anachronistic; they were not a part of text or practice during the time the Vedic corpus was composed. Although there is some textual evidence already in the late Vedic period for beginning personal daily recitation (*svādhyāya*) with an utterance of OM, the practice does not seem to have been generalized and codified until later.[23]

While the orthography adopted by scribes, scholars, and translators to represent OM may vary according to choice or circumstance, influenced by post-Vedic religious, orthographic, iconographic, or scholarly conventions,[24] it frequently masks authentic variations of OM in the oral source texts. The initial sound of the following word often determines whether we find *om, oṁ,* or *oṃ:* preceding a vowel, it is *om* (*óm índravantaḥ prácarata; Maitrāyaṇī Saṃhitā* 4.9.2); preceding other sounds, it is attested variously as *oṃ* or *oṁ* (*oṃ pratiṣṭha; Āpastamba Śrauta Sūtra* 3.20.8). To further complicate things, even when the sound is simply *o* and has no nasal at all, Vedic texts may still classify it under the rubric of OM. Discussions of the *praṇava* of ṚV recitation (e.g., *Kauṣītaki Brāhmaṇa* 11.5; *Śāṅkhāyana Śrauta Sūtra* 1.1.19–22) present *o* as the "pure" (*śuddha*) alternative to *om* ("with *m*," *makāra*). Similarly, the mantra called *āśrāvaṇa,* which has OM as its first term, is attested differently, even in the same text: with *o* (*ó śrāvaya;* MS 1.4.11), or with nasal (*óṁ śrāvaya;* MS 4.1.11). Such variations prompted at least one premodern debate about the preferred pronunciation of the sound, wherein the three variants *om, o,* and *oṁ* are considered (*Jaiminīya Upaniṣad Brāhmaṇa* 1.24.3).[25]

Further variations stem from the conventions for reciting or singing OM. Like other Vedic mantras, OM is connected to any of a number of "recitational practices"[26] that dictate its use in performance. For example, OM often undergoes *pluti,* the lengthening of a vowel to three morae (*mātrā*), represented by the numeral "3": *o*3*m, o*3*ṃ* (e.g., *ó*3*ṃ prátiṣṭha, Vājasaneyi Saṃhitā* 2.13).[27] Another example is the addition of OM to an existing mantra, where the syllable is embedded in the morphology of an underlying word so that it replaces one or more syllables. Consider the *praṇava,* the technique whereby OM is substituted in performance (but not attested in the source text itself) for the final syllable of certain Ṛgvedic verses: a verse ending in *jinvati* becomes, in recitation, *jinvato*3*m* (or *jinvato*3).[28] Other cases attest only the outcome of adding OM in recitation, while the unmodified mantra remains unattested: the mantra *śóṁsāvom* (*Aitareya Brāhmaṇa* 3.12.1) represents the completed transformation, using OM, of an underlying dual imperative (*śáṁsāva,* "let us both recite!").[29]

The manifold recitational practices involving OM point to a key difficulty in navigating the syllable's history. More often than not, OM is unattested in the source texts and only becomes evident through applying the rules of recitation laid out in the *Śrauta Sūtra*s. In this way, most instances of OM in *śrauta* ritual remain hidden, never surfacing in concordances and rarely discussed in the secondary literature. Active intervention on our part is required if we are to listen to OM's history: to make this history audible again we must reconstruct ritual performance on the basis of ancient models. This intervention takes two basic forms, best when judiciously combined in the manner pioneered by Staal: first, philological reconstruction based on the close study and comparison of texts; second, informed consultation with modern insiders, such as the Nampūtiri Brahmins of Kerala, who have maintained a faithful oral tradition.

In sum, the form of OM in mantras and ritual contexts is highly variable and remains in flux throughout the Vedic period. Aiming at a unitary sound with a "primary" or "original" form is like shooting at a moving target. There is still no consensus among Indologists as to whether *o, oṃ, oṁ,* or *om* is primary.[30] This multiformity poses a big challenge for the present investigation. Since the texts themselves accept considerable variation under the rubric of OM, what counts as OM in the Veda and what does not? How to circumscribe the liturgical evidence so that we can speak concretely about OM's history? My solution is to opt for inclusive, flexible criteria: if it sounds anything like the range of sounds above, or if a Vedic text classifies a sound with the technical terms associated with OM, I take it into consideration. As far as my own orthography is concerned, I stick to the attested variants when talking about specific examples. When discussing the syllable generally, however, I will continue using the form "OM" as a convenient way to represent the range of variations.

A comprehensive survey of OM in all three Vedic liturgies, the *Ṛgveda*, the *Yajurveda*, and the *Sāmaveda*, is beyond the scope of this article. In the following discussion I pursue Staal's insights by focusing on the Sāmavedic evidence alone.[31] My sources for liturgical OM are those sections of the Vedic corpus that compile and codify the rituals proper, i.e., the mantra sections of the *saṃhitās* (ca. 1000–800 B.C.E.) and the codifications of the *śrauta sūtras* (700–500 B.C.E.). Early on, the project of textualizing Vedic ritual focused on the "union" (*saṃhitā*) of all the mantras in sequence, grouped according to their use in specific rites; later this expanded to include step-by-step instructions, "threads" (*sūtra*) that teach how to recite the mantras and perform the rites. The *Saṃhitās* are the oldest, most authoritative texts in the Vedic corpus, the raw materials of recitation and ritual, while the *Śrauta Sūtras* are the blueprints for putting it all together in performance. Both are indispensable for understanding liturgical OM.

Like all Vedic texts, individual works in these genres were produced by Brahmin families and then transmitted through hereditary, localized lineages of pedagogy and performance, the schools or "branches" (*śākhā*) of the Vedic family tree.[32] While all draw on a shared ritual culture, the various branches preserve differences in praxis that are of great value for comparative study.

The Oldest OMs: Evidence from the *Saṃhitās*

What is the oldest attestation of OM? How is it used in the texts where it first appears? We now turn to the earliest textualizations of OM in the corpus, found in scattered mantras of the *Saṃhitās*. The passages discussed below are candidates for "oldest OM," according to *the texts that have been passed down*. The Vedic corpus as we know it is an accident of history, as many texts and even whole branches have been lost. So even if we are able to pinpoint the oldest OMs by comparing the testimony of the oldest extant texts, it does not follow that these mantras necessarily represent the "original" uses of the syllable, but only the oldest to which we have access.

OM in the *Sāmaveda Saṃhitā*s

The most ancient attestations of OM come in the *Saṃhitā*s of the *Sāmaveda* and the *Yajurveda*. Because these collections of mantras are stratified compilations, containing material from different times, it is difficult to date them with absolute certainty. The OMs we will discuss all appear in the "Village Songs" (*grāmegeyagāna*) and the "Wilderness Songs" (*araṇyegeyagāna*),[33] identified by Willem Caland as the archaic core of the SV corpus.[34] Michael Witzel has placed a proto-version of this core ("Ur-Sāmaveda Saṃhitā") before that of the oldest YV *Saṃhitā*s, ca. 1000 B.C.E.[35] Therefore, the relative dating of the strata of the Vedic corpus would suggest that the OMs in the SV are older than those in the YV. If this is true, then the SV *Saṃhitā*s furnish us with the oldest attested OMs in South Asia.

SV traditions come down to us in three branches: the *Kauthuma* and the *Rāṇāyanīya*, the recensions of which are nearly identical; and the *Jaiminīya*, which is somewhat different from the other two and probably contains the most archaic material.[36] The *Kauthuma-Rāṇāyanīya Saṃhitā* has been published in the Bibliotheca Indica (BI) edition of Satyavrata Sāmaśrami Bhaṭṭācārya. Because this edition employs two separate, overlapping systems of reference, I follow Willem Caland and Victor Henry and Asko Parpola in simply referring to the *Kauthuma* songs below by volume and page number.[37] For its part, the *Jaiminīya Saṃhitā* lacks a complete critical edition and must be cobbled together from a range of sources, including printed publications, manuscripts, and oral testimony.[38] Following Staal and Parpola,[39] I adopt the "Kerala" system of reference, which is based on the numbering of songs and melodies transmitted in the oral and manuscript traditions of the Nampūtiri Jaiminīyas.

OM as *Stobha* in the Sāmavedic *Gānas*

In the songs of the SV *Saṃhitā*s OM shows up as a nonlexical vocable, a sound without semantic meaning, much like hundreds of other such sounds found in these songs. The SV *Saṃhitā*s are made up of melodies (*sāman*) and verses (*ṛk*) presented in various formats.[40] To form the songs (*gāna*), the words from the verse sections (*ārcika*) were combined with the melodies and interpolated with various syllables (*stobha*). In some cases, these interpolations are nonlexical, although in other cases they are permutations of words, fragments, or sentences. The *gāna*s have been textualized with *stobha*s already embedded; thus, the *stobha*s are an integral part of the text of the song.[41] For clarity, I refer to these song texts, which consist of verses adapted to the melody by means of the added *stobha*s, as "lyrics."

Open up a page of the *gāna*s at random and you will find *stobha*s repeated on page after page: *hā bu, hā u, hoyi, e,* etc. Also common is *o,* often paired with other syllables, especially *vā*, e.g., *o vā o vā.* Later texts seem to suggest that in certain contexts, the Sāmavedic *o* is understood as a variant of OM.[43] In any event, the frequency of pure *o* as a *stobha* renders a survey of that sound in the SV *Saṃhitā*s unfeasible; suffice it to say that *o* appears again and again. By comparison, *om* and its nasal variants (*oṁ, oṃ*) are among the rarest of *stobha*s, seldom encountered in these texts.[43] For the SV *Saṃhitā*s I focus mostly on these variants of OM, although pure *o* sometimes enters into the discussion.

Richard Simon has discussed OM in the "Village Songs" of the *Kauthuma-Rāṇāyanīya*s (KGG), counting twenty-three cases where OM appears in the initial position of the lyric. The majority of these cases occur at a text division, usually in the first *sāman* in a new chapter, while the corresponding cases in the "Village Songs" of the *Jaiminīya*s (JGG) lack OM. These facts suggest that the initial OM may have been added to the KGG during transmission as a reflex of the post-Vedic practice of beginning recitations and chapters with OM. If this is the case, many of the OMs counted by Simon are anachronistic insertions without any bearing on the Vedic material.[44]

Simon has also observed that when *om* occurs in the non-initial position in the *Kauthuma* "Village" songs, it is always in collocation with the *stobha*s *o vā*, as in this example (BI II: 3):

> *uccātejā / tam dhāsāḥ / om ovā / divisadbhū / miyādā de / om o vā / ugrāṁ śā rmā / om o vā/ mā hā auhovā / śravāi //*

The parallel *Jaiminīya* lyric is nearly identical (JGG 49.1). *Om* in these lyrics resembles other *stobha*s: it punctuates the underlying verse.[45] Consider an adjacent lyric that transforms the same base text in a different way:

> . . . *ugraṁ śā rmā / om o / mahovā / śrā vo hāi //* (KGG = BI II, 3)
> . . . *u graṁ śā rmā / oṃ oṃ ma ho vā śrā vo hā i //* (JGG 49.1)

In spite of some variations in representations of the nasal (*oṃ, om*) and in syllable- and "segment"- (*parvan,* represented by slashes) breaks, the above pair of lyrics is closely parallel and, in phonetic terms, nearly identical. As in the previous example, OM is non-initial, repeated, and collocated with other sounds (among these *o vā*, as Simon observed).[46]

Turning now to the "Wilderness Songs" of the *Kauthuma-Rāṇāyanīyas* (KAG) and the *Jaiminīyas* (JAG), in many of these esoteric songs the lyrics consist entirely of *stobhas* and have no relation to Ṛgvedic verses. Bearing in mind the collocation of *om* and *o vā* already noted, consider a similar sequence where the word *vāk* ("voice, speech") takes the place of the nonlexical syllable *vā* and the word *āyus* ("life") serves as finale. A pair of *sāmans* twice attests the sequence (KAG = BI II, 470–471):

> *hāu / hā / o vāk / (triḥ) / om / om / hā / o vāk / e āyuḥ. . .*[47]

The *Jaiminīya* text is longer but similar (JAG 4.9):

> *hā bu hā bu hā bu hā o vāk hā o vāk hā o vāk / oṃ oṃ oṃ oṃ oṃ oṃ / hā o vāk hā o vāk hā o vāg āyur āyur āyur e āyur e āyur e āyuḥ. . .*

In the next example, OM is attested in the initial position, introducing lyrics made up of the *stobhas o vā, jyotis* ("light"), and *āyus* ("life"), among others (JAG 7.4):

> *oṃ oṃ oṃ āyūr āyūr jyotir jyotir jyotiḥ jyotovā jyotovā jyotovā jytovāhāyi jyotovāhāyi jyotovāhāvuvā. . .*[48]

The *Kauthuma* lyric is almost identical, likewise beginning with three repetitions of *om* (KAG = BI II, 505). As noted above, this initial position calls to mind the post-Vedic convention of beginning a recitation with OM. However, the fact that the present example is attested not just in the *Kauthuma* lyric but also in the more archaic *Jaiminīya* text suggests an authentic Vedic provenance.

Another group of OMs comes in the last 17 songs of the *Jaiminīya* "Wilderness Songs." Each of the songs in the series is built on a single word that introduces the lyric. The final syllable of each introductory word is replaced with *-om;* the word is then repeated three times without *om* and combined with *stobhas*. Thus, for example, using the word *satya* ("truth") (JAG 25.24):[49]

> *satyoṃ / satya ho yi satya ho yi satya hā ā vu vā / e suvar jyotiḥ //*

All 17 *sāmans* are formed with this same pattern, using the same *stobhas*. The introductory words vary but always refer to cosmological or divine entities. None of the *sāmans* is based on a *ṛk;* these songs are composed entirely of *stobhas*, some lexical and some not.

I want to pay closer attention to the sound patterns that occur regularly in these Sāmavedic lyrics with OM. Recall Simon's observation that OM within the lyric of these songs almost always occurs in collocation with *o vā*. Examining our examples more closely, it seems that the collocation *om . . . o vā* noticed by Simon is actually part of a larger pattern that includes other syllables, such as *mā, hā, au, ho, ma,* or *ho.* (Incidentally, these *stobhas* would seem to satisfy Staal's criteria for "universal" and "original" mantras: monosyllables formed by the simple opening and closing of the mouth, sometimes with aspiration). Our examples of OM in the "Village Songs" all contain these *stobhas*, varying only in their repetition and manner of distribution. Omitting the intervening words, we have:

om o vā (x 3) . . . *mā hā auhovā* (KGG = BI II, 3; JGG 49.1)
om o / mahovā (KGG = BI II, 3)
oṃ oṃ ma ho vā (JGG 49.1)

Turning to the "Wilderness Songs," we find that the same pattern holds, with several new variations: the substitution of *vāk* for *vā;* the frequent interpolation of the words *āyus* ("life"), *jyotis* ("light"), and *suvar* ("heaven"); and the addition of *e* before the finale:

hāu hā o vāk (x 3) *om* (x 2) *hā o vāk e āyuḥ* (KAG = BI II, 470–471)
hā o vāk (x 3) / *oṃ* (x 6) / *hā o vāk* (x 3) *āyur* (x 3) *e āyur* (x 3) (JAG 4.9)
oṃ (x 3) *āyur* (x 2) *jyotih* (x 3) . . . *jyotovā* (x 3) . . . *jyotovā hā yi* (x 2) . . . *jyotovā hā vu vā* (KAG = BI II, 505; JAG 7.4)

The same holds true for the special group of 17 *Jaiminīya* songs:

. . . *oṃ* . . . *hā ā vu vā / ē suvar jyotiḥ* (JAG 24.25)

Based on these recurring patterns and collocations of *stobhas* it would seem that we are dealing with variations on a traditional refrain of some kind. The simpler versions in the "Village Songs" are elaborated and transformed in the "Wilderness Songs," even as they retain the same basic structure. OM in the SV *Saṃhitās* is consistently associated with this refrain, which, like a jazz riff or a classical leitmotif, remains stable even as it serves as the basis for ornamentation and augmentation.[50]

So what does it mean to uncover such collocations and patterns associated with the oldest OMs? In the SV *Saṃhitās* we have direct attestations of OM in song lyrics but no indication of a synchronic ritual context to further guide our interpretation. It is difficult to say how these songs with OM were used in the liturgies of their time. However, an important clue for understanding OM's Sāmavedic background comes, somewhat unexpectedly, in the oldest *Saṃhitā* of the Black *Yajurveda.* The *Maitrāyaṇī Saṃhitā* attests a number of mantras that feature OM, one of which is in a Sāmavedic style (MS 4.9.21):[51]

> *nidhā́yo vā́3 nidhā́yo vā́3 nidhā́yo vā́3 oṃ vā́3 oṃ vā́3 oṃ vā́3 e ai oṃ svárṇa-jyotiḥ //*

A. A. MacDonell commented on the repetition of OM and other "unintelligible interjections" in this YV mantra but did not note the resemblance to the Sāmavedic *stobhas*.[52] Presented more schematically, the similarities of this example to the patterns in the "Wilderness Songs" become evident, notably the recurrence of *hā, o vā, oṃ vā, e, s(u)var,* and *jyotiḥ:*

> . . . *hāyo vā* (x 3) *oṃ vā* (x 3) *e ai svarṇajyotiḥ*

I suggest that we have encountered here a Yajurvedic elaboration of the same pattern found in the SV *Saṃhitās*. The MS also helps us hone in on the ritual context, for this mantra appears in a group of mantras belonging to the *pravargya* rite.

A further clue comes in the later *Kaṭha Āraṇyaka* of the Black *Yajurveda,* where fragments of a nearly identical lyric appear, identified by Witzel as a *sāman* sung by the *adhvaryu* at the *pravargya* (KĀ 2.230–231):[53]

> *nídhāyy óvā́ nídhā́yy óvéti vái sā́mnó* [*dgāyati* . . .] *é svàr jyótī3r ít*[*i*].

> "He is set down, *ovā;* he is set down, *ovā.*" . . . [He sings] "*e* heaven light."

The KĀ finale *e svar jyotī3r* brings the lyric even closer to the Sāmavedic "Wilderness Songs." Crucially, KĀ identifies this *sāman* as one of several "unexpressed praise-songs" (*aniruktās stutaya*s) that permit the sacrificer to reach the light of heaven, the sun. This identification suggests that this Yajurvedic lyric is among the earliest identifiable examples of "unexpressed song" (*aniruktagāna*), a style of singing of great moment for the subsequent Sāmavedic history of OM. Another variant of this mantra is found in *Taittirīya Āraṇyaka* 4.40, where it is similarly identified as a *sāman* at the *pravargya.*[54]

I now draw a few preliminary conclusions based on this survey of liturgical OM in the SV *Saṃhitās*. The evidence suggests these ancient musical texts furnish us with the oldest attested OMs in the Veda, and therefore in South Asian religions. This points to the importance of melody in OM's early history: the oldest OMs were not simply recited but sung. In the lyrics of Sāmavedic songs, these oldest OMs are non-lexical vocables, known by the technical name *stobha;* as such, they are meaningless, in the narrow sense of conveying no semantic information. OM in the SV *Saṃhitās* is consistently found in collocation with specific *stobhas*, forming a range of recognizable patterns. The recurrence of the pairing *o(ṃ) vā* in collocation with the ending *s(u)var jyotiḥ* suggests a connection between the OM songs of the SV *Saṃhitās* and certain mantras in a Sāmavedic style found in the YV *Saṃhitās* and later texts. The Yajurvedic sources identify these mantras with OM as "unexpressed," thereby suggesting a further connection with "unexpressed song" (*aniruktagāna*), a style of singing central to next chapter of liturgical OM's Sāmavedic history, as will be discussed below.

OM in Performance: Evidence from the *Śrauta Sūtras*

Having surveyed the oldest instances of OM in the songs of the SV *Saṃhitās*, we now fast forward several centuries to the descriptions of praxis in later texts, especially the systematic codifications of the *Śrauta Sūtras*. With step-by-step guidelines for performing SV in the *soma* sacrifice, these primary texts (along with Caland and Henry's masterful synopsis based on them[55]) give us a much more complete sense of OM in the Sāmavedic liturgy (*audgātram*) than was possible from the fragmentary evidence of the *Saṃhitās*. In certain cases it is necessary to consult additional sources, including other Vedic texts, later ritual manuals (*prayoga*), and the oral testimony of modern singers.

I mostly restrict my discussion to the paradigmatic form of the *soma* sacrifice, the *agniṣṭoma* ("praise of Agni"). The *soma* sacrifice is a set of rites organized around the basic act of pressing, filtering, and drinking the juice of the plant called *soma*. The three pressings of *soma* (morning, midday, and "third") take place on a single day and make up the climactic finale of the multiday sacrifice that is performed for the benefit of a patron, the *yajamāna*, and superintended by the *adhvaryu* priest of the YV. The pressing day features the chanting of elaborate suites of mantras: "praise-songs" (*stuti, stotra*) by the *udgātṛ* and other Sāmavedic priests, and "recitations" (*śastra*) by the *hotṛ* and other Ṛgvedic priests. These two types of chants alternate throughout the day, with five of each in the morning, five at midday, and two in the third service, for a total of 12 of each type.

OM in the SV *Stotra*

The uses of OM in the Sāmavedic liturgy cluster around the *stotras*, sung by a trio of singers led by the *udgātṛ*. An individual *stotra* is made up of repetitions called *stotriyās*, each formed from the union of a specified melody (*sāman*) with verses (*ṛk*). The number of repetitions is fixed for each *stotra*. Most *stotra*s use the same melody throughout all repetitions, although some use several melodies. A *stotriyā* is further divisible into five portions, each of which is sung by one or more of the three principal SV singers: the *prastāva* by the *prastotṛ*, the *udgītha* by the *udgātṛ*, the *pratihāra* by the *pratihartṛ*, the *upadrava* by the *udgātṛ*, and the *nidhana* by the trio together. The fivefold division is expanded to seven in performance by the addition of the *hiṃkāra* sung by all together before certain *prastāva*s, and the *ādi*, the insertion of OM before the *udgītha*.[56]

The most significant attestations of OM occur in the *stotra*s set to the *gāyatra* melody, especially those sung in the "unexpressed" (*anirukta*) style. However, the *gāyatra* is scarcely treated in the *Saṃhitā*s and *Śrauta Sūtra*s of SV,[57] a fact that Asko Parpola, in a personal communication, explained as a function of the extreme secrecy surrounding the melody. Tellingly, as will be seen below, the most sustained treatment of the ritual performance of the *gāyatra-sāman* comes in an esoteric Sāmavedic text in the style of the *Āraṇyaka*s and early *Upaniṣad*s.

Prastāva

The "prelude" (*prastāva*), whenever it is sung to the *gāyatra* melody, has *-om* in place of the final syllable of the underlying verse. *Prastāva*s with OM therefore correspond to all occurrences of the *gāyatra* in the *soma* sacrifice: that is, OM occurs as the final syllable of the preludes in all five *stotra*s of the morning service (1–5), and in the first three repetitions of the *pavamānastotra*s in the midday and third services (6, 11).[58] According to the codifications of the *Kauthuma-Rāṇāyanīya*s as reconstructed by Caland,[59] the first *ājyastotra* features three *prastāva*s, all ending in *-om* (lyrics from CH §155):

> *agna āyāhi vītayom* /. . .
> *taṃ tvā samidbhir aṅgirom* /. . .
> *sa naḥ pṛthuśravāyiyom* /. . .[60]

Staal, on the basis of the testimony of modern Nampūtiri singers, provides the corresponding *Jaiminīya* lyrics,[62] which also end in *-om*.

Ādi and *Udgītha*

As the *prastotṛ* finishes the prelude, the *udgātṛ* begins his *udgītha* by singing OM, an addition to the lyric that applies to all *stotra*s regardless of melody. Consider the second *pṛṣṭhastotra*, sung to the *vāmadevya* melody in the manner of the *Kauthuma-Rāṇāyanīya*s (lyrics from CH §203):

om ū tī sadāvṛdhaḥ sa khā au ho hā yi kayā śacāyi . . .[62]

This introduction of the *udgītha* with OM is known as the *ādānam*, "taking up," or the *ādi*, "beginning."[63] Adding OM in this manner is strictly a recitational practice; though never recorded in SV *Saṃhitā*s it is codified in the *Śrauta Sūtra*s of the *Kauthuma-Rāṇāyanīya*s. According to these texts, the basic form of this practice involves the addition of *om* to precede the first syllable of the *udgītha* (*Lāṭyāyana Śrauta Sūtra* 6.10.13); other options include replacing the first syllable entirely with *om*, or replacing it only when it begins with a vowel (LŚS 6.10.14–17).[64] For their part, the *Jaiminīya*s refer to the *ādi* in their *Brāhmaṇa* and *Upaniṣad* but seem not to have codified its performance uniformly; thus it is difficult to say exactly how the *Jaiminīya ādi* was performed.[65] It is clear enough, however, that the *Jaiminīya*s and *Kauthuma*s alike regard the *ādi* as generally referring to the use of OM at the start of the *udgītha*, although there are variants mentioned in specific contexts (e.g., *oṃ vāk* in the *rathaṃtarastotra;* see below).

Aniruktagāna

In the performance of many *stotra*s the lyrics are further transformed. I now take up "unexpressed song" (*aniruktagāna*), the style of singing noted above with reference to its antecedents in the YV and SV *Saṃhitā*s. In *aniruktagāna* the *prastāva* is sung as usual, but the lyrics of other portions are partly or wholly replaced by monosyllables such as *o, om, vā, hum,* and *bhā*. According to a *Brāhmaṇa* of the *Kauthuma-Rāṇāyanīya*s (PB 7.1.8), all *stotra*s sung to the *gāyatra* melody must be performed this way, a pronouncement borne out by the testimony of later authorities (CH §134g n38).

By way of example, consider the *bahiṣpavamānastotra,* which is made up of nine repetitions sung to the *gāyatra* melody. The Ṛgvedic source verse for the second repetition runs (ṚV 9.11.3):[66]

sá naḥ pavasva śáṃ gáve śáṃ jánāya śám árvate /
śáṃ rājann óṣadhībhiyaḥ //

"Purify yourself as weal for our cow, weal for our people, weal for our charger, weal for our plants, O king."

Let's explore how this text is transformed into unexpressed form, guided by a *Śrauta Sūtra* of the *Kauthuma-Rāṇāyanīya*s (LŚS 7.10.15–20). The *prastotṛ* sings his *prastāva* in the usual fashion, setting the first eight syllables to the melody, with text unchanged save for the substitution of *-om* over its last syllable: *sa naḥ pavasva śaṃ gavom.*[67] Next, the *udgātṛ,* taking up his portion with the customary *ādi* (*om*), sings the remainder, even those portions usually handled by the other singers. The *Śrauta Sūtra* teaches that he should approach his part in two ways, silently and audibly. "Mentally" (*manasā;* LŚS 7.10.20)—that is, in silence—he runs through the text in its "expressed" or "versified" form, known by the technical terms *nirukta-* or *ārcikagāna* (lyrics from CH §134g):

> *udgītha: oṁ śā2ṃ jā2nā2ya śam arvātāyi śaṁ rājā1 no2 ṣādhā*1212 /
> *pratihāra: hum ā* /
> *upadrava: bhāyo* /
> *nidhana: suvā*345*ḥ* //

Out loud, however, he sings in the unexpressed style, which entails replacing all the syllables of the *udgītha* with yet more OMs. While the *Śrauta Sūtra* speaks here of "the sound *om*" (*oṃkāra;* LŚS 7.10.20), the detailed testimony of the later authorities suggests that specifically the non-nasal form (*o*) is intended. These *o* sounds correspond exactly to the syllables in the underlying verse, which the singer is in the process of playing back in his mind. His audible singing runs as follows:[68]

> *udgītha: om o*2 *o*2 *o*2 *o o o o o o o o*1 *o*2 *o o*1212 /
> *pratihāra: hum ā* /
> *upadrava: o o* /
> *nidhana: ā* 345 //

The *udgātṛ*'s mentalization has its counterpart in the participation of the silent *pratihartṛ,* who is enjoined not to sing his portion (*pratihāra*) out loud but simply to contemplate it mentally (LŚS 7.11.4). The numerals within the lyrics in this example are part of a complex notational system found in *Kauthuma-Rāṇāyanīya* manuscripts, which also includes superscript numerals (not reproduced here). These superscript and in-line characters interact to convey aspects of melody and rhythm.[69] Note that the distribution of the in-line numbers remains consistent in both the expressed and unexpressed versions; by orienting ourselves with these it is clear that there is a one-to-one replacement of each syllable with an *o* sound.

The *Jaiminīya* teachings about the unexpressed *gāyatra* melody are not found in its *Śrauta Sūtra,* where we would expect them; rather, the *Jaiminīya Śrauta Sūtra* defers to the authority of the *Jaiminīya Upaniṣad Brāhmaṇa,* so this is the source we will follow.[70] Assume the same source verse and *stotra* as a starting point. As among the *Kauthuma*s, the *prastotṛ* sings his prelude and the *udgātṛ* sings the unexpressed portions alone in one breath, without help from the other singers (JUB 3.12.3; 3.13.8; 3.3.1).[71]

After the *prastāva,* which is identical in both branches, the unexpressed portion takes a very different form in *Jaiminīya* texts (e.g., JUB 1.2.3):

o vā o vā o vā / hum bhā / o vā //

The *Jaiminīya* version also lacks the conventional division into portions: instead of four, as would be expected after the *prastāva,* it has three, as above (also sometimes given as one undifferentiated whole).[72] The *Jaiminīya* version also lacks the *ādi* (*om*) at the beginning of the *udgītha.* And whereas the *Kauthuma* unexpressed version corresponds to the phrasing of the source verse, the *Jaiminīya* unexpressed *gāyatra* does not.[73] This *Jaiminīya* version of the *sāman,* because it lacks the "body" of the lexical verse, is known as "the bodiless melody" (*aśariraṁ sāma,* JUB 3.29–31).[74]

This lyric (*o vā o vā o vā hum bhā o vā*), in various permutations and in fragments, is an important locus for hermeneutic reflection in *Jaiminīya* circles. In particular, the syllables *o vā,* along with the variants *o vā3c* (1.2.1), *o3 vā3* (1.3.1), *oṁ vā* (4.8.9), and *oṁ vā3c* (4.8.9), are interpreted as cryptic renderings of OM and Vāc, the goddess "Voice."[75] The continuing prominence of these syllables recalls the early evidence of the SV *Saṃhitā*s, where collocations such as *oṃ vā, o vā,* and *om o vā* are frequently encountered. Moreover, it recalls the early attestation of OM in the YV, *oṃ vā* (MS 4.9.21), as part of a lyric grouped with "unexpressed praise-songs" (*aniruktās stutaya*s, KĀ 2.231–232). It seems possible that Sāmavedic and Yajurvedic lyrics with *o*(*m*) *vā* represent early parallels for the unexpressed *gāyatra* of the *Jaiminīya*s.

My discussion of *aniruktagāna* has concentrated on those *stotra*s sung to the *gāyatra* melody, with its characteristic forms: the replacement of verse syllables by *o* sounds among the *Kauthuma*s, and the replacing of the entire verse by *o vā o vā o vā. . .* among the *Jaiminīya*s. But *aniruktagāna* applies in the singing of *stotra*s with other melodies, the precise forms of which are difficult to describe, since we lack unambiguous codifications and examples from Vedic texts.[76] One well attested form is the *pṛṣṭhastotra* sung to the *rathaṃtara* melody. Consider the first repetition of this song according to the *Kauthuma-Rāṇāyanīya*s (the unmodified text is lined up below for reference; lyrics from CH §199):[77]

prastāva: hum / ābhi tvā śūra nonumo vā /
udgītha: oṃ vāg bhābhubhābhibhabhebhabhabhībhābhabhabhabhabhabhaḥ
(*ārcikagāna: ādugdhā iva dhenavaḥ īśānam asya jágataḥ*)

The signature of this type of *aniruktagāna* is the "*bha-* sound" (*bhakāra*); the long unexpressed sequence of the *udgītha* is formed by substituting *bh-* for the consonants and adding *bh-* to the vowel-initial syllables of the underlying verse, which the *udgātṛ* chants mentally.[78] The astonishing sequence that he sings out loud as the *udgītha* inspired Barend Faddegon to coin a term cherished by Staal, "ritualistic dadaism."[79]

A feature of *aniruktagāna* evident in our examples is the coalescence of the final syllable of the *prastāva* and the initial syllable of the *udgītha.* In this iteration of the *rathaṃtara* melody the *prastāva* ends with the substitution *o vā,* while the *ādi* of the *udgītha* is *oṃ vāk;* compare iterations of the *gāyatra* melody, where the *prastāva* ends with *-om* and the *udgītha* begins with OM (see above). In this way the transition from one portion to another, and from one singer to another, is bridged by a sequence of similar syllables, either *o vā* > *oṃ vāk* or *-om* > OM. Some authorities even teach that the parts of the two singers must overlap, as one ends and the other begins, suggesting that OM helps achieve a continuity of sound in performance. This continuous flow of sound may have inspired one name for the *anirukta-gāyatra-sāman* in *Jaiminīya* texts, the "endless melody" (*anantaṃ sāma,* JUB 1.35.7–8).[80]

Upagāna

At all the *stotras* sung throughout the day (*Drāhyāyana Śrauta Sūtra* 3.4.1), back-up singers (*upagātāraḥ*) provide accompaniment (*upagāna*), intoning OM and other syllables over and over at a low pitch (*mandra,* LŚS 1.11.24; *nigīta,* JŚS 1.11).[81] The back-up singers may number three, four, six, or more; the *yajamāna* participates, along with other priests, excluding the *adhvaryu* and the *hotṛ.*[82] The precise form of the accompaniment varies. According to one *Kauthuma-Rāṇāyanīya* source (DŚS 3.4.6), the back-up singers sing *ho* and the *yajamāna* sings *om;* another source has the reverse (*Bhāradvāja Śrauta Sūtra* 13.17.9). The *Jaiminīya* authorities consider several options (JUB 1.24.3), deciding in favor of *o* drawn out for 14 beats.[83] One text explains that the function of these back-up singers is to cover the gaps between the portions of the *stotra*—that is, to create a continuous flow of sound pausing only at each verse finale (DŚS 3.4.7–10; LŚS 1.11.26 says that the back-up singers should sing over the gaps but remain silent during the unison parts of the main singers).[84]

Pause to imagine this soundscape: the main singers together begin each round of a given *stotra* with hum, the *prastotṛ* often ends the *prastāva* with *-om,* the *udgātṛ* frequently introduces the *udgītha* with OM and substitutes OM sounds for many of its syllables, and at least four back-up singers continuously sing *ho* and *om*—it all adds up to a chorus of rounded-mouth vowels and nasals, projecting a veritable wall of sound.

OM Beyond the SV *Stotras*

While the *stotras* provide an unparalleled density of OMs, there are several other Sāmavedic contexts for liturgical OM in the *soma* sacrifice.

Viśvarūpagāna and *Jyotirgāna*

At his own discretion, the *udgātṛ* may sing a solo repertoire during the predawn hours of the pressing day. Set to the *gāyatra* melody, these solos attest the features I have already noted for the *gāyatra* in the *stotras*: substitution of *-om* for the eighth syllable (analogous to the final syllable of the *prastāva*) and the application of *aniruktagāna* with OM. The solo called "song of all forms" (*viśvarūpagāna*) praises the goddess Vāc (Voice) and her omniform creative potency. According to the *Kauthuma-Rāṇāyanīyas*, this song begins with an *-om* substitution at the end of the first phrase (*yuñje vācam śatapadom*) and proceeds in unexpressed style, with the *yajamāna* following along mentally (CH §120, BI V: 336; LŚS 1.8.9, DŚS 2.4.11–12).[85] The same sources teach that the "song of all forms" must be followed by the "song of the lights" (*jyotirgāna;* LŚS1.8.13–16, DŚS 2.4.17–24).[86] Each repetition of *jyotirgana* begins with an eight-syllable sequence of repeated paired words arranged in a chiasmus, with *-om* substituting for the final syllable. The central pair is "light" (*jyotis*); the framing pairs are Agni, Indra, and Sūrya (lyrics from CH §132e; cf. BI V, 337):

agnir jyotir jyotir agnom. . .
indro jyotir jyoir indrom. . .
sūryo jyotir jyotiḥ sūryom. . .

For their part, the *Jaiminīyas* resist the singing of the *viśvarūpa,* objecting that it constitutes a "thirteenth *stotra,*" and as such disrupts the numerical balance of the twelve *stotras*, whose 190 *stotriyās* are evenly divisible by ten (JŚS 1.8.6). (Perhaps for this reason, the *Jaiminīya* codification of *viśvarūpagāna* mentions only that the *udgātṛ* "utters" [*āha;* JŚS 1.8.15] the verses and does not necessarily sing them.) As for *jyotirgāna,* JS does not attest the verses of "the lights," nor does JŚS address the practice.

Subrahmaṇyā

The fourth Sāmavedic officiant, the *subrahmaṇya,* does not sing any of the *stotras*. He takes his name from his chief task, which is to proclaim the "call for *subrahmaṇyā*" (*subrahmaṇyāhvānam;* JŚS 1.3) on the days leading up to the climactic pressing day: *subrahmaṇyom!* The call has several variants across branches both in its form (ending *-oṃ, -o3m, -o3ṃ*) and in the number of repetitions.[87] Several texts agree that *subrahmaṇyā* ("with a fine formulation") is an epithet of the goddess Vāc (Voice) (JB 2.78; AB 6.3). The *subrahmaṇya* priest first delivers his call during the procession of the *soma* after its purchase (LŚS 1.2.20; DŚS 1.2.27); according to the *Jaiminīyas*, in this iteration the call is "unexpressed" (*anirukta*), in the sense of not being addressed to specific deities besides Vāc (JŚS 1.3.2). On most other occasions, the call is "expressed" (*nirukta*) in the name of Indra: immediately after the call, the *subrahmaṇya* recites a litany describing that god's exploits and inviting him along with other "gods and Brahmins" to the sacrifice (e.g., JŚS 1.3.14; LŚS 1.3.1a; DŚS 1.3.2;[88] CH §49). Morphologically, *subrahmaṇyom* could result from an exceptional *sandhi:*[89] the independent syllable *om* would combine with the final *-ā* of *subrahmaṇyā* to yield the present form.[90] But the form can also be analyzed as the substitution of *-o*(3)*m* for the final syllable,[91] a practice observed elsewhere in SV singing, as in our next example.

Vyāhṛtisāmans

Although I have largely restricted myself in this study to the paradigmatic *soma* sacrifice, I conclude this survey of OM in the Sāmavedic liturgies with a brief excursus beyond the basic paradigm. I now take up an elaboration of the *soma* sacrifice called the *agnicayana*, the ritual of "building the fire altar" that was the focal point of Staal's decades of work on Vedic ritual. According to the *Jaiminīya* tradition, the foundation, building, and consecration of the altar are accompanied by a lengthy selection of solo *sāmans* sung by the *udgātṛ*. Seventeen of these are the "melodies of utterances" (*vyāhṛtisāmans*), the lyrics of which follow the set pattern of beginning with a cosmological term with *-om* substituted for the final syllable: *sūryom* ("sun"), *candrom* ("moon"), *nākom* ("vault of the sky"), and so on. None of these *sāmans* has a Ṛgvedic source verse; they are composed entirely of *stobhas*.[92]

Of the 17 *vyāhṛtisāmans*, five have the additional similarity of "ending with *svar jyotiḥ*" (*svarjyotirnidhanāni;* JŚS).[93] While I have briefly discussed these melodies and lyrics above in my exploration of the SV *Saṃhitās*, by revisiting them now we can fill in further details as to their form and liturgical context. Five different objects are deposited under and on top of the bricks of the altar during its construction. Corresponding to each object is one of these five *sāmans*.[94] For instance, when the "golden man" (*hiraṇmayapuruṣa*) is deposited in the ground below where the altar will be, the *udgātṛ* sings a variation on the word "man"[95] (*puruṣa*):

puruṣom / puruṣa ho yi puruṣa ho yi puruṣa hā a vu vā/ ē suvar jyotiḥ //

When a golden breastplate (*rukma*) is deposited, the source word is "truth" (*satya*).[96] The remaining source words are the three cosmological terms of the *vyāhṛti* mantra, *bhūr bhuvas suvar* ("earth, atmosphere, heaven"; hence the name of the entire group). These three come in sequence, corresponding to placing of pebbles on the lowest ("earth"), middle ("atmosphere"), and top ("sky") layers of the five-tiered altar:[97]

bhūrom . . . e suvar jyotiḥ
bhuvom . . . e suvar jyotiḥ
suvom . . . e suvar jyotiḥ

These five songs echo the *sāman*s drawn from Yajurvedic sources on the *pravargya*,[98] which similarly attest OM in collocation with the recurring finale *s(u)var jyotiḥ*.

This concludes my survey of OM in the Sāmavedic liturgies as codified in the *Śrauta Sūtra*s and related texts. Overall, the results are consistent with the broader profile of liturgical OM's multiformity in the Vedic corpus: the syllable is attested in a range of forms and several different contexts. And yet patterns emerge against this background of multiformity. The first is melody: OM in the Sāmavedic liturgies is always sung. The second is meaninglessness: OM in these songs is always a *stobha*, a nonlexical vocable that conveys no semantic information. The third is repetition: where OM is called for, it comes again and again, interspersed with phonologically similar sounds. The fourth is substitution: OM often substitutes for one or more syllables of an underlying text. The fifth is interpolation: OM may be embedded as an extra syllable within an existing lyric. The sixth is accompaniment: OM is sung in overlapping fashion by two or more singers to provide a continuous flow of sound. The seventh is location: OM clusters most densely in the twelve *stotra*s of the pressing day, especially those sung to the *gāyatra* melody in the style of *aniruktagāna*. These patterns shape a series of performances where OM and related syllables form a wall of sound emanating from the sacrificial ground.

Listening in this way, it is not surprising that Sāmavedic interpretive texts were the first to claim that "this syllable is indeed this whole world" (JB 2.10). In the context of singing the Sāmavedic liturgy, this is not a symbolic claim but an experiential one—the overwhelming sound of *Sāmaveda* in performance is OM! No doubt this is what Frits Staal had in mind when he called OM the "result" of Sāmavedic practice: although there are many sources for OM in Vedic texts and rituals, Sāmavedic ritual performance amplifies OM to an astonishing degree.

Melody, Mantra, and Meaninglessness

I now circle back to some of the issues raised at the start of this study. This detailed survey of liturgical OM according to the Sāmavedic evidence shows that there is indeed a strong relation between OM and *Sāmaveda.* Although the scope of this study has prevented me from comparing the Ṛgvedic and Yajurvedic evidence in detail, the fact remains that OM is absent from the ṚV *Saṃhitā* and attested only a handful of times in the YV *Saṃhitā*s. The oldest usages of OM in the Vedic corpus are most likely those attested in the songs of the SV *Saṃhitā*s, a circumstance that speaks to the great importance of melody in the history of OM. These instances of OM are all nonlexical vocables—that is, they are meaningless sounds denoted by the technical term *stobha.* As such, these OMs are found repeated in collocation with certain other *stobha*s, often in recurring patterns. Variations of *oṃ vā* (*o vā, oṃ vāk,* etc.) are consistent and primary, although elaborate secondary patterns also occur. One such elaboration is the ending of the song with the finale *svar jyotiḥ,* which connects the Sāmavedic iterations to Yajurvedic examples identifiable as "unexpressed" (*anirukta*) singing.

All the features of these oldest uses of OM persist in the *Śrauta Sūtra*s and related texts in which OM remains a meaningless *stobha* that recurs in set patterns and as a prominent feature of "unexpressed song." Alongside these inherited features, the detailed testimony of the later texts reveal others, notably the substitution and interpolation of OM into existing mantras; the use of OM (and similar sounds) as accompaniment; and the dense clustering of OMs in one liturgical context in particular, the Sāmavedic *stotra.*

To what extent can the approach used in this study serve as a blueprint for continuing explorations into OM's history? Following Staal, I chose to concentrate on OM in the Sāmavedic liturgies and to ignore the discursive construction of OM in the interpretive genres of Vedic texts. This choice was inspired by the arrangement of the Vedic corpus: by respecting the indigenous separation between liturgy and discourse, I set out to understand aspects of the history of OM that emerge only when ritual is treated as a category unto itself. I trust that the richness, complexity, and coherence of the liturgical evidence laid out above goes some way toward justifying my approach, and, by extension, offers some small validation for Staal's vision. I have no wish to diminish the place of meaning and interpretation in the history of OM; rather, I expect that by establishing the liturgical facts of the history of OM we are in a better position to explore the interpretive discourses on the syllable. It is precisely in confronting such discourses of Sāmavedic traditions, where we find the most ancient, copious, and sustained hermeneutic reflections on OM in the capacity of "sacred syllable" (e.g., in JB, JUB, and the *Chandogya Upaniṣad*),[99] that our hard-won liturgical expertise will come in handy. Going forward, the Ṛgvedic and Yajurvedic liturgies should be subject to similar scrutiny. The liturgical facts about OM in ṚV and YV will illuminate the corresponding discourses we find in the interpretive texts of these Vedas.

By way of conclusion, I can't resist pointing out that the arc of liturgical OM's development in the Sāmavedic sources closely parallels Staal's scenario for OM as an "original mantra." Recall that he imagined a prehistory in which OM (and other monosyllables) originated as elemental vocalizations preceding the evolution of language. In similar fashion, the earliest Sāmavedic evidence attests OM as a *stobha,* a nonlexical vocable that is arrayed in flexible but fixed patterns with other syllables of the same type. Once language had evolved, Staal suggests, such archaisms remained in the form of "mantras couched in language." Along these lines, the early Sāmavedic patterns with OM sometimes also include the collocation of meaningful words and phrases. Finally, Staal conceives of ritual as a conduit for preserving and transmitting this prelinguistic inheritance. In a corresponding way, the later Sāmavedic ritual evidence shows an ongoing tendency to handle OM as a prelinguistic element, using it to create new patterns of repetition, substitution, interpolation, and the like, without regard to language. And while it may never be proven that prehistoric cavedwellers were humming OM before they could talk, Frits Staal's work shows that the potential for this prehistory is encoded in the melodies and mantras of the Vedic liturgies.

Notes

1 The present study is excerpted from my 2015 dissertation, "This Whole World is OM: Song, Soteriology, and the Emergence of the Sacred Syllable in South Asia,"currently under prepation as a monograph. In this work I attempt a comprehensive inquiry into the first thousand years of the history of OM.

2 Frits Staal, *Rules Without Meaning: Ritual, Mantras and the Human Sciences* (New York: Peter Lang, 1989), pp. 274–276; cf. Annette Wilke and Oliver Moebus, *Sound and Communication: An Aesthetic Cultural History of Sanskrit Hinduism* (Berlin: De Gruyter, 2011), pp. 439–440.

[3] Roman Jakobson, "Why 'Mama' and 'Papa'?", in *Selected Writings, Vol. I: Phonological Studies* (The Hague: Mouton, 1962), p. 541.

[4] Staal, *Rules Without Meaning*, pp. 274–275.

[5] Staal, *Rules Without Meaning*, p. 262.

[6] Staal, *Rules Without Meaning*, p. 262.

[7] Staal, *Rules Without Meaning*, p. 276.

[8] Staal, *Rules Without Meaning*, p. 274.

[9] Cf. Norman W. Brown, "The Creative Role of Vāc in the Rig Veda," in J. C. Heesterman et al., eds., *Pratidānam: Indian, Iranian, and Indo-European Studies Presented to Franciscus Bernardus Jacobus Kuiper on His Sixtieth Birthday* (The Hague and Paris: Mouton, 1968), pp. 393–397; George Thompson, "The Pursuit of Hidden Tracks in Vedic," *Indo-Iranian Journal* 38 (1995): 1–30.

[10] Cf. J. A. B. van Buitenen, "Akṣara," *Journal of the American Oriental Society* 79/3 (1959): 176–187.

[11] Staal, *Rules Without Meaning*, p. 274.

[12] George Thompson, "The Pursuit of Hidden Tracks in Vedic," pp. 25–26, and "On Mantras and Frits Staal," *Journal of Ritual Studies* 9/2 (1995): 35; Asko Parpola, "On the Etymology and Primary Meaning of the Sacred Syllable OM," in Asko Parpola, ed., *Proceedings of the Nordic South Asia Conference, Helsinki 1980* (Helsinki: Finnish Oriental Society, 1981), p. 206.

[13] For a sympathetic critique, see Thompson, "On Mantras and Frits Staal."

[14] Steven Mithen, *The Singing Neanderthals: The Origins of Music, Language, Mind and Body* (Cambridge, MA: Harvard University Press, 2006), p. 138.

[15] Mithen, *The Singing Neanderthals*, pp. 12, 277, 287n8, 332n18.

[16] Parpola, "On the Etymology and Primary Meaning of the Sacred Syllable OM"; A. B. Keith, "OM," in James Hastings, ed., *Encyclopedia of Religion and Ethics* (New York: Charles Scribner's Sons, 1917), vol. ix, pp. 490–492; Hans Heinrich Hock, "On the Origin and Early Development of the Sacred Sanskrit Syllable OM*," in *Perspectives on Indo-European Language, Culture and Religion: Studies in Honor of Edgar C. Polomé, Journal of Indo-European Studies* 7 (McLean, VA: Institute for the Study of Man, 1991), vol. I, pp. 89–110; Maurice Bloomfield, "On the Etymology of the Particle *oṁ*," *Proceedings of the American Oriental Society, 1889, Journal of the American Oriental Society* 14 (1890): cl–clii; Karl Hoffmann, *Aufsätze zur Indoiranistik* (Wiesbaden: Dr. Ludwig Reichert Verlag, 1976), vol. II.

[17] Gerety, "This Whole World is OM."

[18] Frits Staal, "How a Psychoactive Substance Becomes a Ritual: The Case of Soma," *Social Research* 68/3 (2001): 752–753; emphasis added.

[19] Cf. Gerety, "This Whole World is OM."

[20] Frits Staal, "A Theory of Ritual?", p. 131. Paper presented at the South Asia Graduate Student Colloquium, Yale University, New Haven, CT, October 2009.

21 Etymological studies of OM have accepted the primacy of the ritual evidence, using the liturgies as the chief basis for arguments about the syllable's etymology and meaning. To Parpola's list of the etymological literature on OM in "On the Etymology and Primary Meaning of the Sacred Syllable OM," pp. 195–196, we should add Hock, "On the Origin and Early Development of the Sacred Sanskrit Syllable OM*," and Joshua Katz, "Gods and Vowels," in J. Virgilio García and Angel Ruiz, eds., *Poetic Language and Religion in Greece and Rome* (Newcastle on Tyne, UK: Cambridge Scholars Publishing, 2013), pp. 2–28. The few studies of OM in theological discourses have also acknowledged the relevance of the ritual evidence; Keith, "OM"; Dermot Killingley, "Oṃ: the Sacred Syllable in the Veda," in Julius J. Lipner, ed., *A Net Cast Wide: Investigations into Indian Thought In Memory of David Friedman* (Newcastle upon Tyne: Grevatt & Grevatt, 1988), pp. 14–33; Wilke and Moebus, *Sound and Communication.*

22 A study of the history of OM's orthography and iconography, with attention to regional and religious variations, is a clear desideratum.

23 See *Taittirīya Āraṇyaka* 2.11.4; cf. *Mānava-Dharma-Śāstra* 2.74.

24 For instance, Pāṇini's grammar has shaped the post-Vedic legacy of OM by codifying the practice of applying *pluti* to OM at the beginning of a Vedic recitation (Pāṇini 8.2.87); and by devising a rule to justify the exceptional euphonic combination of *om* with a preceding *a/ā,* as in the Sāmavedic invocation *subrahmaṇyom* (which can be analyzed as *subrahmaṇyā + om;* Pāṇini 6.1.95); cf. Louis Renou, *La Grammaire de Pāṇini: texte Sanskrit, traduction française, avec extraits des commentaires* (Paris: Ecole Française d'Extreme-orient, 1966), 2 vols.

25 Cf. Parpola, "On the Etymology and Primary Meaning of the Sacred Syllable OM," p. 198; Jacob Wackernagel, *Altindische Grammatik* (Göttingen, Vandenhoeck und Rupricht, 1896,) vol. I, p. 302. Masato Fujii, "The Bahiṣpavamāna Ritual of the Jaiminīyas," *Machikaneyama Ronso* 20 (1986): 11, notes that all manuscripts of the JUB mention only *om, o,* and *o* as the three options (excluding *oṁ*), and he suggests that the difference between the latter two apparently identical *o* sounds lies in how they are sung.

26 Hock, "On the Origin and Early Development of the Sacred Sanskrit Syllable OM*," pp. 90, 99, 102–105.

27 In direct speech the *pluta* grade communicates emphasis, as in a question, call, or greeting; in ritual contexts it is applied to certain syllables of some mantras. See Klaus Strunk, *Typische Merkmale von Fragesätzen und die altindische "Pluti"* (Munich: Verlag der Bayerischen Akademie der Wissenschaften, 1983), pp. 24, 34–35; W. Dwight Whitney, *Sanskrit Grammar* (Boston: Ginn & Company, 1889, second ed.), p. 79; Wackernagel, *Altindische Grammatik,* vol. I, p. 297.

28 Alfred Hillebrandt, *Das altindische Neu- und Vollmondsopfer in seiner einfachsten Form* (Jena: G. Fischer, 1879), p. 107.

29 Cf. Hoffmann, *Aufsätze zur Indoiranistik,* pp. 552–554; Hock, "On the Origin and Early Development of the Sacred Sanskrit Syllable OM*," pp. 99–100.

30 According to some, e.g., Wackernagel, *Altindische Grammatik,* vol. I, p. 302, pure *o* is the *"Grundform,"* with *oṁ* resulting from the Vedic phonological tendency

to nasalize an extended vowel; Rudolf von Roth, *Zur Literatur und Geschichte des Weda* (Stuttgart: A. Liesching, 1846); Bloomfield, "On the Etymology of the Particle *oṁ*"; Hock, "On the Origin and Early Development of the Sacred Sanskrit Syllable OM*." According to others, for example, Parpola, "On the Etymology and Primary Meaning of the Sacred Syllable OM," p. 198, *om* is the underlying form, itself based on Sansrkit *ām* ("yes") pronounced in a special liturgical register; Albrecht Weber, *Indische Studien* (Berlin: F. Dümmler, 1853), vol. II; Otto von Böhtlingk and Rudolf Roth, *Sanskrit-wörterbuch* (St. Petersburg: Kaiserlichen akademie der wissenschaften, 1855), 7 vols.

31 For the Ṛgvedic and Yajurvedic liturgies, as well as a thoroughgoing study of OM's many meanings in the Vedas, see Gerety, "This Whole World is OM."

32 Michael Witzel, "On the Localisation of Vedic Texts and Schools (Materials on Vedic Śākhās 7)," in G. Pollet, ed., *India and the Ancient World: History, Trade and Culture before A.D. 650, P. H. L. Eggermont Jubilee Volume* (Leuven: Departement Oriëntalistiek, 1987), pp. 173–213, and "The Development of the Vedic Canon and its Schools: The Social and Political Milieu (Materials on Vedic Śākhās 8)," in Michael Witzel, ed., *Inside the Texts, Beyond the Texts: New Approaches to the Study of the Vedas* (Cambridge, MA: Department of Sanskrit and Indian Studies, Harvard University, 1997), pp. 257–345; Louis Renou, *Les écoles védiques et la formation du Véda* (Paris: Imprimerie National, 1947).

33 On these divisions, see note 40 below.

34 Willem Caland, trans., *Pañcaviṃśa-Brāhmaṇa: The Brāhmaṇa of Twenty Five Chapters* (Calcutta: Asiatic Society of Bengal, 1931), pp. xi, xiv–xvii.

35 Witzel, "The Development of the Vedic Canon and its Schools," pp. 268–270.

36 On the *śākhā*s of the SV, see Renou, *Les écoles védiques et la formation du Véda*, pp. 87–129; Masato Fujii, "The Jaiminīya Sāmaveda Traditions and Manuscripts in South India," in Saraju Rath, ed., *Aspects of Manuscript Culture in Ancient India* (Leiden: Brill, 2012), p. 100.

37 Satyavrata Sāmaśrami Bhaṭṭācārya, ed., *Sāma Veda Saṃhitā with the Commentary of Sāyaṇa Ācārya* (Calcutta: Asiatic Society of Bengal, 1874–1878), 5 vols.; Willem Caland and Victor Henry, *L'Agniṣṭoma: description complète de la forme normale du sacrifice de soma dans le culte védique* (Paris: Ernst Laroux, 1907), 2 vols.; Asko Parpola, "The Śrautasūtras of Lāṭyāyana and Drāhyāyaṇa and their Commentaries," *Commentationes Humanarum Litterarum: Societas Scientiarum Fennica* 43/2 (1969): 1–273.

38 The printed sources include Willem Caland, ed., *Die Jaiminīya-Samhitā mit einer Einleitung über die Sāmavedaliteratur* (Breslau: M. & H. Marcus, 1907); Raghu Vira, *Sāma Veda of the Jaiminīyas* (Lahore: International Academy of Indian Culture, 1938); Vibhūtibhūṣaṇa Bhaṭṭācārya, ed., *Jaiminīya Sāmagāna* (Varanasi: Sampurnanand Sanskrit Vishvavidyalaya, 1976); T. N. Makara Bhushanam, *Ārana Gānam of Talavakara Sakha of Jaiminiya Samam* (Chennai: Veda Rakshana Nidhi Trust, n.d. [2000]); and K. A. Ravindran, ed., *Jaiminīya-sāmavedasaṃhitā: Text of Kerala Tradition* (Delhi: Nag Publishers, 2013), 2 vols. Significant evidence comes from the oral testimony of modern Nampūtiri Brahmins of the Jaiminīya branch, recorded in notebooks. These handwritten

"paper manuscripts" were produced in the early 1970s by the highly respected singer Muṭṭattukāṭṭu Māmaṇṇu Iṭṭi Ravi Nampūtiri and his students (Muṭṭattukāṭṭu Māmaṇṇu, n.d.); see Fujii, "The Jaiminīya Sāmaveda Traditions and Manuscripts," p. 112; Asko Parpola, "The Literature and Study of the Jaiminīya Sāmaveda in Retrospect and Prospect," *Studia Orientalia* 43/6 (1973): 21; Finnian M. M. Gerety, "Survivals and Revivals: The Transmission of Jaiminīya Sāmaveda in Modern South India," in Jan Houben, Julieta Rotaru, and Michael Witzel, eds., *The Vedic Śākhās: Past, Present, Future* (Cambridge, MA: Department of South Asian Studies, Harvard University, forthcoming), p. 21.

39 Frits Staal, *Agni: The Vedic Ritual of the Fire Altar* (Berkeley: Asian Humanities Press, 1983), vol. 1, pp. 276–277; Asko Parpola, "The Passages of the *Jaiminīya Śrautasūtra* Dealing with the Agnicayana, Together with Bhavatrāta's Commentary," in Frits Staal, ed., *Agni: The Vedic Ritual of the Fire Altar,* vol. 2, p. 701.

40 The basic division is into compilations of verses alone (*ārcika*), taken from ṚV but arranged in a different order; and compilations of songs (*gāna*), consisting of melodies (*sāmans*) and adapted "source" (*yoni*) verses. These categories are presented in primary (*pūrva-*), paradigmatic (*prakṛti-*) form, as well as in secondary (*uttara-*), modified (*vikṛti-*) form. The *pūrvārcika* contains verses organized by deity (Agni, Indra, Soma), set to melodies in the "village songs" (*grāmegeyagāna;* GG). Next is a set of verses known as the *āraṇyakasaṃhitā* corresponding to the "wilderness songs" (*araṇyegeyagāna;* AG). (Collectively, the GG and AG are known as the *pūrva-* or *prakṛtigāna.*) The *uttarārcika* presents the same verses (plus some others) arranged according to their use in the *soma* sacrifice. These are set to melodies in the *ūhagāna* (including some songs of the GG) and the *rahasya-* or *ūhyagāna* (including some of the AG), known together as the *uttaragāna.* On the arrangement of the SV *Saṃhitās*, see Caland, *Pañcaviṃśa-Brāhmaṇa,* pp. i–ii; Renou, *Les écoles védiques et la formation du Véda,* p. 92; J. F. Staal, *Nambudiri Veda Recitation* ('S-Gravenhage: Mouton & Co, 1961), p. 64; Parpola, "The Literature and Study of the Jaiminīya Sāmaveda in Retrospect and Prospect," pp. 25–26; Wayne Howard, *Sāmavedic Chant* (New Haven, CT and London: Yale University Press, 1977), pp. 8–9.

41 The term *stobha* is first attested in MS 4.7.3; useful definitions are found in the *Śabarabhāṣya* on Jaimini's *Mīmāṃsasūtra* 39 (Jha 1936, III, 1533) and Mādhava's *Jaiminīya-Nyāya-Mālā-Vistara* (9.2.11 on verse 18, quoted in Sāyaṇa's commentary in BI I, 13). See also Hillebrandt, *Das altindische Neu- und Vollmondsopfer in seiner einfachsten Form,* p. 100; Barend Faddegon, "Ritualistic Dadaism," in Sten Konow, ed., *Acta Orientalia* (Leiden: E. J. Brill, 1927), vol. 5, part 3, p. 179; J. M. van der Hoogt, *The Vedic Chant Studied in its Textual and Melodic Form* (Wageningen, Holland: H. Veenman & Sons' Press, 1929), p. 1; Caland, *Pañcaviṃśa-Brāhmaṇa,* p. ix; Louis Renou, *Vocabulaire du Rituel Védique* (Paris: Libraire C. Klincksieck, 1954), s.v. *stobha;* Staal, *Nambudiri Veda Recitation,* p. 64, and "Vedic Mantras," in Harvey P. Alper, ed., *Understanding Mantras* (Albany, NY: State University of New York Press, 1989), p. 56; Jan Gonda, *Vedic Literature: Saṃhitās and Brāhmaṇas. A History of Indian Literature* (Wiesbaden: Harassowitz, 1975), vol. 1, fasc. 1, pp. 315–316; Howard, *Sāmavedic Chant,* vol. 11, p. 539.

It has been speculated (e.g., Hillebrandt, *Das altindische Neu- und Vollmondsopfer in seiner einfachsten Form,* p. 100) that *stobha*s arose when an existing corpus of melody was merged with a selection of ṚV verses: in order to fill out the places where the two did not coalesce *stobha*s were interpolated as "filler"; Hock "On the Origin and Early Development of the Sacred Sanskrit Syllable OM*," p. 17. I follow van der Hoogt, *The Vedic Chant Studied in its Textual and Melodic Form,* p. 72, in refuting this. These nonlexical syllables are an integral part of the SV corpus as it is handed down; indeed, many songs do not depend on verses at all but consist entirely of *stobha*s!

42 Masato Fujii, "The *Gāyatra-Sāman:* Chanting Innovations in Sāmavedic Brāhmaṇas and Upaniṣad," *Zinbun* 42 (2009–2010): 27.

43 Finding OM in the *gāna*s is like looking for a needle in a haystack—none of the *gāna*s are in concordances or digitized and some remain unpublished. Because of this inaccessibility I cannot claim to have examined every single instance of OM in the Sāmavedic corpus.

44 Although Richard Simon, *Das Pañcavidhasūtra* (Breslau: Verlag von M. & H. Marcus, 1913), p. 2n4, gives no citations in support of this total, I have been able to track down many of the OM-initial *sāman*s in KGG to which he refers: BI I, 91, 208, 249, 286, 314, 369, 400, 489; BI II, 2, 14, 30, 55, 91, 224.

45 The verse, from the SV *pūrvārcika* (*Jaiminīya* 1.49.1, in Vira, *Sāma Veda of the Jaiminīyas*, p. 35; *Kauthuma-Rāṇāyanīya* I.5.2.4.1 in Theodor Benfey, ed., *Die Hymnen des Sāmaveda* [Leipzig: F. A. Brockhaus, 1848], p. 49), is based on ṚV 9.61.10 (cf. *Pañcaviṃśa Brāhmaṇa* 12.3.1): *uccā́ te jātám ándhaso diví ṣad bhū́mi ā́ dade / ugrá śárma máhi śrávaḥ //*; "It was born high above from your stalk; though it was in heaven, on earth it took for itself mighty shelter and great fame"; Stephanie Jamison and Joel Brereton, trans., *The Rigveda: The Earliest Religious Poetry of India* (New York: Oxford University Press, 2014), 3 vols.

46 At least one other *sāman* with OM in GG also meets these criteria: KGG = BI II, 4; JGG 49.1. Another attests *om* a single time next to *ovā,* but in separate *parvan*s (KGG = BI II, 5); the parallel *Jaiminīya* text (JGG 49.1) lacks *om.*

47 *Triḥ,* printed with parentheses in KAG/BI, indicates that what precedes it should be sung "three times," as is confirmed in the corresponding *Jaiminīya* example, where *hā o vāk* appears three times in a row. However Staal, *Nambudiri Veda Recitation,* pp. 76–79, presents this and other numerical expressions (*dviḥ,* "two times") as part of the lyric in his small edition of selected *Jaiminīya sāman*s.

48 Staal's unpublished notes on the Nampūtiri performance of the 1975 *agnicayana* connect this *sāman* to the *pravargya* rite (photocopy of Staal's notes courtesy of Masato Fujii).

49 Staal, *Agni: The Vedic Ritual of the Fire Altar,* vol. I, p. 411.

50 This argument should be checked against a musicological analysis of the songs to determine to what extent these lyrical patterns conform to melodic patterns. The best musicological work on Sāmavedic recitation remains the impressive oeuvre of Wayne Howard, *Sāmavedic Chant;* "The Body of the Bodiless Gāyatra," *Indo-Iranian Journal* 30 (1987): 161–173; and "The Music of Nambudiri Unexpressed Chant (aniruktagāna)," in Frits Staal, ed., *Agni: The*

Vedic Ritual of the Fire Altar (Berkeley: Asian Humanities Press, 1983), vol. 2, pp. 311–342.

51 The others are MS 1.4.11; 4.1.11; 4.5.2; 4.9.2, 9.

52 A. A. MacDonell, *A History of Sanskrit Literature* (London: William Heinemann, 1900), p. 183. Cf. Hock, "On the Origin and Early Development of the Sacred Sanskrit Syllable OM*," p. 97.

53 Michael Witzel, ed. and trans., *Kaṭha-Āraṇyaka: Critical Edition with a Translation into German and an Introduction* (Cambridge, MA: Department of Sanskrit and Indian Studies, 2004), p. 93.

54 TĀ 4.40: *nidhāyyo 'vāpi nidhāyyo 'vāpi nidhāyyo 'vāpi / e asme asme / suvarṇajyotiḥ //.* Sāyaṇa's commentary on TĀ 4.40; Rājendralāla Mitra, *The Taittirīya Āraṇyaka of the Black Yajur Veda with the Commentary of Sāyaṇācārya* (Calcutta: C.B. Lewis, Baptist Mission Press, 1864), vol. I, pp. 558–559, calls the syllables of the text *stobha*s and identifies the mantra as a *sāman* sung by the *adhvaryu*. J. A. B. Van Buitenen, *The Pravargya, An Ancient Indian Iconic Ritual* (Poona: Deccan College Postgraduate and Research Institute, 1968), p. 150, links the TĀ version of the *sāman* to an optional *sūtra* on the *pravargya* (ĀpŚS 15.19.11), stating that if the *udgātṛ* does not sing the *puruṣa-sāman,* then the *adhvaryu* should make up for this lack by singing the present one. On the *puruṣa-sāman,* see Staal, *Agni: The Vedic Ritual of the Fire Altar,* vol. I, p. 417, and "Vedic Mantras," p. 55, as well as the following discussion.

55 Caland and Henry, *L'Agniṣṭoma.*

56 On the fundamentals of SV singing in the *soma* sacrifices, see Julius Eggeling, trans., *The Śatapatha-Brāhmaṇa According to the Text of the Mādhyandina School* (Oxford: Clarendon Press, 1885), Part II, pp. 307n5, 310n1, 325n2; Hillebrandt, *Das altindische Neu- und Vollmondsopfer in seiner einfachsten Form,* pp. 99–101; van der Hoogt, *The Vedic Chant Studied in its Textual and Melodic Form,* p. 22; Renou, *Vocabulaire du Rituel Védique,* pp. 168–169; Staal, "The Twelve Ritual Chants of the Nambudiri Agniṣṭoma," in J. C. Heesterman, et al., eds., *Pratidānam: Indian, Iranian, and Indo-European Studies Presented to Franciscus Bernardus Jacobus Kuiper on His Sixtieth Birthday* (The Hague and Paris: Mouton, 1968), pp. 412–413; Staal, *Agni: The Vedic Ritual of the Fire Altar,* vol. I, pp. 602–603; Parpola, "The Śrautasūtras of Lāṭyāyana and Drāhyāyaṇa and Their Commentaries," pp. 12–13; Howard, *Sāmavedic Chant,* pp. 16–24.

The *hiṃkāra* encompasses a range of sounds (*hum, hiṃ, hṃ*) and is used in a variety of liturgical contexts; cf. A. C. Burnell, ed., *The Ārsheyabrāhmaṇa, being the Fourth Brāhmaṇa of the Sāma Veda* (Mangalore: Stolz & Hirner, 1876), p. xlv. For its use at the beginning of certain "rounds" (*paryāya*s) of *stotra*s, see Staal, *Nambudiri Veda Recitation,* p. 69, citing Simon, *Das Pañcavidhasūtra,* p. 3, n. 5; Parpola, "The Śrautasūtras of Lāṭyāyana and Drāhyāyaṇa and Their Commentaries," p. 12.

57 For the *gāyatra* melody in Sāmavedic texts, see Fujii, "The *Gāyatra-Sāman,*" p. 1, n. 1.

58 Wayne Howard notes that "all *prastāva*s of all settings of the *gāyatra* conclude with this syllable [OM]," including the Sāmavedic rendition of the *gāyatrī*

mantra; "The Music of Nambudiri Unexpressed Chant (aniruktagāna)," p. 316; cf. Howard, *Sāmavedic Chant*, p. 514; JAG 25.39. See also Staal, *Nambudiri Veda Recitation*, pp. 67–68, and "The Twelve Ritual Chants of the Nambudiri Agniṣṭoma," p. 416 ff; C. G. Kashikar, *Śrautakośa* (Poona: Vaidika Saṁśodhana Maṇḍala, 1970), vol. II, Sanskrit Section Part I, p. 278 ff; Parpola, "On the Etymology and Primary Meaning of the Sacred Syllable OM," p. 201; Staal, *Agni: The Vedic Ritual of the Fire Altar*, vol. I, p. 10, n. 39.

59 To reconstruct these (and other) *gāyatra* song-texts of the *Kauthuma-Rāṇāyaṇīyas*, Caland depends on unspecified *prayoga*s (CH §134g), as well as the *pariśiṣṭa* to the *uttarārcika* (BI V, 601; Asko Parpola, personal communication, December 2013.

60 The verses, from the SV *uttarārcika* (*Jaiminīya* 3.2.1–3 in Vira, *Sāma Veda of the Jaiminīyas*, p. 51; *Kauthuma-Rāṇāyanīya* II.1.1.4.1–3 in Benfey, *Die Hymnen des Sāmaveda*, p. 62) correspond to ṚV 6.16.10a: *ágna ā́ yāhi vītáye. . . .* , "Agni . . . travel hither to pursue. . ."; 11a: *tám tvā samídbhir aṅgiro. . .* , "You, *aṅgiras*, with kindling sticks. . ."; 12a: *sá naḥ pṛthú śravā́yiyam. . .* , ". . . for us a broad, praiseworthy. . . "; Jamison and Brereton, trans., *The Rigveda: The Earliest Religious Poetry of India*.

61 Staal, "The Twelve Ritual Chants of the Nambudiri Agniṣṭoma," p. 417.

62 The verse, from SV *uttarārcika* (*Jaiminīya* 3.4.3 in Vira, *Sāma Veda of the Jaiminīyas*, p. 53; *Kauthuma-Rāṇāyanīya* II.1.1.12.1 in Benfey, *Die Hymnen des Sāmaveda*, p. 64) corresponds to ṚV 4.31.1: *káyā naś citrá ā́ bhuvad ūtXsadā́vṛdhaḥ sákhā / káyā śáciṣṭhayā vṛtā́ //*; "With what help will our brilliant, ever-strengthening comrade be there for us—with what most powerful troop?"; Jamison and Brereton, trans., *The Rigveda: The Earliest Religious Poetry of India*.

63 Cf. *Pratihāra sūtra*, fol. 3a, quoted in Simon, *Das Pañcavidhasūtra*, which uses the suffix *-ādi*, "beginning with." Bhavatrāta, in his commentary on JŚS, also terms the practice *ādi;* Parpola, "On the Etymology and Primary Meaning of the Sacred Syllable OM," p. 202. Cf. also Eggeling, trans., *The Śatapatha-Brāhmaṇa*, p. 310, n. 1; Hillebrandt, *Das altindische Neu- und Vollmondsopfer in seiner einfachsten Form*, p. 100; Parpola, "The Śrautasūtras of Lāṭyāyana and Drāhyāyaṇa and Their Commentaries," p. 12; Howard, *Sāmavedic Chant*, pp. 18, 530, who calls it *praṇava*.

64 "The taking up (*ādānam*) of the *udgītha* of all [*sāman*s] is by means of the sound *om*"; LŚS 6.10.13; H. G. Ranade, ed., *Lāṭyāyana-Śrauta-Sūtra* (Delhi: Motilal Banarsidass, 1998). Several sūtras on how to implement this broad rule follow: rival opinions for and against the practice of *om* replacing the first syllable of the *udgītha* entirely (14–15); initial vocalic syllables should be replaced by *om*, while consonantal ones should be preceded by it (16); *om* should be treated as an "addition" (*āgantu*) in all situations (17). Caland always treats *om* as an addition to the lyric.

65 A *Jaiminīya* text contains an early reference to this practice (*Jaiminīya Brāhmaṇa* 1.322), discussing the "taking up" (*ā* + *dā*) of OM as an addition to the *stotra*. JUB also contains numerous references to the *ādi*, 1.11.7; 1.12.4; 1.19.2; 1.31.2, 5; 1.58.9; 1.59.6; 2.2.9; 4.10.3, 13, yet none of these describe its form.

66 Jamison and Brereton, trans., *The Rigveda: The Earliest Religious Poetry of India.* Corresponding to SV *uttarārcika: Jaiminīya* 3.1.5 in Vira, *Sāma Veda of the Jaiminīyas,* p. 51; *Kauthuma-Rāṇāyanīya* II.1.1.1.3 in Benfey, *Die Hymnen des Sāma-veda,* p. 62.

67 LŚS (7.10.19) indicates variations in the final syllable: for instance, the final word *naraḥ* from the first repetition might be rendered as *naro3m, naro*3, or *nara*3; cf. Hock,"On the Origin and Early Development of the Sacred Sanskrit Syllable OM*," p. 103.

68 C. G. Kashikar, *Śrautakośa* (Poona: Vaidika Saṁśodhana Maṇḍala, 1970), vol. II, Sanskrit Section Part I, p. 278.

69 For details, consult Howard, *Sāmavedic Chant,* pp. 12 ff, 29–31, 43–44.

70 Although JUB is the primary authority for the form and codification of the *anirukta-gāyatra;* Fujii, "The *Gāyatra-Sāman,*" p. 28, n. 97, and "On the Formation and Transmission of the Jaiminīya-Upaniṣad-Brāhmaṇa," in Michael Witzel, ed., *Inside the Texts, Beyond the Texts: New Approaches to the Study of the Vedas* (Cambridge, MA: Department of Sanskrit and Indian Studies, Harvard University, 1997), p. 90, n. 6, some manuscripts of the JS also attest this form at the end of JAG (25.39); Fujii, "On the Formation and Transmission of the Jaiminīya-Upaniṣad-Brāhmaṇa," p. 91, n. 10; Parpola, "The Passages of the Jaiminīya Śrautasūtra," p. 708.

On the *Jaiminīya* unexpressed *gāyatra,* see Staal, "The Twelve Ritual Chants of the Nambudiri Agniṣṭoma," pp. 416–420, 425, and Staal, *Agni: The Vedic Ritual of the Fire Altar,* vol. I, p, 603; Howard, *Sāmavedic Chant,* pp. 504–505; Masato Fujii, "On the Unexpressed *gāyatra-sāman* in the Jaiminīya-Upaniṣad-Brāhmaṇa," *Journal of Indian and Buddhist Studies* 32/2 (1984): 1123–1121 (1–3); "The Bahiṣpavamāna Ritual of the Jaiminīyas," pp. 13–16; "The *Gāyatra-Sāman,*" pp. 6–8, 24–28.

71 Howard, "The Body of the Bodiless Gāyatra," p. 166.

72 On the normative fivefold division, see note 40. JUB divides it into two overall portions: the *prastāva* and everything after it, which it terms the *gīta,* or "singing" (JUB 3.38.9). The text further subdivides the *gīta* into *udgītha, pratihāra,* and *nidhana,* contributing the basis for the triple division adopted above. In this analysis, only the *upadrava* is lacking. See Staal, "The Twelve Ritual Chants of the Nambudiri Agniṣṭoma," p. 415 ff, and *Agni: The Vedic Ritual of the Fire Altar,* vol. I, pp. 602–604; Fujii, "On the Unexpressed gāyatra-sāman in the Jaiminīya-Upaniṣad-Brāhmaṇa," pp. 1–2, and "The Bahiṣpavamāna Ritual of the Jaiminīyas," pp. 15–16; Howard,"The Music of Nambudiri Unexpressed Chant (aniruktagāna)," p. 318, and "The Body of the Bodiless Gāyatra," pp. 166–171.

73 Still, variations were known to the Jaiminīya tradition, as in the rival versions mentioned in JUB 1.2.3, 4.8.9, and 4.14.12.

74 Cf. Fujii, "On the Unexpressed gāyatra-sāman in the Jaiminīya-Upaniṣad-Brāhmaṇa."

75 Fujii, "On the Unexpressed gāyatra-sāman in the Jaiminīya-Upaniṣad-Brāhmaṇa," p. 28.

76 The living tradition of the Nampūtiri Jaiminīyas furnishes us with a range of otherwise unattested examples of *aniruktagāna* in performance, characterized as the sporadic but systematic replacement of individual syllables with *o* sounds; cf. the modern performances transcribed by Staal, "The Twelve Ritual Chants of the Nambudiri Agniṣṭoma," pp. 419–422; Howard, "The Music of Nambudiri Unexpressed Chant (aniruktagāna)," pp. 328–334.

77 The verse, from SV *uttarārcika* (*Jaiminīya* 3.4.1 in Vira, *Sāma Veda of the Jaiminīyas,* p. 53; *Kauthuma-Rāṇāyanīya* II.1.1.11.1 in Benfey, *Die Hymnen des Sāmaveda,* p. 62), corresponds to ṚV 7.32.22abc: *abhí tvā śūra nonumo ádugdhā iva dhenávaḥ / īśānam asyá jágataḥ suvardṛ́śam. . . ,* "We keep bellowing to you, O champion, like unmilked cows—to you . . . who see [like] the sun, lord of this moving [world]. . . "; Jamison and Brereton, trans., *The Rigveda: The Earliest Religious Poetry of India.*

78 For the *Kauthuma-Rāṇāyanīya* praxis, see Parpola, "The Śrautasūtras of Lāṭyāyana and Drāhyāyaṇa and Their Commentaries," p. 242, n. 2, on LŚS 2.9.12–14a, DŚS 6.1.16; Caland, *Pañcaviṃśa-Brāhmaṇa,* p. 151, n. 1, on PB 7.7.13. For the *Jaiminīya* praxis, see Staal, "The Twelve Ritual Chants of the Nambudiri Agniṣṭoma," p. 422; Howard, "The Music of Nambudiri Unexpressed Chant (aniruktagāna)," pp. 325–326.

79 Faddegon, "Ritualistic Dadaism"; cf. Staal, *Rules Without Meaning,* p. 227.

80 Howard, "The Body of the Bodiless Gāyatra," p. 166; cf. Staal, "The Twelve Ritual Chants of the Nambudiri Agniṣṭoma," p. 429.

81 On *upagāna,* see Parpola, "The Śrautasūtras of Lāṭyāyana and Drāhyāyaṇa and Their Commentaries," pp. 156–162; Fujii, "The Bahiṣpavamāna Ritual of the Jaiminīyas," pp. 9–12.

82 Fujii, "The Bahiṣpavamāna Ritual of the Jaiminīyas," p. 21, n. 6.

83 Bhavatrāta on JŚS 1.11; cf. Fujii, "The Bahiṣpavamāna Ritual of the Jaiminīyas," p. 11.

84 Cf. the testimony of a lost *Brāhmaṇa* quoted at DŚS 3.4.2; Parpola, "The Śrautasūtras of Lāṭyāyana and Drāhyāyaṇa and Their Commentaries," pp. 157–158.

85 Parpola, "The Śrautasūtras of Lāṭyāyana and Drāhyāyaṇa and Their Commentaries," pp. 122–123.

86 Parpola, "The Śrautasūtras of Lāṭyāyana and Drāhyāyaṇa and Their Commentaries," pp. 124–127.

87 On LŚS 1.3.1a and DŚS 1.3.2, see Parpola, "The Śrautasūtras of Lāṭyāyana and Drāhyāyaṇa and Their Commentaries," p. 47n2.

88 Cf. Parpola, "The Śrautasūtras of Lāṭyāyana and Drāhyāyaṇa and Their Commentaries," p. 48.

89 Cf. Pāṇini's codification in note 24.

90 On ŚB 3.3.4.17, see Strunk, *Typische Merkmale von Fragesätzen und die altindische "Pluti,"* p. 34, n. 52. In support of the analysis that OM is a free-standing, invocatory syllable there is an inversion of the call, *oṃ subrahmaṇyā,* mentioned in JB 2.78 as a practice used by "some" (*eke*).

91 Hock, "On the Origin and Early Development of the Sacred Sanskrit Syllable OM*," pp. 104–105.

92 For a list of these 17 *sāmans*, referred to as "moon chants" after the Nampūtiri name for the "Wilderness Songs," see the table in Staal, *Agni: The Vedic Ritual of the Fire Altar,* vol. I, p. 533; cf. Staal, "Moon Chants, Space Fillers, and Flow of Milk," in *Surabhi: Sreekrishna Sarma Felicitation Volume* (Tirupati: Prof. E. R. Sreekrishna Sarma Felicitation Committee, 1983).

93 Cited by Parpola, "The Passages of the Jaiminīya Śrautasūtra," p. 707.

94 The *Kauthuma-Rāṇāyanīya*s also record the *vyāhṛtisāman*s in a similar context (BI V, 486–488); cf. Parpola, "The Passages of the Jaiminīya Śrautasūtra," p. 709, but with the *prastotṛ* (p. 707) or the *yajamāna* as the singer; cf. *Śatapatha Brāhmaṇa* 8.7.4.1–6; Julius Eggeling, trans., *The Śatapatha-Brāhmaṇa According to the Text of the Mādhyandina School, Part IV* (Oxford: Clarendon Press, 1897), p. 145, n. 1.

95 Staal, *Agni: The Vedic Ritual of the Fire Altar,* vol. I, pp. 414, 417.

96 Staal, *Agni: The Vedic Ritual of the Fire Altar,* vol. I, p. 417.

97 Staal, *Agni: The Vedic Ritual of the Fire Altar,* vol. I, pp. 419, 461, 505.

98 Cf. Parpola, "The Passages of the Jaiminīya Śrautasūtra," p. 707.

99 See Gerety, "This Whole World is OM."

Abbreviations

AB	*Aitareya Brāhmaṇa*
AG	*Araṇyegeyagāna*
ĀpŚS	*Āpastamba Śrauta Sūtra*
BI	*Kauthuma-Rāṇāyanīya Saṃhitā.* Satyavrata Sāmaśrami Bhaṭṭācārya, ed., *Sāma Veda Saṃhitā with the Commentary of Sāyaṇa Ācārya,* 5 vols. Bibliotheca Indica 71. Calcutta: Asiatic Society of Bengal, 1874–1878.
CH	Willem Caland and Victor Henry, *L'Agniṣṭoma: description complète de la forme normale du sacrifice de soma dans le culte védique*, 2 vols. Paris: Ernst Laroux, 1907.
DŚS	*Drāhyāyana Śrauta Sūtra*
GG	*Grāmegeyagāna*
JUB	*Jaiminīya Upaniṣad Brāhmaṇa*
JB	*Jaiminīya Brāhmaṇa*
JAG	*Jaiminīya Araṇyegeyagāna*
JGG	*Jaiminīya Grāmegeyagāna*
JŚS	*Jaiminīya Śrauta Sūtra*
JS	*Jaiminīya Saṃhitā*
KAG	*Kauthuma-Rāṇāyanīya Araṇyegeyagāna*
KGG	*Kauthuma-Rāṇāyanīya Grāmegeyagāna*
KĀ	*Kaṭha Āraṇyaka*
LŚS	*Lāṭyāyana Śrauta Sūtra*

MS *Maitrāyaṇī Saṃhitā*

PB *Pañcaviṃśa Brāhmaṇa*

ṚV *Ṛgveda*. Barend A. Van Nooten and Gary B. Holland, eds., *Rigveda: A Metrically Restored Text*. Cambridge, MA: Department of Sanskrit and Indian Studies, 1994.

SV *Sāmaveda*

TĀ *Taittirīya Āraṇyaka*

YV *Yajurveda*

References

Aufrecht, Theodor, ed. *Das Aitareya Brāhmaṇa*. Bonn: Adolph Marcus, 1879.

Benfey, Theodor, ed. *Die Hymnen des Sāmaveda*. Leipzig: F. A. Brockhaus, 1848.

Bhaṭṭācārya, Satyavrata Sāmaśrami, ed. *Sāma Veda Saṃhitā with the Commentary of Sāyaṇa Ācārya*, 5 vols. Bibliotheca Indica 71. Calcutta: Asiatic Society of Bengal, 1874–1878.

Bhaṭṭācārya, Vibhūtibhūṣaṇa, ed. *Jaiminīya Sāmagāna*. Sarasvatī-Bhavana-Granthamālā 109. Varanasi: Sampurnanand Sanskrit Vishvavidyalaya, 1976.

Bhushanam, T. N. Makara. *Ārana Gānam of Talavakara Sakha of Jaiminiya Samam*. Chennai: Veda Rakshana Nidhi Trust, n.d. (2000).

Bloomfield, Maurice. "On the Etymology of the Particle *oṁ*," *Proceedings of the American Oriental Society, 1889, Journal of the American Oriental Society* 14 (1890): cl–clii.

Böhtlingk, Otto von, and Rudolf Roth. *Sanskrit-wörterbuch*, 7 vols. St. Petersburg: Kaiserlichen akademie der wissenschaften, 1855–1875.

Brown, Norman W. "The Creative Role of Vāc in the Rig Veda," in J. C. Heesterman, et al., eds., *Pratidānam: Indian, Iranian, and Indo-European Studies Presented to Franciscus Bernardus Jacobus Kuiper on His Sixtieth Birthday*, pp. 393–397. The Hague and Paris: Mouton, 1968.

Buitenen, J. A. B. van. "Akṣara," *Journal of the American Oriental Society* 79/3 (1959): 176–187.

—. *The Pravargya, An Ancient Indian Iconic Ritual*. Poona: Deccan College Postgraduate and Research Institute, 1968.

Burnell, A. C., ed. *The Ārsheyabrāhmaṇa, being the Fourth Brāhmaṇa of the Sāma Veda*. Mangalore: Stolz & Hirner, 1876.

Caland, Willem, ed. *Die Jaiminīya-Samhitā mit einer Einleitung über die Sāmavedaliteratur*. Breslau: M. & H. Marcus, 1907.

—, trans. *Pañcaviṃśa-Brāhmaṇa: The Brāhmaṇa of Twenty Five Chapters*. Bibliotheca Indica 255. Calcutta: Asiatic Society of Bengal, 1931.

Caland, Willem, and Victor Henry. *L'Agniṣṭoma: description complète de la forme normale du sacrifice de soma dans le culte védique*, 2 vols. Paris: Ernst Laroux, 1907.

Eggeling, Julius, trans. *The Śatapatha-Brāhmaṇa According to the Text of the Mādhyandina School, Part II*. Sacred Books of the East 26. Oxford: Clarendon Press, 1885.

—, trans. *The Śatapatha-Brāhmaṇa According to the Text of the Mādhyandina School, Part IV.* Sacred Books of the East 43. Oxford: Clarendon Press, 1897.

Faddegon, Barend. "Ritualistic Dadaism," in Sten Konow, ed., *Acta Orientalia,* vol. 5, part 3, pp. 177–196. Leiden: E. J. Brill, 1927.

Fujii, Masato, ed. *Jaiminīya-Upaniṣad-Brāhmaṇa.* Unpublished critical edition, n.d.

—. "On the Formation and Transmission of the Jaiminīya-Upaniṣad-Brāhmaṇa," in Michael Witzel, ed., *Inside the Texts, Beyond the Texts: New Approaches to the Study of the Vedas,* pp. 89–102. Cambridge, MA: Department of Sanskrit and Indian Studies, Harvard University, 1997.

—. "On the Unexpressed *gāyatra-sāman* in the Jaiminīya-Upaniṣad-Brāhmaṇa," *Journal of Indian and Buddhist Studies* 32/2 (1984): 1123–1121 (1–3).

—. "The Bahiṣpavamāna Ritual of the Jaiminīyas," *Machikaneyama Ronso* (*Philosophy, Osaka University*) 20 (1986): 3–25.

—. "The *Gāyatra-Sāman:* Chanting Innovations in Sāmavedic Brāhmaṇas and Upaniṣad," *Zinbun* 42 (2009–2010): 1–37.

—. "The Jaiminīya Sāmaveda Traditions and Manuscripts in South India," in Saraju Rath, ed., *Aspects of Manuscript Culture in Ancient India,* pp. 99–118. Leiden: Brill, 2012.

Gaastra, Dieuke, ed. and trans. *Bijdrage tot de kennis van het vedische ritueel: Jaiminīya Śrautasūtra.* Leiden: E. J. Brill, 1906.

Garbe, R., ed. *The Śrauta Sūtra of Āpastamba.* Bibliotheca Indica. Calcutta: Asiatic Society of Bengal, 1882–1892.

Gerety, Finnian M. M. "Survivals and Revivals: The Transmission of Jaiminīya Sāmaveda in Modern South India," in Jan Houben, Julieta Rotaru, and Michael Witzel, eds., *The Vedic Śākhās: Past, Present, Future.* Harvard Oriental Series, Opera Minora 9. Cambridge, MA: Department of South Asian Studies, Harvard University, forthcoming.

—. "This Whole World is OM: Song, Soteriology, and the Emergence of the Sacred Syllable in South Asia." PhD. dissertation, Department of South Asian Studies, Harvard University, 2015.

Gonda, Jan. *Vedic Literature: Saṃhitās and Brāhmaṇas. A History of Indian Literature,* vol. 1, fasc. 1. Wiesbaden: Harassowitz, 1975.

Heesterman, J. C., et al., eds. *Pratidānam: Indian, Iranian, and Indo-European Studies Presented to Franciscus Bernardus Jacobus Kuiper on His Sixtieth Birthday.* The Hague and Paris: Mouton, 1968.

Hillebrandt, Alfred. *Das altindische Neu- und Vollmondsopfer in seiner einfachsten Form.* Jena: G. Fischer, 1879.

—. *Ritual-Litteratur, Vedische Opfer und Zauber.* Strassburg: K. J. Trübner, 1897.

—, ed. *Śāṅkhāyanaśrautasūtram,* 2 vols. Calcutta: Asiatic Society, 1885–1899.

Hock, Hans Heinrich. "On the Origin and Early Development of the Sacred Sanskrit Syllable OM*," in *Perspectives on Indo-European Language, Culture and Religion: Studies in Honor of Edgar C. Polomé,* vol. I, pp. 89–110. *Journal of Indo-European Studies* 7. McLean, VA: Institute for the Study of Man, 1991.

Hoffmann, Karl. *Aufsätze zur Indoiranistik,* vol. II. Johanna Narten, ed. Wiesbaden: Dr. Ludwig Reichert Verlag, 1976.

Hoogt, J. M. van der. *The Vedic Chant Studied in its Textual and Melodic Form.* Wageningen, Holland: H. Veenman & Sons' Press, 1929.

Howard, Wayne. *Sāmavedic Chant.* New Haven, CT and London: Yale University Press, 1977.

—. "The Body of the Bodiless Gāyatra," Indo-Iranian Journal 30 (1987): 161–173.

—. "The Music of Nambudiri Unexpressed Chant (aniruktagāna)," in Frits Staal, ed., *Agni: The Vedic Ritual of the Fire Altar,* vol. II, pp. 311–342. Berkeley: Asian Humanities Press, 1983.

Jakobson, Roman. "Why 'Mama' and 'Papa'?", in *Selected Writings, Vol. I: Phonological Studies,* pp. 538–545. The Hague: Mouton, 1962.

Jamison, Stephanie, and Joel Brereton, trans. *The Rigveda: The Earliest Religious Poetry of India,* 3 vols. New York: Oxford University Press, 2014.

Jha, Gaṅganātha, trans. *Śabarabhāṣya on Jaimini's Mīmāṃsasūtra,* vol. III. Baroda: Oriental Institute, 1936.

Kashikar, C. G. *Śrautakośa,* Vol. II, Sanskrit Section Part I. Poona: Vaidika Saṁśodhana Maṇḍala, 1970.

—, ed. and trans. *The Śrauta, Paitṛmedhika and Pariśeṣa Sūtras of Bharadvāja,* 2 vols. Poona: Vaidika Saṁśodhana Maṇḍala, 1964.

Katz, Joshua. "Gods and Vowels," in J. Virgilio García and Angel Ruiz, eds., *Poetic Language and Religion in Greece and Rome,* pp. 2–28. Newcastle-on-Tyne, UK: Cambridge Scholars Publishing, 2013.

Keith, A. B. "OM," in James Hastings, ed., *Encyclopedia of Religion and Ethics,* vol. IX, pp. 490–492. New York: Charles Scribner's Sons, 1917.

Killingley, Dermot. "Oṃ: the Sacred Syllable in the Veda," in Julius J. Lipner, ed., *A Net Cast Wide: Investigations into Indian Thought In Memory of David Friedman,* pp. 14–33. Newcastle-on-Tyne: Grevatt & Grevatt, 1988.

MacDonell, A. A. *A History of Sanskrit Literature.* London: William Heinemann, 1900.

Mithen, Steven. *The Singing Neanderthals: The Origins of Music, Language, Mind and Body.* Cambridge, MA: Harvard University Press, 2006.

Mitra, Rājendralāla. *The Taittirīya Āraṇyaka of the Black Yajur Veda with the Commentary of Sāyaṇācārya,* 2 vols. Calcutta: C. B. Lewis, Baptist Mission Press, 1864–1872.

Muṭṭattukāṭṭu Māmaṇṇu, Iṭṭi Ravi Nampūtiri. Text of *Jaiminīya Sāmaveda* in handwritten notebooks (n.d.). From the personal collection of Asko Parpola, PDF from a photocopy courtesy of Masato Fujii.

Nooten, Barend A. van, and Gary B. Holland, eds. *Rigveda: A Metrically Restored Text.* Harvard Oriental Series 50. Cambridge, MA: Department of Sanskrit and Indian Studies, 1994.

Oertel, H., ed. and trans. "The Jaiminīya- or Talavakāra-Upaniṣad-Brāhmaṇa," *Journal of the American Oriental Society* 16 (1896): 79–260.

Olivelle, Patrick, ed. and trans. *Manu's Code of Law: A Critical Edition and Translation of the Mānava-Dharma-Śāstra.* New York: Oxford University Press, 2005.

—, ed. and trans. *The Early Upaniṣads: Annotated Text and Translation.* New York: Oxford University Press, 1998.

Parpola, Asko. "On the Etymology and Primary Meaning of the Sacred Syllable OM," in Asko Parpola, ed., *Proceedings of the Nordic South Asia Conference, Helsinki 1980,* pp. 195–214. Studia Orientalia 50. Helsinki: Finnish Oriental Society, 1981.

—, ed. *The Jaiminīya-Śrauta-Sūtra with a Commentary by Bhavatrāta.* Unpublished manuscript, n.d.

—. "The Literature and Study of the Jaiminīya Sāmaveda in Retrospect and Prospect," *Studia Orientalia* 43/6 (1973): 1–33.

—. "The Passages of the Jaiminīya Śrautasūtra Dealing with the Agnicayana, Together with Bhavatrāta's Commentary," in Frits Staal, ed., *Agni: The Vedic Ritual of the Fire Altar,* vol. 2, pp. 700–736. Berkeley: Asian Humanities Press, 1983.

—. "The Śrautasūtras of Lāṭyāyana and Drāhyāyaṇa and their Commentaries," *Commentationes Humanarum Litterarum: Societas Scientiarum Fennica* 43/2 (1969): 1–273.

Ranade, H. G., ed. and trans. *Lāṭyāyana-Śrauta-Sūtra.* Kalāmūlaśāstra Series 27–29. Delhi: Motilal Banarsidass, 1998.

Ravindran, K. A., ed. *Jaiminīyasāmavedasaṃhitā: Text of Kerala Tradition,* 2 vols. Prakashika Series 11. Delhi: Nag Publishers, 2013.

Renou, Louis. *La Grammaire de Pāṇini: texte Sanscrit, traduction française, avec extraits des commentaires,* 2 vols. Paris: École Française d'Extrême-orient, 1966.

—. *Les écoles védiques et la formation du Véda.* Paris: Imprimerie National, 1947.

—. *Vocabulaire du Rituel Védique.* Collection de Vocabulaires Techniques du Sanskrit I. Paris: Libraire C. Klincksieck, 1954.

Reuter, J. N., ed. *The Śrautasūtra of Drāhyāyana. Acta Societas Scientiarum Fennicae* 25/11 (1904).

Roth, Rudolf von. *Zur Literatur und Geschichte des Weda.* Stuttgart: A. Liesching, 1846.

Schroeder, Leopold von. *Maitrāyaṇī Saṃhitā: die Saṃhitā der Maitrāyaṇīya-Śākhā,* 4 vols. Wiesbaden: F. Steiner, 1970–1972. Originally published 1881–1886.

Simon, Richard. *Das Pañcavidhasūtra.* Indische Forschungen 5. Breslau: Verlag von M. & H. Marcus, 1913.

Sreekrishnasharma, E. R., ed. *Kauṣītaki-Brāhmaṇa,* 3 vols. Wiesbaden, F. Steiner, 1968–1976.

Staal, Frits, ed. *Agni: The Vedic Ritual of the Fire Altar,* 2 vols. Berkeley: Asian Humanities Press, 1983.

—. "A Theory of Ritual?" Paper presented at the South Asia Graduate Student Colloquium, Yale University, New Haven, CT, October 2009.

—. "How a Psychoactive Substance Becomes a Ritual: The Case of Soma," *Social Research* 68/3 (2001): 745–778.

—. "Moon Chants, Space Fillers, and Flow of Milk," in *Surabhi: Sreekrishna Sarma Felicitation Volume,* pp. 17–30. Tirupati: Prof. E. R. Sreekrishna Sarma Felicitation Committee, 1983.

—. *Nambudiri Veda Recitation.* Disputationes Rheno-Trajectinae 5. 'S-Gravenhage: Mouton & Co, 1961.

—. *Rules Without Meaning: Ritual, Mantras, and the Human Sciences.* New York: Peter Lang, 1989.

—. "The Twelve Ritual Chants of the Nambudiri Agniṣṭoma," in J. C. Heesterman, et al., eds., *Pratidānam: Indian, Iranian, and Indo-European Studies Presented to Franciscus Bernardus Jacobus Kuiper on His Sixtieth Birthday,* pp. 409–429. The Hague and Paris: Mouton, 1968.

—. "Vedic Mantras," in Harvey P. Alper, ed., *Understanding Mantras,* pp. 48–95. Albany, NY: State University of New York Press, 1989.

Strunk, Klaus. *Typische Merkmale von Fragesätzen und die altindische "Pluti."* Munich: Verlag der Bayerischen Akademie der Wissenschaften, 1983.

Thompson, George. "On Mantras and Frits Staal," *Journal of Ritual Studies* 9/2 (1995): 23–44.

—. "The Pursuit of Hidden Tracks in Vedic," *Indo-Iranian Journal* 38 (1995): 1–30.

Vedāntavāgīśa, Ānandacandra, ed. *Śrautasūtra of Lāṭyāyana with the Commentary of Agniswāmi.* Bibliotheca Indica 63. Calcutta: Asiatic Society of Bengal, 1872.

—, ed. *Tāṇḍya-Mahā-Brāhmaṇa (= Pañcaviṃśa Brāhmaṇa),* 2 vols. Bibliotheca Indica 62. Calcutta: Asiatic Society of Bengal, 1870–1874.

Vira, Raghu. *Sāma Veda of the Jaiminīyas.* Sarasvati Vihara Series 3. Lahore: International Academy of Indian Culture, 1938.

Vira, Raghu, and Lokesh Chandra, eds. *Jaiminīya Brāhmaṇa of the Sāmaveda.* Sarasvati-vihara Series 31. Nagpur: International Academy of Indian Culture, 1954.

Wackernagel, Jacob. *Altindische Grammatik,* vol. I. Göttingen, Vandenhoeck und Ruprecht, 1896.

Weber, Albrecht, ed. *Die Taittirīya Saṃhitā.* Indische Studien XI and XII. Leipzig: F. A. Brockhaus, 1871–1872.

—. *Indische Studien,* vol. II. Berlin: F. Dümmler, 1853.

—. *The White Yajurveda (The Vājasaneyi-Saṃhitā in the Mādhyaṃdina- and Kāṇva Śākhā),* 3 vols. Berlin: F. Dümmler, 1852–1859.

Whitney, W. Dwight. *Sanskrit Grammar.* Boston: Ginn & Company, 1889, second ed.

Wilke, Annette, and Oliver Moebus. *Sound and Communication: An Aesthetic Cultural History of Sanskrit Hinduism.* Berlin: De Gruyter, 2011.

Witzel, Michael, ed. *Inside the Texts, Beyond the Texts: New Approaches to the Study of the Vedas.* Harvard Oriental Series, Opera Minora 2. Cambridge, MA: Department of Sanskrit and Indian Studies, Harvard University, 1997.

—, ed. and trans. *Kaṭha-Āraṇyaka: Critical Edition with a Translation into German and an Introduction.* Harvard Oriental Series 65. Cambridge, MA: Department of Sanskrit and Indian Studies, 2004.

—. "On the Localisation of Vedic Texts and Schools (Materials on Vedic Śākhās 7)," in G. Pollet, ed., *India and the Ancient World: History, Trade and Culture before A.D. 650. P. H. L. Eggermont Jubilee Volume,* pp. 173–213. Orientalia Lovaniensia Analecta 25. Leuven: Departement Oriëntalistiek, 1987.

—. "The Development of the Vedic Canon and its Schools: The Social and Political Milieu (Materials on Vedic Śākhās 8)," in Michael Witzel, ed., *Inside the Texts, Beyond the Texts: New Approaches to the Study of the Vedas*, pp. 257–345. Cambridge, MA: Department of Sanskrit and Indian Studies, Harvard University, 1997.

Poet as Seer, Poetry as Seen: Reflections on Visualization as a Critical Element in the Conceptualization of *Kāvya*

Robert P. Goldman
University of California, Berkeley

keśy àgním keśī́ viṣáṃ keśī́ bibharti ródasī /
keśī́ víśvaṃ svár dṛśé keśī́dáṃ jyótir ucyate //[1]

The wild-haired sage contains the fire within, imbibes the drug, contains the heavens and the earth. The wild-haired sage contains all the world for its illumination and so the wild-haired sage is said to be the light itself.

When I first came to know Frits Staal, back in the dear dead days of late 1960s to early 1970s Berkeley, as his junior colleague in what was then the Department of Near Eastern Studies, we had many interesting and wide-ranging conversations in all manner of academic and (rather lively) social settings. At that time, as I remember, he used to talk with some animation about the figure of the *keśin,* the *Ṛgveda*'s mysterious and enigmatic sage or seer who—like many of us back then—wore his hair long and wild and seemed in no way averse to heightening or expanding his consciousness through the ingestion of a variety mind-altering substances.[2] I think that Frits saw something irresistible in this *keśin,* stoned on his own sagehood (*únmaditā maúneyena*),[3] so in fond memory of him and those times (*te hi no divasā gatāḥ*) I offer this discussion of the Vedic seer so dear to Frits' heart.

All students of Sanskrit literature are surely familiar with the common distinction made between *śravyakāvya,* audible poetry, poetry that is to be recited aloud and imbibed entirely through the auditory faculty; and *dṛśyakāvya,* poetry that is to be enjoyed both aurally and visually, i.e., poetic drama. But this facile distinction has perhaps served to obscure the degree to which, in the classical understanding of the production and consumption of literature, all poetry is seen to be in large measure as much a visual as auditory phenomenon on the part of both the *kavi,* who composes poetry, and the *sahṛdaya,* who relishes it, as it is something whose sonorous use of language is to be relished.

In order to get a sense of how deeply the visual is imbedded in the formation of the poetic in the Sanskrit tradition, it will be helpful to examine briefly three critical genres of literature in which the idea of the poet as seer and poetry as a linguistic representation of what the poet has seen is established and developed into the concept that the skill of the most gifted poets enables the audience who hears his or her poetry to similarly visualize what he or she has seen. These three genres are the Vedic *saṃhitā,* the epics, and the corpus of classical poetry that becomes the object of scientific scrutiny on the part of the *alaṅkāraśāstrin*s.

The centrality of vision, especially a particular heightened form of vision referred to by such terms as *dhīḥ, divyacakṣuḥ, pratibhā,* and *darśana* in poetic, religious, yogic, and philosophical texts from the earliest recoverable periods of Indian literature, has been studied by a number of scholars,[4] not least by Jan Gonda in his meticulous and magisterial studies, *The Vision of the Vedic Poets* and *Eye and Gaze in the Veda.*[5] The present brief offering owes much to these scholars but seeks to focus more precisely on not only what the *kavi* "sees"—that is, the object of the poetic gaze, i.e., the *kāvya,* the thing to be poetically rendered—but how he or she sees it and how it may be visually as well as aurally received by its intended audience.

Let me begin, as most modern histories of Sanskrit literature do, with the Veda. While the metrical portions of the large corpus of Vedic texts, particularly the *saṃhitā*s, contain in many passages material that most people today would regard as highly poetic, the *sūkta*s themselves, because of their unique nature and purpose, were not generally subjected to analysis as poetry by the authors of the a*laṅkāraśāstra.*[6]

Nonetheless we cannot ignore the fact that the terms used for those inspired sages to whom the sacred texts were revealed are referred to by the overlapping terms *ṛṣi, draṣṭṛ,* and *kavi.*[7] All of these terms refer to people gifted with a special kind of sight or insight; the first and the third types have played seminal roles in the traditional history of Indian poetry as they also refer to the inspired sages who produced what are regarded as the earliest and perhaps greatest of all the major poetic compositions, the *Rāmāyaṇa* of Vālmīki and the *Mahābhārata* of Vyāsa. The final term, *kavi,* becomes the standard term for "poet" in later Sanskrit discourse and, indeed, in many of the modern languages of India.

One might question, however: is not the entire Vedic corpus of texts generically referred to as *śruti,* "that which was heard"? This is true, but the term is never used in contradistinction with *dṛṣṭi* or any term indicating sight in the way that *śravya* does, as mentioned in the earlier example. Instead, it is used—in a very different sphere of reference—to contrast with the term *smṛti,* in order to distinguish texts that were directly revealed to or seen by the inspired Vedic seers, *ṛṣi*s or *sūri*s, from those which, although they still convey the truths derived from the known and even perhaps unknown Vedas, have been remembered, composed, and handed down by human authors. Thus, for example, the *Nirukta* explicitly defines the Vedic *ṛṣi*s as those who see the mantras.[8] In this connection, we may note that the same issue arises in the case of the seers of the *Sāmaveda* who see the ritual chants, which are themselves modifications of the Vedic stanzas (*ṛk*s). In a recent paper Giacomo Benedetti notes:

> In the *Pañcaviṃśa Brāhmaṇa,* as is natural for a *Brāhmaṇa* of the *Sāmaveda,* the *ṛṣi* is essentially the person who could see a Sāman, a Vedic "melody" or "chant," and who received a specific benefit from that. So, we could say that the main aspect is the second one, the creation of religious poetry, but, as usual in the *Brāhmaṇa*s, through "vision" (the third aspect). However, since the Sāman has a *ṛc* or Ṛgvedic "strophe," as a base, we should think that what is "seen" by the Ṛṣi are not words in a metrical form, but the way to arrange in a Sāmavedic chant some verses already seen and revealed by a Ṛgvedic Ṛṣi. Having seen this chant, the Ṛṣi can apply it in the ritual.[9]

In any case, what might we understand if we take the position that the sacred mantras were "heard" by the seers? Was it that in an exalted state the *ṛṣi*s somehow heard the hymns being recited aloud and then memorized them? Not a very likely scenario, I would suggest. First of all, since the Veda is believed to have existed before the phenomenal world, who would have recited them in the first instance? Then too, what would be so special about hearing a text recited? As Bruno Lo Turco correctly notes:

> [T]he central faculty of both (the *ṛṣi* and the *kavi*) has to do, unexpectedly, with sight rather than with hearing or speech. The *ṛṣi* observes the Veda rather than listening to it. . . . The Veda, or a part of it, is captured in a momentary glance. The sequential nature of the words serves only to reveal the Veda to an ordinary listener, that is the non-*ṛṣi.*[10]

In the later literature there are occasional references to figures being granted the faculty of supersensory hearing along with many of the supernatural powers, such as clairvoyance, that are regularly associated with advanced spiritual adepts. In a noteworthy example, Vyāsa grants Sañjaya a number of supernatural powers along with supersensory vision. The latter lists them as follows:

dṛṣṭiś cātīndriyā rājan dūrāc chravaṇam eva ca /
paracittasya vijñānam atītānāgatasya ca //[11]

Vision exceeding the (ordinary) senses, hearing things from afar, knowledge of the thoughts of others as well as of what is past and what is yet to come, your majesty.

In general, however, whenever there is an instance of someone being granted a supernormal sense it is that of *divyadṛṣṭi, divyacakṣuḥ,* or *pratibhā*—divine sight.

This being so, what exactly is it that the Vedic seers saw? Surely it was not some large, written text floating in the air before them. So what can it mean to say that someone "sees" a mantra, a *sūkta,* or a poem? It can only mean that through some extraordinary gift of divine sight the seer witnessed the personages and events described in the hymn, things that are invisible to the normal sense of sight, and he then rendered the description in metrical form. This is surely what is indicated when, for example, the great Āṅgirasa seer, Dīrghatamas, who, according to the legend of his birth as narrated in the *Mahābhārata* was born blind, begins his famous and enigmatic *"asya vāmasya"* hymn (*Ṛgveda* 1.164.1) by saying *átrāpaśyaṃ viśpátiṃ saptáputram,* "I saw the Lord of the Peoples with his seven sons."[12]

Since, according to tradition, the sage was deprived of normal vision, it is only through some special form of sight, described by Gonda as "praeternormal and spiritual vision,"[13] that he is able to visualize and describe the Sun God in this way. So, as this example may serve to show, what the poet sees is not what an ordinary person sees in the world around him or her but rather, through an exalted form of vision, something that may be remote both in distance and time and may not ever have been actually witnessed by any ordinary person. Examples of this supernatural form of vision are explicitly found throughout the Vedic *saṃhitā*s. Thus we find:

tád víṣṇoḥ paramám padáṃ sádā paśyanti sūráyaḥ divī́va cákṣur ā́ tatam[14]

The seers always see Viṣṇu's highest abode, for their vision extends to the heavens.

Even the all-important Vedic Goddess of speech, Vāc herself, the personified medium of the mantras, is represented in visual form as in the well-known hymn where it is made clear that only certain specially empowered people can see her.

> *utá tvaḥ páśyan ná dadarśa vā́cam utá tvaḥ śṛṇván ná śṛṇoti enām*
> *utó tv asmai tanúvaṃ ví sasre jāyéva pátya uśatī́ suvā́sāḥ*[15]
>
> One person, though he can see, has not seen Speech. Another, though he can hear, has not heard Her. Yet to another she reveals herself as does a beautifully clothed wife, filled with desire, to her husband.

Several highly illuminating examples of the focused vision vouchsafed to specific Vedic *ṛṣi*s are noted by Benedetti in his study of the objects and contexts of such vision in the *Pañcaviṃśa Brāhmaṇa.*[16] As this text belongs to the *Sāmaveda* tradition, it seems only natural that the seers' visions of the heavenly world and so forth should be mediated by their prior visions of specific *sāmans*. One case cited by Benedetti shows that through a particular visualization a certain seer may acquire a special vision of a heavenly being, and this vision is denied to others along with the rewards such a vision can bring.[17]

> *ṛṣayo vā indraṃ pratyakṣaṃ nāpaśyan sa vasiṣṭho 'kāmayata katham indraṃ pratyakṣaṃ paśyeyam iti sa etan nihavam apaśyat tato vai sa indraṃ pratyakṣam apaśyat. . . .*[18]
>
> The *ṛṣi*s could not see Indra directly. But Vasiṣṭha desired, "How might I see Indra directly?" He visualized the Nihava (*sāman*). Then he saw Indra directly.

Again, the same text states that the ṛṣi Asita Daivala obtained a vision of the three worlds:

> *asito vā etena daivalas trayāṇāṃ lokānāṃ dṛṣṭim apaśyat.*[19]

Examples of this kind are very numerous and can be cited almost without limit.

Indeed, we must understand that even in the absence of explicit references to vision or visualization, this faculty underlies the entire Vedic revelation. So, to give yet another well-known example, when the *ṛṣi* Hiraṇyastūpa Āṅgirasa announces at *Ṛgveda* 1.32.1 that he will proclaim Indra's feats of valor, *índrasya nú vīríyāṇi prá vocam,* and then proceeds to give a graphic and highly visually descriptive account of the god's heroic battle with the demon Vṛtra, it seems clear that he is poetically rendering the events in the hymn as he himself witnessed them.

This conception of the exalted vision of the poet-seer is explicitly described and elaborated in the next, post-Vedic, genre of the poetry of the ancient *ṛṣi*s who were the authors of the great Sanskrit epic poems, the

Mahābhārata and the *Rāmāyaṇa*. This theme of the inspired sage employing a special form of vision to view directly things that are beyond the sensory or intellectual capacities of ordinary mortals is particularly critical to the account of the composition of the massive, ancient epic of India, Vyāsa's grand poetic history of the *Somavaṃśa*, the *Mahābhārata*, and it plays a significant role in the epic story itself. Consider, for example, the following description of the Vyāsa's preparation for undertaking his encyclopedic poetic history:

dharmakāmārthaśāstrāṇi śāstrāṇi vividhāni ca /
lokayātravidhānaṃ ca saṃbhūtaṃ dṛṣṭavān ṛṣiḥ //
itihāsāḥ savaiyākhyā vividhāḥ śrutayo 'pi ca /
iha sarvam anutkrāntam uktaṃ granthasya lakṣaṇam //[20]

The seer saw all together the authoritative texts on righteousness, desire, and polity as well as the various other scientific texts and the rules for worldly behavior and the histories along with their commentaries and the various Vedic scriptures. All of this has been set forth here omitting nothing and this is indeed the distinctive characteristic of this text.

In other words, the seer had a direct vision not only of all the epic events but also of all the Vedic and śāstraic literature necessary for him to compose it authoritatively.

The central tale of the *Mahābhārata* also presents several well-known examples of individuals receiving the gift of special vision that enables them to see directly events that are remote or even are utterly beyond the perceptive capacities of ordinary or even extraordinary humans.[21] Thus Vyāsa offers Dhṛtarāṣṭra the power of this special vision so that the blind king can observe for himself the battle at Kurukṣetra. The king, however, does not wish to witness the slaughter of his kinsmen and expresses instead a desire only for the less intense auditory report of the events. Vyāsa therefore confers the gift of special, transcendent vision, *divyaṃ cakṣuh*, upon Sañjaya, enabling him to serve as history's first war correspondent as he reports the events taking place on the killing fields of Kurukṣetra to the blind king:

Vyāsa uvāca:
yadi tv icchasi saṃgrāme draṣṭum enaṃ viśāṃ pate /
cakṣur dadāni te hanta yuddham etan niśāmaya //
Dhṛtarāṣṭra uvāca:
na rocaye jñātivadhaṃ draṣṭuṃ brahmarṣisattama /
yuddham etat tv aśeṣeṇa śṛṇuyāṃ tava tejasā //

Vaiśaṃpāyana uvāca:
tasminn anicchati draṣṭuṃ saṃgrāmaṃ śrotum icchati /
varāṇām īśvaro dātā saṃjayāya varaṃ dadau //
Vyāsa uvāca:
eṣa te saṃjayo rājan yuddham etad vadiṣyati /
etasya sarvaṃ saṃgrāme na parokṣaṃ bhaviṣyati //
cakṣuṣā saṃjayo rājan divyenaiṣa samanvitaḥ /
kathayiṣyati te yuddhaṃ sarvajñaś ca bhaviṣyati //[22]

Vyāsa said: "If you wish to see this battle, Lord of the Peoples, I will give you a special vision and you can witness it for yourself."

Dhṛtarāṣṭra said: "I do not want to see the slaughter of my kinsmen, foremost of Brahman seers. Through your blazing power, though, I would hear all about the battle."

Vaiśaṃpāyana said: "Since he did not want to see the battle but only to hear about it, the Lord, granter of boons, gave that boon to Sañjaya."

Vyāsa said: "Sañjaya here will narrate the war to you, your majesty. Nothing in this battle will be beyond his vision. Endowed with divine sight, your majesty, he will narrate the war to you. For, your majesty, he will become omniscient."[23]

Of course, by far the best-known example of the gift of supernormal vision in the *Mahābhārata* is found in the famous passage in the *Bhagavadgītā,* where Lord Kṛṣṇa grants this supernormal faculty of vision to Arjuna so that he can see Kṛṣṇa's terrifying cosmic form, which cannot be perceived with the ordinary human eye. Kṛṣṇa tells Arjuna:

na tu māṃ śakṣyase draṣṭum anenaiva svacakṣuṣā /
divyaṃ dadāmi te cakṣuḥ paśya me yogam aiśvaram //[24]

But you cannot see me with your own vision. So I shall grant you a divine vision. Now behold my cosmic power.[25]

As Gonda, Lo Turco, Benedetti, and others have observed, it is clear that in some of the earliest references to the process of poetic composition the critical factor is a heightened form of vision of the poet-seer that may be innate[26] or given as a gift by some divine personage, and which enables the *kavi* to actually see the events that he or she will then render into polished, poetic speech.[27]

In this context the *Rāmāyaṇa* is especially central to the history of poetry and poetics in India precisely because its legendary author, the seer Vālmīki, is widely regarded as the founding creator of the art of literary (as opposed to liturgical) poetry. He is revered as the Ādikavi, the First

Poet, whose immensely influential and widely imitated work is regarded as the first poem, the *Ādikāvya,* a work that has served as a model for poets from the time of its creation onward.

In the opening *sarga* of the poem's *upodghāta,* or preface (*Rāmāyaṇa* 1.1–4), as it has come down to us, Vālmīki is told a very brief summary of the career of the epic hero Rāma, a version that runs only to some sixty-eight *śloka*s (*Rāmāyaṇa* 1.1.8–76) in the Critical Edition of the poem.[28] This rather dry account gives only the roughest outline of Rāma's biography, trials, and adventures. How, then, did the poet come to know so much about the events in the life of the hero, his family, friends, and enemies—some of which had not yet taken place at the time of the poem's composition—so that he was able to render it in intimate and elaborate descriptive detail in a vast poetic composition of some 24,000 *śloka*s?

According to the epic itself, the sage directly witnessed all of the events, public and private, that transpired in the careers of Rāma, Sītā, and all the numerous major and minor figures in the epic story though a special, yogic, inner vision, the capacity for which was granted him by no less a figure than the Creator, Lord Brahmā himself. The god instructs the sage as follows:

> *dharmātmano guṇavato loke rāmasya dhīmataḥ /*
> *vṛttaṃ kathaya dhīrasya te nāradāc chrutam //*
> *rahasyaṃ ca prakāśaṃ ca yad vṛttaṃ tasya dhīmataḥ /*
> *rāmasya sahasaumitre rākṣasāṇāṃ ca sarvaṣaḥ //*
> *vaidehyāś caiva yad vṛttaṃ prakāśaṃ yadi va rahaḥ /*
> *na te vāg anṛtā kāvye kācid atra bhaviṣyate //*[29]

> You must tell the world the story of the righteous, virtuous, wise, and steadfast Rāma, just as you heard it from Nārada, the full story, public and private, of that wise man. For all that befell wise Rāma, Saumitri, the *rākṣasa*s, and Vaidehī, whether in public or private, will be revealed to you, even those events of which you are ignorant. No utterance of yours in this poem shall be false.

By means of this special vision the seer witnessed all the events of Rāma's life and of the lives of all those that affected it—no matter how long ago and far away those events occurred, or even it they had yet to take place—as clearly and directly as one might perceive an *āmalaka* fruit placed in the palm of one's hand. As the poem puts it:

> *tataḥ paśyati dharmātmā tat sarvaṃ yogam āsthitaḥ /*
> *purā yat tatra nirvṛttaṃ pāṇāv āmalakaṃ yathā //*
> *tat sarvaṃ tattvato dṛṣṭvā dharmeṇa sa mahādyutiḥ /*
> *abhirāmasya rāmasya caritaṃ kartum udyataḥ //*[30]

> Then the righteous seer, concentrating in yoga, saw everything that had transpired [in Rāma's life] as clearly as an *āmalaka* fruit placed in the palm of one's hand. And only after that illustrious sage had witnessed it all did he begin to compose the biography of delightful Rāma.[31]

The special heightened vision that enables the *ṛṣi* or *kavi* to witness things that are beyond the power of normal mortal sight is not the only supernormal power these individuals possess.[32] The seer or spiritual adept is not merely the recipient of this special vision, he or she is also the conduit who, through his or her visually inspired speech, actually confers this vision on those who become the audience for the performance of the poetry thus created.[33]

After its well-known account of the creation of the first poem, discussed earlier, the *upodghāta* of the *Vālmīki Rāmāyaṇa* goes on to describe its first performances. The twin bards Lava and Kuśa, who have learned the poem at the feet of their guru, Vālmīki, first sing it publicly before an audience described as consisting of those who were themselves pure-minded seers (*ṛṣīṇāṃ bhāvitātmanām,* 1.4.13). Upon hearing the verses sung, the audience expresses its reaction in visual terms, remarking that it seems as if they can actually see the events described in the poem.

> *te prītamanasaḥ sarve munayo dharmavatsalāḥ /*
> *praśaśaṃsuḥ praśastavyau gāyamānau kuśīlavau //*
> *aho gītasya mādhuryaṃ ślokānāṃ ca viśeṣataḥ /*
> *ciranirvṛttam apy etat pratyakṣam iva darśitam //*[34]
>
> Then all those sages, who delighted in righteousness, praised with delighted hearts those two bards, so worthy of praise, saying, "O! The sweetness of the singing and especially of the poetry! Although all this took place so long ago it is as though we see it before our very eyes."

This conception of the audience of the poem, those who hear it performed, as simultaneously seeing the events and scenes it renders into poetic language is repeated in the *Uttarakāṇḍa,* when the author describes the reaction of Śatrughna's troops as they overhear Lava and Kuśa reciting Vālmīki's composition at the latter's ashram. It appears that they, too, are able to visualize the events as the bards sing of them.

> *padānugāś ca ye rājñas tāṃ śrutvā gītasampadam /*
> *avāṅmukhāś ca dīnāś ca āścaryam iti cābruvan //*
> *parasparaṃ ca te tatra sainikāḥ saṃbabhāṣire /*
> *kim idaṃ kva ca vartāmo māyeyaṃ svapnadarśanam //*[35]
>
> And as for those who were the king's followers, when they heard the magnificence of the singing, they were despondent and hung their heads, and

said: "This is wonderful!" And the soldiers who were there said to one another: "What is this? Where are we? Is this an illusion or a vision in a dream?"

The concept of the visualization, or, more precisely the revisualization, of poetic narrative on the part of the listening audience[36] is given an interesting twist by the poet-playwright Bhavabhūti, in the famous *citradarśana* scene that dominates the first act of his *Uttararāmacarita*. Here in the royal picture gallery, the narrative, once visualized by Vālmīki and revisualized through his poetry by the seers who heard it recited by his disciples, is now made graphically visual to the human eye in the form of a series of paintings. The sight of these representations of what are, in a sense, painted poetry has the same effect on the audience in the play that the early recitation of the *Rāmāyaṇa* had on its original audiences. The viewers of the paintings, here Rāma, Sītā, and Lakṣmaṇa, not only see the events depicted but feel as if they are actually experiencing these events as if they were taking place once again right before their eyes. Viewing a portrait of Daśaratha's sons in their wedding garb, Sītā remarks:

> *ede khu takkālakidagodāṇamaṅgalā cattāro bhādaro viāhadikkhidā tumhe. amho jāṇāmi tassiṃ jevva padese tassiṃ jevva kāle vattāmi. (ete khalu tatkālakṛtagodāna maṅgalāś catvāro bhrātaro vivāhadīkṣitā yuyam. aho jānāmi, tasminn eva pradeśe tasminn eva kāle varte).*[37]
>
> Here you four brothers are rendered auspicious through the tonsures just done and consecrated for the marriage ceremony. Oh! I feel that I am back in that very same time and place.

Similarly Rāma, looking at the same picture, says:

> *samayaḥ sa vartata ivaiṣa yatra māṃ*
> *samanandayat sumukhi gautamārpitaḥ /*
> *ayam āgṛhītakamanīyakaṅkanas*
> *tava mūrtimān iva mahotsavaḥ karaḥ //*[38]
>
> It seems to be that very time, fair-faced one, when your hand, presented to me by Gautama and wearing those ravishing bangles, filled me with as much delight as if it had been a festival in bodily form.

Here Bhavabhūti's audience—the spectators or readers of the play—are made, through the descriptive details in the paintings and in the play within a play, to visualize the scenes in the paintings through the language of the poet in which he expresses the visualization on the part of his characters.

With this conception of the visual in the production and consumption of poetry, it is little wonder that the works of the celebrated poets and playwrights of the Sanskrit literary tradition emphasize so heavily the visually evocative capacity of language by employing densely figured visual descriptions and comparisons that deploy their arsenal of *alaṅkāras*, such as *upamā* and *rūpaka,* as well as devices such as the type of elaborate description known as *jāti* or *svabhāvokti.* It is as if the *kavis* want their audiences, through hearing their poetic speech, to visualize or actually "see" the figures, scenes, and events they are rendering in verse or prose. Of particular note here is the extreme degree to which these ubiquitous comparisons are made through the use of verbal forms that depend on the visual, with meanings such as "to look like," "to appear as," "to seem," "to shine," etc., verbal roots such as √*dṛś,* √*bhā,* √*rāj,* and √*dīp,* and center on qualities that either are physical and actually visible or, when they are moral or spiritual, that can be rendered in visual terms through the use of roots such as √*dīp, saṃ* + *pra* + √*kāś,* and the like. Even when the verb establishing *aupamya* is simply the copula √*bhū,* √*as,* √*vṛt,* etc., the comparison is a visual one to a disproportionate extent.

This characteristic of Sanskrit poetry, its sheer visuality, is clearly notable at the earliest stages, when it is recognized by the authorities on *alaṅkāraśāstra,* most notably in the *Rāmāyaṇa* itself. To a great extent, this visuality is the feature that accounts most significantly for the epic's reputation as not only a piece of *itihāsa* but as the foundational text of Indian *kāvya,* or *belles lettres.*

A few out of virtually numberless possible examples may suffice to demonstrate this. Here, for example, is the First Poet's description of the battlefield outside the walls of Laṅkā, followed by our translation of the passage:[39]

vānarāṇāṃ śarīrais tu rākṣasānāṃ ca medinī /
babhūva nicitā ghorā patitair iva parvataiḥ //
sā mahī rudhiraugheṇa pracchannā saṃprakāśate /
saṃchannā mādhave māsi palāśair iva puṣpitaiḥ //
hatavīraughavaprāṃ tu bhagnāyudhamahādrumām /
śoṇitaughamahātoyāṃ yamasāgarayāminīm //
yakṛtplīhamahāpaṅkāṃ vinikīrṇāntraśaivalām/
bhinnakāyaśiromīnām aṅgāvayavaśāḍvalām //
gṛdhrahaṃsagaṇākīrṇāṃ kaṅkasārasasevitām /
medaḥphenasamākīrṇām ārtasvanitanisvanām //
tāṃ kāpuruṣadustārāṃ yuddhabhūmīmayīṃ nadīm /
nadīm iva ghanāpāye haṃsasārasasevitām //[40]

Heaped up with the corpses of monkeys and *rākṣasas*, as if covered with fallen mountains, the earth looked ghastly. The ground, covered with torrents

> of blood, looked as if it were covered with blossoming *palāśa* trees in the month of Mādhava. Indeed, the battleground resembled a river. Masses of slain heroes formed its banks, and shattered weapons its great trees. Torrents of blood made up its broad waters, and the ocean to which it flowed was Yama. Livers and spleens made up its deep mud, scattered entrails its waterweeds. Severed heads and trunks made up its fish; pieces of limbs its grass. It was crowded with vultures in place of flocks of *haṃsa*s, and it was swarming with adjutant storks instead of *sārasa* cranes. It was covered with fat in place of foam, and the cries of the wounded took the place of its gurgling. It was not to be forded by the faint of heart. Truly, it looked like a river swarming with *haṃsa*s and *sārasa* cranes at the end of the rains.

Or consider the following descriptions of Sītā when she is first seen by Hanumān in Rāvaṇa's *aśokavana:*

> *tāṃ nīlakeśīṃ bimboṣṭhīṃ sumadhyamāṃ supratiṣṭhitām /*
> *sītāṃ padmapalāśākṣīṃ manmathasya ratiṃ yathā //*
> *malapaṅkadharāṃ dīnāṃ maṇḍanārhām amaṇḍitām /*
> *prabhāṃ nakṣatrarājasya kālameghair ivāvṛtām //*[41]
>
> Her hair was jet black; her lips like *bimba* fruit. Her waist was lovely and her posture was perfect. Her eyes were like lotus petals and she looked like Rati, wife of Manmatha. . . . Dejected, covered with dirt and grime, and devoid of ornaments—though she was worthy of them—she resembled the light of the moon, king of stars, obscured by black storm clouds.[42]

This early tradition is closely followed and indeed further developed by even the most sophisticated and highly figurative of the later exponents of the poetic art. Again, there are far too many examples to mention inclusively, but a good one, chosen more or less at random, would be Māgha's florid verbal portrait of *devarṣi* Nārada as he descends from the heavens to meet Lord Kṛṣṇa, in the opening verses of the *Śiśupālavadha:*

> *nisargacitrojjvalasūkṣmapakṣmaṇā lasadbisacchedasitāṅgasaṅginā /*
> *cakāsataṃ cārucamūrucarmaṇā kuthena nāgendram ivendravāhanam //*[43]
>
> Him (Nārada) who, by virtue of the exquisite deerskin with its naturally speckled fine and glossy fur and which clung tightly to his body, which was like a bright segment of a lotus stalk, looked as radiant as Indra's mount, the lord of elephants, in his multicolored blanket.

The intense and unrelenting visuality of the language is impossible to ignore.

While it is true that much of world poetry has considerable visual descriptive content, there are few if any literary cultures other than that of premodern India in which the very idea of poetic creation is so firmly rooted in construction of a special, inspired, and even divine form of sight. This divine sight constitutes the essential gift without which the would-be poet cannot truly and profoundly know or "see" his or her subject matter and render it with such clarity and dense visual detail. The hearers and readers of the product of this special insight or inspiration are thus able to also perceive it too, as clearly as if an *āmalaka* fruit is placed in the palm of our hand.

Notes

1 *Ṛgveda* 10.136.1.

2 At issue here, of course, is the meaning of the term *viṣa,* normally, "poison," in verses 1 and 7 of *Ṛgveda* 10.136, which the *keśin* is said to imbibe alone (vs. 1) and also along with Rudra (vs. 7). The rather straitlaced Sāyaṇācārya, who *ad loc* takes the term *keśin* to refer to the deities of fire, wind, and the sun (*keśino 'gnir vāyuḥ sūryaś ca*) takes viṣa to refer simply to water (*udakanāmaitat*), and in this he has been followed by Ralph T. H. Griffith, who translates it as "moisture"; *The Hymns of the Ṛgveda: Translated with a Popular Commentary* (Delhi: Motilal Banarsidass, 1973), p. 636. Karl Friedrich Geldner, however, renders "den Gifttrank" but glosses in a note, "Das Gift ist der narkotische Trank, durch den er sich in den ekstatischen Zustand versetzt"; *Der Rig-Veda: aus dem Sanskrit ins Deutsche Übersetzt und mit einem laufenden Kommentar versehen. Dritter Teil: Neunter bis zehnter Liederkreis* (Cambridge, MA and London: Harvard University Press, 1978), p. 369. Geldner has been followed by Wendy Doniger O'Flaherty, who renders "the drug"; *The Rig Veda: An Anthology* (London: Penguin Classics, 1981 p. 137. Like Geldner and O'Flaherty (and, of course, Frits himself), I prefer the latter sense of the term.

3 *Ṛgveda* 10.136.3.

4 For example, Diana Eck, *Darśan: Seeing the Divine Image in India* (New York: Columbia University Press, 1996); Robert Goldman, "Review of Jan Gonda's *Eye and Gaze in the Veda,*" *Journal of the Oriental Institute* (Baroda) 21/1–2 (1971): 142–146; Jan Gonda, *The Vision of the Vedic Poets* (Utrecht: Mouton, 1963) and *Eye and Gaze in the Veda* (Amsterdam: Royal Netherlands Academy of Arts and Sciences, 1968); Greg Bailey, "The Significance of the Divine Eye as a Means of Spiritual Vision in Ancient Indian Religion," *Journal of Studies in Mysticism* 2/2 (1979): 86–97; S. K. Belvalkar, "Sañjaya's 'Eye Divine,'" *Annals of the Bhandarkar Oriental Research Institute* 27/3–4 (1946): 310–331; Bruno Lo Turco, "The Construction of Nature: Ṛṣis and Kavis," *Pandanus* 9 (2009): 33–44; Giacomo Benedetti, "The Objects and Contexts of Vision of the Ṛṣis in the Pañcaviṃśa Brāhmaṇa," in Hans Henrich Hock and Radhavallabh Tripathi, eds., *Vedic Studies: Language, Culture, and Philosophy. Proceedings of the 15th World Sanskrit Conference 1* (New Delhi: Rashtriya Sanskrit Sansthan and D. K. Printworld, 2014), pp. 179–194, etc.

5 Gonda, *The Vision of the Vedic Poets* and *Eye and Gaze in the Veda.*

[6] The issue here, as stated famously by Abhinavagupta, is that although the purpose of all edifying composition is education (*vyutpatti*) concerning the four principal aims of life (*caturvarga*), the predominant virtue of true poetry—that is, of *kāvya*—is pleasure or delight (*prīti, ānanda*), as opposed to instruction. This leads Abhinavagupta to his well-known set of comparisons in which he states that while the Vedas teach like a (school)master and the epics like a friend, only poetry teaches in the manner of a wife:

śrotṝṇāṃ ca vyutpattiprītī yady api staḥ . . . tathāpi tatra prītir eva pradhānam / anyathā prabhusammitebhyo vedādibhyo mitrasammitebhyaś cetihāsādibhyo vyutpattihetubhyaḥ ko 'sya kāvyarūpasya vyutpattihetor jāyāsammitatvalakṣaṇo viśeṣa iti pradhānyenānanda evoktaḥ / caturvargavyutpatter api cānanda eva pāryantikaṃ mukhyaṃ phalam / Dhvanyālokalocana 1.1 (p. 66).

[7] Lo Turco argues that the *kavi* in the post Vedic period assumes the functions of the Vedic *ṛṣi:* "the *kavi* is the true heir of the *ṛṣi*"*;* "The Construction of Nature: Ṛṣis and Kavis," pp. 36–37. Nonetheless, it is clear at least by the time of the epics that little if any distinction is made between seer and poet.

[8] *ṛsayo mantradraṣṭāro evam uccāvacair abhiprāyair ṛsīnāṃ mantradṛṣṭayo bhavanti.* Cf. *Nirukta* 7.3; H. M. Bhadkamkar, ed. *The Nirukta of Yāska (with Nighaṇṭu), Edited with Durga's Commentary* (Bombay: Government Central Press, 1918, 1942). Cf. *Bṛhaddevatā* 1.3:

tadvidāṃ tadabhiprāyān ṛṣīṇāṃ mantradṛṣṭiṣu /
vijñāpayanti vijñānaṃ karmāṇi vividhāni ca //

[9] Benedetti, "The Objects and Contexts of Vision of the Ṛṣis," p. 179.

[10] Lo Turco,"The Construction of Nature: Ṛṣis and Kavis," pp. 37–38.

[11] *Mahābhārata* 6.16.8. For a full scholarly discussion of this passage and the interesting issues it raises, see S. K. Belvalkar, "Sañjaya's 'Eye Divine,'" *Annals of the Bhandarkar Oriental Research Institute* 27/3–4 (1946): 310–331.

[12] *Ṛgveda* 1.164.1. For an analysis of this important hymn and the role of the seer's vision in it, see W. Norman Brown, "Agni, Sun, Sacrifice, and Vāc: A Sacerdotal Ode by Dīrghatamas (Rig Veda 1.164)," Journal of the American Oriental Society, 88/2 (1968): pp. 199–218.

[13] Jan Gonda, The Vision of the Vedic Poets (Utrecht: Mouton, 1963; New Delhi: Munshiram Manoharlal Publishers Ltd., 1984, reprint), p. 29.

[14] *Ṛgveda* 1.22.20.

[15] *Ṛgveda* 10.71.4.

[16] Benedetti, "The Objects and Contexts of Vision of the Ṛṣis," pp. 179–194.

[17] Benedetti, "The Objects and Contexts of Vision of the Ṛṣis," pp. 181–182.

[18] *Pañcaviṃśa Brāhmaṇa* XV.5.24.

[19] *Pañcaviṃśa Brāhmaṇa* XIV.11.19.

[20] *Mahābhārata* 1.1.47–48. All references to the *Mahābhārata* are to V. S. Sukthankar, et al., eds., *The Mahābhārata: Critical Edition,* 24 vols. (Poona: Bhandarkar Oriental Research Institute, 1933–1970).

21 Other figures who receive the gift of supersensory sight include the blindfolded queen Gāndhārī, who uses it to visualize and report on the grim aftermath of the Kurukṣetra war, and the lamentations of the surviving women in the *Strīparvan*. On this, see Kevin McGrath, *JAYA: Performance in Epic Mahābhārata* (Boston and Washington, DC: Ilex Foundation: The Center for Hellenic Studies, Trustees for Harvard University, 2011), pp. 17–20.

22 *Mahābhārata* 6.2. 9–10.

23 It is true, as Belvalkar points out ("Sañjaya's 'Eye Divine,'" pp. 131–317), that Sañjaya does not acquire all of his information about the battle remotely but actually visits the field of action in person. Nonetheless, the sights, sounds, and thoughts (not to mention dreams) he experiences there are far beyond the capacity of normal human senses. For example, through his supersensory powers as well as the ability to fly (*ākāśe gatiḥ śubhā*), he is able to hear the sounds of the dead rising to the heavens and witness and report on Arjuna and Kṛṣṇa's dream journey to Mt. Mandara to see Lord Śiva. Belvalkar, of course, ultimately argues that Sañjaya would have been fully competent to report the events of the Bhārata war to Dhṛtarāṣṭra even without the faculty of divyacakṣuḥ, and that this motif was added largely to heighten Vyāsa's own reputation for reportorial accuracy; "Sañjaya's 'Eye Divine,'" pp. 329–331. But this largely ignores the recurrence of this theme throughout the literature.

24 *Bhagavadgītā* 11.8.

25 Note Belvalkar's rationalization of Arjuna's divine vision of the Lord's *aiśvara* form, which he regards more as an act of the devotional imagination rather than of supersensory vision; "Sañjaya's 'Eye Divine,'" pp. 320–321.

26 See Lo Turco, "The Construction of Nature: Ṛṣis and Kavis," p. 38.

27 Lo Turco quotes Bhaṭṭa Tauta to the effect that in the case of poetic composition vision, *darśana,* must precede description, *varṇana;* "The Construction of Nature: Ṛṣis and Kavis," p. 36.

28 All references to the *Rāmāyaṇa,* unless otherwise specified, are to G. H. Bhatt and U. P. Shah, eds., *The Vālmīki Rāmāyaṇa: Critical Edition,* 7 vols. (Baroda: Oriental Institute, University of Baroda, 1960–1975).

29 *Rāmāyaṇa* 1.2.31–34ab. Compare the very similar wording in the *Mahābhārata,* where Vyāsa describes what Sañjaya will be able to visualize with the divine sight he will receive from him (*Mahābhārata* 5.2.11.):

prakāśaṃ vā rahasyaṃ vā rātrau vā yadi vā divā /
manasā cintitam api sarvaṃ vetsyati saṃjayaḥ //

Sañjaya will come to know everything, whether public or private, by day or by night even if it is merely thought of in (someone's) mind.

30 Shastri Shrinivas Katti Mudholkar, ed., *Rāmāyaṇ of Vālmīki,* 7 vols. (Bombay: Gujarati Printing Press, 1914–1920), 1.3.6–7.

31 It is clear that the special vision granted to the epic seers is regarded as in no way different from that vouchsafed to the Vedic ṛṣis, and that the poetry they produce as a result of their divine sight is, in fact, itself a form of Vedic

speech—in other words, of the Supreme Spirit in auditory form (*śabdabrahman*). Consider the way in which the character Ātreyī in Bhavabhūti's famous play *Uttararāmacarita* recounts the story of Vālmiki's acquisition of this power and his commission to create the First Poem, the *Rāmāyaṇa* (*Uttararāmacarita* after 2.5):

> *tena khalu punaḥ samayena taṃ bhagavantam āvirbhūtaśabdaprakāśam ṛṣim upasaṅgamya bhagavān bhūtabhāvanaḥ padmayonir avocat–ṛṣe prabuddho 'si vāgātmani brahmaṇi, tad brūhi rāmacaritam. avyāhatajyotir ārṣaṃ te pratibhācakṣuḥ. ādyaḥ kavir asīty uktvā tatraivāntarhitaḥ. atha bhagavān prācetasaḥ prathamaṃ manuṣyeṣu śabdabrahmaṇas tādṛśaṃ vivartam itihāsaṃ rāmāyaṇaṃ praṇināya.*
>
> And at around that time the Creator of all beings, the lotus-born Lord (Brahmā), approached the blessed seer to whom the illumination of the Supreme Spirit as Speech had been revealed and said, "Seer, you have been enlightened with respect to the Supreme Spirit in the form of Speech. Therefore you must narrate the life of Rāma. Your seer's eye of divine insight will be such that its penetrating light will meet no obstacle. For you are the First Poet." When he had spoken in this fashion, he vanished then and there. Then, the blessed son of Pracetas, for the first time among men, composed such a history, the *Rāmāyaṇa* that is really but a modified form of the Supreme Spirit as Speech.

It is also a commonplace in the Sanskritic literary and religious traditions to regard the epics, which are considered to be the work of divinely inspired *ṛṣis*, to be equal or nearly equal to the Vedas themselves. This can easily be seen in the *phalaśruti* passages that appear at the end of most manuscripts of the poems. Thus we find the *Mahābhārata* frequently referred to as the "Fifth Veda" (*pañcamo vedaḥ*), the "Veda of Kṛṣṇa" (*kārṣṇo vedaḥ*), and "equal to the Vedas" (*vedasaṃmita; Mahābhārata* 18.5.43). On this, see James L. Fitzgerald, "India's Fifth Veda: The Mahābhārata's Presentation of Itself," *Journal of South Asian Literature* 20/1 (Winter–Spring 1985): Part I: *Essays on the Mahābhārata*, pp. 125–140.

The same is true in the case of the *Rāmāyaṇa*, as can be seen in the Vulgate editions (e.g., 1.111.4), and in the sectarian tradition according to which the entire poem is a grand expansion of the sacred *Gāyatrī Mantra* whose twenty-four syllables are said to be found, one by one, at intervals of a thousand *śloka*s in Vālmīki's text. On this issue, see B. N. Bhatt, "Estimating the Traditions of the Vālmīki Rāmāyaṇa by the Presence or Absence of the Syllables of Gāyatrī in Them," *Journal of the Oriental Institute of Baroda* 26/2 (1976): 145–161; Sheldon I. Pollock, *The Rāmāyaṇa of Vālmīki: An Epic of Ancient India, Vol. II: Ayodhyākāṇḍa* (Princeton, NJ: Princeton University Press, 1986), pp. 395, 450, 494; Robert Goldman and Sally J. Sutherland Goldman, *The Rāmāyaṇa of Vālmīki: An Epic of Ancient India, Vol. V: Sundarakāṇḍa* (Princeton, NJ: Princeton University Press, 1996), pp. 3, 301, 390, 423.

32 The various texts in which the power of supernatural vision is demonstrated naturally differ as to what precisely serves as the source of this power. In the

Ṛgveda, as Gonda has shown in *The Vision of the Vedic Poets,* pp. 32–33, the source of the seers' inspiration and vision can be the purified *soma.* In the *Brāhmaṇa* literature, it may be, as Benedetti, has shown in "The Objects and Contexts of Vision of the Ṛṣis," pp. 179–194, the practice of *tapas,* asceticism, or even a preliminary vision of a *sāman.* Ascetic practices, especially those associated with yoga, come to be viewed as one of the major sources of transcendental knowledge, as shown throughout the narrative literature and in such texts as the *Yogasūtra*s 3.25–26; see Pandit Dhundhiraj Śāstri, ed., *Yogasūtram of Maharṣi Patañjali* (Benaras: Jai Krishnadas-Haridas Gupta, 1931).

Elsewhere, especially in the epics, the power of supernatural sight is often viewed as a gift to be granted permanently or temporarily to a person by a divinity or spiritually advanced human. For a further discussion of the faculty of supernatural vision and how it may be acquired as represented in Hindu and Buddhist literature, see Greg Bailey, "The Significance of the Divine Eye as a Means of Spiritual Vision in Ancient Indian Religion," *Journal of Studies in Mysticism* 2/2 (1979): 86–97. For a more technical discussion of this subject, see David Gordon White, *Sinister Yogis* (Chicago: University of Chicago Press, 2009), pp. 151–161.

33 The capacity of the seer or poet not only to perceive visions but to actually generate them in others is no doubt connected to the primordial *ṛṣi*s' cosmogonic power, which enables them to bring things into existence. This power is mentioned in numerous places in the Vedic corpus. For a learned discussion of this, see Lo Turco, "The Construction of Nature: Ṛṣis and Kavis." Compare also Bhavabhūti's well-known verse, according to which reality itself must accord with the speech of the primal seers (*Uttararāmacarita* 1.10):

laukikānāṃ hi sādhūnām arthaṃ vāg anuvartate /
ṛṣīṇāṃ punar ādyānāṃ vācam artho 'nudhāvati //

In the case of virtuous worldly people, their speech conforms to the facts. But in the case of the primordial seers, the facts follow their words.

34 *Rāmāyaṇa* 1.4.15–16.

35 The passage appears as *Rāmāyaṇa* 7, Appendix 1, No. 9, lines 28–22, but we believe that it should have been included in the critically established text. See Sally S. Goldman, "Critical Evidence: Vālmīki's *Uttarakāṇḍa* and the Critical Edition," in Adam Bowles and Alf Hiltebeitel, eds., *Epic Studies Volume: Proceedings of the XVth World Sanskrit Conference* (New Delhi: Rashtriya Sanskrit Sansthan and Printworld, 2015), pp. 298–324.

36 McGrath, seeing Dhṛtarāṣṭra's reception of the verbal report of the battle of Kurukṣetra given to him by the divinely sighted Sañjaya, provocatively likens the king's response to the imaginative catharsis Aristotle posited of the audience of Greek tragedy (*JAYA: Performance in Epic Mahābhārata,* p. 18):

In the *Poetics* of Aristotle, *kátharsis* for a watching audience classical Athenian theatre is said to occur when the spectator imagines in his or her mind's eye events described by a messenger: these typically refer to the horrid and pitiful death of a hero or heroine. It is by virtue of such *imagination,* where the audience *visualizes* what it is that they are *hearing*, that *kâtharsis* actually occurs, for there is no viewing of the violence itself, onstage. I would propose that Dhṛtarāṣṭra is in a similar position—in terms of poetic experience—as a member of an audience in fifth-century Athenian state theatre: in his blindness he imagines and in fact experiences the emotions of those thoughts. What Dhṛtarāṣṭra hears—as the poet Saṃjaya describes—functions similarly: the old king sees by virtue of intellection, not by means of material sensory perception. This is in fact how an audience for the battle books receives the epic as a whole, for Dhṛtarāṣṭra is the *ideal* audience insofar as he is the *first* of listeners.

Of course, a significant difference between the Indian, and, for that matter, the Greek epics and drama is that the former represents violence very graphically, while the latter does not depict violence at all.

37 *Uttararāmacarita* prose following 1.17.

38 *Uttararāmacarita* 1.18.

39 Robert Goldman, Sally. J. Sutherland Goldman, and B. A. van Nooten, *The Rāmāyaṇa of Vālmīki: An Epic of Ancient India, Vol. VI: Yuddhakāṇḍa* (Princeton, NJ: Princeton University Press, 2009), p. 247. [or Robert P. Goldman, et al]

40 *Rāmāyaṇa* 6.46.23–28.

41 *Rāmāyaṇa* 5.13.28, 35.

42 Goldman and Goldman, *The Rāmāyaṇa of Vālmīki: An Epic of Ancient India, Volume V: Sundarakāṇḍa*, p. 155.

43 *Śiśupālavadha* 1.8.

References

Primary Sources

Bhadkamkar, Hari Mahadev, ed. *The Nirukta of Yāska (with Nighaṇṭu), Edited with Durga's Commentary.* Bombay Sanskrit and Prakrit Series, nos. 73 and 85. Bombay: Government Central Press, 1918, 1942.

Bhatt, G. H., and U. P. Shah, eds. *The Vālmīki Rāmāyaṇa: Critical Edition,* 7 vols. Baroda: Oriental Institute, University of Baroda, 1960–1975.

Dhvanyāloka of Shri Anandavardhanacharya with the Lochan Commentary by Shri Abhinava Gupta along with Full Hindi Translation of Both the Texts and the Tarawati Vyakhya by Dr. Ram Sagar Tripathi. Delhi: Motilal Banarsidass, 1963.

Kane, P. V., and C. N. Joshi, trans. and notes. *Uttarāmacarita of Bhavabhūti,* with the commentary of Ghanaśyāma. Delhi: Motilal Banarsidass, 1971.

Mudholkar, Shastri Shrinivas Katti, ed. *Rāmāyaṇ of Vālmīki,* 7 vols. With three commentaries called *Tilaka, Shiromani,* and *Bhooshana.* Bombay: Gujarati Printing Press, 1914–1920.

Paṇśīkar, Wāsudeva Laxmaṇ Śāstrī, ed. *The Śiśupālavadha of Māgha,* with the commentary *Sarvaṃkaṣā* of Mallinātha. Bombay: Nirnaya Sagar Press, 1902.

Ṛgveda-Saṃhitā, 5 vols. With the commentary of Sāyaṇācārya. Poona: Vaidic Samshodhan Mandal, 1933.

Ṛgvedasaṃhitā Śrīmatsāyaṇācāryaviracitabhāṣyasametā. Poona: Vaidikasaṃśodhanamaṇḍala, 1933.

Sadhale, Shastri Gajanana Shambhu, ed. *The Bhagavad-Gita with Eleven Commentaries.* Bombay: Gujarati Press, 1935–1938.

Śāstri, Pandit Dhundhiraj, ed. *Yogasūtram of Maharṣi Patañjali.* With the *Yogapradīpaka* commentary of Paṇḍit Baladewa Miśra. Benaras: Jai Krishnadas-Haridas Gupta, 1931.

Sukthankar, V. S., et al., eds. *Mahābhārata: Critical Edition,* 24 vols. Poona: Bhandarkar Oriental Research Institute, 1933–1970.

Tokunaga, Muneo, ed. *The Bṛhaddevatā: Text Reconstructed from the Manuscripts of the Shorter Recension with Introduction, Explanatory Notes, and Indices.* Kyoto: Rinsen Book Co., 1997.

Secondary Sources

Bailey, Greg. "The Significance of the Divine Eye as a Means of Spiritual Vision in Ancient Indian Religion," *Journal of Studies in Mysticism* 2/2 (1979): 86–97.

Benedetti, Giacomo. "The Objects and Contexts of Vision of the Ṛṣis in the Pañcaviṃśa Brāhmaṇa," in Hans Henrich Hock and Radhavallabh Tripathi, eds., *Vedic Studies: Language, Culture, and Philosophy. Proceedings of the 15th World Sanskrit Conference 1,* pp. 179–184. New Delhi: Rashtriya Sanskrit Sansthan and D. K. Printworld, 2014.

Belvalkar, S. K. "Sañjaya's 'Eye Divine,'" *Annals of the Bhandarkar Oriental Research Institute* 27/3–4 (1946): 310–331.

Bhatt, B. N. "Estimating the Traditions of the Vālmīki Rāmāyaṇa by the Presence or Absence of the Syllables of Gāyatrī in Them," *Journal of the Oriental Institute of Baroda* 26/2 (1976): 145–161.

Brown, W. Norman. "Agni, Sun, Sacrifice, and Vāc: A Sacerdotal Ode by Dīrghatamas (Rig Veda 1.164)," *Journal of the American Oriental Society,* 88/2 (1968): pp. 199–218.

Eck, Diana. *Darśan: Seeing the Divine Image in India.* New York: Columbia University Press, 1996.

Fitzgerald, James L. "India's Fifth Veda: The Mahābhārata's Presentation of Itself," *Journal of South Asian Literature* 20/1 (Winter–Spring 1985): *Part I: Essays on the Mahābhārata,* pp. 125–140.

Geldner, Karl Friedrich. *Der Rig-Veda: aus dem Sanskrit ins Deutsche Übersetzt und mit einem laufenden Kommentar versehen. Dritter Teil: Neunter bis zehnter Liederkreis.* Cambridge, MA and London: Harvard University Press, 1978.

Goldman, Robert. "Review of Jan Gonda's *Eye and Gaze in the Veda,*" *Journal of the Oriental Institute* (Baroda) 21/1–2 (1971): 142–146.

Goldman, Robert, Sally J. Sutherland Goldman, and B. A. van Nooten. *The Rāmāyaṇa of Vālmīki: An Epic of Ancient India, Vol. VI: Yuddhakāṇḍa.* Princeton, NJ: Princeton University Press, 2009.

Goldman, Robert, and Sally J. Sutherland Goldman. *The Rāmāyaṇa of Vālmīki: An Epic of Ancient India, Vol. V: Sundarakāṇḍa.* Princeton, NJ: Princeton University Press, 1996.

Goldman, Sally Sutherland. "Critical Evidence: Vālmīki's *Uttarakāṇḍa* and the Critical Edition," in Adam Bowles and Alf Hiltebeitel, eds., *Epic Studies Volume. Proceedings of the XVth World Sanskrit Conference,* pp. 298–324. New Delhi: Rashtriya Sanskrit Sansthan, forthcoming.

Gonda, Jan. *Eye and Gaze in the Veda.* Verhandelingen der Koninklijke Nederlandse Akademie van Wetanschappen, Afd. Letterkunde, 75.1. Amsterdam: Royal Netherlands Academy of Arts and Sciences, 1968.

—. *The Vision of the Vedic Poets.* Disputationes Rheno Trajectinae 8. Utrecht: Mouton, 1963. New Delhi: Munshiram Manoharlal Publishers Ltd., 1984, reprint.

Griffith, Ralph T. H. *The Hymns of the Ṛgveda: Translated with a Popular Commentary.* J. L. Shastri, ed. Delhi. Motilal Banarsidass, 1973.

Lo Turco, Bruno. "The Construction of Nature: Ṛṣis and Kavis," *Pandanus* 9 (2009): 33–44.

McGrath, Kevin. *JAYA: Performance in Epic Mahābhārata.* Boston and Washington, DC: Ilex Foundation: The Center for Hellenic Studies, Trustees for Harvard University, 2011.

Nooten, Barend A. van, and Gary B. Holland. *Rig Veda: A Metrically Restored Text with Introduction and Notes.* Cambridge, MA and London: Department of Sanskrit and Indian Studies, Harvard University and Harvard University Press, 1994.

O'Flaherty, Wendy Doniger. *The Rig Veda: An Anthology.* London: Penguin Classics, 1981.

Pollock, Sheldon I. *The Rāmāyaṇa of Vālmīki: An Epic of Ancient India, Vol. II: Ayodhyākāṇḍa.* Princeton, NJ: Princeton University Press, 1986.

White, David Gordon. *Sinister Yogis.* Chicago: University of Chicago Press, 2009.

The Monstrous Feminine: *Rākṣasīs* and Other Others—The Archaic Mother of Bhāsa's *Madhyamavyāyoga*[1]

Sally J. Sutherland Goldman
University of California, Berkeley

Bhāsa, the purported author of the Trivandrum plays, is one of the more controversial playwrights of the Sanskrit tradition. The authenticity of his authorship has been critically examined by a number of well-known and influential scholars, as has his date, assuming he was the author of the Trivandrum plays. Scholarship on the date of Bhāsa has given rise to numerous theories, which have variously placed his work from a period prior to Pāṇini (because of the number of non-Pāṇinian forms)[2] to ranging from the seventh or eighth centuries,[3] or as late as the eleventh century C.E.[4] In fact, it seems as if there are as many dates for Bhāsa as there are scholars who have written on the subject.

Scholarship generally falls into three groups: (1) early (pre-Pāṇiṇi), (2) pre-Kālidāsa, or (3) around the seventh to eighth centuries C.E.[5] A reasonable consensus is that the playwright flourished between the time of Aśvaghoṣa and Kālidāsa.[6] Sushil K. De is perhaps the most insightful of Bhāsa's critics when he reminds us that we should not lose sight of the fact that these plays were a product of their environment.[7] As with other Sanskrit plays as they were handed down from one generation to the next, words, verses, and even sections of the plays were bound to have been lost, added, or revised. Thus issues of authorship and dating will always be open to criticism, controversy, and revision.

Despite the intense scholarly attention paid to the structural similarity of the Trivandrum plays, their authorship, and their author's date, little attention has been given over to serious analysis of the plays themselves. And while some scholars (see, for example, A. Berriedale Keith and De) have exercised themselves a great deal over whether or not the plays fit into the structure of the traditional *nāṭaka* or follow exactly the plot of their original "epic" stories or other prototypes, the plays as literary and performative pieces seem largely to get bypassed.[8]

With the aim of addressing this lack, in this paper I will examine one of the lesser plays of Bhāsa, the *Madhymavyāyoga*,[9] focusing less on the play's history and more on its role as a work of literature and performative dramatic art. I will concentrate on two interrelated issues: structure and meaning. Through the mechanism of the first the second will be analyzed, with an eye toward understanding some of the psychological and sociological underpinnings of the world that informed Bhāsa's *vyāgoga*.[10]

The play is quite short, one act, and tells the story of a brahman family, a father, a mother, and their three sons, traveling in a *rākṣasa*-haunted forest on their way to a sacrifice. It so happens that this is the very forest in which the Pāṇḍavas are living out their exile,[11] and it is also the home of the *rākṣasī* Hiḍimbā and her son Ghaṭotkaca. The background of the story is an episode from the *Mahābhārata* in which Bhīma meets and "marries" the *rākṣasī* Hiḍimbā, which, one assumes, was well known to the audience of the play. Their union results in the birth of a son, the half-human, half-demon Ghaṭotkaca.[12]

After the opening verse, a verse in praise of Viṣṇu (Hari) in his Vāmana *avatāra*, the *sūtradhāra*, or stage manager, hears a sound offstage, *aye kiṃ nu khalu . . . śabda iva śrūyate*, and assumes that it could be no other than the voice of a brahman. He again hears words coming from behind the curtain (*nepathye*), *bhos tāta ko nu khalv eṣaḥ*, "Oh! Father! Who indeed is this?"

This type of opening is common to Bhāsa's dramas. The *sūtradhāra* is on stage to introduce the play and its characters. He supposedly hears an unexpected noise offstage, questions what it could be, and then realizes that it concerns the events of the play (as, for example, the crowds being driven away in the *Svāpnavāsavadattam*). The audience is led to believe that the play being performed here and now is actually an ongoing story, in which we are being allowed momentarily to participate vicariously. The effect is not dissimilar from the modern film technique of the "fade-in." The transition functions to merge reality with fantasy and to draw the audience into the story.[13]

Visually, we see only the *sūtradhāra*. But the audience hears the first clues about the theme, tone, and subject matter of the play when the word *bhoḥ* is uttered. Shivaram V. Apte, in his *Practical Sanskrit-English Dictionary*, understands this word only as a vocative particle used when addressing people: "O, sir, oh, hello, ah." But the word *bhoḥ* can, and does in this instance, also carry the intent of sorrow and/or interrogation. According to T. Gaṇapati Śāstrī, the word *bhoḥ* has already been spoken once, by the eldest son. However, while this utterance was not heard by the audience, it has, apparently, been heard by the *sūtradhāra*. The second time *bhoḥ* is uttered—the first time the audience hears it—Gaṇapati Śāstrī understands it to have been spoken by the middle son, and the third time (the line following verse two) by the youngest son. The assumption of the first utterance is not unreasonable, if we are to understand that the gradual descent of the audience into the story is marked largely by the use of this word *bhoḥ*.

The *sūtradhāra*, hearing the question, understands the situation (*bhavatu vijñātam*) and says:

> *bhoḥ śabdoccāraṇād asya brāhmaṇo 'yaṃ na saṃśayaḥ /*
> *trāsyate nirviśaṅkena kenacit pāpacetasā* // (2)[14]
>
> From his uttering of the word *bhoḥ* there is no doubt that he is a brahman. He is frightened by some fearless, evil-minded creature.

The word *bhoḥ* once again echoes in the audience's ears. In the editions of the text by Chintaman R. Devadhar and T. Gaṇapati Śāstrī it is the very first word of the verse, and serves to tell the audience that the previous use of the word was by no means accidental. *Bhoḥ* is thus a syllable pregnant with meaning. Just uttering this word tells the audience, at least according to the *sūtradhāra*, that the person addressed or speaking is a brahman. This is reasonable, for according to the *Manusmṛti*, the word *bhoḥ* is peculiar to brahmans.[15] The word carries the meaning of "concern," "worry," or "anxiety" here as well. This is made clear in the second line of the verse, where the *sūtradhāra* lets the audience know that the brahman is being harassed by some evil creature. The exact nature of the evil creature will be revealed to us only upon the third and final use of the word *bhoḥ*, which follows the verse.

The *sūtradhāra*, hearing the third occurrence of the word *bhoḥ* here, presumably uttered by the youngest of the sons, now fully understands the situation. As the stage manager, he is understood to be an omniscient being, one who has special insights into the nature of the world as depicted in the drama. With the words *hanta dṛdhaṃ vijñātam*, again assuring the audience that he has understood what has happened, the *sūtradhāra* then sets the scene:

> *pāṇḍavamadhyamasyātmajo hiḍimbāraṇisaṃbhūto rākṣasāgnir akṛtavairaṃ brāhmaṇajanaṃ vitrāsayati.*
>
> This is the son of the middle Pāṇḍava, the fire of the *rākṣasa*s, the one born of the kindling-stick Hiḍimbā; it is he who harasses the brahman folks, who are without animosity toward him.

The sentence is fraught with meaning for the audience. We hear for the first time the words *pāṇḍava-, -madhyama-, -ātmaja,* and *hiḍimbā-,* all of which serve as indicators of the plot to come. We discover that the creature just described as *pāpacetasā* is none other than the son of the middle Pāṇḍava, Bhīmasena, and Hiḍimbā. The word *pāṇḍava-* not only identifies the family of the harasser for the audience, but additionally in connection with the word *madhyama,* the middle one, brings to mind Bhīmasena. As the son born between Yudhiṣṭhira and Arjuna, Bhīma is considered the middle son of Kuntī, and it is this Pāṇḍava who will figure prominently in the play. That the son is described in terms of the father is not only important in the light of later plot developments, it also immediately serves to raise a doubt in the audience's mind about why the son of a Pāṇḍava would harass brahmans. While the word *madhyama* conjures up the image of Bhīma, it additionally anticipates the character of the middle son of the old brahman, who will play a vital role in the *vyāyoga.* Finally, the character of Hiḍimbā is introduced. Here, like the patronymic reference to Bhīma, the matronymic is only used to provide a family lineage. Hiḍimbā is, of course, a *rākṣasī.* This, in part, explains the nature of her son.

The *sthāpanā* concludes with a verse describing the brahman family in what must be understood as culturally normative terms.

> *bhrāntaiḥ*[16] *sutaiḥ parivṛtas taruṇaiḥ sadāraiḥ*[17]
> *vṛddho dvijo niśicarānucaraḥ sa eṣaḥ /*
> *vyāghrānusāracakito vṛṣabhaḥ sadhenuḥ*
> *santrastavatsaka ivākulatām upaiti /* (3)
>
> Like a bull, along with his cow and frightened calves, who is pursued by a tiger, this old brahman, along with his wife surrounded by his confused sons, is followed by a night roamer just, becomes agitated.

The father is the bull, the mother the cow, the sons the calves. The association of the family members with bulls, cows, and calves resonates strongly with the audience as these three are among the most powerfully cathected symbols of virility, motherhood, and devotion to one's children, respectively, in traditional Indian society. The verse has placed the threatening figure of Ghaṭotkaca in conflict with the ideal family and other institutions and symbols that mark traditional brāhmaṇic patriarchy. Film theorist Robin Wood has used very similar terms to define the modern horror film, which for him, as Creed has noted, "consistently places the monster in conflict with the family, the couple and the institutions of patriarchal capitalism."[18] As the story unfolds we have the half-human, half-demon figure of Ghaṭotkaca posing just such a threat to the nuclear family, thus giving rise to the traditional *rasa* of the horror-drama, *bhayānaka.*[19]

The transition complete, the scene is set and the play commences. What is remarkable about this *sthāpanā* (and, I would argue, others of Bhāsa as well) is the simplicity with which Bhāsa uses language to provide a transition from the realm of the everyday world into the play. The play by its nature is a *dṛśyakāvya,* but it is through the use of words that Bhāsa constructs the transition. Its simplicity, too, is deceiving, for while the words are sparse they convey multivalent meanings. The *sthāpanā* has not only specifically set the scene of the play. In establishing the boundaries of good and evil, *rākṣasa* verses human, it introduces a paradox: the son whose mother is a *rākṣasī,* and thus by definition evil, and whose father is the son of the wind god, one of the greatest warriors on earth, whose purpose is to uphold dharma. That the feminine here is marked as evil is no accident.[20] I will return to this point below.

Bhāsa carefully introduces the character of Ghaṭotkaca, the son of Bhīma and Hiḍimbā, to represent a troubled and deeply conflicted young man. He is frightening, threatening, intimidating, and potentially filled with evil. Yet he is not without redeeming features although they are largely obscured at the outset of the *vyāyoga.* The old brahman intuits that the young demon is not totally evil, for he hears some concern in his voice, and indicates this as he tells his terrified wife and sons, *brāhmaṇi, na bhetavyaṃ na bhetavyam, putrakāḥ! na bhetavyam, savimarṣā hy asya vāṇī,* "Do not fear, brahman lady, do not fear! Do not fear, my sons! His voice is concerned."[21] This, of course, proves to be the case, as the young demon answers *bho kaṣṭam,* "Oh! Alas!" and we discover the source of his conflict. Bhāsa has once again employed the word *bhoḥ.* Here it is put in the mouth of Ghaṭotkaca, who, despite his *rākṣasa* origins, speaks flawless Sanskrit. The word *kaṣṭam* as an *avyaya* carries the meaning of "woe! alas! alack! or pity!" According to Gaṇapati Śāstrī these words and the verse that follows must be understood as *svagatam,* an aside. He understands this because (1) the demon would not make his true feelings known to the brahman family, and (2) because the brahman, as suggested by his response, appears totally unaware of the words just spoken.[22] Given this and the future developments in the play, Gaṇapati Śāstrī is probably correct in this assumption. Bhāsa, having introduced this element of concern, quickly clarifies it, as he has the young demon say:

jānāmi sarvatra sadā ca nāma dvijottamāḥ pūjatamāḥ pṛthivyām /
akāryam etac ca mayādya kāryaṃ mātur niyogād apanītaśaṅkām // (9)

I know that always and everywhere those best of the twice-borns are the most highly revered on earth. Today, however, disregarding all doubts, I must do this deed that ought not to be done, on account of my mother's command.

The conflict hinted at by the *sūtradhāra* in the *sthāpanā* is now made explicit. Ghaṭotkaca knows what he ought to do, but he cannot go against the word of his mother. Suddenly the entire nature and structure of the drama has changed. No longer is this just a story of a young *rākṣasa* boy out harassing a brahman family; it is about a child whose loyalty, like his parentage, is divided. On the one side is the mother, the *rākṣasī,* who must at all costs be obeyed, even though she is aligned with evil and wrongdoing. On the other side, the father represents the patriarchal world of traditional brāhmaṇic India. That the action plays out in a forest and the brahman family is on its way to a sacrifice serves only to intensify the conflict. Note how Bhāsa makes clear to the audience that evil although manifested in the son, originates in the mother.[23] She has only been referenced twice in the play, once by name and once by function (*hiḍimbāraṇī . . . mātuḥ*) and yet her evil presence permeates the *vyāyoga.* Note, too, that while the audience, which has in some sense taken over the omniscient perspective of the *sūtradhāra,* is aware of this evil feminine threat, the brahman family is yet unaware of her presence.

Realizing that they are doomed and that even the Pāṇḍavas, who have taken up temporary residence in the forest, cannot help (since they too have been called off to a sacrifice, in this case Dhaumya's Śatakumbha sacrifice),[24] the old brahman petitions for their freedom: *asty asmākaṃ mokṣaḥ.* Ghaṭotkaca allows the possibility of release but on one condition (*mokṣo 'sti samayataḥ*). He then tells of his mission:

asti me tatrabhavatī jananī. tayāham ājñāptaḥ: putra mamopavāsanisargārtham asmin vanapradeśe kaścin māṇuṣaḥ parimṛgyānetavya iti.

I have a very respected mother. She has ordered me: "Son! In order to break my fast, in the region of this forest, having sought out some male human, bring him to me."

It is at this juncture that full nature of the threat is made apparent to the audience and the brahman family as well. The threat originates from a *rākṣasī* who wants to consume human (*mānuṣaḥ*), specifically male, flesh. Ghaṭotkaca is only doing his mother's bidding.

The *rākṣasī* is a commonplace of the epic literature. Though the female counterpart of the *rākṣasa*, she is often more frightening. As with the male *rākṣasa*, what is most pronounced about the *rākṣasī* is sexual excess, but carefully set in juxtaposition to her libidinal drive is her need to devour,[25] and this is not uncommonly expressed as a desire to consume humans, or more specifically human blood. This can be understood as an expression of sexuality, especially of excessive libidinal urges, as has been well established so I need not elaborate it further here.[26]

Like other *rākṣasī* figures, such as Śūrpaṇakhā, Surasā, and Siṃhikā, Hiḍimbā too desires to "eat." Her voracious oral consumptive urges can also be seen as representative of her libidinal desires. This intersection between libidinal and gustatory urges are seen in the earliest extant story of Hiḍimbā, known from the *Mahābhārata*. The story is told first in the *Ādiparvan* (1.139–143). Following the fire in the lacquer house, the Pāṇḍava brothers hide in the forest with their mother, Kuntī. As they sleep in the forest the *rākṣasa* Hiḍimba spies them. The *rākṣasa*'s hunger and his proclivity for devouring human flesh are among the first things we learn about him. Among other things he is described as *mānuṣamāṃsādaḥ, piśitepsuḥ,*[27] and *kṣudhārtaḥ*. Hiḍimba, smelling the odor of humans, orders[28] his sister—his female counterpart, as reflected in her name, Hidimbā—to fetch them.

The self-description provided in the passage is important in that it marks the *rākṣasa* as an eater of human flesh: *aṣṭau daṃṣṭrāḥ sutīkṣṇāgrāś cirasyāpātaduḥsahāḥ,* "His eight fangs, with their extremely sharp points, are unbearable for long from the first attack."[29] He describes the manner in which he will consume the humans:

> *ākramya mānuṣaṃ kaṇṭham ācchidya dhamanīm api /*
> *uṣṇaṃ navaṃ prapāsyāmi phenilaṃ rudhiraṃ bahu /*[30]
>
> Having seized the human's throat, I will severe its arteries and drink the abundant, fresh, warm, foamy blood!

The description is clearly reminiscent of the vampire of Western myth, who sucks the blood from its victims with long, pointed fangs.

Hiḍimbā rushes to do her brother's bidding but when she sees Bhīma, rather than "eating him up" she is consumed with lust.[31] Seeing his unparalleled beauty, she falls in love with him (13). Moreover, she decides that he is the right husband for her (*bhartā yukto bhaven mama*); after rationalizing that one's love for one's husband is stronger than that for one's brother, (15) she says:

muhūrtam iva tṛptiś ca bhaved bhrātur mamaiva ca /
hatair etair ahatvā tu modayiṣye śāśvatīḥ samāḥ //[32]

With them slain, my brother's appetite and mine will be sated for only a while; but not having killed them, I will be infatuated for endless years.

Here we see the two notions of gustatory and sexual satiation intersect. Hiḍimbā cannot have both—in fact, she does not need both, for the libidinal urge supplants the gustatory. It is this intersection of the libidinal drive and the need to consume allows for a comparison of the figure of the *rākṣasa* with the Western vampire. I would argue that the figures of the *rākṣasa* and *rākṣasī* in the traditional Sanskrit literary corpus depicts these creatures in a manner not dissimilar from the depiction of the vampire, both male and female, in the Western literary and cinematic tradition. Barbara Creed has noted this connection between the need to consume and the libidinal drive in reference to the Western female vampire:

> The female vampire is abject because she disrupts identity and order; driven by her lust for blood, she does not respect the dictates of the law which set down the rules of proper sexual conduct. Like the male, the female vampire also represents abjection because she crosses the boundary between the living and the dead, the human and animal. . . . The vampire's animalism is made explicit in her bloodlust and the growth of the two pointed fangs.[33]

Like the vampire, the *rākṣasī,* a creature that, in Julia Kristeva's terms, "disturbs identity, system, and order," is a figure that represents abjection.[34]

The intersection of libidinal and gustatory desire creates a tension that Bhāsa employs in his drama to draw his character of Hiḍimbā. At the opening of the story the two traits that are most crucial in her construction are: (1) that she is a *rākṣasī,* which for the audience immediately associates her with negative libidinal and gustatory urges, and who, like the female vampire, is abject as she disrupts identity and order; and (2) that she is a mother, a fact also known from the epic story. This bivalence is reflected in Kristeva's expanded construction of the Freudian Oedipal mother—sometimes referred to as the "archaic mother"—as "the fecund mother and the phanasmatic mother who constitutes the abyss which is so crucial in the formation of subjectivity."[35] This abyss is "the cannibalizing black hole from which all life comes and to which all life returns" and is represented as a source of "deepest terror."

Bhāsa uses his construction of Hiḍimbā as the bivalent archaic mother to generate horror in his audience, not so much by a physical presence or description of her but rather through a representation of her desires and the space that she occupies. Her haunt is the dark forest, impenetrable and dangerous.

> *idaṃ hi śūnyaṃ timirotkaraprabhair nagaprakārair avaruddhadikpatham /*
> *khagair mṛgaiś cāpi samākulāntaraṃ vanaṃ nivāsābhimataṃ manasvīnām //* (10)[36]
>
> This desolate forest, with its paths [that lead] to the [outer] regions blocked by a variety of hills, which appear like masses of darkness, and with its interior regions dense with birds and beasts, is desired as a residence only by determined men.

Roger Dadoun, in his analysis of the film *Dracula* (dir. Tod Browning, 1931), understands the archaic mother as "a non-presence."[37] For both Dadoun and Creed, the signifiers of the archaic mother in the Dracula films are the spaces that Dracula inhabits:

> [T]he small, enclosed village, the pathway through the forest that leads like an umbilical cord to the castle, the central place of enclosure with its winding stairways, spider webs, dark vaults, worm-eaten staircases, dust and damp earth.[38]

Similarly, Bhāsa depicts the symbolism of the archaic mother in his description of the womblike abode of the *rākṣasa,* through which the brahman family is traveling: encircled by mountains, which appear as "masses of darkness, with the only paths that lead to the outer world blocked, filled with terrifying creatures, dark and isolated." For Bhāsa however, the nonpresent mother is more than a symbolic representation of space, she is an omnipotent figure. Her physical presence is denied but her existence is very real. Dadoun suggests that the archaic mother exists as a "non-presence," which should be "understood as a very archaic mode of presence." Bhāsa's use of the mother allows us to clearly imagine what this means, as Hiḍimbā looms at the margins of the play, never visible, yet never out of our consciousness.[39]

One must also keep in mind that as Bhāsa creates the nonpresent presence of the archaic mother, he absents the father, at least in the minds of the audience. The father, here Bhīma, is supposed to be present but, in fact, is absent at this point in the play. In the *Mahābhārata* episode, Hiḍimbā, shortly after the birth of their son Ghaṭotkaca, leaves Bhīma.[40] Bhāsa reinforces that absence. As noted above, the Pāṇḍavas, although temporarily residing in the forest, have been called away. Bhīma has been left to protect the *āśrama.* But at this moment even he is temporarily absent: *sa cāpy asyāṃ velāyāṃ vyāyāmaparicayārthaṃ viprakṛṣṭadeśastha iti śrūyate* (11.7), "One hears that at this time, he, too, has gone to some distant place in order to engage in physical exercise." The absence of the patriarch marks the disintegration of the nuclear family, a situation set in marked contrast to the tightly integrated and intact brahman family under threat. With the male's absence the female's libidinal and gustatory urges reassert themselves. Or, put in more Freudian terms, it is in this absence that the phallic, sexualized woman is able to reassert herself. That this subversion of order is played out in the context of the family, where the father can no longer control the mother, whose everpresent gustatory/libidinal urges (re)surface, creates an even more terrifying and threatening scenario.

In his discussion of *Dracula,* Dadoun argues that the vampire acts "on behalf of the mother."[41] In the midst of the dark castle, Dracula emerges, "with his black cape, pointed teeth, rigid body—carried like an erect phallus—piercing eyes and penetrating look." Dracula is the fetish form, "a substitute for the mother's penis."[42] Now consider Bhāsa's description of Ghaṭotkaca. He appears in the midst of dark, impenetrable forest, quite literally out on his mother's errand. He is described as having long, yellow eyes blazing from the cavity between knitted eyebrows; a massive, broad chest; a complexion like a mass of darkness; protruding fangs; huge, white arms, like the trunks of the best elephants; and so forth.[43] Like Dracula, Ghaṭotkaca, too, can be understood as the projection of the absent maternal phallus.

Against this "nonpresent presence" of the archaic mother, the phallic son Ghaṭotkaca makes his demand, which places him in a monstrous conflict with the normative nuclear family he has been denied:

> *patnyā cāritraśālinyā dviputro mokṣam icchasi /*
> *balābalaṃ parijñāya putram ekaṃ visarjaya //* (12)
>
> If you desire to be set free along with your virtuous wife and two of your sons, then, considering the pros and cons [of the situation], give up one son.

The brahman first offers himself in lieu of his sons, but he is rejected as too old. The mother then offers herself up, but she is rejected because she is a woman. Only a young brahman boy will do. The three sons in turn offer themselves to save the family. But the father is too attached to the elder son and cannot let him go. Similarly, the mother is too attached to the youngest son and cannot bear to see him devoured by the demon. Only the second son, called both Dvitīya, "Second," and Madhyama, "Middle," is left, and he poignantly asks, *pitror aniṣṭaḥ kasyedānīṃ priyaḥ*? (19.4), "Unwanted by my parents, who loves me now?"[44]

The theme of the unloved and unwanted middle child has antecedents in the Śunaḥśepha story, known in its earliest version in *Aitareya Brāhmaṇa* 7.15.14–18.[45] There the story tells of a king named Hariścandra, who desired a son and begs for one from Varuṇa. His boon is granted on the condition that the son will be offered as a human sacrifice to the god. A son, Rohita, is born, but when he learns of his father's promise he runs away. Rohita eventually encounters an impoverished sage named Ajīgarta, who has three sons. Rohita offers the sage money in exchange for one his sons who could be sacrificed in his place. Ajīgarta agrees but will not give up his eldest son, and the mother refuses to give up the youngest. This leaves the middle son, named Śunaḥśepha, who is exchanged for one hundred cows. No one can be found to actually carry out the sacrificial offering, so finally Ajīgarta agrees, again for more money, to carry out the act. Śunaḥśepha takes recourse in the gods who release him. Ajīgarta demands his son back, but Śunaḥśepha refuses to return and instead takes refuge with the sage Viśvāmitra.[46] The similarity between the episodes is clear, though unlike Ajīgarta, Bhāsa's brahman father is emotionally distraught at the decision to give up his son.

While we can see the Śunaḥśepha episode as a possible source for Bhāsa's theme of the unloved middle child, this thematic element as well as the story itself can also be found to have parallels elsewhere in the literature. The other most probable source of Bhāsa's play, as noted by Devadhar, is the story of the demon Baka in the *Mahābhārata*.[47] Here, too, the theme of the unwanted "middle" child is hinted at in connection with none other than our play's hero, Bhīmasena. The story of Baka, like Bhāsa's, stresses the conflicted emotions of a brahman family forced to make a horrific decision to give up one of its children to a demon to save the lives of the rest of the family. The location of the *Mahābhārata* story of Baka is also significant, in that it is placed immediately after the account of the slaying of Hiḍimba by Bhīma and the birth of Ghaṭotkaca.[48]

The Bakāsura episode, while it thematically has much in common with Bhāsa's play, is, nevertheless, quite different in the structure of its narrative. In the story of Bakāsura, the brahman family has only two children; the eldest, still quite young, is a daughter, while the younger child is a very young boy, still crawling. Even so, there are strong similarities. Here, as in Bhāsa's tale, the family must give up one of its children to sate the hunger of a *rākṣasa*. Bhīma becomes, as it were, a surrogate third child, the "middle son" who is given up, here by his mother.

In fact, Bhīma is Kuntī's middle son, and she is willing to offer him up in order to save the brahman family. Note, too, that as in Bhāsa's play, it is the mother's command that must be obeyed and her judgment, although at first questioned by Yudhiṣṭhira, is never really doubted.

To Madhyama's pitiful words, *kasyedānīṃ priyaḥ,* Ghaṭotkaca replies, *ahaṃ prīto 'smi* (19.4).[49] The fact that it is Ghaṭotkaca, and not Madhyama's mother or father, who answers only further intensifies the young boy's plight. In his commentary T. Gaṇapati Śāstrī clearly connects the expression of love with the gustatory urges of the *rākṣasa*s, specifically Hiḍimbā. He explains the phrase [*tvayi*] *manmātṛbhakṣaṇīyatām ātmano 'ṅgīkṛtavati* as "In reference to you (*tvayi*) who have allowed yourself to be food for my mother."[50]

Before he is taken away Madhyama has only one wish—that he might have a sip of water (22.7–8). His wish is granted, but Ghaṭotkaca cautions him to be quick. ~~But~~ Madhyama tarries a bit too long, and Ghaṭotkaca begins to fret: *atikrāmati maṭur āhārakālaḥ* (24.1–2), "The time for my mother's meal is passing." He asks the brahman to call his son (24.2–3), but the old man refuses: *āḥ atirākṣasaṃ khalu te vacanam,* "Oh! His words go beyond those of even a *rākṣasa*" (24.4).[51] Ghaṭotkaca then asks for the name of his son, but this too the old brahman refuses to provide (24.6). However, upon asking the elder son the demon is given the middle son's name, Madhyama ("the middle one") (24.9). Ghaṭotkaca then calls the young boy (24.10–11). Bhīma, also known as Madhyama, engaged in his exercises, hears the call and takes it to be meant for him (25).

Bhīma enters. The character of Bhīma as represented in the epic tradition underlies Bhāsa's construction of his play in a number of ways. We have already touched upon Bhīma as the *madhyama,* middle son, of Kuntī, a role that is explicated and overdetermined in the story of Baka discussed above. In Bhāsa's play, Bhīma is also a patriarchal figure, husband of Hiḍimbā and father of Ghaṭotkaca. Bhīma is additionally associated with excessive consumption.[52] He is called *vṛkodara;* his appetite is never sated and this becomes his fatal flaw as the epic draws to a conclusion. When Bhīma, fallen to the ground, lies dying at the end of the epic, Yudhiṣṭhira reminds him, *atibhuktaṃ ca bhavatā,* "You ate too much."[53] Moreover, and not insignificantly for Bhāsa's play, is Bhīma's history as the son of Vāyu, the wind god. He is the most fierce and powerful of the Pāṇḍavas, the great warrior, slayer of *rākṣasa*s (virtually all the *rākṣasa*s encountered by the Pāṇḍavas in the epic are killed by Bhīma). Bhīma is the one Pāṇḍava brother who is most susceptible to his emotions, particularly his anger. His rage at the insult carried out upon Draupadī in the Sabhāparvan leads to Bhīma swearing to split open the Duryodhana's chest and drink his blood.[54] The association of Bhīma with the consumption of blood cannot be ignored in light of his association with the *rākṣasī* Hiḍimbā, whose inherent nature is to consume human flesh and blood. Perhaps the *raison d'etre* for his dreadful oath can be traced back to Bhīma's relationship with Hiḍimbā. Their intimate relationship, acting much like a vampire's bite, would have in some way infected him, as it were, thereby leading him to behave in a manner that echoes the vampire-like actions of a *rākṣasa*.[55]

Bhīma's entrance into the story now sets up an Oedipal struggle between father and son, while the nonpresent mother hovers on the outskirts of the narrative. As in the original Oedipal myth, the son is unaware that this person who confronts him is his father. Bhīma, too, does not at first recognize his son, Ghaṭotkaca. And while Ghaṭotkaca remains stubbornly adamant in his refusal to acknowledge that Bhīma might be his father, Bhīma soon realizes the true identity of Ghaṭotkaca. The description of both characters, each of whom admires and respects the other's prowess, resonates with phallic imagery. Thus in verse 26, Bhīma, on first seeing Ghaṭotkaca, notes his leonine fangs, his thick neck, his hawklike nose, his adamantine waist, his long and muscular arms, and he compares his gait to that of a bull among elephants.[56] In verse 27, Ghaṭotkaca, when first spying Bhīma, notes that his form, like that of a lion, is strong and virile; his arms are long like plantain trees and his sides are well-tapered.[57] Nevertheless Ghaṭotkaca is at least unconsciously aware of a familial relationship; for he ends his verse with the words *netre mamāharati bandhur ivāgato 'yam,* "He attracts my eyes to him as if he were a relative." The phrase *bandhur iva,* "like a relative," indicates subliminal recognition of or desire for such a relationship by Ghaṭotkaca, while for the audience it reinforces their kinship.

Bhīma declares himself as Madhyama (verses 28, 29), and upon being apprised of the situation, demands that Ghaṭotkaca release the brahman family. Ghaṭotkaca refuses, citing once again his duty to his mother. The struggle now becomes one between son and father over control of feminine, here represented as the command of the mother (*mātur ājñā*).

Ghaṭotkaca says:

> *na mucyate,*
> *mucyatām iti visrabdhaṃ bravīti yadi me pitā /*
> *na mucyate tathā hy eṣa gṛhīto mātur ājñayā //* (36)
>
> I will not release him: Even if my father in confidence asked me to release him, I would not. For he has been captured by my mother's command.

Bhīmasena responds:

> *(ātmagatam) kathaṃ mātur āñjety aho guruśuśrūṣuḥ khalu ayaṃ tapasvī* (36ab)
>
> (To himself:) How is this? [He says] "At the command of my mother?" The wretched fellow is obedient to his elders (mother).
>
> *mātā kila manūsyāṇām daivatānāṃ ca daivatam /*
> *mātur ājñāṃ puraskṛtya vayam etām daśāṃ gatāḥ //* (37)
>
> Indeed, among men the mother is deity among deities. Having given precedence to the mother's command, we have arrived at this condition.

Bhīma's words are explicitly intended to refer to Hiḍimbā and her role as Ghaṭotkaca's mother. Their import in the construction of the larger Pāṇḍava world, however—that is, with reference to Kuntī—is not lost on the audience, nor is the conflict arising from situating one's mother in a position of divinity and yet being required to commit an action that is considered to transgress the boundaries of proper behavior.[58] The identification of the mother as a divinity, in contrast to her role as a demon, allows for the expression of a counterphobic reaction. As Mark Winokur reminds us, the phantasmic mother resides in no other mother than our own:

> [Dadoun's] argument remains a paradigmatic psychoanalytic account, in the sense that the source of anxiety remains with the mother, not the commodity or the racial other.[59]

The mother, although absent up until this point in the play, is real, as are the conflicted emotions that one has toward her.

Bhīma then demands to know who his mother is and, discovering that the boy is none other than his son by Hiḍimbā, offers himself as victim in lieu of the brahman's son. But Bhīma refuses to accompany him until Ghaṭotkaca can best him in battle. There now ensues a fight between father and son for the affection and/or possession of the mother. Bhīma attempts to make himself known to Ghaṭotkaca, but Ghaṭotkaca does not or is not willing to understand that Bhīma is his father, and enters battle with him. The conflict is played out in phallic imagery. Bhīma's only weapon is his right arm, which can be understood to represent the phallus (verse 42). Ghaṭotkaca uproots huge trees to use as weapons, much in the manner of Baka in the *Mahābhārata* story,[60] and finally he uproots the peak of a mountain. Yet neither the tree trunks nor the mountaintop, despite their phallic form, firmness, and size, faze Bhīma for even a moment and the contest resorts to hand-to-hand combat.

Bhīma, much to his own astonishment, is actually bound by the strength of Ghaṭotkaca's arms (*vīryam ullaṅghya bāhvor,* verse 42). He breaks free. Neither can defeat the other; Ghaṭotkaca resorts to a magical weapon that he has acquired though his mother's favor, so it too can be understood as phallic projection of the archaic mother. The verse uttered here by Ghaṭotkaca is telling, as it compares Bhīma, ensnared by this magic *pāśa,* to a very phallic yet impotent *śakradhvaja,* "flagstaff of Śakra":

> *māyāpāśena baddhas tvaṃ vivaśo na gamiṣyasi /*
> *rājase rajjubhir baddhaḥ śakradhvaja ivotsave //* (47)
>
> Captured up by my magic noose, helpless, you cannot move, and you look resplendent, like the flagpole of Śakra held by ropes on the festival day.

Bhīma possesses an anti-*pāśa* mantra (*māyāpāśamokṣaḥ mantraḥ*), which he has acquired from none other than Śiva, whose defining symbol is the *liṅgam* (phallus). Due to the power of this magical weapon, more powerful than the maternal weapon of Ghaṭotkaca, Bhīma is finally able to break his bonds (*patitaḥ pāśaḥ*), thus gaining victory over his son while symbolically castrating him. Much as Dadoun understands that Dracula has identified with the archaic mother and attributes to her a nonexistent phallus, so we can understand that Ghaṭotkaca has identified with his mother, whose imagined phallus, the *pāśa,* is here rendered impotent. The destruction of the *pāśa* is the destruction of the imagined archaic mother. The resolution of the story is now obvious. Bhīma, emerging victorious, nevertheless agrees to accompany Ghaṭotkaca, who has reminded him of his earlier promise, to see Hiḍimbā.

It is only at this point in the *vyāyoga* that Hiḍimbā can and does physically appear on stage. With the destruction of the imagined archaic mother, she, the actual benign mother, can now safely appear. She is no longer a nonpresent presence, as it were, and, once in the company of her husband, she is no longer in need of a human victim to consume. Moreover, she no longer functions as a manifestation of the imagined archaic phallic mother but is instead now representative of the real and present mother, and as such she is no longer a threat. With her libidinal needs sated by the presence of her husband, her gustatory urges disappear. As if to confirm this, Bhīma says *jātyā rākṣasī, na samudācāreṇa* (49.3), "She is a *rākṣasī* by birth, but not by behavior." At this juncture, Bhāsa reintroduces the word *bhoḥ* into his play. The word returns to haunt us, calling us, as it were, back into the real world. Following Bhīma's comment about Hiḍimbā's behavior, she identifies Bhīma as Ghaṭotkaca's father:

ummatta! abhivādehi pidaraṃ, "My wild child! Honor you father!"(49.4). This identification signals the reintegration of the nuclear family, thereby marking the beginning of the end of the story. Ghaṭotkaca responds with *bhos tāta*, "O father!"(49.6), the very same phrase that begins our descent at the opening of the play. These words mark Ghaṭotkaca's own transformation. He has become a properly deferential son, securely situated within the nuclear family, much like the young brahman boys at the opening of the play.

Once reunited with his father, or, put it another way, subordinated to his patriarchal power, Ghaṭotkaca is no longer a threat. He begs his father's forgiveness, *putracāpalaṃ kṣantum arhasi* ("please forgive your son's insolence") (50.1–2), and is blessed by both his father and the old brahman (50.3–5; 50.10). The brahman praises Bhīma with the words *bho vṛkodara! rakṣitam asmatkulaṃ svakulam uddhṛtaṃ ca* (50.12), "O wolf-belly, you have protected our family and saved your own!"

The word *bhoḥ* appears for the last time, perhaps signaling that the play is drawing to a conclusion. Bhāsa's use here of the epithet *vṛkodara*, "wolf-belly," is also probably significant, as it alludes to Bhīma's *rākṣasa*-like voracity, which in all likelihood resonates humorously with the audience, given the plot of the play. The reference to his saving his family can be understood as the reconstitution of the culturally normative, patriarchal nuclear family, which had been threatened by Bhīma's absence. Bhāsa's *vyāyoga* is thus more than a story of horror and valor, more than merely an entertaining interlude. Rather, the play serves as a metaphor of the destructive nature of the uncontrolled phallic woman, whose power, even in her absence, is a source of horror. With the reintegration of the nuclear family achieved—the mother's demonic libidinal needs controlled, the son's Oedipal drives overpowered, and the triumph of the patriarchy assured—the play comes to a happy conclusion.

Notes

1 The original version of this paper was presented at the World Sanskrit Conference, Turin, Italy, 1997. When considering how I might honor the memory of Frits Staal, who was first my teacher and advisor and later my colleague and friend, I felt that this paper would best reflect how Frits has influenced my work. Over the many years of our friendship, he constantly challenged me to push the boundaries of scholarship, seeking new and different paradigms with which to approach the Sanskrit corpus. Hopefully, I have in some small part succeeded.

2 Vishnu S. Sukthankar, "Studies in Bhāsa," *Journal of the American Oriental Society* 40 (1920): 248. Taruvāgrahārām Gaṇapati Sāstrī, *The Svapnavāsavatta of*

Bhāsa Edited with Notes (Trivandrum: Travancore Government Press, 1912). According to Gaṇapati Sāstrī, Bhāsa "must necessarily be placed not later than the third or second century B.C.," p. xxvii. H. B. Bhide, *The Svapna Vasavadatta of Bhasa Edited with Introduction, Notes, with Sanskrit Commentary* (Bhavnagar: n.p., 1916), pp. 36–37. In his introduction, Bhide places Bhāsa somewhere between 475–417 B.C.E.

3 L. D. Barnett, "Abhasa-Bhasa," *Bulletin of the School of Oriental and African Studies* 3/3 (1924): 519–522, places Bhāsa in the seventh century C.E. Chintaman R. Devadhar is less definite, generally agreeing with Barnett but commenting, "though the question of his time cannot be definitely settled for want of adequate data"; *Plays Ascribed to Bhasa: Their Authenticity and Merits* (Poona: Oriental Book Agency, 1927), p. 62.

4 Sushil K. De, "The Dramas Ascribed to Bhasa," *Indian Historical Quarterly* 15 (1941): 420. See Vishnu S. Sukthankar, "Studies in Bhāsa," *Journal of the American Oriental Society* 40 (1920): 249, n. 4, and "Studies in Bhāsa V. A Bibliographical Note," *Journal of the Bombay Branch of the Royal Asiatic Society* 26 (1921–1923): 233. Jeffrey L. Masson and D. D. Kosambi, *Avimāraka (Love's Enchanted World)* (Delhi: Motilal Banarsidass, 1970), pp. 3–7. Cf. A. D. Pulsalkar, *Bhasa, A Study* (Delhi: Munshiram Manoharlal, 1968), pp. 6–23; Vishnu S. Sukthankar, "Studies in Bhāsa V. A Bibliographical Note," *Journal of the Bombay Branch of the Royal Asiatic Society* 264 (1921–1923): 167–187; Masson and Kosambi, *Avimāraka,* p. 13, n. 2; H. J. H. Tieken, "The So-called Trivandrum Plays Attributed to Bhasa," *Wiener Zeitschrift für die Kunde Südasiens Band* 37 (1993): 6, n. 5.

5 For examples of some early dates, see Moreshwar R. Kāle, who gives 370 B.C.E. in *Introduction to Svapnavāsavadattam* (Bombay: Booksellers' Publishing Co., 1929), pp. xxxvi–xxxviii; Bhide gives 475–417 B.C.E. in *The Svapna Vasavadatta of Bhasa, Introduction;* Gaṇapati Śāstrī gives the third to second centuries B.C.E. in *The Madhyamavyāyoga of Bhāsa with the commentary of Paṇḍit T. Gaṇapati Śāstrī* (Trivandrum: Sridhara Printing House, 1917), Introduction; Sukthankar is more cautious, commenting only on the age of the Prākrit in the plays, "which is much older than any we know from the dramas of the so-called classical period of Sanskrit literature,""Studies in Bhāsa," p. 259. A number of scholars date Bhāsa much later, to the seventh century C.E. or later. See, for example, L. D. Barnett, who gives the seventh century C.E. in "The Matta Vilāsa and 'Bhāsa'," *Bulletin of the School of Oriental Studies* 1/3 (1920): 37; A. Krishna Pisharoti and K. Rama Pisharoti give "not earlier than the eighth century," "Bhāsa's Works—Are They Genuine?", *Bulletin of the School of Oriental Studies* 3/1 (1923): 114; Devadhar, *Plays Ascribed to Bhasa,* p. 62, follows Barnett, and understands seventh century C.E.; Tieken writes, "The conclusions regarding its (the *Pratijñāyaugandharāyaṇa*) date (not older than the Mattavilāsa) . . . and patronage (Pallavas, Narasiṃhavarman II) have provisionally been extended to the other Trivandrum plays," "The So-called Trivandrum Plays Attributed to Bhasa," p. 36.

6 Vishnu S. Sukthankar, "Studies in Bhāsa," *Journal of the American Oriental Society* 40 (1920): passim. Sukthankar understands the Prākrit to be of an age of that of Aśvaghoṣa's; M. Winternitz writes "sometime before Kālidāsa"

in"Bhāsa: What Do We Really Know of Him and his Work?", in Mohammad Shafi, ed., *Woolner Commemoration Volume* (Lahore: Mehar Chand Lachman Das, 1940), p. 309; A. Berriedale Keith, in *The Sanskrit Drama* (Oxford: The Clarendon Press, 1924), p. 95, gives 300 C.E.

8 De, "The Dramas Ascribed to Bhasa," p. 421:

> The studies have now made it reasonable to assume that the Trivandrum plays, whether they are by Bhāsa or by some other playwright, are of the nature of adaptations or abridgments made for the stage, and they have in fact been regularly used as stage-plays in the Kerala country. This very important fact should not be lost sight of in any discussion of the plays. It explains the traditional handing down of the plays without mention of the author's name, in closely resembling prologues, which are probably stage-additions, as well as the coincidence of formal technique and a large number of repetitions and parallels, which recur in these, as also in some other Sanskrit plays of Kerala.

8 There are of course exceptions. See, for example, Jeffrey M. Masson, "A Note on the Sources of Bhāsa's (?) Avimāraka," *Journal of the Oriental Institute of the Maharaja Sayajirao University of Baroda* XIX (1969): 60–74; Robert P. Goldman, "Fathers, Sons, and Gurus: Oedipal Conflict in the Sanskrit Epics," *Journal of Indian Philosophy* 6 (1978): 325–392; Edwin Gerow, "Bhāsa's Ūrubhaṅga and Indian Poetics," *Journal of the American Oriental Society* 105/3 (1985): 405–412; Farley Richmond and Yasmin Richmond, "The Multiple Dimensions of Time and Space in Kūṭiyāṭṭam, the Sanskrit Theatre of Kerala," *Asian Theatre Journal* 2/1 (1985): 50–60. H. J. H. Tieken, in "Three Men in a Row (Studies in the Trivandrum Plays II)," *Wiener Zeitschrift für die Kunde Südasiens* 41 (1997): 17–52, offers a provocative and insightful analysis of a number of the plays with an eye to their ritual implications as well as a new, much later dating of the poems; see also his "The So-called Trivandrum Plays Attributed to Bhasa."

9 The *vyāyoga*, according to the *Nāṭyaśāstra* and other works on drama, is defined as follows: The hero should be a renowned person, the female characters should be few, and the action should cover only one day. There should be many male characters and fighting like in a *Samavakāra* (a type of drama). It should not be as long as that (i.e., a *Samavakāra*), it should be only one act. The hero should not be divine but he should be a royal seer. It should also have various types of fighting. Later *alaṃkāraśāstrin*s added that it should have neither the *garbha* nor *vimarśa sandhi*s; the hero should be of the class styled *dhīroddhata* ("firm and haughty"); wrestling and fighting should not be on account of a woman. Cf. Keith, *The Sanskrit Drama*, p. 347; *Nāṭyaśāstra* 20.90–93, where the *vyāyoga* is defined. See also *Dāśarūpaka* 3.54, *Sāhityadarpaṇa* 514.

10 The play, as is true of all great works, in my opinion, can be read on many levels. I do not intend to suggest that my reading of the story is the only one. Clearly it can, and does, have multiple interpretations. See, for example, Tieken, "Three Men in a Row (Studies in the Trivandrum Plays II)," who reads the story as a covert *upanayana* ritual.

11 It is uncertain whether it is during the first exile or the second that Bhāsa intends his encounter. Hiḍimbā gives birth to Ghaṭotkaca at *Mahābhārata*

1.143.28, during the first exile, at which time, Ghaṭotkaca vows filial piety to Bhīmasena, promising to come to him whenever he is needed (1.143.38). Bhīmasena next encounters Ghaṭotkaca, in the *Araṇyakaparvan,* during the Pāṇḍavas' second exile, when Draupadī, exhausted and unable to keep up with her husbands as they journey to Mount Gandhamādana, faints. Bhīma summons his son, Ghaṭotkaca, to carry his stepmother (*Mahābhārata* 3.144.24–25). Bhāsa, apparently, intends his play to take place at some point during these two events.

12 The story is told in the *Ādiparvan* of the *Mahābhārata* (1.139–143) and then again in a reprise in the *Araṇyakaparvan* (3.130.85–97). All references are to V. S., Sukthankar, et al., eds., *Mabhābhārata: Critical Edition,* 24 vols. (Poona: Bhandarkar Oriental Research Institute, 1933–1970), unless otherwise indicated.

13 See Robert Goldman, "The Serpent and the Rope on Stage: Popular Literary and Philosophical Representations of Reality in Traditional India," *Journal of Indian Philosophy* 14 (1986): 355–356.

14 All citations are from C. R. Devadhar, ed., *Bhāsanāṭakacakram: Plays Ascribed to Bhāsa* (Poona: Oriental Book Agency, 1937; 1962, reprint), pp. 422–439. All translations are the author's unless otherwise indicated.

15 *Manusmṛti* 2.128:

> *avācyo dīkṣito nāmnā yavīyān api yo bhavet /*
> *bho bhavatpūrvakaṃ tv enam abhibhāṣeta dharmavit //*
>
> A person who has been consecrated should not be addressed by name, even if he is younger, a man who knows the law, should speak after him saying, hello sir (*bhoḥ*).

16 V.l. *śrāntaiḥ.*

17 The compound *sadāraiḥ,* "with his wife," technically modifies *sutaiḥ,* "with his sons."

18 Barbara Creed, *The Monstrous-Feminine: Film, Feminism, Psychoanalysis* (London and New York: Routledge, 1993), p. 61. See also Robin Wood "The American Nightmare: Horror in the 70s," in *Hollywood from Vietnam to Reagan* (New York: Columbia University Press, 1986), pp. 70–94.

19 Pulsalkar, *Bhasa, A Study,* p. 208.

20 Sally J. Sutherland Goldman, "Re-siting Sītā: Gender and Narrative in *Vālmīki's Sundarakāṇḍa,*" *Purāṇa* 45/2 (2003): 115–135; "Who's For Dinner? Cannibalistic Urges in the *Mahābhārata,*" paper presented at the Annual Meeting of the American Oriental Society, San Diego, California, March 2004.

21 Here I am reading *-vimarṣā* as v.l. for *vimarśā;* s.v. Monier Monier-Williams, *A Sanskrit-English Dictionary* (Oxford: Oxford University Press, 1899; 1964 reprint).

22 T. Gaṇapati Śāstrī, *The Madhyamavyāyoga of Bhāsa,* p. 34, notes.

23 See Sally J. Sutherland, "The Bad Seed: Senior Wives and Elder Sons," in Sally J. Sutherland, ed., *Bridging Worlds: Studies on Women in South Asia* (Berkeley: Centers for South and Southeast Asia Studies, UC Berkeley, 1991), pp. 24–52.

24 Literally, "the hundred-pot" sacrifice.

[25] See Robert P. Goldman and Sally J. Sutherland Goldman, *The Rāmāyaṇa of Vālmīki: An Epic of Ancient India. Volume V, Sundarakāṇḍa: Introduction, Translation, and Annotation* (Princeton, NJ: Princeton University Press, 1996), pp. 65–68; Robert P. Goldman, "Rāvaṇa's Kitchen: A Testimony of Desire and the Other," in Paula Richman, ed., *Questioning Rāmāyaṇas* (Delhi and Berkeley: Oxford University Press and University of California Press, 2000), pp. 105–116; 374–376; S. Goldman, "Re-siting Sītā: Gender and Narrative in Vālmīk's Sundarakāṇḍa" and "Who's For Dinner? Cannibalistic Urges in the *Mahābhārata*."

[26] S. Goldman, "Nikumbhilā's Grove: *Rākṣasa* Rites in *Vālmīki's Rāmāyaṇa*," in J. L. Brockington, ed., *Battle, Bards and Brāhmins* (Delhi: Motilal Banarsidass, 2012), pp. 255–275; S. Goldman, "Who's For Dinner? Cannibalistic Urges in the *Mahābhārata*" and "Re-siting Sītā: Gender and Narrative in Vālmīk's Sundarakāṇḍa"; R. Goldman, "Rāvaṇa's Kitchen: A Testimony of Desire and the Other"; Creed, *The Monstrous-Feminine.*

[27] The word *piśita* means "flesh" but it clearly refers to human flesh in such usages as *pīsītāśanaḥ, piśitāśaḥ, piśitāśin,* and *piśitābhuk,* all of which refer to demons that are flesh-eaters, or man-eaters. See Vaman Shivaram Apte, *The Practical Sanskrit-English Dictionary* (Poona: Prasad Prakashan, 1957–1959), s.v.

[28] MBh 1.139.4–10:

duṣṭo mānuṣamāṃsādo mahākāyo mahābalaḥ /
āghrāya mānuṣaṃ gandhaṃ bhaginīm idam abravīt //
upapannaś cirasyādya bhakṣo mama manaḥpriyaḥ /
snehasravān prasravati jihvā paryeti me mukham //
aṣṭau daṃṣṭrāḥ sutīkṣṇāgrāś cirasyāpātaduḥsahāḥ /
deheṣu majjayiṣyāmi snigdheṣu piśiteṣu ca //
ākramya mānuṣaṃ kaṇṭham ācchidya dhamanīm api /
uṣṇaṃ navaṃ prapāsyāmi phenilaṃ rudhiraṃ bahu //
gaccha jānīhi ke tv ete śerate vanam āśritāḥ /
mānuṣo balavān gandho ghrāṇam tarpayatīva me //
hatvaitān mānuṣān sarvān ānayasva mamāntikam /
asmadviṣayasuptebhyo naitebhyo bhayam asti te //
eṣāṃ māṃsāni saṃskṛtya mānuṣāṇāṃ yatheṣṭataḥ /
bhakṣayiṣyāva sahitau kuru tūrṇaṃ vaco mama //

That wicked, gargantuan, and powerful consumer of human flesh, having smelled the odor of a human, spoke to his sister: (4) "Today after such a long time, I have come across some food dear to my heart. My tongue salivates with the juice of delicate things and licks all around my face. (5) My eight fangs, with their so sharp points, are unbearable from the first attack, after such a long time; I will eat these bodies and their most delicate flesh. (6) Having seized the human's throat, I will sever his arteries and drink his abundant, fresh, warm, foamy blood! (7) Go, discover who these sleeping forest-resorting men. The strong, powerful human odor as it were satisfies my nose. (8) Having killed all of these humans, bring them back to me. Have no fear of those who sleep in our realm. (9) Having prepared the flesh of these humans as we like it, together we will eat it. Quickly obey my words." (10)

[29] MBh 1.39.6ab.

[30] MBh 1.39.7.

[31] The passage parallels the passion experienced by Śūrpaṇakhā upon seeing the two Rāghavas, however, the resolution is far from the same; *Rāmāyaṇa*

(Rām) 3.17.16. All references are to G. H. Bhatt and U. P. Shah, gen. eds., *The Vālmīki Rāmāyaṇa: Critical Edition,* 7 vols. (Baroda: Oriental Institute, 1960–1975), unless otherwise noted.

32 MBh 1.139.16.

33 Creed, *The Monstrous-Feminine,* p. 61. In this connection, Creed has noted the lesbian nature of the female vampire in the Western film, a point of departure I feel with the *rākṣasī* in the brāhmaṇic tradition. Certain lesbian overtones exist in a few stories, but the norm would be the female *rākṣasa* attacking a male victim, and thus maintaining a counternormative but nevertheless heterosexual relationship. One counterexample to this, a clear example of same-sex desire, is found in the *Sundarakāṇḍa* of the *Vālmīki Rāmāyaṇa,* where the *rākṣasīs* express their strong desire to consume Sītā; Rām 5.23.34–41 and notes.

34 Julia Kristeva, in *Powers of Horrors: An Essay on Abjection* (New York: Columbia University Press, 1982), provides a hypothesis for the analysis of the representation of the woman as monstrous. She suggests a way of situating the monstrous feminine in the horror film in relation to the maternal figure and what she terms "abjection," that which does not "respect borders, positions, rules" [but] "disturbs identity, system, order" (p. 4).

35 Creed, *The Monstrous-Feminine,* p. 25.

36 According to G. Śāstrī, the phrase "by determined men (*manasvīnām*)" refers to the Pāṇḍavas.

37 Roger Dadoun, "Fetishism in the Horror Film," in James Donald, ed., *Fantasy and the Cinem*a (London: British Film Institute, 1989), p. 52

38 Creed, *The Monstrous-Feminine,* p. 20; Dadoun, "Fetishism in the Horror Film," p. 52.

39 Creed, *The Monstrous-Feminine,* p. 20, Dadoun, "Fetishism in the Horror Film," pp. 53–54.

40 MBh 1.143.36.

41 Creed, *The Monstrous-Feminine,* p. 21.

42 Dadoun, "Fetishism in the Horror Film," pp. 52–55; Creed, *The Monstrous-Feminine,* p. 20.

43 Bhāsa introduces Ghaṭotkaca at the very opening of his story, immediately following the close of the *sthāpanā,* or introductory scene. Each male member of the family, starting with the father, asks, "Who is he?" and follows by saying a verse that describes the *rākṣasa*'s physical appearance. The mother of the three boys, called only *brāhmaṇī,* speaks last, and, as is typical in Sanskrit *kāvya,* she speaks in prose and in Prākṛta (*ayya ko eso amhāaṃ sandāvei,* "My lord! Who is this that torments us?"). Dadoun, "Fetishism in the Horror Film," p. 55, draws our attention in particular to the importance of Dracula's fangs and penetrating eyes, physical features of Ghaṭotkaca that Bhāsa highlights in his verses:

[brāhmaṇaḥ]—bhoḥ ko nu khalv eṣaḥ:
taruṇavikaraprakīrṇakeśo bhrukuṭipuṭojjvalapiṅgalāyatākṣaḥ /
sataḍid iva ghanaḥ sakaṇṭhasūtro yuganidhane pratimākṛtir harasya // 4

[The Brahman]—Oh! Who, indeed, is he who—with hair scattered about like the [red] rays of the morning sun, with his long, yellow eyes blazing from the cavity between his knitted eyebrows [and] with his [golden] necklace around his neck like a cloud with lightning, [is] the very image of Hara at the cosmic dissolution?

[*prathamaḥ*]—*ko nu khalv eṣaḥ:*
grahayugalanibhākṣaḥ pīnavistīrṇavakṣāḥ kanakakapilakeśaḥ pītakauśeyavāsāḥ /
timiranivahavarṇaḥ pāṇḍuroddhṛttadaṃṣṭro nava iva jalagarbho līyamānendulekhaḥ // 5

[First]—Who, indeed, is he who—with eyes like a pair of planets, with his massive and broad chest, with his golden, yellow (*pīta-* v.l. *pīna-*) hair, with color is that of a mass of darkness, and with fangs protruding (reading *-uddhṛta-* for *udvṛta*) and white—[appears like] a new stormcloud into which the digits of the moon disappear?

[*dvitīyaḥ*]—*bhos tāta! ka eṣaḥ bhoḥ*
kalabhadaśanadaṃṣṭro lāṅgalākāranāsaḥ karivarakarabāhur nīlajīmūtavarṇaḥ /
hutahutavahadīpto yaḥ sthito bhāti bhīmas tripurapuranihantuḥ śaṅkarasyeva roṣaḥ // 6

[Second (= Madhyama, "Middle")]—Oh, Daddy! Oh, who is he who—has fangs like the tusks of a young bull elephant, a nose the shape of a plow, arms, which are [huge like] the trunks of the best among elephants, and a complexion [like] that of a stormcloud? [Who is he,] who like the blazing fire into which an oblation has been offered, stands there terrifying (*bhīmaḥ*) like the anger of Śaṅkara and the destroyer of the city of Tripura?

[*tṛtīyaḥ*]—*bhos tāta. ko nu khlav ayam asmān pīḍayati:*
vajrapāto 'calendrāṇāṃ śyenaḥ sarvapatatriṇām /
mṛgendro mṛgasaṅghānāṃ mṛtyuḥ puruṣavigrahaḥ // 7

[Third]—Oh Daddy! Who indeed is this one who torments us?
He is the strike of the thunderbolt to the best among mountains, he is the hawk among birds, he is a lion among the herds of deer, he is death in human form.

44 Cf. Śunaḥśepha's words to Viśvāmitra, Rām 1.60.20.

45 See R. Goldman, "Fathers, Sons, and Gurus: Oedipal Conflict in the Sanskrit Epics," pp. 348–349. The story is narrated in the *Rāmāyaṇa* as well (Rām 1.60–61) and *Bhāgavatapurāṇa* 9.7. It is referred to at MBh 13.3.6.

46 The story continues, and Viśvāmitra, adopting Śunaḥśepha as his son, considers Śunaḥśepha as his eldest son, thereby displacing the 50 elder boys. Viśvāmitra asks his sons to accept this arrangement, but they refuse and Viśvāmitra curses them to fall from their current high status. The Oedipal implications of the story have been thoroughly discussed; see R. Goldman, "Fathers, Sons, and Gurus: Oedipal Conflict in the Sanskrit Epics," pp. 348–349.

47 Pulsalkar, *Bhasa, A Study,* p. 206, while he understands the plot to be from the imagination of the poet, sees the Śunaḥśepha episode as the underlying source of theme. Devadhar, *Plays Ascribed to Bhasa,* p. 63, on the other hand, understands the Baka episode of the *Mahābhārata* as the probable source of the play, although he to understands it to be largely a creation of the poet.

48 MBh 145–152. The Pāṇḍavas and Kuntī return to the Ekacakra forest, and there they dwell in the house of a brahman. Disguised as brahmans they beg for alms. At night Kuntī would divide the food into two portions, one half for herself and the four brothers, and the rest for Bhīma. One day, when the boys had gone out, Bhīma stayed behind with Kuntī. From inside the house a loud wailing is heard. Kuntī is filled with compassion and wants to help the family. She

goes to the inner apartments where she finds the family—husband, wife, daughter, and son—seated and wailing in grief. The distraught brahman says that it is better that they all go, rather than sacrifice one of them. He says he cannot sacrifice his ever-faithful wife, the mother of his children, nor can he sacrifice his young daughter. Even though some fathers might love their sons more than their daughters, he does not. He would gladly sacrifice himself, but then how would the family survive? The wife offers herself, because she is the most expendable, is old, and has already had the pleasures of a husband and children. Moreover, without a husband she could not protect or sustain the children. It is not against the law for a man to have many wives, but it is against the law for a woman to have more than one husband. The daughter, hearing this, begs to be allowed to sacrifice herself. She argues that she after all will be given away; it might as well be now as later. Finally, the young boy, crawling to each of them in turn, tells his parents and sister not to worry, that he will kill the man-eating *rākṣasa* with a piece of straw.

At this juncture, Kuntī asks what the trouble is. The brahman responds that in this region a man-eating *rākṣasa* named Baka (Bakāsura) haunts the forest and, if sated, protects the forest and surrounding villages and lands. But the *rākṣasa* demands as his price for this protection a cartload of rice, two buffaloes, and the human who brings the food to him. People have provided him with his food in turn, and, after many years, when a man's turn comes, he cannot avoid it. If he tries to escape, the *rākṣasa* kills him, his wife, and children. The brahman tells Kuntī that he and his entire family will go to the *rākṣasa.* Kuntī says not to worry, she has five sons, and one of them will bring the *rākṣasa* his food. The brahman rejects her offer, they debate the subject, and finally the brahman accedes to the plan. Kuntī asks Bhīma to go and he agrees.

When the boys come back, Yudhiṣṭhira intuits that something is going on. He asks his mother what she has done, why has she forsaken her son for another? He finally accuses her of having lost her senses. She reassures him that she has not lost her senses: they have been living off the generosity of the brahman family and she feels that some compensation is in order. She also knows Bhīma's strength and capabilities. Yudhiṣṭhira finally agrees with her course of action.

In the meantime, the next day Bhīma takes the food to the place where the man-eating *rākṣasa* is found. Bhīma calls out the *rākṣasa* and, in a great rage, Baka comes to where Bhīma is standing and sees that Bhīma is eating his food. The *rākṣasa* threatens to kill him, but Bhīma only laughs. The *rākṣasa* lets loose a terrifying yell and rushes Bhīma, who continues to eat. The *rākṣasa* then strikes Bhīma on the back with both fists. Bhīma feels the blow, but he does not look at the *rākṣasa* and continues to eat. The *rākṣasa* then uproots a tree and attacks Bhīma. Bhīma finally finishes eating and makes ready to fight. He grabs the tree that Baka has uprooted. The battle continues. Both contestants heave huge trees at one another. Eventually Bhīma wins and breaks the *rākṣasa* in half, killing him. Thereupon Bhīma deposits the corpse of the demon at the city gates and returns to the brahman's home unnoticed.

49 G. Śāstrī glosses the phrase as *aham . . . prītimān . . . tvayi,* "I am filled with love for you"; *The Madhyamavyāyoga of Bhāsa,* p. 15.

50 "In reference to you (*tvayi*) who have allowed yourself to be food for my mother"; G. Śāstrī, *The Madhyamavyāyoga of Bhāsa*, p. 16.

51 Here following G. Śāstrī, who comments, "The idea is that even a *rākṣasa* would not say such cruel words (*rākṣaso 'pīḍṛśaṃ krūraṃ vacanaṃ na brūyād iti bhāvaḥ*)," *The Madhyamavyāyoga of Bhāsa*, p. 19.

52 S. Goldman, "Who's For Dinner? Cannibalistic Urges in the *Mahābhārata*" and "The Heroic, The Demonic, and the Counter Normative in the Characterization of Vyāsa's Bhīmasena," presented at the Seminar Series, Centre for Historical Studies, School of Social Science, Jawaharlal Nehru University, New Delhi, March 3, 2010.

53 MBh 17.2.2.25; see also MBh 17.2.22–23.

54 MBh 2.61.44–46. Bhāsa was very familiar with this episode as one of his plays, the *Urubhaṅga* ("Breaking of the Thigh") has as its central action the battle between Duryodhana and Bhīma. In the play, however, Bhīma is taken away after the illegal blow and does not drink the blood.

55 S. Goldman, "Who's For Dinner? Cannibalistic Urges in the *Mahābhārata*" and "The Heroic, The Demonic, and the Counter Normative in the Characterization of Vyāsa's Bhīmasena."

56 See also Dadoun, "Fetishism in the Horror Film," pp. 54–55, where the vampire as phallus is discussed.

siṃhāsyaḥ siṃhadaṃṣṭro madhunibhanayanaḥ snigdhagambhīrakaṇṭho
babhrubhrūḥ śyenanāso dviradapatihanur dīrghaviśliṣṭakeśaḥ /
vyūḍhorā vajramadhyo gajavṛṣabhagatir lambapīnāṃsabāhuḥ
suvyaktaṃ rākṣasījo vipulabalayuto lokavīrasya putraḥ // 26

His face is that of a lion; he has the fangs of a lion as well; his eyes are like honey-wine; his neck smooth and thick; his eyebrows are tawny he has the nose of a hawk; his chin is like that of the lord of elephants; and his hair is long (v.l. for *-dīpta-*) and scattered. His chest is broad, his waist is like adamantine, his gait is that of a bull among elephants, his arms are long with muscular shoulders. Clearly this one endowed with such great strength is the son of some worldly hero, yet born of a *rākṣasī*.

57 The passage reads:

siṃhākṛtiḥ kanakatālasamānabāhur madhye tanur garuḍapakṣaviliptapakṣaḥ /
viṣṇur bhaved vikasitāmbujapatranetro netre mamāharati bandhur ivāgato 'yam // 27

He has the form of a lion; his arms are like that of a golden palmyra tree; slender in waist, his sides are tapered like the wings of Garuḍa. He might be Viṣṇu, with his eyes like full-blown lotus petals. He attracts my eyes to him as if he were a relative.

58 A similar inability to transgress one's mother's dictum led to Draupadī's marriage to all five Pāṇḍava brothers in the *Mahābhārata* (MBh 1.182.2). It is also Kuntī whose order must be obeyed in the Baka story, even at the risk of serious danger to oneself.

59 Mark Winokur, "Technologies of Race: Special Effects, Fetish, Film, and the Fifteenth Century," *Genders* 40 (2004); http://www.genders.org/g40/g40_winokur.html, accessed April 2005.

60 See n. 48.

References

Acharya, N. R., ed. *Manusmṛti.* With the commentary *Manavarthamuktāvalī* of Kullāka. Bombay: Nirṇayasāgar Press, 1946, tenth ed.

Āgāśe, Kāśīnāthaśāstri, ed. *Aitareya Brāhmaṇa with Sāyaṇa's Commentary.* Ānandāśrama Sanskrit Series no. 32. Poona: Śnandāśrama Press, 1931.

Ṛg-Veda Aitareya-Brāhmaṇa. Titus—On the basis of the edition by Th. Aufrecht, *Das Aitareya Brāhmaṇa. Mit Auszügen aus dem Commentare von Sāyaṇācarya and anderen Beilagen* (Bonn: n.p., 1897). http://titus.unifrankfurt.de/texte/etcs/ind/aind/ved/rv/ab/ab.htm; accessed September 2013.

Apte, Vaman Shivaram. *The Practical Sanskrit-English Dictionary,* 3 vols. Poona: Prasad Prakashan, 1957–1959.

Barnett, L. D. "Abhasa-Bhasa," *Bulletin of the School of Oriental and African Studies* 3/3 (1924): 519–522.

—."The Matta Vilāsa and 'Bhāsa'," *Bulletin of the School of Oriental Studies* 1/3 (1920): 35–38.

Bhāgavatapurāṇam. With the Commentary Bhāvārthabodhinī of Srīdhara Svāmin. Delhi: Motilal Banarsidass, 1983; 1988, reprint.

Bhatt, G. H., and U. P. Shah, gen. eds. *The Vālmīki Rāmāyaṇa: Critical Edition,* 7 vols. Baroda: Oriental Institute, 1960–1975.

Bhide, H. B. *The Svapna Vasavadatta of Bhasa Edited with Introduction, Notes, with Sanskrit Commentary.* Bhavnagar: n.p., 1916.

Creed, Barbara. *The Monstrous-Feminine: Film, Feminism, Psychoanalysis.* London and New York: Routledge, 1993.

Dadoun, Roger. "Fetishism in the Horror Film," in James Donald, ed., *Fantasy and the Cinema,* pp. 38–61. London: British Film Institute, 1989.

De, Sushil Kumar. "The Dramas Ascribed to Bhasa," *Indian Historical Quarterly* 15 (1941): 415–429.

Devadhar, Chintaman Ramchandra, ed. *Bhāsanāṭakacakram: Plays Ascribed to Bhāsa.* Poona: Oriental Book Agency, 1937; 1962, reprint.

—.*Plays Ascribed to Bhasa: Their Authenticity and Merits.* Poona: Oriental Book Agency, 1927.

Gaṇapati Śāstrī, Taruvāgrahārām, ed. *The Madhyamavyāyoga of Bhāsa with the Commentary of Paṇḍit T. Gaṇapati Śāstrī.* Edited and published by the commentator. Trivandrum: Sridhara Printing House, 1912.

—.*The Svapnavāsavatta of Bhāsa Edited with Notes.* Trivandrum Sanskrit Series vol. VXV. Trivandrum: Travancore Government Press, 1912.

—.*Works (of Bhāsa).* Trivandrum Sanskrit series; nos. 15–17, 20–22, 26, 39, 42. Trivandrum: Travancore Government Press, 1917.

Gerow, Edwin. "Bhāsa's Ūrubhaṅga and Indian Poetics," *Journal of the American Oriental Society* 105/3 (1985): 405–412.

Ghosh, Manomohan, ed. *The Nāṭyaśāstra ascribed to Bharata-muni. Edited with an Introduction and Various Readings, Vol. I (Chapters I–XXVII).* Calcutta: Manish Granthalaya Private Limited, 1967.

Goldman, Robert P. "Fathers, Sons, and Gurus: Oedipal Conflict in the Sanskrit Epics," *Journal of Indian Philosophy* 6 (1978): 325–392.

—. "Rāvaṇa's Kitchen: A Testimony of Desire and the Other," in Paula Richman, ed., *Questioning Rāmāyaṇas*, pp. 105–116; 374–376. Delhi and Berkeley: Oxford University Press and University of California Press, 2000.

—. "The Serpent and the Rope on Stage: Popular Literary and Philosophical Representations of Reality in Traditional India," *Journal of Indian Philosophy* 14 (1986): 349–369.

Goldman, Robert P., and Sally J. Sutherland Goldman. *The Rāmāyaṇa of Vālmīki: An Epic of Ancient India. Volume V, Sundarakāṇḍa: Introduction, Translation, and Annotation.* Princeton, NJ: Princeton University Press, 1996.

Goldman, Sally J. Sutherland. "Nikumbhilā's Grove: *Rākṣasa* Rites in Vālmīki's *Rāmāyaṇa*," in J. L. Brockington, ed., *Battle, Bards and Brāhmins*, pp. 255–275. Papers of the 13th World Sanskrit Conference. Delhi: Motilal Banarsidas, 2012.

—. "Re-siting Sītā: Gender and Narrative in Vālmīki's *Sundarakāṇḍa*," *Purāṇa* 45/2 (2003): 115–135.

—. "The Heroic, The Demonic, and the Counter Normative in the characterization of Vyāsa's Bhīmasena," presented at the Seminar Series, Centre for Historical Studies, School of Social Science, Jawaharlal Nehru University, New Delhi, March 3, 2010.

—. "Who's For Dinner? Cannibalistic Urges in the *Mahābhārata*," paper presented at the Annual Meeting of the American Oriental Society, San Diego, California, March 2004.

Kale, Moreshwar Ramchandra. Introduction, in *Svapnavāsavadatta of Bhasa*, pp. ix–xxxviii. Bombay: Booksellers' Publishing Co., 1929.

—, ed. *Svapnavāsavadatta of Bhasa*. Edited with an exhaustive introduction, a Sanskrit commentary, a literal English translation, critical and copious notes, and useful appendices. Bombay: Booksellers' Publishing Co., 1929.

Keith, Arthur Berriedale. *The Sanskrit Drama*. Oxford: The Clarendon Press, 1924.

Kinjawadekar, Pandit Ramachandrashastri, ed. *Mahābhāratam*. With the Bharata Bhawadeepa by Nīlakaṇṭha. Poona: Shankar Narahar Joshi Chitrashala Press, 1933.

Kristeva, Julia. *Powers of Horror: An Essay on Abjection*. Leon S. Roudiez, trans. New York: Columbia University Press, 1982.

Masson, Jeffrey M. "A Note on the Sources of Bhāsa's (?) Avimāraka," *Journal of the Oriental Institute of the Maharaja Sayajirao University of Baroda* XIX (1969): 60–74.

Masson, Jeffrey L., and D. D. Kosambi. *Avimāraka (Love's Enchanted World)*. Delhi: Motilal Banarsidass, 1970.

Monier-Williams, Monier. *A Sanskrit-English Dictionary*. (1899). Oxford: Oxford University Press, 1964, reprint.

Mudholakar, Shastri Shrinivas Katti, ed. *Rāmāyan of Vālmīki*, 7 vols. With three commentaries called *Tilaka, Shiromani,* and *Bhooshana*. Bombay: Gujarati Printing Press, 1914–1920.

Paṃśīkar, Wāsudeva Laxmaṇ Śāstrī, ed. *Rāmāyaṇa of Vālmīki.* With the commentary (Tilaka) of Rāma. Bombay: Nirṇayasāgar Press, 1930, fourth rev. ed.

Parab, Kāśīnāth Pāṇḍurang, ed. *The Daśarūpaka of Dhanañjaya.* With the commentary of Dhanika. Bombay: Nirṇayasāgar Press, 1897.

Pisharoti, A. Krishna, and K. Rama Pisharoti. "Bhāsa's Works—Are They Genuine?", *Bulletin of the School of Oriental Studies* 3/1 (1923): 107–117.

Pollock, Sheldon I. *The Rāmāyaṇa of Vālmīki: An Epic of Ancient India. Volume III, Araṇyakāṇḍa: The Forest.* Introduction, Translation, and Annotation. Princeton, NJ: Princeton University Press, 1991.

Pulsalker, A. D. *Bhasa, A Study.* Foreword by A. Berriedale Keith. Delhi: Munshiram Manoharlal, 1968, reprint.

Richmond, Farley. "The Bhasa Festival, Trivandrum India," *Asian Theater Journal* 6/1 (Spring 1989): 68–76.

Richmond, Farley, and Yasmin Richmond. "The Multiple Dimensions of Time and Space in Kūṭiyāṭṭam, the Sanskrit Theatre of Kerala," *Asian Theatre Journal* 2/1 (1985): 50–60.

Sahityadarpaṇam of Yogeśvaradatta Śarma Parāśarah Viśvanaātha Kavirāja. Vivṛtiḥ, Vijñapriyā, Kusumapratimā, Lakṣmī, Vivṛtipurtih, Locanam, Vimalā, Rucirā. Dilli: Nag Publishers, 1999, reprint.

Śāstrī, Kṛṣṇa Śaṅkar, ed. *Bhāgavatapurāṇam.* With thirteen commentaries. Ahmedabad: Sribhagavatavidyapitha, 1965.

Shastri, Madhusudan, ed. *Natyasastra of Bharatamuni.* With the commentary (*Abhinavabharati*) of Abhinava Guptacharya. Edited with introduction and the commentaries Madhusudani and Balakreeda. Varanasi: Banaras Hindu University, 1971.

Sukthankar, Vishnu Sitaram. "Studies in Bhāsa," *Journal of the American Oriental Society* 40 (1920): 248–259.

—. "Studies in Bhāsa II. On the Versification of the Metrical Portions of the Dramas," *Journal of the American Oriental Society* 41 (1921): 107–130.

—. "Studies in Bhāsa III. On the Relationship between the Cārudatta and Mṛcchakaṭika," *Journal of the American Oriental Society* 42 (1922): 59–74.

—. "Studies in Bhāsa IV. A Concordance of the Dramas," *Annals of the Bhandarkar Institute* 4 (1923): 167–187.

—. "Studies in Bhāsa V. A Bibliographical Note," *Journal of the Bombay Branch of the Royal Asiatic Society* 26 (1921–1923): 230–249.

—. "The Bhāsa Riddle: A Proposed Solution," *Journal of the Bombay Branch of the Royal Asiatic Society,* n.s. (1925): 126–143.

Sukthankar, V. S., et al., eds. *Mabhābhārata: Critical Edition,* 24 vols. With *Harivaṃśa.* Poona: Bhandarkar Oriental Research Institute, 1933–1970.

Sutherland (Goldman), Sally J. "The Bad Seed: Senior Wives and Elder Sons," in Sally J. Sutherland, ed., *Bridging Worlds: Studies on Women in South Asia,* pp. 24–52. Berkeley: Centers for South and Southeast Asia Studies, University of California, Berkeley, 1991.

Tieken, H. J. H. "On the Use of Rasa in Studies of Sanskrit Drama," *Indo Iranian Journal* 43 (2000): 115–138.

—. "The *Purvaranga,* the *Prastavana,* and the *Sthapaka,*" *Wiener Zeitschrift für die Kunde Südasiens* XLV (2001): 91–124.

—. "The So-called Trivandrum Plays Attributed to Bhasa," *Wiener Zeitschrift für die Kunde Südasiens* Band 37 (1993): 5–44.

—. "Three Men in a Row (Studies in the Trivandrum Plays II)," *Wiener Zeitschrift für die Kunde Südasiens* 41 (1997): 17–52.

Unni, N. P. *Bhāsa Afresh: New Problems in Bhāsa Plays.* Trivandrum: College Book House, 1978. Delhi: Nag Publishers, 1999, reprint.

Winokur, Mark. "Technologies of Race: Special Effects, Fetish, Film, and the Fifteenth Century," Genders 40 (2004). http://www.genders.org/g40/g40_winokur.html; accessed April 2005.

Winternitz, M. "Bhāsa: What Do We Really Know of Him and his Work?", in Mohammad Shafi, ed., *Woolner Commemoration Volume,* pp. 297–308. Lahore: Mehar Chand Lachman Das, 1940.

Wood, Robin. "The American Nightmare: Horror in the 70s," in Robin Wood, *Hollywood from Vietnam to Reagan,* pp. 70–94. New York: Columbia University Press, 1986. New York: Columbia University Press, 2003, reprint, pp. 63–84..

Philosophy as Drama: Amṛtacandra and Abhinavagupta

Phyllis Granoff
Yale University

Introduction

The Digambara philosopher Amṛtacandra was the author of remarkably original commentaries to the much earlier *Pravacanasāra* and *Samayasāra* of Kundakunda, texts that may all be considered foundational for the *adhyātma,* the mystical Jain movement. Amṛtacandra also wrote several independent works, including a verse epitome of the *Samayasāra,* called the *Samayasāra Kalaśa;* a doctrinal text, the *Puruṣārthasiddhyupāya;* and a philosophical work, the *Laghutattvasphoṭa.* Almost nothing is known about him; his conjectured dates range from the early to mid-tenth century.[1] In this paper I argue that Amṛtacandra, in his commentary to the opening verses of the *Pravacanasāra,* reworks ideas found in the writings of two important theorists of drama, Bhaṭṭa Nāyaka and Abhinavagupta, and on that basis should not be placed before the end of the tenth century and more likely to the beginning of the eleventh century.

Amṛtacandra's interest in these dramatic theorists should not surprise us. Indeed, he calls his commentary on the *Samayasāra,* the *Ātmakhyāti,* a drama, or *nāṭaka,* and we shall see that both the *Ātmakhyāti* and the *Kalaśas* are steeped in the language of drama and of aesthetic theory. I begin with his remarks on the benedictory verses of the *Pravacanasāra,* which I believe reflect not only on Abhinavagupta's ideas but also his very language. I conclude with some comments on Amṛtacandra's use of terms from aesthetic theory in the *Ātmakhyāti* and the *Kalaśas.*

The Opening Verses to the *Pravacanasāra*

In his commentary to verse 5 of the *Pravacanasāra,* Amṛtacandra explains that the opening benedictory verses of the text function on two levels.[2]

The first level is the obvious one, involving the duality of self and other, subject and object. At this level a devotee praises the Jinas. The second level eradicates that duality by eliminating the distinction between self and other. It does this through a process that involves an understanding of the interpenetration or close entanglement of self and other. This process is further described as depending on a particular relationship between the two normally polar opposites, the relationship of *bhāvaka* and *bhāvya*. Subsequent commentators and modern translators describe this as a form of meditation, with the *bhāvaka* as the meditator and the *bhāvya* the soul. But Amṛtacandra's language here is strikingly close to that of Abhinavagupta in the *Abhinavabhāratī*, and understanding this may help to clarify what these terms mean. As noted above, it may also help us to date Amṛtacandra. In addition, his evocation of concepts that we consider to be more at home in texts on aesthetics offers further evidence of what I have characterized elsewhere as a medieval Jain eagerness to see all of learning brought together, a trait that I suggest is distinctive of many Jain authors.[3] Finally, I also believe that attention to Amṛtacandra's use of Abhinavagupta's ideas may help us to understand the substance of Abhinavagupta's often elusive text and enrich our understanding of aesthetic theory.

Abhinavagupta, in describing how a drama produces *rasa*, aesthetic pleasure, follows the lead of Bhaṭṭa Nāyaka, whose views he criticizes and refines. Bhaṭṭa Nāyaka had described three levels of response to a play. In the first, labeled *abhidhā* by Bhaṭṭa Nāyaka, the words of the text make known their meaning. In the second, which Bhaṭṭa Nāyaka calls the function of *bhāvaka*, the techniques of the drama result in the removal of delusion, *moha*, and the generalization, or *sādhāraṇīkaraṇa*, of the various aesthetic elements, the *vibhāva*s, etc. This is the process by which *rasa* is brought about. The final stage is enjoyment, *bhoga*, in which the mind is steady, and Bhaṭṭa Nāyaka likens this aesthetic pleasure to the enjoyment of the ultimate, *parabrahma*.[4]

There has been considerable debate about the second stage and what the term "generalization," *sādhāraṇīkaraṇa*, means. Abhinavagupta describes the process in this way:[5]

> The viewer's self is neither entirely obscured nor cognized in its concrete unique details. The same is true of the other (that is, it is neither entirely obscured nor cognized in its concrete unique details).

In other words, the spectator views what is happening as neither specifically happening to himself nor specifically happening to someone else.[6]

Abhinavagupta explains further:[7]

> In the enactment of a drama, particular details, whether they belong to the real world or are imagined by the poet, details such as time and place, the identity of the agent experiencing the action, and so on, which would serve to fix or limit what is happening in the drama, come together. And in coming together they cease entirely to be able to fix or limit the action. And with this the state of commonality is richly enhanced.[8]

In his analysis of the nondual prayer Amṛtacandra describes the process as one in which subject and object are completely entangled with each other; he uses the term *saṃvalana.* Abhinavagupta employs the more usual term *sambandha,* which I translate as "coming together," but the result is the same. Object and subject, self and other, lose their specific identities through this process in such a way that a unique cognition of perfect bliss is the result.[9] Both Amṛtacandra and Abhinavagupta describe a similar process. In Amṛtacandra's dualist understanding of the prayer, there is the subject, the one who prays, and the object of his devotion. Through a special cognitive practice subject and object merge, their differences are eradicated, and this leads finally to the cognition of the nonduality of the soul. For Abhinavagupta, in the beginning the spectator sees him- or herself, the actor, and the character as different from each other, characterized by differing times and places, and distinctive characteristics. Through the various techniques of the drama these differentiating characteristics, juxtaposed with each other, evaporate, so that object and subject, character and actor, and character, actor, and spectator all blend together. The emotions revealed are no longer ordinary ones, tied to a particular time and place or to a specific individual. Abhinavagupta characterizes this experience as pure pleasure.[10]

It is here that I see a striking convergence between Amṛtacandra and the ideas of Abhinavagupta and Bhaṭṭa Nāyaka. For all of them there is a distinctive process called *bhāvanā,* in which the delimiting factors of self and other recede, leaving behind a pure cognition of bliss. If I am correct in seeing in Amṛtacandra a close reflection of the ideas of Bhaṭṭa Nāyaka and Abhinavagupta and the very language of Abhinavagupta, it is clear that he cannot be dated before these two scholars. This would situate him at the earliest in the late tenth and more likely in the eleventh century C.E.[11] Even this later date suggests that new ideas circulated rapidly in medieval India. In fact, the commentary to the benedictory verses of the *Pravacanasāra* is not the only example of Amṛtacandra's attentiveness to these cutting-edge aesthetic theories. The entire *Ātmakhyāti,* his commentary to the *Samayasāra,* and the *Kalaśa*s, his verses on the *Samayasāra,* are steeped in the language and thought of the Sanskrit drama and the new criticism. I offer a few examples below.

Amṛtacandra, the *Nāṭaka,* and the Language of Aesthetic Theory

Amṛtacandra's *Ātmakhyāti* reflects the world of the Sanskrit drama in its very structure.[12] It opens with a section that Amṛtacandra explicitly calls the *pūrvaraṅga,* or prologue, as it is known in classical Indian plays, in which the *sūtradhāra* first steps onto the stage. Amṛtacandra announces his appearance: *atha sūtrāvatāra,* "Now the *sūtradhāra* appears on stage." He sets the stage for the play / text by indicating its subject matter in the first 38 verses. These introductory verses provide a synopsis of the Jain understanding of the soul and the various entities of Jain ontology, soul, not-soul, sin, virtue, the influx of karma, the eradication of karma, bondage and release, and they describe the means to achieve correct knowledge.[13] The *pūravaraṅga* concludes with Kundakunda's verse 38, a clear statement of the nature of the soul: "I am one, pure, in essence knowledge and sentience, without form. Nothing material belongs to me, not even the tiniest thing."[14]

Amṛtacandra divides Kundakunda's text into clear chapters. He tells us that the *pūrvaraṅga* is over and introduces the next act, "Soul and not-soul, joined together as one, enter."[15] This act concludes with the soul and not-soul, now separated from each other, leaving the stage, after Kundakunda's verse 68, which states that the various states in which the soul is said to exist, states of anger, passion, and so on, do not belong to the soul but to the material world and are products of the material karma that results in delusion. They are insentient and completely different from the soul.[16]

The next section of the text examines the concept of agency and action, and Amṛtacandra tells us that after the soul and not-soul, clearly separated from each other, have withdrawn from the stage, they return, this time in the guises of an agent, *kartṛ,* and an object of action, karma.[17] They will withdraw again after verse 144, having discarded their disguises as agent and object of action, for in this section Amṛtacandra thoroughly refutes the notion that the soul makes its own karma. Karma is a purely material process that happens outside the soul; the soul is not the causal agent responsible for its changes. In the next section, karma, which is one, appears on the stage as two actors, sin and virtue.[18]

In this way, each section of the text begins with the appearance on stage of a character; following sin and merit comes *āsrava,* the influx of karma; then *saṃvara,* the prevention of the influx of karma; after him is *nirjarā,* the eradication of karma, followed by bondage, or *bandha,* and *mokṣa,* liberation. The final character to take center stage, after verse 307, is "completely and utterly perfect knowledge," *sarvaviśúddhajñāna.*

The hero of this unusual drama is this last character, also called the light of the soul, *jñānajyotis* (*Kalaśa* 46). This knowledge of the soul is described explicitly in terms taken from works on dramaturgy: it is *paramodātta,* "most noble," and *dhīra,* "steadfast" (*Kalaśa* 46), or *dhīrodātta,* attributes of the *nāyaka* of the Sanskrit theater. It is filled with the overflow of its own *rasa, svarasavisarāpūrṇa* (*Kalaśa* 193).

These are the characters in this drama, but a play also requires the presence of appreciative spectators, of which Amṛtacandra is also acutely aware. The spectators of this drama are those who can experience the soul in its true state. They are called *rasika*s, "connoisseurs" (*Kalaśa* 22), and Amṛtacandra invites them to savor the performance:

> People! Leave off all this delusion that has been with you from birth. Savor that knowledge that is arising, a source of joy to those who know to appreciate it (*rasikānām*). For never will the one soul share the same nature with anything that constitutes the material world.[19]

A drama must also have a dominant aesthetic sentiment. It should come as no surprise that this sentiment is *śānta rasa,* ultimate calm. When the curtain that is delusion is pushed back, the spectators are immersed in *śānta rasa* (*Kalaśa* 32). Amṛtacandra encourages them:

> May you all, all together, at the same moment float upon this feeling of peace that floods the world, as the blessed ocean of knowledge rises, pushing aside the curtain of delusion with its great force.[20]

The experience the audience will have is one of bliss; the play delights the mind (*Kalaśa* 33).[21] The very nature of the soul is knowledge and highest bliss (*Kalaśa* 180).[22] The ultimate experience of the soul is also called *camatkāra,* a common term in treatises on aesthetics for the otherworldly experience of the drama (*Kalaśa* 6), and one to which Abhinavagupta is partial.[23] Perfect knowledge, in a surfeit of that bliss, dances with the all-pervasive expanse of the sky as the stage (*Kalaśa* 162).

The language with which Amṛtacandra describes the soul also has parallels in descriptions of the aesthetic experience. Amṛtacandra's experience of the soul is one in which all notions of object and subject, self and other, are absent and the soul is known as it really is, simply a mass of knowledge, *jñānaghana* (*Kalaśa* 6: *pūrṇajñānaghanasya*), or *avabodhaghana* (*Kalaśa* 13). This recalls Abhinavagupta's description of the state of *sādhāraṇībhāva*. In this state, the particulars of time and place that characterize the self as self and the other as other have been left behind; the perception is characterized by Abhinavagupta with the word *ekaghanatā*—a single dense mass of knowledge.[24] While this terminology is far older than Abhinvagupta and goes back to the *Upaniṣad*s, its use by Abhinavagupta and Amṛtacandra is striking.[25]

We have seen that Amṛtacandra fashions his commentary to the *Samayasāra* as a drama: there is a master of ceremonies, a *sūtradhāra;* there are actors who put on and take off their costumes; there is an audience; and there is a dominant aesthetic flavor. In fact, the entire commentary is pervaded by the language of aesthetic theory. I give only one example here. Amṛtacandra even calls into service the language of *vyabhicāri bhāva* and *sthāyibhāva* to contrast the real nature of the soul as pure knowledge with transitory emotional states that are wrongly identified as essential transformations of the soul. In Sanskrit drama the *vyabhicāri bhāva*s are emotional states that accompany the main emotion (*sthāyibhāva*) and change from time to time. They are an important part of the toolkit a dramatist has at his disposal to create the experience of the drama for the spectator. Amṛtacandra brings in these terms in his commentary to Kundakunda's verse 203. The verse itself seems quite straightforward:

> Leave off the states that belong to the material world and have no place in the soul; take hold of that one permanent and fixed state that is known to be the soul's natural state.[26]

Amṛtacandra gives this concept a new character by describing those "material" states of anger, passion, and so on as akin to the *vyabhicāri bhāva*s of the drama. He takes this simple verse, which urges its audience to understand that the soul is something other than the material world, and puts it into the language of the aesthetic theory. These states do not belong to the soul, he says; they are momentary, *kṣaṇika,* and he further describes them as *vyabhicāriṇo bhāvā,* "transient emotional states." They are also described as *aniyatatvāvasthā,* "conditions that are not constant or natural to the soul." By contrast, there is only one state of the soul that is natural to it and always present. This is knowledge, which is constantly experienced and permanent.

While these ideas are familiar, the language Amṛtacandra employs here is distinctive. Knowledge, he says, is the *sthāyibhāva* of the soul; it is *svādya,* that which is to be experienced, and it is furthermore experienced as the one absolutely real *rasa, paramārtharasatayā svadamānaṃ jñānam ekam evedaṃ svādyam.* In the verse (*Kalaśa* 13) that follows immediately on this commentary, Amṛtacandra repeats that the soul alone is the one solid entity to be savored.[27]

It should be clear from these references that Amṛtacandra has found in theoretical reflections on aesthetic experience and the practice of the drama powerful tools to express the truths of Jain philosophy. I have argued elsewhere that this openness to other branches of knowledge might be considered a hallmark of medieval Jain authors, but even among them Amṛtacandra is unique. I suspect that he has found in Abhinavagupta more than just an interesting or different way of expressing himself; he has also found a rich resonance to his own thought, and at the same time he remains fully committed to a very different understanding of reality. In conclusion, I offer some comments on the significance of Amṛtacandra's very unusual framing of his philosophical commentary.

Conclusions

In the history of *Alaṅkāraśāstra,* as scholars today understand it, two moments stand out for the convergence of religious/philosophical thinking and speculation on the nature of the aesthetic experience. One of them, of course, revolves around Abhinavagupta and Bhaṭṭa Nāyaka, for whom the experience of a work of poetry, performed or read, is tantamount to the experience of the soul, the goal of the religious quest. The second moment is usually placed much later, in the sixteenth century with the Vaiṣṇava Gosvāmins, particularly Rūpa Gosvāmin, whose *Ujjvalanīlamaṇi,* a text on aesthetics, defined Vaiṣṇava aesthetic theory. For the Gosvāmins the drama itself becomes a mode of worship, a means of access to the divine drama of Kṛṣṇa and his companions. No longer mere spectators, devotees become active participants in that drama. Worshiping Kṛṣṇa by dressing like him and imitating his actions finds its source in the *Bhāgavata Purāṇa,* where in the absence of Kṛṣṇa the *gopī*s act out Kṛṣṇa's deeds. One *gopī* pretends to be the demonness Pūtanā and suckles another woman, who is pretending to be Kṛṣṇa. Another cries like a baby and kicks her friend, who is playing the role of the cart that Kṛṣṇa overturned. Kṛṣṇa's entire life cycle is reenacted and the reenacted scenes become a means for the *gopī*s to be in Kṛṣṇa's presence, even in his absence. Kṛṣṇa and Balarāma, too, are actors, pretending to be ordinary mortals, while in the very act of creation God is likened to an actor.[28] The theater provides metaphors and similes that are useful for describing how God works in the world, and it also functions more concretely as a means to access his direct presence.

My work on Amṛtacandra is only beginning, but I would like to suggest that he represents a third and very different moment in the relationship between aesthetic theory and religious thought. Unlike either Abhinavagupta or Rūpa Gosvāmin, Amṛtacandra does not see the drama as a direct means to experience the ultimate truth; instead, he sees the theories and practice of the drama as a framework for understanding events that can make the sometimes arcane truths of Jain doctrine accessible to an audience. Thus, such emotional states as anger, passion, and so on are not simply like the *vyabhcāri bhāva*s, they are *vyabhicāri bhāva*s, transitory states that come and go and therefore cannot be the essence of the soul. Devoid of particulars, of anything outside itself, the soul that shines forth is not simply like the undivided experience, the *ekaghanatā,* which ultimately results from the play. It is a solid mass of consciousness.

Of course, Amṛtacandra is not without context. In India there is a strong tradition of allegorical drama, the most famous of which is the *Prabodhacandrodaya* of Kṛṣnamiśra, probably written at the same time or perhaps slightly after Amṛtacandra's works. The *Prabodhacandrodaya* espouses Vedānta and is decidedly hostile to Buddhists and Jains. But Jains also wrote allegorical plays: the *Moharājaparājaya,* "The Defeat of King Delusion," was written by the Jain Yaśaḥpāla in the thirteenth century. Before that, in 906 C.E. a Jain monk, Siddharṣi, composed the *Upamitibhavaprapañcakathā,* the most elaborate and sustained allegory of medieval India.

Amṛtacandra's *Ātmakhyāti* shares with these allegorical dramatists the personification of abstract concepts such as bondage, liberation, and so on, and he was no doubt familiar with allegorical plays. But the *Ātmakhyāti* is really something else. In the end, no matter what Amṛtacandra tells us, it is not merely a play, it is a philosophical commentary. Then again, Amṛtacandra also tells us that drawing such a distinction may be quibbling. When life itself is a grand play, the language of the drama remains an important means for us to understand who we are.

> In this beginningless grand drama of illusion, where we fail to know the difference between the soul and the material world, it is really the material world, characterized by color, touch, and so on, that is the actor. Separate from all of that is this soul, consisting of pure consciousness, completely inimical in nature to the modifications of the material world, such as passion and anger.[29]

Notes

1 For what we do know, see A. N. Upadhye's introduction to the *Pravacanasāra* (Agas: Rājacandra Jaina Śāstramālā, 1934); Padmanabh S. Jaini's introduction to the *Laghutattvasphoṭa* (Ahmedabad: L. D. Institute, 1978), pp. 1–40; and Dr. Uttamacandra Jain, *Ācārya Amṛtacandra vyaktitva evaṃ kartṛtva* (Jaipur: Pandita Todarmal Smarak Trust, 1977), pp. 21–41. I am deeply indebted to Professor Jaini, with whom I first read Amṛtacandra and without whose constant encouragement I would not have completed this paper. He read several drafts and always offered helpful suggestions. I also thank David Shulman and Diwakar Acharya, who also read and commented on earlier versions of this essay.

2 *praṇativandanābhidhānapravṛttadvaitadvāreṇa bhāvyabhāvakajṛmbhitātinirbhareta-retarasaṃvalanabalavilīnanikhilasvaparavibhāgatayā pravṛttādvaitam namaskāram.*

From the *Pravacanasāra,* with Gujarati translation of Himatlāl Jeṭhālāl Śāha (Sonagadh: Śrī Digambara Jaina Svādhyāyamandira Trust, n.d.); accessed July 2013 at http://www.AtmaDharma.com.

3 Phyliss Granoff, "Unspoken Rules of Debate in Medieval India and the Boundaries of Knowledge," in Gérard Colas and Émilie Aussant, eds., volume on Indian Scholasticisms (Paris: École Franciase d'Extrême-Orient, forthcoming).

4 Subodhchandra Mukherjee Śāstrī, ed., *The Nāṭyaśāstra of Bharata, Chapter Six with the Abhinavabhāratī* (1926), pp. 54–55:

caturvidhābhinayarūpeṇa nibiḍanijamohasaṅkaṭanivāraṇakāriṇā vibhāvādisādhāra-ṇīkāraṇātmanābhidhāto dvitīyenāṃśena bhāvakatvavyāpāreṇa bhāvyamāno raso.

5 Śāstrī, ed., *The Nāṭyaśāstra of Bharata,* p. 59: *nātmātyantatiraskṛto na viśeṣata ullikhitah / evaṃ paro pi.*

6 Sheldon Pollock, "What was Bhaṭṭa Nāyaka Saying? The Hermeneutical Transformation of Indian Aesthetics," in Sheldon Pollock, ed., *Epic and Argument in Sanskrit Literary Tradition, Essays in Honor of Robert P. Goldman* (Delhi: Manohar, 2010), pp. 143–184, specifically p. 160, perhaps following the translation of R. Gnoli, *The Aesthetic Experience According to Abhinavagupta* (Varanasi: Chowkhamba Sanskrit Series Office, 1968), p. 56. Pollock translates this as "and the same is true for everyone else," and argues that the sentence means to say that what happens to one spectator happens to everyone in the audience. This is, I think, incorrect. After the word *paro,* "the other," we need to repeat what has just been said for the self, namely that the other, too, is neither entirely obscured nor is it presented to consciousness in all its unique particularity. Abhinavagupta makes this clear when he states explicitly a few sentences later that neither self nor "other," in this case, the actor or the character in the drama, is experienced in all its unique particularity. In other words, for a single spectator the self and other are no longer cognized as such: *tatah sa eṣa svaparaniyatatāvighnāpasāraṇaprakāro vyākhyātaḥ* (Śāstrī, ed., *The Nāṭyaśāstra of Bharata,* p. 62).

The similarity with invariable concomitance is that in invariable concomitance the individual particulars of time and place are also not cognized; there is instead knowledge of "fire" and "smoke" in general. Pollock further argues that the force of this *bhāvanā* is such that the "discourse of both scripture and literature comes to be directed to oneself" (p. 162). This is also problematic: Abhinavagupta is clear that if the spectator sees everything as pertaining to himself he will fail to appreciate the drama as art. A common problem with this is that if the drama presents something sad, the spectator will feel sad, and he may never again return to the theater. In his subsequent explanation Abhinavagupta is explicit in explaining that what is happening with *bhāvanā* is that a major impediment—to think that the emotions generated are either specifically one's own or someone else's—to appreciating the drama is removed. If the spectator regards the feeling of pleasure as his own, he will become distracted with thoughts of how to sustain that pleasure or how to get even more pleasure like the pleasant feeling he has now; if he regards the pleasure as belonging to someone else, then he will be distracted by thoughts of jealousy or will feel indifferent. The various techniques of the stage have been designed to remove this impediment by preventing the spectator from seeing the happiness and suffering portrayed on stage as either belonging to himself or to someone else. In describing these techniques Abhinanavgupta concludes, "Thus has been explained the means to do away with the impediment that comes from seeing things as relating concretely to either the self or another," *tatah sa eṣa svaparaniyatatāvighnāpasāraṇaprakāro vyākhyātaḥ* (Śāstrī, ed., *The Nāṭyaśāstra of Bharata*, p. 62).

The discussion in Lawrence McCrea, *The Teleology of Poetics in Medieval Kashmir* (Cambridge, MA: Harvard University Press, 2008), pp. 382–392, provides a clear summary of Bhaṭṭa Nāyaka's views, as does David Shulman, *More than Real: A History of the Imagination in South India* (Cambridge, MA: Harvard University Press, 2012), pp. 64–67.

The debt owed by Abhinavagupta and Bhaṭṭa Nāyaka to the Mīmāṃsaka philosophers is noted in Prem Swarup Gupta, *Rasagaṅgādhara kā Śāstrīya Adhyayan* (Delhi: Bhārata Prakāśana Mandira, 1962), p. 149, cited by Kājī Añjum Salfi, "Daśarūpaka aur Nāṭyadarpaṇa meṃ rasa-svarūpa evaṃ niṣpatti: eka tulanātmaka vivecana," *Aspects of Jainology* 1 (1987), accessed online September 2, 2014 at http://www.jainlibrary.org/book.php?file=211153. In his article Salfi notes that Dhanañjaya was also heavily influenced by the Mīmāṃsā.

7 Śāstrī, ed., *The Nāṭyaśāstra of Bharata*, p. 59: *tadatra sākṣātkārāṇāyamānatve pariposikā naṭādisāmagrī yasyām vastusatāṃ kāvyārpitānām ca deśakālapramātrādīnām niyamahetūnām anyonyasambandhabalād atyantam apasaraṇe sa eva sādhāraṇībhāvah sutarāṃ puṣyati.*

My phrase "In the enactment of a drama," a loose translation for *naṭādisāmagrī*, "the totality of factors that constitute a play, starting with the actors," is meant to include all the various techniques of acting as well as the actors.

8 There is a variant reading for the passage by Abhinavagupta in the *Kāvyānuśāsana*, p. 98. This has *pratibandha* instead of *sambandha*. R. Gnoli, *The Aesthetic Experience According to Abhinavagupta* (Varanasi: Chowkhamba Sanskrit Series Office, 1968), p. 13, line 21, also has *pratibandha*. The concept is the same: when they are juxtaposed, the details of time, place, agent, etc. clash with each other and cancel one another out. Both readings lead to the same conclusion: de-

tails of time and place that would tie the experience either to a specific actor, character, or spectator are mutually incompatible and cannot coexist. Once they come into contact with each other, they are unable to gain a firm foothold in the spectator's mind.

Somewhat later, in a passage cited in full by another Jain monk, Hemacandra, Abhinavagupta summarizes how all of this works (Śāstrī, ed., *The Nāṭyaśāstra of Bharata,* pp. 71–72); Prof. Rasiklal C. Parikh and Dr. V. M. Kulkarni, *Kāvyānuśāsana (with Alaṃkāracūḍāmani and Viveka) of Ācārya Hemacandra* (Bombay: Śrī Mahāvīra Jaina Vidyālaya, 1964, second rev. ed.), pp. 103–104):

> When the actor puts on things like a crown or a mask the spectator is disabused of his view that the person before him is simply the actor. But because of the firm traces left behind by his earlier cognition (of the actor), even though the words of the drama inform him that the person before him is Rāma, he is not firmly established in that belief, either. Thus he gives up all notions of time and place, etc. associated with either of them. And then, things like horripilation, which he knows to be associated with joy and love, cause him to perceive joy and love, but without any particular connection to a specific time and place. Into this love (*sthāyibhāva rati*) his own self enters, because of previous mental traces of his own. This is why he is not indifferent when he perceives the emotion of love. But he also does not see it as specifically pertaining to himself, which might lead him to want to possess for himself and embrace the object of that love. Nor does he perceive the emotions as specifically pertaining to someone else, whereby he might feel sorrow or hatred. In this way the emotion of love, made common to self and other, being experienced either in a chain of congitions or in one single cognition is the *rasa śṛṅgāra.*

Hemacandra adds words of approval: "As the Honored master Abhinavagupta has said, 'The transformation into a generalized state is accomplished through the vibhāvas, etc.' I am following his views exclusively."

It is worth noting that characters in Sanskrit literature who are watching plays never achieve such an abstract appreciation; they are repeatedly described as becoming overwhelmed by sadness and behaving hysterically; for example, Rāma in the concluding act of the *Uttararāmacarita* and in act 3 of the *Bālarāmayaṇa,* and Nala in act 6 of the *Nalavilāsa* of Hemacandra's disciple, Rāmacandra.

9 Amṛtacandra refers repeatedly to the relationship of *bhāvya-bhāvaka,* for example in his commentary to the *Samayasāra,* verses 32 and 83. It is worth noting that Amṛtacandra is not the only Jain philosopher who is up to date on the latest in aesthetic theory. Hemacandra's *Kāvyānuśāsana* with its commentaries gives evidence of his close engagement with the theories of both Bhaṭṭa Nāyaka and Abhinavagupta, and his summary of the process of aesthetic appreciation in the theater is particularly useful in understanding Abhinavagupta. Hemacandra's disciple Rāmacandra wrote a number of dramas and coauthored with Guṇacandra a text on dramaturgy, the *Nāṭyadarpaṇa,* which is often indebted to Abhinavagupta. See Kājī Añjum Salfi, "Nāṭyadarpaṇa par Abhinavabhāratī Kā Prabhāv," *Aspects of Jainology,* Part 3 (1991), ed. Pandit Dalsukh Malvaniya, accessed online on September 2, 2014: http://www.jainlibrary.org/book.php?file=211251.

10 Śāstrī, ed., *The Nāṭyaśāstra of Bharata,* p. 64.

[11] This is slightly later than the date suggested by Uttamacandra Jain, *Ācārya Amṛtacandra vyaktitva evaṃ kartṛtva*, p. 21.

[12] References are to the edition with Hindi and Gujarati translations, accessed September 2013: http://www.AtmaDharma.com.

[13] Verses 13, 15, and 16.

[14] *aham ekkao khalu suddho daṃsaṇaṇāṇamaiyo sadārūvī*
ṇa vi atthi majjha kiṃ ci vi aṇṇaṃ paramāṇumettaṃ pi // 38.

[15] *Samayasāra with Ātmakhyāti*, with Hindi translation, p. 84: a*tha jīvājīvau ekībhūtau praviśataḥ*. Accessed September 2013, http://www.Atmadharma.com.

[16] *Samayasāra with Ātmakhyāti*, p. 126: *iti jīvājīvau pṛthagbhūtau niṣkrāntau.*

[17] *atha jīvājīvau kartṛkarmaveṣeṇa praviśataḥ.*

[18] *athaikam eva karma dvipātrībhūya puṇyapāparūpeṇa praviśati.*

[19] *tyajatu jagad idānīṃ moham ājanmalīḍhaṃ*
rasayatu rasikānāṃ rocanam jñānam udyat /
iha katham api nātmānatmanā sākam ekaḥ
kila kalayati kāle kvāpi tādātmyavṛttim // 22.

There is a typo here, *kāpi* for k*vāpi*, correct in the Gujarati edition of the *Kalaśa*s (Sonagadh: Śrī Digambara Jaina Svādhyāya Mandir, n.d.), accessed September 2013: http://AtmaDharma.com..

[20] *majjantu nirbharam amī samameva lokā*
ālokam ucchalati śāntarase samastāḥ /
āplāvya vibhramatiraskariṇīṃ bhareṇa
pronmagna eṣa bhagavān avabodhasindhuḥ // 32.

[21] *mano hlādayat.*

[22] *sahajaparamānandasarasaṃ paraṃ pūrṇam jñānam.*

[23] Śāstrī, ed., *The Nāṭyaśāstra of Bharata*, p. 59.

[24] Śāstrī, ed., *The Nāṭyaśāstra of Bharata*, p. 59.

[25] Also *Kalaśa*s 173, 188, etc. I have written about this term in "The Art of the Philosopher: Painting and Sculpture as Metaphor," in Chikafumi Watanabe, et al., eds., *Samskrita-sādhutā: Goodness of Sanskrit: Studies in Honour of Professor Ashok N. Aklujkar* (New Delhi: DK Printworld, 2012), pp. 259–272.

[26] *ādamhi davvabhāve apade mottūṇa giṇha taha ṇiyadaṃ/*
thiram egam imaṃ bhāvaṃ uvalabbhaṃtam sahāveṇa // 203.

[27] It is not incidental that Amṛtacandra also uses the term *aniyatatvāvasthā* for the transient emotional states and *niyatatvāvastha* for the natural state of the soul as knowledge. On the use of these terms, see Salfi, "Daśarūpaka aur Nāṭyadarpaṇa meṃ rasa-svarūpa evaṃ niṣpatti: eka tulanātmaka vivecana."

[28] For example 10.40.3, 10.30.14 ff. On God as actor, see 1.3.37, 11.31.11.

[29] *asminnanādini mahatyavivekanāṭye*
varṇādimān naṭati pudgala eva nānyaḥ.
rāgādipudgalavikāraviruddhaśuddhacaitanyadhātumayamūrtir ayaṃ ca jīvaḥ // 44.

References

Amṛtacandra. *Śrīsamayasāra Kalaśas.* With Gujarati translation by Pandit Candulāl Jobāliyā. Sonagadh: Śrī Digambara Jaina Svādhyāya Mandir, n.d. http://www. AtmaDharma.com.

Granoff, Phyliss. "The Art of the Philosopher: Painting and Sculpture as Metaphor," in Chikafumi Watanabe, et al., eds., *Samskrita-sādhutā: Goodness of Sanskrit: Studies in Honour of Professor Ashok N. Aklujkar,* pp. 259–272. New Delhi: DK Printworld, 2012.

—."Unspoken Rules of Debate in Medieval India and the Boundaries of Knowledge," in Gérard Colas and Émilie Aussant, eds., volume on Indian Scholasticism. Paris: École Francaise d'Extrême-Orient, forthcoming.

Gnoli, R. *The Aesthetic Experience According to Abhinavagupta.* Varanasi: Chowkhamba Sanskrit Series Office, 1968.

Gupta, Prem Swarup. *Rasagaṅgādhara kā Śāstrīya Adhyayan.* Delhi: Bhārata Prakāśana Mandira, 1962.

Jain, Uttamacandra. *Ācārya Amṛtacandra vyaktitva evaṃ kartṛtva.* Jaipur: Pandita Todarmal Smarak Trust, 1977.

Jaini, Padmanabh S. *Laghutattvasphoṭa.* Ahmedabad: L. D. Institute, 1978.

McCrea, Lawrence. *The Teleology of Poetics in Medieval Kashmir.* Cambridge, MA: Harvard University Press, 2008.

Parikh Rasiklal C., and V. M. Kulkarni. *Kāvyānuśāsana (with Alaṃkāracūḍāmani and Viveka).* Bombay: Śrī Mahāvīra Jaina Vidyālaya, 1964, second rev. ed.

Pollock, Sheldon. "What was Bhaṭṭa Nāyaka Saying? The Hermeneutical Transformation of Indian Aesthetics," in Sheldon Pollock, ed., *Epic and Argument in Sanskrit Literary Tradition, Essays in Honor of Robert P. Goldman,* pp. 143–184. Delhi: Manohar, 2010.

Pravacanasāra. With Gujarati translation by Himatlāl Jeṭhālāl Śāha. Sonagadh: Śrī Digambara Jaina Svādhyāyamandira Trust, n.d. http://www. AtmaDharma.com.

Salfi, Kājī Añjum. "Daśarūpaka aur Nāṭyadarpaṇa meṃ rasa-svarūpa evaṃ niṣpatti: eka tulanātmaka vivecana," *Aspects of Jainology* 1 (1987); http://www.jainlibrary.org/ book.php?file=211153.

—."Nāṭyadarpaṇa par Abhinavabhāratī Kā Prabhāv," *Aspects of Jainology,* Part 3 (1991). Pandit Dalsukh Malvaniya, ed. http://www.jainlibrary.org/book.php?file=211251.

Śāstrī Subodhchandra, Mukherjee, ed. *The Nāṭyaśāstra of Bharata, Chapter Six with the Abhinavabhāratī.* Paris, 1926.

Shulman, David. *More than Real: A History of the Imagination in South India.* Cambridge, MA: Harvard University Press, 2012.

Upadhye, A. N. *Pravacanasāra.* Agas: Rājacandra Jaina Śāstramālā, 1934.

The Divine Revolution of *Ṛgveda* X.124: A New Interpretation Beyond Asuras and Devas

Stephanie W. Jamison
University of California, Los Angeles

The short (nine-verse) ākhyāna (dialogue) hymn ṚV X.124 may be one of the most discussed poems in the Ṛgveda; the number, variety, and contradictory nature of its interpretations are truly astounding.[1] These multiple interpretations are of course facilitated by the difficulties that beset many Ṛgvedic dialogue hymns—that the dramatic situation from which the dialogue stems is not defined and that the speakers who are party to the dialogue are not identified. Everything must be deduced from the snatches of competitive or cooperative speech, and, it hardly needs to be said, determining the meaning of these speech snatches depends in great part on our assumptions about the participants in the dialogue and the situation being addressed. In other words, it exemplifies the inherent circularity of much Ṛgvedic interpretation.

What we can say about the poem without drawing on such assumptions? First, that it is divided into two parts: the dialogue portion, with 1st and 2nd ps. reference, ends with verse 6, while the last three verses, couched entirely in the 3rd ps., are in the mouth of the poet.[2] As for the dialogue proper, the hymn begins with an invitation to Agni to become a ritual participant in the sacrifice of the speaker(s), and in the following verses the speaker or speakers proclaim that they are leaving one side to join another. The context appears to be a divine one: Agni, Varuṇa, and Soma are all addressed (in vss. 1, 5, and 6 respectively), and those three, as well as Indra and Vṛtra, are mentioned in the 3rd person. But what is most intriguing, at least superficially, is that both an *ásura* and *ásura*-s in the plural are mentioned (vss. 3 and 5 respectively), and the latter, the plural Asuras / 'lords' [/*ásura*-s], are on the losing end of things, while the speaker of verse 2 identifies himself as a Deva and announces his departure from a or the *á-deva-* 'non-god' / 'un-godly, godless'.

This configuration has been too tempting to ignore, and at least since the nineteenth century the dominant interpretation has situated the hymn within the rivalry of Asuras and Devas so prominent in Middle Vedic literature, continuing into the epic and beyond. This interpretation in part goes back to Sāyaṇa, but it was made more piquant for modern Western scholars by the apparent mirror-image ideological matching of the Indic Deva/Asura competition with the Old Iranian Ahura (Mazdā), chief of the pantheon, and his eternal opponents, the demonized daēuuas. There is only one thing that obstructs this delicious etymological superimposition, and that one thing is the Ṛgveda. For, as has long been (more or less) known and as was shown at length and in detail by Wash Edward Hale (Ásura *in Early Vedic Religion,* 1986), the Ṛgveda has almost no trace of this neat bisection of the supernatural population,[3] and in fact in the Ṛgveda the word *ásura-* is regularly used positively and applied to beings who are also identified as *devá*s. Thus, despite the chorus of formidable voices in favor of an Asura/Deva interpretation of X.124—and this includes, inter alia, Geldner, Bergaigne, Hillebrandt, Norman Brown, Kuiper, Oberlies[4]—such an interpretation ill fits the Ṛgveda, even the late Ṛgveda, to which textual stratum this hymn belongs.

The only scholar that I know of who departs significantly from this paradigm is Brereton, whose paper on the hymn, presented in 2003, still languishes unpublished in conference-volume limbo (see n. 1). His treatment is intriguing, original, bold, and persuasive in many ways. Instead of seeing the hymn as set in mythological time and space, he provides it with a contemporary ritual context, interpreting it as responding to the crisis caused by the death of a sacrificer, whose ritual fire was therefore extinguished. The successor to this dead sacrificer calls on the extinguished fire to return, to serve as *his* ritual fire. As the new sacrificer is also the new king, he assumes the role of Indra and also asks Varuṇa to offer his help.

Proferes (also n. 1) also largely frees himself from the Asura/Deva paradigm, but does position the hymn in the mythological realm, taking it as an account of Indra's rise to power and (in the last three verses) his royal unction—again a persuasive reading of some parts of the hymn. The interpretations of Brereton and Proferes converge in their view that someone—either the god Indra or his human counterpart—is assuming the kingship, by ritual means.

Given that the hymn has been so very well trodden and given, especially, that I find several of the newer treatments of it quite appealing, it may seem mischievous to produce yet another one here. I do so because none of the interpretations can account for everything in the hymn—nor will mine—and because there are certain qualities of the hymn that seem to have escaped everyone's notice.

But I will begin by sketching the trajectory of the hymn, mostly according to the traditional interpretation, and highlighting the evidence that best supports the old Asura/Deva interpretation—though I do not in fact subscribe to that interpretation. In the first verse a speaker (by most accounts Indra [though Sāyaṇa ascribes it to unidentified ṛṣis]) calls to Agni to "come to this sacrifice of ours" (1a: *imáṃ no agna úpa yajñám éhi*), in order to become our oblation-bearer (1c: *áso havyavā́ṭ*. . .). The speaker remarks that Agni has lain for a long time "in long darkness" (*dīrgháṃ támaḥ*). Verse 2 contains Agni's reply (or presumably Agni's—the speaker is not identified), which establishes the side-switching scenario.

> X.124.2 *ádevād deváḥ pracátā gúhā yán prapáśyamāno amṛtatvám emi*
> *śiváṃ yát sántam áśivo jáhāmi svā́t sakhyā́d áraṇīṃ nā́bhim emi*

> [Agni:] Going in concealment and hiding, I go, as a god, from the non-god / godless, foreseeing immortality for myself.
> When I unkindly leave (him), though he is kindly disposed, from my own fellowship I go to an alien lineage.

Note the telling initial phrase *ádevād deváḥ* "from the/a non-god/godless, as a god" and the other indications of the disfavored and favored sides, especially *svā́t sakhyā́d áraṇīṃ nā́bhim*. . . "from my own fellowship to an alien lineage." Verse three continues the dichotomy. For the third time in two verses we find a phrase consisting of a verb of motion plus an ablative of origin sharply contrasting with an accusative of goal (or equivalent, in 2ab), this time pāda d: *ayajñiyā́d yajñíyam bhāgám emi* "From the one without sacrifice I go to a sacrificial portion." The identity of the verse 3 speaker is disputed: Geldner assigns the verse to Agni, but others, including Doniger,[5] Proferes, and me, to Varuṇa (who will figure by name in the next verse). This verse also contains the first mention of an Asura, pāda c: *śáṃsāmi pitré ásurāya śévam* "I proclaim (him) as kindly to the Father Asura [/Lordly Father]." This expression follows upon, and seemingly contradicts or corrects, Agni's statement in the previous verse (pāda c) *śiváṃ yát sántam áśivo jáhāmi* "When I unkindly leave (him), though he is kindly disposed. . ." There Agni identified himself as unkindly to the kindly being he left behind, whereas here the speaker (Varuṇa?) seems to assert that Agni *is* kindly to the Father Asura. The patterned contrasting statements invite us to identify the kindly abandoned creature in vs. 2 with the Father Asura in vs. 3.

Verse 4 also contains an abandonment scenario, though without an ablative (pāda b): *índraṃ vr̥ṇānáḥ pitáraṃ jahāmi* "Choosing Indra, I leave the father." The father is presumably the same Father Asura of the preceding verse, though again the identity of the speaker is in dispute, with Geldner favoring Agni; Doniger, Proferes and me opting for Soma. The trio of Agni, Soma, and Varuṇa appear together in the second half of this verse, followed by the climactic declaration "the kingship has made a revolution."

X.124.4cd *agníḥ sómo váruṇas té cyavante paryā́vard rāṣṭráṃ tád avāmy āyán*

Agni, Soma, Varuṇa—they bestir themselves. The kingship has made a revolution; I help it (along), by coming here.

After this decisive political change brought about by the apparent defection of the three named gods, Indra (by most accounts) speaks the next two verses, in which he proclaims the loss of the Asuras' (or lords') powers (5a), invites Varuṇa to share (or take over) rule (5b, d), and calls on Soma to emerge so that the two can smash Vr̥tra (6c):

X.124.5a *nírmāyā u tyé ásurā abhūvan*

These Asuras (/lords) have lost their magic powers.

X.124.5b, d *tvā́ṃ ca mā varuṇa kāmáyāse*
. . . , *máma rāṣṭrásyā́dhipatyam éhi*

And if you, Varuṇa, will love me,
. . . , come here to the overlordship of my kingdom.

X.124.6c *hánāva vr̥tráṃ niréhi soma*

Let us two smash Vr̥tra—come forth, Soma!

As noted above, the dialogue ends with verse 6. The remaining verses, in the poet's voice, describe the happy results. Varuṇa releases the waters and the rivers flow (vs. 7), peacefully and happily associated with Indra (vss. 8-9), whom they freely choose.

This synopsis of the hymn shows why the Asura/Deva interpretation has been so attractive and so tenacious. The repeated abandonment of one side by a series of gods; the naming of Father Asura as the abandoned figure, possibly identified as a "non-god"; the pronouncement of the Asuras' loss of māyā; and the "revolution" of kingship—all these factors make this interpretation hard to wriggle out of, without aggressive reinterpretation of the key phrases. The subject of the hymn seems to be nothing less than a radical political and religious reconfiguration, with shifting alliances leading to a fundamental realignment of the major divinities and to a new sacrificial order and a new rule, and the terms *devá* and *ásura* provide tempting hooks on which to hang the new alignment. But, in addition to the lack of evidence for a Deva/Asura rivalry in the ṚV already discussed, there are important counterindications in the hymn itself—not least the passage where Agni asserts his identity as a god even as he is leaving his own kin-group, supposedly the Asuras.

But I want to draw attention to a different issue, a remarkable tone found in the hymn that stands out in a ṚVic context. Whoever the two opposing parties in this revolution were, the power shift from one to the other was remarkably peaceful, especially for the Ṛgveda where most conflicts have violence as their defining characteristic. This peacefulness is emphasized throughout the hymn. As we already noted, Agni refers to the non-god he left as "being kindly disposed" (*śivá*), apologetically describing himself as "unkind" (*áśiva*) in leaving (vs. 2c). Varuṇa seems to counter this in vs. 3c by proclaiming that Agni was indeed kind (*śéva*). The narrative verses that follow the dialogue highlight the theme of peace even more. In vs. 7 Varuṇa is said to have released the waters "without an excess of power" (*áprabhūtī*) and the waters thus released "make peace with each other" (*kṣémaṃ kr̥ṇvānā́ḥ*) like co-wives.[6] In vs. 8 Indra "dwells peacefully" (*tā́ īm ā́ kṣeti*) amid his subjects, the waters, who "follow" (*sacante*) his power and freely "choose him as clans choose a king" (*tā́ īṃ víśo ná rā́jānaṃ vr̥ṇānā́ḥ*). In vs. 9 Indra, symbolically a goose, is the "yokemate" (*sayújam*) of the waters and he "roams in fellowship" (*sakhyé cárantam*) with them.

The only violence in the hymn is prospective and will turn out to have positive effects: the smashing of Vr̥tra foreseen by Indra in vs. 6, once Soma has allied himself with Indra. The hymn is all about negotiation and a sort of sacrificial horse-trading: see Indra's offers of important roles to Agni (1c), Varuṇa (5d), and Soma (6d). Indra even begs Varuṇa to "love" him (5b). The principal figures "choose" their side and their ruler (Soma in 4b and even the female rivers in 8b) and make their own moves, as emphasized by the repeated verbs of motion: "come!" [*éhi*] 1a; "going . . . I go, . . . I leave, . . . I go" [. . . *yán . . . emi; . . . jáhāmi . . . emi*] 2; "I go" [*emi*] 3d; "I leave... they bestir themselves ... (I) coming here" [. . . *jahāmi, . . . cyavante, . . . āyán*] 4; "come!" [*éhi*] 5d; "come forth!" [*niréhi*] 6c. The peaceful and voluntary nature of the change in alliances—the lack of retaliation by the deserted side, the lack of interest in pursuing their advantage and crushing their opponents by the winning side—distinguishes this episode not only from almost every other such situation in the Ṛgveda but also from the perpetual conflict and reflexive hostility between Asuras and Devas in Middle Vedic literature (see also the ṚV passages in n. 3), an indication, perhaps, that that rivalry is not the context in which to interpret this hymn.

Although, given the apparent failure of so many Ṛgvedic interpreters to identify the deserted party successfully, it is foolhardy to suggest my own candidate, I will make an essay in that direction. Here I will start from a paradox that has always puzzled me, "always" being since I first learned about the kinship of the Indo-European languages and first encountered the phrasal equation that changed my life and set me on this path, the trio of divine figures represented in Sanskrit *dyaúṣ pitā́,* Greek Zeus pater, and Latin Jūpiter, all stemming from Proto-Indo-European **dyḗus ph₂tḗr* 'Father Sky/Heaven'. The paradox is that, though in Greek and to an even greater extent in Latin the name has lost transparency,[7] the power and charisma of the god remain strong in those traditions: he is the head of the pantheon and not just by courtesy. He wields real power. Whereas in Sanskrit the name is entirely transparent, but as a divinity Father Heaven is a marginal figure, most often paired with Mother Earth and offered some fairly pallid reverence. There are no hymns addressed only to him. Almost the only narrative mythology associated with him is the brutal rape of his daughter, but this is alluded to rarely in the text (I.71.5, 8; X.61.5-7). What has happened to rob him of the position that his linguistic brothers hold onto so successfully in Greek and Latin?

I would suggest that the "revolution" referred to in our hymn involves the peaceful passing of power from the old dominant divinity, Father Heaven, inherited from Indo-European times, to a newer set of ritually oriented, human-centered gods, especially Indra. Note first that the figure most clearly left behind by the deserting divinities is a "father"—qualified once as Father Asura/lordly father (3c), once just as father (4b). Here I would like to shift the focus in the resonant phrase *pitré ásurāya* from *ásura-* to *pitár-*, suggesting that the "father" is the more important half and that its referent here is Dyaus. Dyaus is elsewhere called *ásura-* (at least I.131.1 *dyaúr ásuraḥ,* possibly also III.53.7=X.67.2), and of course the collocation *dyaúṣ pitā́* is what we're starting from (cf., e.g., I.71.5, I.89.4, I.90.7, I.164.33, I.191.6, IV.1.10, VI.51.5). The word "father" is also elsewhere used to refer clearly to Dyaus, though without naming him (X.61.6-7; this is the incest story).

One strain of thinking about Dyauṣ Pitar and his brothers in Greek and Latin is that the power differential between the Indic figure and Zeus and Jūpiter that I recently mentioned is not a paradox at all—in the way that I have just configured it—that in fact it is the very transparency of his name that has doomed Father Heaven to eclipse, as it were. His identification with heaven-the-place keeps him trapped there, while Zeus and Jūpiter, freed from nomenclatural confinement, can amass further qualities and powers that are untethered to a heavenly location. See especially Oberlies (*Religion des Ṛgveda* I, 258-61), citing also von Bradke and Haudry. Without this ability to shape-shift, our Dyauṣ Pitar sees his original supreme power pass to more nimble gods who are able to act in geographical and conceptual spheres closer to mankind.

I think we can see the geographical relocation reflected in a verse of X.124 that I have not yet cited, the final one of the dialogue portion, where Indra says:

> X.124.6ab *idáṃ svàr idám íd āsa vāmám, ayám prakāśá urv àntárikṣam*

> Here is the sun—it alone used to be the thing of value. (But now) there is this coming to light—the broad midspace.

(See Oberlies, p. 367, though I do not subscribe to the details of the cosmology he sees behind this.) The sun, elsewhere identified as the son of Heaven and Earth, was originally the major celestial feature, located in heaven (*diví,* as is frequently said, e.g., in the following verse). In my reading of the verse Indra points to the sun and acknowledges its previous preeminence on the scale of value,[8] but suggests that it is now matched or rivaled by the light of the broad midspace—the midspace where so much of what makes life possible on earth is concentrated, particularly rain-making, to be alluded to in Varuṇa's release of the waters in the following verse (7b).

But even more important than the change of location is the conceptual change. As Vedic religion becomes more and more centered on sacrifice, a distant sky god becomes more and more irrelevant to religious practice, especially as there is a distinct shift in the model for what happens in the sacrifice, how the contact between divine and human is effected. In the ṚV we find two competing models of the sacrificial mechanism. In one the essence of the sacrifice is carried *up* to the gods in heaven by the smoke of the fire, the god Agni. This reminds us of Homeric sacrifices, with the smoke of hecatombs rising towards the divine recipients (e.g., Iliad 1.315-17). In the other, the gods themselves come *down* to our ritual ground and partake of the sacrifice there, while being joyfully welcomed and hospitably entertained. The two models seem to coexist without conflict in the text despite the contradiction. For example, in the first hymn in the ṚV, the Agni hymn I.1, vs. 4 expresses the "going-to-heaven" model: "whatever sacrifice you surround on all sides, Agni, just that one goes to the gods" (*ágne yáṃ yajñám adhvarám viśvátaḥ paribhū́r asi / sá íd devéṣu gachati*), while the "gods-come-to us" model is found in vs. 2 ("he will convey the gods here," *sá devā́m̐ éhá vakṣati*) and vs. 5 ("the god will come here with the gods," *devó devébhir ā́ gamat*). But, although there seems to be no ideological conflict between the two, one of them seems to become increasingly dominant, or so is my impression—namely, the "come here" model, which invites the epiphany of the god or gods. This is certainly the model found in the "classical" śrauta sacrifice of the Middle Vedic period.

And, to put it baldly and rather simplistically, it's hard for Father Heaven to get around—much less leave the sky and come to our ritual ground on earth to participate in the sacrifice. Although Heaven and Earth are occasionally invited to the sacrifice, these invitations are rare and not insistent—as though the poets and sacrificers realized that pushing it might sound ludicrous. The clearest (and almost only[9]) example is the following, esp. the second hemistich:

> VII.53.2 *prá pūrvajé pitárā návyasībhir, gīrbhiḥ kṛṇudhvaṃ sádane ṛtásya ā́ no dyāvāpṛthivī daívyena, jánena yātam máhi vāṃ várūtham*

> With newer hymns bring forward into the seat of truth (= ritual ground) the two ancient-born fathers [= H+E].
> O Heaven and Earth, drive here to us with the divine folk. Great is your protection.

And it was an experiment that was not repeated. Not surprisingly this second half verse is a variant of numerous similar invitations issued to the far more mobile twin gods, the Aśvins[10] (e.g., VII.72.2 *ā́ no devébhir úpa yātam arvā́k*), adopted into a short Heaven-and-Earth hymn. It is just as well not to think too hard about what kind of "driving" Heaven and Earth could do.

Although the "going-to-heaven" model is never abandoned in the ṚV, the epiphany model seems to me the more prominent one, and gods that could participate in either will be favored over those who are limited to one or the other. Indra, who figures prominently in our hymn, is of course the god whose epiphany is most desired in the ṚV and whose potential absence is most worrisome, as hymn after hymn attests. Two of the other three gods mentioned in the hymn by name, Agni and Soma, are the embodiments of the two most crucial sacrificial substances. In the hymn Indra[11] issues invitations to both these gods, with specific reference to sacrifice and to oblations; significantly, these invitations to Agni and Soma frame the dialogue portion of the hymn. In vs. 1 Indra calls to Agni to come to the sacrifice (1a) and become oblation-conveyor (*havya-vā́ṭ*)(1c). In vs. 6, after having proposed that Indra and Soma jointly smite Vṛtra (*hánāva vṛtrám̐ niréhi soma* "Let us two smite Vṛtra. Come forth, Soma!"), he promises that "we (all)" will sacrifice to Soma, with the paradoxical statement

> X.124.6d *havíṣ ṭvā sántaṃ havíṣā yajāma*
>
> We shall sacrifice to you with an oblation, though you yourself are an oblation.

This statement is tellingly parallel to the famous one in the Puruṣasūkta X.90.16a *yajñéna yajñám ayajanta devā́ḥ* "The gods sacrificed to the sacrifice with a sacrifice" (in my reading; others would translate "the gods performed the sacrifice with a/the sacrifice"[12]). These two statements express a kind of endless loop, an inescapable reflexivity: the object of worship and the means of worship are identical (sacrifice and sacrifice, soma and soma). This tight internal and grammatical circularity is situated within a larger, though not explicitly expressed, circularity: in X.90 it is the gods—the ordinary *object* of worship—who are performing the sacrifice. In X.124 it is Indra (by most lights) who invites Agni to participate in "this our sacrifice" (*imáṃ naḥ . . . yajñám,* 1a); when examined, this is a phrase of radical ambiguity. The first reading is that the 1st ps. "I" of Indra and unspecified others are performing the sacrifice, but a second and not outlandish reading is "the sacrifice performed *for* us."[13] The "us" in both cases presumably being other gods. Similarly, in vs. 6, when Indra tells Soma "we will sacrifice to you," clearly Indra and unspecified others, again presumably gods, are performing the sacrifice, but Soma is a god and Indra is thus promising that the gods will sacrifice to one of themselves.

What I am groping towards saying here is that X.124 is "about" the primal instituting of the sacrifice, which in its first instantiation was a closed circle—created by the gods to worship themselves.[14] Before this institution there was no sacrifice, at least as the hymn presents it or, to be honest, as I interpret what the hymn presents. I would thus suggest that in the ṚVic conceptual universe, Father Asura (or as I think of him the lordly Father Heaven) was a revered figure but did not receive yajña (which didn't yet exist). (To forestall the obvious questions, I'm not claiming that the yajña is an invention of the Ṛgveda; it was of course deeply embedded in the Indo-Iranian religious system, given the importance of the cognate *yasna* in the Avestan religious texts and the endless Younger Avestan litanies of praise structured by the repeated verb *yazamaide* "we worship." Our hymn simply presents a mythological narrative of Ur-time and of the establishment of the institutions that have existed from time immemorial.)

In any case it is in this way that I interpret the ablative of starting point, accusative of goal phrases: they express the transition from the original divine situation, with Father Heaven as the central figure, to the new yajña-centered configuration of gods. The clearest of these ablative/accusative constructions is 3d *ayajñiyā́d emi* "From him/that without sacrifice I go to a sacrificial portion/share in the sacrifice."[15] Potentially more troubling for my hypothesis is the statement in 2ab *ádevād deváḥ . . . emi* "As a god, I go from the non-god/godless." If the starting point, the figure that is left behind, is Dyauṣ pitar, how can he be *ádeva-*? After all, the word *devá-* itself is a morphological derivative of the root noun that gives him that name, *div-/dyu-*. But in fact this conundrum is easily solved, and the solution is aided by this derivational relationship: Dyauṣ pitar is, in fact, *not* a god; he is the father of the gods. They are both linguistically and conceptually derived from him. As far as I can tell, the word *devá-* is never used of Dyaus in the ṚV. His parental status, as father of the gods, is of course signalled by the title Pitar, but also by the bahuvrīhi *deváputra-* 'having the gods as sons' several times applied to Heaven and Earth; e.g.,

> I.159.1 . . . *dyā́vā . . . pṛthivī́ . . .*
> *devébhir yé deváputre sudáṃsasā, . . . vā́ryāṇi prabhū́ṣataḥ*

> Heaven and Earth, the two of wondrous power who, having gods as sons, together with the gods tender things of value. . .

Notice that the fact that Heaven and Earth perform the action "together with the gods" implies that they are not gods themselves.[16] Dyaus is also on a number of occasions called the father or begetter of particular gods, especially Dawn (*divó duhitár-*, very common, e.g., I.92.5), Sūrya (e.g., X.37.1), the Aśvins (e.g., I.181.4), and indeed Indra (e.g., somewhat ambiguously, IV.17.4). Agni is also called the son of Heaven (III.25.1), and if Agni is the speaker of the statement "I, as god, go from the non-god/godless. . ." followed in the same verse by "I go from my own fellowship to an alien lineage" (2d *svā́t sakhyā́d áraṇiṃ nā́bhim emi*), there is no contradiction between those two statements: the non-god from whom he, the god, departs can still belong to "his own fellowship," since his father is not a god but only the begetter of gods.

Under this interpretation Agni's destination, *áraṇīm nā́bhim* "an alien lineage," is initially puzzling, since he's supposed to be joining his brother gods. This is not the place for a thorough investigation of the word *áraṇa-* and its relatives, but it seems generally to refer to 'foreign' or 'alien' places and people primarily in terms of physical distance and separation from familiar surroundings, not kinship or natural affinity. In this case the very fact that Agni is moving from his original place to one quite distinct might be enough to condition the use of this word. But I also think it is a word play. The differently accented *aráṇī* is the word for the kindling sticks rubbed together to produce the ritual fire (i.e., Agni). Since, as I argue, Agni has been in a presacrificial state, that is, unkindled (see the "long darkness" of 1d), the feminine *áraṇīm* 'alien' may pun on the fem. (usually dual) *aráṇī* 'kindling sticks', and refer to his transition to being kindled in order to take on his sacrificial role. Another word play is likely found in the word *nā́bhi-*. This word, literally 'navel', is used not only of kinship affiliation, as apparently here, but also and more commonly to refer to the ritual ground (e.g. VIII.12.32, 13.2) and indeed the ritual fire itself (e.g., III.17.4, VI.7.2) as the conceptual navel or center of the universe. So, in going to the *nā́bhi-* Agni again is depicted as leaving a presacrificial state to arrive at a place for sacrifice.

The hypothesis that the gods are leaving a pre-sacrificial state in order to embark on the practice of sacrifice also fits with several other features ascribed to the various gods. In verse 1 Agni is said to "have lain for a long time in long darkness" (1d: *jyóg evá dīrgháṃ táma ā́śayiṣṭhāḥ*), while in vs. 4 Soma (if he is the speaker) says about the father "I have 'done' many years within him" (4a: *bahvī́ḥ sámā akaram antár asmin*). For these quintessentially sacrificial gods the absence of sacrifice has condemned them to torpor and inaction, darkness and confinement.[17] Sacrifice will free them to fulfill their natures.

In vs. 3 Varuṇa (again, if he is the speaker), on seeing that Agni has become "the guest of the other branch" (3a: *páśyann anyásyā átithiṃ vayā́yāḥ*), proclaims that he himself "measure[s] out the many domains of truth" (3b: *ṛtásya dhā́ma ví mime purū́ṇi*). Although the resonant phrases "domains of truth" and "measure out" have various applications in the ṚV, both physical and ethical, here I would suggest that Varuṇa is performing the initial measuring of the ritual ground. "Domain of truth" is clearly used for the place of sacrifice in IV.7.7 and most likely VII.36.5, and the word *dhā́man-* by itself frequently applies to the same place, especially in Agni and Soma hymns. The root √*mā* 'measure', with or without the preverb *ví* (as here), is used a number of times to describe the "measuring (out) of the sacrifice," esp. in Maṇḍala X. Cf. X.110.11 *sadyó jātó vy àmimīta yajñám* "Just born, he [= Agni] measured out the sacrifice at once" and VIII.13.30 *mímīte yajñám ānuṣák. . .* "he measures the sacrifice in proper order." Thus, like Agni and Soma, Varuṇa is deeply engaged in the original institution of the sacrifice. He is also invited by Indra (vs. 5) to "the overlordship of my [=Indra's] kingdom" (5d: *máma rāṣṭrásyā́dhipatyam éhi*),[18] which reminds us of the famous and much discussed hymn IV.42, where, at least on the surface, Indra and Varuṇa put forward competing claims to kingship. The complementary powers of those two on view in IV.42 seem to be reflected here as well, and the change to a more human-centered religious system that I see reflected in our hymn engages both gods: Indra protecting men physically and aiding them in conflict (the much-discussed Kriegskönig of Oberlies and others), while Varuṇa provides the ethical dimension in peaceful situations (the complementary Friedenskönig). That Indra *invites* Varuṇa, whose "love" he seeks, rather than engaging in provocative boasting as in IV.42, reflects the general peaceable tone of the hymn that I remarked on much earlier. It is especially striking that it is the hyper-hostile war god Indra who entreats Varuṇa with coaxing words. The cooperative nature of their relationship in this hymn is also suggested by the apparent part played by Varuṇa in an exploit ordinarily attributed only to Indra. In vs. 6 Indra invites Soma to come out so they can both smash Vṛtra (*hánāva vṛtráṃ niréhi soma*), which ordinarily in the ṚV precipitates Indra's release of the rivers/waters. But in vs. 7 it's *Varuṇa* who's credited with this release (*áprabhūtī váruṇo nír apáḥ sṛjat*). Of course, Varuna has control over the waters elsewhere, especially rain, but the switch in agency seems deliberate in the Vṛtra context.

As for the posited transition from Father Heaven to the gods and especially Indra, there is in fact some evidence for the transfer of divine power from Heaven to the gods elsewhere in the ṚV, in passages where Heaven (and Earth) defer to Indra and his might. Such passages are not uncommon with other gods demonstrating submission to Indra, however, and so it is possible to take these descriptions as simply providing an extravagant rhetorical measure of Indra's vast power: he's so formidable that even Heaven gives way to him. Nonetheless I think we should give them some credence as representing an actual mythological situation—particularly the following passage where Heaven is identified as *dyaúr ásuraḥ*:

> I.131.1ab *índrāya hí dyaúr ásuro ánamnaténdrāya mahī́ pṛthivī́ várīmabhiḥ*
>
> Because to Indra the lordly Heaven has constantly bowed, and to Indra the great Earth (has bowed) with her expanses.

Even more telling is the next passage, which describes the passing of "dominion" (*kṣatrám*) from Heaven and Earth to Indra, a power transfer that is characterized by "magnanimity":

> IV.17.1 *tvám mahā́m̐ indra túbhyaṃ ha kṣā́ ánu kṣatrám maṃhánā manyata dyaúḥ*
>
> You, Indra, are great. To you did Earth, to you did Heaven magnanimously yield dominion.[19]

A similar and even more explicit statement about *Varuṇa's* assumption of kingship is found in the following passage, not too far from our hymn—though it has to be said that the hymn in which it is found is pretty impossible and the purport of the quoted passage may not be what I claim:

> X.132.4 *asā́v anyó asura sūyata dyaús, tváṃ víśveṣāṃ varuṇāsi rā́jā*
>
> The one, yonder Heaven, was consecrated (as king), but (the other, namely) you, lord Varuṇa, are (now) king of all.

Particularly noteworthy is the fact that the vocative asura is found in the first pāda, sandwiched between *asaú* and *dyaúḥ*, but presumably must be read with the other vocative, *varuṇa* in pāda b. It is as if the poet wants to associate the word with both figures: Heaven by word order and Varuṇa by grammar.

To summarize, it seems possible that the old sky-centered religion focused on the inherited paternal divinity Dyaus quietly gave way to one located in realms closer to men, where divinities concerned themselves with issues important to mankind, such as the release of the waters (vss. 7-8), and actively sought the praise and sacrificial offerings of men (vs. 9 and, by implication, throughout the hymn). Dyaus Pitar remained a revered figure, honored as father and the original progenitor (*janitár-*), but he played little or no role in the sacrificial system. There was thus no violent rupture in the social or religious fabric, just a peaceful fading into well- but perfunctorily honored irrelevance for Dyaus, displaced by ritual-centered gods like Agni and Soma and those deeply involved with men's affairs, ethically (Varuṇa) or martially (Indra).

Although there remain a number of loose ends in this interpretation of the hymn, two in particular stand out—and, I think, can be dealt with together. First, I earlier said that the primal sacrifice as established was a closed loop performed by gods for gods, but in the last paragraph I depicted the gods seeking the sacrifices of *men*. How did humans get inserted into the picture; what is the source of the human/divine interchange? Second, I have barely said anything about the last three verses of the hymn.

I do not have a definitive, hymn-internal answer for the first question, but I suggest that this may be what the last three (non-dialogue) verses (7–9) are, in part, about. The killing of Vṛtra, which is urged by Indra in 6c, brings about the release of the waters (7b), which in turn makes human life possible, as we know from elsewhere in the ṚV. But there is no direct mention of humans in what follows, only of waters and rivers and their mutually beneficial relationship with each other and with Indra. Nonetheless, this relationship is expressed in terms appropriate to humans: the waters stand for the mortal subjects of the king, who is represented by Indra; as already noted, the waters dwell with each other peacefully, choose their king as clans do, and abide by their choice and defer to his power. In other words, these verses establish an "as if" situation: the audience finds itself inhabiting a recognizably human social context, quite explicitly so, though the actual referents are waters, standing in for humans. The poet transitions from primordial time, inhabited only by divinities talking to each other, to something configured very like present time, though its denizens are still, superficially, mythological figures.

In this ambiguous context, I would suggest that there is an indirect transfer of sacrificial responsibility in the last three verses, signalled by a kind of ring composition. After the institution of the primal sacrifice effected in the first six verses, in the first half of verse 7 Varuṇa (pāda b) and, by implication but without naming him, Indra (pāda a) perform cosmos-altering deeds.

> X.124.7ab *kavíḥ kavitvā́ diví rūpám ā́sajad, áprabhūtī váruṇo nír apáḥ sṛjat*
>
> The poet with his poetic craft has fastened the form (of the sun?) in heaven; without excess of power Varuṇa released the waters.

The first pāda is a verbal variant on one of Indra's standard actions, putting the sun in heaven (see n. 8); as noted above, the second deed is usually credited also to Indra, though Varuṇa's association with water and rain makes him also a candidate for performing it. What is striking is that the unnamed Indra is called a *kaví* 'poet' and it is by his 'poetic craft' (*kavitvā́*) that he performs the action.[20] The phrase *kavíḥ kavitvā́* opens this second part of the hymn. The plural *kaváyaḥ* is almost the last word of the hymn (9d *índraṃ ní cikyuḥ kaváyo manīṣā́* "The poets discerned Indra through their inspired thought"). Matching the instrumental *kavitvā́* 'poetic craft' in 7a is the functional equivalent instrumental *manīṣā́* 'inspired thought', such that the three-verse sequence begins and ends with strict parallelism. But while Indra is the kavi in 7a, he is quite definitely not one of the kavis of 9d, since he appears in that pāda in a different case (acc.), as the object of their discerning. These kavis must be *human* poet-sacrificers, offering the praise he seeks (9c *anuṣṭubham ánu* "in pursuit of the verse of praise"). Without calling attention to it, the composer of X.124 has modulated from the gods-worshiping-gods model, with Indra as a kavi, to one in which other, presumably human, kavis offer praise and sacrifice *to* the god(s). The closed circle is broken and the human/divine dynamic established, but the verbal identitification of Indra and the human kavis implies that the current model of sacrifice derives from the older one depicted earlier in the hymn and that the human officiants are occupying formerly divine roles.

Appendix
Sanskrit Text of Ṛgveda X.124

1. *imáṃ no agna úpa yajñám éhi páñcayāmaṃ trivŕ̥taṃ saptátantum /*
áso havyavā́ḷ utá naḥ purogā́ jyóg evá dīrgháṃ táma ā́śayiṣṭhāḥ //

2. *ádevād deváḥ pracátā gúhā yán prapáśyamāno amr̥tatvám emi /*
śiváṃ yát sántam áśivo jáhāmi svā́t sakhyā́d áraṇīṃ nā́bhim emi //

3. *páśyann anyásyā átithiṃ vayā́yā r̥tásya dhā́ma ví mime purū́ṇi /*
śáṃsāmi pitré ásurāya śévam ayajñiyā́d yajñíyam bhāgám emi //

4. *bahvī́ḥ sámā akaram antár asminn índraṃ vr̥ṇānáḥ pitáraṃ jahāmi /*
agníḥ sómo váruṇas té cyavante paryā́vard rāṣṭráṃ tád avāmy āyán //

5. *nírmāyā u tyé ásurā abhūvan tváṃ ca mā varuṇa kāmáyāse /*
r̥téna rājann ánr̥taṃ viviñcán máma rāṣṭrásyā́dhipatyam éhi //

6. *idáṃ svàr idám íd āsa vāmám ayám prakāśá uR̥V àntárikṣam /*
hánāva vr̥tráṃ niréhi soma havíṣ ṭvā sántaṃ havíṣā yajāma //

7. *kavíḥ kavitvā́ diví rūpám ā́sajad áprabhūtī váruṇo nír apáḥ sr̥jat /*
kṣémaṃ kr̥ṇvānā́ jánayo ná síndhavas tā́ asya várṇaṃ śúcayo bharibhrati //

8. *tā́ asya jyéṣṭham indriyáṃ sacante tā́ īm ā́ kṣeti svadháyā mádantīḥ /*
tā́ īṃ víśo ná rā́jānaṃ vr̥ṇānā́ bībhatsúvo ápa vr̥trā́d atiṣṭhan //

9. *bībhatsū́nāṃ sayújaṃ haṃsám āhur apā́ṃ divyā́nāṃ sakhyé cárantam /*
anuṣṭúbham ánu carcūryámāṇam índraṃ ní cikyuḥ kaváyo manīṣā́ //

Notes

1 This paper expands on and gives supporting evidence for my translation and interpretation of this hymn in Stephanie W. Jamison and Joel P. Brereton, trs., *The Rigveda: The Earliest Religious Poetry of India. An English Translation,* 3 vols. (New York: Oxford Univ. Press, 2014), 1597–1601. The amount of secondary literature devoted to this hymn is little short of amazing, and for want of space (and inclination) I will not attempt to survey it. For a brief characterization of many of these treatments see Wash Edward Hale, Ásura- *in Early Vedic Religion* (Delhi: Motilal Banarsidass, 1986), 86-92, and for a recent and intriguing interpretation see Theodore Proferes, *Vedic Ideals of Sovereignty and the Poetics of Power* (New Haven: American Oriental Society, 2007), 106–13, as well as the unfortunately as-yet-unpublished treatment of Joel Brereton, to appear in the Proceedings of the World Sanskrit Conference in Helsinki in July 2003, a précis of which is found in Jamison-Brereton, *Rigveda,* 1599–1600.

2 The full text of the hymn is given at the end of the paper, to show the relationships of the various parts quoted piecemeal in the body of the text. The translations given in the body of the text match those in Jamison-Brereton, with some adjustments.

3 A few passages in the late R̥V do make unequivocal reference to the conflict: X.53.4 *yénā́surām̐ abhí devā́ ā́sāma* ". . . by which we gods will overcome the Asuras"; X.157.4 *hatvā́ya devā́ ásurān yád ā́yan* "The gods having smashed the Asuras when they came. . . ."

4 Karl Friedrich Geldner: see his long introduction and his tr. of the hymn ad loc., *Der Rig-Veda aus dem Sanskrit ins Deutsche übersetzt und mit einem laufenden Kommentar versehen* (Cambridge, Mass.: Harvard Univ. Press, 1951); Abel Bergaigne, *La religion védique d'après les hymnes du R̥igvéda,* 4 vols. (Paris: F. Vieweg, 1878–97); Engl. tr. *Vedic Religion,* tr. V. G. Paranjpe (Delhi: Motilal Banarsidass, 1978), vol. 3: 148–55 (cited after tr.); Alfred Hillebrandt, *Vedische Mythologie,* 3 vols. (Breslau: Verlag von M. & H. Marcus, 1902), vol. 3: 69–70; W. Norman Brown, "Proselytizing the Asuras," *JAOS* 39 (1919): 100; F. B. J. Kuiper: e.g., "The Basic Concept of Vedic Religion," *History of Religion* 15 (1975): 107–20, *Varuṇa and Vidūṣaka: On the Origin of the Sanskrit Drama* (Amsterdam: North Holland Publishing Co., 1979), 8–13; Thomas Oberlies, *Die Religion des R̥gveda,* pt. 1: *Das religiöse System des R̥gveda* (Vienna: DeNobili, 1998), 391.

5 Wendy Doniger [O'Flaherty], *The Rig Veda: An Anthology* (Harmondsworth, UK: Penguin Books, 1981 [rpt. 2005]), 110–12.

6 Since co-wives are notoriously *un*peaceful towards each other (see ṚV X.145, 159), this is a signal achievement.

7 However, Ben Fortson pointed out to me [p.c., 3/14] that some older Latin forms are more transparent and also suggested the possibility that Jupiter owes many of his traits to reinterpretation à la grecque.

8 And in fact Indra is credited with placing the sun in heaven in passages too numerous to list (e.g., I.7.3 *ā́ sū́ryaṃ rohayad diví* "he made the sun mount in heaven," etc. etc.), indeed in the paraphrase also in the next verse, X.124.7.

9 Cf. also IV.56.1. There may be others scattered about. They are also sometimes offered sacrifice without being explicitly urged to come to the ritual ground; e.g., X.81.6 *svayáṃ yajasva pṛthivī́m utá dyā́m* "by yourself sacrifice to Earth and Heaven" (addressee is Viśvakarman).

10 Also Mitra and Varuṇa (e.g., VII.66.17–19), Indra and Vāyu (VII.91.5).

11 At least in my reading and that of most of others; however, not Brereton for vs. 1, and even in vs. 6 he thinks it's the sacrificer impersonating Indra, as it were.

12 In fact, the existence of this parallel in X.124 seems to me to tip the balance in the interpretation of the far more famous X.90.16.

13 A possibility that is of course aided by the grammatical ambiguity of enclitic *naḥ,* which can be either genitive or dative (in addition to the presumably excluded accusative—though technically a translation of *imáṃ naḥúpa yajñám éhi* as "come to us, to this sacrifice," with two parallel goals in the accusative, is possible).

14 Proferes also argues that the hymn depicts the primal sacrifice.

15 Note that *yajñíyam bhāgám* occurs several times (I.20.8, I.161.6, II.23.2, III.60.1). In all but one passage (II.23.2) it refers to the share the Ṛbhus win by their hard work and miraculous results; in III.60.1 they attain this share by their *māyā́-*. Since the Ṛbhus are (demi-)gods who originally did not have a share in the sacrifice but earned one by their deeds (see esp. Brereton, "Gods' Work: The Ṛbhus in the *Ṛgveda,*" in *Indologica: T. Ya. Elizarenkova Memorial Volume,* Book II, ed. L. Kulikov and M. Rusanov [Moscow: Izdatelstvo RGGU 40, 2012], 111–34), the phrase is apt here, since it is applied to a similar radical change from lacking the sacrifice entirely to possessing a share in it.

16 I do have to admit that Heaven and Earth together, both by name and when designated by the fem. *ródasī* 'two world-halves', can occasionally be called (du.) *devī́* 'two goddesses'; note that it is always feminine, and so Dyaus has been subsumed into the pairing. Cf., e.g., X.64.14 *té hí dyā́vāpṛthivī́ mātárā mahī́, devī́ devā́ñ jánmanā yajñíye itáḥ* "For Heaven and Earth, the two great mothers, the goddesses worthy of the sacrifice, proceed by virtue of their kinship with the gods" (note both the heavily feminine and maternal context and the implied distinction between the gods and their mothers); VII.97.8 *devī́ devásya ródasī jánitrī, bṛ́haspátiṃ vāvṛdhatur mahitvā́* "The two goddesses, the world-halves, begetters of the god, strengthened Bṛhaspati with their greatness" (again note the maternal emphasis). (Cf. also I.106.3, IV.56.2.)

[17] A point also made in somewhat different terms by Proferes (pp. 108–9).

[18] What exactly this means is hotly debated, but the precise sense is not important for this discussion.

[19] Other passages are VI.18.15, 72.3.

[20] Indra is of course called a *kaví-* elsewhere (e.g., I.11.4), though it is not one of his standing epithets. The stem *kavitvá-* is found only here in Vedic.

The Meaning of Ritual in the *Brāhmaṇas*

Joanna Jurewicz
University of Warsaw

In his famous and provocative essay "The Meaninglessness of Ritual,"[1] Fritz Staal argues that ritual has no meaning outside itself, that its only meaning lies in the performance and in the strict observance of the rules of the rite. Thus understood, ritual would be another example of human autothelic activity, similar to play and games. Years later, Michael Witzel published "Meaningful Ritual: Vedic, Medieval, and Contemporary Concepts in the Nepalese Agnihotra Ritual,"[2] in which he argues that it is possible to see a coherent structure of the *agnihotra* rite, still performed today in Nepal, and that it is possible to explain its various elements and discern links between the ritual, the world, and the human psyche.

I think both scholars are right. It is very probable that many actual performers of ritual do not know the meaning of the rites they perform, and moreover they are likely not very much interested in it. In fact, such is the nature of many everyday activities we perform: we do them because we think they should be done or because we were taught to do them. Sometimes, while raising a child, talking with a teenager, or when we meet someone from a different culture, we are asked, often with surprise or irritation, "Why? What for?" And just as often, we actually we do not know the answer.

On the other hand, to make the world meaningful seems to be one of the main psychospiritual needs of human beings.[3] Even if the meaning is encoded in the activity itself, which should be performed well regardless of why or what for, we cannot say that the act has no meaning at all. What is more, for many philosophers and theologians who attempt to explain the nature of ritual, looking for the meaning of particular ritual activities would be external to the mere performance. The ancient Indian composers of the *Brāhmaṇas* are one of the best examples of this. I would even say that the search for the meaning of ritual was their *raison d'etre,* if not their obsession. The question remains of to what extent the later tradition and the performers were and are aware of these attempts.

In this paper I would like to show some aspects of these search-for-meaning efforts, and that these efforts require mental abilities that are common to human beings. I will analyze some passages from the exegesis of the *agnihotra* rite as presented in the *Śatapathabrāhmaṇa* (ŚB) 2.2.4–2.4.1[4] Apart from the philological methodology, I will apply the methodology of cognitive linguistics in order to reconstruct these mental strategies.

Cognitive linguistics is a branch of linguistics that investigates the relationship between verbal and nonverbal signs, thinking, and experience. It postulates that thinking is not independent from experience, rather the opposite: it is embodied, i.e., motivated by experience, both in universal and cultural dimensions.[5] It also proposes three models of mental operations performed by human beings, both in comprehension of the perceived data and in discourse: conceptual metonymy, conceptual metaphor, and conceptual blending.[6] The motivating influence of experience and the mental operations are reflected in the signs, so it is possible to reconstruct them through analysis of the signs.

I will first show that ancient Vedic ritual thinking is also embodied; second, that it is possible to reconstruct these mental strategies; and third, that this reconstruction opens for us a way to understanding the Vedic mind.[7] My general aim is to show the efforts to make ritual meaningful and that these efforts can be seen as an example of the general human ability to create sense in the world around us.

Embodiment: Experience

In the first two sections I will analyze the examples that demonstrate that even very abstract concepts are grounded in the experience of the authors of ŚB.

The main cosmogony that explains the necessity of the *agnihotra* rite (ŚB 2.2.4.1–9) is based on the everyday human experience of fire. Prajāpati creates fire but has no fuel for it; in the meantime, the fire grows bigger and bigger until it finally threatens Prajāpati's existence in its enormity. Prajāpati tries to appease the fire with milk, but it takes some time before he learns how to safely sustain the fire. This experience with fire is used to conceive and express a very complex concept of God, for whom creation is dangerous and who can even be annihilated during the process, unless a safe way of manifesting this dangerous creative power is found.[8] This is conceived of in terms of the safe way to maintain the fire, which is realized on the cosmic level in the world's functioning and on the ritual level in the *agnihotra.*

The experience with fire is used elsewhere in the exegesis of the *agnihotra.* For example, according to ŚB 2.3.31 ff, Prajāpati creates fire that begins to burn everything around it, so the creatures try to trample it. It turns out that the human being is the only creature who can safely maintain fire and use it for his own good. This is the reason for performing the *agnihotra:* in the daily performance of the rite the fire is kept by the sacrifice, who is brought back to life after his death by the cremation fire.[9] Thus, everyday mindful activity with fire, which should be maintained but should not be allowed to burn out of control, is used to explain the nature and aim of ritual performances.

The experience used in the religious and ritual exegesis can even refer to the behavior of the animals. This is the basis for the explanation of why the *sāman* should be pronounced with the sound *"hiṁ!"* In ŚB 2.2.4.12 it is said that three gods, Agni, Vāyu, and Sūrya, who were created by Prajāpati when he appeased his dangerous energy in their creative act, go forward and eastward. They then produce a cow, which gazes at them and utters *"hiṁ!"* The gods realize that this is *"hiṁ!"*, the syllable that should be pronounced at the end of the *sāman.* The forward/eastward movement in the ritual is based on the experience of a similar movement by the nomadic Aryans.[10] During this migration the Aryans seized the resources of their enemies, including cattle.[11] This concept of expansion is used to conceive of creation: the forward/eastward movement became the movement through which the world developed. In the *Ṛgveda* (ṚV), dawns, rivers, thoughts, and speech were all conceived of in terms of cows, as these are the elements of the world that make life and cognition possible.[12]

This conceptual frame is evoked by the exegesis of ŚB and further elaborated according to the experience of its composers. Here only one cow is mentioned (and not entire herds, as in ṚV) and the everyday experience of cattle husbandry is recalled: when a cow with a full udder sees a human being, it lows because it wants to be milked. I would argue that the sound *"hiṁ!"* uttered by the cow on seeing the gods is the onomatopoeic sound of this commonplace lowing.[13] This everyday experience serves as an explanation of the creation of a part of ritual speech.

The activities that are used to explain complex and abstract concepts are very simple, common to all human beings who live with fire and take care of cattle. The mechanism that allows us to use everyday concepts in thinking is called conceptual metaphor (discussed below), widely common in religious and ritual thinking. When Jesus describes God as a shepherd who looks for his lost sheep, or as a good father who cares for his children, or when, during the Last Supper, he instructs his disciples on how they should commemorate him, he also refers to simple, everyday experiences, obvious to everyone in his community. This is done in order to explain very complex concepts, such as the notion of a loving God and the miracle of transubstantiation that takes place during the Holy Mass.[14]

Embodiment: Tradition

The second kind of background for thinking is cultural tradition, which, for the composers of ŚB, is preserved in the Vedas. We have already seen that it was necessary to refer to ṚV in order to better understand the meaning of the gods producing a cow, although ṚV was not recalled explicitly there. But there are more direct references. For example, the composer of ŚB quotes verbatim ṚV 1.89.9 (ŚB 2.3.3.6). The reason he does so is that in the preceding sentence (ŚB 2.3.3.5) he has explained the nature of the mutual dependence between the human being and fire (mentioned above): the human being sustains the fire during his life, and when he dies the cremation fire sustains him. Thus fire, the "son" of the human being, now becomes his father (*sá eṣá putraḥ sán pitā́ bhavati*). In ṚV 1.89.9, quoted in ŚB, there is a similar expression (*putrā́so yátra pitáro bhávanti*), and the whole stanza refers to the immortality gained by the human being. In ṚV, immortality equals a lifetime of one hundred years. In ŚB, immortality is attained after death, thanks to the daily performance of the *agnihotra* rite and proper cremation of the body at death.

I would argue, however, that the expression *sá eṣá putraḥ sán pitā́ bhavati* evokes the whole Ṛgvedic concept of the mutual relationship between father and son, according to which the father either becomes his own son (e.g., ṚV 1.69.2b: *pári prájātaḥ krátvā babhūtha bhúvo devā́nām pitā́ putraḥ sán*), or his own grandson (ṚV 6.16.35a: *gárbhe mātúṣ pitúṣ pitā́*) ; ṚV 1.69.2b is even phonetically similar to the formulation in ŚB (*putraṃ̐ sán pitā́ bhavati*). In these terms, the poets of the ṚV express the ambivalent reality, in terms of the fire, that the creative act (as a father) manifests its part (as a son) and then is born again within its manifested part (the son becomes the father).[15]

This metaphysics is preserved in the exegesis of the *agnihotra* in ŚB. According to the main cosmogony, mentioned above, the creation of Prajāpati's ambivalent self is conceived in terms of the fire that comes from Prajāpati's mouth as his internal contents (ŚB 2.2.4.1). So Prajāpati is the father of fire. Then it is said that thanks to the proper offering of his milky aspect into his fiery aspect, Prajāpati "reproduced himself, and saved himself from Agni, Death, as he was about to devour him" (ŚB 2.2.4.7: *sá hutvā́ prajā́patiḥ / pra cā́jāyatātsyatáś cāgnér mṛtyór ātmā́nam atrāyata*), so he became the son of the fire.[16] Thus the ŚB composers could base their text on the earlier tradition and, at the same time, modify it according to their needs. The mutual relationship between the human being and fire, which is reenacted during *agnihotra* and *antyeṣṭi* rites, is the ritual expression of the mutual relationship between creator and creation, conceived of as constant tension between the existence and nonexistence of both.

Another reference to ṚV was probably so obvious to the composer of ŚB that in the verse that explains why milk that comes from the cow's udder is warm, he did not feel the need to refer directly to any concrete Ṛgvedic passage:

> *tā́m u hāgnír abhídadhyau / mithunyánayā syā́m íti tā́ṁ sámbabhūva tásyāṁ rétaḥ prā́siñcat tát páyo 'bhavat tásmād etád āmā́yāṁ gávi satyā́ṁ śṛtám agnér hí rétas tásmād yádi kṛṣṇā́yāṁ yádi róhiṇyāṁ śuklám evá bhavaty agnísaṁkāśam agnér hí rétas tásmāt prathamadugdhám uṣṇám bhavaty agnér hí rétaḥ* / (2.2.4.15)
>
> Now, Agni coveted her,[17] "May I unite with her," he thought. He united with her, and his seed became that milk of hers: hence, while the cow is raw, that milk in her is cooked (warm), for it is Agni's seed; and therefore also, whether it is in a black or a red [cow], it is ever white, and shining like fire, it being Agni's seed. Hence it is warm when first milked; for it is Agni's seed.

However, it is impossible to understand this explanation without reference to ṚV, in which the expression *āmā́su pákvam* (or its variants) is repeated in several stanzas,[18] e.g.:

> *āmā́su cid dadhiṣe pakvám antáḥ páyaḥ kṛṣṇā́su rúśad róhiṇīṣu* (1.62.9c)
>
> You placed the boiled, shining milk in the raw, black, and red ones.
>
> *ayáṁ góṣu śácyā pakvám antáḥ* (6.44.24c)
>
> . . . skillfully [he placed] the boiled [milk] in the cows. . .

The following Ṛgvedic stanza does not use exactly the same expression *āmā́su pákvam,* it only evokes the concept of the boiled milk in the raw cows, but its linguistic form is very similar to that of ŚB 2.2.4.15:

> *tuvám etád adhārayaḥ kṛṣṇā́su róhiṇīṣu ca páruṣṇīṣu rúśat páyaḥ* (8.93.13a)
>
> You kept this milk in the black, red, and spotted ones.

The contexts of these uses of the expression *āmā́su pákvam* in ṚV allows us to reconstruct the meaning of the concept expressed by it, which is the creation of the manifest aspect of reality within the unmanifest and their coexistence: boiled milk refers to the manifest aspect, raw cow to the unmanifest one.[19] In ṚV, the agent who places boiled milk in the raw cow is most often Indra, but the fiery nature of milk is implied.[20] The exegetical bent of ŚB is clear: it leaves no doubt that milk is a part of fire, as its seed. On the other hand, the reference to Ṛgvedic metaphysics again allows the ŚB composers to express the mutual relationship between creator and creation and show that it is preserved on the consecutive stages of the cosmogonic activity. On one hand, Agni is the father of the cow because he has produced it. On the other hand, Agni is born from the cow as its milk, so he is its son.[21]

The references to ṚV show the continuity of the conceptual tradition. Thanks to this, the *agnihotra* could be inscribed within the Ṛgvedic concepts as their ritual realization.

Models of Mental Operations: The Metonymic Model

In the following sections I will discuss the models of mental operations characteristic of human thinking that are used by the ŚB composers. This cognitive analysis will shed more light on the conceptual mechanisms, identification and symbolization, that are prevalent in religious and ritual thinking. As we will see, the models proposed by cognitive linguistics allow us to see the structure of these mechanisms and the reasons for their conceptual power.

Conceptual metonymy is a model of thinking that operates within one concept (which in cognitive linguistics is called the conceptual domain, and this one element provides access to the whole concept or another element.[22] For example, there is metonymy that operates within the concept of a container with content. This metonymy is of two kinds. In the first case the concept of container gives access to the concept of contents (*Container for Contents*). Thanks to this metonymy, we can meaningfully say "I've drunk a bottle," instead of "I've drunk a bottle of wine." In the second case, the concept of contents gives access to the concept of container (*Contents for Container*), and thanks to this metonymy we can be sure that we will be understood when we ask at the table, "Pass me the salt, please," instead of "Pass me the salt cellar, please."[23]

Metonymy is a fundamental mechanism of symbolization: the symbolic sign is a concept that leads the thought of its recipient toward the whole conceptual domain, which is typically extremely complex and abstract. For example, the sign of the cross gives access to the huge conceptual domain of Christ, his death and resurrection, and the religion founded on the basis of his teachings. As we will see below, conceptual metonymy also motivates identifications.

For the analysis of metonymies in the ŚB I have chosen the following passage:

> *té hocuḥ / bhadráṁ vā́ idám ajījanāmahi yé gā́m ájījanāmahi yajñó hy èvèyáṁ nó hy ṙte gór yajñás tāyaté 'nnaṁ hy èvèyāṁ yád dhí kíṁ cā́nnaṁ gaúr evá tád íti /* (2.2.4.13)
>
> They said, "Auspicious, indeed, is what we have produced here, who have produced the cow: for, truly, she is the sacrifice, and without her no sacrifice is performed; she is also the food, for the cow, indeed, is all food."

The text identifies the cow with the sacrifice and with food. Of course, if we assume that the composers of ŚB were sane people, we understand that these identifications are not ontological statements: a cow is not actually a sacrifice and it is not all food. In the light of cognitive linguistic methodology, both identifications are metonymic. The first metonymy can be schematically presented as *Cow for Sacrifice,* the second as *Cow for Food.*

Let us begin with the metonymy *Cow for Sacrifice.* This is explained by the composer in the following way: the cow is the sacrifice because there is no sacrifice without a cow. Thus understood, "cow" is the essence of the sacrifice (both conceptually and ritually), its indispensable element without which there would be no sacrifice at all. In cognitive research it has been shown that the relationship between an entity and its essence is conceived of in terms of a substance present within an object that is conceived of as a container.[24] As I have mentioned above, there is the metonymy *Content for Container* and *Container for Content.* The sentence "She (cow) is the sacrifice" (*yajño hy èvèyāṁ*) is motivated by the metonymy *Contents for Container* (*Cow for Sacrifice*), which reflects the metonymic thinking *Essence for Substance.*

The second sentence, "The cow is all food" (*yád dhí kíṁ cā́nnaṁ gaúr evá tád*), is motivated in the following way. Experientially, food in ancient India was connected with the cow, because cattle provided meat, milk, and dairy products—cream, butter, and clarified butter (ghee). In the case of meat eating, the sentence "The cow is all food" is motivated by the same metonymy as in the English sentence, "We're having chicken for dinner today," when in fact we may only eat the legs or wings of a chicken.[25] Thus the concept "cow" gives the recipient access to the concept "meat."

In the case of milk, it depends on how the relationship between "cow" and "milk" is conceived. Let us assume that milk is conceived of in terms of being a product, with a cow as its producer.[26] In the framework of this conceptualization the sentence "The cow is all food" (*yád dhí kíṁ cā́nnaṁ gaúr evá tád*) is motivated by the metonymy *Producer for Product,* which also motivates such English sentences as "I drive a Ford," where the brand name "Ford" stands for "car."[27] The concept of cow thus gives us access to the concept of milk. This metonymy is very active in ṚV, in which the word "cow," *gó,* is used in reference to milk.[28]

The metonymic relationship between the cow and its product, milk, operates in the following way. The relationship between milk and cream/butter/clarified butter can be seen as the relationship between material and an object made of that material. Thus understood, the metonymy *Material Constituting an Object for Object* is the same kind of metonymy as that which motivates the English use of the word "wood" to describe a forest.[29] The metonymy *Milk for Clarified Butter* motivates the sentence in the main cosmogony that says that the oblation created by Prajāpati was "either the oblation of milk or of clarified butter because both are milk" (ŚB 2.2.4.4, 2.2.4.5). If the recipient wishes to evoke the concept of cream, butter, or clarified butter via the concept of cow, he must activate the chain of metonymies: *Producer* (cow) *for Product* (milk) and *Material Constituting an Object* (milk) *for Object* (cream/butter/clarified butter). I would argue that the hearer of the sentence "The cow is all food" is required to activate all the abovementioned metonymies in order to see its sense: "cow," as the source of various kinds of food, can be metonymically understood to mean *all* food. The final metonymy that must be evoked in order to understand this sentence is, in my opinion, again Essence for Substance: there is no food without the products of the cow.

Through the use of the metonymic model it is possible to understand the rational ground behind ritual identifications in the *Brāhmaṇa*s. Next I will discuss another model that enhances our comprehension of Brāhmaṇic thinking, the metaphoric one.

Models of Mental Operations: The Metaphoric Model

Conceptual metaphor is a mode of thinking that operates between two concepts, called "conceptual domains," which enables thinking about one concept in terms of another. For example, in Indo-European languages cognition is conceived of in terms of seeing.[30] The conceptual metaphor is reflected in language so that we can meaningfully say, "I see what you mean" when we wish to express that we understand someone else's thought. Complex concepts are usually conceptualized with the aid of various source concepts. Cognition is just such a concept, and it can also be conceptualized, e.g., in terms of "grasping," as reflected in the sentence "Now I've grasped your point."

Metaphor is very important in religious thinking. Human concepts of "god" are always construed metaphorically. Recall Jesus' descriptions of God based in everyday life experience. The elements of the experience are used as the source concepts for the metaphoric conceptualization of a loving God in terms of a shepherd or father; such an understanding of God is basic to Christian theology.[31] Metaphors are also used in philosophy, e.g. the abovementioned metaphor *Cognition is Seeing* is the fundamental metaphor for René Descartes' theory of reason and cognition.[32] Finally, the conceptual metaphor motivates the symbolization, in that the source concept, e.g., "dove," triggers the recipient to think about the target concept: "the Holy Ghost." In the framework of metaphoric mapping, this is: "The Holy Ghost is a dove."

As I have already shown, in the main cosmogony that explains the *agnihotra* everyday activity with fire is used in the description of Prajāpati's cosmogonic activity. Such a description betrays the conceptual metaphor in the framework in which creation is conceived of in terms of kindling the fire, and the world's functioning in terms of properly sustaining the fire. Moreover, in this cosmogony, fire is also conceived of metaphorically as a hungry being that should be fed—more precisely, in terms of a newborn who must be fed with milk.

The conceptualization of fire as a hungry being comes from ṚV,[33] but the exegesis of the *agnihotra* in the ŚB elaborates it in another direction. Here the main topic, the most important from the point of view of the ritual, is the presence of the sun in the fire of an *agnihotrin*. The sun that comes to the *agnihotrin*'s fire is conceived of as a hungry guest. The way fire is presented in the main cosmogony already implies this conceptualization, due to the terrifying character of Agni's presence, which causes Prajāpati to threaten to kill him. When there is no food for a child it is a universally horrible situation, and in the Indian tradition being unable to offer food to a hungry guest in one's home is horrible as well.[34]

The source concept of the guest is elaborated more in the exegesis. For example, in ŚB 2.3.1.7 the sun is called Indra[35] or Prajāpati, and the gods are conceived of in terms of its rays. They enter the fire of an *agnihotrin* (2.3.1.7) as esteemed guests for whom the house should be beautifully arranged before their arrival (2.3.1.8). The *āhavanīya* fire should be prepared before sunset, because it will serve as the home of the gods who will visit, and so it should be properly arranged before they arrive. The oblations, however, are given just after sunset, when the sun and the gods are already present in the fire, and just before sunrise, before the sun and the gods have departed the fire:

> *sá yát sāyam ástamite juhóti / agnā́v evaìbhyá etát práviṣṭebhyo juhoty átha yát prātar ánudite juhoty ápretebhyá evaìbhyá etáj juhoti tásmād uditahomínāṁ víchinnam agnihotrám manyāmaha íti ha smāhā́surir yáthā śūnyám āvasathám āháred eváṁ tád íti* / (2.3.1.9)
>
> Now when he offers in the evening after the sun has set, he thereby offers to them after they have entered his fire-house; and when he offers in the morning before sunrise, he offers to them before they go away. Therefore Āsuri said, "The *agnihotra* of those who offer after sunrise we regard as useless: it is as if one were to take food to an empty dwelling."

The ritual rules are explained in these simple terms. Everyone can easily understand the futility and nonsensical character of bringing food for a guest who has not yet arrived or has already left the house.

The source concept can also be elaborated in such a way that it becomes the argument in the discussion. One such discussion concerns the problem of whether or not the sacrificer should approach the sacrificial fire. Arguments are based on the metaphor *The Sun/The Fire is An Important Person.* The first argument is that the sacrificer should approach the sacrificial fire because it is the giver of cattle (this is explained on the basis of a cosmogony),[36] so one should supplicate the fire for cattle and this boon will be granted to him. The counter-argument is then given: one should not approach the fire, because doing so would be rude, just as a demanding person asks a favor from someone who is higher in the social hierarchy; the higher-status person would finally become annoyed and angry and would not give anything (again, a suitable cosmogony is provided at ŚB 2.3.4.4).

Another argument in favor of approaching the fire introduces the concept of sacrifice: the sacrificial fire, because of its very nature, is supposed to listen to human requests and the sacrificer has the right to pray for its blessings. The next counter-argument brings the discussion back to the concept of asking a socially higher person for favors, discussed above. The reason the sacrificer should not approach the fire is explained by a vivid image of someone who in a pushy way asks a brahmin or *kṣatriya* for a favor and receives nothing, as opposed to someone who is not rude and demanding. The last argument elaborates the source concept in the following way: if someone says to his master that he is dependent on him, the master is obliged to support him. So the sacrificer should approach the sacrificial fire.

All of these arguments are based on the metaphor, the framework of which is that the sun/fire is conceived of as an esteemed, wealthy person who has obligations toward his dependents. In ancient India this was an everyday social experience, obvious to everyone. The concrete source concepts make what would otherwise be a complicated and difficult-to-understand ritual simple and meaningful.[37]

Models of Mental Operations: Conceptual Blending

Conceptual blending is a model of a more complex conceptual operation that occurs between at least two concepts and leads to the emergence of a new concept, called the blend. The blended concept provides additional meaning not present in the input concepts. The model adds another concept, called the generic space, which contains elements shared by the input concepts; usually its content is very schematic and general.[38]

Blends are created by participants of the ritual and in the ritual exegesis. If a blend refers to the objects used in the ritual space, or activities performed there, it consists of at least two input concepts: the concept of an object or activity, and the concept of its ritual meaning. For example, the Holy Communion in the Catholic Church is a blend motivated by two input concepts, bread and the body of Christ. In the blend, created in the minds of the participants of the Mass, the ritual wafer (bread) is (or becomes, through transubstantiation) Christ's body.[39]

Another kind of blend is created when a participant in the ritual situation constitutes one of its input concepts. The next input concepts have to do with what is in the actual interest of the participant, which can either be a future event that is supposed to occur due to the enactment of the ritual, or a past event that is reenacted in the ritual, or a reality beyond the discursive level. In the blend the relevant elements of the input concepts become one, and thus the concept of sacred space is created: the participant of the ritual acts within this space, and, at the same time, he is somewhere else—in the past, in the future, or outside everyday categories.[40] Thus, a participant in the Holy Mass, well versed in the Catholic tradition, construes a blend motivated by the following input concepts: the actual Mass in which he takes part, the last two days of

Christ's life and his resurrection, and the life of the participant and his/her expectations for the future. In the blend, the participant is present, here and now, in the past, as one of the Apostles, and also in the future, which, thanks to the ritual, will unfold according to his expectations.

The same kind of blends can be construed in Vedic ritual. In the *agnihotra* the basic ritual blend occurs when the sacrificer assumes that the sun is present in his fire. He blends two input concepts: the sun and his fire. This blend has a visible ritual realization, the *āhavanīya* fire. The sacrificer is also expected to create a blend in which he is Prajāpati, who successfully creates the world and avoids his own annihilation, and at the same time he is himself, who becomes immortal thanks to the cremation fire. There are other aspects of Vedic ritual rationality that can be disclosed when we utilize the model of conceptual blending.

I would argue that this power of the blend is the ground for treating the sacrifice in the Veda as the model of the world. In the European tradition, a model is never identical with what it represents. When CERN's Large Hadron Collider was about to be activated many people were afraid that it would cause catastrophe, that the subatomic changes taking place in it would incite dramatic physical changes in the world. This could not happen, of course, because the Large Hadron Collider is only a model of some processes that take place in reality.

However, within the ritual blend of the Vedic theoreticians, sacrifice is a model that is identical with the world. Its main function is to reduce the complexity of the world into human scale[41] so that it becomes easy to understand and perform operations in the world. Putting the problem in terms used by Clifford Geertz, the Large Hadron Collider is only a model of the world, while the Vedic sacrifice is both a model of the world and for the world, the mechanism that makes the world work according to human will and activity.[42] Putting the problem in cognitive terms, we can say that while in Western thought the concepts of the Large Hadron Collider and the world are not merged into one blended concept, they would be in Vedic ritualistic thought.

I will first analyze the sacrifice functioning as the model *for* the world. As I have just mentioned, the *āhavanīya* fire is the visible sign of the ritual blend that allows the sacrificer to believe that the sun is present in his fire. According to the exegesis that implicitly assumes the model role of the sacrifice, operations on fire are operations on the real sun. Consider the following example:

átha yát prātar ánudite juhóti / prájanayaty evaìnám etát só 'yáṁ téjo bhūtvā́ vibhrā́jamāna údeti śáśvad dha vaí nódiyād yád asmínn etā́m ā́hutiṁ ná juhuyāt tásmād vā etā́m ā́hutiṁ juhoti / (2.3.1.5)

And when he offers in the morning before sunrise, then he produces that [sun-child] and, having become a light, it rises shining. But, assuredly, it would not rise were he not to make that offering: this is why he performs that offering.

The earlier description, at ŚB 2.3.1.3–4, creates the blend that consists of three input concepts: fire, sun, and hungry child. The relation between the first and second input concepts is the metonymic relation of container (fire) and content (sun), or of cause (fire) and effect (sun) (*Container for Content, Cause for Effect*). The relation between the second and third input concepts is metaphoric: the sun is conceived of in terms of a child (*The Sun is a Child*). In the blend, two milky oblations, poured into fire, are conceived as food for the child, which is the sun (*Oblations are Food*). In this sacrificial "Large Hadron Collider," when the sacrificer pours oblations he is feeding the sun present in his fire, and thus gives it the power to rise in the morning. In the framework of this conceptualization, it seems obvious that if the sacrificer did not make the offerings the sun could not rise. Thus the mysterious cosmic power of the sun by which it rises everyday is explained through the simple activity of feeding a child, an action that is known and easily understood by anyone. The blend also allows the human being to believe in having some control over cosmic processes. Finally, it presents these cosmic processes as the obvious result of human activity.

In the next example, the model character of the *agnihotra* refers to the human body:

tád dugdhvā́dhiśrayati / śṛtám asad íti tád āhur yárhy údantaṁ tárhi juhuyād íti tád vaí nódantaṁ kuryād úpa ha dahed yád údantaṁ kuryā́d áprajajñi vaí réta úpadagdhaṁ tásmān nódantaṁ kuryāt / (2.3.1.14)

Having milked he puts that [milk] on [the *gārhapatya* fire], because it has to be cooked. Here now they say, "When it rises to the brim, then we shall offer it!" He must not, however, let it rise to the brim, since he would burn it if he were to let it rise to the brim; and unproductive indeed is burnt seed: he must not, therefore, let it rise to the brim.

This passage creates a blend that consists of two input concepts. The first is the pot with the milk that is heated on the fire in the ritual; the second is of male sexual arousal. The relation between these two concepts is metonymic and metaphorical. The "seed" is metaphorically conceived of as milk (*Seed is Milk;* ŚB 2.3.1.15). The human being is metonymically reduced to his head (*Head for a Person*),[43] and the head is metaphorically conceived of as the pot (*Head is a Pot*).[44] In the conceptual blend, whatever happens to the milk in the pot also happens to the sacrificer's seed (i.e., sperm): if the milk boils to the brim, the man's seed is also emitted unproductively. Thus the sacrifice is a model not only for the cosmos but also for human physiology.

The following description creates a blend that compresses[45] concepts which are both spatially and temporally remote:

> *tán ná sāmyúdvāsayeta / sāmí hāsmaí sá glāyati sá yáthā haivaìṣá etásmā asmíṁl loké sāmí glā́yaty evám u haivaìṣá etásmā amúṣmiṁl loké sāmí glāyati tásmān ná sāmyúdvāsayeta* / (2.3.3.4)
>
> One must not, therefore, remove it (i.e., the sacrificial fire from the hearth) prematurely, for too soon it languishes for him; and as it languishes for him too soon in this world, even so does it languish for him too soon in yonder world: one must not, therefore, remove it prematurely.

The input concepts of this conceptual blend are the following: the first is the sacrificer in the sacrificial space, the second is the sacrificer in the future. There is the relation of identity between the concept of fire and sacrificer: in the sacrificial space the sacrificer is Prajāpati, who, in turn, is Agni.[46] In the blend, whatever happens to the fire in the sacrificial space now, the same will happen to the sacrificer in the future.

Sacrifice is also the model of the world, and as such it plays an important explanatory role. For example, the fact that the sun (metaphorically conceived of as an embryo; ŚB 2.3.1.4, 2.3.1.5) enters the fire (metaphorically conceived of as a womb) in the evening explains why all living beings go to sleep in the evening: when they sleep, they are also conceived of as being in an embryonic state (ŚB 2.1.3.3). The explanatory power rises exactly in the blend that creates an ontological link between such distant concepts and spheres of reality as the sunset, living beings that sleep, and the situation of an embryo in the womb.

The last example in this section shows how the blend is further elaborated in the exegesis:

> *sā́ yā́ pūrvā́hutiḥ / té devā́ átha yóttarā té manuṣyā̀ átha yát srucí pariśináṣṭi té paśávaḥ* / (2.3.1.16)
>
> Now the first libation (*pūrvā́huti*) represents the gods, and the second (*úttarāhuti*) represents the men, and what remains in the ladle represents cattle.

The passage construes the main blend with two input concepts: the sacrifice and the world of gods and living beings. In the blend, the milk poured in two oblations corresponds to gods and humans, and the milk that remains in the ladle corresponds to cattle. The rules of pouring oblations are set and explained in the following way:

> *sá vái kánīya iva pūrvāmā́hutiṁ juhoti / bhū́yā́ ivóttarām bhū́ya iva srucí páriśinaṣṭi* / (2.3.2.17)
>
> Only a little he offers for the first libation, somewhat more for the second, and still more he leaves in the ladle.
>
> *sá yátkánīya iva pū́rvāmā́hutiṁ juhóti / kánīyāṁso hí devā́ manuṣyè̀bhyó 'tha yád bhū́ya ivóttarām bhū́yāṁso hí manuṣyà̀ devebhyó 'tha yád bhū́ya iva srucí pariśináṣṭi bhū́yāṁso hí paśávo manuṣyè̀bhyáḥ* (2.3.2.18)
>
> The reason why he offers only a little for the first libation is that the gods are fewer than men; and why he offers somewhat more for the second libation is that men are more numerous than gods; and why he leaves still more in the ladle is that cattle are more numerous than men.

The composer creates an analogous relation between the input concepts: the sacrificial space is profiled according to the real space. The rule is that the more entities there are that are receiving the oblation, the more milk is reserved for them. We can presume that the sacrificer thus maintains the cosmic order of gods and living beings, and that the relationship between the world and its sacrificial model is mutual. On the one hand, the sacrificial model patterns the world and preserves the world's structure (of model); on the other hand, observation of the rules in the model guarantees the preservation of the structures in the world (for model). Now the conceptual blend is enriched with the next input concept, the sacrificer in the future:

> *kánīyāṁso ha vā́ asya bhā́ryā bhávanti bhū́yāṁsaḥ paśávo yá eváṁ vidvā́n agnihotráṁ juhóti tád vaí sámṛddhaṁ yásya kánīyāṁso bhā́ryā ásan bhū́yāṁsaḥ paśávaḥ* / (2.3.2.18)
>
> And, verily, whosoever, knowing this, offers the *agnihotra,* his cattle will be more numerous than those [people] that have to be supported by him: for he, indeed, is in a prosperous condition, whose cattle are more numerous than those [who are] dependent on his support.

The blend encompasses present and future; the future preserves the rules of the present and the proportions between living beings. Thanks to the relation of the identity between the sacrificial space and spatial and temporal spaces outside it, the sacrificer can be certain about what will happen to him and to the external world both in the present and in the future.

The blends created during ritual and its exegesis reduces complex cosmic and physiological processes into simple concepts of human scale. In this way, they facilitate understanding the world. They also allow people to believe that they have at least some measure of control over these larger processes. As such, blends play a very important role, from a psychological point of view, for those who are able to feel safe in the world, thanks to these metaphorical concepts. The blends also motivates identifications between the concepts of objects and activities.

How Does the *Agnihotra* Save One from Death?

In this last section I will analyze how meaning is built in a longer passage that presents the argument of why one is compelled to perform the *agnihotra* and how it is possible that doing so frees one from death. This argument appears in the main cosmogony for the first time where it states that Prajāpati saved himself from death by giving a milky part of himself to his fiery part. In the same way, the human being can save himself by giving a substitute for himself to the fire. During his life this substitute is the milk that is poured into fire in the *agnihotra.* When the sacrificer dies, his body, burned in the cremation fire, will serve as the substitute for his immortal part that will survive death (ŚB 2.2.4.7–8). The passage analyzed below explains how it is possible for the *agnihotra* to save the sacrifice from premature death, because it renders possible the sacrificer's use of cosmic forces for his own benefit.

The explanation begins with the identification of the sun with death:

> *tád vā́ eṣá evá mṛtyúḥ / sá eṣá tápati tád yád eṣá evá mṛtyús tásmād yā́ etásmād arvā́cyaḥ prajā́s tā́ mriyanté 'tha yā́ḥ párācyas té devas tásmād u tè 'mṛ́tās tásyemā́ḥ sárvāḥ prajā́ raśmíbhiḥ prāṇéṣv abhíhitās tásmād u raśmáyaḥ prāṇā́n abhyávatāyante* / (2.3.3.7)
>
> Now yonder burning [sun] doubtless is no other than Death; and because he is Death, therefore the creatures that are on this side of him die. But those that are on the other side of him are the gods, and they are therefore immortal. It is by the rays (or *raśmi,* "reins, thongs") of that [sun] that all these creatures are attached to the vital airs (breath or life), and therefore the rays extend down to the vital airs.
>
> *sá yásya kāmáyate / tásya prāṇám ādā́yodeti sá mriyate sá yó haitám mṛtyúm ánatimucyā́thāmúṁ lokám éti yáthā haivàsmíṁl loké ná saṁyátam ādriyáte yadā́ yadaìvá kāmáyaté 'tha māráyaty evám u haivàmúṣmiṁl loké púnaḥ punar evá prámārayati* / (2.3.3.8)

> And the breath of whomsoever he (i.e., the sun) wishes he takes and rises, and that one dies. And whosoever goes to the yonder world not having escaped that Death, him he causes to die again and again in the yonder world, even as in this world one regards not him that is fettered, but puts him to death whenever one wishes.

The identification of the sun with death is based on metonymy *Effect for Cause:* the sun may cause death not only because of its excessive heat, but first of all because it is the cosmic embodiment of the power of time that causes everything to mature and grow old, and finally to die. The track of the sun in the sky divides the world into two parts: the part in which mortal beings inhabit, below the sun, and that of the immortal gods who exist above the sun. The rays of the sun sustain the life of mortal creatures, but the sun may also take them whenever it wants.[47] Moreover, if someone dies without having become free from death (through ritual activities), he will be killed after his death many times over by the merciless sun. Undergoing endless multiple deaths is perhaps the most horrifying prospect for a human being. To die once is terrifying enough, but to die many times? This is the meaning of the *punarmṛtyú.*

But how one can be freed from death before death? It is possible due to the *agnihotra,* during which a human being can harness cosmic processes for his own benefit:

> *sá yát sāyam ástamite dvé ā́hutī juhóti / tád etā́bhyām pū́rvābhyām padbhyā́m etásmin mṛtyaú prátitiṣṭhaty átha yát prātaránudite dvé ā́hutī juhóti tád etā́bhyām áparābhyām padbhyā́m etásmin mṛtyaú prátitiṣṭhita sá enam eṣá udyánn evā̀dāyódeti tád etám mṛtyúm átimucyate saìṣā̀gnihotré mṛtyor átimuktir áti ha vaí púnar mṛtyúm mucyate yá evám etā́m agnihotré mṛtyor átimuktiṁ véda* / (2.3.3.9)
>
> Now when, in the evening after sunset, he offers two libations, then he firmly plants himself on that Death with those forefeet of his; and when, in the morning before sunrise, he offers two libations, then he plants himself on that Death with those hindfeet of his. And when he (i.e., the sun) rises, then, in rising, he takes him up and thus he (i.e., the sacrificer) escapes that Death. This, then, is the release from death in the *agnihotra:* and, verily, he who knows the release from death in the *agnihotra* is freed from death again and again.

In the evening, when the sun enters the fire of an *agnihotrin,* he offers two libations. This act enables him to, as it were, catch the sun in his hands. Thus he is able to keep the sun in his fire for the whole night. Then, in the morning, he again offers two oblations and thus he (metaphorically) stands on the sun with his feet. When the sun rises it takes him up, and the sacrificer travels on it to reach the immortal sphere.

The identification between the two oblations and the sacrificer's hands and feet is implied here. I would argue that this identification is based on metonymy: *Oblations for Hands.* This metonymy is complex and consists of two metonymic sub-mappings. The first metonymy is *A Ladle for Oblation* (a specific realization of the metonymy *Container for Content*).[48] The second metonymy, *Hand for a Ladle,* is more culturally entrenched. It is attested in the following passage:

> *átha srucā́ úpadadhāti / bāhū́ vaí srucaú bāhū́ evā̀smínn etát prátidadhāti té yát srucaú bhávataḥ srucaú hí bāhū́ idám evá kapúchalamayáṁ daṇḍó dvé bhavato dvaú hī̀maú bāhū́ pārśváta úpadadhāti pārśváto hī̀maú bāhū́* / (7.4.1.36)
>
> He then lays down two offering spoons, the offering spoons are arms: it is his arms he thus restores to him (i.e., Agni). And as to why offering spoons [are laid down], it is because the arms are offering spoons, that bowl and the handle are two, for there are two of these arms. He lays them down at the [left and right] sides, for these arms [of ours] are at the sides.

When the recipient activates the metonymic chain *A Ladle for Oblation, Hand for a Ladle,* he creates a blend whose framework is the two oblations that are the two hands and legs of the *agnihotrin,* who catches the sun disc with them and flies upon it above the mortal sphere.

The blend created by the whole passage analyzed above has up to this point consisted of the following input concepts. The first is the sacrificer who performs the *agnihotra,* and the second is the day-night cycle of the sun. One could ask, however, why the sun is called *mṛtyú* here, and why the recipient has to activate its concept not directly but via the metonymy *Effect for Cause* discussed above. The concept of death is what leads the thought of the recipient to the concept of the sun. In my opinion, calling the sun *mṛtyú* in this passage is very well considered. First, the composer can explicitly express that the operations performed on the fire are the operations performed upon death. Second, if the recipient activates the Vedic conceptualization of the sun in terms of a horse or bull[49] and enriches the blend with one of these concepts, he will understand victory over death in the vivid terms of taming a horse or bull: the sacrificer catches death, stands on it, and goes wherever he wants, just as with a tamed horse or bull. He is thus freed from death before his death.

This blend is elaborated in the next passage:

> *yáthā vā́ íṣor ánīkam / eváṁ yajñā́nām agníhotraṁ yéna vā́ íṣor ánīkam éti sárvā vaí ténéṣur ety eténo hāsya sárve yajñakratáva etám mṛtyúm átimuktā́ḥ* / (2.3.3.10)
>
> What the arrowhead is to the arrow, that the *agnihotra* is to sacrifices. For

whither the head of the arrow flies, thither the whole arrow flies: and so are all his works of sacrifice freed by this [*agnihotra*] from that Death.

The next input concept of the blend is an arrow. The input concept of sacrifice is enlarged with the concept of all the sacrifices performed during the sacrificer's life, which are conceived of as an arrow, with the *agnihotra* as the arrowhead. In the blend, the sacrificer flies above the sun (into immortality) on the arrow made of all the sacrifices he performed during his life, led by the *agnihotra,* the arrowhead. I would go even further and argue that in this blend the sacrificer himself becomes the arrow that comprises all of his ritual deeds performed until this moment, and the arrowhead is his own head.

When the sacrificer reaches the other side of the sun, he becomes free from the influence of time and his sacrificial body, made of his ritual deeds, is not destroyed by it:

ahorātré ha vā́ amúṣmiṁl loké pariplávamāne / púruṣasya sukṛtáṁ kṣiṇuto 'rvā́cī́naṁ vā́ áto ahorātré tátho hāsyā́horātré sukṛtáṁ ná kṣiṇutaḥ / (2.3.3.11)

Now day and night, revolving, destroy [the fruit of] man's righteousness in the yonder world. But day and night are on this side [of the sun] from him [after he has gone up to heaven]; and so day and night do not destroy [the fruit of] his righteousness.

In order to describe this freedom from the influence of time, the composer adds the next input concept, riding on a chariot:

sa yáthā rathopasthé tíṣṭhan / upáriṣṭād rathacakré palyáṁyamāne upāvékṣetaivám parástād arvā́cī́no 'horātré upā́vekṣate ná ha vā́ asyāhorātré sukṛtáṁ kṣiṇuto yá evám etā́m ahorātráyor átimuktiṁ véda / (2.3.3.12)

And as, while standing inside a chariot, one would look down from above on the revolving chariot wheels, even so does he look down from on high upon day and night: and, verily, day and night destroy not the reward of him who thus knows that release from day and night.

There is a conceptual metonymic link between the chariot and the arrow mentioned in the previous passage: the weapon used by chariot-mounted warriors was the bow and arrow. The metonymy *Arrow for the Warrior on the Chariot* strengthens the coherence of the blend built by this description. The coherence of the blend is strengthened even more in the Veda by the sun conceived of not only in terms of a horse/bull but also in terms of a chariot.[50] In the blend the sun is the chariot, and day and night are its two wheels.[51] Thus the earlier description of the sacrificer who catches the sun and flies up on it conceptually agrees with the description of him riding in a chariot. The *agnihotrin* who rides on the sun is conceived of as a warrior riding in a chariot, the wheels of which revolve below him and cannot crush him, unlike those who are below the chariot, whose bodies are destroyed.[52]

This analysis shows that the description of the power of the *agnihotra* is very well considered. All the images are developed coherently and there are no unnecessary or redundant thoughts or words. The composer draws from the cultural heritage but transforms it in such a way in order to convince his audience about the beneficial values of the *agnihotra* rite.

We can see the rationality that lies behind human conceptual mechanisms: within the frames of the blend built by the description, the links between ritual, cosmos, and sacrificer are clear and obvious. The same kind of rationality is apparent in modern science, which, for example, explains genetic processes in terms of the coding and transmission of information.[53]

At the same time, the composer construes his description in such a way that he can lead his recipient through images that refer to concrete experiences and that change and unfold in logically ordered sequences. The first image is of taming a bull or horse, in terms of which victory over death is conceived: one takes hold of an animal with his hands and then tries to mount it. The concept of a horse belongs to the complex concept of a chariot-mounted warrior who fights with bow and arrow; in the next sequence, the recipient's thought should focus on the concept of an arrow in terms of which the sacrificer, endowed with his sacrificial body, is conceived. In the following sequence, the recipient is invited to focus on the concept of the chariot in terms of which the sun in the sky is conceived. Finally, in a retrospective, overall view, he may understand catching the sun/death and standing upon it in terms of ascending a chariot: one first grasps it with his hands and then climbs up on it using his legs. These simple images give a reasonable, easily understood basis for the extremely complex concept of freeing oneself from death before one's actual death.

Conclusion

I hope to show that the composers of ŚB want the ritual to be meaningful; they present and explain its final aim and the aim of its particular activities. At the same time, they employ simple, human-scale images in order to express very complex and abstract concepts. The basic assumption of cognitive linguistics and the models of mental operations proposed by it allow us to reconstruct how the meaning of ritual is construed. It is worth adding that the mental operations analyzed by cognitive linguistics are usually performed unconsciously, automatically, and effortlessly. This fact reinforces the natural character of thinking about the influence of ritual.[54]

At thus point I would like to once again recall Frits Staal's provocative paper, "The Meaninglessness of Ritual." I consider his comparison of ritual to play to be very accurate, and my analysis in this paper confirms this accuracy. Staal saw the similarity between ritual and play in their autothelic character. However, there are additional similarities between ritual and play. As Johan Huizinga and Roger Caillois have shown, the strict observance of rules is another important aspect of play.[55]

The similarity between ritual and play can also be seen in the fact that in both activities objects and acts have different meanings from those accepted in everyday life.[56] The person "who knows thus" (*evaṁvíd*), the sacrificer and the priests, similarly to those who play, enter a reality in which nothing means itself. And actually it does not matter if the meaning lies outside the ritual (as for the composers of ŚB) or not (as Staal assumes). If a sacrificer pours two oblations of milk into the fire because he has been taught to do so by his father, or because he wishes to catch the sun and become immortal—in either case, the activity has no sense outside of the sacrificial space, in the world of ordinary reality in which pouring milk into fire is simply wasting it. If a sacrificer is just taught to perform the ritual, his play consists of the strict observation of the rules. If he is *evaṁvíd*, his play involves his understanding the meaning of this apparently useless activity that is hidden to those who are outside the play. It follows, then, that there are more similarities between ritual and play. Staal's intuition surely needs more investigation that may perhaps lead us toward a general analysis of the role of play in ancient Indian philosophical and ritual thought.

Notes

1 Fritz Staal, "The Meaninglessness of Ritual," *Numen* 26/1 (1979): 2–22.

2 Michael Witzel, "Meaningful Ritual: Vedic, Medieval, and Contemporary Concepts in the Nepalese Agnihotra Ritual," in Albert W. Van den Hoek, Dirk H. A. Kolff, and M. S. Oort, eds., *Ritual, State, and History in South Asia: Essays in Honour of J. C. Heesterman* (Leiden: E. J. Brill, 1992), pp. 774–825.

3 Mark Johnson, *The Body in the Mind: The Bodily Basis of Meaning, Imagination, and Reason* (Chicago and London: University of Chicago Press, 1987); Clifford Geertz, *Interpretacja kultur: Wybrane eseje* (Kraków: Wydawnictwo Uniwersytetu Jagiellońskiego, 2005).

4 For an analysis and interpretation of the *agnihotra* in early Vedic texts, see H. W. Bodewitz, *The Daily Evening and Morning Offerings (Agnihotra) According to the Brāhmaṇas* (Leiden: E. J. Brill, 1976). For a description of the *agnihotra* in the *Śrautasūtras*, see Paul Émile Dumont, *L'Agnihotra. Description de l'agnihotra dans le ritual védique* (Baltimore, MD: The John Hopkins Press, 1939).

5 George Lakoff and Mark Turner, *More Than Cool Reason: A Field Guide To Poetic Metaphor* (Chicago: University of Chicago Press, 1987).

6 For conceptual metonymy and metaphor, see George Lakoff and Mark Johnson, *Metaphors We Live By* (Chicago: University of Chicago Press, 1980); Lakoff and Turner, *More Than Cool Reason.* For conceptual blending, see Gilles Fauconnier and Mark Turner, *The Way We Think: Conceptual Blending and the Mind's Hidden Complexities* (New York: Basic Books, 2003).

7 Cf. Michael Witzel, "On Magical Thought in the Veda," inaugural lecture (Leiden: Universitaire Pers, 1979) and "How to Enter the Vedic Mind? Strategies in Translating a Brahmana Text," in Enrica Garzilli, ed., *Translating, Translations, Translators: From India to the West* (Cambridge, MA: Department of Sanskrit and Indian Studies, Harvard University, 1996), pp. 163–176.

8 Cf. Joanna Jurewicz, "Prajāpati, the Fire, and the Pañcāgnividyā," in Piotr Balcerowicz and Marek Mejor, eds., *Essays in Indian Philosophy, Religion and Literature* (Delhi: Motilal Banarsidass, 2004), pp. 45–60. The model of mental ability that allows us to conceive one concept in terms of another is called conceptual metaphor (see the section "Models of Mental Operations: The Metaphoric Model").

9 The mutual relationship between the fire of the *agnihotra*/the cremation fire and the human being is why the *Jaiminīya Brāhmaṇa* inserts a description of the cremation in the middle of its description of the *agnihotra* (1.45–50); they are separated in H. W. Bodewitz, *Jaiminīya Brāhmaṇa I, 1–65. Translation and Commentary with A Study of Agnihotra and Prāṇāgnihotra* (Leiden: E. J. Brill, 1973).

10 J. C. Heesterman, "Other Folk's Fire," in J. F. Staal, ed., *Agni: The Vedic Ritual of the Fire Altar* (Berkeley: Asian Humanities Press, 1983), vol. 2, pp. 76–94.

11 Joanna Jurewicz, *Fire and Cognition in the Ṛgveda* (Warszawa: Dom Wydawniczy Elipsa, 2010), p. 98 ff.

12 Jurewicz, *Fire and Cognition in the Ṛgveda,* pp. 99–101, 84–86.

13 A cow bellowing the sound *hiṁ* when it has been separated from its calf is mentioned in ṚV 1.124.27–28.

14 Eve E. Sweetser and Mary Therese DesCamp, "Metaphors for God: Why and How Do Our Choices Matter for Humans? The Application of Contemporary Cognitive Linguistic Research to the Debate on God and Metaphor," *Pastoral Psychology* 53/3 (2005): 207–238; Jesper Sørensen, *A Cognitive Theory of Magic* (Lanham, New York, Toronto, and Plymouth, UK: Altamira Press, 2007).

15 Cf. Jurewicz, *Fire and Cognition in the Ṛgveda,* p. 201 ff.

16 This is more explicit in the cosmogonies of the *agnicayana,* where Prajāpati dies and is revived by fire, e.g., ŚB 6.1.2.12–13.

17 The bellowing cow created by Agni, Vāyu, and Sūrya.

[18] Jurewicz, *Fire and Cognition in the Ṛgveda,* p. 215 ff.

[19] This is again metaphorical conceptualization; see the section "Models of Mental Operations: The Metaphoric Model."

[20] Jurewicz, *Fire and Cognition in the Ṛgveda,* p. 218 ff.

[21] Jurewicz, *Fire and Cognition in the Ṛgveda,* p. 222 ff.

[22] In cognitive linguistics the concept in which metonymy operates is called the conceptual domain. The concept that is reached via metonymic mapping is called the target domain, and the concept that gives access to the target concept is called the vehicle. Cf. Lakoff and Johnson, *Metaphors We Live By;* Günter Radden and Zoltan Kövecses, "Towards a Theory of Metonymy," in Klaus-Uwe Panther and Günter Radden, eds., *Metonymy in Language and Thought* (Amsterdam and Philadephia: John Benjamins Publishing Co., 1999).

[23] Radden and Kövecses, "Towards a Theory of Metonymy," p. 41, give the following examples: "the bottle is sour" for "milk" (*Container for Content*) or "the milk tipped over" (*Content for Container*).

[24] Lakoff and Johnson, *Philosophy in the Flesh,* p. 347; George Lakoff, *Moral Politics: How Liberals and Conservatives Think* (Chicago and London: University of Chicago Press, 2002), p. 87 ff. The mechanism that allows for thinking about the abstract concept of essence in terms of a material object, such as the content of a container, is conceptual metaphor; see the section "Models of Mental Operations: The Metaphoric Model."

[25] Cf. Radden and Kövecses, "Towards a Theory of Metonymy," p. 48. This is the metonymy *Material Constituting an Object for an Object.*

[26] Milk can also be seen as a part of a cow; the metonymy then is *Whole for Part.*

[27] Radden and Kövecses, "Towards a Theory of Metonymy," p. 39.

[28] E.g., ṚV 9.45.3b, 9.46.4c, 9.50.5b; Alexander Lubotsky, *A Ṛgvedic Word-Concordance* (New Haven, CT: American Oriental Society, 1997), vol. 1, p. 480, passim.

[29] Radden and Kövecses, "Towards a Theory of Metonymy," p. 32.

[30] See Eve E. Sweetser, *From Etymology to Pragmatics: Metaphorical and Cultural Aspects of Semantic Structure* (Cambridge: Cambridge University Press, 1990). The concept that lends its categories is called the source domain (in this example, "seeing"), while the concept that is conceived of in terms of these categories is called the target domain (in this case, "cognition").

[31] See Sweetser and DesCamp, "Metaphors for God: Why and How Do Our Choices Matter for Humans?"

[32] Lakoff and Johnson, *Philosophy in the Flesh,* p. 393 ff .

[33] Jurewicz, *Fire and Cognition in the Ṛgveda,* pp. 325ff; cf. pp. 124–125, 208–209.

[34] Cf. a description of the guest in the later *Kaṭha Upaniṣad* 1.7: *vaśvanāraḥ praviśati atithir brāhmaṇo gṛhān / tasyaitāṁ śānti kurvanti hara vaivasvatodakam //;* "The guest is like fire who needs to be appeased with water, otherwise it will burn the house."

35 Agni is presented in the *Ṛgveda* as radiant, e.g., ṚV 1.52.6; cf. Jurewicz, *Fire and Cognition in the Ṛgveda*, p. 360. In ŚB 6.1.1.2 the middle breath of reality kindles the vital airs and because of this it is called Indra.

36 In ŚB 2.3.4.1–2 the gods throw cattle and other animals into the fire, and the fire disappears with them during the night. The gods then ask the fire to give back the animals and the fire gives them back.

37 Another example: the way in which the conception is understood becomes the pattern for understanding the ritual (ŚB 2.3.1.32–35).

38 The concepts involved in blending are called mental spaces. The concepts that are blended are called input spaces, and the general concept, the elements of which are shared by the input spaces, is called the generic space. The concept that emerges is called the blend.

39 Cf. Sørensen, *A Cognitive Theory of Magic.*

40 Eve E. Sweetser, "Blended Spaces and Performativity," *Cognitive Linguistics* 11, 3/4 (2000): 305–333.

41 Fauconnier and Turner, in *The Way We Think,* pp. 312, 346–348, argue that this is one of the most important aims of conceptual blending; cf. Fauconnier and Turner, "Compression and Global Insight," *Cognitive Linguistics* 11/3–4 (2000): 283–304.

42 Cf. Geertz, I*nterpretacja kultur,* pp. 115–116.

43 For the notion of head as human being, cf. Lakoff and Johnson, *Metaphors We Live By,* p. 37.

44 Cf. Jurewicz, *Fire and Cognition in the Ṛgveda,* pp. 167, 257, 379, 400.

45 Compression is one of the most important mechanisms of conceptual blending; cf. Fauconnier and Turner, "Compression and Global Insight" and *The Way We Think,* pp. 312, 346–350.

46 The identity of the sacrificer with the fire is motivated by the cultural assumptions expressed in the exegesis of the *agnihotra:* the sacrificer is identified with Prajāpati (Agni), the personification of fire.

47 *Jaiminīya Upaniṣad* 1.46 depicts one of the seasons that serve as the guardians of the sun as a personified being wielding a hammer (*kūþahasta*) with which he strikes the dead person.

48 In Poland, we may say to a child [when giving medicine?], "Eat one spoon for the health of your mummy."

49 Jurewicz, *Fire and Cognition in the Ṛgveda,* pp. 158, 160, 168, 187 passim.

50 Jurewicz, *Fire and Cognition in the Ṛgveda,* pp. 53, 54, 117, 217 passim.

51 Both metaphors well entrenched in the Veda; cf. ṚV 1.164.11–14; *Atharvaveda* 19.53.1–2.

52 The blend is further elaborated according to exegetical needs: *Svargaloka is a House, Agnihotra is a Door to the House, Agnihotra is a Boat that Carries to the House, Sacrificial Fires are Oars.*

53 See Elena Semino, *Metaphor in Discourse* (Cambridge: Cambridge University Press, 2008).

[54] As Lakoff and Turner write in *More Than Cool Reason*, pp. 62–63:

> Once we learn a conceptual metaphor, it too is just there, conventionalized, a ready and powerful conceptual tool—automatic, effortless, and largely unconscious. The things most alive in our conceptual system are those things that we use constantly, unconsciously, and automatically. . . . Anything that we rely on constantly, unconsciously, and automatically is so much part of us that it cannot be easily resisted, in large measure because it is barely even noticed. To the extent that we use a conceptual schema or a conceptual metaphor, we accept its validity. Consequently, when someone else uses it, we are predisposed to accept its validity. For this reason, conventionalized schemas and metaphors have *persuasive* power over us.

[55] Johan Huizinga, *Homo ludens: Zabawa jako źródło kultury* (Warszawa: Czytelnik, 1985), pp. 25–27; Roger Caillois, *Żywioł i ład* (Warszawa: Państwowy Instytut Wydawniczy, 1973), pp. 304–305, 306. (Caillois is also evoked in Staal, "The Meaninglessness of Ritual," p. 10.) The differences between the theories of these two scholars are not relevant to the present discussion.

[56] Huizinga, *Homo ludens*, pp. 27–28; Caillois, *Żywioł i ład*, pp. 302–303, 306.

References

Bodewitz, H. W. *Jaiminīya Brāhmaṇa I, 1–65. Translation and Commentary with A Study of Agnihotra and Prāṇāgnihotra.* Leiden: E. J. Brill, 1973.

—. *The Daily Evening and Morning Offerings (Agnihotra) According to the Brāhmanas.* Leiden: E. J. Brill, 1976.

Caillois, Roger. *Żywioł i ład.* Warszawa: Państwowy Instytut Wydawniczy, 1973. Polish translation of a selection of papers from *Le myth et l'homme* (1938), *L'homme et le sacré* (1950), *Instincts et societé* (1964), and *Les jeux et les hommes* (1958).

Dumont, Paul Émile. *L'Agnihotra. Description de l'agnihotra dans le ritual védique.* Baltimore, MD: The John Hopkins Press, 1939.

Fauconnier, Gilles, and Mark Turner. "Compression and Global Insight," *Cognitive Linguistics* 11/3–4 (2000): 283–304.

—. *The Way We Think: Conceptual Blending and the Mind's Hidden Complexities.* New York: Basic Books, 2003.

Geertz, Clifford. *Interpretacja kultur: Wybrane eseje.* Kraków: Wydawnictwo Uniwersytetu Jagiellońskiego, 2005. Polish translation of *The Interpretations of Cultures: Selected Essays by Clifford Geertz.* New York: Basic Books, 1973.

Heesterman, J. C. "Other Folk's Fire," in J. F. Staal, ed., in collaboration with C. V. Somayajipad and M. Itti Ravi Nambudiri, *Agni: The Vedic Ritual of the Fire Altar*, vol. 2, pp. 76–94. Berkeley: Asian Humanities Press, 1983.

Huizinga, Johan. *Homo ludens: Zabawa jako źródło kultury.* Warszawa: Czytelnik, 1985. Polish translation of *Homo ludens: Proeve eener bepaling van het spel-element der cultuur*, in L. Brummel, et al., eds., *Johan Huizinga: Verzamelde werken V (Cultuurgeschiedenis III)*, pp. 26–246. Haarlem: H. D. Tjeenk Willink & Zoon, 1950.

Johnson, Mark. *The Body in the Mind: The Bodily Basis of Meaning, Imagination, and Reason.* Chicago and London: University of Chicago Press, 1987.

Jurewicz, Joanna. *Fire and Cognition in the Ṛgveda.* Warszawa: Dom Wydawniczy Elipsa, 2010.

—."Prajāpati, the Fire, and the *Pañcāgnividyā*," in Piotr Balcerowicz and Marek Mejor, eds., *Essays in Indian Philosophy, Religion and Literature*, pp. 45–60. Delhi: Motilal Banarsidass, 2004.

Lakoff, George. *Moral Politics: How Liberals and Conservatives Think.* Chicago and London: University of Chicago Press, 2002.

—. *Women, Fire, and Dangerous Things: What Categories Reveal about the Mind.* Chicago and London: University of Chicago Press, 1987.

Lakoff, George, and Mark Johnson. *Metaphors We Live By.* Chicago: University of Chicago Press, 1980.

—. *Philosophy in the Flesh: The Embodied Mind and Its Challenge to Western Thought.* New York: Basic Books, 1999.

Lakoff, George, and Mark Turner. *More Than Cool Reason: A Field Guide To Poetic Metaphor.* Chicago: University of Chicago Press, 1989.

Lubotsky, Alexander. *A Ṛgvedic Word-Concordance*, 2 vols. New Haven, CT: American Oriental Society, 1997.

Radden, Günter, and Zoltan Kövecses. "Towards a Theory of Metonymy," in Klaus- Uwe Panther and Günter Radden, eds., *Metonymy in Language and Thought*, pp. 17–59. Amsterdam and Philadephia: John Benjamins Publishing Co., 1999.

Semino, Elena. *Metaphor in Discourse.* Cambridge: Cambridge University Press, 2008.

Sørensen, Jesper. *A Cognitive Theory of Magic.* Lanham, New York, Toronto, and Plymouth UK: Altamira Press, 2007.

Staal, Frits. "The Meaninglessness of Ritual," *Numen* 26/1 (1979): 2–22.

Sweetser, Eve E. "Blended Spaces and Performativity," *Cognitive Linguistics* 11, 3/4 (2000): 305–333.

—. *From Etymology to Pragmatics. Metaphorical and Cultural Aspects of Semantic Structure.* Cambridge: Cambridge University Press, 1990.

Sweetser, Eve E., and Mary Therese DesCamp. "Metaphors for God: Why and How Do Our Choices Matter for Humans? The Application of Contemporary Cognitive Linguistic Research to the Debate on God and Metaphor," *Pastoral Psychology* 53/3 (2005): 207–238.

Witzel, Michael. "How to Enter the Vedic Mind? Strategies in Translating a Brahmana Text," in Enrica Garzilli, ed., *Translating, Translations, Translators: From India to the West*, pp. 163–176. Harvard Oriental Series, Opera Minora 1. Cambridge, MA: Department of Sanskrit and Indian Studies, Harvard University, 1996.

—."Meaningful Ritual: Vedic, Medieval, and Contemporary Concepts in the Nepalese Agnihotra Ritual," in Albert W. Van den Hoek, Dirk H. A. Kolff, and M. S. Oort, eds., *Ritual, State, and History in South Asia: Essays in Honour of J. C. Heesterman*, pp. 774–825. Leiden: E. J. Brill, 1992.

—. "On Magical Thought in the Veda," inaugural lecture. Leiden: Universitaire Pers, 1979. Accessed online: http://www.people.fas.harvard.edu/~witzel/Magical_Thought.pdf.

Eroticism in Hindu Texts and Modern Hindus

P. Pratap Kumar
Emeritus Professor,
University of KwaZulu Natal, South Africa

Introduction

In a recent online discussion of religion in South Asia list one scholar asked to find a verse that he came across in his research on the Mahābhārata. Here is how he made the request:

> I am hoping someone can tell me the origin of this (rather vulgar, sorry) verse cited by Nilakantha in his commentary on MBh 3:116:8: *sundaraṃ puruṣaṃ dṛṣṭvā bhrātaram pitaraṃ sutam / yonir dravati nārīṇāṃ satyaṃ satyaṃ janārdana //.*

I was particularly interested in the apologetic manner in which he qualified his request. It represented a typically English sense of "public decency"—in public one does not use language that sounds offensive to the listeners. When Lord Macaulay introduced English education in India, his desire was to introduce Indians to English customs and habits so that they would become "civilized." Whether or not English education "civilized" Indians, there is certainly evidence to suggest that Indian moral sensibilities have certainly been affected by the long presence of the English in India. Whether or not English education is the direct cause of the Indian reluctance to speak of matters of a sexual nature in public, contemporary Indian society certainly reflects an ambivalent and mixed bag of social conventions in this regard. On the one hand, Indian audiences can enjoy an erotic dance display on stage in traditional dance forms, and nowadays on the celluloid screens of Bollywood. On the other hand, no one in contemporary Indian society behaves in an openly sexual manner or speaks about sexual matters in open discussion, especially within traditional circles.

While this is generally the case, a host of Hindu texts are replete with erotic discussions and these texts are often considered religious and hence sacred. A lay Hindu is generally oblivious to these references in

Hindu texts, primarily due to ignorance about the texts, and pandits generally avoid commenting extensively on them. For instance, both Śaṅkara and Rāmānuja make no comment on the reference of an explicit discussion about sexual intercourse between a man and woman in the *Brihadāraṇyaka Upaniṣad* (6.4.1 ff). This seeming avoidance and reluctance to comment on such matters might reflect the orthodox traditional mindset and might have resulted in concealing them from lay readers or listeners, particularly in the context of religious devotion. Such avoidance of erotic texts found in sacred books is not peculiar to Hinduism. Relative reluctance to read or talk about the Song of Solomon in the Bible also speaks directly to the commonly held view that pious religious folk tend to avoid such erotic texts.

But once the very same religious texts became available to a larger academic public that may or may not be Hindu, let alone orthodox, it became inevitable for these matters to be brought out into public discourse. This inevitably resulted in a surprised and shocked response from the practicing Hindu lay public, particularly from the educated middle class, on realizing that their religious texts contained such erotic discussions. So, the question is: how should Hindu intellectuals as well as the lay public make sense of these so-called concealed matters of eroticism? The general lay response has been denial of the presence of such matters in their religious texts, as evidenced in the saga of the student protest around an essay by Professor A. K. Ramanujan that was made a core essay for the B.A. Honours degree program in the History Department of Delhi University.[1] The denial is further amplified by anger and frustration and casting blame on "foreign" and "Western" attempts to "distort" Hindu culture. In an academic discussion, avoidance of or reluctance to discuss matters that may cause some participants discomfort is not really an option, as this would mean that scholarly criticality and rigor are compromised and academic freedom curtailed. Therefore, let me first outline some evidence of eroticism within Hindu sacred texts. I shall be selective, as the idea is to mainly offer some examples of what there is rather than being exhaustive on the matter concerned.

Eroticism in Hindu Texts

In Hindu texts, most of the allusions to sexual metaphors and encounters seem to occur in the context of the creation of the universe or the creative powers of the gods or progeny for humans. It is not uncommon for Hindu texts to depict gods in a most ambivalent manner. In the ancient texts, such depictions carried metaphors of sexual intercourse. In the *Ṛgveda, inter alia,* there is a reference to the sky god (Dyaus) having sexual intercourse with his daughter, the dawn goddess (Uṣas) (ṚV X.lxi.4–7).[2] This topic is elaborated in the *Aitareya Brāhmaṇa* (3:33): Prajāpati becomes a deer and chases his daughter, who has changed to an antelope; he has sexual intercourse with her, which of course angered the gods, who then placed a curse on him; later he was punished by Rudra, who was born out of him (Prajāpati). As A. Berriedale Keith points out, this Prajāpati in later Upaniṣadic texts becomes transformed into Brahman in the neuter gender:

> Prajāpati might, it is clear, have become a much greater figure had it not been for the fact that the philosophic spirit which conceived him soon went beyond the original idea and transformed the male, as too personal for the expression of the absolute, into the neuter Brahman Svayaṃbhu ("Self-Existent Prayer").[3]

Whether this transformation of Prajāpati into Brahman has anything to do with overcoming the sexual connotations associated with him is not clear.[4] As Jan Gonda points out, however, Prajāpati does become the "originator" of expiation (*prāyaścitta*) rituals in the *Grihya Sūtra* literature.[5] It is also not surprising that Prajāpati becomes integral to the wedding rituals performed according to the *Grihya Sūtras*. Here he is propitiated to ensure that the couple will have offspring.[6] Not surprisingly, in the Upaniṣadic texts there are explicit details of sexual matters, again in relation to offspring. The *Brihadāraṇyaka Upaniṣad* (BU) contains details of a ritualized procedure for how a woman must submit to her male partner for sexual intercourse even without her consent in order to obtain progeny (BU 6.4.1 ff). The text begins with the *Ṛgveda* allusion and speaks first about Prajāpati creating a woman and having intercourse with her, as he needed a base for his semen. Here the symbolism is elaborated—the vulva of the woman becomes "the sacrificial ground; her pubic hair is the sacred grass; her labia majora are the *soma* press; her labia minora are the fire blazing at the center" (BU 6.4.3). From this, a ritual doctrine is developed:

> A man who engages in sexual intercourse *with this knowledge* obtains as great a world as a man who performs a *soma* sacrifice, and he appropriates to himself the merits of the women[7] with whom he has sex. The women, on the other hand, appropriate to themselves the merits of a man who engages in sexual intercourse with them *without this knowledge.* (BU 6.4.3; emphasis added)

What follows from here includes detailed instructions for a man who wants to have sex with a woman whether or not she wishes to. The procedures explained in a ritualized manner are clear for when the man wants to have sex with a woman who accepts willingly, or when she refuses when he wants to impregnate her (BU 6.4.6–12).[8] In modern times this would be defined as rape, but not so in the language of the ancient texts. It is important to note that all of the erotic references in these early texts are significantly in the context of the rituals associated with progeny, and no other sense seems possible.

In the epic literature, both the epics contain copious details of sexual encounters between humans and gods, and among humans. The genealogy of the Kuru dynasty in the *Mahābhārata* begins with the amorous dalliance of Viśvāmitra[9] and Menaka (the celestial being), who was sent by Indra to distract the sage from his ascetic practice.[10] In contemporary society, a woman seeking to have a child by the husband of another woman might be construed as an adulterer. But Sarmiṣṭha, the maid of Devayāni, seeks to have a child by Devayāni's husband, Yayāti. The willing Yayāti expresses fear that he might have to lie about the liaison to his wife. Sarmiṣṭha gives a brief lesson in ethics: it is acceptable to lie in the following five cases: in joking, in regard to women, marriage, threat to life, and when faced with losing all of one's possessions (Mbh 1.77.16–17). Above all, she pleads with him to help her preserve her virtue by giving her a child (Mbh 1.77.20–21). But here is the shocker to the modern mind—eventually Sarmiṣṭha has three children by Yayāti, and once the secret comes out and she is confronted by Devayāni, Sarmiṣṭha responds, "A friend's husband is, according to usage, one's own husband as well" (Mbh 1.77.20). After several long genealogical narratives, the *Mahābhārata* story comes to the main narrative, which opens with a sex scene: King Mahābhiṣa in the company of the gods is carried away by the nakedness of the river goddess (Gaṅgā), which was caused by the wind god (Vāyu). Consequently, both the king and the river goddess are cursed to become humans (Mbh 1.91).

The intrinsic relationship between sexual dalliance and being cursed plays out in the *Mahābhārata* in many places, and emanating from these are the ethics of expediency, as illustrated in the example cited above from MBH 1.77.16. Again, consistent with the older textual tradition, the allusions to erotic exploits are primarily in the context of progeny. An interesting instance in this regard is the story of Pāṇḍu[11] having children by other men (celestial beings) who have intercourse with his wife. His first wife, Kunti, initially refuses to concede to Pāṇḍu's request, insisting that she would only be loyal to him. But Pāṇḍu explains that in the old custom women could have any number of men and the practice of women settling with one man is attributed to Śvetaketu, son of Uddālaka. When another sage, Vaśiṣṭa,[12] comes to take away Uddālaka's wife, his son Śvetaketu tries to stop his mother from being taken away by a stranger, but Uddālaka restrains him. Śvetaketu, unhappy about the situation, declares that from then on all women should have only one man for a husband and likewise, men should also be loyal to their wives (note the plural!). This is known ever since as the law of Śvetaketu (Mbh 1.113.17–20).

There is generally a tendency in the *Rāmāyaṇa* to depict most of its characters as virtuous and ethical. As mentioned in note 8, Vaśiṣṭa of the *Mahābhārata* is a wife-stealer, yet in the *Rāmāyaṇa* he is the most virtuous sage. Kṛṣṇa in the *Mahābhārata* is portrayed most erotically, yet he is often seen to flout ethics in the interest of securing the victory of the Pāṇḍava brothers, while Rāma in the *Rāmāyaṇa* is a righteous and well-behaved prince. There is an extraordinary emphasis of asceticism in the *Rāmāyaṇa* text; for instance, note the story of Sāgara and his descendants, who one after the other practice asceticism and go to the world of Indra. This eventually culminates in a tradition of royal asceticism in which Bhagīratha is depicted as royal ascetic who brings Gaṅgā down to the earth (Rām 1.38–44; 1.44.17).

Even after clearly emphasizing the ascetic tradition strongly, the *Rāmāyaṇa* also dwells at some length on the sexual encounters between Viśvāmitra and Menaka, who was sent by the gods to distract him. Later it also refers to Indra's failed attempt in sending the celestial Raṃbha to undo the ascetic power of Viśvāmitra (Rām 1.63.20, 1.64.1). In another instance, Indra, king of the gods, takes on the form of the sage Gautama and copulates with Gautama's wife, Ahalya. It is interesting to note that although Ahalya realizes that it is Indra, the king of the gods in disguise, she falls for his attraction and willingly agrees to his sexual advances. What is also important to note is that the poet does not hesitate to use highly sensual language appropriate for the scene, e.g., Indra addresses the hermit's wife as a "well-formed one" (*susamāhite*) and says, "O, the one with well-formed hips, I am very satisfied" (*suśroni parituṣṭo'smi*) (Rām 1.48.18–22)

Furthermore, the *Rāmāyaṇa* is not averse to the practice of offering meat and liquor—aspects that are often integral to erotic discussions—as is befitting an important guest. During Bharata's journey in search of Rāma, in order to persuade him to return to Ayodhya from his exile, Guha, a local tribal king, offers fish, meat, and honey in his honor (Rām

2.84.10); later, when Bharata reaches the hermitage of Bharadvāja, the hermit offers him the choicest of liquors: "Let *maireyam* (liquor extracted from a palm tree) and other refined liquor flow (*suniṣṭitām surām*)" (Rām 2.91.15). Nothing that is generally associated with so-called extraneous behavior seems to be excluded from Hindu texts.

Not only written texts but also a host of other visually represented "texts" also mediate erotic images of Hindu gods and goddesses. The reliefs on the exteriors of the Khajurāho temples illustrate the most elaborate *Kāmasūtra* texts created by the Candela dynasties. The imposing fortresses built by their fellow Rajputs, the Bundelas, are situated not far from the Khajurāho temples: the two complexes sit next to each other, one symbolizing the power of eroticism and sensuality, the other the power of the warriors. In both places it is Śiva who is depicted—Śiva as the erotic god and Śiva as the great ascetic warrior. One is an inversion of the other, yet they are shown together without contradiction.[13] In fact, the Bundelas, from their impenetrable fortresses, protected the erotic temples at the Khajurāho site from invading Afghan warriors. The clue to the presence of such inversions may be in what Stella Kramrisch points to:

> [T]heir images are stationed on the temple walls for the purpose of attracting the eye, the senses, and the mind of the devotee, so that he concentrates on them and becomes oblivious of all distraction. By contemplating their enthralling presence he is led into the temple.[14]

Kramrisch generally subscribes to the idea that there is an inner and meta-meaning to the outer text or sculpture: "The configurations of Indian sculpture are based on what the eye sees, but proceed beyond empirical truth to express the metaphysical."[15] But, in the few lines quoted above, she hones in on an interesting idea from the viewpoint of the notion of inversion: "oblivious of all distraction," "he is led into the temple." In other words, what seems to be distracting by itself is now the focal point for further investigation. No longer averse to spirituality as such, it is what I would refer to as "inverted forms of esoteric spirituality," to borrow Ralph Slotten's phrase.[16]

Making Sense of Eroticism in Hindu Texts

The modern Hindu disquiet regarding the existence of eroticism in Hindu texts has been illustrated in a number of recent incidents related to banning academic works by Western scholars, e.g., Paul Courtright's 1989 book on Gaṇeśa and Jeffrey Kripal's 1998 book on Kālī. There have been other incidents as well, such as James Laine's 2003 book on Śivaji. More recently, Wendi Doniger's *Hindus: An Alternative History* (2009) is another example of a book that became the object of Hindu disquiet regarding eroticism and the kind of explanations proffered by some Western scholars.[17]

In general, there is a sense that regional versions of some of the Hindu texts, such as the epics and mythological texts, have been rendered in such a way that allusions to incidents or events, particularly erotic references that were received awkwardly in later times, were either deleted or modified. In this regard, not only allusions to eroticism in texts but also other references to seemingly unethical behavior have been suppressed, especially in the regional traditions. G. P. Deshpande reminds us of one such example in the wake of the rightwing Hindu nationalists' attack on the Muslim mosque in Ayodhya in 1992:

> I am certain that these pop-Hindus do not know, for example, that when Tulsidas wrote the *Rāmāyaṇa,* he removed the story of Shambuka altogether. Shambuka was a Shudra who had undertaken to do *tapasya*! The shastras did not permit it. Hence Ram killed him. Tulsidas found this quite uncomfortable. He could not justify Ram there and therefore he removed the story. The story appears in the original *Rāmāyaṇa* by Valmiki. Tulsidas was apologetic about it and expunged it from his text.[18]

Nevertheless, in the Sanskritic tradition as well as in various regional traditions, the authors of Hindu texts used sexual metaphors consciously to construct a worldview in which the mundane and the spiritual coexisted comfortably side by side, especially in the context of rituals related to progeny. They do not seem to have seen any incongruity in using such language and metaphors, which to a modern reader may seem inappropriate. There is a plethora of institutions and organizations that offer teachings of Hinduism today that quite consciously obfuscate such references in the Hindu religious texts, as noted above. None of the texts I referred to above are *Kāmasūtra*-type texts that could easily be associated with such erotic language and metaphor; they are the mainstream religious texts that are often read and discoursed on in religious contexts with utmost devotion.

There is sufficient evidence within the Hindu tradition for the transformation of outward ritual practices that involved sexual activity and the consumption of meat and wine. In the early history of Hinduism, the advent of both Buddhism and Jainism may have influenced such changes. In later periods, Brāhmanism became increasingly ritualistically orthodox by eliminating, suppressing, or sublimating what seemed unacceptable or was intended for private discourse only, e.g., the Smārta Brāhmans transforming the left-handed *Kaula Tantra* into a sublimated Śrī Vidya practice, which might have been effected by or around the time of the Advaita philosopher Śaṅkara. Even so, almost all esoteric traditions required strict ritual initiation and a dedicated practice under the supervision of a teacher. Western scholarship has long pointed out the role of the works of Karl Marx, Sigmund Freud, Friedrich Nietzsche, Claude Lévi-Strauss, and Noam Chomsky in bringing to the fore the "phenomenon of concealment" that brings with it a profound sense of secrecy or privacy.[19] Within the Indian tradition, the extent to which esoteric sexual practices among Baul poets have been sublimated by the later Bengali literary tradition, dominated by intellectuals such as Rabindranath Tagore, has been pointed out by Charles H. Capwell.[20]

Such sublimation of incongruent (or uncomfortable for certain sensibilities) aspects in Hindu texts is not necessarily a modern phenomenon. We can identify at least two ways in which erotic aspects have been reinterpreted in ways that would not seem incongruent to the lay or orthodox Hindu: devotionalism and tantrism. Ascribing spiritual meanings to erotic references within Hindu texts has been one of the most fruitful ways Hindus can find them to be coherent within their traditions. As such, we can find a whole genre of *bhakti* literature within Śaivism and particularly in Vaiṣṇavism that interprets erotic aspects in terms of spiritual meanings. The *Bhāgavata Purāṇa* (aka *Śrīmad Bhāgavatam*) is a good illustration of how Kṛṣṇa's erotic relationships with a host of his female companions, especially with Rādhā, are seen as an intensely devotional relationship between God and his devotee. Devotionalism, with its spiritual emphasis, has fundamentally influenced the modern Hindu view of such erotic references to the extent that today, even when such erotic images are discussed, the modern Hindu seems not to be embarrassed in the midst of other cultures. It is therefore easy to understand why devotees visiting temples and witnessing erotic images on the temple walls or listening to devotional songs in vernaculars that contain erotic descriptions of gods and goddesses are unashamed by them and seem least embarrassed.

One of the most famous songs in praise of Lord Veṅkateśvara that is performed regularly at the Śrī Veṅkateśvara temple in Tirupati is clearly a good example of how a strongly devotional attitude on the part of devotees overtakes any erotic meanings of the songs they hear. One of the verses reads: "Don't look at Śrīdevī naughtily; don't make Alamēlumaṅga jealous; make both dear wives sit on either side, arousing, caressing, and delighting."[21] Eroticism such as this built into devotional poetry is common and does not seem to cause any discomfort among devotees. With all its eroticism in the Bhāgavata Purāṇa, Kṛṣṇa devotees read the text with no uneasiness. In Hinduism, if eroticism is made integral to devotionalism/spirituality, asceticism is seen as its counterbalance. If Kṛṣṇa devotionalism is seen as the paragon of *viraha bhakti*,[22] both Śiva and his cognate deity Skandha/Subrahmaṇya (Murukaṉ in Tamil tradition) offer ascetic options to Hindu devotees. Within the Viṣṇu incarnation complex, both Kṛṣṇa and Rāma as two different images—one as the erotic and the other more inclined toward the ascetic—sit side by side with no contradiction. Rāma is depicted as an illustration of the ascetic tendency in Hindu practice, although in the North Indian context Rāma devotionalism is as intense as Kṛṣṇa devotionalism is in the south and around the western and eastern coastal regions of India. As such, devotionalism, both in the form of the erotic as well as the ascetic mode, have been a useful way to make sense of and accommodate seemingly incongruent aspects of Hinduism.

Modern Hindus thus have come to receive the gradually evolved sublimated traditions, and it is perhaps not fair to suggest that there has been any conscious attempt on the part of Hindus to obfuscate or suppress erotic texts within Hinduism. What scholars who engage in reading texts using linguistic and other modern scientific methods perhaps should take into account is that the average Hindu is not exposed to or is not privileged to read the innumerable texts that may have shaped his or her worldview. They are instead exposed to various devotional discourses within which some of the texts are embedded.

Here lies perhaps one of the most crucial differences between how a born Hindu encounters his or her religious tradition and how an outside scholar, whether of Indian or Western background, is exposed to Hinduism. Born Hindus are generally introduced to their religion (as is common in the case of virtually all religious communities) through family traditions and localized cultural expressions. In contrast, the outside scholar invariably begins by learning the languages of the Hindu traditions and, in most cases, he or she begins with Sanskrit, which is considered the primary medium to enter Hindu texts. They then begin to read some basic texts such as the *Bhagavadgītā* and the *Rāmāyaṇa*. A significant number of Western scholars who teach Hinduism mostly at the undergraduate level remain at this basic level of entrance into the Hindu worldview, while a few specialists undertake more detailed reading of advanced texts. Again, even there the specialists tend to read the texts only of their specific areas, e.g., those who specialize in Vedic texts rarely read other, later compositions, tantra specialists read mostly tantric texts, and so on. Naturally, a scholar's view of Hinduism is shaped by what they read, and scholar-specialists may also tend to think that born Hindus do not know as much as they do, which in a way is true—at least in terms of in-depth scholarly study. But from the point of view of a practicing Hindu who is born into his or her tradition, he or she does not indeed need to know the various texts, as they sufficiently rely on what has been passed on to them by their families and the communities among whom they practice their tradition. Thus, there exists a tension between how a born Hindu comes to his or her tradition and how scholars come to understand Hinduism. Neither can be faulted for their entrée into and subsequent understanding of Hinduism. It is interesting to note that both groups rely on their respective sets of conventions and traditions—scholars on scholarly conventions and native practitioners on the oral and informal knowledge of their traditions. This tension between the two—the academic community and the native Hindu communities—is important to recognize in order to examine the issue of whether or not a conscious or unconscious obfuscation of some aspects of Hinduism took place.

The second form of making sense of erotic and other seemingly incongruent aspects of Hinduism are the tantric-oriented forms that internalize the meanings of ritual and privatize their performance. Because such "esoteric" rituals are accessed mainly only by initiated devotees and the general public is not permitted to read about or witness them, general knowledge of tantrism is certainly limited to publicly available sources. Although today many tantric texts have been translated and are available in the public domain, the general public is less aware of them, largely because their orientation to Hindu practice revolves around temples and other neo-Hindu organizations that distribute certain types of theistic Hinduism to which the general public can relate.

The issue of obfuscation of texts that detail aspects considered uncomfortable by contemporary Hindus is often attributed to Hindu nationalist organizations, which responded to what they perceived as the incursion of Western or nonnative Indian value systems, specifically Christianity and Islam. Some scholars have pointed out that Hindu nationalism is in fact an historical byproduct of colonialism, specifically eighteenth- and nineteenth-century European Romantic and Enlightenment ideas.[23] Modern Hinduism is also attributed to influences from

Western Orientalists and Christian missionaries. However, some scholars have argued against the attribution of influence solely from Western Orientalists and Christian missionaries by discussing the roles played by Indian intellectuals themselves.[24]

Although Indian texts such as the *Upaniṣads*, the epics, and the mythological texts have certain pedagogical significance in offering spiritual and ethical guidance to Hindus, it would be erroneous to see their role primarily from that point of view. The Indian texts are also performative, especially in the context of ritual, and therefore derive their significance as texts of ritual procedures. But they can also be read as texts that offer poetic imagination and entertainment within a religious context. In recent years, particularly since the time of such scholars as Radhakrishṇan[25] there has been a proliferation of attempts to defend the ethical component of Hindu texts, against the outside critique that ethics is not central to the Hindu tradition.[26] There is nothing problematic about looking for ethical imperatives in Hindu texts, but inadvertently such attempts have rationalized Hindu texts to the extent that it has culminated in the popular mind that the sole purpose of these texts is to offer moral lessons.

This trend of rationalizing Hindu texts through moral ideas perhaps could be attributed to the emergence of neo-Vedānta–based Hindu discourse. Against the charge levied by some inside scholars (e.g., Agehananda Bharati and others) that neo-Hinduism produced "inauthentic" Hinduism, Brian Hatcher offers a history of neo-Vedānta that profusely uses ideas from East and West eclectically.[27] Hatcher's work makes abundantly clear the extent to which neo-Vedānta has played a role in constructing a discourse on Hinduism through appropriating skillfully, in order to make something that has been denounced from Christian and Islamic influences a more palatable Hindu view, and hence suitable for public consumption. In the process of this rationalization based on an eclectic approach, what is evident, as Hatcher puts it, are "apparent betrayals of meaning and errors of memory occasioned by the eclectic's selective habits of borrowing."[28] Inadvertently, however, this new discourse on Hinduism has become the handmaid of Hindutva ideology.

There seems to be something natural about how Hinduism places two completely extreme elements next to each other. The poets of the Hindu texts from the Vedas to the epics and even to the present time effortlessly move from highly erotic narratives to very devout and morally uplifting statements. In other words, for them the erotic narratives are not necessarily repugnant (or titillating) as they might be for a modern person with Victorian moral proclivities. If this were not the case, for instance, the entire *Mahābhārata* epic narrative would not have been possible. By emphasizing the moral and ethical lessons of the *Gītā* in particular, or the *Mahābhārata* in general, we might lose the many diverse motifs in the epic narratives and the many social and cultural roles the narratives may have played. The proliferation of the ethical treatment of the many Hindu texts and the tendency to draw broad ethical comparisons with works of the Western intellectual traditions[29] inadvertently ignores the natural tendencies of Indian intellectuals and poets to weave together seemingly extraneous elements into a coherent whole.

In the language of ritual, Brahmanical authors do not seem to think in moral terms. For instance, as mentioned earlier in *Aitareya Brāhmaṇa* 3:33, when Prajāpati engages in what has been termed incest, the text actually uses the term *akritam,* meaning that which is not to be done, i.e., taboo. The language is very ritualized and not moralistic.[30] The *Aitareya Brāhmaṇa* is preoccupied more with the ritual procedures emanating from the Prajāpati episode, which is only alluded to in the *Ṛgveda* but is substantially elaborated in the *Aitareya Brāhmaṇa* for ritual purposes.

Conclusion

Simply because people in modern times are embarrassed by the presence of erotic passages within devotional texts does not and need not mean that the original authors were similarly embarrassed or viewed such content as untoward in any way. We modern Hindus seem to find such erotic references shameful and embarrassing. Yet the artistic profundity present in these texts need not be sacrificed at the altar of a supposed "sacred ethics" that may well be influenced by nonindigenous values. To put it another way, think of the artists who sculpted the beautiful images on the pillars of the Khajurāho temples. These skilled artists went to great lengths to carve the images of the many nude figures of men and women with great attention to detail. Surely if they were embarrassed by or ashamed of such subject matter, they could not have produced such excellent, expressive work. Embarrassment or a feeling of shame is only in our viewing of it today. It is unnecessary to postulate moral implications when there might be none. In any case, at the level of ritual, devotees are generally oblivious to the erotic symbols and expressions and conduct the rituals almost mechanically. This does not mean they are unaware of the mythic narratives, especially those that circulate in the sthalapurāṇas. In other words, both ritual and legend or myth are equally potent and significant statements, and one does not necessarily need both for meaning to be obtained, although it is helpful if there is a correlation between the two.

While from a practitioner's point of view it is understandable to engage in emotional, theological, and devotional treatment of texts, such treatment need not see academic and intellectual analyses of texts as in any way prejudicial to their religious and devotional engagement. Excessive theologizing and ethicizing of the texts from a narrow perspective can impede intellectual honesty and integrity in dealing with a variety of possible motifs within them. There must be room in society for doubting theology and its metaphysics, an essentially hermeneutical tool known as "suspicion," or what Pierre Bourdieu calls "radical doubt."[31] After all, religion is not only about otherworldly matters, it is also, as Bourdieu suggests, a social field—regardless of believers' claims that religious ideas are derived from a higher source. The domination, intimidation, and violence often associated with religion, as seen in the case of the Delhi University incident, is demonstrable and socially traceable. I therefore share in Bourdieu's view that religion, in this case Hinduism, can be and is assailable, and need not be protected under the guise of religious sentiment that can in fact foster religious intolerance.

Let me conclude by echoing the sentiment Bourdieu phrases so well, quoted by Terry Rey: "Nothing in the social world is unassailable in this regard—not art, not education, not sociology, and certainly not religion."[32] And I add the following from the *Mahābhārata,* in the words of Śakuntala, addressing her husband who had forgotten that she was his wife:

> A hundred horse sacrifices had once been weighed against Truth, and Truth was found heavier than a hundred horse sacrifices. O king, Truth, I ween, may be equal to the study of the entire Vedas and ablutions in all holy places. There is no virtue equal to Truth: there is nothing superior to Truth. O king, Truth is God himself; Truth is the highest vow.[33]

Notes

1 In 2004 the Department of History at Delhi University included as a compulsory reading in its undergraduate degree program an essay by Prof. A. K. Ramanujan, "Three Hundred Ramayanas: Five Examples and Three Thoughts on Translation." According to some commentators, the arrangement was for a period of four years, i.e., up to the 2008 academic year. In 2008, Delhi University's Council decided to continue it. But in October 2011 the Council decided to remove Ramanujan's essay from the reading list, allegedly due to pressure from rightwing Hindu protestors on campus. However, according to some members of the university, the decision to act

was precipitated by a court action brought by rightwing supporters and a court order to the Council to internally settle the matter and report back to the court in a matter of days. Some commentators countered the criticism leveled against the Council that it had introduced the item relating to the essay at the last minute, allegedly to push the issue in favor of dropping the essay from the curriculum, asserting that the Vice Chancellor's last-minute introduction of the item was not intentional but that he was forced to do so under pressure from the court to act quickly. Whatever the case, the ensuing debate on the saga went global through both mainstream media and social media.

2 It is interesting to note that ṚV 10:61 verses 4–9 were deleted from the electronic text of Ralph T. H. Griffith's translation, *The Hymns of the Rigveda* (Benares: E. J. Lazarus & Co., 1896, second ed.), 2 vols.; http://www.sacred-texts.com/hin/rigveda/index.htm, even though in the original Griffith translated the verses into Latin, not English!

3 For Prajāpati's identification with Brahmā, see *Aitareya Upaniṣad* 3:3. See A. Berriedale Keith, *Indian Mythology, The Mythology of All Races*, vol. 6 (Boston: Marshall Jones Company, 1917), chap. 3. www.rbedrosian.com/keithint.htm, accessed March, 30, 2015.

4 In the *Mahābhārata* version of the creation story, Prajāpati is identified with the creator god Brahmā (Mhb 1.1.28–30).

5 Jan Gonda, "Prajāpati and 'Prāyaścitta,'" *Journal of the Royal Asiatic Society of Great Britain and Ireland* 1 (1983): 49.

6 Jan Gonda, "The Popular Prajāpati," *History of Religions* 22/2 (November 1982): 131.

7 It is interesting to note the plural here: one man is allowed many wives, but a woman is allowed only one husband.

8 The *Mahābhārata*'s comment on this situation is that if a woman refuses to have children with her husband she becomes sinful (Mhb 1.113.19). The *Rāmāyaṇa* agrees with this tradition of Prativrata (1.1.91).

9 As a result, Menaka gives birth to a daughter, Sakuntala, and from her union with Dushanta the Bharata dynasty was established (Mhb 1.66–69). The story makes a point that Viśvāmitra was a *kṣatriya* and became a *brāhmaṇa*. Viśvāmitra's story is much more elaborate in the *Rāmāyaṇa* (Rām). According to the *Rāmāyaṇa,* after he was involved with Menaka, Viśvāmitra realizes that he was deceived by the gods and he goes off to the northern regions to perform further ascetic practices, after which Brahmā bestows upon him the status of a Brahma sage. Indra, fearing for his own status, then sends Raṃbha to distract Viśvāmitra (Rām 1.63.20, 1.64.1). Nevertheless, in the *Mahābhārata* Viśvāmitra becomes the progenitor of the Kuru dynasty by default.

The episode of Viśvāmitra producing an offspring with Menaka is absent in the *Rāmāyaṇa* story, nor is he depicted as having sexual union with Raṃbha when he finds out about Indra's deception (Rām 1.64.10–11). Implicitly, the *Mahābhārata* affirms the purity of the *kṣatriya* lineage of the Kurus. In the *Rāmāyaṇa* it is certainly clear from the way Vaśiṣṭa treats Viśvāmitra that he (Viśvāmitra) would still have been a *kṣatriya* (before becoming a *brāhmaṇa*) (Rām

1.52.6, where Viśvāmitra is referred to as *rājānam* Viśvāmitram; in verse 7 Vaśiṣṭa clearly addresses him as *rājan* when inquiring about his welfare).

In another narrative, the *Mahābhārata* also affirms that marriage between a *kṣatriya* and a *brāhmaṇa* is legitimate; e.g., the marriage of Yayāti (a *kṣatriya*) and Devayāni (daughter of a *brāhmaṇa*) (Mbh 1.77). In another story that appears earlier in the epic the very same celestial Menaka has another child, a daughter, by a Gandharava king, Viśvavasu. She was called Prāmadavara and was raised by the sage Sthūlakeśa; later she is married to Ruru (son of Prāmati), the great grandson of the sage Bhrigu (Mbh 1.8). The *Mahābhārata* is replete with stories of sexual union between humans and celestials, as though the two worlds have constantly coalesced.

10 The *Rāmāyaṇa* version of the encounter of Viśvāmitra and Menaka attributes it to the gods (*surānām karma*) in general and not particularly to Indra (Rām 1.63.11).

11 Pāṇḍu could not father children because of a curse placed on him by a sage who was having sexual intercourse with his wife in the form of an antelope, and was killed by Pāṇḍu's arrow. (The idea of taking the forms of deer/antelope as a medium to have sexual intercourse, either among the gods or among humans, seems to occur infrequently and does not involve modern ethical issues surrounding such images.) Note the underlying theme of Rudra's arrow piercing Prajāpati in the form of antelope, and Pāṇḍu's arrow piercing the brahman and his wife in the form of antelope. In both cases, the sexual act has not yet been completed. The seed is withheld. In the *Aitareya Brāhmaṇa* account, Prajāpati's seed (semen) is preserved by the gods to produce the other creatures. In the case of the epic narrative, the brahman's seed is withheld, which creates a consequence for Pāṇḍu being deprived of his seed entirely, thus requiring the gods to intervene later to offer their seed. The sage curses Pāṇḍu: because he interrupted their sexual intercourse and thereby prevented the creation of progeny, he, too, will face the same fate if he has intercourse with his wives (Mbh 1.109.50–30)

Compare this with the story of Śiva and Uma in the *Rāmāyaṇa,* as told by Viśvāmitra to Rāma. The gods, fearing that Śiva's prolonged intercourse with Uma will result in progeny that might fill the whole world and destroy it, request Śiva to hold his semen within himself. But Śiva has already reached the stage of ejaculation and needs to deposit the overflowing semen somewhere, so he spills it onto the earth, on the gods' recommendation. The place where the semen was deposited becomes a reed lake from which Skanda emerges (because he was suckled by the celestial Krittikas, Skanda is also known as Kārtikeya). In the meantime, Uma, upset about the interruption of her intercourse with Śiva, which deprives her of having a son, promptly places a curse on all the gods that they cannot have children with their wives. She also places a curse on the goddess of the earth that she will be wife to many and will not have happiness from her children (Rām 1.36.20–24).

12 It is difficult to establish whether the wife-stealing Vaśiṣṭa in this story is the same figure as in the *Rāmāyaṇa,* the family priest of King Dasaratha, hailed as the best of sages (*munisārdulam*) (Rām 2.3.5). It's as if there is a shortage of sages, as seemingly sages with the very same names appear again and again,

not only in the two epics but also in various other *Purāṇa* texts. The Vaśiṣṭa of the *Rāmāyaṇa* is portrayed as most virtuous. Viśvāmitra gives weapons to Rāma in the *Rāmāyaṇa* (Rām 1.27.2 ff) and to Karṇa in the *Mahābhārata*.

13 Gabriella Eichinger Ferro-Luzzi discusses the inversion of symbols, especially in the context of erotic depictions, in "The Female Lingam: Interchangeable Symbols and Paradoxical Associations of Hindu Gods and Goddesses (and Comments and Reply)," *Current Anthropology* 21/1 (February 1980): 45–68.

14 Stella Kramrisch, *Indian Sculpture in The Philadelphia Museum of Art* (Philadelphia: University of Pennsylvania, 1961), p. 19.

15 Kramrisch, *Indian Sculpture in The Philadelphia Museum of Art*, p. 24.

16 Ralph Slotten, "Exoteric and Esoteric Modes of Apprehension," *Sociological Analysis* 38/3 (Autumn 1977): 193.

17 Paul B. Courtright, *Ganesa: Lord of Obstacles, Lord of Beginnings* (Oxford: Oxford University Press, 1989); Jeffrey J. Kripal, *Kali Child: The Mystical and the Erotic in the Life and Teachings of Rāmakṛṣṇa* (Chicago: University of Chicago Press, 1998); James W. Laine, *Śivaji: Hindu King in Islamic India* (Oxford: Oxford University Press, 2003); Wendy Doniger, *The Hindus: An Alternative History* (New York: Penguin Press, 2009).

18 G. P. Deshpande, "Polity and Culture in the Wake of Ayodhya," *Economic and Political Weekly* 28/6 (February 6, 1993): 217.

19 Slotten, "Exoteric and Esoteric Modes of Apprehension," p. 186.

20 Charles H. Capwell, "The Esoteric Belief of the Bauls of Bengal," *The Journal of Asian Studies* 33/2 (February 1974): 255–264.

21 In Telugu: *śrīdevivaṅkaku cilipigācūḍaku; alamēlumaṅgaku alukarānīyaku; muddhu satuliddarini iruvaipulājerci; muripiñci lāliñci mucchaṭalatēlci // śeṣaśailāvāsa //.*

22 Friedhelm Hardy, *Viraha-Bhakti: The Early History of Kṛṣṇa Devotion in South India* (Oxford: Oxford University Press, 1983).

23 Chetan Bhatt, *Hindu Nationalism: Origins, Ideologies, and Modern Myths* (New York: Berg Publications, 2001).

24 Brian K. Pennington, *Was Hinduism Invented? Britons, Indians and Colonial Construction of Religion* (Oxford: Oxford University Press, 2005).

25 S. Radhakṛṣṇan, "Hindu Dharma," *International Journal of Ethics* 33/1 (1922): 1–22.

26 See, among a host of recent books discussing business ethics for modern times, Arti Dhand, "The Dharma of Ethics, the Ethics of Dharma: Quizzing the Ideals of Hinduism," *The Journal of Religious Ethics* 30/3 (Fall 2002): 347–372; Bina Gupta, "'Bhagavad Gītā' as Duty and Virtue Ethics: Some Reflections," *The Journal of Religious Ethics* 34/3 (September 2006): 373–395; Arvind Sharma, "The Puruṣārthas: An Axiological Exploration of Hinduism," *The Journal of Religious Ethics* 27/2 (Summer 1999): 223–256.

27 Brian A. Hatcher, *Eclecticism and Modern Hindu Discourse* (Oxford: Oxford University Press, 1999).

28 Hatcher, *Eclecticism and Modern Hindu Discourse*, p. 27.

[29] See, for example, Gupta, "'Bhagavad Gītā' as Duty and Virtue Ethics: Some Reflections."

[30] Martin I. Haug points out, in *Aitareya Brāhmaṇa of Rigveda* (Allahabad: Sudindra Nath Vasu, 1922), p. 148:

> [T]he mentioning of the word *papman* in connection with Prajāpati, was, no doubt, regarded by the author, as very inauspicious. Even the incestuous act committed by Prajāpati, he does not call *pāpa,* sin, or *doṣa,* fault, but only *akritam,* "what ought not to be done," which is the very milder term by which a crime can be mentioned.

[31] Pierre Bourdieu, "Genesis and Structure of the Religious Field," Jenny B. Burnside, Craig Calhoun, and Leah Florence, trans., *Comparative Social Research* 13 (1991): 1–44.

[32] Terry Rey, *Bourdieu on Religion: Imposing Faith and Legitimacy* (London: Equinox, 2007), p. 58.

[33] Mhb 1:69:22–25: *aśvamedha sahasraṃ ca satyaṃ ca tulayā dhṛtam aśvamedha sahasrād dhi satyam eva viśiṣyate.*

References

Bernstein, Richard. *The East, the West, and Sex: A History of Erotic Encounters.* New York: Random House, 2009.

Bhatt, Chetan. *Hindu Nationalism: Origins, Ideologies, and Modern Myths.* New York: Berg Publications, 2001.

Bourdieu, Pierre. "Genesis and Structure of the Religious Field," Jenny B. Burnside, Craig Calhoun, and Leah Florence, trans., *Comparative Social Research* 13 (1991): 1–44.

Capwell, Charles H. "The Esoteric Belief of the Bauls of Bengal," *The Journal of Asian Studies* 33/2 (February 1974): 255–264.

Courtright, Paul B. *Ganesa: Lord of Obstacles, Lord of Beginnings.* Oxford: Oxford University Press, 1989.

Deshpande, G. P. "Polity and Culture in the Wake of Ayodhya," *Economic and Political Weekly* 28/6 (February 6, 1993): 215–218.

Dhand, Arti. "The Dharma of Ethics, the Ethics of Dharma: Quizzing the Ideals of Hinduism," *The Journal of Religious Ethics* 30/3 (Fall 2002): 347–372.

Doniger, Wendy. *The Hindus: An Alternative History.* New York: Penguin Press, 2009.

Ferro-Luzzi, Gabriella Eichinger. "The Female Lingam: Interchangeable Symbols and Paradoxical Associations of Hindu Gods and Goddesses (and Comments and Reply)," *Current Anthropology* 21/1 (February 1980): 45–68.

Freilich, Morris. "Myth, Method, and Madness," *Current Anthropology* 16 (1975): 207–226.

Ganguli, Kisari Mohan, trans. *The Mahabharata of Krishna-Dwaipayana Vyasa Translated into English Prose.* Calcutta: Pratap Chandra Roy, 1883–1896. Digitized by sacred-texts.com, 2003. Redaction from Distributed Proofing, Juliet Sutherland, Project Manager.

Gonda, Jan. "Prajāpati and 'Prāyaścitta,'" *Journal of the Royal Asiatic Society of Great Britain and Ireland* 1 (1983): 32–54.

—. "The Popular Prajāpati," *History of Religions* 22/2 (November 1982): 129–149.

Griffith, Ralph T. H., trans. *The Hymns of the Rigveda*, 2 vols. Benares: E. J. Lazarus & Co., 1896, second ed. http://www.sacred-texts.com/hin/rigveda/index.htm, accessed October, 14, 2014.

Gupta, Bina. "'Bhagavad Gītā' as Duty and Virtue Ethics: Some Reflections," *The Journal of Religious Ethics* 34/3 (September 2006): 373–395.

Hardy, Friedhelm. *Viraha-Bhakti: The Early History of Kṛṣṇa Devotion in South India*. Oxford: Oxford University Press, 1983.

Hatcher, Brian A. *Eclecticism and Modern Hindu Discourse.* Oxford: Oxford University Press, 1999.

Haug, Martin I., ed. *Aitareya Brāhmaṇa of Rigveda.* Allahabad: Sudindra Nath Vasu, 1922.

Keith, A. Berriedale. *Indian Mythology, Mythologies of All Races*, vol. 6. Boston: Marshall Jones Company, 1917. Electronic text in HTML formatting by Robert Bedrosian, 2009; www. rbedrosian.com/keithint.htm, accessed March, 30 2015.

Kramrisch, Stella. *Indian Sculpture in The Philadelphia Museum of Art.* Philadelphia: University of Pennsylvania, 1961.

Kripal, Jeffrey J. *Kali Child: The Mystical and the Erotic in the Life and Teachings of Rāmakṛṣṇa.* Chicago: University of Chicago Press, 1998.

Laine, James W. *Śivaji: Hindu King in Islamic India.* Oxford: Oxford University Press, 2003.

Lele, Jayant. "Saffronisation of Shiv Sena: Political Economy of City, State and Nation," *Economic and Political Weekly* 30/25 (June 24, 1995): 1520–1528.

Lerner, Martin. "Some Unpublished Sculpture from Harshagiri," *The Bulletin of the Cleveland Museum of Art* 56/10 (December 1969): 354–364.

Madhavananda, Swami, trans. *The Brihadaranyaka Upanishad, with commentary by Śaṅkaracharya.* Almora, India: Advaita Ashrāma, 1950.

Nanda, Meera. "Breaking the Spell of Dharma: Case for Indian Enlightenment," *Economic and Political Weekly* 36/27 (July 7–13, 2001): 2551–2566.

Pennington, Brian K. *Was Hinduism Invented? Britons, Indians and Colonial Construction of Religion.* Oxford: Oxford University Press, 2005.

Radhakṛṣṇan, S. "Hindu Dharma," *International Journal of Ethics* 33/1 (1922): 1–22.

Rāmāyaṇa. http://sacred-texts.com/hin/rys/index.htm, accessed October 14, 2014.

Rey, Terry. *Bourdieu on Religion: Imposing Faith and Legitimacy.* London: Equinox, 2007.

Sharma, Arvind. "The Puruṣārthas: An Axiological Exploration of Hinduism," *The Journal of Religious Ethics* 27/2 (Summer 1999): 223–256.

Slotten, Ralph. "Exoteric and Esoteric Modes of Apprehension," *Sociological Analysis* 38/3 (Autumn 1977): 185–208.

Universal Knowledge: Swami Vivekananda on the Vedas

Jeffery D. Long
Elizabethtown College

> My teaching is my own interpretation of our ancient books, in the light which my Master shed upon them. I claim no supernatural authority. Whatever in my teaching may appeal to the highest intelligence and be accepted by thinking people, the adoption of that will be my reward.
>
> —Swami Vivekananda[1]

Swami Vivekananda's Approach to the Vedas

It is doubtful that any modern Hindu spiritual teacher has had greater influence on the self-understanding of contemporary Hindus than Swami Vivekananda. Although certainly not without his critics and detractors, even during his short lifetime, he has been credited with a major renaissance and reform of Hinduism, with being a major inspiration for the movement for Indian independence, and with opening the Hindu tradition to non-Indian practitioners. He is also seen as an important catalyst for the rise of Hindu nationalism, and is often cited by Prime Minister Narendra Modi as his personal hero and inspiration.

The recent celebration of the sesquicentennial of Swami Vivekananda's birth was the occasion for countless events, primarily in India but also globally.[2] It gave rise to numerous publications and to the creation of two academic chairs in his name, at the University of Chicago and the University of Southern California. It was also not without controversy, most notably when the Council for a Parliament of the World's Religions withdrew support from a major sesquicentennial event in Chicago, citing as its rationale the fact that this event was also sponsored by Hindu nationalist organizations with which it did not wish to be associated. This controversy points to the contested nature of Swami Vivekananda's legacy, and the tensions that exist between his proclamations of universal religious acceptance and pluralism and his status as an inspirational figure to the Hindu nationalist movement.

Taking into account Swami Vivekananda's prominence and influence, it should come as no surprise that his interpretations of the Vedas have had a more profound impact on the self-understanding of many contemporary Hindus than have the Vedas themselves. In this essay I do not seek to advance, much less prove, this thesis. I do, however, seek to show that many popular Hindu conceptions about the Vedas are echoed, and may indeed have their source, in the teachings of this important Hindu master.

The Vedas constitute a notoriously vast and complex literature. These ancient texts have been composed over the course of many centuries—indeed, over the course of a millennium, if one uses the term Veda to refer not only to the early *Saṃhitā* literature but also to the *Brāhmaṇa*s, *Āraṇyaka*s, and *Upaniṣad*s. The precise meaning and import of these texts were contested even many centuries ago. Attempts to interpret the Vedas have given rise to such diverse schools of thought as the ritualistic Pūrva Mīmāṃsā system, the nondual or Advaita Vedānta of Śaṅkara, and the numerous theistic and devotional systems, such as Viśiṣṭādvaita, Dvaita, Bhedābheda, and Acintya Bhedābheda (to name only a few). To read the Vedas is always to approach them through a particular interpretive lens, whether as a ritual specialist in the lineage of Jaimini, a seeker for *mokṣa* in the tradition of Śaṅkara, or as a modern academic Indologist with an eye on the reconstruction of ancient history and culture.

As the quotation cited at the start of this essay indicates, Swami Vivekananda saw the Vedas through the eyes of a spiritual seeker under the training of a master, in his case, Sri Ramakrishna Paramahansa. Ramakrishna was not a Vedic scholar in a conventional sense, neither in a traditionalist sense or a modern academic one. Vivekananda once said of him, "I am the disciple of a man who could not write his own name, and I am not worthy to undo his shoes."[3] Vivekananda clearly held Ramakrishna in the highest possible esteem as the central inspirational figure of his life, but the light that Vivekananda saw his Master as shedding upon the Vedas was not the light of the intellect but of a life lived in direct awareness of ultimate reality.

This theme of direct awareness and a direct experience of the nature of being is, in many ways, definitive of Swami Vivekananda's approach to the Vedas, as well as of modern Hinduism. This sense is further borne out by the remainder of this quote:

> I claim no supernatural authority. Whatever in my teaching may appeal to the highest intelligence and be accepted by thinking people, the adoption of that will be my reward.[4]

This is a thoroughly modern (or modernist) approach to truth: not through the presumed authority of a text—the Veda as *śabda pramāṇa*—but through reason reflecting on experience. It is the experience that is primary. The text illustrates and illuminates that direct experience.

To be sure, to call this approach modern is not to suggest that it is without ancient Indian precedent. Indeed, a portion of the *Bhagavadgītā* suggests a similar outlook:

> Some people please themselves by debating the Vedas. They recite the florid Vedic chants, but they have no insight, while ever saying that only the Vedas matter! In their hearts they are driven by desire and are eager for heaven. Their words promise rebirth as the fruit of their actions. Their talk is all about their elaborate rituals whose purpose is to gain pleasure and power. They are obsessed with pleasure and power! The words of the Vedas deprive them of good sense. They lack the insight that is based on firm resolve, and they do not gain insight even when engaged in intense concentration. . . . As useful as a water tank is when there is flooding in all directions, that is how useful the Vedas are for a Brahmin who has true insight.[5]

In the context of the *Gītā,* the emphasis is upon the priority of genuine, direct insight over what might be called "mere book-learning." Specifically, what is criticized is the aim of ritualistic interpreters of the Vedas, which is not liberation, *mokṣa* or *mukti,* from the cycle of rebirth, but rather a better rebirth in a heavenly realm (*svārga*), as well as the fulfillment of other, more this-worldly goals promised by the Vedas as the fruit of proper ritual conduct.

For one who has true insight, such finite goals have no appeal. Only insight (*vijñāna*) leads to liberation: the realization of infinite being, consciousness, and bliss (*sat-chit-ānanda*). One who has this insight no longer has any need of the Vedas. The Vedas may make one aware of the need for such insight but once the insight has arisen, one has arrived at one's destination. The road map to that destination is no longer needed.

Similarly, the Jain and Buddhist *śramaṇa* traditions aim at the cultivation of direct experience of the ultimate nature of reality, seeing authoritative teaching as a means to an end, rather than a value in and of itself, such as when the Buddha famously instructs his disciples to "be a light unto yourselves."

Modernity refers not so much to a period of history as to a mode of thought. This mode of thought, in contrast with what might be called a traditional or premodern mode, is the approach to knowledge not through an external authority, such as a text, institution, or teacher, but ultimately through the light of one's own reason, reflecting on experience. External authorities may well be necessary at an early stage of the journey, for example, when a beginning student of science must rely upon a textbook and a teacher to learn the basic principles that she will eventually employ on her own in the search for knowledge. Reliance on an external authority (text or teacher), however, is merely an aid to the eventual, direct experience that will give rise to true, as opposed to merely derivative, knowledge. This is Swami Vivekananda's approach to the Vedas.

The Eternal Veda and the Written Vedas

Swami Vivekananda's approach is well summarized in the following quotation from a lecture given at Harvard in 1896:

> The Vedas teach three things: the Ātman is first to be heard, then to be reasoned, and then to be meditated upon. When we first hear it, we must reason on it, so that we don't believe it ignorantly but knowingly; and after reasoning what it is, we must meditate upon it, and then realize it. And that is religion. Belief is no part of religion. We say that religion is a superconscious state.[6]

This is clearly a reference to the three stages of realization taught in the Advaita Vedānta tradition of Śaṅkarācārya: *śravaṇam* (hearing), *mananam* (thinking, reasoning), and *nidhidhyāsana* (contemplation). It is equally clearly an illustration of Vivekananda's emphasis on direct awareness over belief in an external authority. As in the teaching of Śaṅkara, the Vedas, for Vivekananda, are an essential source of knowledge. Without them, one would never initially hear about the Ātman—the divine Self within. They are, one could say, a catalyst for knowledge.

Simply hearing and believing what one has heard, however, is not sufficient for reaching the goal of liberation, for which the seeker desirous of liberation, the *mumukṣin,* strives. This is a sharp contrast, not so much with the approach of Śaṅkara, on whose thought Vivekananda elaborates, but with the religious traditions with which Vivekananda's American audience would have been familiar, in which belief in the exact words of scripture, despite not having been present to witness the events to which these words attest, is the *sine qua non* of the religious life. One must next apply reason to the words of scripture. Do they make sense? Are they coherent with one's reason and experience? Do they answer any questions or explain any phenomena that would otherwise remain mysterious? Once one is satisfied that the teachings do, indeed, meet these criteria, one moves to the stage of contemplation. This is not simply to engage with these teachings intellectually, which has already been done in the second stage. It is to move from *jñāna* to *vijnāna,* from knowledge to realization. It is only this final state that Vivekananda is content to grant the title religion. "Belief is no part of religion. We say that religion is a superconscious state."

Reflecting further upon this theme of a superconscious awareness, and connecting it with the Vedas, Vivekananda says in his work "Hinduism and Sri Ramakrishna":

> Rishihood, the power of supersensuous perception of the Vedas, is real religion. Until this develops in the life of an initiate, religion is a mere empty word to him or her, and it is to be understood that the initiate has not taken yet the first step in religion.[7]

Again, we see the theme of direct perception that goes beyond intellectual knowledge as the ultimately desired state, and as constitutive of religion in the truest and fullest sense of the word. One does not stop at believing what one has been taught. One reflects on it, ensuring that it has been fully understood, then moving on to direct perception of it.

Vivekananda's wording, "the power of supersensuous perception of the Vedas," is also interesting here. The Vedas are not simply the catalyst for direct realization; they also, in some sense, constitute its object:

> Truth is of two kinds: (1) that which is known through the five ordinary senses and by reasoning based thereon; (2) that which is known through the subtle, supersensuous power of yoga. Knowledge acquired by the first means is called science; and knowledge acquired by the second is called the Vedas.[8]

This is one of the more radical moves taken by Swami Vivekananda in his approach to the Vedas. He identifies them not simply with the set of texts that go by this name but with the sum total of spiritual truth:

> The whole body of supersensuous truths, having no beginning or end, and called by the name of the Vedas, is ever-existent. The Creator Himself is creating, preserving, and destroying the universe with the help of these truths. The person in whom this supersensuous power is manifested is called a Rishi, and the supersensuous truths which he realizes are called the Vedas.[9]

Interestingly, by identifying the Vedas with the sum total of supersensuous truths, Swami Vivekananda is able to affirm the traditional doctrine that the Vedas are *apauruṣeya,* not man-made. It is not at all clear how a set of texts, composed at a definite time and place, can be said to be eternal and not created by human beings, i.e., not the construct of the human mind. If, however, the term *veda* refers to eternal truth, of which any given text is but a manifestation, or to which it is a guide, it becomes easier to see the Vedas in this fashion.

This raises the question, however, of the relationship between Vedas as the sum total of eternal truths and the particular set of texts that go by this name. Swami Vivekananda sees the Veda as eternal truth reflected in the scriptures of many religions, and this perspective enables his ideas about religious pluralism and universal religion:

> The Hindus found their creed upon the ancient Vedas, a word derived from vid, "to know." These are a series of books which, to our minds, contain the essence of all religion. But we do not think they alone contain the truths. They teach us the immortality of the soul.[10]

Vivekananda does not see the books collectively called the Vedas to be the sole repository of eternal truth. Spiritual truth can be found anywhere, because the Ātman is everywhere:

> Who is independent? Not our body, for it depends upon external conditions; nor our mind, because the thoughts of which it is composed are caused. It is our soul that is independent. The Vedas say that the whole world is a mixture of independence and dependence, of freedom and slavery, but through it all shines the soul independent, immortal, pure, perfect, holy.[11]

Yet the Vedas do hold a special position for Swami Vivekananda, for he sees these texts as the preeminent manifestation of eternal truth:

> Although the supersensuous vision of truths is to be met with in some measure in our Puranas and Itihasas and in the religious scriptures of other races, still the fourfold scripture known among the Aryan race as the Vedas being the first, the most complete, and the most undistorted collection of spiritual truths, deserve to occupy the highest place among all scriptures, command the respect of all nations of the earth, and furnish the rationale of all their respective scriptures.[12]

This passage clarifies why Swami Vivekananda's approach to religious diversity, while in many respects pluralistic, can best be categorized as a form of what is often termed inclusivism; he does take a particular religious scripture to be the criterion by which the truths found in all traditions are to be assessed and evaluated. While the texts known as the Vedas are not to be strictly identified with the eternal Veda, which must be realized directly (and could conceivably serve as a corrective even to the written Vedas), they are proposed as the most reliable guide to the realization of eternal truth.

This inclusivist nature of Swami Vivekananda's approach to religious diversity, which places the Vedas at the top of a hierarchy of religious approaches, is made even more explicit in the following passage from a lecture given in Brooklyn in 1894:

> The idea of an objective God is not untrue—in fact, every idea of God, and hence every religion, is true, as each is but a different stage in the journey, the aim of which is the perfect conception of the Vedas. Hence, too, Hindus not only tolerate but accept every religion, praying in the mosques of the Muslims, worshiping before the fire of the Zoroastrians, and kneeling before the cross of the Christians, knowing that all the religions, from the lowest fetishism to the highest absolutism, mean so many attempts of the human soul to grasp and realize the infinite, each determined by the conditions of its birth and association, and each of them marking a stage of progress. We gather all these flowers and bind them with the twine of love, making a wonderful bouquet of worship.[13]

Again, even the Vedas, which contain "the most complete and the most undistorted collection of spiritual truths," which "deserve to occupy the highest place among all scriptures," and whose "perfect conception" of divinity is the aim of every religion, must be superseded by direct realization:

> The Vedas are the only scriptures that again and again declare that you must go beyond them. The Vedas say that they were written just for the child mind; and when you have grown, you must go beyond them.[14]

Some Additional Reflections

Swami Vivekananda did not wholeheartedly reject the widespread Hindu use of images in worship (*mūrtipūjā*) after the fashion of earlier Hindu reformers, such as the founding figures of the Brahmo Samāj, including Rammohan Roy and Devendranath Tagore, or the founder of the Ārya Samāj, Swami Dayananda Saraswati. He could hardly do so, given that his master, Sri Ramakrishna, had profound fondness for this practice and frequently used it to attain the heights of spiritual realization. At the same time, the imprint on his mind of the Brahmo Samāj, of which he was a practicing member at the time of his first meeting with Ramakrishna, and his leaning toward a nondualistic spirituality, led him to see the use of images as generally necessary only for those who were at an earlier stage of the journey to realization. Additionally, taking into account his American audience's largely Christian background, it should come as no surprise that in some contexts Vivekananda downplayed the use of images, mentioning the fact that the Vedas do not endorse this practice—a lesson he would have learned well from the Brahmo Samāj. Interestingly, he attributes the widespread use of images in contemporary Hinduism, indirectly, to the nontheistic teaching of Buddhism:

> The result of Buddha's constant inveighing against a personal God was the introduction of images into India. In the Vedas they knew them not, because they saw God everywhere, but the reaction against the loss of God as Creator and Friend was to make images, and Buddha became an image—so too with Jesus. The range of images is from wood and stone to Jesus and Buddha.[15]

Finally, Vivekananda sees the Vedas as texts capable of giving inspiration in times of self-doubt. In his role as a catalyst for the movement for Indian independence, and for instilling a sense of pride in the people of India (particularly among Hindus), he would cite the Vedas in a way akin to that of a motivational speaker using positive affirmations to inspire an audience:

> Wake up, stop not until the goal is reached," say the Vedas. Up, up, the long night is passing, the day is approaching, the wave has risen, nothing will be able to resist its tidal fury. The spirit, my boys, the spirit; the love, my children, the love; the faith, the belief; and fear not! The greatest sin is fear.[16]

Again, in the "motivational speaker" mode (which has made Vivekananda's works popular in business circles in contemporary India and numerous "management institutes" bearing his name have sprung up):

> The condemnation of all weakness—this is the idea in all our teachings which I like, either in philosophy, or in religion, or in work. If you read the Vedas, you will find this word always repeated—fearlessness—fear nothing. Fear is a sign of weakness. We must go about our duties without taking notice of the sneers and the ridicule of the world.[17]

Conclusion

For Swami Vivekananda, the term Veda refers primarily to the sum total of what he terms "supersensuous truths." This enables him to affirm the traditional claim that they are *apauruṣeya,* eternal and not man-made. These truths can be perceived directly through a yogic process of mental purification, culminating in the state of "rishihood," in which one fully comprehends the ultimate purpose of religion: not belief, nor even intellectual knowledge, but an experiential realization of the eternal truths of existence. These truths can be perceived by anyone, because their ultimate object (and subject), the Ātman, is within all beings. This is the basis for Vivekananda's famous religious pluralism, his affirmation, in the spirit of his master, Sri Ramakrishna, of the truth and salvific efficacy of all religions.

On closer inspection, this pluralism is revealed to be a form of inclusivity. While they cannot be identified in any exclusive or perfect way with eternal truth, the set of texts known as the Vedas are the most perfect expression of this truth of any existing scripture, including those of other religions, as well as the later texts of Hinduism, such as the *Purāṇa*s and *Itihāsa*s (the *Rāmāyaṇa* and *Mahābhārata*). The Vedic texts therefore constitute a criterion in against which other, less perfect scriptures may be measured.

And yet the Vedic texts themselves are not the absolute truth. They are the entry point, the doorway through which one enters the spiritual journey. They require further thought and reflection (*mananam*) in order for their claims to be accepted, and meditative contemplation (*nidhidhyāsana*) in order for their truths to be realized directly.

With his interpretation of the Vedas Swami Vivekananda establishes a template by which many contemporary Hindus understand the Hindu tradition as, in one sense, universal and comprehensive in scope, and even able to accommodate the truths of other traditions, and yet at the same time bearing a distinctive and predominant role for Hindu textual traditions in the larger economy of humanity's realization of its potential divinity. It also enables him to define Hinduism in contrast with other traditions that see faith in a scriptural revelation as the be-all and end-all of the spiritual life, rather than as a mere entry point. In this sense, one can see in Vivekananda's interpretation of the Vedas the roots of the tension between those who see him primarily as a disciple of universal acceptance and those who see him primarily as an Indian, and specifically Hindu, cultural hero. He is, in fact, both at the same time—teaching that there is truth in all religions, yet stopping short of a relativism that would leave no distinctive space for the Vedic tradition and its claims.

Notes

[1] Swami Vivekananda, *The Complete Works of Swami Vivekananda* (Kolkata: Advaita Ashrama, 1979), vol. 5, p. 186.

[2] The celebration of the sesquicentennial of Swami Vivekananda's birth actually spanned more than one calendar year, from late 2012 to mid-2014.

[3] Vivekananda, *The Complete Works,* vol. 9, p. 330.

[4] Vivekananda, *The Complete Works,* vol. 9, p. 330.

[5] George Thompson, trans., *The Bhagavad Gita: A New Translation* (New York: North Point Press, 2008), 2:42–44, 46.

[6] Vivekananda, *The Complete Works,* vol. 5, pp. 302–303.

[7] Vivekananda, *The Complete Works,* vol. 6, p. 181.

[8] Vivekananda, *The Complete Works,* vol. 6, p. 181.

[9] Vivekananda, *The Complete Works,* vol. 6, p. 181.

[10] Vivekananda, *The Complete Works,* vol. 1, p. 329.

[11] Vivekananda, *The Complete Works,* vol. 1, p. 330.

[12] Vivekananda, *The Complete Works,* vol. 6, p. 182.

[13] Vivekananda, *The Complete Works,* vol. 1, pp. 331–332.

[14] Vivekananda, *The Complete Works,* vol. 5, p. 311.

[15] Vivekananda, *The Complete Works,* vol. 7, pp. 21–22.

[16] Vivekananda, *The Complete Works,* vol. 5, p. 35.

[17] Vivekananda, *The Complete Works,* vol. 1, p. 47.

References

Thompson, George, trans. *The Bhagavad Gita: A New Translation.* New York: North Point Press, 2008.

Vivekananda, Swami. *The Complete Works of Swami Vivekananda,* 9 vols. Kolkata: Advaita Ashrama, 1979.

Vedic Turtles and Their Visiting Cards: Doing Vedas with Frits

Thennilapuram Mahadevan
Howard University

We all know of Frits Staal's many laserlike insights that go to the heart of the various disciplines he found time to master, always expressed with the brevity and lucidity of a sutra from Bodhāyana: "Rationality is independent of literacy"; "Artificial Language is more generous than Natural Language"; "Could **Panini**'s *lopa* suggest *śūnya* and thus the Hindu Zero?"; "Mantras are meaningless"; "The Vedic Oral Tradition is a case of 'turtles all the way'"; "The *abhivādaye* greeting ['I salute you'] is a Brahman's Visiting Card."[1]

It has been my good fortune to work on the last two gems in this list, the "Vedic turtles" and how these turtles come by the "visiting cards" that convey their Vedic bona fides. Was there a first turtle? If so, can it be located in time and place, or is it only the last vague residue of an infinite regression? And how, at our end, some 3,000 years later, does a "visiting card" come to convey its bearer's Vedic allegiances?

The Three Vedic Markers

To start with, what is a Vedic "visiting card"? Obviously, it is not the familiar printed card we carry, though it serves the same purpose of presenting the bearer as a professional with training and expertise in a field, in this case, that of the Vedic rituals. It is not a physical object but rather a ritual act of a preliterate world, a tableaux declamation of the bearer's Vedic credentials, as intelligible in its social register as is the its modern, print-world real counterpart, a business or name card. As I seem poised to figure personally in this narrative, my visiting card would declaim, "Greetings. Of Kāśyapa-Āvatsāra-Naidruva, the three-*ṛṣi pravara* of the Kāśyapa *gotra* and of the *Baudhāyana Sūtra*, a student of *Yajus śākhā*, I, Śrī Mahadeva Śarma, bow to you."[2]

The three-*ṛṣi pravara* marks a biological patriliny of the *gotra* bearer, traced in the above declamation ultimately to a *ṛṣi* of the name "Kāśyapa," a sort of the idiom's "first turtle," with verses in the *Ṛgveda* (I.99 ff), followed by his descendant Avatsāra (ṚV 5.54 ff) and his descendant, Nidhruva (ṚV 9.63).[3] The three make up a patrilineal *ṛṣi pravara*, a term that literally means a "summons" to perform a Vedic ritual[4]—that is, a Vedic elect. It is one of approximately 50 such lineages, all with verses in the *Ṛgveda*, as both individual and family collections and subsequently fused together, when the individual and family collections are edited into a ten-*maṇḍala Ṛgveda*, as its global agency ca. 1000 B.C.E. Let us note that in oral tradition texts and their agencies are irrevocably linked, *sine qua non*. As we now know, this Vedic oral agency is the nucleus of the historical brahmans, incubated over the next six generations or so, through the evolution of the Classical Ritual, ca. 850 B.C.E., as the familiar "caste" group, which is now forever closed by endogamy (marital kinship to only another *gotra* affiliate) and exogamy (but not to one of one's own *gotra*).[5] All historical brahmans quite literally originate here, wherever they are found today, and what Frits used to call "Vedic fieldwork" reveals no single-*gotra* brahman settlements—at least four of these constitute the actual case of the brahman *agrahāram*s of the peninsula. As well, altogether 36 of the putative approximately 50 lineages are attested in the peninsula; and, of extraordinary interest, they are of different sizes, with the Bhāradvājas flagrantly always number one, while the Kāśyapa, Vaiśvāmitra(-Aghamarṣaṇa Kauśika *pravara*), Jāmadagnya Bhargava, and Kaundinya-Vāsiṣṭhas lines form the bulk at formation as well as historically.[6]

If the *gotra* marker thus relates to survival and biology, the sūtra designation in the card marks one's *Paideia* patrimony.[7] This, maximally and ideally, would constitute the mastery of both texts and their *brāhmaṇa* praxes in ritual, in my case, of the Baudhāyana school: the *Taittrīya Saṃhitā-Taittirīya Brāhmaṇa-Taittirīya Āraṇyaka-Taittirīya Upaniṣad-Baudhāyana Sūtra*. In its bare essence, the sūtra is like a diploma on the wall of a doctor's office, advertising a profession, a livelihood, and, in a brahman *agrahāram*, security, comfort, and even affluence, but in return, covenanted to be the physical repository of the Vedic texts, totaling some 5 million syllables, all orally composed and transmitted successfully with the fidelity of an electronic recording for over 3,000 years.[8] We see that there must be a system, and not only prodigious individuals, behind its success. The sūtra label systematically and fastidiously fashions its adherent's daily life; the *Paideia* practices and institutions of his sūtra textures him, minutely and absolutely, amounting in orthopraxic cases to a sort of physical imprisonment. A *śrotriya* brahman thus followed no other profession.[9]

(I must add here the unexpressed other half of my visiting card: my mother's natal Parāśara *gotra*, with the three-*ṛṣi* (Vāsiṣṭha-Śāktya-Pārāśara) *pravara* and the *Āśvalāyana Sūtra* of the *Ṛgveda*. A ritual, called *gotrodbhava*, installed her at my parents' wedding into the Kāśyapa fold and she later gave birth to nine Kāśyapa children, the four sons remaining Kāśyapa throughout their lifetimes and begetting more Kāśyapas, while the remaining five daughters (one deceased before marriage) were all Kāśyapas going into their marriages but through the same *gotrodbhava* ritual they joined, respectively, the Pārāśarya *gotra-Āśvalāyana Sūtra*, the Vaiśvāmitra (Āghamarṣaṇa) *gotra-Āśvalāyana Sūtra*, the Ātri (Gaviṣṭhira) *gotra-Āśvalāyana Sūtra*, and the Bhāradvāja (Bārhaspatya-Āṅgirasa) *gotra-Baudhāyana Sūtra*. I have elaborated this scenario a little to underscore the commonplace reality, even banality, of one generation past, in which large families were the norm and strict Vedic biology prevailed to bring them about, efficiently and competently, in the *agrahāram*s of the peninsula in the early part of the twentieth century—a system that was surely much more entrenched in the historical past. We should thus envision distinctive brahman communities in these *agrahārams*, numerous enough to meet the *gotra* rules of endogamy and exogamy and thus the gotra patriliny and also the *Paideia* patrimony, a profession, so as to endure, even prosper. We cannot conceive of any other way in which Vedic visiting cards have remained viable for nearly 3,000 years than this physical evidence from the past, more probative than Aryan bones, if indeed such were ever found.)

Frits brought into play a third Vedic marker in addition to the *gotra* and sūtra affiliations in the lives of the brahmans, an experience-near sign of the Geertzian scheme,[10] the easily visible hair accouterments[11] of brahman males that are not recorded in the visiting cards. In the peninsula the hair tuft worn at the front of a shaven head, the *pūrvaśikhā,* and one at the back, like a ponytail, the *aparaśikhā,* are both long-known in the *Gazetteer* ethnology of British India[12] but only as stray factoids about brahmans and not as, what Frits intuited, a wider Vedic marker. It is more like an umbrella, cohering groups of the two Geertz experience-far markers, *gotra* and sūtra affiliations. This suddenly brings into view large collections of individuals, indeed whole populations, that can and must be studied systematically and historically, as has been called for by Michael Witzel.[13]

The Vedic markers thus universally characterize the brahmans as Vedic oral agents: the *gotra* patriliny determines from the start the biological destiny; the sūtra patrimony dictates the mundane means of livelihood; and the *śikhā* marks a broader visible category, unlike the *gotra* and sūtra markers. We can now definitively identify a brahman in the essential and indispensable criteria, which are of such inertia that even after vacating the *Padeia* patrimony for other livelihoods, abandoning the traditional *śikhā* accouterments, an individual can remain a brahman. A vast majority of brahmans are no longer, strictly speaking, Vedic oral agents—further made so because gotra marriages are still sufficiently common and binding.

Vedic Fieldwork

Frits Staal addresses many of these questions in his first publication, *Nambudiri Veda Recitation,*[14] and my subsequent investigations have merely been to connect the dots, from many field trips, urged by Witzel's famous "back to the village" Mao call.[15] I daresay that my connecting some of the dots was made possible only by being privy or emic to the civilization under study. I can say with no exaggeration that Staal's *Nambudiri Veda Recitation* is to Vedic civilization what, to borrow from his bank of yen, the *śivasūtra* is to Pāṇinian grammar: a simulacrum.

My tribute to Frits, then, is a test case, an example, of such a dot followed up to reveal the "big picture," opening to a philological understanding of the Vedic civilization, to wit, through its texts and their oral adjuncts. Frits notes, as in a taxonomical discourse about the Vedic schools he found in the peninsula, that among the Aparaśikhā Tamil brahmans, the *Āpastaṃba Sūtra* of the *Kṛṣṇa Yajurveda* is the dominant adherence, while it is unknown among the Malayalam-speaking Nambudiri brahmans, over the mountains to the west, who follow only the *Baudhāyana* and *Vādhūla Sūtra*s of that *saṃhitā.*

This puzzled me in regard to my own visiting card. While I spoke Tamil I was not an *Āpastaṃba Sūtra* adherent, but rather of the *Baudhāyana* school, like the Malayalam-speaking Nambudiri brahmans. (I discovered later that the *Baudhāyana Sūtra* does occur among the Aparaśikhā Tamil brahmans as well, a miniscule presence; the sūtra itself is referred to as the *Pravacana Sūtra,* after the mode of oral traditions of the *Brāhmaṇa* texts, "pronouncement" or "announcement"[16]—the sūtra is the oldest, and thus indeed proximal to the *Brāhmaṇa* texts.)

I raised this question with Frits when Alf Hiltebeitel, our foremost living *Mahābhārata* scholar, brought him to George Washington University in Washington D.C., for spring semester 2001. During this semester I saw Frits at every seminar meeting, on Wednesdays, and also every

Saturday, at his apartment, where we talked for the entire day over cheap, good red wine (Cote du Ventoux, Vidal Fleury), a variety of cheeses, and the then-famous Breadline French baguettes. I had by then worked through his *Nambudiri Veda Recitation* and *Agni: The Vedic Ritual of the Fire Altar* (I am perhaps the only person who ever photocopied the entire two-volume Agni),[17] and many of his journal articles. Indeed, I had become a bit of a "Frits" groupie with my own stock of Staaliana, so much so that Frits began to refer to me at some point as his "mind."

Although we did not solve my sūtra problem until later, we began to catch up on the underlying issues, the grand scale of the Vedic oral traditions, evidenced by some 11 Vedic schools in the peninsula alone, a good percentage of which are still quite worthy of their visiting cards. Discussion of the Vedas filled the day. It began to seem as if we were "doing" the Vedas, the way physicists do physics, despite my lack of formal Indological training—or perhaps because of it: I took nothing for granted and Frits never showed condescension at my wayward doubts and queries. For instance, how does a *Yajus* adherent like myself, or a *Sāma* adherent like his great friend Māmuṇṇu Iṭṭi Ravi Nambutiri, of the Bhāradvāja *gotra* (Bhāradvāja-Bārhaspatya-Āṅgirasa *gotra pravara*) come to have a *gotra* patriliny that goes back to the ṚV, like my Kāśyapa, or Iṭṭi Ravi's Bhāradvāja? Or how can the *Caraṇavyūha* number 1,000 schools for the *Sāmaveda*? Is it an admission that because of the extraordinary complexity of the oral traditions of the *Sāmaveda* (and no Vedist was ever more conscious of this than Frits), every *sāma* chanter is a school unto himself? Frits certainly thought of Iṭṭi Ravi as one in a thousand.

At semester's end, in summer 2001, he sent me off to India with an armload of addresses, to do what he called "Vedic fieldwork," suggesting that I start with my own sūtra question for a field-level investigation. I thus set off, as may not be entirely unbecoming a *Bodhāyana Sūtra* adherent, *prāṇmukhaḥ pradakṣiṇaṃ yajñopavīti daivāni karmāṇi karoti* ("facing east, turning to the right, invested with the sacred thread, he performs the divine rites"), seeking to arrive at Frits' maxim of *sarvatomukham* ("facing all directions").[18]

This was my first trip "back to the village." Regarding my sūtra aporia, I started with my mother, the sort of source who "just knew" things, due to being deeply immersed in the ways and mores of a Vedic *agrahāram*[19]—and indeed she sometimes knew about things that were lying hidden in plain sight. Both *gotra* and sūtra affiliations of the different families in an *agrahāram* are public knowledge, from the *saṃskāra* or *gṛhya* rituals, which literally reveal the sūtra adherences of individual families and their *gotra* affiliations, at weddings. For instance, something as routine as the annual *upākarma* ritual (the changing of the sacred thread) is performed publicly, at the temple tank (in place of a river as in the Vedic tradition), but the ritual is performed differently, and even on different days, for different sūtra adherents, so that the contents of the individual Vedic visiting cards of the *agrahāram* are pretty much in the public domain. That is, in the emic domain.

The *ex cathedra* answer from my mother was, "There is no *Āpastaṃba Sūtra* among us," compounding my earlier dilemma but also opening up new avenues. This led me to search for the "us" in my mother's answer: Tamil-speaking brahmans who were not of the *Āpastaṃba Sūtra*—and also, at once, it opened "privy" and emic doors that were often closed to an etic outsider. The brahman problem became almost a Rubik's cube, with many moveable items: sūtra, *śikhā,* domicile, language. The answer was that "we" make up a very small group of brahmans known as Cōḻiyar, from long residence in the Cōḻa area of Tamil Nadu; these Cōḻiyar brahmans wear a *pūrvaśikhā* tuft, like the Nambudiri brahmans. Indeed, the *śikhā* had fallen into disuse, perhaps by the 1920s. My father, Ramanujan, the first of his Kāśyapa forbears to venture outside the Vedic fold, was told by his British Jesuit professor, around 1920 at St. Joseph's College in Trichi (an institution of some prestige in South India), that his hair tuft was "most inconvenient." A few years before this he experienced the trauma of having to cut off his generous tuft for a trip to Cambridge, England.

Frits already knew all this broadly, but the emic dots refused to connect. For instance, he puzzled over the *pūrvaśikhā* tuft of the Tamil-speaking Cōḻiya group, noting its occurrence also among the Malayalam-speaking Nambudiri Pūrvaśikhās. In *Nambudiri Veda Recitation* he records other similarities between the two groups: both, for instance, follow the Jaiminīya school of the *Sāmaveda* (*Sāmaveda* 68). As we know, through the 1970s Witzel showed that the *Āgniveśya Sūtra* of a Cōḻiya group at Avaṭaiyār Koil in Tanjavur, Tamil Nadu, is the same as the Vādhūla school of a distinct Nambudiri group in Irinjalakkuda, in Kerala, confirmed by Asko Parpola,[20] leading us to the surmise that the two groups have been long separated and now speak different languages, dialects of an once-parental Tamil language.

Perhaps because of their obscurity and small size, Frits seems to have put away in his mind the Cōḻiya group as a "limit" case of brahman survival; he hearkens back to the group in his book *Mantras between Fire and Water*[21] some 30 years after his first encounter with them, when trying to adjudicate the question of whether the Bali "brahman" priests were indeed brahmans, as they were known locally. The Cōḻiyas, he notes, are equally obscure, small, and remote, but they possess robust visiting cards—the *gotra* and sūtra markers, absent among the Bali brahmans—leading him to conclude that the latter were not true brahmans in the Vedic sense.

We have thus two brahman groups in the peninsula but at two different areas, that speak different languages yet are united in different Veda *śākhā*s: exclusively Baudhāyana or Vadhūla (= Āgniveśya) if *Yajus* adherents; Jaiminīya, if Sāmavedis. In addition, both possess a common *śikhā* accouterment. Are we then looking at a once common entity? Why the split? And when? Why two languages, Malayalam over the Western Ghats to west and to the Arabian Sea, and Tamil east over the mountains all the way to Bay of Bengal? More dots, in other words, are created when "doing Vedas."

It becomes clear in hindsight that these and associated questions can be resolved only through further Vedic fieldwork and deeper understanding of the three Vedic markers: first, the Geertz experience-near *śikhā* or *kuṭumi* (in Tamil) and thus glaringly missing in the visiting cards; second, the Geertz experience-far categories of *gotra* and sūtra markers. Several field trips began to reveal the Tamil-speaking Pūrvaśikhā brahmans as a sovereign group. Beginning with the core Cōḻiya group in the Cōḻa and the Tonṭaimaṇṭalam area to the north (the Sri Rangam and Tiruveḷḷarai agrahārams) and the Pāṇṭiyan kingdom in the south-southeast (the Vēṃbattūr, Kaṭayanallūr, and Vallanāṭu *agrahārams*); and, in the modern period, the scattered Palakkad *agrahārams* (Koḻunthirap-Puḷḷi, Chembai) to the north of Kerala and in the Trivandrum area in the south. A very important Vaiṣṇava adjunct to the Cōḻiya Pūrvaśikhās is found in the Trichi-Sri Rangam area (Tiruvellarai, Anbil) and around Madurai (Tiruvillip-Puttūr and Tiruk-Kōṣttiyūr) in the Pāṇṭiyan lands.

Frits had already noted this Cōḻiya Vaiṣṇava adjunct in Tinturepparai on the banks of the Tāmṛavarṇi River in southeast Tamil country. All three brahman Āḻvārs of the canonical 11 come from this group, founding thus the Āḻvār phase of the great Śrī Vaiṣṇava movement of the Tamil country, besides being the conduit of the Sanskrit sources of the Vaiṣṇava *métier*.[22] Likewise, another Pūrvaśikhā group, the Chidambaram Dīkṣitars, plays an equally crucial role in the rise of the Nāyan-Mār Śaivism in the area. I found yet another Pūrvaśikhā group in the Mukkāṇi, or Cutantira, brahmans of the Tiruchendur Subrahmania, or Murukan, a temple on the east coast.

It becomes possible now to do an unthinkable thing—to put a number behind the entire Tamil Pūrvaśikhā group in the peninsula, in both Tamil Nadu and Kerala: perhaps 20,000 in all.[23] Not only was there not one *Āpastaṃba Sūtra* adherent among them,[24] my first dot, but when connected with other discovered data revealing an entire population linked by set of common Vedic texts. A "big picture." Moreover, these texts were in remarkable alignment with the Vedic schools of the Malayalam-speaking Nambudiri Pūrvaśikhās, with the sole exception of the Kauṣītaki school of the *Ṛgveda*, found among the Nambudiri Pūrvaśikhās but not among their Tamil-speaking brethren, or not yet then. In 2002, at the advent of the Internet age, through many emails, it became a wager between Frits and me, with him challenging me to find a *Kauṣītaki Sūtra* adherent among the Tamil Pūrvaśikhā brahmans, like finding a new element in the Periodic Table. With 100,000, a number Frits, Vinod Bhattatiripad,[25] and I had estimated for the Malayalam-speaking Nambudiri brahmans, we have more than 120,000 Pūrvaśikhā brahmans. An entire branch of brahmans comes into view through their Vedic texts; a rationally conceived group rises before our eyes.

The *Kauṣītaki Sūtra* of the ṚV soon turned up in fieldwork among the Tamil Cōḻiya group, eight families in Parali *agrahāram* in Palghat (with roots in the Tamil *agrahāram*s Kaliyākuṭi and Ālaṅguṭi in the Kumbakonam area along the Kāvēri River), as well as the evidence to explain the regional distributions of the Pūrvaśikhā Vedic schools, not just their present several locations but perhaps their once-common original home in the past, the latter from Witzel's localizations of the Vedic schools where they first formed.[26] Frits saw in this a breakthrough in Vedic studies.[27] All of the Pūrvaśikhā schools "formed" in south-southeast Pāñcāla land, not far from Kosala in the north, took shape over perhaps three centuries, from 850 to 500 B.C.E., not *ab ovo* but from a recursionary *Paideia* capital brought with them from Kurukṣetra. There were enough to perform the final morph of the Classical Ritual, the 1975 *agnicayana* at Pāññāl, organized and recorded by Frits.

That such a Vedic event occurred at Kurukṣetra under the Tura Kāvaṣeya-Janamejaya Pārikṣita *brahmakṣatra* aegis is self-evident: all later brahman groups, all the way down the peninsula, possess this paradigm, so as to suggest a "Big Bang"-like dispersal from Kurukṣetra during and after the formation of the *agnicayana*. These distributions reveal themselves, later, as *caraṇa*s, or schools, found in a radius from the center at Kurukṣetra: the *Kaṭha YV caraṇa*s in the north and northwest, in Kashmir; the *Maitrāyanī YV* school in the west-southwest; the Pūrvaśikhā *caraṇa*s in the south-southeast, all the way to the Kosala borders; and finally the Gotama Rāhūgaṇa-Videha Māṭhava *brahmakṣatra* grid radiation to the Videha area, beyond the recently heteroprax Sadānīra River, as the *Śatapatabrāhmaṇa* tells us, all of the *Śukla YV caraṇa*s rising among them, which were in time adopted by the Magadha imperium in the sixth century B.C.E. This last item, besides providing us with a reason for the departure to the peninsula of the Pūrvaśikhā *Kṛṣṇa YV* groups, the *Baudhāyana-Vādhūla* schools, with their Classical Ritual cohorts, the *Kauṣītaki-Āśvalāyna ṚV* and the *Jaiminīya SV* schools. The Pūrvaśikhā brahmans are then evidenced in the Sangam-era peninsula (50 B.C.E. to 300 C.E.).[28]

Although we can't exactly place them regionally in peninsula at this time, we know that these brahmans came to possess a *brahmakṣatra* relationship with the three chieftains of the Tamil realm, referred to as *mūvēndar*s ("three Indras"): a Cōḷa chieftain performing the *rājasūya;* a Pāṇṭiyan adding on the Vedic epithet to his name, *paliyākacālai,* "of the sacrificial hall," from hosting numerous Vedic rituals. The Irumpurai Ceras made huge land grants to these brahmans in the Karur area, on the Amarāvatī River. With the well-known Kaḷabhra Interregnum of Tamil history, the Pūrvaśikhā group seems to fragment and is later found in its present location. All of the historical branches acknowledge the duress of the breakup in the legends and *sthalapurāṇa*s of their new homes.

The Nambudiri Pūrvśikhās, most likely in the patronage in the Karūr area of the Cera Irumpurai chieftains, moved to Malabar over the Palghat Gap and settled on both banks of the Niḷa River, later naming it the Bhāratap-Puḷa, upon reaching, as it were, the end of the Bhāratavarṣaa. They were led there by Mēḻattōl Agnihotri and his 99 *agniṣṭoma*s, who sanctified the land with Agni, in the manner of his *Śatapathabrāhmaṇa* forbear, Gotama Rāhūgaṇa, ca. 850–500 B.C.E. All the Pūrvaśikhā brahmans remaining behind in the Tamil country possess a *sthalapurāṇa* of a journey as a group to what were to become their historical settlements, *agraharām*s, echoing the duress: 3,700 for the Cōḻiya Pūrvaśikhās of Tiruveḷḷarai; 3,000 for the Chidambaram Dīkṣitars; 2,000 for the Tiruchendur Mukkāṇis; and 300 each for the Avaṭaiyār Koil and Tinturepparai Cōḻiyas. They all arrive at their destinations to find one family missing and the relevant *bhakti* deity (Viṣṇu, Śiva, or Subrahmanya-Muruka) appears to take its place.

An equally vivid "big picture," even bizarrely symmetrical, emerges for the Aparaśikhā brahmans when we subject their Vedic schools to the same scrutiny as above, relating their Vedic schools to their original loci in Witzel's localization scheme. To begin with, these schools, also *Kṛṣṇa YV,* date close to half a millennium after the Pūrvaśikhā schools, and they crystallize around the *Āpastaṃba* and closely related *Bhāradvāja* and *Śāṭyāṣāḍa/Hiraṇyakeśi Sūtra*s, on the banks of the Yamanā River around Mathurā and eastward toward the Gaṅga, in the Doab, 300 B.C.E. These groups must have gained great benefits from the Gupta revival of Vedism in the fourth century C.E., almost a millennium afterward, so that when we encounter them in our story they show themselves, as is evidenced in later data about them, to be at the height of their Vedic prowess: more than 10 percent of them are seen to have *Śrauta* credentials in the Copper Plate epigraphy detailing their migration southward. The first recorded arrival of an *Āpastaṃba* adherent in the peninsula is Jyeṣṭa Śarman of the Gautama *gotra* of the Vēsantha (Jalapuram) Copper Plates of the Pallava king Simhavarman II, issued in his nineteenth regnal year, in the fifth century C.E., granting the village of Vēsantha.[29] Beginning as a trickle and still in the north, in the Toṇṭaimaṇṭalam area, just south of the Vēṇkaṭa hills, it becomes a spate over the successive seventh through eleventh centuries C.E., debouching into the Kāvēri delta through the sixteenth century.[30]

Keeping to Frits' premise that a brahman is essentially a Vedic oral agent, it can be shown that some 1,500 Aparaśikhā brahmans migrated to the Tamil country from the fifth through seventeenth centuries C.E., purely as Frits' Vedic oral agents. Their names, sūtra, and *gotra* affiliations, their Vedic credentials, really our Vedic visiting card, but "printed" in a one-of-a-kind migration record in the world, the famed Copper Plate epigraphy of the Pallava (fifth to tenth centuries C.E.), are the Cōḻa (tenth to thirteenth centuries C.E.); the Pāṇṭiyan (thirteenth to fourteenth centuries C.E.); and the Tanjāvūr Nāyakas (fourteenth to sixteenth centuries C.E.). This is really a monument to history in unhistorical India. The real number, counting unfound Copper Plates, may well be ten times the found number of 1,500, giving us a total of 15,000 (grown now close to a million individuals, quite possibly the largest single brahman concentration of the subcontinent.) I coined them "Burton Stein brahmans," much to Frits' delight, as he knew and liked the historian's work on the brahman-peasant relationship in the Tamil country, showing that these newly arrived brahmans built up a vigorous, even hegemonic, presence in South India. They have a Web-presence now as Tam-Bram.

Where Do We Go From Here?

Many points made above were still in the future when Frits and I met in Trichur for the 2003 *agniṣṭoma,* but a broad "big picture" about the brahmans in the peninsula seemed within our grasp, when tracked through their Vedic markers. We adumbrated this thesis in our joint article,[31] written over a week the following summer at Frits' house in the Oakland hills, with San Francisco Bay and its bridges in view. An overall vindication of the stratigraphy thesis reached above through the Vedic markers soon came from the textual history of the *Mahābhārata* (and the *Rāmāyaṇa*) and the history of the Śrī Vaiṣṇava movement in the peninsula, but I am ahead of myself.

What I have tried to show here is that Frits' two "thick" insights about brahmans as the agents of the Vedic oral traditions, the "turtles" of the idiom, stop them from infinite regression. On the contrary, they acquire (oral) visiting cards attesting to a 3,000-year *Paideia* system, lucidly narrating their story. In fact, investigation of the other item found in the visiting cards, that of the *gotra* affiliations of the brahmans, takes us, when the relevant dots are connected, literally to the spawning grounds of the "turtles" in the Linguistic Area in Greater Punjab, ca. sixteenth to eleventh centuries B.C.E. Each "turtle" is one of the fifty-odd areal poetic agencies of the ṚV—my Kaśyapa and Iṭṭi Ravi's Bharadvāja forbears among them. With the global TMS, these human agencies, along with their individual and family *saṃhitās*, have also been edited together, as the global Vedic oral agency, a "One Tolkien ring," or rather the "One and Future Ring." Two "impossible" things seem to happen now: first, through the next six generations, from 1000 to 850 B.C.E., over the Yamunā-Dṛṣadvatī Doab to Kurukṣetra, the Classical Ritual incubates these fifty-odd groups into a *gotra* patriliny with the twin endogamy-exogamy rules. Second, through the same period, the performance of the Classical Ritual, possible now through the *pravara* summons, transforms the entire *gotra* patriliny into tri-Vedic adherents, specialists in view of the work of the Classical Ritual, of *YV-ādhvaryavam, ṚV-hautram,* and *SV-audgātram*—the precise or specific sūtra patrimony forming over time during school canonizations.[32] My Kāśyapa forbear went into the TMS as a Ṛgvedi, singing soma hymns, and came out a YV adherent, becoming in time a Baudhāyani, as did Iṭṭi Ravi's forbear, who entered the TMS as a Bharadvāja Ṛgvedi but exited as a Sāmavedi, and in time becoming a Jaiminīya.

That is to say, Frits' sūtras are not dead ends. One can "do Vedas" with them and with no sense of envy. Consider for instance the one about the generosity—a case of giving back more than it took—of "artificial" languages (which included for Frits "numbers," or numeracy in general) as against "natural" language. The Indic *paribhāṣa* tradition is Frits' immediate example of an Artificial Language, but the idea is extensible to the irreducible metrical discourse of the Indo-European Oral Traditions, the dactylic hexameter discourse of Homeric epics; the 8–8–8 syllable-verse (GA), the 10-10-10–10 syllable-verse (TR), the 11–11–11–11 syllable-verse (JG) of the Vedic oral tradition (from an Indo-Iranian past), variously described in our time as *kunstsprache,* a poetic idiom or, most massively, the "Language of the Gods," in clear elitist contrast to the "Language of Mortals," Mr. Higgins' "squashed cabbage leaves."

Anthropologists have characterized this "spoken poetry" as its foremost adaptive trait. The PIE oral traditions spread it through "elite recruitment" of and from host societies in their paths,[33] most vividly illustrated in the admixture between the Āryan Vedic-speaking tribes and clans and the South Asian tribes and clans of the area, giving rise to the Linguistic Area.

In ongoing work I argue that an essential Frits difference characterizes the contrast between the two major historical vectors of the IE oral tradition, namely, the oral fidelity of the transmission, ignored largely in the Western vector but a cardinal rule in the Indo-Iranian vector and achieved practically by the *Paideia*-instituted *padapāṭha* analysis of the human sound, to ensure an exact audio recording-like transmission—fidelity, both lexical and phonetic. It is striking that it is an Indo-Iranian trait, pointing to a radical schism in the PIE oral traditions, like the erstwhile *centum-śatem* feature, and, as I show, we are soon able to tease out an or the Āryan vector of the Punjab from the sixteenth to eleventh centuries B.C.E., with new ethos and features, such as the string of some 19 *dānastutis* in the TMS-ṚV[34]—this entire vector, evolving in the Linguistic Area of the Greater Punjab, becomes unarguably the most successful radiation of the Indo-European Language and its Artificial Language—the "metrical discourse" joined at the hip to its agency, forever. Such an arrival of self-ascribed Āryans, ca. sixteenth century B.C.E., over the Mujāvat and Hindu Kush mountains and down the Khyber and Bolan passes, always held great romance for Frits.

A final cue from Frits to us is to reckon boldly with the evidence that the Vedic oral tradition was never really interrupted by literacy, which to this day, as Frits' peninsular brahmans, both Tamil- and Malayalam-speaking, illustrate. To be sure, literacy eventually arose in post-Vedic period in India, ca. fourth century B.C.E., and when it did, its graph was pre-cast from the *padapāṭha* analysis of the human sound, already developed to ensure phonetic fidelity comparable to that of a audio recording. Thus, as we know, its alphabet is not arbitrary and illogical (remember that rationality is independent of literacy); indeed, it is not a "salad of letters," as in the Greek-Latin alphabet, but rather an exact topological mirror of the human vocal apparatus, giving us a syllabary that has for three millennia rivaled the modern IPA. This was in fact one of Frits' pet mantras: the Vedic-Sanskrit alphabet is to its linguistics what *śivasūtra* is to Pāṇinian grammar: mutually explicable algorithms.

Frits' premise that a brahman is a priori a Vedic oral agent, with visiting cards and all, embeds, enmeshes, and entangles our subject so deeply into the entire Vedic system as to render him into an object, an impersonal cog in a vast machine kept well oiled through *gotra* patriliny and sūtra patrimony. As has been suggested, it is an automaton,[35] but an automaton that is a product of verifiable biological adaptations. Many deductions one arrives at here are Holmsian: the least improbable remainders after we eliminate all impossible clauses in the syllogism. The institution of the gotra patriliny seems altogether impossible on its face: quite literally, that a breeding stock of the original fifty-odd poetic agencies of the TMS, ca. 1000 B.C.E. could be locked in without escape on one hand or, on the other, allowing no new recruits, going back in this respect to its earlier ethos in the linguistic area, when "elite recruitment" was a key policy in the interaction between the incoming Vedic Āryans and indigenous South Asian peoples. Yet from fieldwork evidence we see, each Vedic oral agency that forms in the half millennium from the sixteenth to eleventh centuries B.C.E. is subjected to selective breeding, as mandated by the *gotra* laws, first from 1100 to 850 B.C.E., roughly six generations, then perpetuated into a longitudinal chain of some 150 generations, as in Frits' regressive turtles, all pointing to a biological explanation, an example of exaption,[36] or the spandrel of evolutionary biology. That is to say, an objective nonanatomical mutation—the skill or ability with artificial language in the production of metrical language—dictates that the exaption will result in a "species" or caste category, the brahman, whether or not every member of the speciation possesses the skill.

Likewise, it is equally "impossible," as in the Holmsian syllogism, that a *sūtra patrimony can found in brahmans from Kashmir to Kerala and Gujarat to Bengal, when the field evidence shows it to be otherwise. What remains should be true, so that the fixed, exact audio recording-like transmission of the *Paideia* patrimony must be true. Anything less does not adequately justify its survival and success, especially in light of being able to haul up a veritable coelacanth,[37] like Frits' 1975 *agnicayana*, from the depths of time. The ritual was known to have existed, for A. B. Keith and Arthur Macdonnell[38] in the early part of the twentieth century, and for Willem Caland, Frits' great mentor, but it was not seen outside the milieu of Frits' Vedic agents, and occurred thousands of miles away from its first performance in Kurukṣetra, ca. 850 B.C.E., at the aegis of the Tura Kāvaṣeya-Janamejaya Pārikṣita *brahmakṣatra* grid. The ritual requires the entire sum of Vedic knowledge as of 850 B.C.E. for its performance—enough to make any physicist giddy with envy.

The *Pitṛu* Ritual for Frits, or Frits Floats into the Western Ocean?

I last saw Frits at the Olappamanna Mana, his hosts from the 1960s, a great "Renaissance" Nambudiri home in Veḷḷinēḷi, Palghat district, close to the Kuntī River. The Kuntī, a stream in summer, becomes a raging river in the monsoon season, on its way to join the Bhāratap-Puḻa, or Niḷa, River, no doubt its true name. As he was ill and rather unhappy, Frits had decided to go back to Thailand before the end of the "second" Pāññāl *atirātram* in 2011. Almost playing to a topos of "back to Pāññāḷ," we had all gathered in a well-appointed hotel by the river, as Witzel notes in his article in this volume,[40] really quite speechless as the entire phenomenon began to unfold. Frits too was speechless, in his case literally so as he was suffering from severe bronchitis. (I have a pocketful of Frits' notes from this event, written in enviable penmanship.)

I had once narrated to Frits my trip to Varanasi to immerse my mother's last remains in the Gaṅga, primarily in order to highlight a "ritual" episode as an ongoing recursion, not unlike the "dull number" episode between Godfrey H. Hardy and the ill Ramanujan, in which Hardy noted the license plate number of the taxicab he had taken to the hospital, 1729, and Ramanujan joyfully exclaimed on the far-from-dull character of the number. My host-priest at Varanasi, like me also from Palghat and Tamil-speaking, was as an *Āpastaṃba* by birth, an Aparaśikhā brahman, long settled at Hanuman Ghat in Varanasi. He had to dust up his *Baudhāyana Gṛhya Sūtra* textbook, used for *Āpastaṃba* visitors, and he let me know in no uncertain terms that his *Āpastaṃba Sūtra* was "modern" and as such suitable for "officegoers." He assured me that the ritual for my mother the next day, the *pārvaṇa śrāddha,* would be over for *Āpastaṃba*-following officegoers by noon or even earlier, but for me, as a Baudhāyani adherent, it would continue well into the afternoon, with 26 *piṇḍa*s against the three of the *Āpastaṃba.* This was indeed was the case. The entire story delighted Frits, as the *Bodhāyana* was his favorite *sūtrakāra,* navigating one from *prāṇmukha* to *sarvatomukha.*

A tacit understanding had arisen between Frits and I that I might do something like this, a Vedic parting, for him but on the Niḷa River, always immediate to the Vedas of his Nambudiris. I received the news of Frits' death in an email from Karin Staal, his niece in Amsterdam (with whom I had already been in contact about her impending visit to Thailand and her inability to contact him). Hearing from his son about Frits' death, I raised the matter of performing the ritual with Frits' ashes, and he readily agreed. I arrived in Calicut (Kōḻikkoḍ) with the container of ashes in June 2012.

Vinod Bhattatiripad met us at the airport, and there was very nearly a press event outside the airport buildings. We traveled in a motorcade to Tirunāvāya, the famous ritual site on the Bhāratap-Puḻa-Niḷa River, designated for obsequies for the departed with all the frills, close to the thoroughness dictated by the *Bodhāyana*. I had not anticipated such a major public event and had rather naively thought that the ritual would be a quiet immersion ceremony at Pāññāḷ, with Frits' close friends, after which we would adjourn to enjoy a glass of Vidal Fleury Rhone, a bottle of which I had brought with me. Instead a full Vedic ritual unfolded and I submitted to the occasion, becoming a small pawn in the recursionary maze of rituals so well described by Frits. I took off my shirt and trousers and changed into the orthoprax "unstitched" clothing, and descended the steps all the way down to the river. After the rice, *tulasī* (Indian basil), and sesame oblations, I sat on the steps, completely soaked from the three ritual immersions in the river, and placed the urn with Frits' remains on the water's surface. On standing up from the river, looking west, I watched as the flower-embellished urn floated away to the western ocean.

Notes

1 Some of these "sutras" appear in Frits' writings: "Artificial Languages across Sciences and Civilizations," *Journal of Indian Philosophy* 34 (2006): 89–141; *The Fidelity of Oral Tradition and the Origins of Science* (Amsterdam: North-Holland Publishing Co., 1986).

The "visiting card" came up in 2005 when I played an audiotape of an *abhivādaye* while we were riding in a car in New York with Alf Hiltebeitel—proving to Frits that I had found the *Kauṣītaki Sūtra* of the ṚV among the Cōḻiya Pūrvaśikhās. My choice of a Bodhāyana sūtra for a measure of sense and brevity is linked to Frits'great partiality to Bodhāyana, especially for his mathematical praxis in his *Śulba Sūtra,* mensurational acumen, needed to lay out the ritual enclosures of the Classical Ritual, action of the ritual moving east-west facing rising sun, but through different geometrical shapes. A personal moment for me in this regard is the question put to Frits by a boy from my *agraharam* at the Mūlaṅgōde *atirātram* in 2007: Was Pythagoras' theorem not Bodhāyana's, as he was being taught in school in the new nationalist idiom? Frits answered the boy in loud affirmation.

2 The Sanskrit text would read: *abhivādaye. kāśyapa āvatsāra naidhruva triarṣeya pravarān vitaḥ Kaśyapa gotraḥ Baudhāyana Sūtraḥ yaju śākhāadhyāyi Śrī Mahādeva Śarmaḥ nāma aham asmi bho.* See G. S. Ghurye, *Caste and Race in India* (Mumbai: Popular Prakashan, 2008, reprint) for a discussion of the *abhivādaye* liturgy, including a full text of the liturgy.

3 I give below the Kāśyapa singers of the ṚV:

Kāśyapas (Kāśyapa-Āvatsāra-Naidhruva)	41 hymns; 352 verses
Kāśyapa Mārica	1.99 (1 hymn; 1 verse)
	9.64 (1 hymn; 30 verses)
	9.91-92 (2 hymns; 12 verses)
	9.113–114 (2 hymns; 15 verses)
	9.67.4–6 (0 hymn; 3 verses)
	10.137.2 (0 hymn; 1 verse)
Avatsāra Kāśyapa	5.44 (1 hymn; 15 verses)
	9.53–60 (8 hymns; 32 verses)
Nidhruvi Kāśyapa	9.63 (1 hymn; 30 verses)
Asita and Devala Kāśyapa	9.5–24 (20 hymns; 164 verses)
Rebha Kāśyapa	8.97 (1 hymn; 15 verses)
Raibha-Kāśyapas	9.99–100 (2 hymns; 17 verses)
Bhūtāṃśa Kāśyapa	10.106 (1 hymn; 11 verses)
Vivṛhan Kāśyapa	10.163 (1 hymn; 6 verses)

See Thennilapuram Mahadevan, "The Three Rails of the *Mahābhārata* Textual Tradition," *Journal of Vaishnava Studies* 19/2 (2011): 23–69, for a complete breakdown of the *Ṛgveda* along these lines. See also Mahadevan, "The Institution of *Gotra*, The *Ṛgveda*, and the Brahmans," in Joel B. Brereton, ed., *The Vedas in Indian Culture an History: Proceedings of the Fourth International Vedic Workshop*, Austin, Texas, 2007; "Textual Support for Early Integrity of the *Mahābhārata* from its Southern Recension," paper presented to the 14th World Sanskrit Conference, Kyoto, 2009; "The Southern Recension the *Mahābhārata:* The *Harivaṃśa* and Alvār Vaishnaivism," in Vishwa Adluri, ed., *Ways and Reasons for Thinking about the Mahābhārata as a Whole* (Pune: Bhandarkar Oriental Institute, 2013), pp. 87–128.

Several sources exist for a measure of the *censu:* a mainstay in 2000s was the Sunday Hindu matrimonials, close to 250, each listing the *gotra* affiliations. *The Śrutivāṇi,* a matrimonial trade publication from Trichur, Kerala, is very useful for the brahman diaspora of Palghat. We shall never have a real census of brahmans, although it has often been called for from Bhandarkar downward. But reasonable areal asymptotes can be had. See note 6.

4 Arthur A. Macdonell, *A Practical Sanskrit Dictionary with Transliterature, Accentuation and Etymological Analysis Throughout* (London: Oxford University Press, 1929), s.v. 181.

5 I make the argument that the Anukramaṇī Index of the *Ṛgveda* is a reliable and in some instances historical list of the *ṛṣi*-composers of the *Ṛgveda.* We can identify around 50 poetic families coming together with their individual and family collections to edit a text and its oral agency. These names pass on as

the later (850 B.C.E.) *gotra* labels, closing the agency through the endogamy-exogamy mandates of the *gotra* institution. It could be said that the historical brahmans date from this time onward, 700 B.C.E. We have good evidence that a social caste of brahman did not exist before or during the edition of the ten-*maṇḍala saṃhitā;* however, we have also evidence that they formed over a six-generation span, along the Jamunā-Dṛṣadvatī, creating and created by the Classical Ritual.

6 Over the last 10 years I have created a virtual *gotra* census for the peninsula, addressing a long-standing lacuna. An estimate of the original sizes of each founding agency appears in the *Pravara* List of the Appendix of the *Baudhāyana Śrauta Sūtra* (eighth to sixth centuries B.C.E.), southeast Pāñcāla area, not far from Kosala, with close correlation with extant *gotra* census of present day brahmans.

7 Remarkably, this constitutes the very definition of *paideia* in the Greek context, as set of skills signifying a "profession"; Warner Jaeger, *Paideia: The Ideals of Greek Culture* (Oxford: Basil Blackwell, 1943), vol. II, pp. 129–130. Countering the Sophist claim that rhetoric is a *techne,* Plato compares it with a skill, like music, requiring and maintained by constant practice. As Jaeger notes, "Our word art does not adequately reproduce the sense of the Greek word. . . . Like art *techne* emphasizes practical use. But art for us implies individual creation subject to no rule, whereas *techne* has the sense of well-established knowledge and ability, which we associate with *technique* or *profession*. . . . The Greeks used [the word] for any profession based on special knowledge—not only painting and sculpture, architecture and music, but just as much, or even more, medicine, strategy, or helmsmanship" (p. 129; emphasis in original).

8 Michael Witzel, in "Tracing the Vedic Dialects," in Collette Caillat, ed., *Dialectes dans les litterratures indo-aryennes* (Paris: Edition-Diffusion de Bocard, 1989), pp. 131–132, provides the *akṣara* content of some 32 texts, counting the 397,265 *akṣara*s of the ṚV as a base figure, roughly giving us a total of 5.5 million *akṣaras*.

9 No doubt this will be disputed in light of the picture of brahmans in India and overseas, adhering to practically any occupation possible or available. But the claim is still a dogma, in the sense that all other vocations for a brahmans are anachronistic Entire discourses concern the *śṛotriya* brahmans, stipulating their release from salt taxes (2.12.33: *śrotriyāstapakhinio viṣṭayaśva bhaktala vaṇam hareyuḥ*); exempting their properties from royal appropriation in times of national emergencies (5.2.37: *pāsaṇḍa saṃghdravyama śrotriyopabhogyam deva dravyam vā kṛtyakarāḥ pretasya dugdhgṛhasya vāhiste nyastamitypareśu*). A prince, unjustly treated by his father, may secretly rob temples but not what belongs to a *śrotriya* (1.18.9: *pāsaṇḍa saṃghdravyama śrotriyopabhogyam vā devadravyamāṇḍya vidhvādravyam vā gūḍamanu praviśya sārthyāna pātrāni ca madamarasayogenātisaṃghāyāpaharet*), and he should grant lands to the *śrotriya*s exempt from tax and fines (2.1.7: *ṛtvigārya purohita śrotriyebhyo brahma deyanya daṇḍkārṇyabhirūpadāyadakani prayaccet*). Indeed, in the *Arthaśāstra, śrotriya* is not an adjective modifying a subject, as in *śṛotriya* brahmans, but a substantive in itself, a professional group, distinguished as such from what

L. N. Rangarajan calls "general Brahmans," *Kautilya: The Arthashastra* (Delhi: Penguin Books, 1992, reprint), p. 46.

10 Clifford Geertz, *The Interpretation of Cultures: Selected Essays* (New York: Basic Books, 1973), pp. 377–378.

11 Many *śikhā* accouterments are attested in the Vedic period with some relation to the *gotra* marker; see John Brough, "The Early History of the Gotras," *Journal of the Royal Asiatic Society* (1946): 32–90. For the peninsula, the British *Gazetteer* sources are still very useful. Edgar Thurston, in *Castes and Tribes of Southern India* (Delhi: Cosmo, 1975, reprint), vol. I, p. 393; vol. II, pp. 152–241, formally acknowledges and discourses on this distinction, although distinctly from an *aparaśikhā* perspective. For instance, the Thurston informants mention the *pūrvaśikhā* as noteworthy. All of Thurston's "native informants" see the *pūrvaśikhā* mode as exceptional. K. Rangachari is listed on the title page as Thurston's assistant, and he was almost certainly the compiler of the information on the brahmans of the Tamil and Telugu country. M. N. Subramania Aiyar is mentioned as the informant for the Nambudiri section in the Thurston volumes (vol. II, p. 154). L. K. Anantha Krishna Iyer, in *The Cochin Tribes and Castes* (London: Luzac & Co., 1909–1912), vol. II, pp. 171–188, is strong on the Nambudiris. All these are, anecdotally, Aparaśikhā brahmans, in particular from the *vaṭama* and *bṛhatcaraṇam* sections of the Aparaśikhā group, what I characterize (see note 23) as the "Burton Stein brahmans," the brahmans of the Tamil country (including the *vaṭakalai* section of the Śrī Vaiṣṇava brahmans) to take to Western education earliest, beginning indeed their lives earlier in the Tamil country under the Pallava-Cōḷa patronage from ca. fifth century C.E. onward. The distinction between the two types of kuṭumis has been further elaborated by V. Raghavan, *The Present Position of Vedic Recitation and Vedic Sakhas* (Kumbakonam: Veda Dharma Paripalana Sabha, 1962); Frits Staal, *Nambudiri Veda Recitation* (The Hague: Mouton, 1961); Asko Parpola, "The Literature and Study of the Jaiminiya Sāmaveda: In Retrospect and Prospect," *Studia Orientalia* 53 (1973): 3–33; "On the Jaiminiya and Vādhūla Traditions of South India and the Pāṇḍu/Pāṇḍava Problem," *Studia Orientalia* 55 (1984): 429–468.

12 Thurston, *Castes and Tribes of Southern India*; Iyer, *The Cochin Tribes and Castes*.

13 Michael Witzel, in his article "On Indian Historical Writing: The Role of the Vaṃśāvalīs," *Journal of the Japanese Association for South Asian Studies* 2 (1990): 1–57, calls for a radically Vedic approach to brahman history, away from the old *vaṃśāvali* (lineage) lists of lineages.

14 Staal, *Nambudiri Veda Recitation*.

15 Witzel's "Mao call" of 1999: "Why not on your next trip to India? They may be just next door, outside of 1986 377-Nagpur, Tanjore or Ahmedabad. Not to forget that some of these reciters may have settled at Benares. . . ."

16 Macdonell, *A Practical Sanskrit Dictionary*, s.v. 181.

17 Frits Staal, *Agni: The Vedic Ritual of the Fire Altar*, 2 vols. (Berkeley: Asian Humanities Press, 1983); *Nambudiri Veda Recitation*.

18 *Prāṇmukhā* to *sarvatomukhaḥ* constituted for Frits the *Baudhāyana* paradigm,

starting "facing east" and arriving "facing all directions," rearticulating the Ṛgvedic idea of brahman, the truth statement that anchors *ṛk,* one might say the Vedic paradigm. Staal, "From *Prāṅmukham* to *Sarvatomukham:* A Thread through the *Śrauta* Maze," in Arlo Griffiths and Jan E. M. Houben, eds., *The Vedas: Texts, Language & Ritual: Proceedings of the Third International Vedic Workshop, Leiden 2002* (Groningen: Egbert Forsten, 2004), pp. 521–555.

19 *Agraharams*, now in deep decay, were the settlements of Tamil-speaking brahmans of the peninsula, 50 to 300 households of different *gotra* and sūtra affiliations. The Nambudiri brahmans of Kerala lived in rather isolated houses, belonging to different *grāmams*. See Staal, *Nambudiri Veda Recitation*.

20 Parpola, "On the Jaiminiya and Vādhūla Traditions of South India and the Pāṇḍu/Pāṇḍava Problem."

21 Frits Staal, *Mantras between Fire and Water: Reflections on a Balinese Rite* (Amsterdam: Koninklikje Nederlandse Akademie van Wetenschappen, 1995). This book is about Staal's attempt to collect the hand mudrās used in rituals in Bali. The citation occurs in Appendix II, pp. 91–10: "Were the Brahmins of Southeast Asia Brahmins?" To a great extent, this would also apply to Thailand, Cambodia, and Laos.

22 Friedhelm Hardy, in *Virahabhakti: The Early Kistory of Kṛṣṇa Devotion in South India* (Delhi: Oxford University Press, 1983), shows beyond doubt that this is the case: as he notes on p. 413, "I would strongly doubt that the Āḻvārs were familiar with the versions [of the Kṛṣṇa story] found in Br/ViP (*Brahma* and *Viṣṇupuraṇa*s). . . . [I]t seems fairly certain [that Periyāḻvār] cannot have known the BhP (*Bhāgvatapurāṇa*) either" (interpolations and parenthetical glosses added). Posing the question "Where does Periyāḻvār take his mythical themes (*bālacarita; gopi métier*)?", Hardy answers, "We know that the *Harivaṃśa* most probably was one of his sources." As I have shown, the *Mahābhārata* (Appendix I, no. 21): 386–422) is substantively derived from *adhyāya*s 38, 41, 42 of *Harivaṃśa*—but in the peninsula, among the Pūrvaśikhā circles.

23 Arriving at an exact number of a given community is South India is forever imperiled now by the "vote bank" politics. What can be a number for the Brahman population of the Tamil Nadu, the so-called Tam-Bram entity of Websites? After much reflection I would estimate it around a million or less.

24 Of course, this can be questioned: can I claim 100 percent? I would venture to wager, yes, as in the case of the exception proving the rule. Among brahman distributions, it is not exceptional that a family with a specific visiting card may find itself in another brahman settlement of another set of Vedic visiting cards. It is not unknown that the family may accept the host *Veda Sūtra:* that is, a Baydhāyani living among the *Āpastaṃba* brahmans may accept the latter as their praxes sūtra. There is one such *Āpastaṃba* adherent in the Nambudiri community. In another such case of proving the rule, in January 2014 I passed through a well-known Aparaśikhā *agraharam,* Koduvāyūr in Palghat District. I was introduced there to an "*Apastaṃba* Cōḻiya." I stewed in the taxi, puzzling, wondering if there could be a hole in my argument. Later the same day, while questioning some "elders," I found out that the mother of this man was indeed a Cōḻiya woman from my village, who had married

an *Āpastamba* brahman of the Vatama group from a nearby village; for the time period, this was not at all common.

25 Vinod Bhattatiripad is the convener of Nambudiri.com.

26 Michael Witzel, "Tracing the Vedic Dialects," in Collette Caillat, ed., *Dialectes dans les littératures indo-aryennes,* (Paris: Edition-Diffusion de Bocard, 1989), pp. 97–265, and "Ṛgvedic History: Poets, Chieftains, Polities," in George Erdosy, ed., *The Indo-Aryans of Ancient South Asia* (Berlin: Walter de Gruyter, 1995), pp. 307–352, provides a panorama of Vedic India, starting at ṚV (Level 1, W), YV and SV (Level 2–>3; W>C), spreading eastward onto *Brāhmaṇa* texts, Level 3–5 (C–>E), and culminating in E Level 5.

27 Staal was emphatic on this point in "shop talk" about the field of Vedic studies. He saw the ritual aspect of the Vedic tradition coming downstream from Willem Caland through his own work on ritual and on the other side, the philological aspect of the Vedic tradition, coming down from F. B. J. Kuiper and Murray B. Emeneau through Witzel, the two constituting a synthesis, as in my work.

28 Witzel, "Ṛgvedic History: Poets, Chieftains, Polities."

29 T. V. Mahalingam, ed., *Inscriptions of the Pallavas* (New Delhi: Indian Council of Historical Research, 1983), pp. 52–54, item 7.

30 Burton Stein, in *Peasant State and Society in Medieval South India* (Delhi: Oxford University Press, 1980), p. 4, gives a fuller treatment of this thesis that the Coromandal Brahmadeya village was a keystone of Coromandal culture: "[D]uring the Chola age, we are afforded the first view . . . of how wealthy and powerful peasants, Brahmans, great chiefs and kings . . . shaped a highly variegated landscape to their distinctive purposes. And the arrangements established . . . during the Chola period persisted into the modern age notwithstanding political, social and cultural developments which transformed many crucial aspects of South Indian life."

31 Thennilapuram Mahadevan and Frits Staal, "The Turning Point in a Living Tradition: Somayagam 2003," *Electronic Journal of Vedic Studies* 10/2 (2003).

32 Witzel's entire series, "Materials on Veda Śākhās" is useful, in particular the eighth, "The Development of the Vedic Canon and Its Schools: The Social and Political Milieu," in Michael Witzel, ed., *Inside the Texts—Beyond Texts: New Approaches to the Study of the Vedas* (Cambridge, MA: Department of Sanskrit and Indian Studies, Harvard University, 1997), pp. 257–345.

33 David W. Anthony, *The Horse, the Wheel, and Language: How Bronze-Age Riders from the Eurasian Steppes Shaped the Modern World* (Princeton, NJ: Princeton University Press, 2010), sees the domestication of horses the "the most dramatic moment" (pp. 18–19) of the PIE migrations, 4800 BP. The IE speakers offered the host population "attractive opportunities to participate in their language" (pp. 15–16). Anthony further argues against nineteenth-century Āryanistic thinking in general, noting that "the term *Āryan* (italics in the original) should be confined only to this Indo-Aryan branch of the IE family" (p. 9).

34 In ongoing work, I show that these *dānastuti*s are a special feature of Vedic poetry, as such marking the cementing of the *brahmakṣatra* grid underlying the

Vedic state, in verses addressed by the *ṛṣi*-singer to his *kṣatra* patron, in praise of gifts received. As we know, such praise poetry was a feature of the IE Oral Traditions (see Calvert Watkins, *How to Kill a Dragon: Aspects of Indo-European Poetics* [New York and Oxford: Oxford University Press, 1995]), but in the Vedic example, it points to a special status of the *bráhma* element, a *primus inter pares,* in the Vedic state—modulating the "Hindu" state profoundly of this model.

35 Stephanie Jamison, *Sacrificed Wife/Sacrificer's Wife: Women, Ritual, and Hospitality in Ancient India* (New York: Oxford University Press, 1996).

36 Stephen Jay Gould's definition of "spandrel" in *Questioning the Millennium: A Rationalist's Guide to a Precisely Arbitrary Countdown* (New York: Harmony Books, 1997), is a useful starting point: "Evolutionary Biology needs such an explicit term for features arising as byproduct, rather than adaptations, whatever their subsequent exaptive utility." As we know, Noam Chomsky already interprets language as a spandrel, almost 90 percent of it introspective, or I Language, an autonomous system doing its thing in neural computations, as does the digestive or the visual systems. The metrical Artificial Languages, both Western and Eastern, push the idea further: the need of a special skill set and its cultivation as a *Paideia* byproduct. What we see in the Indic case takes the whole process to its limit, the audiorecording-like transmission of the human sound, demands its *padapāṭha* analysis and a genetically closed caste, almost inert automatons, and demanding an entire civilization to anchor it.

37 I owe this happy imagery to Greg Nagy, from a 2015 colloquium at the Center for Hellenic Studies, Washington DC.

38 In Arthur Macdonnell's case we have an interesting "ships passing in the night" story. In 1913 he was at Bolgatty Palace, the home of the British Resident at Cochin, meeting with and mentoring a Cochin prince and urging him to write about the local Brahmans and their Vedic traditions, while at the same time the Vedic rituals were taking place just a few miles to the north. The prince was certainly knowledgeable. Macdonnell published an account in the *Journal of the Royal Asiatic Society.*

39 See Michael Witzel, "Reminiscences of Frits Staal and the *Agnicayana,*" pp. 601–622.

References

Anthony, David W. *The Horse, the Wheel, and Language: How Bronze-Age Riders from the Eurasian Steppes Shaped the Modern World.* Princeton, NJ: Princeton University Press, 2010.

Arunachalam, M. *The Kaḷabhras in the Pāṇṭiyan Country and Their Impact on the*

Brough, John. "The Early History of the Gotras," *Journal of the Royal Asiatic Society* (1946): 32–90.

Ehlers, Gerald. "A Note on Pūrvaśikhā," *Electronic Journal of Vedic Studies* 10/4 (October 2003).

Ehret, Christopher. "Language Change and the Material Correlates of Language and Ethnic Shift," *Antiquity* 62 (1988): 564–574.

Geertz, Clifford. *The Interpretation of Cultures: Selected Essays.* New York: Basic Books, 1973.

Ghurye, G. S. *Caste and Race in India* (1932). Bombay (Mumbai): Popular Prakashan, 2008, reprint.

Gould, Stephen Jay. *Questioning the Millennium: A Rationalist's Guide to a Precisely Arbitrary Countdown.* New York, Harmony Books, 1997.

Hardy, Friedhelm. *Virahabhakti: The Early Kistory of Kṛṣṇa Devotion in South India.* Delhi: Oxford University Press, 1983.

Hart, George. *The Poems of Ancient Tamil.* Berkeley: University of California Press, 1975.

Hart, George, and Hank Heifetz. *The Four Hundred Songs of War and Wisdom.* New York: Columbia University Press, 1999.

Ikari, Y. "A Survey of the New Manuscripts of the Vādhūla School—MSS. of K1 and K4," *Zinbun: Annals of the Institute for Research in Humanities* 33, Kyoto University (1998): 1–30.

Iyer, L. K. Anantha Krishna. *The Cochin Tribes and Castes,* 2 vols. London, Luzac & Co., 1909–1912.

Jaeger, Warner. *Paideia: The Ideals of Greek Culture,* Vol. II. Oxford: Basil Blackwell, 1943.

Jagadeesan, N. *History of Srīvaiśnavism in the Tamil Country: Post Ramanuja.* Madurai: Koovai Publishers, 1977.

Jamison, Stephanie. *Sacrificed Wife/Sacrificer's Wife: Women, Ritual, and Hospitality in Ancient India.* New York: Oxford University Press, 1996.

Krishnan, K. G. *Karandai Tamil Sangam Plates of Rajendrachola I.* Delhi: Archeological Survey of India, 1983.

Macdonell, Arthur A. *A Practical Sanskrit Dictionary with Transliterature, Accentuation and Etymological Analysis Throughout.* London: Oxford University Press, 1929.

Mahadevan, Iravagtam. *Early Tamil Epigraphy: From the Earliest Times to the Eighth Century CE.* Chennai: Crea A, 2003.

—. "From Orality to Literacy: The Case of the Tamil Society," *Studies in History* (n.s.) 11/2 (1995): 173–188.

Mahadevan, Thennilapuram. "Brahmans and the Sanskrit Epics: Their Migrations to the South." Paper presented to the University Seminar on South Asia, George Washington University, 2003.

—. "On the Southern Recension of the *Mahābhārata,* Brahman Migrations, and Brāhmī Paleography," *Electronic Journal of Vedic Studies* 15/2 (2008): 1–143.

—. "Textual Support for Early Integrity of the *Mahābhārata* from its Southern Recension." Paper presented to the 14th World Sanskrit Conference, Kyoto, 2009.

—. "The Institution of *Gotra,* The *Ṛgveda,* and the Brahmans," in Joel B. Brereton, ed., *The Vedas in Indian Culture an History: Proceedings of the Fourth International Vedic Workshop,* Austin, TX, 2007.

—."The Southern Recension the *Mahābhārata:* The *Harivaṃśa* and Alvār Vaishnaivism," in Vishwa Adluri, ed., *Ways and Reasons for Thinking about the Mahābhārata as a Whole* (Pune: Bhandarkar Oriental Institute, 2013) pp. 87–128.

—."The Three Rails of the *Mahābhārata* Textual Tradition," *Journal of Vaishnava Studies* 19/2 (2011): 23–69.

Mahadevan, Thennilapuram, and Frits Staal. "The Turning Point in a Living Tradition: Somayagam 2003," *Electronic Journal of Vedic Studies* 10/2 (2003).

Mahalingam, T. V., ed. *Inscriptions of the Pallavas.* New Delhi: Indian Council of Historical Research, 1988.

—.*Kāñcīpuram in Early South Indian History.* Bombay: Asia Publishing House, 1969.

Marr, J. R. *The Eight Anthologies: A Study in Early Tamil Literature.* Madras: Institute of Asian Studies, 1985.

Narayanankutti, Melangath. *Saṅgak-kālacharitam.* Trivandrum: Kerala Bhasha Institute, 2003.

Parpola, Asko. "On the Jaiminiya and Vādhūla Traditions of South India and the Pāṇḍu/Pāṇḍava Problem," *Studia Orientalia* 55 (1984): 429–468.

—."The Literature and Study of the Jaiminiya Sāmaveda: In Retrospect and Prospect," *Studia Orientalia* 53 (1973): 3–33.

—.*The Śrautasūtras of Laṭyāyana and Drāhyāyaṇa and Their Commentaries: An English Translation and Study.* Helsinki: Helsingfors, 1968.

Raghavan, V. *The Present Position of Vedic Recitation and Vedic Sakhas.* Kumbakonam: Veda Dharma Paripalana Sabha, 1962.

Rangarajan, L. N., ed. and trans. *Kautilya: The Arthashastra* (1987). Delhi: Penguin Books, 1992, reprint.

Renou, Louis. "The Vedic Schools and the Epigraphy," in Vishva Bandhu, ed., *Siddhabhāratī*, pp. 214–221. Hoshiarpur: V. V. R. Institute, 1950.

Salomon, Richard. *Indian Epigraphy. A Guide to the Study of Inscriptions in Sanskrit, Prakrit, and the Other Indo-Aryan Languages.* New York: Oxford University Press, 1998.

Staal, Frits. *Agni: The Vedic Ritual of the Fire Altar,* 2 vols. Berkeley: Asian Humanities Press, 1983.

—."From *Prāṅmukham* to *Sarvatomukham:* A Thread through the *Śrauta* Maze," in Arlo Griffiths and Jan E. M. Houben, eds., *The Vedas: Texts, Language & Ritual: Proceedings of the Third International Vedic Workshop, Leiden 2002,* pp. 521–555. Groningen Oriental Studies 20. Groningen: Egbert Forsten, 2004.

—.*Mantras between Fire and Water: Reflections on a Balinese Rite.* Appendix by Dick van der Meij. Amsterdam: Koninklikje Nederlandse Akademie van Wetenschappen, 1995.

—.*Nambudiri Veda Recitation.* The Hague: Mouton, 1961.

—.*Rules without Meaning: Ritual, Mantras, and the Human Sciences.* New York: Lang, 1989.

—.*The Fidelity of the Oral Tradition and the Origins of Science.* Amsterdam: North Holland Publishing Company, 1986.

—. "The Independence of Rationality from Literacy," *European Journal of Sociology* 30 (1989): 301–310.

Stein, Burton. "Brahman and Peasant in Early South Indian History," *The Adyar Library Bulletin* 31/32 (1968): 229–269.

—. *Peasant State and Society in Medieval South India.* Delhi: Oxford University Press, 1980.

Thurston, Edgar. *Castes and Tribes of Southern India,* 7 vols. (1909). Delhi: Cosmo, 1975, reprint.

Watkins, Calvert. *How to Kill a Dragon: Aspects of Indo-European Poetics.* New York and Oxford: Oxford University Press, 1995.

Witzel, Michael. "Meaningful Ritual: Vedic, Medieval, and Contemporary Concepts in the Nepalese Agnihotra Ritual," in Albert W. Van den Hoek, Dirk H. A. Kolff, and M. S. Oort, eds., *Ritual, State, and History in South Asia: Essays in Honour of J. C. Heesterman,* pp. 774–825. Leiden: E. J. Brill, 1992.

—. "On Indian Historical Writing: The Role of the Vaṃśāvalīs," *Journal of the Japanese Association for South Asian Studies* 2 (1990): 1–57.

—. "On the Origin of the Literary Device of the 'Frame Story' in Old Indian Literature," in Harry Falk, ed., *Hinduismus and Buddhismus: Festscrift für Ultrich Scneider,* pp. 380–414. Freiburg: Hedwig Falk, 1987.

—. "Ṛgvedic History: Poets, Chieftains, Polities," in George Erdosy, ed., *The Indo-Aryans of Ancient South Asia,* pp. 307–352. Berlin: Walter de Gruyter, 1995.

—. "Substrate Language in Old Indo-Aryan (Ṛgvedic, Middle, Late)," *Electronic Journal of Vedic Studies* 5/1 (August 1999): 1–67.

—. "The Development of the Vedic Canon and Its Schools: The Social and Political Milieu," (Materials on Veda Śākhās 8), in Michael Witzel, ed., *Inside the Texts—Beyond Texts: New Approaches to the Study of the Vedas,* pp. 257–345. Harvard Oriental Series, Opera Minora 2. Cambridge, MA: Department of Sanskrit and Indian Studies, Harvard University, 1997.

—. "Tracing the Vedic Dialects," in Collette Caillat, ed., *Dialectes dans les littératures indo-aryennes.* Acts of the Colloque International, Paris, September 16–18, 1986. Publicationes de L'Institut de Civilisation Indienne, Series 8, Fasc. 55, pp. 97–265. Paris: Edition-Diffusion de Bocard, 1989.

—. "Vaidics and Vedic Religion," *Indology List,* May 13, 1999.

Notes sur les joutes védiques

Boris Oguibénine
Université de Strasbourg

Dans mon livre *La déesse Uṣas. Recherches sur le sacrifice de la parole dans le Ṛgveda*[1] j'ai proposé une explication du rôle et du pouvoir de la parole dans la religion sacrificielle du *Ṛgveda.* L'essentiel en est que la parole védique prend corps et existence dans une ambiance de joute, de rivalité et de violence ritualisées. Elle présente le sacré, le labeur du poète officiant étant semé d'embûches. Les obstacles rendant diffiiciles le travail poétique sont de nature intérieure et extérieure: le poète se doit d'être prompt à créer une parole efficace (surmonter la résistance que constitue l'Enigme sacrée, réussir la maîtrise des règles poétique); il doit satisfaire son patron, le commanditaire du sacrifice (car il lui est impératif de se faire attribuer la *dakṣiṇā,* la récompense qui affirmera son statut de poète), contrecarrer les vélleités adverses que lui opposent ses confrères (être le meilleur à parler du *bráhman*), enfin oeuvrer à réaffirmer la valeur du sacrifice védique malgré l'hostilité de ses ennemis non-védiques et non-sacrifiants. Dans les recherches sur la religion du Veda, les voix de Paul Thieme et de Louis Renou ont toujours été les plus écoutées. Renou notamment s'est maintes fois prononcé sur la nature et la finalité de la joute védique, mais certaines de ses vues ont été très vivement, et à mon sens fructueusement, discutées par Thieme. F. B. J. Kuiper a, à sa manière, pris part à ce débat. Les notes qui suivent sont destinées à faire le point sur ces controverses qui m'ont beaucoup inspirées et qui m'ont permis, si jamais la tâche n'est pas impossible, de comprendre davantage l'univers conceptuel complexe des hymnes du *Ṛgveda.*

1

Le sacrifiant védique a deux aspects, intimement liés: il est combattant et antagoniste. Il a recours à la parole de louange quand il affronte son homologue intestin (ce qui est très vraisemblablement dénoté par le terme *vívāc* lorsqu'il désigne non l'action de se disputer, mais l'agent de la dispute ou de la controverse verbales, par un transfert courant dans le *R̥gveda*).[2] Le sacrifiant est aussi assimilé au guerrier quand ses actions visent à combattre et à éliminer son homologue extérieur.[3] Le sacrifice est en effet considéré comme confrontation (du poète avec ses dieux) et affrontement (des poètes entre eux, des patrons du sacrifice rivaux) et il n'est pass étonnant que sa presentation ait pris pour modèle l'éthos guerrier. Celui-ci s'impose car le sacrifice du poète officiant, son acte d'offrande de la parole, est teinté de violence, sinon d'effort par lequel il vise à se démarquer de son rival pour le déposséder et pour attirer à soi les dieux. C'est ainsi que, dans la vision du poète officiant, son rival est compromis: il est inefficace (*sthirápīta*, "raidi et gras"), il est appelé 'celui qui se meut avec sa fiction inféconde' (10.71.5: *ádhenvā carati māyáyaiṣáḥ*),[4] il est dénigré autant que le redoutable adversaire guerrier.

L'officiant ne sera évidemment jamais dit "guerrier" expressément. Le symbolisme védique opère une distinction entre le sacrifiant-en-général (*yájamāna-*, "le sacrifiant-laïc" selon la suggestion de Renou dans sa traduction de 1.24.11),[5] personnage à vocation guerrière et le poète officiant à coloration guerrière. Les moyens à la disposition de chacun de ces protagonstes ne sont pas les mêmes, chacun est aux prises avec son propre adversaire et fait face à son propre combat, avec les armes qui répondent à la situation.

2

Dans son étude "The Ancient Aryan Verbal Contest" et dans son ouvrage *Varuṇa and Vidūṣaka*,[6] Kuiper exposait sa théorie où l'accent avait été mis sur les relations étroites des disputes vebales des poètes védiques avec d'autres formes des duels opposant des partenaires divers quant à leur nature (dieux, héros montant les chars attelés de chevaux, guerriers de camps adverses, etc.). La nature des controverses est variée, mais ells sont conçues sur un même modèle.

Un autre point important de cette théorie est que ces disputes et combats reprennent à leur manière le symbolisme de la cérémonie que les ethnographes appellent le potlatch. Marcle Mauss et Gerrit J. Held l'ont abusivement reconnue pour institution fondamentale de la civilisation indienne et même indo-aryenne.[7]

Les hypothèses de Kuiper me semblent fort intéressantes surtout en ce qu'elles éclairent les relations, en effet décisives, organisant plusieurs formes de disputes de divers plans, mais je ne trouve pas entièrement convaincantes ses constructions concernant la période hivernale, seule appelant les combats et les compétitions. Autant qu'on puisse constater, chaque fois que Kuiper se prononce sur ce moment précis de l'année,[8] ce ne sont pour lui que des hypothèses qui restent à vérifier.

Or, en faisant abstraction de l'hypothèse du rituel du solstice d'hiver, il apparaît (j'ai essayé de le montrer dans mon livre sur Uṣas cité ci-dessus ainsi que dans mes *Essais sur la culture védique et indo-européenne*) que les disputes verbales et autres formes de compétition védiques sont d'une importance bien plus générale. Il serait, en conséquence, trop restrictif de les mettre en corrélation exclusive avec un prétendu rituel d'hiver dont en réalité rien ne prouve l'existence dans la religion du *Ṛgveda.* L'explication gagnera en prenant en compte le caractère essentiel de la performance rituelle et liturgique des poètes officiants védiques: c'est une expression de leurs efforts pour le rétablissement du cosmos (et Kuiper a raison de valoriser le rapport entre l'activité sacerdotale et le renouveau cosmique) et c'est, sous forme de louanges des dieux, quand les poètes s'opposent en rivaux dans une vívāc et s'assimilent aux guerriers, que prend corps le principe même de leur participation au processus sacrificiel.

À une autre occasion, en évoquant le personnage d'Uṣas, déesse des disputes et des compétitions, Kuiper s'interroge: "Où les biens (distribués comme les *vāja-* lors du ritual d'Uṣas)[9] sont-ils conquis, si une guerre ordinaire est exclue?"[10] J'ai proposé une réponse à cette question dans le chapitre *"Vāja et dakṣiṇā"* des *Essais sur la culture védique et indo-européenne.* La corrélation cosmogonique des *vívāc* védiques décisive pour Kuiper—et elle est en effet incontestable, même si la nature de ces disputes s'explique, me semble-t-il, autrement, dans un cadre plus vaste—est reprise par lui dans son analyse de la *vívāc* entre Varuṇa et Indra.[11] La conclusion de Kuiper sur l'attribution à Varuṇa de la maîtrise des eaux dans le nouveau règne des dieux inauguré par Indra est sans doute justifiée (c'est en dehors de la présente discussion), mais voyons de plus près ce qu'est la *vívāc.*

Il peut bien s'agir de la répartition des secteurs du cosmos sur lesquels règnera chaque divinité, sans qu'effectivement, comme le montre Kuiper, Varuṇa soit subordonné à Indra, mais il est intéressant de préciser quel devait être le contexte rituel de la dispute des deux dieux.

Cette dispute aboutissant à la répartition des zones de pouvoir (4.42 et 10.124.5) doit bien refléter la nature de chacun de ces dieux. Si en 4.42 c'est encore Varuṇa qui énonce ses mérites,[12] il est normal (et cela ne contredit pas la conclusion finale de Kuiper) qu'il rappelle son lien avec l'eau (4.42.4a: *ahám apó apinvam ukṣámāṇāḥ,* "c'est moi qui ai gonflé les eaux arrosantes"). Le dialogue est cependant bel et bien une *vívāc* qui a pour but final la victoire sur son adversaire son "refoulement" et même son assujettissement ou apprivoisement: 3.34.10: *nunudé vívācó 'thābhavad damitābhíkratūnām,* "(Indra) a repoussé les disputants, il est ainsi devenu le dompteur des arrogants qui élèvent leur force spirituelle (au-dessus des autres)."[13] L'objet d'une *vívāc* est aussi la démonstration de la suprématie sur l'adversaire au moyen d'un *bráhman* bien composé et énoncé. Il n'est donc pas étonnant que, dans la série des *bráhman,* des formulations portant sur leurs actes et pouvoirs respectifs, Indra et Varuṇa fassent apparaître les différences de leurs natures. Immédiatement après Varuṇa proclamant ses droits sur les eaux —si tel est le sens du mot *ádhipatyam*[14]— c'est au tour d'Indra d'annoncer, dans un style ne dévoilant que les "connexions" de (ou les allusions à) sa nature de guerrier, comme c'est l'usage dans les bráhman: 4.42.5: *mām náraḥ sváśvā vājáyanto mām vṛtaḥ samáraṇe havante/ kṛṇómy ājím maghávāhám índra íyarmi reṇúm abhíbhūty-ojāḥ,* "C'est moi qu'appellent les hommes aux bons chevaux, aspirant aux prix de compétition, moi, quand ils sont encerclés dans un combat ; je suscite le combat, moi, Indra le généreux, je soulève la poussière, moi, qui possède la force supérieure."[15]

Ainsi, s'il est un contexte rituel-cadre de la dispute des deux dieux, il est identique au rituel des disputes poétiques confrontant, au plan des hommes, les poètes officiants. Ce rituel—j'entends encore le comportement codifié et institualisé—devait se dérouler selon les mêmes règles que la contestation réciproque des officiants recherchant chacun l'octroi des privilèges. La présentation de cette contestation est souvent chargée d'allusions explicites aux affrontements guerriers, comme le sont les discours d'Indra et de Varuṇa: celui-ci proclame, dès le début de l'hymne 4.42 son statut de guerrier à la tête d'un domaine royal (v. 4.42.1a: *máma dvitā́ rāṣṭrám̐ kṣatríyasya,* "c'est à moi en effet qu'est ce domaine royal, [à moi] le [roi] guerrier"). Il y proclame également sa nature royale (4.42.2a: *ahám̐ rā́jā*)[16] liée évidemment le plus étroitement à la guerre, à la maîtrise et à la domination cosmiques (4.42.3–4). Il n'est certes pas sans importance que le dialogue évoqué ici soit celui des dieux—ce qui permet à Kuiper de développer sa présentation du conflit entre Indra et Varuṇa—mais le *Ṛgveda* pratique aisément la transposition d'usages et de modèles de comportement du plan humain au plan divin et inversement. Il ne semble donc pas nécessaire de maintenir l'hypothèse du rituel du Nouvel An, selon Kuiper, période de la crise cosmique favorisant les disputes rituelles, verbales et autres. À noter encore que, dans son plus récent ouvrage, Kuiper hésite, comme auparavant, sur le fait que le *Ṛgveda* soit une collection d'hymnes créés pour célébrer la période des disputes: "[T]his collection of hymns was in essence . . . designed for the celebration of the New Year period of contests. This cannot be definitely proved. . . ."[17]

En résumant brièvement les acquis de ma recherché (notamment dans *La déesse Uṣas*), je crois avoir montré, sans référence au rituel saisonnier, sans avoir recours à la théorie de Kuiper, que le sacrifiant védique avait à affronter deux types d'adversaires, à l'intérieur et à l'extérieur de la société védique. S'il devait faire face à l'adversaire extérieur, la victoire sur celui-ci devait changer en mieux sa position au sein de la sodalité (des poètes, des guerriers) tandis que la victoire sur l'adversaire intérieur apportait (au poète officiant, au sacrifiant-en-général) des changements à la société védique.

3

Ill existe une perspective où les conjectures de Kuiper trouvent un écho favorable, si ce n'est une approbation. Vladimir Toporov prend acte de ces remarques de Kuiper (qui incluent une longue citation de la thèse de G. W. Locher, *The Serpent in Kwakiutl Religion*[18]):

> The fact that the *Ṛgveda* often associates the ideas of war and contest allows us to conjecture that war, no less than present-giving, contests and chariot-races, was thought of as stimulating the creative forces of the Cosmos during the winter ritual. . . . "[T]he whole exchange traffic of the potlatch is, really, nothing but one great sacrifical rite. . . . But then the act [of giving away of copper pieces in the potlatch] was also a rebirth rite, a passing on to a new phase of life. . . . As a matter of fact, the very principle of the potlatch is intimately bound with the root idea of the winter ritual. . . . Besides the conception of sacrifice, also the idea of combat belongs to the most essential elements of the potlatch complex" (Locher).

Kuiper conclut alors:

> This explains why the poet of III.34, after mentioning the battles between Aryans and Dasyus in st. 9, immediately passes on to their mythic prototype. . . . The Old Aryan winter ritual was indeed a mere replica of the primordial *vívāc-* between the cosmic powers of nether world and upper world. . . .[19]

Or ces remarques servent d'appui à Toporov pour reconstruire la strate archaïque des rituels funéraires chez les anciens Prussiens dont une partie importante était la triple destruction: *destruction par crémation* des effets personnels du défunt (armes, vêtemetns, etc.), *consommation/destruction* de la nourriture et des boissons, enfin la *destruction par répartition* des biens du défunt parmi les participants aux concours hippiques accompagnant les funérailles.

Le commentaire de Toporov mérite qu'on le cite presque in extenso:

> On aura vu que le motif de destruction dans une situation liminaire pour le défunt qui passe de ce monde à l'autre monde, à une vie nouvelle, reprend une caractéristique [essentielle] du plan macrocosmique: destruction de l'univers à la jonction de l'année qui passe et du Nouvel An. . . . S'il en ainsi, il est naturel d'admettre que les compétitions [dont les concours hippiques] précédant la crémation du défunt, en tant que variante institualisée de la contestation en général. . . , n'est autre chose que la réplique "microcosmique" de la confrontation "macrocosmique" qui a lieu lors du passage d'une année à l'autre où le démiurge, aux prises avec son adversaire incarnant le chaos et la mort, l'emporte sur celui-ci en établissant une nouvelle organisation. Dans cette confrontation, comme dans le duel d'Indra et de Vṛtra [dans le *Ṛgveda*] et dans les guerres entre les Aryens et les Dasyus, reproduisant, pour les Aryens, cet événement mythologique des "premiers" temps, la destruction, la dévastation et leur compensation est un des principaux motifs (ce qui rapprochent encore la dispute-contestation "cosmique" et les compétitions lors des rites funéraires).[20]

Soit, mais on cherchera en vain quelques témoignages védiques sur la destruction des biens identique à celle lors du potlatch (en dépit de cette affirmation de Kuiper, "Many data provided by the Rigveda are strongly reminiscent of the winter ritual of the North American Kwakiutl, the most conspicuous characteristic of which was the potlatch-ceremony"[21]). En effet, un exemple parmi d'autres: la lecture de 6.47.6 donnée par Kuiper ainsi que son explication (nullement évidentes): *piba . . . sómam indra vṛtrahā́ . . . samaré vásūnām,* "bois le soma, ô Indra, [toi] le meurtrier de Vṛtra," lors de la confluence des richesses' est commenté ainsi:

> [T]he ritual act of invigorating the god is closely associated with a reference to a present-giving, which may be the god's annual renewal of life, but which may equally well be an actual war or a ceremonial contest of the potlatch type, in which wealth was won (or lost).[22]

Il est assez arbitraire de voir dans la combinaison *samará vásūnām,* "in der Anhäufung von Schätzen" (selon Karl F. Geldner que cite Kuiper sans donner sa propre traduction[23]) la remise de présents lors du potlatch (et encore moins la destruction des biens) alors que visiblement cette combinaison est accolée à la désignation d'Indra, meurtrier du monstre, pour préciser que ce meurtre ouvre justement l'accès aux richesses: on a là l'explicitation suffisamment claire du grand mythe védique sans rapport avec le potlatch.

Pour Kuiper, la déesse Uṣas est la déesse du potlatch. Or plusieurs question se posent inévitablement quand on relit son argumentation. Une fois examinées les strophes 7.78.5, 6.46.9. 5.86.6, 1.124.10, 5.79.4 (sur certaines desquelles, dans le meme ordre[24]), il conclut, du reste tout à fait judicieusement, que les dieux (dont Indra et Uṣas) et les patrons du sacrifice étant désignés comme généreux (*maghávan-*), il est clair que les patrons avaient la fonction sociale de distribution des biens (des *maghá-*) identique à la même function religieuse des dieux; mais son autre conclusion est fort arbitraire, ce qu'il semble reconnaître:

> It is indeed unbelievable that the *surís* (les patrons, cf. le terme allemand *Lohnherren,* "patrons de remuneration") should have had the title of *maghávan-* during the whole year: even the reiteration of Indra's cosmogonical act must have been restricted to one well-defined period, viz. the beginning of the new year" (mais les poètes officiants s'exerçaient justement et percevaient leur salaire rituel, la *dákṣiṇā,* continûment, sans que leur performances soient associées à une période quelconque!). Although it is admittedly very difficult to trace, behind the mythological allusions and identifications, the real events which the Vedic poets had in mind, this assumption allows us to arrive at a fuller and more concrete understanding of many hymns.[25]

Je pense, soit dit en passant, qu'en effet nous n'arriverons jamais à saisir complètement la réalité védique à travers les hymnes, mais nous pouvons rétablir un système cohérent du symbolisme véhiculé par ces textes, en respectant toutefois les données lexicales, souvent difficilement définissables: or, là encore, même si 7.32.14–15 évoque l'octroi des biens par les patrons "au moment décisif du *vṛtrahátya,* du meurtre de Vṛtra" ou "quand l'enjeu arrive à décision" (*pā́rye diví* selon Renou[26]), peut-on suivre Kuiper qui s'interroge après avoir cité ces strophes: "Does not this ritual reiteration of the god's *vṛtrahátya* clearly refer to a winter ceremony. . . ?", et accepter que "the present-giving has probably been a weapon in the social contest, which then must also have taken place in the same period of crisis, about the beginning of the new year"?[27] Il a pourtant été établi que, dans le système symbolique du *Ṛgveda,* les poètes officiants étaient gratifiés de *dákṣiṇā* en fonction de leur réussite aux compétitions, aux joutes, qui devaient avoir lieu sans être liées aux rites saisonniers.[28] On peut supposer que le rituel (qui conjugait parole et libation, prière orale et offrandes matérielles) présenté dans les hymnes ṛgvédiques, avait servi de modèle pour les pratiques rituelles ultérieures car les textes post-ṛgvédiques se réfèrent explicitement au *Ṛgveda*. Quel seraient alors les raisons pour que les liens entre le rituel et le prétendu potlatch effectué lors du passage au Nouvel An auraient été exposés de manière cryptée, insuffisamment explicites?

4

Je crois utile de suggérer ici quelques modifications à la lecture des extraits du *Ṛgveda* rappelés dans l'étude de Kuiper, "The Ancient Aryan Verbal Contest." Ces modifications visent moins à opposer à la théorie de Kuiper une interpretation incompatible avec la sienne qu'à compléter celle-ci dans une direction qui est précisément compatible avec sa partie essentielle.

> 6.33.2: *tvā́m hìndravase vívāco hávante carṣaṇáyaḥ śurasātau / tvā́ṃ víprebhiḥ ví paṇimr aśā́yas tvóta ít sánitā vā́jam árvā,* "C'est toi, ô Indra, que les peuples qui s'affrontent en disputants appellent au secours lors du combat des héros. Tu as [agissant de concert] avec les orateurs-inspirés, dispersé les Paṇi [les miserable]. Le coursier gagne son prix-de-compétition grâce à ton soutien.

S'il est ici question des opposants (ou des disputants) qui manient la parole (cf. encore les *vívācas* de 3.34.10)[29] invoquant l'assistance d'Indra lors de leur combat (Kuiper comprend *śū́rasāti-*, "obtainment of valiant sons"), deux séries d'événements sont habilement juxtaposées et probablement assimilées les unes aux autres: il s'agit de deux variétés d'activité, celle des guerriers marquée de la présence d'Indra, dieu de la guerre, et le faire sacrificiel des poètes laudateurs comparé au coursier qui gagne son prix ou, pour le dire autrement, d'un rapprochement de deux variétés du sacrifice qui s'éclairent mutuellement, où Indra, dieu guerrier par excellence, agit sur deux plans associés, la guerre et l'activité des poètes inspirés. On ne peut éluder une question controversée à laquelle diverses réponses ont été ébauchées: s'agit-il des opposants appartenant à un groupe social homogène, des disputes intestines des sacrifiants donc, ou bien d'affrontements d'adeptes d'Indra et de leurs adversaires extérieurs? Kuiper ne se prononce pas sur le terme *carṣaṇí-*.[30] En partant de 3.34.10, il conclut par cette réflexion qui est peut-être la clé de sa conception du lien entre les disputes verbales inaugurant le Nouvel An et le rituel d'hiver:

> If we are ready to admit that the Vedic people were speaking about something definite and did not merely repeat ancient poetic formulas devoid of

real sense, these words can only be taken to refer to a winter ritual, a ceremonial . . . contest inaugurating the new year."[31]

Mais même en admettant que 3.34.10 parle "about something definite," l'hypothèse du rituel du nouvel an ne semble pas nécessaire.

Kuiper fait suivre sa lecture de 6.33.2 de son interpretation sur le plan cosmique de 7.30.2:

> *hávanta u tvā hávyaṃ vívāci tanū́ṣu śū́rāḥ sū́ryasya sātaú/ tvā́ṃ víśveṣu sényo jáneṣu tvā́ṃ vṛtrā́ṇi randhayā suhántu,* "Les héros t'invoquent, toi digne d'invocation dans une dispute [verbale], dans un combat pour leurs corps, pour gagner le soleil. Parmi toutes les populations tu es le guerrier [par excellence]; livre-[nous nos] ennemis pour [les] abattre à [notre] aise!"[32]

Il est encore possible que les participants d'une dispute verbale et les héros guerriers ne soient pas ici distingués, car les hymnes sont délibérément ambigus. Je ne peux suivre Kuiper que sur un point: il y est effectivement question de l'affrontement en vue de s'approprier les biens obtenus habituellement par voie de sacrifice (intégrité corporelle, soleil, victoire sur l'adversaire), mais il est aussi probable que le vocabulaire guerrier (*sénya-*, "guerrier," peut-être "lanceur de fleches," *randh-*, "livrer au pouvoir ennemi,"[33] *suhántu-*, "aisé à abattre") y soit employé afin d'assimiler le conflit ou la rivalité intestine et la guerre menée aux confins de l'univers sacrificielle védique.

> 7.23.2: *áyāmi ghóṣa indra devájāmir irajyánta yác churúdho vívāci / nahí svám ā́yuś cikité jáneṣu tā́nī́d áṃhāṃsy áti parṣy asmā́n,* "Le cri familier, parent des dieux, a été tendu [vers toi] ô Indra ! Les biens ont été mis à disposition [des disputants) lors de [leur] dispute [riteulle]. Parmi les hommes, nul ne connaît sa proper durée-de-vie. Porte-nous au-delà des limites étroites [de cette durée]!"

Malgré l'incertutude du sens due surtout au verbe difficile *irajy-*, "diriger, ordonner, commander," mais en admettant que les *śurúdh-*, "les biens, la nourriture" (et "la durée-de-vie"?) sont livrés lors ou à la suite d'une compétition des poètes (selon Oldenberg[34]), c'est bien cette compétition engagée sous sa forme belliqueuse qui est comparée à un *samaryá-*, "confrontation guerrière." Kuiper le dit aussi clairement et rappelle judicieusement 7.23.1:

> *úd u bráhmāṇy airata śravasyéndraṃ samaryé mahayā vasiṣṭha / . . . upaśrotā́ ma ī́vato vācā́ṃsi,* "Les formules-sacrées se sont élevées, elles qui recherchent la renommée. Magnifie Indra, ô Vasiṣṭha lors de [ton] affrontement [avec le rival]. [Puisse Indra] prêter son ouïe à quelqu'un comme moi."[35]

Il faut relever ici tout particulièrement l'évocation des formules-sacrées et du pouvoir du poète de se faire entendre auprès du dieu qu'il célèbre. Il est certain aussi, et Kuiper le dit, que la confrontation guerrière est rapprochée ici d'une situation de crise où a lieu la dispute rituelle des poètes officiants employant leurs moyens éprouvés (en 7.23.2, *ghóṣadevájāmi-* est un appel aux dieux que le poète nomme "[leur] parent," cf. d'autres traductions de cette combinaison de mots: "das den Göttern vertraute Geschrei," "das Getön, dem die Götter verschwistert sind," "the cry that is the gods' kinsman."[36] La crise, bien que périodique, est sentie comme une menace permanente; elle est évoquée par le terme *áṃhas* qui n'est pas sans lien avec les *vṛtrā́ṇi*, "ennemis," mais aussi "obstacles hostiles" affaiblis ou dépassés grâce à Indra. C'est sans doue une crise cosmique, elle est résolue par l'intervention de ce dieu supprimant les entraves extérieures 7.23.3:

> *yujé ráthaṃ gavéṣaṇaṃ háribhyām úpa bráhmāṇi jujuṣāṇám asthuḥ / ví bādhiṣṭa syá ródasī mahitvéndro vṛtrā́ṇi apratī́ jaghanvā́n,* "Les formules-sacrées se sont approchées de celui qui s'en réjouit, pour que soit attelé aux alezans le char allant à la quête des vaches. Indra a repoussé les deux Mondes par sa puissance, lui le meurtrier des ennemis qui n'avaient pas [d'adversaire] à leur taille."[37]

Quelles sont alors les raisons impératives pour expliquer *śurúdh-* comme un terme technique de la terminologie du potlatch qui se rattacherait, ici encore, à un rituel de l'inauguration du Nouvel An?[38]

6.45.28 est une strophe évoquant les chants de louange célébrant Indra: *imā́ u tvā suté-sute nákṣante girvaṇo gíraḥ,* "Vers toi viennent lors de chaque pressurage ces chants de louange, ô toi désireux de louanges," et c'est 6.45.29,[39] strophe où il est question d'une compétition poétique, qui en offre une espèce de commentaire: *purūtámam puraṇā́ṃ stotṝṇā́ṃ vívāci / vā́jebhir vājayatā́m,* "[Ces chants s'approchent de toi] du meilleur, lors de la compétition de nombreux [poètes], qui se disputent autour des prix-de-compétition."[40] Je pense que l'auteur de ces strophes les rattache l'une à l'autre, notamment par l'emploi des termes des courses de chars (*vā́ja-*, le dénominatif *vājay-*), cette autre forme de compétition, assimilable à la joute verbale.[41] Kuiper observe également que ces deux formes de confrontation sont intimement apparentées, v. les strophes 2, 12, et 15 du même hymne et, pour leur évocation similtanée, 1.178.3: Indra y est présenté comme un héros vainqueur dans les combats, écoutant le poète en détresse, poussant en avant le char de l'adorateur, entonnant ses chants à lui. On a là deux formes de compétition, deux façons d'Indra d'intervenir aux côtés de son laudateur, deux orientations complémentaires propres au dedans (joute poétique) et au dehors (guerres extérieurs) du processus sacrificiel. Ces deu formes se complètent autant qu'elles s'assimilent. Dès lors, pourquoi rejeter[42] ce que Geldner[43] appelait "Opferkonkurrenz"? Quelles sont les raisons d'attribuer le double patronage d'Indra à deux aspects différents d'un dieu prétendûment présidant au rituel d'hiver ? V. encore 1.178.4 où réapparaissent les mêmes aspirations des laudateurs et du sacrifiant-laïc, protégés par Indra, dieu des joutes poétiques et dieu-guerrier, célébré dans les combats et dans les disputes verbales (*samaryé . . . stavate vívāci*), et cf. Kuiper pour une lecture selon ses hypothèses sur le rituel d'hiver, cadre des compétitions.[44]

5

On sait que Paul Thieme avait mis en garde les lecteurs de Louis Renou: le danger serait la tendance de Renou à séculariser la poésie du *Ṛgveda,* notamment en évaluant le rôle attribué aux joutes rituelles des poètes officiants.[45] On se demande, dit Thieme, à quelles occasions ces disputes littéraires avaient eu lieu, si ells avaient accompagné de grands sacrifices, comme Renou semble avoir affirmé;[46] il serait difficile, dit encore Thieme, d'admettre cette hypothèse impossible à vérifier et qui veut que le *Ṛgveda* soit le produit de tels exercices purement littéraires. Il conviendrait, en revanche, selon Thieme, d'établir quel est le contenu authentiquement religieux des hymnes. La donnée la plus immédiate pourrait favoriser une telle recherche: la poésie védique a été créée pour accompagner les rites sacrificiels (en tout cas, en ce qui concerne les hymnes les plus anciens); de surcroît, la conviction du poète était que son oeuvre chantée rendait le sacrifice efficace. Les hymnes ne sont donc pas uniquement des témoignages de l'habileté et de la compétence littéraire des poètes et si toutefois on insistait sur l'importance des compétitions, cellesci sont d'abord et surtout des compétitions de performances rituelles rivales ainsi que des compétitions de discours rivaux accompagnant des rites rivalisants.

Thieme a sans doute raison d'inciter à la recherche du contenu spécifique religieux de la poésie védique. Il me semble cependant que ses thèses sont susceptibles de développements allant dans le sens même de ses critiques des thèses de Renou, lesquelles—qu'on n'y voie pas de contradiction—ne me paraissent pas entièrement injustifiées.

Seule une partie des vues de Kuiper sur les competitions védiques me semble acceptable dont notamment l'importance qu'il attache aux disputes de diverses sortes dans la religion du *Ṛgveda*.[47] En effet, j'ai essayé de montrer dans mes *Essais sur la culture védique et indo-européenne* et dans *La déesse Uṣas* que les disputes verbales, lieu de la création littéraire, devaient servir de modèle pour la structuration des affrontements en dehors de la sphère de la parole alors que la parole poétique était cette offrande par laquelle ses auteurs mettaient en marche le processus sacrificiel.

Renou faisait état des joutes et des tournois et ne leur attribuait qu'une valeur littéraire. Or il me semble que l'importance de cette valeur est exagérée. D'ailleurs, seuls quelques accents placés ici et là font la différence de sa conception d'avec celle de Thieme. Il suffit de changer ces accents, de ne pas accorder, par exemple, trop d'importance à ce que Renou appelle la nature littéraire des hymnes pour trouver des points communs aux deux conceptions.

Si le faire sacrificiel englobe les chants, on n'insistera jamais assez sur le fait que la nature même du *Ṛgveda* et sa religion sont étroitement liées. Leur lien est plus profond que ne saurait l'être le lien unissant tout autre discours et le message qu'il véhicule. Pour le poète védique appelé à officier, chanter, parler, énoncer n'est pas foncièrement distinct de "agir, faire, sacrifier par d'autres moyens que la parole." Selon une analyse récente, l'activité sacrificielle et rituelle en général est, d'un côté, désignée par le verbe *kṛ-*, "faire, produire, fabriquer,"[48] et ses dérivés, et de l'autre côté, le *bráhman* est autant dit, parlé et chanté que fait et fabriqué, v. Renou et tout particulièrement 8.32.17: *pánya íd úpa gāyata pánya ukthā́ni śaṃsata brahmā́ kṛṇota pánya ít*, "Chantez pour [Indra] l'admirable, dites des récitations pour [Indra] l'admirable, faites les *bráhman* pour [Indra] l'admirable,"[49] où sont alignés les verbes *gā-*, *śaṃs-*, "chanter, reciter," et *kṛ-*. Selon Renou et Silburn:

> le *bráhman* est une forme d'activité qui sans doute se manifeste par excellence dans la chose dite, qui éventuellement se mélange aux noms des parties chantées ou murmurées de la diction religieuse. . . .[50]

La parole liturgique dont le *bráhman* est une des expressions essentielles (Thieme le reconnaît également: "*bráhman* . . . eben nur Sprüche, Hymnen usw"[51]) est "agie," elle est activité en même temps qu'elle denote l'activité. La formule et le rite se rejoignent,[52] la parole est autant acte que l'acte d'offrande oblatoire.

Il est vrai que Thieme ne reconnaît pas le rôle structurant des conflits entre les poètes, conflits qui servent de forme à leur concurrence. Il ne fait mention des conflits qu'en passant: la seule rivalité observable est, pour lui, celle des participants des rites accompagnés de discours des poètes. En conclura-t-on que la première rivalité entraîne la seconde qui n'est alors que subalterne?

La conception de Thieme du contenu religieux du *Ṛgveda* a cet avantage principal que son interprétation des termes *bráhman* et *ṛtá-* se tiennent réciproquement: le *bráhman-* est la formulation par le langage poétique, sa nature se précise par l'effet magique ou miraculeux que produit cette formulation, alors que celle-ci est l'instrument de l'énonciation du *ṛtá-*, "vérité."[53]

Si Thieme, dans ses explications du fonctionement de la parole védique, tend à exclure l'idée d'affrontement des poètes entre eux ou tout au moins à la minimiser, Renou propose une interprétation différente. L'idée des disputes verbales rituelles et des joutes poétiques y est la pierre angulaire. Pour lui, le *bráhman* est "cette forme de pensée à énigme consistant à poser une corrélation, une identification explicative."[54] C'est aussi, pour les auteurs védiques, le moyen de reveler les faits de corrélation entre le microcosme et le macrocosme, d'où l'idée de *ṛtá*, "le résultat des corrrélations, le produit de l'adaptation," de "l'agencement" entre ces deux variantes du cosmos.[55] Or la notion meme d'énigme posée par Renou est intimement liée à son interpretation du *ṛtá*,[56] de même que le type de discours énoncé lors des compétitions oratoires "qui comporte la maîtrise des équivalences" est pour Renou défini par le *ṛtú-*, "repartition fonctionnelle," des choses dans leur réalité au sens de la classification répartitive.[57]

D'autres différences entre les deux conceptions sont encore plus instructives. Elles tiennent aux representations générales que les deux auteurs ont de la religion védique et peutêtre de la religion tout court. Selon Renou, la religion védique privilégie comme une catégorie essentielle ce "réseau d'interrelations et d'identifications primitives dont était tissée la substance des hymnes." C'est avec ces interrelations et identifications que l'homme opère pour établir "les equations entre le monde rituel et le monde mythique, entre l'ordre humain et l'ordre divin"[58] Or, pour Thieme, la vérité du *bráhman* est ce contenu qui ne peut être contesté ni par le bon sens ni par les témoins oculaires, cette vérité n'est confirmée que par le miracle, lequel se produira du fait que la vérité est énoncée sous une forme poétique ("kunstvoll geformt") et qu'elle est chantée. C'est ce miracle qui rendra vraisemblables et acceptables les vérités qui sont elles-mêmes paradoxales et qui ne peuvent être ni démontrées ni appréhendées par les non-initiés. On voit par où passe la différence entre Thieme et Renou: pour Thieme, il s'agit plus du mode de l'énonciation de la vérité qui determine l'essentiel de la religion védique, alors que pour Renou, ce sont les conditions socio-religieuses de la formulation de la vérité qui comptent davantage. Ces conditions induisent le recours aux énigmes qui défient la sagacité du concurrent et qui recèlent des paradoxes parce qu'elles établissent des relations secretes connues d'initiés et qui énoncent le contenu du *ṛtá-*.[59] Il n'est pas sans intérêt que aussi bien Thieme que Renou trouvent des témoignages de la continuité entre la pensée védique et la spéculation bouddhique. Thieme, à la suite de H. Lüders, mais en le modifiant sur quelques points, voit un exemple de la continuité dans la conception de *satyakriyā*, "énonciation d'une vérité qui provoque une conséquence, pour la plupart du temps immédiate, dans le monde materiel"[60] Renou de son côté pense que ce que les auteurs védiques désignaient par "connexion" se retrouve dans la pensée bouddhique comme "cause" (*nidāna*).[60]

Si Thieme reconnaît le fait de compétition des poètes et des officiants du rite: "where there are contests they are . . . contests of rivaling ritual performances and of rivaling word power accompanying rivaling rites,"[62] il ne lui attribue pas la valeur d'un *principe structurant* du symbolisme védique. Les disputes sont pour lui un fait secondaire sans valeur intrinsèque. Mais il me semble qu'un fragment important, sinon central, de la religion védique se présente de manière cohérente dès lors qu'on reconnaît le rôle de la parole poétique et de ses vicissitudes saisis dans le cadre de la confrontation ou de la contestation mutuelle des poètes officiants-sacrifiants, élément qui structure leur vision formulée par des énoncés-énigmes dont parlait Renou. Même si ces énoncés révèlent des représentations qui peuvent paraître paradoxales, on admettra qu'elles traduisent la richesse conceptuelle du système symbolique propre aux hymnes védiques, à la lecture souvent déconcertante. *In fine:* que serait le *Ṛgveda* si ses hymnes ne reproduisaient pas les énoncés *différents* des *ṛṣi* védiques cherchant, à travers et au cours de leurs rivalités et joutes, à appréhender le *bráhman*, si les hymnes s'étaient contenté de présenter une fois pour toutes ce qu'est ce *bráhman*, sans exposer ses multiples tentatives et approches traduites dans ses 1,017 hymnes?

Notes

1 Boris Oguibénine, *La déesse Uṣas. Recherches sur le sacrifice de la parole dans le Ṛgveda* (Louvain: Peeters, 1988).

2 Le nom *vívāc-*, "contestation, joute verbale," est féminin, mais il est masculine au sens de "opposant, adversaire dans la contestation."

3 Pour plus de développements, v. mes *Essais sur la culture védique et indo-européenne* (Pisa: Giardini, 1985), p. 81 (English translation: *Essays on Vedic and Indo-European Culure* [New Delhi, Motilal Banarsidass, 1998], pp. 96–97). Particulièrement sur ces deux figures majeures du culte védique, Oguibénine,

"La religion du sacrifce védique et le sort de l'officiant et du guerrier dans l'Inde brâhmanique," in M. Giacomarra e E. Marchetta, eds., *Mito, Storia, Società* (Palermo: STASS, 1987), pp. 193–209.

4 Louis Renou, *Hymnes spéculatifs du Veda* (Paris: Gallimard, 1956), p. 72, et ses commentaires en *Études védiques et pāṇinéennes* (Paris: Editions E. de Broccard, 1955–1969), vol. XVI, p. 141.

5 Renou, *Études védiques et paninéennes,* vol. VII, p. 94.

6 F. B. J. Kuiper, "The Ancient Aryan Verbal Contest," *Indo-Iranian Journal* 4 (1960): 217–281 (je me référerai essentiellement à cette étude désignée dans la suite par Kuiper suivi du numéro de la page); *Varuṇa and Vidūṣaka: On the Origin of the Sanskrit Drama* (Amsterdam: North-Holland Publishing Co., 1979), pp. 22 et ss., p. 30.

7 Marcel Mauss, "Essai sur le don. Forme et raison de l'exchange dans les sociétés archaïques," in Marcel Mauss, *Sociologie et anthropologie* (Paris: Presses Universitaires de France, 1973), pp. 143–279; Gerrit J. Held, *The Mahābhārata: An Ethnological Study* (Leiden: K. Paul, Trench, Trubner & Co. Ltd., 1935). Le terme de potlatch prend ainsi valeur de métaterme à portée générale apte à servir en matière, pourtant si délicate et malléable, de comparaison des religions et des pratiques symboliques. Ce terme a dû être adopté par Kuiper en raison de la présence présumée chez les Indiens védiques et les Indiens Kwakiutl du sacrifice de solstice d'hiver symbolisant le passage vers une nouvelle phase de vie, de la présence aussi des representations courantes chez les uns et les autres, du prestige, des honneurs rendus et des prix conquis. On peut relever dans un ouvrage d'anthropologie que dans les cérémonies de potlatch "un hôte distribue des richesses aux invités qu'il réunit pour valider, par leur présence, son accession au nouveau titre ou son passage à un nouveau statut," Claude Lévi-Strauss, *La voie des masques* (Paris: Plon, 1979), p. 21. Il est possible toutefois que des rapprochements basés sur la paradigmatisation d'une pratique soient utiles, mais on constate que les différences entre les pratiques des Indiens védiques et ceux d'Amérique sont, dans ce cas, trop importantes pour qu'on ait recours au terme de potlatch en tant que catégorie efficace pour l'analyse des faits védiques. Il serait intéressant de savoir si les spécialistes des religions amérindiennes pourraient retrouver des éléments du potlatch dans les hymnes védiques. Cf. les remarques dubitatives de Hanns-Peter Schmidt, *Bṛhaspati und Indra: Untersuchungen zur vedischen Mythologie aund Kulturgeschichte* (Wiesbaden: O. Harassowitz, 1968), p. 192, p. 54, mais v. Jean Haudry, *La religion cosmique des Indo-Européens* (Milano-Paris: Archè-Les Belles Lettres, 1987), p. 67–78 (où l'idée de potlatch est retenue et étendue à l'indo-européen).

8 Kuiper, "The Ancient Aryan Verbal Contest," pp. 221–224, 238–240; *Varuṇa and Vidūṣaka,* p. 38.

9 Si on se demande si ce ritual existait effectivement à l'epoque du *Ṛgveda,* je précise que je n'insiste pas sur le terme "rituel," mais qu'il s'agit d'une performance codifiée, instituée en des formes particulières et propres à ce qu'on peut appeler la religion de la déesse Uṣas.

10 Kuiper, "The Ancient Aryan Verbal Contest," p. 239.

11 Kuiper, *Varuṇa and Vidūṣaka*, pp. 22–23, 43.

12 Selon Renou, *Études védiques et pāṇinéennes*, vol. V, p. 97; vol. VII, p. 78, mais contrairement à l'interprétation de Kuiper, *Varuṇa and Vidūṣaka*, p. 23.

13 Cf. la traduction de Renou, *Études védiques et pāṇinéennes*, vol. XVII, p. 77.

14 Kuiper, *Varuṇa and Vidūṣaka*, pp. 22–23; p. 25, n. 73.

15 Sur les figures stylistiques *kṛ ājím*, "susciter le combat," et *ar- reṇúm*, "soulever la poussière," et leur parallélisme servant à évoquer l'une par l'autre, v. *Essais sur la culture védique et indo-européenne*, p. 36, où sont discutées les "connexions" d'Indra à la guerre. Les "connexions" sont à entendre au sens que donnent à ce terme Renou et Lilien Silburn, "Sur la notion de *bráhman*," *Journal Asiatique* 236/237 (1948–1949): 7–46 (= Louis Renou, *L'Inde fondamentale* [Paris: Hermann, Collection Savoir, 1978], pp. 83–116), cf. Renou, "'Connexions' en védique, 'cause' en bouddhique," in *L'Inde fondamentale*, pp. 149–153.

16 Les paroles de Varuṇa 4.42.1: *rājāmi kṛṣṭér upamásya vavréḥ*, "je régis le peuple de la strate la plus élevée" (Renou, *Études védiques et pāṇinéennes*, vol. V, p. 97) témoignent aussi de son statut de roi-guerrier (cf. mes remarques, *Essais sur la culture védique et indo-européenne*, pp. 47–48, n. 28).

17 Kuiper, *Varuṇa and Vidūṣaka*, p. 43.

18 Gottfried W. Locher, *The Serpent in Kwakiutl Religion: A Study in Primitive Culture* (Leiden: E. J. Brill, 1932).

19 Kuiper, *Varuṇa and Vidūṣaka*.

20 Vladimir N. Toporov, *Recherches en étymologie et sémantique, Volume I: Théorie et quelques-unes de ses applications* (Moscow: Jazyki slavjanskoj kul'tury, 2005), p. 547. Voir aussi Boris Oguibénine and Nataliya Yanchevskaya, "Reconstructing Features of Indo-European Mythology of Death and Funeral Rituals from Baltic, Slavic, and Buddhist Parallels," in Wim M. J. van Binsbergen and Eric Venbrux, eds., *New Perspectives on Myth, Proceedings of the Second Annual Conference of the International Association for Comparative Mythology, Ravenstein (The Netherlands), 19–21 August, 2008* (Haarlem: Shikanda, 2010), pp. 59–73.

21 Kuiper, *Varuṇa and Vidūṣaka*.

22 Kuiper, *Varuṇa and Vidūṣaka*.

23 Karl F. Geldner, *Der Rig-Veda Aus Dem Sanskrit ins Deutsche Übersetzt und Mit Einem Laufenden Kommentar Versehen* (Cambridge, MA: Harvard University Press, 1951).

24 Oguibénine, *La déesse Uṣas*, pp. 98, 81, 96.

25 Kuiper, "The Ancient Aryan Verbal Contest."

26 Renou, *Études védiques et pāṇinéennes*, vol. VII, p. 84.

27 Kuiper, "The Ancient Aryan Verbal Contest."

28 Voir Oguibénine, *La déesse Uṣas*, Index général, p. 220, s.v. *compétition*.

29 Et cf encore Renou, *Études védiques et pāṇinéennes*, vol. XVII, p. 77; Kuiper, "The Ancient Aryan Verbal Contest," p. 269. Pour resumer 3.34.9–10 (cf. déjà ci-dessus), ces strophes présentent Indra terrassant les *dásyu*, ennemis extérieurs, au profit des *arya*, ses adeptes; Indra gagne les coursiers, le soleil, les

vaches, l'or, les plantes, les jours et les nuits, les arbres, l'espace médian, il brise la caverne de Vala, il refoule les disputants (*vívācas,* "the challengers," selon la traduction de Stephanie W. Jamison and Joel P. Brereton, *The Rigveda* [London: Oxford University Press, 2014], vol. 1, p. 516; *vívācas,* ici, est un terme ambigu et complexe, ces contestataires ou disputants pouvant être intestins et/ou extérieurs) et dompte ceux qui dressent leur pouvoir-spirituel contre lui. Kuiper y voit un exemple de concomitance de l'exploit d'Indra et des performances des héros qui s'assimilent à Indra. C'est aussi un renvoi clair aux héros luttant lors des conflits intestins comparés au combat cosmique d'Indra. On y met l'accent, encore selon Kuiper, sur la stimulation de l'activité cosmique du dieu par les affrontements des humains entre eux. Seule la référence péremptoire au potlatch amérindien autorise Kuiper à dire, avec toute la prudence d'ailleurs, que "although it is advisable in principle to omit all reconstructions of possibly underlying ideas which are not explicitly stated in our texts, the fact that the Rigveda often associates the ideas of war and contest allows us to conjecture that war . . . was thought of as stimulating the creative forces of the Cosmos during the winter ritual"; "The Ancient Aryan Verbal Contest," p. 269. Il me semble que la référence au rituel d'hiver est forcée, elle est justement du ressort du nonévoqué explicitement dans les hymnes védiques.

30 L'examen de ce terme par Paul Thieme, *Kleine Schriften* (Wiesbaden: F. Steiner, 1971), vol. I, pp. 247–258; et Bernfried Schlerath, *Das Königtum im Rig- und Atharvaveda* (Wiesbaden: F. Steiner, 1960), p. 35, n. 7 et seq. amène à reconnaître dans 6.33.2 une description du conflit des opposants des groupes sociaux étrangers les uns aux autres et en état de guerre. La traduction du début de la strophe par Jamison and Brereton, *The Rigveda,* vol. 1, p. 817: "For the separate peoples, disputants, call [separately] on you for help at the contest of champions," va dans le meme sens.

31 Kuiper, "The Ancient Aryan Verbal Contest," p. 271.

32 Kuiper, "The Ancient Aryan Verbal Contest," p. 271.

33 Cf. Renou, *Études védiques et pāṇinéennes,* vol. X, p. 78, sur *radhrá-.*

34 Hermann Oldenburg, *Ṛgveda. Textkritische un exegetische Noten,* 2 vols. (Berlin: Weidmannsche buchhandlung, 1909–1912).

35 Kuiper, "The Ancient Aryan Verbal Contest."

36 Geldner, *Der Rig-Veda Aus Dem Sanskrit*; Oldenburg, *Ṛgveda. Textkritische un exegetische Noten;* Jamison and Brereton, *The Rigveda.* Cf. Louis Renou, *Études sur le vocabulaire du Ṛgveda* (Pondichéry: Institut Francais d'indologie, 1958), pp. 49–50.

37 Une analyse de 7.23.3 dans son contexte cosmogonique est proposée dans ma *Structure d'un mythe védique: le mythe cosmogonique dans le «Rgveda»* (The Hague and Paris: Mouton, 1973), pp. 60–61.

38 Kuiper, "The Ancient Aryan Verbal Contest," p. 270.

39 Kuiper, "The Ancient Aryan Verbal Contest," p. 272.

40 Cette strophe est traduite un peu différemment dans *La déesse Uṣas,* p. 155, n. 42, où l'on trouvera des réflexions sur la dispute verbale.

[41] Cf. Tatyana Y. Elizarenkova, "Notes on the Contests in the Ṛgveda," *Annals of the Bhandarkar Oriental Research Institute* 68 (1987): 101: "[I]t is sometimes not so easy to tell from the vague contexts of the RV, whether the chariot-races or the contest of poetic prayers is meant." Cf. pp. 102, 103–104, sur les courses de chars comme modèle pour toute contestation, compétition ou concours (dont les disputes verbales et les actes de guerre) et sur le mot *rátha-*, "char," substitut symbolique du chant poétique, notamment en 2.31.1. Elizarenkova note (pp. 101–102) que la terminologie védique des compétitions est d'origine indo-européenne et que sa majeure partie trouve des correspondances étymologiques hors du domaine indo-iranien. Sous ce rapport, on peut signaler qu'un essai sur la religion de Zarathustra s'inspirant de l'étude de Kuiper des faits avestiques dans "The Ancient Aryan Verbal Contest" montre que dans cette religion avaient largement cours des notions relevant de la pratique des joutes verbales: "combattre avec la prière," "répondre aux énigmes posées par des représentants des forces du Mal," "exercer son éloquence pour combattre les propos mensongers." Zarathustra y est présenté en guerrier éloquent qui défait Angra Mainyu, Esprit Malin (v. D. L. Bishop, "Zarathustra as Victor in the Verbal Contest," *Journal of Ancient Near Eastern Society of Columbian University* 9 [1977]: 5–9, n. 9.

On ne dira jamais assez combien est complexe le terme *vā́ja-* que l'on ne peut rendre par un seul mot. V. *La déesse Uṣas,* pp. 103–108, et l'index, p. 224.

[42] Kuiper, "The Ancient Aryan Verbal Contest," p. 273.

[43] Karl F. Geldner, *Vedische Studien* (Stuttgart: W. Kohlhammer, 1892), vol. II, p. 163.

[44] Kuiper, "The Ancient Aryan Verbal Contest," p. 273.

[45] Les critiques de Thieme sont exposées dans son compte-rendu de Renou, *Études védiques et pāṇinéennes,* vol. I; Thieme, *Kleine Schriften,* vol. 2, pp. 722–727, et cf. son étude "Bráhman" en *Kleine Schriften,* vol. 1, pp. 100–138.

[46] V. Renou, *L'Inde fondamentale,* p. 51.

[47] Cf. Kuiper, "The Ancient Aryan Verbal Contest," pp. 217–218: tout en accordant à Thieme la nécessité de la recherche du contenu religieux du *Ṛgveda,* ce sont les disputes rituelles elles-mêmes qui, pour lui, sont des phénomènes sociaux et religieux. Je ne peux que le suivre, à m'en tenir uniquement à la valeur des disputes prises en elles-mêmes sans les subordonner au rituel du Nouvel An.

[48] Sur le sens de ce verbe dans les hymnes, v. mes remarques préliminaires en *Annuaire de l'École Pratique des Hautes Études, Sciences Religieuses* 85 (1976–1977): 192. V. surtout les observations de Karl Hoffmann sur le nom de la lignée des officiants védiques Kaṇva, dérivé de kṛ- prenant le sens de "agir magiquement, faire qqch. à qqn./qqch." dans le contexte de la liturgie chantée dont un exemple clair est 8.37.7ab: *śyāvā́śvasya rébhatas táthā śṛṇu/ yáthā́śṛṇor átreḥ kármāṇi kṛṇvatáḥ,* "Écoute [ô Indra] Śyāvāśva chantant [tes louanges], de même que tu as écouté Atri accomplissant ses actes [rituels]!"; Hoffmann, *Aufsätze zur Indoiranistik* (Wiesbaden: Reichert, 1975), vol. 1, pp. 15–28, notamment p. 24.

[49] Renou, *L'Inde fondamentale,* pp. 84–85.

[50] Renou, *L'Inde fondamentale,* p. 85.

51 Thieme, *Kleine Schriften*, vol. I, p. 106.

52 Renou, *L'Inde fondamentale*, p. 63.

53 Thieme, *Kleine Schriften*, vol. I, p. 120.

54 Renou, *L'Inde fondamentale*, p. 88.

55 Renou, *L'Inde fondamentale*, pp. 58, 92.

56 Renou, *L'Inde fondamentale*, pp. 58–59: "[L]e poète-sacrifiant . . . pense que son effort crée le *ṛtá-* ou du moins en assure le maintien. Le *ṛtá-* . . . résulte des corrélations. . . ; certains hymnes nous présentent ces corrélations sous forme d'énigmes . . . qu'on appelle des bráhmans . . . il s'agit pour le poète, qui est censé participer à un tournoi oratoire. . . , d'exprimer sous forme d'énigmes des images traduisant une corrélation; et aussi, en tant que spectateur d'un tournoi, de comprendre, d'interpréter correctement un bráhman proposé par ses concurrents."

57 Renou, *L'Inde fondamentale*, p. 123.

58 Renou, "'Connexions' en védique, 'cause' en bouddhique," p. 149.

59 D'où encore une différence entre les deux auteurs, assez importante: si Renou traduit *ṛtá-* par "ordre cosmique," Thieme affirme: "Dass *ṛtá* die Wahrheit und nichts als Wahrheit bezeichnet, muss nach Erörtungen von Lüders, *Varuṇa* I 13 ff. endgültig sicher stehen"; *Kleine Schriften*, vol. I, p. 119, n. 2.

60 H. Lüders, *Varuṇa* (Göttingen: Vandenhoeck & Ruprecht, 1951) vol. I, p. 15; cf. Thieme, *Kleine Schriften*, vol. I, p. 117.

61 Renou, "'Connexions' en védique, 'cause' en bouddhique," pp. 149–153. J'ai relevé et montré l'importance de la notion de lien explicative dans le *Ṛgveda*, v. mes *Essais sur la culture védique et indo-européenne*, pp. 121–130 (ch. 4, "Le signifiant et le signifié dans le sacrifice védique").

62 Thieme, *Kleine Schriften*, vol. II, p. 724.

References

Bishop, D. L. "Zarathustra as Victor in the Verbal Contest," *Journal of Ancient Near Eastern Society of Columbia University* 9 (1977): 5–9.

Elizarenkova, Tatyana Y. "Notes on Contests in the Ṛgveda," *Annals of the Bhandarkar Oriental Research Institute* 68 (1987): 99–109.

Haudry, Jean. *La religion cosmique des Indo-Européens.* Milano-Paris: Archè-Les Belles Lettres, 1987.

Held, Gerrit J. *The Mahābhārata: An Ethnological Study.* Leiden: K. Paul, Trench, Trubner & Co. Ltd., 1935.

Hoffmann, Karl. *Aufsätze zur Indoiranistik*, vol. 1. Wiesbaden: Reichert, 1975.

Geldner, Karl F. *Der Rig-Veda Aus Dem Sanskrit ins Deutsche Übersetzt und Mit Einem Laufenden Kommentar Versehen.* Harvard Oriental Series, vols. 33–35. Cambridge, MA: Harvard University Press, 1951.

—. *Vedische Studien*, 2 vols. Stuttgart: W. Kohlhammer, 1892.

Jamison, Stephanie W., and Joel P. Brereton. *The Rigveda,* 3 vols. London: Oxford University Press, 2014.

Kuiper, F. B. J. "The Ancient Aryan Verbal Contest," *Indo-Iranian Journal* 4 (1960): 217–281.

—. *Varuṇa and Vidūṣaka: On the Origin of the Sanskrit Drama.* Amsterdam: North-Holland Publishing Co., 1979.

Lévi-Strauss, Claude. *La voie des masques.* Paris: Plon, 1979.

Locher, Gottfried W. *The Serpent in Kwakiutl Religion: A Study in Primitive Culture.* Leiden: E. J. Brill, 1932.

Luders, H. *Varuṇa,* 2 vols. Göttingen: Vandenhoeck & Ruprecht, 1951–1959.

Mauss, Marcel. "Essai sur le don. Forme et raison de l'exchange dans les sociétés archaïques," in Marcel Mauss, *Sociologie et anthropologie,* pp. 143–279. Paris: Presses Universitaires de France, 1973.

Oguibénine, Boris. *Annuaire de l'École Pratique des Hautes Études, Sciences Religieuses* 85 (1976–1977).

—. *Essais sur la culture védique et indo-européenne.* Pisa: Giardini, 1985. English translation: *Essays on Vedic and Indo-European Culure.* New Delhi, Motilal Banarsidass, 1998.

—. *La déesse Uṣas. Recherches sur le sacrifice de la parole dans le Ṛgveda.* Louvain: Peeters, 1988.

—. "La religion du sacrifice védique et le sort de l'officiant et du guerrier dans l'Inde brâhmanique," in M. Giacomarra and E. Marchetta, eds., *Mito, Storia, Società,* pp. 193–209. Quaderni del Circolo Semiologico Siciliano 22–23. Palermo: STASS, 1987.

—. *Structure d'un mythe védique: le mythe cosmogonique dans le «Rgveda».* The Hague and Paris: Mouton, 1973.

Oguibénine, Boris, and Nataliya Yanchevskaya. "Reconstructing Features of Indo-European Mythology of Death and Funeral Rituals from Baltic, Slavic, and Buddhist Parallels," in Wim M. J. van Binsbergen and Eric Venbrux, eds., *New Perspectives on Myth, Proceedings of the Second Annual Conference of the International Association for Comparative Mythology, Ravenstein (The Netherlands), 19–21 August, 2008,* pp. 59–73. Papers in Intercultural Philosophy and Transcontinental Studies 5. Haarlem: Shikanda, 2010.

Oldenburg, Hermann. *Ṛgveda. Textkritische un exegetische Noten,* 2 vols. Abhandlungen der Königlichen Gesellschaft der Wissenschaften zu Göttingen. Philologisch-historische. Berlin: Weidmannsche buchhandlung, 1909–1912.

Renou, Louis. *Études sur le vocabulaire du Ṛgveda.* Pondichéry: Institut Francais d'indologie, 1958.

—. *Études védiques et pāṇinéennes,* 17 vols. Paris: Editions E. de Broccard, 1955–1969.

—. *Hymnes spéculatifs du Veda.* Paris: Gallimard, 1956.

—. *L'Inde fondamentale.* Charles Malamoud, ed. Paris: Hermann, Collection Savoir, 1978.

Schmidt, Hanns-Peter. *Bṛhaspati und Indra: Untersuchungen zur vedischen Mythologie aund Kulturgeschichte.* Wiesbaden: O Harassowitz, 1968.

Schlerath, Bernfried. *Das Königtum im Rig- und Atharvaveda*. Wiesbaden: F. Steiner, 1960.

Silburn, Lilien. "Sur la notion de bráhman," *Journal asiatique* 236–237 (1948–1949): 7–46.

Thieme, Paul. *Kleine Schriften*, Volume I. Wiesbaden: F. Steiner, 1971.

—. *Kleine Schriften*, Volume II. Stuutgart: F. Steiner, 1995.

Toporov, Vladimir N. *Recherches en étymologie et sémantique, Volume I: Théorie et quelques-unes de ses applications*. Moscow: Jazyki slavjanskoj kul'tury, 2005.

The Shadow of Kālī Over the Goddess Kāmākṣī and Her City

Carl Olson
Allegheny College, Pennsylvania

While touring the south Indian city of Kāñcīpuram in January 1998, a lay temple assistant related a story to our party that captured my attention. It told of the arrival of Kālī, a horrible, frightening crone, to the city. According to the temple guide, when Kālī, the fearsome, ugly hag, arrived from the north, Śiva transformed her into a beautiful maiden named Kāmākṣī, who was placed in charge of protecting the city of Kāñcīpuram, a city sacred to both Śiva and Viṣṇu. In fact, Kāñcīpuram is divided into Śaiva and Vaiṣṇava parts, both of which are protected by the goddess Kāmākṣī. The Śaiva part of the city, called "Big Kāñchi," includes the larger temples such as the Kailāsanātha, the Ekāmrēśvarar, the Kāmākṣī Amman, and the Vaikuntaperumāl, while the Vaiṣṇava part of the city, called "Little Kāñchi," is an area on the eastern extremity of the city centered around the Śrī Varadarājaswāmi temple.[1] There is also a significant Jain community in the city with its own temples, along with a Buddhist monastery that dates to the thirteenth century. Even though I have not been able to textually confirm the apparent folk story related by our temple guide, I became intrigued by the implications of the transformation of the ugly and horrifying Kālī into a paradigm of beauty.

Kālī, depicted as the terrifying crone in either myth or iconography, represents the extreme of corporeal ugliness, a form called Dakṣiṇakālikā.[2] The term *dakṣiṇā* is rich with significance for the Hindu religious tradition because it represents the ancient Vedic sacrificial altar located in the southern direction that is used for offerings to ancestors. The south is the direction of death, and the southern altar of the ancient Vedic sacrificial cult is also intended to protect and ward off evil influences that emanate from this evil and ominous direction.[3] The term *dakṣiṇā* also means sacrificial gift, and this meaning is closely tied to *śraddhā* (faith).[4] With respect to Kālī, *dakṣiṇā* represents death, danger, darkness, and dread, and yet it also suggests that underlying these dismal features the goddess is a bestower of gifts. At the other aesthetic extreme is a goddess like Kāmākṣī, who epitomizes the Indian ideal of feminine beauty. How is it possible for such apparently very different types of goddesses to become identified?

The scholar Stanley N. Kurtz claims that the Hindu goddess is a unified deity: "So far from representing split mother images, the Goddess seems repeatedly to affirm the unity of all aspects of the maternal."[5] Embarking on a study of Santoshi Ma and how she should be classified as a goddess, Kurtz concludes that she is not a new goddess or a divine figure divorced from other divine figures. He relates how he came to realize that the problem is how to classify all goddesses. Based on claims by Hindu devotees of both genders that "all goddesses are one," Kurtz's insightful investigation of the Indian extended family and how children are raised by several mothers leads him to conclude that each particular goddess is merely a manifestation of a single great goddess.[6] As a consequence of his position, there can be no new or unique goddess figure, because any new figure is incorporated into a living matrix of the complex of a paradigmatic goddess figure. It is this fundamental unity that clarifies all differences.

But where is it possible to locate Kurtz's work within the context of the psychology of religion? Peter Connolly offers a helpful distinction between hard and soft psychological approaches. The former approach attempts to approximate the rigor of the natural sciences by using experimentation and mathematical analysis, while with the latter approach the observer engages with subjects in social settings, joining them in activities and talking with them.[7] Based on his methodological approach, Kurtz fits into the soft approach, according to the distinction made by Connolly.

Although this distinction is not by itself to be construed as a negative assessment of Kurtz's approach to the subject, I argue in this essay that Kurtz accepts the claim of unity among goddesses much too literally and uncritically. Moreover, this essay will call Kurtz's basic assertion into question by looking at the relationship between the greater all-Indian figure of Kālī and the more regional goddess Kāmākṣī, along with the local goddess Lalitā. Any attempt to classify Hindu goddesses according to some preconceived unity is called into question by examining the actual historical, cultural, and aesthetic context of the three goddesses.

Obviously, if Kālī can assume the comely guise of Kāmākṣī in southern India, and she appears as beautiful to Bengali poets and her other devotees, the form of Kālī as Dakṣiṇakālikā is merely her most terrible and frightening manifestation and does not exhaust her aesthetic possibilities. Nonetheless, the Dakṣiṇakālikā manifestation of Kālī is a powerful, awe-inspiring image of the goddess. This form of Kālī represents her with a dark complexion, emaciated skin, eyes red with blood (*Mahābhārata* [Mbh] 10.1.65), sunken reddish eyes,[8] or with a third eye in the middle of her forehead, an attempt to suggest her transcendental wisdom, which parallels that of her consort Śiva. The mouth of the goddess is detailed by the composer(s) of the *Devī Māhātmya*[9] section of the *Mārkeṇḍaya Purāṇa,* which describes its width, the lolling tongue, the gaping mouth that swallows elephants, horses, men, and demons, the sharp teeth in which demons are crushed, and swallowing the blood of the demon Raktabīja and other demonic figures.[10] Within the Indian cultural context, this orgy of eating flesh and drinking blood is closely associated with sexual activity; the symbolism of food is intimately connected to sexuality in the Indian consciousness.[11] Kālī's wide, bloodstained mouth with protruding, sharp fangs represents the devouring cavity of her body, which stands in sharp contrast to her lower cavity, the womb that gives life. The life-taking and life-giving aspects of these respective cavities form a circle that connects the upper and lower parts of the body. The symbolism is of a terrible goddess in a bloody cycle of life and death that mutually sustain each other in a wet, overflowing orgy of blood, the primal liquid of life. This suggests that the devouring mouth of Kālī is symbolically akin to the *vagina dentata,* a consumer of the flesh and blood of the penis.

If we grant that Kālī is a pan-Indian goddess, I propose in this paper to examine what happens when a pan-Hindu goddess casts a shadow on, or influences, a local goddess such as Kāmākṣī, who had become identified historically to Lalitā prior to the advent of the pan-Indian goddess. If Kālī's influence on Kāmākṣī was so marked, why is it that the latter did not become externally ugly and frightening, more Kālī-like, rather than the other way around? Moreover, what does the relationship between a pan-Hindu goddess and a local goddess suggest about the importance of location in Hinduism? Why is there not an aesthetic unity among the three goddesses if "all goddesses are one," as Kurtz asserts?

In order to offer provisional answers to these kinds of questions, I will review briefly the nature of Lalitā and Kāmākṣī, the significance of Kāmākṣī's connection to a particular south Indian city, and compare the aesthetic extremes represented by the two sets of goddess figures. This is followed by a brief discussion of what Indian aesthetic theory suggests about the arrival of Kālī in a southern city. This general approach will be a direct response to the claims made in Kurtz's work about the unity of goddesses, and to his methodological approach to the subject.

The Beautiful Exterior and the Dark Interior of Lalitā

Before it is possible to discuss the patron goddess of Kāñcīpuram, it is wise to review the exploits and physical description of the goddess Lalitā, as she is considered to be a form of Kāmākṣī.[12] These two goddesses share outward physical beauty and certain interior dark features. Although they do not share the apparent ugliness of Dakṣiṇakālikā, Lalitā and Kāmākṣī do share some of Kālī's wrathful, terrifying, powerfully feminine features. In fact, Lalitā shares with Kālī the ability to destroy demons with feminine energy (*śakti*) that manifests many of the overpowering and horrifying aspects of Dakṣiṇakālikā.

The narrative of Lalitā is given in the *Brahmānda Purāṇa,* in a section of the text called the *Lalitā Māhātmya,* which is a parallel to the *Devī Māhātmya* of the *Markaṇḍeya Purāṇa* in terms of the overall structure of their narratives. With respect to body symbolism and general countenance of the goddess described in the *Brahmānda Purāṇa,* Lalitā is the exact opposite of Kālī in her Dakṣiṇakālikā form: Lalitā is forever youthful at sixteen years of age, possesses a reddish color; her nails are likened to the splendor of sandal paste and the lotus, her thighs are so lovely that they excite even the god of love (Kāma), her lips are like red silk cloth, her hips and buttocks are well developed, her navel is depressed like a whirlpool, her waist is slender and gives the impression of breaking due to the weight of her plump breasts, her hands are soft, her neck is beautiful, her circular face is lustrous and enhanced by her red lips, perfect teeth, and large eyes (4.4.37.68–77). The single facial feature that she shares in common with Kālī is the third eye on her forehead, a facial feature that her spouse Śiva also possesses (4.4.37.80). Lalitā's four arms hold, respectively, a white lotus and a piece of sugarcane in her right hands, and in the left hands a noose (*pāśa*), a goad (*ankuśa*), and arrows (4. 4.5. 1). Thus her right hands hold symbols of her role as mother of the universe that reflect her creative nature, while her left hands represent her connections with her roles as protector, guide, destroyer, and mistress of death. Another description in the text (4.4.10.90) emphasizes her martial nature by stating that she holds the noose, goad, bow (*dhanus*), and *śakti* (feminine energy and power). In comparison to the predominance of the demonic left or destructive side of Kālī and her frightful ugliness, the right side of Lalitā and her beauty tend to dominate her divine character after the destructive activities are concluded.

The primary purpose for the origin of Lalitā in the Hindu pantheon is modeled on the exploits of Durgā in the *Devī Māhātmya*. According to the *Brahmānda Purāṇa* (4.4.10.88), Lalitā is destined to kill Bhandāsura and protect the triple cosmos. This scenario tends to support David Dean Shulman's claim that the myth of the slaying of the buffalo-demon is the archetypal goddess myth of India.[13] Both future antagonists—demon and goddess—are born from fire. The demon is born of the fire associated with the anger of Rudra (4.4.12.1), while Lalitā originated from the fire of a divine sacrificial fire (4.4.10.88). Against the demonic forces of Bandāsura, Lalitā leads an army of women (*śakti*s) that emanate from different parts of her body and symbols associated with her by means of her creative and deceptive power of *māyā*.

Some of these female *śakti*s share common features with Kālī in her Dakṣiṇakākilā manifestation. A *śakti* of the goddess' chariot named Dandanāyikā is described as having curved teeth and a dark complexion (4.4.20.5). Other emanations possess dreadful or fiery eyes (4.4.20.8). Some *śakti*s with hideous countenances and sharp teeth eat the flesh and bones, and even drink the blood and semen of their fallen enemies (4.4.20.15–26). Their eyes roll about in their sockets from the blood and liquor they enjoy consuming in a state of perpetual inebriation and continuous laughter. This description of some of the *śakti*s reveals an army of man-eating and perhaps even a man-hating, feminine force. There are times in the text when this feminine force appears as either impersonal or personal forces that will consume the vital fluids—blood and semen—of men.

Consistent with Kālī's tantric background and the shadow of her apparent influence on a goddess associated with a specific city, and her darker and more frightening features, the *śakti*s consume forbidden things such as flesh, blood, liquor, and semen. This gruesome buffet of flesh and vital bodily fluids of male figures reflects a popular male prejudice concerning women in traditional Indian culture, which views all women as vampiresses prepared to drain men of their vital bodily fluids. This is especially true of draining men of their semen, a bodily fluid representing the essence of maleness, even though it is only the final product of the process of digestion.

According to the *Brahmānda Purāṇa*, the feminine force of the *śakti*s confronts a male chauvinist force of boastful, prideful, and egotistical fools who are convinced that women are stupid and are deluded into assuming that they can play the traditional heroic, military roles of men (4.4.21.73). The male demons are, of course, too self-assured, and their misogynist attitudes motivate them to underestimate their female opponents. The author of this text possesses a keen sense of humor; he or she is able to expose social and sexual tensions in Indian society within the genre of mythology, and accomplishes this task in a clever, insightful, and humorous manner by demonstrating how an army of chauvinist males can be defeated by feminine forces that do not even truly exist.

By means of their own power of *māyā* and out of frustration associated with their defeat in combat, the demonic male generals create a feminine demon named Sarpinī, who possesses a smoky complexion and a huge belly, and she creates many types of poisonous serpents from different parts of her own body (4.4.28.16–28). When any of these serpents are cut they multiply, much like the demon Raktabīja in the *Devī Māhātmya.* These multiplying serpents are counteracted by the goddess Nakulī (mongoose), who is able to create a multitude of mongooses to defeat the army of serpents (4.423.51–56). While the demonness is female, the serpents to which she gives birth are symbolically male, phallic figures, which are then eaten by the feminine mongooses. This entire narrative scenario represents apparently a playful, mythological scenario of fellatio and subsequent emasculation.

Another important aspect of this cosmic battle between the demonic, evil, masculine forces and the righteous, feminine forces is that the war is performed in the spirit of *līlā* (play). This is evident by the words and attitude of the forever nine-year-old daughter of Lalitā named Bālā, or Kumārikā, who wants to join in the fun by engaging in the battle (4.426.80).

At one point in this cosmic conflict, the demons begin to gain an advantage through the creation of a *yantra* (mystical diagram), which is thrown into the camp of the *śakti*s, causing them to become mentally dejected and confused. They begin to adopt an attitude of renunciation by discarding their weapons, much like the despondent Arjuna of the *Bhagavadgītā* (4.40–42). To counter the magical *yantra* Lalitā creates Ganeśa, a pot-bellied, broken-tusked, elephant-headed, and celibate deity, from her laughter in order to destroy it. Once Ganeśa achieves his task, the goddess grants him the boon of being the first to be worshiped at a temple before any other deities (4.427.104). What is interesting about the creation of Ganeśa, the "remover of obstacles," within the overall context of the narrative is that because he is a eunuch and comic figure his birth does not contradict the feminine nature of the army of the goddess nor the spirit of *līlā* (play) in which the battle is being waged.[14]

In a confrontation that is modeled on the slaying of the buffalo demon by the goddess Durgā, Lalitā finally slays Bhandāsura in a battle matching the forces of good against those of evil. When the demon discharges a missile, symbolic of some evil, the goddess counters with a counter-missile symbolic of something good. For instance, darkness is countered by the sun, heresy by truth, blindness by sight, fear by courage, and destruction of memory by its retention (4.429.62–89). From another perspective, the goddess' actions and her victory over evil recall Indra's victory over the demonic serpent Vṛtra in the *Ṛgveda* (1.32.1–15). While Indra requires a phallic weapon like a *vajra* (thunderbolt) to defeat his demonic foe, the mere thumbnail of Lalitā's right hand is sufficient for her conquest, while her other fingernails form the origin of the ten major incarnations of Viṣṇu (4.4.29.91).

Not only do Lalitā and Kālī both have the ability to kill demons but the *Brahmānda Purāṇa* (4.4.30.14; 4.4.30.29) also makes clear that Lalitā assumes the form of Kālī, mistress of death, although she is able to do this without adopting the terrible or ugly features associated with Kālī's Dakṣiṇakālikā form. The śaktis, feminine forces that emanate from Lalitā's body, represent the dark, mysterious, frightening features that connect her to similar features in Kālī, in which they are more overt in the mistress of time. Thus, beneath her beautiful external appearance, Lalitā possesses destructive and malevolent potential. Moreover, an apparently benign nature falsely suggested by her beauty is merely a mask she wears in order to hide the malevolent side of her nature. Dakṣiṇakālikā, however, is the exact opposite of Lalitā: her horrifying external physical features hide the more benign and maternal features she possesses, which are acknowledged by genuine devotees.

On the surface, this review of the goddess Lalitā seems to support Kurtz's position to some extent. While Lalitā's story seems to conform to the paradigmatic act of Durgā's destruction of the buffalo demon, this does not necessarily prove a unity between Durgā and Lilatā. It is equally plausible that a local, tribal goddess like Lalitā acquired some of the characteristics of a pan-Indian goddess without losing her local identity and uniqueness. According to Kurtz, the emphasis upon the unity of the goddess is based

> in the craving for narcissistic merger with the mother-part of an effort to recover the early period when the self of the mother and that of the child were not clearly distinguished.[15]

This kind of assertion is an interesting and suggestive form of psychological speculation, but it cannot and is not really verified by Kurtz, even though he uses his own firsthand accounts with respect to his study of actual Hindu extended families. At this crucial point, Kurtz's work represents the more speculative approach of the psychology of religion, in contrast to those whose work is more objective and verifiable. The problematic nature of verification in Kurtz's theory is suggested by numerous questions that go unanswered. Does the child conceive these in-law mothers as his or her mother? Does the biological mother of the child consider her child to be also the cultural offspring of the extended family? Do the in-law mothers grasp their own interactions with the children of other members of the extended family to be their own children in any genuine sense? What about the psychological development of young females? These kinds of questions are never really answered with firsthand responses from the subjects of Kurtz's study.

Moreover, the mythological evidence with respect to Lalitā seems to suggest that this specific figure's nature is decidedly demonic. Kurtz traces the demonic features of such a goddess to the presence of the mother-in-law in the Indian extended family. If Durgā represents the good biological mother, the goddess Kālī or Lalitā manifests, for instance, the demonic mother-in-law for Kurtz.[16] There are a couple of problems with this kind of assertion: Kurtz presupposes that all mothers-in-law are demonic and that the child's actual mother is always good. Although he seems to be aware of the problematic nature of these types of distinctions when he claims that contrary maternal images coexist in a more complex unity,[17] the all-encompassing kinds of statements made by Kurtz simplify an actually more complex situation, which will become evident as I unfold the story in this essay.

The Goddess of Kāñcīpuram

According to the *Lalitā Māhātmya* (4.4.12.1) of the *Brahmānda Purāṇa,* the goddess Lalitā is rewarded for her exploits by the god Brahmā with two epithets: Kāmākṣī and Kāmeśvarī. After Lalitā's exploits are related in the text, the goddess Kāmākṣī emerges as an independent figure from Lalitā, but the former shares the latter's beauty, and even that of Lakṣmī, as Lalitā had previously been the goddess of good fortune in an earlier incarnation. In fact, Kāmākṣī is the origin of the *śakti*s, Śrī, Brahmā, Vāc (goddess of speech), and Śiva (4.5.5–7). Like other great gods and goddesses of the Hindu tradition, she creates, sustains, and destroys the world through the gods Brahmā, Viṣṇu, and Śiva (4.5.40.8).

Even though there is an attempt to win universal status for Kāmākṣī by the author of this part of the *Brahmānda Purāṇa,* she is closely identified in the Hindu religious tradition with the city of Kāñcīpuram, which is considered one of India's seven sacred cities and the only one that is located in the southern part of the country. This intimate connection between the goddess and the city is evident in the myth of Pārvatī's playful closing of the eyes (sun and moon) of Śiva, which plunges the cosmos into darkness and causes the human inhabitants of earth to abandon their sacrifices to the gods and ancestors. For this unintended transgression, Śiva makes Pārvatī perform penance as an expiation for her sin by sending her first to the sacred city of Kāśī, and eventually to Kāñci to propitiate Kāmākṣī (4.5. 0.10–16).

In another myth, Kāmākṣī helps Śiva rid himself of the curse of brahminicide because he had beheadied the god Brahmā with his fingernail, to which the god's head had become stuck. After visiting many sacred sites and performing various forms of penance, Śiva finally receives a vision of Kāmākṣī, who graciously removes the skull from the god's fingernail, near the city of Kāñci in the vicinity of the river Kampā (4.5.40.52–86). Not only is Śiva is saved from sin, confusion, and ignorance by the goddess in this myth, the city of Kāñci becomes identical to the sacred city of Kāśī, which is especially sacred to the male deity.

Kāñcīpuram is the former capital of the Pallava dynasty, a center of Jain, Buddhist, and Hindu culture, and the location of a monastery established, according to tradition, by the famous Advaita Vedānta philosopher Śaṅkara. The city is located about forty-four miles west of Chennai, a large south Indian city located on the Bay of Bengal. The term *kāñci* means "waist girdle," which suggests that Kāñcīpuram means "Town of the Waist Girdle" or "Town of the *Kāñci* Tree."[18] The city's temples are considered to be the homes of gods that form a single extended family. The temples and divine icons are built facing the direction of the king's palace, making the royalty a part of the divine extended family.[19]

Kāñci, which is divided into Vaiṣṇava and Śaiva sections, as mentioned above, is ruled entirely by the goddess Kāmākṣī. The *Bhāgavata Purāṇa* (10.79.4–15) connects the name of the city with Kāmakoti, a designation of the goddess Kāmākṣī,[20] although Friedhelm Hardy connects the term to a Sanskrit term suggesting "store-room; treasury; enclosed area; inner apartment."[21] The *Padma Purāṇa* refers to it as a place of purification (6.253.17–21) and a sacred place of pilgrimage that is equal to other holy places (6.204.37). The territory guarded by the goddess is akin to a sacrificial arena and the anchoring point of a cosmogony. In the former case, the territory of Kāñci is akin to the *vedi* (altar) of the Vedic sacrificial plot; the latter is represented by the presence of a cave, a tradition preserved by the Tamil legends of Kāñci by the cave within the heart of the temple of Kāmākṣī.[22] Similar to Mīnākṣī in the city of Madurai and Śivakāmāsundarī in the city of Cidambaram, Kāmākṣī is specific to Kāñcīpuram and serves as its patroness.

According to the *Kāñcipurāṇam* (3.2), the city of Kāñcipuram was built by the deity Brahmā; he called it beautiful, and a sage called it more sacred than Benares (63.217–18). In part, the Kāñcipurāṇam is a text that represents a series of stories about the establishment of the various *liṅga* in the city, which chronicles the growth of the city's sanctity. From another perspective, the text is a local rendition of how chaos is transformed into cosmos. In fact, even the gods participate in the establishment of the *liṅga* in one case to atone for their neglect of Śiva after he saved the cosmos by swallowing the poison produced at the churning of the ocean (12.60). In a liberal spirit, the text gives two derivations of the name of the city. According to one version, *ka* signifies the "supreme being" and *añci* conveys the sense of "to venerate," which means that the city is the place of veneration of Ka, suggesting the goddess (62.35–36). Another interpretation claims that Kāñci is the navel of women because the city is considered to be the navel of the goddess of the earth, whose name is similar to the name of Kāñci (62.36–39). Either derivation of the name of the city closely ties it to the goddess Kāmākṣī.

In her mythology the goddess Kāmākṣī is closely identified with Kāma, deity of desire and arch-enemy of the ascetic Śiva. According to the *Brahmānda Purāṇa* (4.4.30.35–55), after the death of the demon Bhandāsura at the hands of Lalitā, representing the goddess of Kāñci at this point in the story, Kāma, who had been born as the demon after being burned to ashes by Śiva, is rendered bodiless, to the consternation of his wife, Rati, who petitions the goddess to restore him to life. Kāma, who is reborn invisible from a side-glance of the goddess, acknowledges his filial relationship to the goddess and he is able to wound the meditating Śiva. This causes Śiva to abandon his ascetic practices, become infatuated with Pārvatī, marry her, and father a son named Kumāra, who is destined to lead the gods against the demon Tāraka. Kāmākṣī is thus not merely the reviver of Kāma. By means of her close association with him she inherits some of Kāma's attributes, which can be witnessed by her icon in her temple in Kāñcipuram. Her iconographical form depicts her holding a sugarcane bow and five flower-arrows in her lower left and right hands, respectively. In her upper left and right hands she holds a *pāśa* (noose) and an *ankuśa* (goad). The implements in her lower hands indicate her appropriation of some of Kāma's attributes.

This close association between Kāma and Kāmākṣī helps to explain the mythical origin of her name, "having the eyes of desire." The *Kāñcī-māhātmya* (23.1–35) relates a story about the origin of Kāmākṣī's eyes that begins with Śiva laughing at Pārvati after defeating her at a game of dice, which prompts his wife to respond with charges of cheating and derogatory remarks about her husband's character, behavior, and appearance. Insulted, Śiva curses his wife to become black and have three eyes. Begging his forgiveness, and in order to free herself from the curse, Śiva informs Pārvatī that she must become Kāmākṣī and have her eyes.

According to a Tamil myth, Kāmākṣī's third eye can function much like the third eye of Kālī or Śiva and burn a victim to ashes. This myth relates the narrative of Kāttavarāyan, a trickster figure created by Śiva to guard his mother's garden, who is destined to be impaled on a stake when seeking his mother Kāmākṣī, who is engaged in asceticism on the banks of the Kampā River. While wandering toward his mother, the hungry Kāttavarāyan kills a bird sitting in a tree; as it falls, the bird cries out to the goddess for help. Opening the third eye located on her forehead, Kāmākṣī reduces her son to ash, from which grows a branch and then an infant. Due to Śiva's curse, which destined Kāttavarāyan to be impaled and caused Kāmākṣī to lose her place in the left half of the body of the god, the goddess attempts to divert her son's amorous attention from a beautiful maiden and save him from his eventual terrible death (which, paradoxically, is the only way in which Kāmākṣī can be restored to the body of her consort).

Kāttavarāyan is cursed for stealing the clothing of the Seven Maidens as they bathe in the ocean of milk. Fleeing the pursuing maidens, Kāttavarāyan runs to his mother, who transforms him into an infant, and she reduces the demanding maidens into seven stones with her third eye. Eveline Masilamani-Meyer helps bring this scenario into perspective, describing Śiva's action: "He curses her to be a demon, an evil spirit, in other words to become a goddess on earth, dangerous as an evil spirit."[23] Kāmākṣī in this myth also displays her dual role of mother and destroyer, nurturer and devourer.

From one perspective, Kāmākṣī's destruction of her son tends to undermine Kurtz's equation of all mothers with goodness. The destruction of her son and the transformation of the maidens, who are sources of temptation for her son and represent competition with the mother for her son's affection, seem to suggest what Kurtz calls the "Durgā complex," a Hindu stage of childhood development corresponding to the Oedipal complex in the West:

> In the Durga complex, the tension between the boy's tie to the natural mother and his tie to the collective women of the joint family is played out through images of self-castration.[24]

Kurtz does not conceive of this process as something negative; it is rather a healthy development connected to a voluntary renunciation of the incestuous relationship in favor of a more mature psychic development. The Durgā complex is problematic because it introduces a "macroreduction" that moves Kurtz's theory and similar types toward a hierarchical monism.[25]

From a different perspective, Kāttavarāyan seeks his mother, a scenario that does not support Kurtz's notion of the *ek-hi* phase of male psychological development. He explains that "The crucial work of the *ek-hi* phase lies in the gradual realization by the child that his true mother is a collectivity."[26] If the child's initial attachment to its mother is broken as one matures and accepts a collective motherhood, Kāttavaryan's action runs counter to mature development depicted by Kurtz. Even if one generously grants that Kāttavarāyan is a mythological exception to the rule, Kurtz does not supply real proof for his position by providing tests results of case studies with actual children.

It is also possible to raise the following types of questions: What about those children not raised in an extended family setting? Is there any measurable difference between the emotional intensity of a child's affection for his or her biological mother versus in-law mothers? Unfortunately, Kurtz does not attempt to empirically measure the thinking of the children, biological mothers, or extended family members. These kinds of shortcomings in Kurtz's structuralist/psychoanalysis methodological synthesis tend to cast a negative light over his comments about goddesses.

As her name indicates, Kāmākṣī is intimately connected to Kāma, the chief antagonist of the ascetic Śiva, and her mythology often depicts her aiding the deity of desire. The *Kāmākāīvilāsa* (14.9–66), for instance, reports how she restored Kāma's burned body after he worshiped her at her shrine. With the help of Kāmākṣī, Kāma is able to overcome Śiva, who searches for the goddess. Finally, Śiva locates the goddess at Kāñci, and asks her to satisfy his desires, which she refuses to do. Having decided to rape her, the goddess defends herself by creating an army of Kāmas, which motivates Śiva to counter with a force of Rudras who reduce the Kāmas to ashes only to be revived by the goddess. After Śiva is defeated, he is lead by Kāma to beg from the goddess, who takes pity on the god and tells him to take refuge by mediating on her. Then, Kāmākṣī reveals herself in all her beauty to Śiva, who responds by circumambulating her shrine, the Kāmakoti in the inner sanctum of her temple in the city of Kāñci. This local tradition transforms Śiva into a pilgrim of the goddess and places him at the mercy of the erotic powers of Kāma, who is made invincible by Kāmākṣī. This is evident by the name Kāmeśvara by which Śiva is known in Kāñci. This evidence appears to suggest the victory and ascendance of feminine forces over the predominant masculine forces, or to suggest, at least, competing cultural forces.

The episode of Śiva's defeat by Kāmākṣī contradicts Lawrence A. Babb's claim that masculine divinity tends to act as a restraining factor over the potentially destructiveness of feminine divinity, a mode of restraint that is accomplished by entering into a conjugal relationship.[27] Frédérique Apfel Marglin calls into question the negative connotations about female sexuality suggested by Babb's position because a positive assessment of female sexuality is expressed by auspiciousness, which enables one to see that sexual intercourse and menstruation, although normally considered impure, are auspicious. In contrast to Babb's position, Marglin writes:

> From all these observations we can conclude that it is not the inherently dangerous and malevolent nature of female sexuality that needs to be tamed and controlled by the male in order to transform it into benevolent wifely submission, since such an inherent nature does not exist. The character of single goddesses is ambivalent because their śakti, their potency, can go in two directions.[28]

According to Marglin, female power, which is antihierarchical, is positive and valued because it brings the fertilizing rains that maintains life. Marglin claims that the power of the single goddess is derived from her celibacy, and it is not due to any inherent danger in her female sexuality.[29] The myths of Lalitā's victory over masculine forces and Kāmākṣī's humbling of Śiva would appear to contradict Marglin's position to some degree. Since *śakti* is a potent power, it is inherently dangerous. In fact, any masculine, feminine, or neuter form of power is potentially dangerous.[30] Moreover, there is abundant evidence of the dangerous power possessed and exercised by married goddess figures, which is often exerted in anger.

There is further evidence suggesting the ascendance of feminine forces when Kāmākṣī is credited with saving the *liṅga* of Śiva. In a narrative similar to the story in the *Skanda Purāṇa* (3.1.44.82–117), where Sītā, wife of the heroic Rāma, creates a *liṅga* made of sand, Kāmākṣī creates a sand *liṅga* at Kāñcipuram, according to the *Kāmāīvilāsa* (8.30), and she protects it from the floodwaters. By attracting a great god to a local shrine and establishing him at a given location, Kāmākṣī is acting like a chthonic goddess. Shulman makes this general observation:

> It is the goddess, who is identified with the earth and with all that is indigenous and unique in the site of the shrine, who is responsible for effecting the link between the deity and his local home. In this sense the goddess is associated with the ancient concept of pratiṣṭhā., the firm ground of stability that makes life possible in the midst of chaos; the goddess provides the god with pratiṣṭhā in the one spot that is not subject to change or destruction, the center of the universe, the shrine.[31]

Not only does Kāmākṣī locate and protect the god within the shrine, she provides the very basis for worship of the male deity. If ordinary life is like a boat in a sea of disorder and chaos, the goddess, a repository of feminine power, serves as a safe haven and support for life, as well as a creator of life as prefigured by her creation of the sand *liṅga.* For a localized goddess like Kāmākṣī, this means that her creative and supportive efforts tie her to the earth and a given local. This localization of the cult and role of the goddess is symbolized, according to the *Kāñcipurāṇam* (63.364–401), by the marks of Kāmākṣī's breasts and jewelry left on the sand *liṅga.* This type of evidence does not, however, appear to directly connect her to Kālī and support the story of the lay temple assistant about Kālī's transformation into the goddess of Kāñci. It also does not support Kurtz's claim of the sameness of all goddesses, even though an Indological authority such as Jan Gonda views Kāmākṣī as a form of Durgā.[32] Nonetheless, other evidence gives greater support to the connection between these two goddess figures.

C. R. Srinivasan calls attention to a folk belief in the area of Kāñci that Kāmākṣī takes the form of Kālī at night and causes havoc.[33] According to the tradition, Śaṅkara, the eminent Advaita Vedānta philosopher and resident of Kāñci, interceded for the concerned, frightened citizens by performing penance in order to please the goddess and restrain her from terrifying the populace. The deep devotion of the philosopher pleased the goddess who assured him that she would not leave her temple without his permission. At the present time, there is a life-size stone image of Śaṅkara very close to the sanctum in the Kāmākṣī temple. When the *utsavamūrti* of the goddess is taken from her sanctuary on festival occasions for a journey through her kingdom the barriers pause before the statute of Śaṅkara. This scenario provides direct evidence of a connection between the two goddesses.

Further evidence of a connection can be discovered in the sacrificial sphere and the call for a blood sacrifice. Thurston tells a story about the rivalry between two castes, the Seniyans (weavers) and the Pallis or Vanniyams (farmers). Some magically adept weavers created spells to stop the Pallis from parading through the streets of Kāñci with their annual car festival to the local deities. Then, unscrupulous Seniyans went to the king to complain about the public nuisance caused by the Pallis' blocking traffic. In turn, the Pallis blamed the Seniyans for placing a spell on their festival cars. The unsympathetic king claimed that they could counteract any such spells, prescribed a particular time for the festival cars to be removed from the road, and affirmed that failure to comply with his mandate would result in the expulsion of the caste from his kingdom. Due to the pressure of the king's threat and the hopelessness of the situation, the Pallis turned to Kāmākṣī for assistance, who appeared to an elder of the caste and informed him how to identify a member of the caste who could remove the spells. The man identified was Ramasawmy Naikan, a minister of the king, who discovered spirits around each of the wheels of the cars by means of his clairvoyant powers. After praying to the goddess for help in defeating these malevolent spirits in her temple, Kāmākṣī appeared to her devotee to give him instructions, a remedy that horrified the Pallis because it involved the propitiatory sacrifice of a woman pregnant with her first child. In order to placate the outraged Pallis, Naikan agreed to sacrifice his own wife, who was pregnant with her first child. This heroic gesture pleased the goddess and the spells of the Seniyans instantly collapsed.[34] This Kālī-like insistence on a sacrifice was also found by Carl Gustav Diehl in an advertisement in the *Madras Mail* in 1951 for a sacrifice in Tanjore to the goddess that would promote peace, prosperity, and communal harmony.[35] Such insistence by the goddess for sacrifice is more suggestive of a link in the mind of the local populace with Kālī.

From the scholarly perspective of Kurtz, what occurs with the interaction between Kālī and Kāmākṣī is not the development of a new goddess, but the greater goddess (Kālī) encompasses a local figure who serves as a partial form of the pan-Indian goddess. There can be no new or unique goddess figure for Kurtz because any new figure is "born into the living matrix of this complex larger Goddess."[36] In contrast to Kurtz, we have demonstrated that Kāmāksī possessed her own well-defined nature before her connection with Kālī. This scenario suggests a more complex and dynamic situation that often depends on local, regional, and pan-Indian circumstances about which it is very difficult to draw accurate generalizations. It is insufficient to base a system of goddess classification on both "the tensions and constraints of the kinship system, and at a still deeper level, in the structure of the Hindu psyche."[37] This type of methological approach is reductionistic in a twofold sense: structualist and psychological. This double methological stance neglects the historical or time dimension that is more apt to manifest the dynamic aspect of the interaction of a greater goddess with a local figure. Kurtz's synchronic approach needs to be balanced by an equally diachronic approach. Kurtz admits to blending two Western perspectives in order to transform them into something new and to discern the viewpoint of a foreign culture. Moreover, this type of an approach raises questions about the wisdom of superimposing alien methods upon Indian culture that are in part additionally very subjective. Although in fairness to Kurtz, he does claim to be sensitive to the issue of imposing a Western explanatory system like psychoanalysis upon an alien culture.

Comparison of Aesthetic Extremes

This essay has called attention to the shadow of Dakṣiṇakālikā over the city of Kāñcīpuram and its patron goddess Kāmākṣī. I have also called attention to extreme nature of Kālī's grotesque ugliness. Her disheveled hair, her red sunken eyes, gaping mouth, fangs dripping with blood, lolling tongue, and sagging breasts are all symbolic in their own way of death and the ultimate victory of time, even though she also paradoxically represents with her *śakti* the forces of life. The overall impression left by Kālī's red eyes, sharp teeth, gaping mouth, bodily appendages, and grotesque costume of severed hands and heads is extreme horror. The extreme ugliness of Dakṣiṇakālikā tends to stupefy one's rational mind and jars one's imagination, which suggests that the body symbolism of Kālī is akin to a trace that is continually coming into and instantaneously passing out of existence. Since her body symbolism is so extreme, mere mortals can never get a complete cognitive, imaginative, or perceptual grasp of Kālī. In other words, she eludes us by her extremity.

In contrast to Kālī, the extremity of beauty is represented by Lalitā/Kāmākṣī, whose comely appearance is extolled by poets and devotees. In this sense Dakṣiṇakālikā and Lalitā/Kāmākṣī appear to be exact opposites. Although Lalitā/Kāmākṣī is externally beautiful, she embodies internal ominous and ugly features, which suggests the shadow of Dakṣiṇakālikā upon these identified goddesses. The *śakti*s created from the body of Lalitā recall some of Dakṣiṇakālikā's grotesque features. And we have referred to the folk belief about Kāmākṣī becoming the goddess Kālī at night, which suggests that there is a darker side of the nature of the goddess of Kāñcīpuram. The shadow cast by Kālī over these local goddesses does not suggest any identity with the pan-Indian figure as Kurtz wants to assert.

Besides her grotesque appearance, Dakṣiṇakālikā is sexually extreme. From one perspective, it is Kālī and her *śakti* that brings the prone, lifeless Śiva to life by the touch of her feet. The image of Kālī with a sword in her hand, while standing or straddling the prone ascetic god in a superior sexual position, suggests a close connection between sex, creative power, and violence. The *Kāmasūtra* (2.3.1, 33) recognizes, for instance, the role of violence in sexuality, and it even describes sexual activity as a kind of combat (2.7.1). The kind of unrestrained sexuality of Kālī that is being suggested is symbolized in part by her disheveled hair and tongue.

In a manner similar to Dakṣiṇakālikā, Lalitā is also sexually extreme when she creates her feminine army to battle the misogynist army of male demons and drinks the defeated foe's blood and semen. Kāmākṣī's close association with Kāma, her restoring him to life, and her name suggest sexual extremeness. Not only is Kāmākṣī the protector of the liṅga, but she can also create an army of Kāmas to counter Śiva's army of Rudras and halt his attempt to rape her. Thus, behind a benign exterior appearance, Lalitā and Kāmākṣī are potentially sexually extreme.

In addition to the extremes of ugliness and sexuality, another extreme represented by the bodily symbolism of Dakṣiṇakālikā is death. Her emaciated skin, gaping and all consuming mouth, her swallowing of blood, and her sharp fangs are suggestive of death. The earrings consisting of corpses, the ring of skulls for a necklace, severed hands that adorn her waist, her disheveled hair, sagging breasts, and threatening sword are also manifestations of her close association with death and destruction. Although other gods and goddesses are connected to death in some manner, it is the Dakṣiṇakālikā form of the goddess with her close association with ghosts and ghouls and cremation grounds that is indicative of Kālī's extreme and intimate association with death and the cycle of time.

Just as Lalitā and Kāmākṣī share to some extent Dakṣiṇakālikā's association with ugliness and sexuality, they also share her connection to death. From the commencement of her career, Lalitā is destined to slay the demonic Bhandāsura. Both the demon and the goddess are born from fire, although Lalitā is born of the sacrificial fire that suggests not only death but also rebirth. The *śaktis* created by Lalitā are directly connected to death because they drink not only liquor but also blood and semen, fluids normally associated with life. The specific bodily fluids of blood and semen are connected to *rasa,* the liquid element and support of life in general.[38] If we consider the Indian medical science of Āyurveda (science of longevity), *rasāyana* (path of *rasa*) is its seventh branch, and represents a holistic approach to increasing bodily longevity by using techniques intended to rejuvenate the body that includes a combination of plant and mineral elixirs with clinical therapeutic techniques. From its early association with waters and liquids in general in the *Ṛg Veda* (1.105.2), *rasa* evolved into the fluid essence of the universe and the support of all bodily constituents (*dhātus*).[39] With respect to the goddesses Lalitā and Kāmākṣī, their connection to vital bodily fluids in their mythology intimately connects these united figures with the very essence and pulsating flow of life itself. Thus, the goddesses are not only associated with death, but they are paradoxically also connected to the flow of life.

Both Lalitā and Kāmākṣī are depicted holding a goad, arrows, and a noose, which are items that can be used to cause pain, kill, or lead the dead away in the case of the latter article, although the goad can also be used to guide souls to liberation. In her mythology, Kāmākṣī reduces her own son to ashes and reduces the Seven Maidens to seven stones by means of the deadly power of her third eye. And dissimilar to Lalitā with whom she is identified, Kāmākṣī destroys a demon, according to the *Kāñcipurāṇam* (61.1–23), who drinks the blood and semen of the gods, rendering the deities impotent and disinterested in sexual relations with their wives. The goddess kills the demon with a single arrow, recreates the gods, reunites them with their wives, and re-establishes the gods in their proper work. These types of deeds connect Kāmākṣī with the extremes of violence, death and destruction, which are so reminiscent of Dakṣiṇakālikā. And like Kālī, the destructive deeds of Kāmākṣī result in this particular case in the restoration of vitality and life for other divine beings. Moreover, since Kāmākṣī is directly connected to Lalitā, she is both a consumer of and releaser of vital bodily fluids.

Even if the three goddesses share features like ugliness, sexual extremes, and death, this does not equate to any unity as Kurtz is quick to claim in his book. Although it is impossible to identify accurately all the features that Lalitā and Kāmākṣī might have historically inherited from Kālī due to inadequate historical evidence, it is probably more historically accurate to view Lalitā and Kāmākṣī as developing their own specific identity before becoming closely associated with each other and later connected with and influenced by Kālī. Kurtz explains the diversity among goddesses as due to child rearing practices.[40] This type of methodological approach reminds one of Durkheim's claims that society explains religion. Moreover, the aesthetic extremes manifested by these goddesses tend to undermine the symmetrical distinction made by Kurtz between the good mother and the demonic mother-in-law because the three goddesses do not fit perfectly into this type of reductionistic categorization.

Concluding Comments

Within the context of this essay, we have witnessed a twofold transformation of Dakṣiṇakālikā in the southern city of Kāñcīpuram: an earlier historical example of the softening of the image of Dakṣiṇakālikā from a terrifying crone into a beautiful goddess and a transformation of two local goddesses into a pan-Indian goddess by a process of identification of Kālī with Kāmākṣī and Lalitā, two local goddess figures that were probably identified with each other before their connection with Kālī. Although it is not unusual in the religious history of India to identify Sanskritic gods and goddesses with local and regional deities, it is difficult to completely discern why south Indians would associate a local goddess with a goddess like Dakṣiṇakālikā and her ugly features. It is apparent that south Indians perceived something beneath the external horrifying features of Kālī that appealed to them. But by associating Kālī with one or more local goddesses, the southerners softened her more horrible and aesthetically less attractive aspects because they were unable to fully embrace a goddess figure whose body symbolism represents the extreme of disorder, or at least the threat of it, for a goddess who would protect a city with an inherent promise of order and stability. Thus the historical and mythological evidence seems to suggest that the process of benignly altering or softening the harsh features of Kālī predates the devotional poetry of Bengali devotees of the goddess, although it is difficult to precisely determine why this occurred at Kāñcīpuram with specifically Kāmākṣī. This scenario suggests also a more dynamic situation than that depicted by Kurtz with respect to the interaction between the various goddesses, even though the historical record is not entirely lucid on this interaction.

It is possible, however, to attempt to offer a plausible scenario of what may have happened in the southern city of Kāñcīpuram. It is possible, for instance, that Lalitā was a goddess of some forest tribe who became intimately associated with the goddess of the local city of Kāñci, who may also have been the goddess of some tribal group living in the adjacent area or forest. It is also possible to surmise that the arrival of Kālī from the north to a southern city, which was open to influences from the north, grafted Kālī onto an already existing local goddess, who previously became connected to a fierce and beautiful figure. From the perspective of the Kāñcīpurāṇam, if the city of Kāñcīpuram owes its sacredness to the establishment of liṅgas of Śiva, the advent of Kālī and her identification with Kāmākṣī is a cultural process in which Kālī, a spouse of a great god like Śiva, is united with her husband in a city consecrated by his iconic symbol. For the local goddess Kāmākṣī, it means that she shares to some extent in the pan-Indian nature of the great goddess, even though she retains her identity to a particular place or city. In other words, Kāmākṣī is Kāñcīpuram, and the city of Kāñci is Kāmākṣī. This type of identity suggests a hierarchical structure with Kāmākṣī presiding over the synchronic structure. There is a certain arbitrariness related to the boundaries of Kāñcīpuram established by its early human inhabitants, but the goddess gives the place stability, certitude, long term endurance, and well-being by guaranteeing the locative specificity and sacredness of the site by infusing her power into it.

In a sense, Kāmākṣī's identity with Kālī represents the diachronic aspect of this religious process. In his study of the Central Himalayan goddess Nandadevi, William S. Sax makes a statement about marriage practices in this region of India that is appropriate in its spirit to the goddess Kālī because "places and persons mutually determine each other; the bride has moved to a new place, hence she is transformed."[41] For a pan-Hindu goddess, the importance of location can be expressed as follows: "Kālī in one place is both the same and different from Kālī in another place."[42] It is almost as if Kālī as the diachronic aspect of the process is necessary for the ultimate unity of sameness and difference of the place called Kāñcīpuram.

Although we have seen that Lalitā/Kāmākṣī share certain fierce and dark features with Kālī, why did these more local figures not inherit the ugly features of Kālī? Why did they remain beautiful? We can speculate that the terrible Dakṣiṇakālikā offended the aesthetic sensibilities of the Tamils, and the inhabitants of southern India were actually among the initiators of the process of altering or softening the fierce image of Kālī.

According to the Kashmiri Śaiva philosopher Abhinavagupta, suggestive meaning *(dhvani)*, which is to be distinguished from conventional (*abhidhā*) and secondary (*laksanā*) forms of meaning, takes precedence over the literal sense of a word, and embodies an evocative kind of meaning that transcends primary denotation and metaphor.[43] The reason that the suggestive takes precedent over the denotative or conventional kind of meaning is due to the nature of dhvani itself, which embodies the essence of poetry, for instance, and represents the cause of beauty.[44] *Dhvani* is directly connected to *rasa*, an undifferentiated mass of aesthetic delight that is evoked by *dhvani*.[45] When a person experiences *rasa* and its enjoyment (*bhoga*) becomes a real possibility or can be asserted to be inevitable. This pleasure of relishing *rasa*, which possesses the characteristics of melting, expansion, and radiance, is not produced, for instance, by the words of poetry or the viewing of iconic forms of art, but it rather emerges from the cessation of ignorance.[46] It is possible that the Dakṣiṇakālikā form of Kālī, although very suggestive of meaning, did not evoke the element of aesthetic delight (*rasa*) among south Indians, who appeared to prefer the extreme of the beautiful over that of ugliness, even though Laitā/Kāmākṣī indubitably possessed certain interior dark features.

From prior statements about the close connection between Dakṣiṇakālikā and Lalitā/Kāmākṣī with bodily fluids, we can recognize an obvious and ironical association between the aesthetic meaning of *rasa* and its more primordial reference to the liquid essence of life in the form of semen, blood, herbal remedies, and *soma*, the hallucinogenic drink of immortality. Just as the aesthetic meaning of *rasa* evokes notions of pleasure, the historically earlier meaning of the term suggests fluids that support all life. And just as post-Vedic references regard blood as female in distinction to solids, which are considered male, and metaphorically appears as male semen or as its seed substitute,[47] the goddesses are associated with pain and pleasure, destruction and creativity, the cycle of death and rebirth and the flow of life, bondage and liberation, stability and transformation, and ugliness and beauty. In short, the nature and activities of these goddesses are woven into the very fabric of the pulsating existence of the universe and the flux of human life, providing support for the continued existence of the universe and its inhabitants.

If devotees of Kālī can find beauty and motherly features in her terrible form, it seems reasonable to view this fascinating goddess as an inversion of Indian ideals of beauty. It is also possible to grasp a beautiful goddess like Lalitā/Kāmākṣī as an inversion of Indian ideals of the ugly because of her interior dark and ominous features. Thus, external beauty is no guarantee of a benign goddess, nor does a lack of external beauty mean that a goddess necessarily lacks inner loveliness and the possibility of evolving into a beautiful goddess. Extremes can become norms or hidden under the mask of beauty, and ugliness can cover an interior beauty that becomes revealed to genuine devotees.

With respect to Lalitā, Kāmākṣī, and Kālī, we possess suggestive evidence of the interaction of two local goddesses with a pan-Indian goddess. The historical and mythological evidence suggests a much more complex scenario than the unity of all goddesses depicted by Kurtz. Even though it is an interesting and suggestive study that correctly places emphasis on the importance of the joint family, Kurtz's theory is highly speculative and lacks any genuine data supported by empirical testing that would support his thesis. Kurtz is not completely wrong, however, because we have acknowledged a connection between two local goddesses with an all-Indian conception. However, Kurtz's acceptance of the claim that "all goddesses are one" oversimplifies a more complex situation and tends to obscure the unique features and adventures of the local figures. As David Kinsley[48] and, following him, Kathleen M. Erndl[49] have shown, many Hindu goddesses do not fit into neat categories. Moreover, by using what he calls the "Durgā complex," Kurtz indicates two things: that the Oedipus complex of Freud is not universal and that the Durgā complex is culturally specific to India. However, Kurtz does not make it clear whether or not his Durgā complex is part of the experience of a non-neurotic individual's experience of childhood. Thus Kurtz stretches credulity when he makes the Durgā complex the universal foundation for the claim that "all goddesses are one." This kind of position tends to exclude other possible factors.

Notes

1 K. V. Raman, *Śrī Varadarājaswāmi Temple—Kañchi* (New Delhi: Abhinav Publications, 1974).

2 N. N. Bhattacharya, *History of Tantric Religion* (New Delhi: Manohar Publications, 1982), pp. 349–356. See also David R. Kinsley, *The Sword and the Flute: Kālī and Kṛṣṇa, Dark Visions of the Terrible and the Sublime in Hindu Mythology* (Berkeley: University of California Press, 1975) and *Hindu Goddesses: Visions of the Divine Feminine in the Hindu Religious Tradition* (Berkeley: University of California Press, 1986).

3 Jan Gonda, *Die Religionen Indiens I: Veda und älterer Hinduismus* (Stuttgart: W. Kohlhammer, 1960), pp. 140–141.

4 Jan Gonda, *Change and Continuity in Indian Religion* (The Hague: Mouton & Company, 1965), pp. 19–22.

5 Stanley N. Kurtz, *All the Mothers Are One: Hindu India and the Cultural Reshaping of Psychoanalysis* (New York: Columbia University Press, 1992), p. 99.

[6] Kurtz, *All the Mothers Are One*, p. 5.

[7] Peter Connolly, "Psychological Approaches," in Peter Connolly, *Approaches to the Study of Religion* (London and New York: Cassell, 1999), p. 144.

[8] Eden F. Pargiter, trans., *The Mārkaṇḍeya Purāṇa* (Delhi: Indological Book House, 1969), 87.7.

[9] See Thomas B. Coburn, *Devī Māhātmya: The Crystallization of the Goddess Tradition* (Delhi: Motilal Banarsidass, 1984).

[10] Pargiter, trans., *The Mārkaṇḍaya Purāṇa*, 87.5–8, 9–10, 12; 88.9, 56.

[11] Sudhir Kakar, *Intimate Relations: Exploring Indian Sexuality* (Chicago: University of Chicago Press, 1989), p. 91.

[12] V. R. R. Dikshitar, *The Lalitā Cult* (Delhi: Motilal Banarsidass Publishers, 1942), p. 30.

[13] David Dean Shulman, "The Murderous Bride: Tamil Versions of the Myth of Devī and the Buffalo-Demon," *History of Religions* 16/2 (1976): 120–146.

[14] Paul R. Courtright, *Ganeśa: Lord of Obstacles, Lord of Beginnings* (Oxford: Oxford University Press, 1985), pp. 110–111.

[15] Kurtz, *All the Mothers Are One*, pp. 99–100.

[16] Kurtz, *All the Mothers Are One*, p. 111.

[17] Kurtz, *All the Mothers Are One*, p. 110.

[18] D. Dennis Hudson, "Ruling in the Gaze of God: Thoughts on Kancipuram's Maṇḍala," in Martha Ann Selby and Indira Visvanathan Peterson, eds., *Tamil Geographies: Cultural Construction of Space and Place in South India* (Albany, NY: State University of New York Press, 2008), p. 109.

[19] D. Dennis Hudson, *Krishna's Mandala: Bhagavata Religion and Beyond* (New Delhi: Oxford University Press, 2010), pp. 49, 56.

[20] R. Dessigane, et al., *Les legends çivaites de Kañcipuram: Analyse de texts et iconographie* (Pondichéry: Institut Français de Indologie, 1964), pp. i–vi.

[21] Friedhelm Hardy, *Viraha-Bhakti: The Early History of Kṛṣṇa Devotion in South India* (Delhi: Oxford University Press, 1983), p. 643.

[22] Marie-Claude Porcher, "La representation de l'espace dans le Kāñcīmāhātmya," in Jean-Claude Galey, ed., *L'espace du temple: Espaces, itinéraries, médiations* (Paris: Éditions de l'École des Hautes Études en Sciences Sociales, 1985), p. 25.

[23] Eveline Masilamani-Meyer, "The Changing Face of Kāttavarāyan," in Alf Hiltelbeitel, ed., *Criminal Gods and Demon Devotees: Essays on the Guardians of Popular Hinduism* (Albany, NY: State University of New York Press, 1989), p. 89.

[24] Kurtz, *All the Mothers Are One*, p. 10.

[25] Ivan Strenski, *Religion in Relation: Method, Application and Moral Location* (Columbia, SC: University of South Carolina Press, 1993), p. 44.

[26] Kurtz, *All the Mothers Are One*, p. 143.

[27] Lawrence A. Babb, *The Divine Hierarchy: Popular Hinduism in Central India*

(New York: Columbia University Press, 1975), p. 229, and "Marriage and Malevolence: The Uses of Sexual Opposition in a Hindu Pantheon," *Ethnology* 9/2 (1970): 137–148.

28 Frédérique Apfel Marglin, "Female Sexuality in the Hindu World," in Clarissa W. Atkinson, Constance H. Buchanan, and Margaret Miles, eds., *Immaculate and Powerful: The Female in Sacred Image and Social Reality* (Boston: Beacon Press, 1985), p. 56.

29 Marglin, "Female Sexuality in the Hindu World," p. 56.

30 Gerardus van der Leeuw, *Religion in Essence and Manifestation* (New York: Harper & Row, 1963), vol. 1, p. 44. See also Mircea Eliade, *The Sacred and the Profane* (New York: Harcourt, Brace, & Company, 1959).

31 Shulman, *Tamil Temple Myths*, p. 51.

32 Jan Gonda, *Die Religionen Indiens II: Der jüngere Hinduismus* (Stuttgart: W. Kohlhammer, 1963), p. 14.

33 C. R. Srinivasan, *Kanchipuram through the Ages* (Delhi: Agam Kala Prakashan, 1979), p. 246.

34 Edgar Thurston, *Castes and Tribes of Southern India* (Madras: Government Press, 1909), vol. 6, pp. 25–26.

35 Carl Gustav Diehl, *Instrument and Purpose: Studies on Rites and Rituals in South India* (Lund: CWK Gleerup, 1956), p. 266.

36 Kurtz, *All the Mothers Are One*, p.16.

37 Kurtz, *All the Mothers Are One*, p. 20.

38 Jean Filliozat, *La Doctrine classique de la medicine indienne, ses origins et ses parallèles grecs* (Paris: Imprimerie nationale, 1949), p. 126.

39 David Gordon White, *The Alchemical Body: Siddha Traditions in Medieval India* (Chicago and London: University of Chicago Press, 1996), pp. 184–185.

40 Kurtz, *All the Mothers Are One*, p. 9.

41 William S. Sax, *Mountain Goddess: Gender and Politics in a Himalayan Pilgrimage* (Oxford: Oxford University Press, 1991), p. 78.

42 Kathleen M. Erndl, *Victory to the Mother: The Hindu Goddess of Northwest India in Myth, Ritual, and Symbol* (Oxford: Oxford University Press, 1993), p. 60. The importance of location is made evident in D. Dennis Hudson, *The Body of God: An Emperor's Palace for Krishna in Eighth-Century Kanchipuram* (Oxford: Oxford University Press, 2008).

43 Daniel H. H. Ingalls, Jeffrey Moussaieff Mason, and M. V. Patwardhan, trans., *The Dhvanyāloka of Ānandavardhana with the Locana of Abhinavagupta* (London: Cambridge University Press, 1990), 2.1.

44 Ingalls, Mason, and Patwardhan, trans., *The Dhvanyāloka of Ānandavardhana*, 1.1.

45 Ingalls, Mason, and Patwardhan, trans., *The Dhvanyāloka of Ānandavardhana*, 1.4.

46 Ingalls, Mason, and Patwardhan, trans., *The Dhvanyāloka of Ānandavardhana*, 2.4.

47 Wendy Doniger O'Flaherty, *Women, Androgynes, and Other Mythical Beasts* (Chicago and London: University of Chicago Press, 1980), p. 33.

[48] Kinsley, *Hindu Goddesses*, p. 35.

[49] Erndl, *Victory to the Mother*, p. 158.

References

Babb, Lawrence A. "Marriage and Malevolence: The Uses of Sexual Opposition in a Hindu Pantheon," *Ethnology* 9/2 (1970): 137–148.

—. *The Divine Hierarchy: Popular Hinduism in Central India.* New York: Columbia University Press, 1975.

Bhattacharya, N. N. *History of Tantric Religion.* New Delhi: Manohar Publications, 1982.

Coburn, Thomas B. *Devī Māhātmya: The Crystallization of the Goddess Tradition.* Delhi: Motilal Banarsidass, 1984.

Connolly, Peter. "Psychological Approaches," in Peter Connolly, *Approaches to the Study of Religion*, pp. 135–192. London and New York: Cassell, 1999.

Courtright, Paul R. *Ganeśa: Lord of Obstacles, Lord of Beginnings.* Oxford: Oxford University Press, 1985.

Dessigane, R., et al. *Les legends çivaites de Kañcipuram: Analyse de texts et iconographie.* Pondichéry: Institut Français de Indologie, 1964.

Diehl, Carl Gustav. *Instrument and Purpose: Studies on Rites and Rituals in South India.* Lund: CWK Gleerup, 1956.

Dikshitar, V. R. R. *The Lalitā Cult.* Delhi: Motilal Banarsidass Publishers, 1942.

Eliade, Mircea. *The Sacred and the Profane.* Willard R. Trask, trans. New York: Harcourt, Brace, & Company, 1959.

Erndl, Kathleen M. *Victory to the Mother: The Hindu Goddess of Northwest India in Myth, Ritual, and Symbol.* Oxford: Oxford University Press, 1993.

Filliozat, Jean. *La Doctrine classique de la medicine indienne, ses origins et ses parallèles grecs.* Paris: Imprimerie nationale, 1949.

Gonda, Jan. *Change and Continuity in Indian Religion.* The Hague: Mouton & Company, 1965.

—. *Die Religionen Indiens I: Veda und älterer Hinduismus.* Stuttgart: W. Kohlhammer, 1960.

—. *Die Religionen Indiens II: Der jüngere Hinduismus.* Stuttgart: W. Kohlhammer, 1963.

Hardy, Friedhelm. *Viraha-Bhakti: The Early History of Kṛṣṇa Devotion in South India.* Delhi: Oxford University Press, 1983.

Hudson, D. Dennis. *Krishna's Mandala: Bhagavata Religion and Beyond.* New Delhi: Oxford University Press, 2010.

—. "Ruling in the Gaze of God: Thoughts on Kancipuram's Maṇḍala," in Martha Ann Selby and Indira Visvanathan Peterson, eds., *Tamil Geographies: Cultural Construction of Space and Place in South India*, pp. 87–116. Albany, NY: State University of New York Press, 2008.

—. *The Body of God: An Emperor's Palace for Krishna in Eighth-Century Kanchipuram.* Oxford: Oxford University Press, 2008.

Ingalls, Daniel H. H., Jeffrey Moussaieff Mason, and M. V. Patwardhan, trans. *The Dhvanyāloka of Ānandavardhana with the Locana of Abhinavagupta*. Harvard Oriental Series Vol. 49. London: Cambridge University Press, 1990.

Kakar, Sudhir. *Intimate Relations: Exploring Indian Sexuality*. Chicago: University of Chicago Press, 1989.

Kinsley, David R. Hindu *Goddesses: Visions of the Divine Feminine in the Hindu Religious Tradition*. Berkeley: University of California Press, 1986.

—.*The Sword and the Flute: Kālī and Kṛṣṇa, Dark Visions of the Terrible and the Sublime in Hindu Mythology*. Berkeley: University of California Press, 1975

Kurtz, Stanley N. *All the Mothers Are One: Hindu India and the Cultural Reshaping of Psychoanalysis*. New York: Columbia University Press, 1992.

Leeuw, Gerardus van der. *Religion in Essence and Manifestation*, 2 vols. New York: Harper & Row, 1963.

Marglin, Frédérique Apfel. "Female Sexuality in the Hindu World," in Clarissa W. Atkinson, Constance H. Buchanan, and Margaret Miles, eds., *Immaculate and Powerful: The Female in Sacred Image and Social Reality*, pp. 39–59. Harvard Women's Studies in Religion Series. Boston: Beacon Press, 1985.

Masilamani-Meyer, Eveline. "The Changing Face of Kāttavarāyan," in Alf Hiltelbeitel, ed., *Criminal Gods and Demon Devotees: Essays on the Guardians of Popular Hinduism*, pp. 69–104. Albany, NY: State University of New York Press, 1989.

Pargiter, Eden F., trans. *The Mārkaṇḍeya Purāṇa*. Delhi: Indological Book House, 1969.

Porcher, Marie-Claude. "La representation de l'espace dans le Kāñcīmāhātmya," in Jean-Claude Galey, ed., *L'espace du temple: Espaces, itinéraries, médiations*, pp. 23–51. Paris: Éditions de l'École des Hautes Études en Sciences Sociales, 1985.

Raman, K. V. *Śrī Varadarājaswāmi Temple—Kañchi*. New Delhi: Abhinav Publications, 1974.

Sax, William S. *Mountain Goddess: Gender and Politics in a Himalayan Pilgrimage*. Oxford: Oxford University Press, 1991.

Shulman, David Dean. "The Murderous Bride: Tamil Versions of the Myth of Devī and the Buffalo-Demon," *History of Religions* 16/2 (1976): 120–146.

Srinivasan, C. R. *Kanchipuram through the Ages*. Delhi: Agam Kala Prakashan, 1979.

Strenski, Ivan. *Religion in Relation: Method, Application and Moral Location*. Columbia, SC: University of South Carolina Press, 1993.

Thurston, Edgar. *Castes and Tribes of Southern India*, 7 vols. Madras: Government Press, 1909.

White, David Gordon. *The Alchemical Body: Siddha Traditions in Medieval India*. Chicago and London: University of Chicago Press, 1996.

For Frits Staal: On Mantras

André Padoux
Centre National de la Recherche Scientifique, Paris

I do not recall exactly when I first met Frits Staal, but it was long ago. We were together in Weimar (then part of the German People's Republic) in 1979. We must have talked about mantras, but my main memory of him at that time of a particular incident. Some French participants of the conference went to the restaurant of the Hotel Elefant and, ignoring the local custom, walked toward a free table without waiting to be invited to do so by the maitre d'hotel. He was furious and wanted to expel us, shouting *"Raus!"* ("get out!"). Now, to say *"Raus!"* to French citizens who, a few years earlier, had lived in occupied France was really a provocation and asking for trouble. Fortunately, Frits Staal (who spoke excellent French) was with us and diplomatically restored peace.

We must have also both attended other Sanskrit conferences, but I haven't retained any memory of them. On the other hand, I remember well a "tantric conference" held in 1992 in Menlo Park, California, after which Frits drove me in his sports car to his very nice house overlooking UC Berkeley. This was a very friendly and extremely pleasant experience. Frits was in Paris in spring 1984, giving talks at the University of Paris X–Nanterre, which I attended and found very interesting and thought-provoking. These talks were later published by the Collège de France in *Jouer avec le Feu: Pratique et théorie du rituel védique.*[1]

I am quite ignorant of Vedism, one of Staal's main fields of study, but ritual and mantras are in my field of research. Mantras were the theme of his last talk, which was entitled in the book, very characteristically (and not unambitiously), "Hommes et oiseaux chanteurs: Les mantra védiques et les origines du langage et de la religion." He took up again and developed the main themes of this last talk, as well as the more general theme of the nature of ritual, in his very remarkable (and sometimes deliberately provocative) *Ritual and Mantras: Rules without Meaning.*[2]

Frits had already written on Vedic mantras in his contribution to *Understanding Mantras* edited by Harvey P. Alper,[3] who was a dear friend of mine. I worked with Harvey on the book and contributed the Conclusion, "Mantras—What Are They?"[4] I did not come to any precise conclusion about the nature of mantras, both because to make a conclusive statement on mantras when considering them from the Vedas through tantra and into modern times, which was the scope of the book, was simply not possible. In any case, given what I then knew of the subject, it would have been very presumptuous to attempt such a conclusion. Even now, twenty-five years later, I would not proffer a categorical conclusion, though my view of mantras is somewhat clearer and more simple—perhaps one would say simplistic, as I tend to see mantras mainly as a magical use of language or sounds.

I did not express any disagreement with Staal in *Understanding Mantras* for the simple reason that I had (and still have) scarce knowledge of Vedic matters. I would therefore not make bold to contradict him, and in fact I had no reason to do so. I merely underlined somewhat more than he had that the term "mantra," when used for the Vedas, has a larger meaning than in Hinduism, since it is used generally for the Vedic hymns, not merely for specific stereotyped ritual formulas. The recitation of the Veda is deemed to be useful and effective, as Staal points out, only when its phonetic form is strictly followed, which is a basic trait of Puranic or tantric mantras. The precise phonetic form of mantras, however, is to be strictly respected, but generally a possible "musical" aspect is not referred to, as it is for the Vedic recitation, which is a veritable psalmody.

My disagreement with Staal—which never diminished my friendliness toward him nor my admiration for his work—arose five years later when I listened to his 1994 lectures at the University of Paris X–Nanterre, and continued after I read some of his later papers, especially his 1996 book, *Ritual and Mantras: Rules without Meaning.* This disagreement concerns both Staal's conception of ritual and his view of the nature of mantras. The origin of our differing views can probably be found in our different intellectual backgrounds and training: Staal studied logic, mathematics, and linguistic theory, while I read in law, philosophy, literature, and anthropology. Then, too, our different fields of research may have contributed to our parting of the ways: the Vedas and tantra are two very different worlds.

Staal's first Paris lecture begins with a quotation from Émile Durkheim's *Les formes élémentaires de la vie religieuse,* to the effect that religious phenomena come by nature under two categories: belief (*croyances*) and rites/ritual, both of which are defined by the nature of their objects. The object, and therefore the nature, of ritual is found in belief. Durkheim adds: "Ritual can therefore only be defined after belief has been defined,"[5] a point with which Staal categorically differs—for him, ritual has no definite object. Staal sees ritual as an interesting subject from the phonological, syntactic, semantic, or pragmatic points of view. The structure of a particular ritual is an interesting object, and to know what actions are performed, which mantras are uttered, is an interesting subject—but to hope to find meaning in all of this is useless. For him, rituals are outwardly manifested unconscious structures that have grown like crystals or nervous systems in the human mind, and while study of them is possible it is beyond the scope of anthropology. Which is to say, if I understand his view, that rituals are not to be studied as forms of human behavior, consciously alive and present in a particular context, but as mere objective material facts.

Mantras were the subject of the last of Staal's Paris lectures, in which he is concerned with Vedic ritual syllables, the so-called *stobha* of the Sāmaveda, such as *phaṭ, hāu,* etc. He notes that they are entirely nonlinguistic, near to musical sounds, and their origin can be found, he believes, in "a prelinguistic past, in the process of biological evolution." In this respect, he believes that mantras are akin to birdsong. Staal notes that birds use song patterns for specific purposes, in particular in forms of behavior, in ritual attitudes, if you like, all of which they have in common with mantras. One may well admit this resemblance. In my view, however, there is a great difference between these processes: birds employ "song" urged by their genetic nature: they live the action as a part of themselves. They have no conscious awareness of what they do. Humans, however, are conscious: they realize what they are doing and they do it because they believe that such actions are useful and effective toward some end. In this case, people may well deceive themselves, they may blindly follow absurd traditional rules, but they are nonetheless conscious of what they are doing, which makes all the difference from the genetically imprinted actions of birds.

It is not unlikely that priests sometimes recite mantras without apparently paying attention to what they are saying, as Staal remarks in passing (I witnessed this once in Pondicherry). Still, a basic, mandatory principle for the person who utters a mantra is to concentrate mentally on what is being uttered—to be conscious of what he is doing. As Kṣmarāja says in his commentary on *Śivasūtra* 2.1:

> The mantra is not a mere conglomerate of different syllables. It is the very mind of the devotee who, through intense awareness of the deity of the mantra, attains identity with that deity.

One might say that this view represents a typically Śaiva nondualistic position, yet it is a generally widespread Indian belief.

It could also be argued that this does not prevent mantras from being meaningless. Some are clearly not meaningless—those that invoke a deity, for instance. But some ancient Indian philosophers of the Mīmāṃsā did say that they are meaningless. This is obviously the case of the monosyllabic mantras, the *bīja* mantras, *oṃ,* the primary one, as well as all such *bīja*s as *hrīṃ, sauḥ,* and so on. However, as the Indologist Louis Renou (who Staal sometimes quoted) once noted, mantras may have no meaning but they have a function, a role, especially in ritual.[6]

Hindu post-Vedic rites consist essentially of the utterance of mantras that are deemed to effectuate a number of ritual actions: to call forth the presence of a deity or to dismiss it, to purify water, to enclose or safeguard a ritual area, etc. Admittedly, the "mantrified" water remains only water; it is not changed into *amṛta*—except for the person who believes it to be. One may well consider this transubstantiation (to use a Catholic term) as purely symbolic. Nonetheless, it is not merely ritually but also sometimes socially meaningful (think of the baptism certificates from Christian churches used in German-occupied Europe to prove to the Nazis that their bearer was not a Jew).

Surely all of this is mere symbols. Yet such symbols are the "the metaphors we live by."[7] Frits Staal, like all of us, surely must, at times during his life, have made use of, suffered from, or profited by the social power of words. I could add that mantras (at least some) may well be "nonsense syllables" (to quote J. N. Farquhar)[8] but they can also be prayers, animated by and charged with the faith of believers.

While this discussion may seem entirely critical, I do not wish it to be taken so. First, it would be unfair, to say the least, to criticize Frits Staal when he is no longer among us, nor do I wish to criticize a friend. I have expressed some disagreements between our views of ritual and mantras, the study of which he considered to be beyond anthropology, while I believe it to be a proper subject of anthropological research. I never found his approach useless—far from it. Considering the babbling of babies as analogous to mantras may also show that ritual behavior and play with the sounds of language are deeply ingrained elements in human nature. To have pointed this out is thus useful; it puts things in perspective and diminishes our pride—not a bad thing.

One cannot but regret in this respect that Frits Staal left us, or stopped working effectively, too early to be aware of recent developments in the neurosciences, as well as of the views of the *Daseinsanalyse* of Ludwig Binswanger, et al.,[9] based on the treatment of schizophrenia, which reveal the presence of language in the depths of the human mind. Indian mantrikas or philosophers of grammar (Bhartrihari) explain this by the basic presence in humans of *vāc*, the Word, "ruler of gods," a notion of which our dear friend Frits would surely not have approved, even as it reinforces some of his views and intuitions. We have also discovered that the supposedly incoherent babbling of newborns is not, for them, without meaning because it expresses their reactions to the outside world.

I would add, however, that as deeply ingrained in us as language is, images seem to reside at a deeper level of consciousness than does speech (this has also been shown by an analytical approach). In fact, in daily life (not to mention dreams), we think more in images than in words—don't we? Rather than merely opposing Frits Staal's views, I would like to show that he explored a different aspect of that fundamental human element, the mind. Had he been aware of later developments he would certainly have contributed to the ongoing study of the subject with his usual very personal, original, and thought-provoking views.

Notes

1 Frits Staal, *Jouer avec le Feu: Pratique et théorie du rituel védique*. Publications De L'Institut De Civilisation Indienne (French Edition) (Paris: De Boccard, 1990).

2 Frits Staal, *Ritual and Mantras: Rules without Meaning* (Delhi: Motilal Banarsidass, 1996).

3 Frits Staal, "Vedic Mantras," in Harvey P. Alper, ed., *Understanding Mantras* (Albany: State University of New York Press, 1989), pp. 48–95.

4 Andre Padoux, "Mantras—What Are They?", in Harvey P. Alper, ed., *Understanding Mantras* (Albany, NY: State University of New York Press, 1989), pp. 295–318. This book is now out of print (though available online) but was reprinted, *Understanding Mantras* (Third Edition) (New Delhi: Motilal Banarsidass, 2012). This edition includes a Working Bibliography for the Study of Mantra and a Bibliographical List, both by Harvey P. Alper (pp. 327–530), which are, as has been said, "a tremendous piece of work—almost publishable by itself."

5 Émile Durkheim, *Les Formes Élémentaires de la Vie Religieuse. Le Système Totémique en Australie* (Paris: Les Presses Universitaires de France, 1968).

6 Louis Renou, *Etudes védiques et paninéennes* (Paris: Institut de Civilisation Indienne, 1955–1969), Fascicule 6, "Le destin du Veda en Inde."

7 George Lakoff and Mark Johnson, *Metaphors We Live By* (Chicago: University of Chicago Press Books, 1980, 2003). See also John L. Austin, *How to Do Things*

with Words: The William James Lectures Delivered at Harvard University in 1955. J. O. Urmson and Marina Sbisà, eds. (Oxford: Clarendon Press, 1962).

8 John N. Farquhar, *An Outline of the Religious Literature of India* (London: Oxford University Press, 1920), p. 201.

9 Ludwig Binswanger, *Grundformen und Erkenntnis menschlichen Daseins* (Zürich: Niehans, 1942).

References

Austin, John L. *How to Do Things with Words: The William James Lectures Delivered at Harvard University in 1955.* J. O. Urmson and Marina Sbisà, eds. Oxford: Clarendon Press, 1962

Binswanger, Ludwig. *Grundformen und Erkenntnis menschlichen Daseins.* Zürich: Niehans, 1942.

Durkheim, Émile. *Les Formes Élémentaires de la Vie Religieuse. Le Système Totémique en Australie.* Paris: Les Presses Universitaires de France, 1968.

Farquhar, John N. *An Outline of the Religious Literature of India.* London: Oxford University Press, 1920.

Lakoff, George, and Mark Johnson. *Metaphors We Live By.* Chicago: University of Chicago Press Books, 1980, 2003.

Padoux, André. "Mantras—What Are They?", in Harvey P. Alper, ed., *Understanding Mantras* (Third Edition), pp. 295–318. New Delhi: Motilal Banarsidass, 2012.

Renou, Louis. *Etudes védiques et paninéennes,* 17 vols. Paris: Institut de Civilisation Indienne, 1955–1969.

Staal, Frits. *Jouer avec le Feu: Pratique et théorie du rituel védique.* Publications De L'Institut De Civilisation Indienne (French Edition) Paris: De Boccard, 1990.

—. *Ritual and Mantras: Rules without Meaning.* Delhi: Motilal Banarsidass, 1996.

—. "Vedic Mantras," in Harvey P. Alper, ed., *Understanding Mantras,* pp. 48–95. Albany: State University of New York Press, 1989.

On the Date of Bhavatrāta, the *Jaiminīya* Commentator

Sudalaimuthu Palaniappan

Introduction

Bhavatrāta, the commentator of the *Jaiminīya Śrautasūtra*, occupies an important place in the history of the Vedic tradition of Kerala. Scholars have identified Bhavatrāta with Bhavarāta mentioned in the *Avantisundarīkathā* by Daṇḍin who was in the court of the Pallava king Narasimhavarman I (630–68 C.E.).[1] This identification, made despite the difference in names, has been used to assign the date of the migration of Bhavatrāta's grandfather from the Cōḻa country into the Cēra country and the composition of the above-mentioned commentary. This identification has also been used to categorize the openness of Kerala's Nambudiri Brahmans to accept a brahman from Tamil Nadu into their ranks in their earlier history. As we carefully look into this issue more closely, it becomes obvious that this identification is unwarranted on the basis of available evidence, and all conclusions deriving from this identification need to be revised.

Genealogical Problems in Identifying Bhavatrāta with Bhavarāta

While discussing Bhavatrāta's commentary on the *Jaiminīya Śrautasūtra* in his 1983 article, Asko Parpola writes:[2]

> In the introductory verses, Bhavatrāta mentions his compassionate father Mātṛdatta, who was a trivedin. Daṇḍin, who lived around A.D. 700,[3] speaks in very much the same terms of his friend, the great Vedic scholar Mātṛdatta, whose father and son were both called Bhavarāta (sic), the former a Kalpasūtraṭīkākāra from Kerala.[4]

It is obvious that the names indicated by Dandin are:

Bhavarāta—grandfather
Mātṛdatta—father, the friend of Daṇḍin
Bhavarāta—son

While Parpola was careful to note the name Bhavarāta as given by Daṇḍin for Mātṛdatta's father, K. K. Raja gives the name of Mātṛdatta's father as Bhavatrāta in his 1983 article:

> In the seventh century Daṇḍin refers in his Avantisundarīkatha to some Brahmin friends in Kerala such as Mātṛdatta, a poet who wrote some commentaries, and his father, Bhavatrāta.[5]

Parpola's 1984 article, "On the Jaiminīya and Vādhūla Traditions of South India and the Pāṇḍu/Pāṇḍava Problem," provides more details regarding Bhavatrāta:

> The migration of Tamil Jaiminīyas to Kerala had started considerably earlier, around the sixth century, for Bhavatrāta in the introductory verses of his commentary on the Jaiminīya-Śrautasūtra mentions that his paternal grandfather Hastiśarman came to Kerala from the village of Vasiṣṭhakuṭi in the Cōḻa country, described by him as an ancient settlement of Sāmavedins descended from the sage Maṭhara belonging to the Kāśyapa gotra; in Kerala Hastiśarman married the daughter of Brahmadatta from the line of Viśvāmitra, who became Bhavatrāta's teacher: his father Mātṛdatta mastered fully the Sāma-, Ṛg- and Yajurvedas, śruti as well as smṛti, but was apparently too busy to teach him, since Bhavatrāta says that he was held in high regard by kings and was much consulted by the brahmans.[6]

So we have the following genealogy given by Bhavatrāta:

> Hastiśarman—grandfather
> Mātṛdatta—father
> Bhavatrāta—son

The following table compares the names of Bhavarāta's and Bhavatrāta's genealogies as given by Daṇḍin and Bhavatrāta.

Table 1. Names of Bhavarāta's and Bhavatrāta's Genealogies

	Bhavarāta's lineage given by Daṇḍin	Bhavatrāta's lineage in his own words
Grandfather	Bhavarāta	Hastiśarman
Father	Mātṛdatta	Mātṛdatta
Son	Bhavarāta	Bhavatrāta

Only the names of the father in the two lineages are identical. It is surprising that scholars so readily identified Daṇḍin's Bhavarāta, the grandfather, with Hastiśarman, the grandfather of Bhavatrāta. They also discounted the difference in names between Bhavarāta and Bhavatrāta. It is as if the scholars have assumed that Hastiśarman changed his name to Bhavatrāta on moving to Kerala!

When we look at the inscriptional evidence regarding the name Vasiṣṭhakuṭi for the village from where Bhavatrāta's grandfather migrated to Kerala, the identification of Bhavarāta with Bhavatrāta becomes even more untenable.

Inscriptional Data Concerning Vasiṣṭhakuṭi

Vasiṣṭhakuṭi was also called Tiṭṭaikuṭi historically and is called Tiṭṭakuṭi (also written as Tiṭṭagudi) today. It is located near Vriddhachalam in the Cuddalore district of Tamil Nadu. The Vaidyanāthasvāmin temple and the Sukhāsana Perumāḷ temple in Tiṭṭakuṭi have 28 inscriptions of the Cōḻa, Pāṇṭiya, and Vijayanagara dynasties. Of these, datable inscriptions range from Cōḻa Rājadhirāja II's inscription of ca. 1168 C.E. to Vijayanagara's Vīra-Bhūpati's inscription of 1420 C.E.[7] For over 200 years from 1168 C.E., the inscriptional record had only Tiṭṭaikuṭi embedded in full locational descriptions such as Vaṭakarai Virutarājabhayaṅkara Vaḷanāṭṭu Meṟkānāṭṭu Brahmadeyam Tiṭṭaikuṭiyāṉa Tiruccirrampalaccaturvetimaṅkalam or Tiṭṭaikuṭiyāṉa Tiruccirrampalaccaturvvetimaṅkalam or other variants.[8] Here Vaṭakarai refers to the location of Tiṭṭaikuṭi alias Tiruccirrampalaccaturvetimaṅkalam in Virutarājabhayaṅkara Vaḷanāṭu, a major Cōḻa administrative unit, on the northern bank of the river Veḷḷāṟu (also written as Vellar). Meṟkānāṭu referred to a minor administrative unit within Virutarājabhayaṅkara Vaḷanāṭu. It is only in the inscription of Viruppana (who was also called Virupākṣa and was the son of Harihara II of the Saṅgama dynasty of Vijayanagara) of 1399 C.E. the name Śrīvasiṣṭhakuṭiāṉa Vidyāraṇyapuram (meaning Śrīvasiṣṭhakuṭi alias Vidyāraṇyapuram) was mentioned for the first and only time in the epigraphic record.[9] (Two later inscriptions only use Tiṭṭaikuṭi and not Vasiṣṭhakuti.) The identity of this Śrīvasiṣṭhakuṭi with Tiṭṭaikuṭi is confirmed by the inscription of Vīra-Bhūpati (1420 C.E.),[10] which referred to Tiṭṭaikuṭiāṉa Vidyāraṇyapuram.

Table 2 presents select inscriptions belonging to Cōḻa, Pāṇṭiya, and Vijayanagara kings mentioning Tiṭṭaikuṭi or Vasiṣṭakuṭi. One can see minor variations in spelling between the inscriptions for essentially the same name, mostly depending on whether Sanskrit phonemes are naturalized into Tamil or not. For instance, we see Virutarāja- as well as Virutarāca-.

Table 2. Select Inscriptions Mentioning Tiṭṭaikuṭi and Vasiṣṭhakuṭi

Full Name of Tiṭṭaikuṭi and Vasiṣṭhakuṭi as Occurring in Inscriptions	King	Date	Inscription No. in *South Indian Inscriptions*, v. 8
Vaṭakarai Virutarājabhayaṅkaravaḷanāṭṭu Meṟkānāṭṭtu brahmadeyam Tiṭṭaikuṭiyāṉa Tirucccirrampalacaturvvedimaṅkalam	Cōḻa Rājādhirāja II	1168 C.E.	291
Tiṭṭaikuṭiyāṉa Tirucccirram-palaccaturvvetimaṅkalam	Māṟavarman Vīra-Pāṇṭiya	1358 C.E.	300
Vaṭakarai Virutarācapayaṅkara Vaḷanāṭṭu Meṟkānāṭṭtu brahmadeyam Tiṭṭaikuṭiyāṉa Tirucccirrampalaccaturvvetimaṅkalam	Kampaṇa	1372 C.E.	282
Śrīvasiṣṭhakuṭiāṉa Vidyāraṇyapuram	Viruppaṇa	1399 C.E.	286
Tiṭṭaikuṭiāṉa Vidyāraṇyapuram	Vīra-Bhūpati	1420 C.E.	275

Even the Vijayanagara inscription of Kampaṇa of 1372 C.E.[11] has only Tiṭṭaikuṭi. So, it is most likely that Viruppaṇa was the ruler, under whom was created the name Śrīvasiṣṭhakuṭiāṉa Vidyāraṇyapuram (Śrīvasiṣṭhakuṭi alias Vidyāraṇyapuram). Viruppaṇa's high regard for Vidyāraṇya, of the Sringeri mutt, is known from his undated inscription in the Śrīraṅganātha temple in Śrīraṅgam.[12] So, it is not surprising that he would want to memorialize the Sringeri pontiff by renaming a village.

While new names for old places are not all that uncommon historically, when inscriptions want to refer to a place with two names, they use the format "name 1 alias name 2," i.e., as in Tiṭṭaikuṭi āṉa Tirucciṟṟampalaccaturvetimaṅkalam. Here Tiṭṭaikuṭi was most probably the old name, where Tamil *tiṭṭai* means "rising ground"[13] and Tamil *kuti* means "village, town."[14] In other words, the original name of the village meant that it was a village or town on a rising ground.[15] Later another name was given to the village when it was possibly converted to a *brahmadeya,* a village granted to the Brahmans. When that happened, the convention was to refer to it as Tiṭṭaikuṭiāṉa Tirucciṟṟampalaccaturvetimaṅkalam. While this makes logical sense, what seems to have happened between 1372 and 1399 is extraordinary. When the new name Vidyāraṇyapuram was created, the old name Tiṭṭakuṭi was most probably changed to Vasiṣṭhakuṭi too! After all, there is no other epigraphic record of the village Tiṭṭaikuṭi ever having been called Vasiṣṭhakuṭi.

This leads one to speculate what could have motivated the change of the name from Tiṭṭaikuṭi to Vasiṣṭhakuti. To answer this query, we have to consider the biography of Vidyāraṇya. Discussing the epigraphic and literary evidence regarding Vidyāraṇya and the Vijayanagara kingdom, Herman Kulke writes:

> All this evidence leaves us in no doubt about the important and most influential role which Vidyāraṇya played as guru, scholar and mahant after he took charge of Sringeri in about 1374/75.[16]

Viruppaṇa's father, Harihara II, became a devotee of Vidyāraṇya after he ascended the throne of Vijayanagara in 1377.[17] Vidyāraṇya died in 1386 C.E.[18] and Harihara II established an agrahāra called Vidyāraṇyapura near Sringeri in 1386 C.E.[19] Viruppaṇa had been Mahāmaṇḍaleśvara of the Tamil country from 1377 to 1400 C.E.[20] Viruppaṇa probably wanted to honor Vidyāraṇya even more by comparing him to Vasiṣṭha, who was the family guru to Daśaratha, the father of Rāma, the hero of the Rāmāyaṇa. So, Viruppaṇa or one of his officials not only created a new name, Vidyāraṇyapuram, but also most probably etymologized the old name Tiṭṭaikuṭi to Vasiṣṭhakuti sometime between 1386 and 1399 C.E.

In this context, it is good to remember what Colin P. Masica notes elsewhere in a different context:

> [M]aking a borrowed work look native . . . was unfortunately the special forte of the old Sanskrit lexicographers. Aided by a precocious discovery of the laws of sound change and the assumption that all languages were corruptions of Sanskrit, they were able not only to turn Prakrit and Modern Indo-Aryan forms "back into" Sanskrit but also to manufacture plausible-looking Sanskrit out of material that had never been Sanskrit.[21]

Only in this case, Viruppaṇa or some other official of his must have backformed the hybrid name Vasiṣṭhakuṭi out of the original Tamil name Tiṭṭaikuṭi. Whoever did this must have been well aware of the fact that the Sanskrit name Vasiṣṭha can be naturalized into Tamil as Vatiṭṭa in the absence of masculine ending "n."[22] When we consider that Tiṭṭaikuṭi becomes colloquially Tiṭṭakuṭi, one can see the Sanskritizers' effort of making Tiṭṭakuṭi seem to be nothing but a corrupt form resulting from Vasiṣṭhakuṭi > Vatiṭṭakuṭi > Tiṭṭakuṭi with the loss of the initial syllable, "Va."

As mentioned above, today Tiṭṭaikuṭi is called Tiṭṭakuṭi and there is a part of Tiṭṭakuṭi called Vatiṭṭapuram—not Vatiṭṭakuṭi. The name Vatiṭṭapuram seems to combine Vatiṭṭa- (<Vasiṣṭha) from Vaṣiṣṭhakuṭi and –puram from Vidyaraṇyapuram. Vatiṭṭapuram seems to be clearly a post-1399 C.E. name since it combines parts of the two names that are mentioned for the first time in the inscription of 1399 C.E.

A question might arise as to whether it was not possible for the name Tiṭṭaikuṭi to have been derived from Vasiṣṭhakuṭi at all. As we noted earlier, the name Vatiṭṭaṉ occurs in the Kamparāmāyaṇam, a Tamil literary text. As a Tamil literary text, the Kamparāmāyaṇam eschews the use of non-Tamil phonemes, and naturalizes non-Tamil phonemes into Tamil phonemes. But the case of Tamil inscriptions is very different. Tamil inscriptions use significant number of Sanskrit words rendered in Grantha script, interspersing Grantha letters even in the middle of Tamil words. In such a situation, there is no barrier against the use of a name such as Vasiṣṭhakuṭi in the several inscriptions that mention Tiṭṭaikuṭi. So the logical inference for the lack of occurrence of the name Vasiṣṭhakuṭi in inscriptions before 1399 C.E. could only be that the name did not exist earlier.

This means that Hastiśarman could not have gone to Kerala from Vasiṣṭhakuṭi in the Cōḻa country before 1372 C.E., when the inscription issued under Kampaṇa still called present-day Tiṭṭakuṭi as Tiṭṭaikuṭi. So, I do not think the identification of Bhavatrāta, the author of the commentary on Jaiminīya Śrautasūtra, with Bhavarāta, the person mentioned by Daṇḍin in his Avantisundarīkathā, is justified.

In support of his identification of Bhavatrāta, Parpola also described several legends prevailing in Kerala that suggested Bhavatrāta lived several centuries earlier than the fourteenth century C.E.:[23]

> This information matches with several other data. In 1971, I wished to check whether any Jaiminīyas were left in Vasiṣṭhakuṭi and found some of them still living in the present-day village of Tiṭṭakuṭi in South Arcot district. In Kerala, on the other hand, Śrī Īṭṭi Ravi told me many unwritten legends about Bhavatrāta. Bhavatrāta is definitely considered to have been a Nambudiri and he is associated especially with the Naripparra mana (no. 9): it is only this and the three neighboring manas that belong to the Kāśyapa gotra and it is only in these houses that the uncommon name Bhavatrāta is current (traditionally, the first son of a Nambudiri is given the name of his

> paternal grandfather, the second son that of his maternal grandfather, and the third son that of his father). Moreover, Bhavatrāta is said to have been the grandson of Mēḻattōḷ Agnihotri, a famous culture hero of Kerala, a performer of 99 śrauta sacrifices during his lifetime, traditionally dated to 343–378 A.D.[24] Bhavatrāta allegedly functioned as the Subrahmaṇya priest in Agnihotri's sacrifices; the Yajñeśvara temple associated with the site of those sacrifices is in the immediate vicinity of the Naripaṟṟa mana. According to a medieval commentary written by Nīlakaṇṭa Nambudiri of the Kūtallūr mana of Nāgaśreṇi (Nāreri), his father Brahmadatta belonging to the Viśvāmitra gotra is a descendant of that Yajñeśvara Agnihotri:[25] the name Brahmadatta (going down in the family line) and his gotra match with those of Bhavatrāta's grandfather.

Raja provides more details regarding some of the legends regarding Mēḻattōḻ Agnihotri, who was also referred to as Yajñesvara Agnihotri:

> According to popular tradition the first person to perform sacrifices in Kerala was Mēḻattōḻ Agnihotri, the son of the legendary sage Vararuci. It is said that Vararuci married a low-caste girl unwittingly and had twelve children by her, each being brought up in a different community. The eldest child, Mēḻattōḻ Agnihotri, performed 99 sacrifices on the banks of the Nīlā (Bhāratappuḻa). The dates of his birth and death are traditionally given as 343 and 378 (represented by the Kali dates given in the chronograms *yajñasthānam saṃrakṣyam* and *purudhīsamāśrayaḥ*). Much credence cannot be given to the tradition about Vararuci, although a similar scandal about Vararuci is mentioned by Bhoja in his *Śṛngāraprakāśa*.[26] A similar story is also popular in Tamilnāḍ.[27]

The Tamil story mentioned by Raja occurs in a text called the *Kapilarakaval*.[28] According to the story, a Brahman named Pakavaṉ married a Pulaiya woman named Āti and had seven children, each of whom was brought up in a different community. The eldest of the children, Kapilaṉ, was brought up in a Brahman family. Two of his siblings were Auvai, and Vaḷḷuvar. Kapilaṉ, Auvai, and Vaḷḷuvar were ancient poets of Tamil Nadu and no historicity can be attributed to this story. Justifiably, K. K. Raja did not give much credence to the tradition about Mēḻattōḻ Agnihotri too. Also, the legendary fourth-century date of Mēḻattōḷ, traditionally considered to be the maternal grandfather of Bhavatrāta, does not fit with the seventh-century date attributed to Bhavatrāta if he is identified with Bhavarāta. So, one cannot put much faith into the historicity of these legends. In fact, one can argue that these legends were possibly created to produce an ancient Nambudiri pedigree for a non-Nambudiri Brahman from the Cōḻa country.

Any conclusions regarding the date of the movement of Sāma Vedic traditions or Brahmans from the Cōḻa country to Kerala based on Bhavatrāta's commentary need to be revised despite whatever legends that might prevail among Nambudiri families regarding Bhavatrāta.[29]

Based on his identification of Bhavarāta with Bhavatrāta, Parpola had come to the following conclusions regarding the relations between Kerala Nambudiris and immigrant Tamil Brahmans:

> Bhavatrāta's grandfather belonged to the early Tamil immigrants, who were still treated as equals and also accepted into marriage. Inscriptions from the 9th century suggest that owing to Cōḻa invasions, Brahman students carried weapons[30] From these times the relations between the immigrant Tamil Brahmans and the Nambudiris have not been so cordial, and at least in the case of the Jaiminīyas the two groups have kept strictly separate.[31]

Thennilapuram Mahadevan uses Parpola's conclusions as additional evidence for his theory of tracing the origin of Kerala's Nambudiris to locations that are presently in Tamil Nadu. Discussing the term *paviḻiyam* for the Āśvalāyana tradition, Mahadevan notes:

> Today, the term has survived only among the Nambudiri Pūrvaśikhās, designating the Āśvalāyana tradition, placing the Nambudiri Pūrvaśikhās thus in north-eastern part of the Tamil country as late as the 8th century C.E. . . . We know as well that a Vedic ritualist like Hastiśarman—of Kāśyapa gotra and Jaiminīya Sūtra—of Vasiṣṭhakuṭi, thus with the historical identity of a Śōḻiya Pūrvaśikhā and from the southern parts of the Toṇṭaimaṇṭalam area in the Tamil country, could arrive at Kerala and become a "Nambudiri" Pūrvaśikhā there in roughly the same period: the impediment of the language and the alienation from long separation having not yet arisen.[32]

Based on the revised date of Bhavatrāta's grandfather's migration to Kerala proposed here, we have to conclude that cordial relationship between at least a section of Malayalam Nambudiris and Tamil Brahmans must have existed well into the fourteenth century C.E. Also, whatever other facts one may point to regarding the original home of Nambudiris, one cannot rely on the assumption that Bhavatrāta's grandfather migrated to Kerala from the Cōḻa country in the seventh century C.E. Finally, we have to conclude that most probably Bhavatrāta belonged to the fifteenth century C.E.

Conclusions

Earlier scholars' identification of Bhavatrāta with Bhavarāta mentioned by Daṇḍin ignores the difference in the names of the grandfathers,

Hastiśarman vs. Bhavarāta as well as the difference in names between Bhavatrāta and Bhavarāta. When we look at the epigraphic records related to Vasiṣṭhakuṭi, from where Bhavatrāta's grandfather had migrated, we find that there was no record of the name Vasiṣṭhakuṭi prior to the late fourteenth century and all earlier inscriptions use the name Tiṭṭaikuṭi. It is most probably due to a desire on the part of Viruppaṇa, the Vijayanagara Mahāmaṇḍaleśvara, to honor Vidyāraṇya, the pontiff of Sringeri, Tiṭṭakuṭi was Sanskritized and renamed Vasiṣṭhakuti alias Vidyaraṇyapuram. This means earlier views regarding the history of Sāma Vedic traditions in Kerala based on Bhavatrāta's seventh-century C.E. date have to be revised based on Bhavatrāta's fourteenth-century date proposed here.

Notes

1 K. A. Nilakanta Sastri, *A History of South India,* 4th ed. (Madras: Oxford University Press, 1975, 1987, seventh impression), p. 345.

2 Asko Parpola, "The Passages of the *Jaiminīya Śrautasūtra* Dealing with the *Agnicayana,* together with Bhavatrāta's Commentary: The Sanskrit Text, and English Translation, and Notes," in Frits Staal, ed., *Agni: The Vedic Ritual of the Fire Altar* (Berkeley: Asian Humanities Press, 1983), vol. 2, p. 700.

3 See Śuranad Kunjan Pillai, *Avantisundarī of Ācārya Daṇḍin* (Trivandrum: University of Travancore, 1954), p. 23.

4 See S. K. Pillai, *Avantisundarī of Ācārya Daṇḍin,* p. 13, II.21 ff.

5 K. K. Raja, "Sanskrit and Malayalam References from Kerala," in Frits Staal, ed., *Agni: The Vedic Ritual of the Fire Altar* (Berkeley: Asian Humanities Press, 1983), vol. 2, p. 307.

6 Asko Parpola, "On the Jaiminīya and Vādhūla Traditions of South India and the Pāṇḍu/Pāṇḍava Problem," *Studia Orientalia* 55/22 (1984): 445.

7 *South Indian Inscriptions* (Mysore: Archaeological Survey of India, 1937, 2001, reprint), inscription nos. 273–300, vol. 8, pp. 397–400.

8 Tamil *āṉa* means "alias" and *-nāṭṭu* is the oblique form of *-nāṭu.*

9 *South Indian Inscriptions,* no. 286, vol. 8, p. 400.

10 *South Indian Inscriptions,* no. 275, vol. 8, p. 400.

11 *South Indian Inscriptions,* no. 282, vol. 8, p. 399.

12 *South Indian Inscriptions,* no. 294, vol. 24.

13 T. Burrow and M. B. Emeneau, *A Dravidian Etymological Dictionary* (Oxford: Clarendon Press, 1984, second ed.), no. 3221.

14 S. Vaiyapuri Pillai, ed., *Tamil Lexicon,* 6 vols. and supplement (Madras: University of Madras, 1924–1939).

15 As a name of a place, Tiṭṭakuṭi is not unique. We find another Tiṭṭakuṭi near Pattukkottai in the Tanjavur district of Tamil Nadu as well.

[16] Herman Kulke, "Mahārājas, Mahants, and Historians: Reflections on the Historiography of Early Vijayanagara and Sringeri," in Anna Libera Dallapiccola, ed., in collaboration with Stephanie Zingel-Ave Lallemant, *Vijayanagara—City and Empire: New Currents of Research* (Stuttgart: Steiner Verlag Wiesbaden GMBH, 1985), p. 132.

[17] Kulke, "Mahārājas, Mahants and Historians," p. 131.

[18] Kulke, "Mahārājas, Mahants and Historians," p. 131.

[19] Leela Prasad, *Poetics of Conduct: Oral Narrative and Moral Being in a South Indian Town* (New York: Columbia University Press, 2007), p. 44.

[20] A. Krishnaswami, *The Tamil Country Under Vijayanagar* (Annamalainagar: Annamalai University, 1964), p. 71.

[21] Colin P. Masica, "Aryan and Non-Aryan Elements in North Indian Agriculture," in Madhav M. Deshpande and Peter Edwin Hook, eds., *Aryan and Non-Aryan in India* (Ann Arbor: Center for South and Southeast Asian Studies, University of Michigan, 1979), p. 60.

[22] S. V. Pillai, ed., *Tamil Lexicon,* gives the name Vatiṭṭaṉ with the masculine suffix *ṉ* occurring in the *Kamparāmāyanam.* The name Vasiṣṭha is also naturalized as Vaciṭṭaṉ.

[23] Parpola, "On the Jaiminīya and Vādhūla Traditions of South India," p. 446.

[24] On *agnihotri,* cf. Raja, "Sanskrit and Malayalam References from Kerala," p. 304f.

[25] Raja, "Sanskrit and Malayalam References from Kerala," p. 304f.

[26] See V. Raghavan, *Bhoja's Śṛṅgāraprakāśa* (Madras: Self-published, 1963), p. 829.

[27] Raja, "Sanskrit and Malayalam References from Kerala," p. 304.

[28] A. V. Subramaniya Aiyar, *Kapilarahaval: A Tamil Poem on Caste* (Madras: n.p., 1975), pp. 103–105.

[29] Parpola, "On the Jaiminīya and Vādhūla Traditions of South India," p. 446.

[30] Cf. Raja, "Sanskrit and Malayalam References from Kerala," p. 302.

[31] Parpola, "On the Jaiminīya and Vādhūla Traditions of South India," p. 446.

[32] Thennilapuram P. Mahadevan, "On the Southern Recension of the *Mahābhārata,* Brahman Migrations, and Brāhmi Paleography," *Electronic Journal of Vedic Studies* 15/2 (2008): 34.

References

Aiyar, A. V. Subramaniya. *Kapilarahaval: A Tamil Poem on Caste.* Madras: Self-published, 1975.

Burrow, T., and M. B. Emeneau. *Dravidian Etymological Dictionary.* Oxford: Clarendon Press, 1984, second ed.

Krishnaswami, A. *The Tamil Country under Vijayanagar.* Annamalainagar: Annamalai University, 1964.

Kulke, Herman. "Mahārājas, Mahants, and Historians. Reflections on the Historiography of Early Vijayanagara and Sringeri," in Anna Libera Dallapiccola, ed., in collaboration with Stephanie Zingel-Ave Lallemant, *Vijayanagara—City and Empire: New Currents of Research,* pp. 120-143. Stuttgart: Steiner Verlag Wiesbaden GMBH, 1985,

Masica, Colin P. "Aryan and Non-Aryan Elements in North Indian Agriculture," in Madhav M. Deshpande and Peter Edwin Hook, eds., *Aryan and Non-Aryan in India,* pp. 55–151. Ann Arbor, MI: Center for South and Southeast Asian Studies, University of Michigan, 1979.

Mahadevan, Thennilapuram P. "On the Southern Recension of the *Mahābhārata,* Brahman Migrations, and Brāhmi Paleography," *Electronic Journal of Vedic Studies* 15/2 (2008).

Parpola, Asko. "On the Jaiminīya and Vādhūla Traditions of South India and the Pāṇḍu/Pāṇḍava Problem," *Studia Orientalia* 55/22 (1984): 429–468.

—. "The Passages of the *Jaiminīya Śrautasūtra* dealing with the *Agnicayana,* together with Bhavatrāta's Commentary: The Sanskrit Text, an English Translation, and Notes," in Frits Staal, ed., *Agni: The Vedic Ritual of the Fire Altar,* vol. 2, pp. 700–736. Berkeley: Asian Humanities Press, 1983.

Pillai, Śuranad Kunjan. *Avantisundarī of Ācārya Daṇḍin.* Trivandrum Sanskrit Series 172. Trivandrum: University of Travancore, 1954. Quoted in Asko Parpola, "The Passages of the *Jaiminīya Śrautasūtra* Dealing with the *Agnicayana,* together with Bhavatrāta's Commentary," in Frits Staal, ed., *Agni: The Vedic Ritual of the Fire Altar,* vol. 2, p. 700. Berkeley: Asian Humanities Press, 1983.

Pillai, S. Vaiyapuri, ed. *Tamil Lexicon,* 6 vols. and supplement. Madras: University of Madras, 1924–1939.

Prasad, Leela. *Poetics of Conduct: Oral Narrative and Moral Being in a South Indian Town.* New York: Columbia University Press, 2007.

Raghavan, V. *Bhoja's Śṛngāraprakāśa.* Madras: Self-published, 1963. Quoted in K. K. Raja, "Sanskrit and Malayalam References from Kerala," in Frits Staal, ed, *Agni: The Vedic Ritual of the Fire Altar,* vol. 2, p. 304. Berkeley: Asian Humanities Press, 1983.

Raja, K. K. "Sanskrit and Malayalam References from Kerala," in Frits Staal, ed., *Agni: The Vedic Ritual of the Fire Altar,* vol. 2, pp. 300–310. Berkeley: Asian Humanities Press, 1983.

Sastri, K. A. Nilakanta. *A History of South India.* Madras: Oxford University Press, 1975, 1987, fourth ed.

South Indian Inscriptions, vols. 8, 24. Mysore: Archaeological Survey of India, 1982.

Meetings with Frits Staal

Asko Parpola
University of Helsinki

While working on my Ph.D. dissertation[1] I discovered a manuscript containing parts of the *Jaiminīya Śrautasūtra* that were believed to be long lost.[2] On my first trip to India I wanted to search for more material on that text on which I am still working. In October 1970, I therefore wrote to Frits Staal, who had studied the living Vedic traditions of South India, especially among the Nambudiri Brahmins of Kerala, some of whom belonged to the Jaiminīya branch of *Sāmaveda*.[3] Staal straightaway wrote to my future guru in *Jaiminīya Sāmaveda*, Śrī Iṭṭi Ravi Nambūdiri, telling that he would be coming to Kerala again in February 1971, probably together with me. A copy of Staal's letter to Iṭṭi Ravi, with a note addressed to me, is reproduced on the next page.

Staal came to Madras later than planned. Immediately after his arrival I went to see him at Woodland's Hotel on March 9. The meeting was amicable but very brief. Staal suggested collaboration in publishing the songs of the *Jaiminīya Sāmaveda*, in particular the totally unknown *Ūha-* and *Ūhya-Gānas* that survived in oral tradition in Kerala. His plans however had changed so that he would be leaving for Varanasi in a few days, and would not be able to come with me to Kerala. On the day of my departure, March 12, he came riding a motorcycle with his friend to give me last-minute detailed advice on how to reach the village of Panjal (photo, right). I went to Kerala briefly a second time in May to collect the audiotapes of the *Jaiminīya Gānas* that Śrī Iṭṭi Ravi Nambūdiri had chanted at Frits's request with the tape recorder that Frits had left with him. Before sending the tapes on to Staal to Berkeley, I copied them in Copenhagen where I was working at that time, and

Frits Staal and Asko Parpola, Madras, 1971.

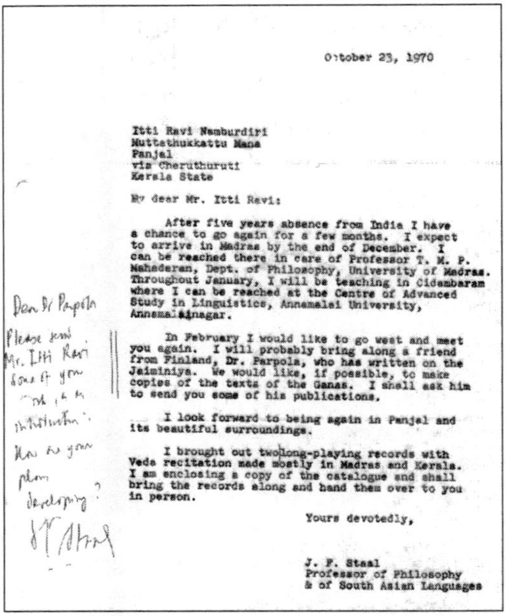

O:tober 23, 1970

Itti Ravi Namburdiri
Muttathukkattu Mana
Panjal
via Cheruthuruti
Kerala State

My dear Mr. Itti Ravi:

After five years absence from India I have a chance to go again for a few months. I expect to arrive in Madras by the end of December. I can be reached there in care of Professor T. M. P. Mahaderan, Dept. of Philosophy, University of Madras. Throughout January, I will be teaching in Cidambaram where I can be reached at the Centre of Advanced Study in Linguistics, Annamalai University, Annamalaiinagar.

In February I would like to go west and meet you again. I will probably bring along a friend from Finland, Dr. Parpola, who has written on the Jaiminiya. We would like, if possible, to make copies of the texts of the Ganas. I shall ask him to send you some of his publications.

I look forward to being again in Panjal and its beautiful surroundings.

I brought out twolong-playing records with Veda recitation made mostly in Madras and Kerala. I am enclosing a copy of the catalogue and shall bring the records along and hand them over to you in person.

Yours devotedly,

J. F. Staal
Professor of Philosophy
& of South Asian Languages

Dear Dr Parpola
Please send Mr. Itti Ravi some of your [illegible]
How are your plans developing?
JF Staal

Letter from Frits Staal, 1970. Staal P201, Department of Philosophy, UC Berkeley.

copies were later deposited in Helsinki and Kyoto as well. The *Jaiminīya Gānas* are still largely unpublished but work on them has been going on: among other things, my colleague and former student Masato Fujii and I have collected much new manuscript material on these and other *Jaiminīya* texts.[4]

Staal and I next met in spring 1973 in Gothenburg, Sweden, where I taught Sanskrit and Gothic for one term during the sabbatical leave of Prof. Gösta Liebert. I had arranged guest lectures by Frits in both Gothenburg and Helsinki. (I could not go with him to Helsinki, but among other instructions I gave him addresses of some philatelist shops. My wife reported that he was very happy after purchasing some rare stamps of Indian princely states.) In Gothenburg Staal invited me to join another project of his, documenting the greatest Vedic sacrificial ritual of Kerala, the *atirātra agnicayana.* For me, acceptance meant an extensive and at times rather frustrating correspondence with many people during the following year, when Staal was otherwise engaged and I was in charge, but eventually the difficulties were overcome and the ambitious venture was successfully realized in April 1975 in Kerala, where I spent two weeks, and Staal spent some more time. The results included a 58-minute documentary film[5] and two monumental volumes, to which I contributed three papers.[6]

Afterward our paths crossed only a few times. Frits loved swimming, as I heard also from my Keralite friends, and he succeeded in getting me into the hotel pool during the 7th World Sanskrit Conference in Leiden in August 1987. He was a bit hurt when I, his friend and protégé, publicly objected to his thesis that "ritual is meaningless." Our next meeting was again in Leiden fifteen years later, at the Third International Vedic

Workshop in 2002, and a final and very cordial meeting took place in 2008 in Chennai, where he attended my public lecture and afterward invited me to the lunch offered by the editor of *The Hindu*.

Asko Parpola and Frits Staal, Chennai, 2008.

For a young Indologist just beginning his career, Frits Staal's trust and friendship was inspiring and encouraging. In the early years of our acquaintance, between 1971 and 1983, we often exchanged letters and publications. I cherish good memories of Frits, one of my teachers and friends, and I thank George Thompson for this opportunity to pay my respects to him.

Notes

1 Asko Parpola, *The Śrautasūtras of Lāṭyāyana and Drāhyāyaṇa and their Commentaries: An English Translation and Study, Vol. I, Part 1: General Introduction and Appendices* (Helsinki: Societas Scientiarum Fennica, 1968).

2 Cf. Asko Parpola, "On the *Jaiminīyaśrautasūtra* and its Annexes," *Orientalia Suecana* 16 (1967): 181–214.

3 Frits Staal, *Nambudiri Veda Recitation* ('s-Gravenhage: Mouton & Co., 1961).

4 Masato Fujii, "The *Jaiminīya Sāmaveda* Traditions and Manuscripts in South India," in Saraju Rath, ed., *Aspects of Manuscript Culture in South India* (Leiden: Brill, 2012), pp. 99–118; Masato Fujii and Asko Parpola, "Manuscripts of the *Jaiminīya Sāmaveda* Traced and Photographed in 2002–2006," in Asko Parpola and Petteri Koskikallio, eds., *Vedic Investigations: Papers of the 12th World Sanskrit Conference, Vol. 1* (Delhi: Motilal Banarsidass, 2016), pp. 127–166.

5 Robert Gardner and J. F. Staal, *Altar of Fire.* Film Study Institute at Harvard University, 1976, 58 min.

6 C. G. Kashikar and Asko Parpola, "*Śrauta* Traditions in Recent Times,"in Frits Staal, ed., *Agni: The Vedic Ritual of the Fire Altar* (Berkeley: Asian Humanities Press, 1983), pp. 193–251; Asko Parpola, "The Passages of the *Jaiminiya Śrautasutra* Dealing with the *Agnicayana,* Together with Bhavatrata's Commentary: The Sanskrit Text, an English Translation, and Notes," in Staal, ed., *Agni: The Vedic Ritual of the Fire Altar,* vol. 2, pp. 700–736; Parpola, "The Pre-Vedic Indian Background of the *Śrauta* Rituals," in Staal, ed., *Agni: The Vedic Ritual of the Fire Altar,* vol. 2, pp. 41–75, pl. 7–8.

References

Fujii, Masato. "The *Jaiminīya Sāmaveda* Traditions and Manuscripts in South India," in Saraju Rath, ed., *Aspects of Manuscript Culture in South India*, pp. 99–118. Indological Library, vol. 40. Leiden: Brill, 2012.

Fujii, Masato, and Asko Parpola. "Manuscripts of the *Jaiminīya Sāmaveda* Traced and Photographed in 2002–2006," in Asko Parpola and Petteri Koskikallio, eds., *Vedic Investigations: Papers of the 12th World Sanskrit Conference, Vol. 1*, pp. 127–166. Delhi: Motilal Banarsidass, 2016.

Gardner, Robert, and J. F. Staal. *Altar of Fire.* Film Study Institute at Harvard University, 1976, 58 min.

Kashikar, C. G., and Asko Parpola. "*Śrauta* Traditions in Recent Times," in: Frits Staal, ed., *Agni: The Vedic Ritual of the Fire Altar,* vol. 2, pp. 193–251. Berkeley: Asian Humanities Press, 1983.

Parpola, Asko. "On the *Jaiminīyaśrautasūtra* and its Annexes," *Orientalia Suecana* 16 (1967): 181–214.

—."The Passages of the *Jaiminiya Srautasutra* Dealing with the *Agnicayana*, Together with Bhavatrata's Commentary: The Sanskrit Text, an English Translation, and Notes," in Frits Staal, ed., *Agni: The Vedic Ritual of the Fire Altar,* vol. 2, pp. 700–736. Berkeley: Asian Humanities Press, 1983.

—."The Pre-Vedic Indian Background of the *Śrauta* Rituals," in Frits Staal, ed., *Agni: The Vedic Ritual of the Fire Altar,* vol. 2, pp. 41–75, pl. 7–8. Berkeley: Asian Humanities Press, 1983.

—.*The Śrautasūtras of Lāṭyāyana and Drāhyāyaṇa and their Commentaries: An English Translation and Study, Vol. I, Part 1: General Introduction and Appendices.* Commentationes Humanarum Litterarum 42, vol. 2. Helsinki: Societas Scientiarum Fennica, 1968.

Staal, J. Frits. ed. *Agni: The Vedic Ritual of the Fire Altar,* 2 vols. Berkeley: Asian Humanities Press, 1983.

—.*Nambudiri Veda Recitation.* 's-Gravenhage: Mouton & Co., 1961.

Jesus Christ, Tantric Deity: Syntax and Semantics in Ritual Change[1]

Richard K. Payne
Institute of Buddhist Studies, Berkeley

Ritual Change

One of the characteristics frequently noted in academic discussions of ritual is resistance to change—either actually evidenced or attributed. It seems obvious, at least to me, that rituals *do* change. Those of us who are old enough may recall the what were then considered radical changes in the Catholic Mass following Vatican II.[2] These included such changes as the use of the vernacular instead of Latin and relocating where the officiant stands so that his actions can be viewed by the laity.

The view of ritual as subject to change has perhaps received increasing attention because it is counter to an older, received view. Catherine Bell notes, for example, that "Part of the dilemma of ritual change lies in the simple fact that rituals tend to present themselves as the unchanging, time-honored customs of an enduring community."[3] She then indicates two reasons for this: the "legitimacy of age and tradition" and the use of ethnographic methods to study oral societies. Such methods generally frame research results in terms of the "ethnographic present," looking at a society synchronically rather than diachronically.[4] Synchronic studies may in turn have been motivated by functionalist theory. With its fundamental argument that social practices exist because they provide social stability, functionalism reinforced a static conception of "primitive" societies and of "primitive" religious practices, a conception that is itself part of the rhetoric of "high modernity."

The analogies made between language and ritual by some scholars suggests another reason—though indirectly from those theories. Discussing the arbitrary character of the linguistic sign, such as phonemic minimal pairs,[5] Terence Hawkes points out that "The very arbitrariness of the linguistic sign protects it from change."[6] Linguistic signs are arbitrary in the sense they have no rationale other than social convention, and are therefore not subject to debate—they simply are. Despite doctrinal or symbolic meaning being attributed to them, rituals are performed in the way that they are because that is the way they are performed. In his rejection of the thesis that rituals are referentially meaningful, Staal makes this point:

> [W]hen we ask a brahmin explicitly why the rituals are performed, we never receive an answer which refers to symbolic activity. There are numerous different answers, such as: we do it because our ancestors did it; because we are eligible to do it; because it is good for society; because it is good; because it is our duty; because it is said to lead to immortality; because it leads to immortality.[7]

I personally experienced this during a festival (*matsuri*) on Mt. Kōya in 1983. When I asked some of the participants, "Why are you doing this?" they responded, "Because we've always done it."

The conception of rituals as static and unchanging, even perhaps as the most conservative factors of a given religious world, is itself located in a conceptual frame in which change is understood as being driven primarily by changes in doctrine. This representation of the relative roles of ritual and doctrine in religion derives from a theological conception of religion.

Several additional factors also support this conception of ritual as static, two of which I briefly note here. The first follows from the Protestant Reformation, when some Protestant advocates argued against the conception of ritual as salvific. This entered popular Western religious culture in the form of the connotation for the term "ritual" as something done purely out of rote or habit, as mere activity done unthinkingly and which lacks any substantive content or meaning.[8] This characterization of ritual was reinforced by the Romantics' emphasis on spontaneity as the guarantor of the authenticity that they valued, in contrast to what they characterized as the inauthenticity of premeditated actions, which were stultifying and constrained the creative spirit.

For religious studies per se, another factor is the influence of the scholarship of Mircea Eliade. Once almost definitive of the field, the influence of his work has faded in academia, though he continues to occupy a zombie-like existence in the popular religious world. One of the areas of Eliade's thought that has been criticized is his theories of ritual. In Eliade's view, rituals are understood by their practitioners as the reactualizion of the deities' actions in *illud tempus.* This reactualizing does not mean copying or simply reenacting, but rather making the actions of the gods at the beginning of time present once again in the timeless realm of the ritual performance itself, technically know as anamneusis. Under this anamnestic theory, because of their divine origins rituals cannot be allowed to change.[9]

Psychological approaches to ritual are a third factor, inasmuch as they still seem to struggle with the pathologizing analogies between ritual and obsessive behavior introduced most famously by Freud.[10] More recently, the cognitive study of religion has given attention to ritual as well, and several influential authors have continued emphasize resistance to change in a fashion very reminiscent to that of Freud.[11]

Frits Staal on Ritual Change

A very different theoretical orientation, one that also suggests that rituals are highly stable, was put forth by Frits Staal. In contrast, for example, to Eliade's crypto-theologizing, Staal was much more scientifically oriented. He has theorized that rituals (and also mantras) do not change, even when transmitted across cultural boundaries.[12] Staal does not, however, hold a conception of ritual as rigidly unchanging, as is the case with some of the understandings just mentioned. Through my own work, he was quite aware of ritual substitutions, such as those found in the Shingon *homa* (Jpn. *goma* 護摩) ritual. *Homa* rites in Japan employ sesame oil (Jpn. *goma abura* 胡麻油) as a substitute for the clarified butter (ghee) used in Vedic and Brahmanic rituals. In other words, for Staal, while rituals are stable—and, in some ways, highly stable—they are not unchanging. His syntactic analysis of ritual allows us to identify such changes, examine them for regularities, and consider the basis for such regularities.

Thus, rituals have proven highly stable forms of practice, even as they have moved across boundaries of language and religious culture.[13] Indeed, ritual has been much more stable than symbolic, theological, or philosophical interpretations, or doctrinal justifications of them—despite the intellectualist presumption that action follows from thought or, more specifically in the realm of religious studies, that doctrine is primary while praxis is derivative.[14]

Inside and Outside the Script

Despite the received view of ritual we no longer need ask whether or not rituals change. Instead, the question now is: How do they change? And, what kind of changes allow us to say that a ritual has changed?[15]

Given the centrality of ritual action to all religious traditions, ritual change is an important part of studying a tradition's history—certainly at least as important as studying doctrinal change. The importance of ritual change raises the question of methodology: how can we go about studying ritual change? and, perhaps more important, how can we study ritual change in a systematic fashion that allows for comparisons between instances of ritual change?

Most studies of ritual change conform to the dominant concerns of contemporary critical theory, tending to focus on change deriving from social, political, economic, institutional, or doctrinal factors.[16] In general, such studies do not examine changes to what might be called the "script" of the ritual, a term I use here to refer not only to a prescriptive ritual text, but as inclusive of all the other injunctions regarding proper ritual performance that are part of a ritual system. Changes based on social or political factors, and so on, mentioned above, are then "extra-script changes"—that is, these types of changes are external to what may be abstracted as the ritual practice as such. In contrast, changes to the script of a ritual, or what may be called "intra-script changes" are changes within a ritual, whether to the instructions recorded in a ritual manual or to the set of injunctions regarding proper performance of a ritual. This terminology maps closely to the distinction Roy Rappaport makes between the self-referential aspects, which he also calls indexical aspects, and the canonic aspects of ritual performance:

> The self-referential represents the immediate, the particular and the vital aspects of events; the canonical, in contrast, represents the general, enduring, or even eternal aspects of universal orders.[17]

Rappaport goes on to note that the canonical aspects are given the "quality of perdurance . . . by the apparent invariance of its mode of transmission."[18] What I am calling here "extra-script" correspond to what Rappaport terms the self-referential or indexical aspects, while "intra-script" correspond to the canonical aspects.[19]

Syntax and Semantics of Ritual

Staal adapted the category of syntax from linguistics to describe one important aspect of ritual. I propose extending that borrowing from linguistics so that ritual changes can be analyzed into two types: ritual syntax and ritual semantics. My thesis is that semantic change is the most frequent kind of change and is much easier to undertake. As with language, syntactic change is less frequent and more difficult to implement. What I expect to accomplish in this essay, however, is simply to establish that there is a relation between syntactic and semantic change and a means for the systematic analysis and description of those changes.

This proposal implicates that there are systematic dynamics by which rituals change, which can be identified and described formally.[20] In addition to semantic and syntactic dynamics, there may be other intra-script changes. It is expected, however, that these would be just as regular as the syntactic and semantic ones studied here, and that comparable appropriations of concepts from linguistics would be equally effective in studying such aspects. The relation between semantics and syntax is complex—changes to one can effect changes to the other. It is not simply the case that syntax is an empty structure into which semantic elements are placed:

Subject / verb / object
Boy / kick / ball, or
Boy / throw / ball, or
Girl / hit / ball, and so on.

Semantic elements are not independent of syntax, nor is syntax unaffected by differing semantic elements. The example given above employs a transitive verb; the use of an intransitive verb would effect the syntactic structure: Boy / run. In the analysis below, we will see how this complex relation between syntax and semantics also plays out in ritual. First, however, I will consider some of the extra-script factors involved in the production of the two *homa*s under examination.

Yogi Chen

The particular instance of ritual change I am examining here is of a set of *homa* rituals composed by Yogi Chen, a Chinese Buddhist who followed tantric Buddhist practices. He moved from China to Kalimpong, where he studied and practiced with the Tibetan expatriate community. By the mid-1970s he again relocated, to Oakland and Berkeley, the East Bay region of the San Francisco Bay Area. Chen became part of the Chinese expatriate community and promoted his own version of tantric Buddhism, including a variety of *homa* rituals. His work is now carried on by Yutang Lin, who has also composed several *homa* texts.

As Nicolas Sihlé notes about texts, they can be "crucial elements of distinctly local constructions of meaning."[21] Considering the nature of the ritual texts he examined, Sihlé argues that they are best seen "as key (albeit all too often neglected) elements situated at the juncture between a local sociocultural universe and the larger world of Tibetan Buddhism."[22] Similarly, Yogi Chen's *homa* rituals function at the intersection of multiple religious dimensions, including the Chinese appropriation of Tibetan tantric practices, Chinese expatriate communities, and the surrounding Christian religious culture of Berkeley, California, in the 1970s. The latter extra-script factor becomes evident in what I will for convenience at times simply refer to as Yogi Chen's "Jesus *homa*."

Analysis of "A Ritual Fire Sacrifice to the Five Saints of Christianity"

The two rituals examined in more detail below, the "Jesus *homa*" and the "Śākyamuni *homa*," are very similar to one another, and are part of the relatively small corpus of *homa* ritual manuals composed by Yogi Chen available in English.[23] In addition to the Jesus[24] and Śākyamuni[25] *homa*s, these include "A Ritual of Fire Sacrifice to the Green Tara,"[26] "A Ritual of Homa to the Healing Buddha,"[27] "Homa Ritual Honoring Bodhisattva Earth Treasure," "A Ritual of Fire Sacrifice to Kurukula,"[28] and "A Ritual of Fire Sacrifice to the God of Wealth (Vaisaravana [sic])."[29] An examination of the outlines of the Jesus and Śākyamuni *homa*s given in the appendices makes the similarities evident, but these are more sharply clarified by the inverted tree diagrams shown below.

Yogi Chen's "Jesus *homa*" is entitled in full "A Ritual of Fire Sacrifice to the Five Saints of Christianity."[30] The "five saints" are arranged in mandala-like fashion on a cross. The text instructs the practitioner to visualize "a big sphere of pure white light on the seat" of the deities in the ritual enclosure.

> This is the Holy Spirit. At the center of this light is Jesus on the Cross. God is above the Cross, while male apostles, like St. Francis is named, are below the Cross. To the right of the Cross is the Holy Mother; to the left are female apostles, like Theresa. These are the five saints we are referring to. Our arrangement of the seat of the Holy Spirit differs from that of Christianity. This eases the correspondence between Holy Spirit and Dharmakaya.[31]

I should note that there is some inconsistency between the mandalic representation described in this visualization and the sequence of offerings made in the course of the ritual per se (Appendix 1, 10d). In addition to this symbolic adaptation of the cross in the form of a mandala,

Chen adapts the form of the *homa* ritual itself in order to make offerings to the "five saints of Christianity."

Content of Yogi Chen's "Jesus *Homa*"

The melding of Christian imagery into this Buddhist ritual is found in a section in which Jesus is identified as an incarnation of Guanyin, and in turn with a monk named Jin Ai. The last action the practitioner is instructed to perform in preparing the seat of the deities (Appendix 1, section 6) is "Then praise Jesus with this stanza":

> You are the incarnation of compassionate Kuan yin,
> Through the ages He appears in various forms for Salvation.
> Once in China as the Holy monk Jin Ai,
> He cut his flesh into stripes [strips?] to inspire others' Bodhicitta,
> His blood became white and paved the way to Pure Land,
> With his heart in his palms, he knelt toward West and died.
> His sacrifice was more supreme than yours,
> This offering to you is in honor of all compassionate monks,
> Thus we worship fully the Holy spirit of Kuan yin.
> Through the Kalpas there are numerous Buddhas and Bodhisattvas
> Whose Holy sacrifices are most worthy of being praised,
> Yet none of these sacrifices is as well known
> As Jesus' Crucifixion.[32]

This stanza of praise is noteworthy in that it both subsumes Jesus into an incarnation of Guanyin and, at the same time, praises the sacrifice of Jin Ai as superior to that of Jesus in the crucifixion, indeed asserting that there are numerous buddhas and bodhisattvas that are not as well known whose sacrifices are worthy of being praised equally or perhaps to an even greater degree. Additionally, the stanza of praise might be understood to homologize the Pure Land with the Christian Heaven. Perhaps underlying this is a Buddhist claim to superiority, something along the lines of, "They talk about Heaven, but we know that is actually a symbol for the Pure Land."

Subsumption and Subjugation: Differing Rhetorical Strategies at the Interface of Religions

With Yogi Chen's Jesus *homa* we see the same religiocultural strategy in late twentieth-century Berkeley as was exercised by tantric Buddhists in medieval China and elsewhere. Just as Amoghavajra and Yi Xing ingested the Northern Dipper into Buddhist ritual praxis by creating new *homa*s that have the Northern Dipper as the central deity[33] (Jpn. *honzon* 本尊), so too does Yogi Chen attempt to ingest Jesus, God, Mary, and the saints. If the Northern Dipper, so central to Daoism and Chinese popular religion, could become a Buddhist deity, then why couldn't Jesus and his "retinue" be subsumed into the Buddhist pantheon?

Although this is admittedly speculative, one can easily imagine that the symbolic reinterpretations of the crucifix into a mandala, the conflation of the "five saints" with the Holy Spirit and the Holy Spirit in turn with the *dharmakāya,* are strategic rhetorical moves that Vajrabodhi and Yi Xing would have appreciated. Similarly, had they been in Yogi Chen's place, might not they have done the same? As tantalizing as such speculations may be, at best they provide only an argument by analogy. The strategic moves involved, however, are fundamentally the same, simply carried forward several centuries and relocated to the West Coast. Despite the speculations, what we see here is something that can perhaps best be described as the subsuming of Jesus and others into a tantric Buddhist ritual context.

In addition to such ritual practices, Buddhist myth also evidences rhetorical strategies in encounters between different traditions, one of which is subjugation. An important instance of this has been studied, for example, by Ronald Davidson.[34] In this case the subjugation of Maheśvara (Śiva) by Vajrapāṇi asserts the superiority of Buddhist tantric practice over Śaiva, while at the same time "This comical tale of direct competition between the Śaiva and Bauddha traditions recognizes the homogeneous nature of many of their rituals and symbols."[35] Subjugation is also an important accomplishment in stories of Padmasambhava's role in the establishment of the buddhadharma in Tibet. The biographies of Padmasambhava tell us that because Śāntarakṣita had been unable to tame the native spirits through the performance of peaceful rites, the monastery at bSam yas could not be completed. King Khri Srong lde btsan then sent messengers requesting Padmasambhava's assistance. Because of his greater tantric powers Padmasambhava was able to bring the local deities under control and the monastery could then be completed.[36]

Analysis of the Yogi Chen *Homa*s

Structually, these are fairly simple *homa* rituals, comprising two sets of offerings in each case. The first is to Agni, while the second is to the chief

Syntactic Structure of *Homa* of Jesus and the Saints

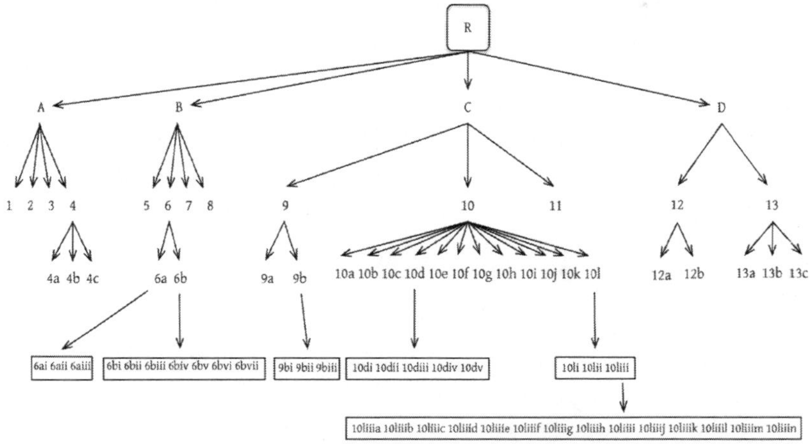

Syntactic Structure of *Homa* of Śākyamuni

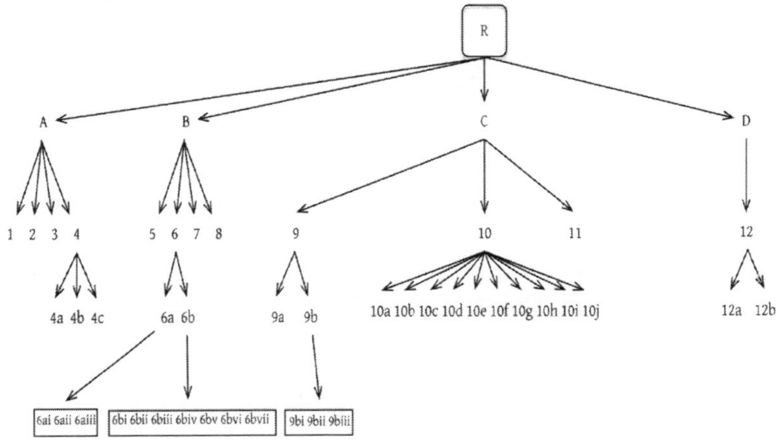

deity (*honzon* 本尊). In one case, the chief deity is Śākyamuni, and in the other it is the "five saints of Christianity." In contrast, Shingon *goma*s typically have five sets of offerings, to Agni, Lord of the Assembly (who varies, depending on who the Chief Deity is), the Chief Deity (the primary buddha, bodhisattva, or other deity evoked in the ritual), the

Celestial Deities (including asterisms of various kinds), and the Worldly Deities (the Vedic gods).

Yogi Chen's *homa*s also differ from typical Shingon *goma* rites in that they do not include any act of ritual identification. While ritual identification (or deity yoga) is widely found in tantric Buddhist rituals, it is not universal. Thus, for example,while Shingon gomas include ritual identification, the Shingon ritual for feeding hungry ghosts does not. According to Charles Orzech, this is a consequence of hungry ghost rituals that derive from different Chinese ritual corpi.[37]

Assymetry, not Terminal Abbreviation

The rituals have been grouped into four segments, identified by the capital letters A through D. The first two, A and B, are general preparations, followed by preparations specific to the performance of the homa as such. Segment C constitutes the *homa* offering acts, beginning with starting the fire through to thanking Agni. The final segment D terminates the ritual.

Both rituals appear to be assymetrical, rather than evidencing terminal abbreviation. Many rituals—indeed, all of those examined in my previous research—have an identifiable central activity that constitutes the central axis of ritual action. In previously studied *homa*s the axial action is ritual identification between the practitioner and the deity. This is normally performed in the midst of making offerings to the chief deity. Terminal abbreviation is characteristic of symmetrical rituals, which repeat the same actions in the second half of the ritual as in the first, but in abbreviated form. Such rituals frequently have shorter ritual actions, fewer ritual actions, or both, in the second half of the performance, that is, those following ritual identification. An example of shortening ritual actions is requiring fewer recitations of a mantra at the end of a ritual than at the beginning. An example of fewer ritual actions might be leaving out the second of a set of three actions performed in the beginning of the ritual when the same set is performed at the end.

In these cases and others in Yogi Chen's *homa* corpus, the terminal sequence is so short that although a ritually central event (the axis) is identifiable, the rituals appear to be assymetrical rather than abbreviated in their second half. In the Śākyamuni *homa* the terminating acts are the dedication of merit (12) in general (12a) and special (12b) forms. The Jesus *homa* adds confession (13), which comprises four acts: recitation of the hundred-syllable *dhāraṇī* of Vajrasattva (13a), confession to Vajrasattva (13b), confession of breaches of *śīla* (moral conduct) (13c), and confession of quarreling about religion (13d). The key characteristic of terminal abbreviation is performing the same ritual acts, though abbreviated in one form or another, at the close of the ritual as at the beginning. In Yogi Chen's *homa*s the closing actions—dedication of merit in the Śākyamuni *homa* and both dedication of merit and confession in the Jesus *homa*—have no corollary in the opening portion of the ritual. Despite my own expectations, these are thus not symetrical rituals that have been abbreviated in their terminal sequence but are, rather, assymetrical rituals.

While it happens that the rituals I examined previously have been structurally symmetrical, there is no reason to believe that either symmetical or asymmetrical rituals are somehow more fundamental, or earlier, or more classic, or have any other sort of precedence over the other. Asymmetrical rituals, including those that have irregularly interrupted sequences of actions, are however equally subject to syntactic analysis, and therefore promise opportunities for developing ritual transformation rules corresponding to syntactic transformation rules.

Embedding

One of the patterns discussed by Staal is the embedding of ritual elements in the creation of more complex rituals from simpler forms.[38] Embedding can be done more than once, in which case it is known as recursive embedding. If such recursion takes place at the same level it is called sequential resursive embedding, while if additional levels are added it is called repeated recursive embedding.[39] In the Śākyamuni *homa* 10.d is the offering of the five grains, while in the Jesus *homa* 10.d is an embedded sequence of five offerings, one to each of the "five saints": the Holy Spirit, the Holy Father, the Holy Son, the Holy Mother, and the Holy Apostles. In addition to sequential recursive embedding, Yogi Chen's Jesus *homa* is also characterized by repeated recursive embedding. Offering the cross to Jesus (10.l) is comprised of three actions: praising the Cross (10.l.i), praying (10.l.ii), and offering crosses (10.l.iii). The last in turn comprises 14 offerings (10.l.iii.a through 10.l.iii.n), one for each of the 14 stations of the cross. This is an instance of repeated recursive embedding—embedding within an embedded sequence of another sequence. This second embedding is diagrammed as a lower level in the inverted tree diagram for the ritual.

Syntax and Semantics, Redux

Staal, in his famous article on the "meaninglessness" of ritual, draws on the syntactic distinction between phrase structure rules and transformational rules. These are different kinds of regular and systematic changes in ordered behaviors, that is, in sentences and in rituals. In Staal's usage the changes identified as instances of phrase structure rules are diagrammed using single arrows (→), while those that are instances of transformational rules are diagrammed using double arrows (⇒). Embedding, discussed above, is an instance of a phrase structure rule; see diagram 1.

Diagram 1
Example of Phrase Structure Rule: Embedding

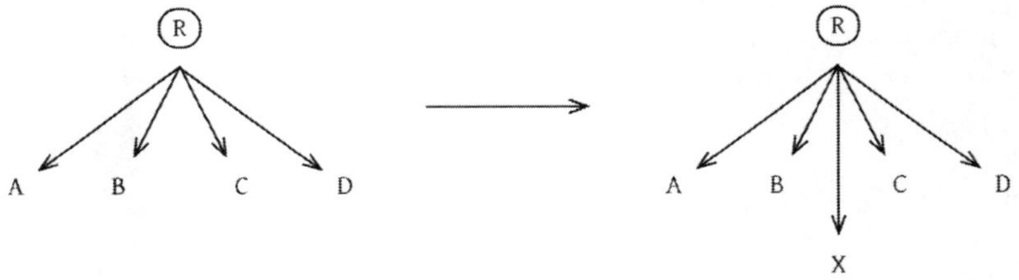

When a change involves more than just the structure of a ritual but also modifies an element within the ritual, then the change is characterized as involving a transformational rule. Staal exemplifies this kind of change with the instance of embedding a second set of recitations of a specific verse. The first recitation calls for 15 verses to be recited, while the new embedded recitation calls for the recitation of 17 verses. While they are otherwise the same, being embedded as the second occurrence involves a modification of the recitation. Staal points out that the modification does not occur just in isolation but rather that "We have to represent the entire configuration."[40] In other words, a transformation rule cannot be represented simply as X → X* since the effect of writing a rule in this form would be that all occurrences of X would be replaced by X*, which is not what occurs.[41] Only in the larger context, the "entire configuration," does such a modification take place. An instance of a transformational rule is shown in diagram 2.

At this level of analysis the relation between syntax and semantics can be studied. In the cases at hand, a semantic change is simultaneously

Diagram 2
Example of Transformation Rule:
Terminal Abbreviation

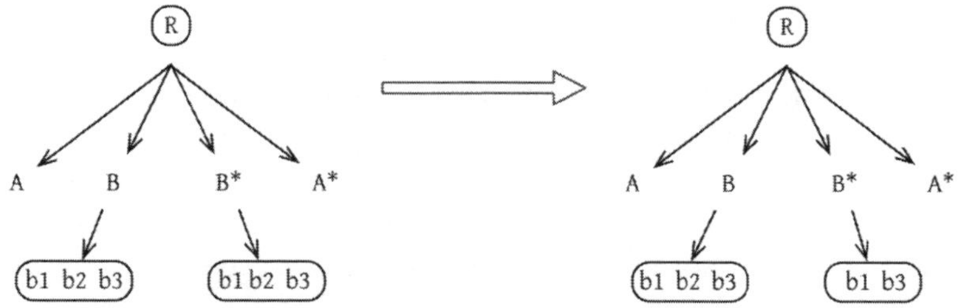

reflected in a syntactic change. Specifically, the role of Jesus and the other "saints of Christianity" leads to the addition of the sequentially embedded set of ritual acts representing the 14 stages of the cross—10.l.iii.a to 10.l.iii.n. I want to emphasize the use mentioned above of the terminology of a semantic change being reflected in a syntactic change. This is intended to indicate that the relationship is not a strongly causal one, which would be the case if a semantic change were to determine a specific syntactic change. In this case, there was no semantic requirement that Yogi Chen make a syntactic change, i.e., embedding the 14 stages of the cross, to his *homa* when he decided to have Jesus as the chief deity. He could just as well have created a *homa* ritual with Jesus as the chief deity without these actions.

On the other hand, neither does this assert that more strongly causal relations are not possible. Other semantic changes could require syntactic changes in a more strongly causal sense. As Ruth M. Kempson notes, it is well recognized in linguistics "that there is an interaction between syntactic properties of sentences and their semantic properties."[42] She gives as example that a change in the order of sentence elements, a syntactic change, creates a change in meaning, a semantic change. For instance, "Bob hit the ball" has a different meaning from "The ball hit Bob." Alternatively, a semantic change, for instance, "Bob *hid* the ball," precludes the semantic inversion indicated in the former instance. In other words, a semantic change can have a strongly causal effect on syntax.

Conclusion

The high degree of similarity between the Śākyamuni and Jesus *homa*s is not surprising, since they were both written by the same person, Yogi Chen. Taken together, however, they are useful for the specific theoretical issue I have explored here: the hypothesis regarding the effects of semantic change on the syntax of a ritual. Semantically, replacing Śākyamuni Buddha with the five saints of Christianity involves changing the symbolic framework of the ritual, a shift that has further symbolic entailments. Within the tantric system itself, for example, different deities entail different mantras. Here, the move to a Christian symbolic framework entails a change in the kinds of offerings being made. Syntactically, the offerings to the five saints and, in particular, the stations of the cross, involve changes to the structure through recursive embedding. Because it includes additional semantic content, Yogi Chen's Jesus *homa* evidences a corresponding syntactic change, the distinctive character of which is made evident by the use of inverted tree diagrams.

Appendix 1. Outline of Yogi Chen's "Five Saints of Christianity" *Homa*

1. Permission of the Earth Goddess
2. Produce *bodhicitta*
3. Bless bell, *vajra,* and drum
4. Protection
    4.a. incantation
    4.b. stanza to the protectors
    4.c. four *huṃ* incantation
5. Bless the offerings
6. Prepare the ritual enclosure:
    6.a. arrange the seat of the fire god (Agni)
        6.a.i. stanza in praise of Agni
        6.a.ii. visualize White Agni
        6.a.iii. welcome Agni
    6.b. arrange the seat of the Five Saints
        6.b.i. visualize the Heavenly Palace
        6.b.ii. stanza for the seat of the Five Saints
        6.b.iii. visualization (mandalic)
        6.b.iv. arrange the seat of Jesus
        6.b.v. welcome Jesus
        6.b.vi. praise Jesus
7. Bless the wood
8. Bless the oil
9. Start the fire
    9.a. bless the fire

- 9.b. offer to Agni (10)
  - 9.b.i. incantation
  - 9.b.ii. praise
  - 9.b.iii. prayer
- 10. Offer to the Five Saints
  - 10.a. bless wine and bread
  - 10.b. praise holy meal
  - 10.c. prayer
  - 10.d. offer to the Five Saints, individually
    - 10.d.i. Holy Spirit
    - 10.d.ii. Holy Father
    - 10.d.iii. Holy Son
    - 10.d.iv. Holy Mother
    - 10.d.v. Holy Apostles
  - 10.e. offer oat meal to the Five Saints, together
  - 10.f. offer fish to the Five Saints, together
  - 10.g. offer sesame seeds
  - 10.h. offer mustard seeds
  - 10.i. offer white silk garment
  - 10.j. offer seven long needles and red and white threads
  - 10.k. offer four pieces of fresh fruit (any kind)
  - 10.l. offer the Cross to Jesus (prepare 14 crosses of two red candles)
    - 10.l.i. praise the Cross
    - 10.l.ii. pray
    - 10.l.iii. offer crosses at the Fourteen Stations of the Cross
      - 10.l.iii.a. condemned to death
      - 10.l.iii.b. bearing the cross
      - 10.l.iii.c. first fall
      - 10.l.iii.d. meet his mother
      - 10.l.iii.e. Simon shares the load
      - 10.l.iii.f. Veronic wipes Jesus' face
      - 10.l.iii.g. second fall
      - 10.l.iii.h. weeping women
      - 10.l.iii.i. third fall
      - 10.l.iii.j. garment stripped
      - 10.l.iii.k. nailed to cross
      - 10.l.iii.l. salvation through death
      - 10.l.iii.m. lay in mother's arms
      - 10.l.iii.n. ascent to heaven
- 11. Give thanks to Agni

12. Dedication of merit
    12.a. general prayer
    12.b. special prayer
13. Confession: One hundred-word incantation (*dhāraṇī*) of Vajrasattva
    13.a. recitation of the hundred syllable *dhāraṇī* of Vajrasattva
    13.b. confession to Vajrasattva
    13.c. confession of breaches of śīla
    13.d confession of quarreling about religion

Appendix 2. Outline of Yogi Chen's Śākyamuni Buddha *Homa*

1. Permission of the Earth Goddess
2. Produce *bodhicitta*
3. Bless bell, *vajra,* and drum
4. Protection
    4.a. incantation
    4.b. stanza to the protectors
    4.c. four *huṃ* incantation
5. Bless the offerings
6. Prepare the ritual enclosure:
    6.a. arrange the seat of the fire god (Agni)
        6.a.i. stanza in praise of Agni
        6.a.ii. visualize White Agni
        6.a.iii. welcome Agni
    6.b. arrange the seat of the Buddha
        6.b.i. recitation
        6.b.ii. visualize Śākyamuni
        6.b.iii. seven-branch praise recitation
        6.b.iv. grateful commemoration stanza
        6.b.v. pleading for blessings
7. Bless the wood
8. Bless the oil
9. Start the fire
    9.a. bless the fire
    9.b. offer to Agni (10)
        9.b.i. incantation
        9.b.ii. praise
        9.b.iii. prayer

10. Offer to Śākyamuni
    10.a. *bodhi* branches
    10.b. black sesame seeds
    10.c. mustard seeds
    10.d. five grains
    10.e. gold leaves (or Bhutanese gold dust)
    10.f. five yards of yellow silk
    10.g. yellow and red flowers
    10.h. other fruits
    10.i. dates
    10.j. eight common offerings
11. Give thanks to Agni
12. Dedication of merit
    12.a. general prayer
    12.b. special prayer

Notes

1 This essay includes material from a paper presented at the conference "Buddhism without Borders," organized by Scott Mitchell and Natalie Quli, to whom I wish to express my thanks, held at the Institute of Buddhist Studies, Berkeley, California, March 2010. Other material from that paper has found its way into "Integrating Christ and the Saints into Buddhist Ritual: The Christian *Homa* of Yogi Chen," *Buddhist–Christian Studies* 35 (2015): 37–48 (also in German translation in *Salzburger Theologische Zeitschrift,* forthcoming); and "Self-Representation and Cultural Expectations: Yogi Chen and Religious Practices of Life-Writing," *Entangled Religions* 3 (2016): 33–82.

2 See Matthias Jung, "Expressive Appropriateness and Pluralism: The Example of Catholic Liturgy after Vatican II," in Jens Kreinath, Constance Hartung, and Annette Deschner, eds., *The Dynamics of Changing Rituals: The Transformation of Religious Rituals within Their Social and Cultural Context* (New York: Peter Lang, 2004), pp. 221–231.

3 Catherine Bell, *Ritual: Perspectives and Dimensions* (Oxford: Oxford University Press, 1997), p. 210.

4 Bell, *Ritual: Perspectives and Dimensions,* p. 210. Bell also mentions in passing the "now discredited constrast between societies 'with history' and those 'without history'" (p. 211) but does not pursue this topic. It is one of the ways modernity was self-constructed as a means of distinguishing the progressive societies of Europe and America from the passive and eternalistic societies, which were then subject to colonization.

5 Phonemic minimal pairs are two words of different meanings that are differentiated from one another by one sound, e.g., "to" and "do" or "grin" and "green."

[6] Terence Hawkes, *Structualism and Semiotics* (Abingdon, Oxford, and New York: Routledge, 2003, second ed.), p. 14.

[7] Frits Staal, "The Meaninglessness of Ritual," *Numen* 26 (1979): 3.

[8] I note at this point that, given the nature of many of the responses to Staal's essay on the "meaninglessness" of ritual (see n. 7), it seems possible that some or perhaps many of Staal's critics mistakenly believed that he was reiterating this kind of claim. A careful reading of Staal's essay, however, reveals that this is not in fact the claim he is making.

[9] An influence in the formation of the older religious studies view may also have been a tendency to depend on classic Roman sources for an understanding of ritual, and, as we know, the Romans tended toward a high degree of legalism.

[10] Ritual is interpreted as a technique for controlling anxiety and as a symptom of obsessive-compulsive disorder; see Wikipedia, s.v. "ritual," http://en.wikipedia.org/wiki/Ritual; accessed Thursday, February 18, 2010.

[11] See, for example, Pierre Liénard and Pascal Boyer, "Whence Collective Rituals? A Cultural Selection Model of Ritualized Behavior," *American Anthropologist* 108/4 (2006): 814–827; and, in fuller exposition, Pascal Boyer and Pierre Liénard, "Why Ritualized Behavior? Precaution Systems and Action Parsing in Developmental, Pathological and Cultural Rituals," *Behavioral and Brain Sciences* 29/6 (2006): 1–56.

[12] See Frits Staal, *Rules Without Meaning: Ritual, Mantras and the Human Sciences* (New York, Peter Lang, 1989).

[13] See Richard K. Payne and Michael Witzel, eds., *Homa Variations: Ritual Change across the Longue Durée* (New York: Oxford University Press, 2016).

[14] This conception of the relation between doctrine and ritual derives from the Protestant Reformation, when the understanding and intentionality of ritual action was deemed more important than proper performance of the ritual. This idea is still the basis for some, if not all, of Protestant liturgical theology, evidenced by impassioned discussions about the propriety of revising liturgical practices. In a study of the history of liturgical revision in the American Episcopal Church, Carl Seaquist, in "Ritual Individuation and Ritual Change," *Method and Theory in the Study of Religion* 21 (2009), notes the importance in those discussions of the idea that "rituals express paricular theological doctrines, which often are made explicit in the spoken component of worship and perhaps also are shown iconically through physical actions" (p. 349).

[15] Seaquist provides a philosophical discussion of these issues in"Ritual Individuation and Ritual Change" (see n. 14).

[16] See, for example, Kreinath, Hartung, and Deschner, eds., *The Dynamics of Changing Rituals;* Jens Kreinath, Jan Snoek, and Michael Strausberg, eds., *Theorizing Rituals: Issues, Topics, Approaches, Concepts* (Leiden and Boston: Brill, 2006).

[17] Roy A. Rappaport, *Ritual and Religion in the Making of Humanity* (Cambridge: Cambridge University Press, 1999), p. 53.

18 Rappaport, *Ritual and Religion in the Making of Humanity*, p. 53.

19 I have no particular disagreement with Rappaport here, other than what seems to me to be the unnecessary difficulties introduced by using the terminology he developed. His terminology is based on a sophisticated philosophical discussion but, in the absence of a full exposition of that discussion, the uninitiated reader may well find his terminology opaque.

20 To the best of my knowledge, an approach that examines rituals in fine enough detail to identify specific dynamics of ritual change is limited to the formal analyses of ritual syntax via the inverted tree diagrams pioneered by Staal, though that was not his main intent in creating these diagrammatic forms.

21 Nicolas Sihlé, "Written Texts at the Juncture of the Local and the Global," in José Ignacio Cabezón, ed., *Tibetan Ritual* (Oxford: Oxford University Press, 2010), p. 36.

22 Sihlé, "Written Texts," p. 37.

23 In addition to English-language *homa* manuals by C. M. Chen, several additional titles and updated versions are available on Yutang Lin's website, http://yogichen.org/gurulin/elist/eng_fil.html; accessed April 6, 2015.

24 C. M. Chen, *Collected Works* 40, no. 122;. http://yogichen.org/cw/cw40/bk122.html; accessed April 6, 2015. Also note two additional files of teachings on this particular rite, *Collected Works* 40, no. 123, http://yogichen.org/cw/cw40/bk123.html, and *Collected Works* 40, no. 124, http://yogichen.org/cw/cw40/bk124.html., both accessed April 6, 2015.

25 Chen, *Collected Works* 40, no. 118,. http://yogichen.org/cw/cw40/bk118.html., accessed April 6, 2015.

26 C. M. Chen, *A Ritual of Fire Sacrifice to Green Tara*, Yutang Lin, trans. (El Cerrito, CA: Yutang Lin, 2002).

27 Chen, *Collected Works* 40, no. 116, http://yogichen.org/cw/cw40/bk116.html; accessed April 6, 2015.

28 Chen, *Collected Works* 40, no. 81, http://yogichen.org/cw/cw32/bk081.html; accessed April 6, 2015.

29 Chen, *Collected Works* 32, no. 80, http://yogichen.org/cw/cw32/bk080.html; accessed April 6, 2015.

30 Chen, *Collected Works* 40, no. 122, http://www.yogichen.org/cw/cw40/bk122.html; accessed December 15, 2009.

31 C. M. Chen, "A Ritual of Fire Sacrifice to the Five Saints of Christianity" *Collected Works* 40, no. 122, http://yogichen.org/cw/cw40/bk122.html; accessed April 6, 2015.

32 Chen, "A Ritual of Fire Sacrifice to the Five Saints of Christianity."

33 *Secret Essentials for Performing Homa to the Seven Stars of the Northern Dipper*, translation attributed to Amoghavajra (T. 1306, *Beidou qi xing huma miyao yigui/Hokuto shichishō goma hiyō giki* 北斗七星護摩祕要儀軌); *Homa Ritual for the Seven Stars of the Northern Dipper*, attributed to Yixing (T. 1310, *Beidou qi xing huma fa/Hokuto shichishō goma hō* 北斗七星護摩法). See Richard K. Payne, "The *Homa* of

the Northern Dipper," in David B. Gray and Ryan Richard Overbey, eds., *Tantric Traditions in Transmission and Translation* (New York: Oxford University Press, 2016), pp. 284–307; Christine Mollier, *Buddhism and Taoism Face to Face: Scripture, Ritual, and Iconographic Exchange in Medieval China* (Honolulu: University of Hawai'i Press, 2009).

[34] Ronald M. Davidson, "Reflections on the Maheśvara Subjugation Myth: Indic Materials, Sa-skya-pa Apologetics, and the Birth of Heruka," *Journal of the International Association of Buddhist Studies* 14/2 (1991): 197–235.

[35] Davidson, "Reflections on the Maheśvara Subjugation Myth," p. 202.

[36] See Lewis Doney, *The Zangs gling ma: The First Padmasambhava Biography* (Andiast, Switzerland: International Institute for Tibetan and Buddhist Studies, 2014), pp. 46–47.

[37] Charles Orzech, personal communication (email), February 2016.

[38] See also Frits Staal, "Ritual Syntax" in M. Nagatomi, et al., eds., *Sanskrit and Indian Studies: Essays in Honor of Daniel H. H. Ingalls* (Dordrecht: Reidel, 1980), pp. 119–142; "Ritual Structure" in Frits Staal, ed., *Agni: The Vedic Ritual of the Fire Altar* (Berkeley: Asian Humanities Press, 1983), vol. 2, pp. 127–134.

[39] These patterns are discussed and diagrammed in Richard K. Payne, "Ritual Syntax and Cognitive Theory," *Pacific World: Journal of the Institute of Buddhist Studies*, 3rd series, no. 6 (Fall 2004): 195–227.

[40] Staal, "The Meaninglessness of Ritual," p. 18.

[41] Despite the abstract character of this kind of analysis, as with linguistics, the undertaking is empirical.

[42] Ruth M. Kempson, *Semantic Theory* (Cambridge: Cambridge University Press, 1977), p. 6.

References

Boyer, Pascal, and Pierre Liénard. "Why Ritualized Behavior? Precaution Systems and Action Parsing in Developmental, Pathological and Cultural Rituals," *Behavioral and Brain Sciences* 29/6 (2006): 1–56.

Chen, C. M. *A Ritual of Fire Sacrifice to Green Tara*. Yutang Lin, trans. El Cerrito, CA: Yutang Lin, 2002.

—. "A Ritual of Fire Sacrifice to the Five Saints of Christianity," *Collected Works* 40, no. 122. http://yogichen.org/cw/cw40/bk122.html.

—. *Collected Works* 32, no. 80. http://yogichen.org/cw/cw32/bk080.html.

—. *Collected Works* 40, no. 81. http://yogichen.org/cw/cw32/bk081.html.

—. *Collected Works* 40, no. 116. http://yogichen.org/cw/cw40/bk116.html.

—. *Collected Works* 40, no. 122. http://www.yogichen.org/cw/cw40/bk122.html.

Davidson, Ronald M. "Reflections on the Maheśvara Subjugation Myth: Indic Materials, Sa-skya-pa Apologetics, and the Birth of Heruka," *Journal of the International Association of Buddhist Studies* 14/2 (1991): 197–235.

Doney, Lewis. *The Zangs gling ma: The First Padmasambhava Biography*. Andiast, Switzerland: International Institute for Tibetan and Buddhist Studies, 2014.

Hawkes, Terence. *Structualism and Semiotics.* Abingdon, Oxford, and New York: Routledge, 2003, second ed.

Jung, Matthias. "Expressive Appropriateness and Pluralism: The Example of Catholic Liturgy after Vatican II," in Jens Kreinath, Constance Hartung, and Annette Deschner, eds., *The Dynamics of Changing Rituals: The Transformation of Religious Rituals within Their Social and Cultural Context*, pp. 221–231. Toronto Studies in Religion, vol. 29. New York: Peter Lang, 2004.

Kempson, Ruth M. *Semantic Theory.* Cambridge: Cambridge University Press, 1977.

Kreinath, Jen, Constance Hartung, and Annette Deschner, eds. *The Dynamics of Changing Rituals: The Transformation of Religious Rituals within Their Social and Cultural Context.* Toronto Studies in Religion, vol. 29. New York: Peter Lang, 2004.

Kreinath, Jens, Jan Snoek, and Michael Strausberg, eds. *Theorizing Rituals: Issues, Topics, Approaches, Concepts.* Leiden and Boston: Brill, 2006.

Liénard, Pierre, and Pascal Boyer. "Whence Collective Rituals? A Cultural Selection Model of Ritualized Behavior," *American Anthropologist* 108/4 (2006): 814–827.

Mollier, Christine. *Buddhism and Taoism Face to Face: Scripture, Ritual, and Iconographic Exchange in Medieval China.* Honolulu: University of Hawai'i Press, 2009.

Payne, Richard K. "Integrating Christ and the Saints into Buddhist Ritual: The Christian *Homa* of Yogi Chen," *Buddhist–Christian Studies* 35 (2015): 37–48.

—. "Ritual Syntax and Cognitive Theory," *Pacific World: Journal of the Institute of Buddhist Studies,* 3rd series, no. 6 (Fall 2004): 195–227.

—. "Self-Representation and Cultural Expectations: Yogi Chen and Religious Practices of Life-Writing," *Entangled Religions* 3 (2016): 33–82.

—. "The *Homa* of the Northern Dipper," in David B. Gray and Ryan Richard Overbey, eds., *Tantric Traditions on the Move: Their Development through Time, and Transmission through Cultural Space,* pp. 284–307. New York: Oxford University Press, 2016.

Payne, Richard K., and Michael Witzel, eds. *Homa Variations: Ritual Change across the Longue Durée.* New York: Oxford University Press, 2016.

Rappaport, Roy A. *Ritual and Religion in the Making of Humanity.* Cambridge: Cambridge University Press, 1999.

Seaquist, Carl. "Ritual Individuation and Ritual Change," *Method and Theory in the Study of Religion* 21 (2009): 340–360.

Sihlé, Nicolas. "Written Texts at the Juncture of the Local and the Global," in José Ignacio Cabezón, ed., *Tibetan Ritual,* pp. 35–52. Oxford: Oxford University Press, 2010.

Staal, Frits, ed. *Agni: The Vedic Ritual of the Fire Altar,* 2 vols. Berkeley: Asian Humanities Press, 1983.

—. "Ritual Syntax" in M. Nagatomi, et al., eds. *Sanskrit and Indian Studies: Essays in Honor of Daniel H. H. Ingalls,* pp. 119–142. Studies of Classical India, vol. II. Dordrecht: Reidel, 1980.

—. "Ritual Structure" in Frits Staal, ed., *Agni: The Vedic Ritual of the Fire Altar,* vol. 2, pp. 127–134. Berkeley: Asian Humanities Press, 1983.
—. *Rules without Meaning: Ritual, Mantras, and the Human Sciences.* Toronto Studies in Religion, vol. 4. New York: Peter Lang, 1989.
—. "The Meaninglessness of Ritual," *Numen* 26 (1979): 2–22.

The *Bhūtasaṃkhyā* Notation: Numbers, Culture, and Language in Sanskrit Mathematical Literature

Alessandra Petrocchi
Cambridge University

Abstract

A method of expressing numbers by means of symbolic words arranged as in place value notation was developed in India in the early centuries of the Common Era. In the *bhūtasaṃkhyā* notation, the digits from 0 to 9 are denoted by certain significant words that connote a numerical association derived from many areas of Indian culture. This paper analyzes this system, taking into account the relation between mathematical representations, culture, and language that contribute to its originality. While looking at the *bhūtasaṃkhyā* as the creative attainment of a process in which the flexibility of the Sanskrit language has been used as a tool that functions in poetic structure and the method of oral transmission of Sanskrit mathematical texts, I argue that it also represents a "constitutively social form" of language, where each sign, embedded in social images, memories, and descriptive information, becomes mathematical "sense-making," insofar it is rooted in the semantic field "Indian culture."

In order to understand cognitive and social functions served by this numerical notation system, I attempt to delineate, with the use of a formalized language typical of mathematical logic, the dialectic between numbers and collective representations in the context of ancient Indian culture.

Introduction

Frits Staal has challenged many dominant ideas about language, logic, ritual geometry, and religious practices with implications far beyond the field of Sanskrit.[1] Among his most influential contributions to Indological studies have been his theories on the grammatical method in

Pāṇini. Explaining the different directions taken by scientific developments in India and in the West, Staal writes that "Pāṇini's method has occupied a place comparable to that held by Euclid's method in Western thought."[2] Comparing the methods employed by the Indian linguist (fourth century B.C.E.) and the Greek mathematician (third century B.C.E.), and defending the thesis that the mathematical method is characteristic of Western philosophy while the grammatical method is characteristic of Indian philosophy, Staal emphasizes that

> mathematics and linguistics share certain features that also occur in other sciences but which are especially well-developed in these two: the expressions are fully explicit, and the system as a whole is as simple as possible. This results in the postulation of a small number of elements which are combined in accordance with rules of various types. In India, these requirements led to the development of the sūtra style, which emphasized rules, and which, having originated in the ritual manuals, culminated in Pāṇini's grammar.[3]

In the context of such an analysis, the relation between mathematics and natural language can be approached from different perspectives. For instance, one can emphasize the language-like attributes of mathematics, pointing out that mathematics is indeed itself a language: an artificial language especially designed for carrying out mathematical activity employing a standard code of conventional symbols to express relations, arguments, and sentences. Moreover, the logic, clarity, and set of formulas that regulate the high level of formality of mathematics similarly evoke the rules and principles governing the syntax of a language. It is interesting to note that research on modern linguistics, computer science, and mathematical logic investigates the formal structure of language using mathematical methods.

Certainly, the development of specific linguistic practices in Sanskrit mathematical texts, and consequently the practice of mathematics, must be situated in relation to the cultural context in which they took shape. I argue that the various forms of expression attested in Sanskrit mathematical texts should be considered in the light of the relation between the oral tradition and written literature in ancient India, which contributes to the originality of these texts.

In the attempt to investigate certain properties of the *bhūtasaṃkhyā* system of notation, an ingenious linguistic code through which the versatility of the Sanskrit language enriched the way of communicating mathematical concepts in the Indian tradition, this paper explores the relation between culture, language, and numbers in Sanskrit mathematical texts. For this purpose, I address the following key questions: How has Sanskrit been adapted to the needs of formal scientific expression? What can we say about the way in which mathematical representations and language, two well-defined meaning-making systems, have interacted in construing mathematical knowledge in the Indian context?

It is not my purpose here to demonstrate how the richness and flexibility of the Sanskrit language have enriched the scientific terminology of mathematics. I have shown elsewhere[4] that the linguistic attainment in this area is fascinating, as it shows not only a wide range of technical terms for denoting concepts and their explanations, but also a variety of ways to convey mathematical meanings.

In order to investigate the role played by the bhūtasaṃkhyā in Sanskrit mathematical treatises, in this article I will particularly refer to the *Gaṇita sāra saṃgraha* by Mahāvīrācārya (ninth century C.E.), which I have selected to serve as the main source for certain theoretical and practical considerations.[5] After delineating a brief history of the *bhūtasaṃkhyā,* I will survey the various methods of expressing numerical values found in this text, and then look more closely at the exceptional list of word-numerals[6] given by the author. In exploring the relation between worldviews, numerical values, and semantic fields that may have contributed to formalize the *bhūtasaṃkhyā* system, I attempt to represent its logical structures by means of the symbolic language typically adopted in modern mathematical linguistics and logic. Though my interest primarily concerns the role played by literary and oral traditions in shaping mathematical writings in all their dimensions, I adopt a perspective that takes into account, within the framework of the Indian context and more particularly of the śāstric branches of learning, the influence of social and cultural factors in the representations of mathematical objects.

Early Occurrences of the Word-numerals System

In order to first investigate the *bhūtasaṃkhyā* as a system of notation and then as a language, I will start by clarifying what a numerical notation system is. In his historical-anthropological analysis, Stephen Chrisomalis defines it as a "visual, relatively permanent, and primarily non-phonetic system for representing numbers."[7] The primary function of a numerical notation as a representational system is to communicate mathematical values. In this regard, I wish to point out that the *bhūtasaṃkhyā,* although it is a structured system for representing numbers based on alphasyllabic numerals, was not designed with mathematical purposes in mind, even though it was mainly employed in mathematical and astronomical works. I will clarify this point in the following sections of this paper.

Before going further with the investigation of this system of notation, let me briefly lay out its historical account. It has been noted by several scholars[8] that by the first half of the first millennium C.E. Sanskrit mathematical and astronomical works had employed mainly two kinds of notation for expressing large numbers consisting of several digits. In the first type of notation, commonly known as *bhūtasaṃkhyā*,[9] the digits from 0 to 9 are expressed as words, while in the second method, called *kaṭapayādi*, they are represented by consonants of the Sanskrit alphabet. Among the two, the *bhūtasaṃkhyā* notation system seems to be older and was employed throughout India from the early centuries of the Common Era on. The first traces of the *bhūtasaṃkhyā* system of numeration, in which numbers are expressed by means of words arranged as in place value notation but following a left-to-right direction,[10] are found in the *Yavanajātaka* by Sphujidhvaja,[11] a third-century C.E. Sanskrit text consisting of an earlier translation into Sanskrit of a Greek astrological text. The emergence of Greco-Indian astrology is part of the cultural fusion that followed the collapse of Alexander's empire at the end of the fourth century B.C.E. During this time, Indian Greeks (called Yavanas in Sanskrit) integrated into Indian culture, adopting Hindu beliefs, taking Sanskrit names, and intermarrying into Indian dynastic families.

Christopher Minkowsky[12] underlines that a new period of Indian astronomy famously began in about the second century C.E. with the appropriation of Greco-Babylonian and Hellenistic astronomical-astrological models, parameters, and interpretative systems. Given this background, the Yavanajātaka represents an Indianized version of traditional Greek astrology, including the first-known occurrence in India of the familiar twelve signs of the Greco-Babylonian zodiac. The *bhūtasaṃkhyā* appears for the first time in this text as a peculiar Indian invention. The function of this verbal notation is to provide synonyms for ordinary words denoting cardinal numbers, such as *eka*, "one," *dvi*, "two," and so on. This system consents to the name of any object or being, associated in nature or by culture with a particular number, to stand for it. In this way, the mathematical referent is expressed without ruining the scansion of the verse.[13]

The *bhūtasaṃkhyā* system was popularly employed in Sanskrit *jyotiḥśāstra* literature[14] as well as in metrics. In this system, the symbolic words that denote numbers, arranged from unit's place onward in a right-to-left sequence,[15] are derived from many sources, including mythology, ritual, the human body, cosmology, poetic convention, and various *śāstras*. We can infer that this notation came into use for practical reasons: it preserves the rhythm of the *ślokas*, avoids inelegant ways of naming numbers, and supports a mnemonic function, linking words with numbers. Such use of word-numerals is present in almost all later mathematical and astronomical works.

In regard to the second method of notation mentioned above, according to S. R. Sarma[16] the first datable occurrence of the *kaṭapayādi* alphabetic notation is in Haridatta's *Grahacārinabandhana,* composed in 683 C.E. Bhibhutibhisan Datta and Avadesh N. Singh[17] place its invention around 500 C.E. and claim that it must have been known to the mathematical-astronomer Āryabhaṭa (ca. late fifth–early sixth centuries C.E.), but there is no textual evidence to support this assertion. The name *kaṭapayādi* is taken from four syllables of the Sanskrit alphabet (*ka, ṭa, pa, ya*) that are assigned to the digit 1 in this system. Vowels have no numerical significance in the *kaṭapayādi* convention, and neither do consonants that appear in conjunction with a following consonant or at the end of a word. Only a consonant that is immediately followed by a vowel has a numerical value. Chrisomalis writes that "structurally this system is an ordinary ciphered-positional and decimal system."[18] Kim Plofker underlines that the

> flexibility of this system means that authors can encode digit sequences in actual Sanskrit words. For example, the word bhavati, "becomes," is decoded as the sequence 4–4–6, implying the number 644.[19]

This way of using code syllables at a symbolic and semantic level ensures that it is always possible to form code words that also carry meaning.

Around 150 years earlier the mathematician-astronomer Āryabhaṭa employed another technique for verbally representing numbers. In his work the Āryabhaṭīya (1.2) he describes an alphanumeric encoding system that depends on the phonetic order of the Sanskrit alphabet, according to which consonants are assigned specific integer values and vowels are used to represent decimal powers. In this way, consonants and vowels are combined into syllables representing numbers. Annette Wilke and Oliver Moebius emphasize, however, that

> in the *kaṭapayādi* system the sensory dimension of the text is emphasized by choosing beautiful words with pleasant associations. This is probably a

major reason why the *kaṭapayādi* system became so popular, while Āryabhaṭa's system died out. It was simpler and aesthetically more satisfying by allowing a greater play with sounds and meanings.[20]

The *Bhūtasaṃkhyā* System in the *Gaṇita Sāra Saṃgraha*

The *Gaṇita Sāra Saṃgraha* (GSS) by Mahāvīrācārya, a Jaina mathematician, is the first-known independent mathematical treatise in Sanskrit to survive in its entirety.[21] According to historians, Mahāvīrācarya lived at the ninth-century Rastrakuta court in Karnataka, indicated by his praise to King Amoghavarṣa.[22] The study of mathematics was very popular among Jaina scholars, as it represents one of the four *anuyoga*s, "auxiliary sciences," that indirectly enable the practitioner to attain *mokṣa,* "liberation." As suggested by the title, which translates as "compendium on the essentials of mathematics," Mahāvīrā's work is an exposition, a summary of the essentials of *gaṇita.* I have shown elsewhere that Mahāvīra organizes various teachings into a self-consistent whole and provides an unprecedented amount of detail about the organization of mathematical topics.[23]

In the first chapter, *saṃjñādhikāra,* which is dedicated to the treatment of technical terms, Mahāvīra gives in ten *śloka*s a large list of names of certain things used to denote numbers in arithmetical notation. Though a more or less extensive use of words as numerals can be found in other mathematical works,[24] to my knowledge no other Sanskrit mathematical text provides such an exceptional list. Mahāvīra seems to have been the only mathematician who collected and arranged in order words used for representing numbers. He seems to have introduced this topic with the word, *saṃkhyāsaṃjñā,* "technical terms for numbers."[25] It is interesting to note that Mahāvīra uses terms and concepts belonging to Jain philosophical and spiritual thought, not only those of general Sanskrit literature.

In the following ten verses, Mahāvīra lists words standing for numbers:[26]

śaśī somaś ca candrendū prāleyāṃśū rajanīkaraḥ //
śvetaṃ himagu rūpañca mṛgāṅkaś ca kalādharaḥ //
dvi dve dvāv ubhau yugalayugmaṃ ca locanaṃ dviyam /
dṛṣṭir natrāmbakaṃ dvandvam akṣicakṣur nayaṃ dṛśau //
haranetraṃ puraṃ lokaṃ trai [tri] ratnaṃ bhuvanatrayam /
guṇe vaḥniḥ śikhī jvalanaḥ pāvakaś ca hutāśanaḥ //
ambodhir viśadhir vārdhiḥ pyodhis sāgaro gatiḥ /
jaladhir bandhaś ca turvedaḥ kaśāyassalilākaraḥ //
iṣur bāṇaṃ śaraṃ śastram bhūtam indriyasāyakam /

pañca vratāni viṣayaḥ karaṇīyastantusāyakaḥ /
ṛtujīvo raso lekhyā dravyaṃ ca ṣaṭukaṃ kharam //
kumāravadanaṃ varṇaṃ śilīmukhapadāni ca //
śailamadrirbhayaṃ[27] *bhūdhro nagācalamunirgiriḥ (sic) /*
aśvāśvipannagā[28] *dvīpaṃ dhāturvyasanamātṛkam (sic) /*
aṣṭau tanurgajaḥ karma vasu vāraṇapuṣkarim //
dviradaṃ dantī digduritaṃ nāgānīkaṃ karī yathā /
nava nandaṃ ca randhraṃ ca padārthaṃ labdhakeśavau //
nidhiratnaṃ grahāṇāṃ ca durganāṃ ca saṅkhyayā /
ākāśaṃ gaganaṃ śūnyam ambaraṃ khaṃ nabho viyat //
anantam antarikṣaṃ ca viṣṇupādaṃ divi smaret //[29] (GSS 1.53–63)

Based on these verses, I present the following correspondence between numbers and words:[30]

(1) *Śaśin, soma, candra, indu, prāleyāṃśu, rajanīkaraḥ, himagu, mṛgāṅka,* and *kalādharaḥ* are synonyms of "moon," which is only one; *śveta,* lit., "white," stands also for "moon," and *rūpa,* "form/shape," denotes the number 1 because everything has only its own one shape.

(2) *Yugala, yugma, dvi,* and *dvaṃdva* mean "pair, couple," and therefore stand for the number 2, as well as *locana, dṛṣi, dṛṣṭi, netra, ambaka, akṣi,* and *cakṣu,* which are synonyms of "eyes." *Naya* means "method"; according to the Jainas there are two methods of knowledge (*pramāṇa* and *naya*).

(3) Haranetra refers to the three eyes of Śiva; *pura,* "city," is linked to the three cities representing three *asuras*, which, as found in the *Purāṇas*, are said to have caused great distress to the gods until Śiva destroyed them. *Triratna,* "three jewels," refers to the three jewels mentioned in Jainism: right perception, right knowledge, and right conduct. *Loka* and *bhuvana* mean "world"; the number of worlds ordinarily counted in Sanskrit literature are three: the upper, lower, and middle worlds. *Guṇa* denotes the three qualities of *sattva, rajas,* and *tamas. Vahni, agni, jvalana, pāvaka,* and *hutāśana* are synonyms for "fire"; there are three kinds of sacrificial fires: *gārhapatya, āhavanīya,* and *dakṣiṇa.*

(4) The words *ambodhi, viśadhi, vārdhi, payodhi, sāgara, jaladhi,* and *salilākaraḥ* mean "ocean." It was believed that there are four oceans, the eastern, southern, northern, and western oceans. The word *gati,* "passage," refers to the "passage into rebirth"; according to Jainism the soul may have four kinds of embodiment (*deva, tiryak, manuṣya,* and *naraka*). *Bandha* is "bondage," of which the Jainas recognize four kinds of spiritual bondage (*prakṛti, sthiti, anubhāva,* and *pradeśa*). The word *kaṣāya,* "attachment to objects," is also connected to Jaina philosophy; there are

four causes of attachment (*krodha, māna, māyā,* and *lobha*). Last, the word *veda* stands for the number 4, referring to the four Vedas.

(5) *Iṣu, bāṇa, śastra, śara,* and *sāyaka* are synonyms for "arrow"; the arrows of the Indian "Cupid" (Kāmadeva) are said to be five. *Bhūta* is one of the five elements; *indriya* denotes one of the five senses; *karaṇīya* and *vrata* refer to the five acts of devotion according to the Jaina religion; and *viṣaya* alludes to the objects cognizable by the five senses.

(6) According to Sanskrit literature there are six seasons (*ṛtu,* "season") and six principal tastes (*rasa*). Dravya concerns the elementary substances, which are six (*jīva, dharma, adharma, padula, kāla,* and *ākāśa*) according to the Jainas. Kumāravadana refers to the six faces of Kumāra (Śiva's son). Śilīmukhapada literally means "leg of a bee," of which there are six; thus the word stands for the number 6.

(7) *Śaila,* as well as *acala, mahīdra, bhūdhra, naga,* and *giri,* are synonyms for "mountain." The geography of the *Pūrana*s recognizes seven principal mountains. *Muni* stands for the seven luminous and eternal sages mentioned in Sanskrit literature. *Aśva* alludes to the seven horses of the sun's chariot; *aśvin* literally means "consisting of horses." *Pannaga* are the seven serpents reckoned in Hindu mythology. *Mātṛkā* stands for the seven goddesses. *Dhātu* refers to the seven constituents of the body.

(8) *Ibha, gajaḥ, vāraṇa, puṣkarī, dvirada, dantī, naga,* and *karī* are synonyms for "elephant"; eight elephants are said to guard the eight cardinal points of the world. *Tanu* means "body," and stands for the number 8, as Śiva's body is considered to be made up of eight elements. There are also eight kinds of karma, according to the Jainas. *Vasu* alludes to the eight classes of Vedic deities. *Dik* means "direction" and stands for the eight cardinal points. *Durita* means "bad action," of which there are eight types, just as there are eight kinds of *karman* ("action"). *Anīka* refers to the eight kinds of armies mentioned in Sanskrit literature.

(9) *Nanda* is the name of a dynasty of nine kings that ruled in Magadha. *Randhra,* "cavity, hole," refers to the nine orifices of the human body. *Padārtha* means "objects"; the Jainas recognize nine categories of things. *Labdha,* "obtained," concerns the attainment of the nine powers recognized in Jaina philosophy. *Keśava,*[31] *nidhi,* and *ratna* are synonyms of "jewel,"[32] while *graha,* "planet," alludes to the nine planets recognized by Indian astronomy.

(10) *Ākāśa, ananta, gagana, ambara, kha, nabha, viyat, antarikṣa, viṣṇupāda, śūnya,* and *dyu* are all synonyms for "sky" (or "space") and stand for the number 0.

The information provided by this list represents a practical device given by Mahāvīra for interpreting the coding-based association of the word-numerals system on which some of his *uddeśaka*s, "sample problems," are further expressed. As he does not use all the words mentioned, the list may have been intended as a technical tool for mathematical students trained in *jyotiṣa* literature.

Let us now look more closely at the way in which the *bhūtasaṃkhyā* system is applied in the GSS. Though actually well distributed throughout the work, it is more commonly used in the second chapter (*parikarmavyavahāra*), devoted to the explanation of the arithmetical operations. In verses 10–17, for instance, certain numbers are said to constitute different families of "necklaces," referring to the arrangement of the figures.

Mahāvīra gives the following *uddeśaka* in *śloka* 13, using the *bhūtasaṃkhyā* system:

> *analābdhihimagumuniśaraduritākṣipayodhisomamāsthāpya* /
> *śailena tu guṇayitvā kathaya tvaṃ rājakaṇṭhikābharaṇam* // (GSS 2.13)
>
> Having written down: 1 (*somam,* "moon"); 4 (*payodhi,* "ocean"); 2 (*akṣi,* "eyes"); 8 (*durita,* "wordly action"); 5 (*śara,* five "arrows"); 7 (*muni,* seven "sages"); 1 (*himagu,* "moon"); 4 (*abdhi,* "ocean"); 3 (*anala,* three sacrifical "fires"); [and] having multiplied [the number so obtained] by 7 (*śailena*), give [the result that is like] a royal necklace.

Therefore, the two numbers expressed by the *bhūtasaṃkhyā* method are 142857143 and 7 respectively, which when multiplied yield "the royal necklace," 1000000001.

Numeral Expressions in the GSS

We have seen so far that the *bhūtasaṃkhyā* is a particular way to express numerical values using a word-numerals association, but there are other methods in which Sanskrit was applied for expressing numbers. For the sake of metrical convenience as well as for aesthetic-expressive needs, various devices are used in Sanskrit mathematical literature. In regard to the GSS one finds, for example:

The additive method, one of the most common in mathematical works:[33]

> *tryadhikadaśatriśatayutāny ekatriṃśatsahasrajambūni* /
> *saikāśītiśatena prahṛtāni narair vadaikāṃśam* // GSS 2.25
>
> 31313 *jambū* fruits have been divided between 181 persons. Give the portion of each.

The number 31313 is here given as (reading from right to left) *ekatriṃśat sahasra* = 31,000 added to (*yutāni*) *try adhika daśatriśata* = 3 added to (*adhika*, lit., "additional") 310 = 313. The number 181 is expressed as *aśītiśata*, which is 180 preceded by *saika* (lit., "with 1"), therefore 181.

The subtractive method is also often used. For instance, in GSS 2.4 the number 139 is expressed as *catvariṃśac caikonaśatādhika*, literally, "100 (*śata*) defective (*ūna*) of 1 added to (*adhika*) 40 (*catvariṃśat*)," therefore (100 - 1) + 40.

The multiplicative system is another method used by Mahāvīra. For instance, the expression *pañcatriṃśac chatasamadhikaṃ saptanighnaṃ sahasram* (GSS 2.35) stands for the number 7,135, given as "1,000 multiplied by 7 (*saptanighnaṃ sahasram*) with the addition (*samadhikaṃ*) of 135 (*pañcatriṃśat śata*)," therefore (1,000 x 7) + 135.

In *śloka* 27 Mahāvīra uses a rather interesting expression for the number 12345654321:

> *ekādiṣaḍantāni krameṇa hīnāni hāṭakāni*
>
> [A number of] pieces of gold [such as] beginning with 1 and ending with 6, and then diminishing in order.

Verse 15 belongs to the *uddeśaka*s mentioned above, in which certain numbers are said to constitute different families of "necklaces":

> *sapta śūnyaṃ dvayaṃ dvandvaṃ pañcaikañ ca pratiṣṭhitam /*
> *trayaḥ saptatisaṇgunyaṃ kaṇṭābharaṇam ādiśet* // 15
>
> The figures 7, 0, 2, 2, 5, and 1 are put down [in order from the units' place] (reading from right to left), then this number, which is multiplied by 73, should be called a necklace (*kaṇṭābharaṇam*).

The product of 15,2207 × 73 is 11,111,111.

It is interesting to note that the first three methods are place value–notation based, meaning that the numbers are expressed accordingly to the their position in the decimal system. By contrast, in the fifth method a certain large number is given as a list of digits, one after one and read from right to left.

If, on the one hand, the variety of these systems represents a particularly elegant way of playing with the beauty of numbers, on the other it clearly allows for dispensing with flexible systems for writing numerical expressions while respecting the literal requirements of the verse.

In light of this, it would take us much too far afield to go into detail about the lexicon and etymology of technical terms used in Sanskrit mathematical texts. For my purpose here, it is enough to highlight that the vocabulary used, typical of an ordinary, "natural" Sanskrit, denotes a wide range of conventional terms that have been fully integrated into mathematical context, with the consequent acquisition of technical meanings. As I have illustrated elsewhere,[34] the result is an established "specialized lexicon," with some of these terms being consistently polysemic.

Means of Knowledge: The "Eight Qualities of a Mathematician"

In focusing attention on the linguistic practices of Sanskrit mathematical texts, I want to suggest that the various systems of writing numerical expressions found in mathematical texts should also be considered as purely functional literary devices to the specific features of Sanskrit literature, where the influence and privileged position of oral transmission is evident even in treatises on technical subjects, often considered as knowledge to be learned by heart. For instance, metrical form and brevity render the mathematical text compact and therefore more easily memorized; at the same time, while reading a Sanskrit mathematical text we can notice that many details are missing in the concise verse-rules, so much that sometimes such texts are difficult to understand. They were probably orally transmitted, and the reasoning beyond mathematical statements were also orally expounded by teachers.

However, it is important to keep in mind that Sanskrit mathematical treatises were often accompanied by long prose commentaries. The role of commentaries[35] was not only to explain the literal meaning of verses but also to convince the reader that they were properly formulated. Commentators usually repeat the compact verse rule in a more articulated and comprehensible prose form, giving sample problems and explaining in more or less detail, according to each author's style, the mathematical procedures, often step by step. The pedagogical goal of a commentary, in representing the perspective of the *mūlākāra,* the "author of the root-text," commented upon, is to guide the audience's reading in such a way that the reader's understanding of the mathematical content is improved.

Another significant aspect is that the validity of the statements are not discussed in Sanskrit mathematical commentaries, because the authority of the śāstric traditional knowledge is considered to be the source and indirectly establishes the texts' truth and accuracy.

In this regard, the role of the mathematical proof in Indian mathematics is a controversial issue among scholars. Although historiography has not paid adequate attention to the role played by the mathematical examples in the Indian tradition, I have shown elsewhere[36] that *uddeśaka*[37] does not presuppose merely the practical execution of an exercise, but rather represents a significant device enabling the construction of an actual proof, and therefore provides a system of knowledge based on deductive syllogism. I argue that in Sanskrit mathematical texts "the sample problem" highlights the relation between the type of text and the kind of proof developed. In my view, sample problems in Sanskrit mathematical texts enable authors to formulate general proofs to mathematical problems.

This point relates closely to the epistemological foundations of ancient Indian mathematics. Textual sources do not help provide a detailed account of the way in which mathematical knowledge was perceived and acquired and, as Plofker has highlighted,[38] there is a great deal of uncertainty concerning how mathematical practitioners were trained and evaluated.

For these reasons, the following passage from GSS is extremely valuable and of great interest. Mahāvīra lists here what he calls the eight "qualities of a mathematician," and in so doing he expresses the view of the tradition of which he was a part on the "means of knowledge" for a mathematician:

> *laghukaraṇohāpohānālasyagrahaṇadhāraṇopāyaiḥ* /
> *vyaktikarāṅkaviśiṣṭair gaṇako' ṣṭābhir guṇair jñeyaḥ* // GSS 1.69
>
> A mathematician is to be known by eight qualities, which are paramount for the manifestation of numbers: concision, [a thorough knowledge of mathematical] procedures, confutation, not indolence, comprehension, memory, and by [ingenious] means of working.

Before looking at the qualities mentioned here, I must point out a problem concerning this verse.[39] I understand *vyaktikarāṅkaviśiṣṭair* to qualify *aṣṭābhir guṇair,* but in Raṅgācārya's translation this represents the eighth and last *guṇa,* "quick method in working."[40] If *laghukaraṇa* is a compound, however, we would find *laghū* instead of *laghu,* since when compounded with forms of the verb *kṛ* the first member (either noun or adjective) ending in a vowel lengthens that vowel.[41] A similar issue occurs in the second line with *vyaktikara,*[42] which should actually be *vyaktīkara.*[43] In my opinion, it is only the first line to list the eight attributes of a mathematician. I thus consider *laghu* as standing for *laghutva* and *karaṇa* as denoting the second *guṇa.*[44]

Having pointed out the ambiguity of this verse and in order to understand to what extent they pertain to the specific activity of a mathematician, let us look more closely at each of these qualities, or *guṇa.* The first *guṇa* is *laghutva,* which indicates the quality of concision, economy expressed as the ability to go straight to the point. The second quality is *karaṇa,* which in Sanskrit mathematical texts means "procedure, method, calculation." It refers here to the algorithmic ability and knowledge a mathematician must possess.

The third quality, *ūha,* "inference,"[45] suggests the idea of a cognitive act, a process of deducing a conclusion from evidence and reasoning, thus "inductive reasoning." This implies a sense of cause and effect, the ability to construct and follow a step-by-step logical argument. Much of mathematics depends on "if this, then that" reasoning, an abstract form of thinking about causes and their effects.

The fourth is *apoha,* lit., "exclusion,"[46] which I understand here as alluding to the ability to remove doubts and confute others' ideas, and therefore refers to the way a mathematician should deal with objections. The fifth is *anālasya,* "not indolence." The sixth is *grahaṇa,* "comprehension": a mathematician should be sharp in learning. The seventh is *dhāraṇā,* "memory." The eighth and last is "[ingenious] means of working," the ability to find solutions, to construct and follow a causal chain of facts or events.

All of these can be recognized as general qualities of intellectual cognition and at the same time, as the author seems to suggest, they should represent the characteristics and the methodological setting of a mathematician. Surprisingly, I have found four of these "*guṇa*s " mentioned in *Arthaśāstra* 6.1.4,[47] which in turn seems to run parallel to the *aṣṭabuddhiguṇa*s, "eight qualities of the intellect," mentioned in Purāṇic texts.[48]

A final consideration concerns the number 8, which is often found in Jaina literature.[49] For instance, according to Jain texts there are eight kinds of fears, eight main types of karma, eight *vargaṇa*s,[50] eight virtues, eight objects of auspiciousness, and eight items used to perform the *pujā* of a *tirthaṅkara* in a Jaina temple.[51]

Culture and Mathematical Representations: The *Bhūtasaṃkhyā* as a Language

A major factor in investigating the *bhūtasaṃkhyā* is to understand the logic process that contributed to the development of this notation system. It can scarcely be ignored that recent research in the field of cognitive psychology would certainly provide an important perspective in understanding processes such as memory, perception, mental imagery, association, concept formation, problem solving, and pattern recognition that influence the elaboration of symbolic representations (such as the *bhūtasaṃkhyā*) in systems of knowledge. In his work *Numerical Notation: A Comparative History,* Stephen Chrisomalis repeatedly points out that the social dimension of numerical notations is intimately linked to a specific historical context, and at the same time implies cognitive factors.

The intriguing *modus operandi* of the *bhūtasaṃkhyā* evokes the relation between language, mathematics, and reality. My arguments in the following discussion draw on principles of cognitive psychology (How does the brain processes information and concept formation?), the philosophy of mathematics (What is a number and what is a mathematical object? How and to what extent mathematical ideas are shaped by cultural and cognitive features?), and the sociology of scientific knowledge (What are the social conditions that affect science?), and I often make use of the formalized mathematical language typical of Western logic and linguistics.

As it is a method in which conventional signs of the language-system "Sanskrit" are used to describe another system of signs, namely the mathematical language of numbers, I propose to consider the *bhūtasaṃkhyā* as a meta-language. The question here is to identify what kind of act is implied when semantically different terms are used as referents for the same numerical value. Adopting the well-known Sausserian categories,[52] we can say, for instance, that in the *bhūtasaṃkhyā* language terms such as *abdhi,* "ocean," and *gati,* "passage," become signifiers of the same signified number 4.[53]

Now, according to what principle did linguistic units that denote two different concepts, such as "ocean" and "passage," develop into mathematical objects? We have seen that the word *agni,* "fire," becomes a symbol of the number 3 because it is associated to the idea of the (Vedic) "three sacrificial fires."

Central to a theory of the *bhūtasaṃkhyā* system as a meta-language is the understanding of the mechanism, which we can observe is based on a sort of "affinity by abstraction," that links concepts to corresponding numerical values. As I mentioned above, while looking at the *bhūtasaṃkhyā* as a representational system of communication the first impulse is to emphasize the so-called "cognitive aspects of meaning," those aspects that go to determine the objects spoken of, and what properties they are said to have. This finds an echo in Donald Davidson's much quoted statement: "What is it for words to mean what they do?"[54] Modern philosophers of language, such as Sara Mills, emphasize that

> meaning is constructed by the system of representation and representation is an essential part of the process by which meaning is produced and exchanged between members of a culture. It does involve the use of language, of signs and images which stand for or represent things. Representation connects meaning and language to culture.[55]

I am not attempting here to apply modern semantic studies to define the way meanings are conveyed through signs in the context of literary Sanskrit practices. Rather, the point I want to put forward is that the *bhūtasaṃkhyā,* which is first of all the result of a poetic-literary strategy in which the referent (a certain number) is denoted by a representational signifier (a word taken from everyday usage), evolved as a social convention through the common practice of a group of initiates.[56] In order to outline my arguments more precisely and to illustrate how we can analyze the logical structure of this system, I will introduce "the use of a mathematical language inspired by the language of contemporary logic,"[57] which helps avoid the ambiguity of the natural language and simplifies the dialectic relation of the constitutive elements of the word-numerals system of notation. If objections such as "Have Indian structures been forced into Western categories? Have modern mathematical logic and a Western conceptual framework been imposed onto the Indian tradition?" are raised, I answer with Staal's words:

> I am not preaching an absolute, unchanging truth; my attempt was a scientific inquiry, hence not final. I was careful not to introduce concepts of Western logic into my language by symbols that stand in one-to-one correspondence to the original expressions. . . . I use symbols merely because they are more precise and unambiguous than ordinary English.[58]

Just as Staal's *Universals: Studies in Indian Logic and Linguistics* illustrates his arguments on language and logic in Indian thought, I believe that the formal symbolic representations of mathematical logic can help in the investigation of the principles of the *bhūtasaṃkhyā.* Moreover, it must be acknowledged that the level of systematization, formalization, and conceptualization that characterize modern mathematics and mathematical linguistics on the one hand, and the structure of the language as well as the methods of Indian logic on the other, draw attention to the relation between mathematics, language, and philosophy.

Number, Object, Quality, and Technical Term: The Four Logical Terms

In the following section I articulate a logical argument consisting of four terms:

(1) *Saṃkhyā,* "number," is in the *bhūtasaṃkhyā* notation that which needs to "be signified" by another element standing for it.

(2) I use the word *bhūta* to denote an animate or inanimate object that, before being adopted as a technical term, is semantically related to the referent conveyed by its literal meaning.

(3) With *saṃjñā* I indicate a "technical term," which I understand as the result of a process by which an object (*bhūta*) has been established to stand for a number.

(4) Last, I call *lakṣaṇa,* lit., "quality, attribute," the characteristic of an "object" that is either socially produced by the process of interaction of the members of the society, or as part of an object by nature. For instance, in the *bhūtasaṃkhyā* system the "object," *akṣi,* "eye," stands for the number 2 because the *lakṣaṇa* of *akṣi* is the fact that human beings have two eyes. This is an inherent "attribute" of the "object" *akṣi.* On the other hand, *naya,* "method," stands also for the number 2 based on the *lakṣaṇa* of *naya,* the two methods of knowledge for the Jainas. This is a "quality" that has been socially attached to the "object" *naya.* Also, *lakṣaṇa* as the *conditio sine qua non* of a certain "object" (*bhūta*) becomes a "technical term" (*saṃjñā*). In a few words, then, when an "object" has such a "quality," the "object" becomes somehow "measurable," and is therefore transformed into a "technical term" (*saṃjñā*) that denotes a "number" (*saṃkhyā*).

Now, let us apply these four logical terms to the word *agni,* which is used in the *bhūtasaṃkhyā* system to stand for the number 3:

(1) The number 3 is the *saṃkhyā.*

(2) *Agni* in its literal meaning of the object "fire" is *bhūta.*

(3) *Lakṣaṇa* is the measurable quality, "three sacrificial fires."

(4) Because the "object" fire bears a *lakṣaṇa* in relation to the number 3, *agni,* "fire," therefore becomes a *saṃjñā* standing for that number.[59]

I suggest that the first, fundamental relation between these terms has the following form:[60]

(1) A (x, y)

This may be read as: "x occurs in y," therefore the relation A is an "occurrence relation."

In relation to our logical argument, where l stands for a "quality" (*lakṣaṇa*) and b for an "object" (*bhūta*), the first relation established is:

(1) A (l, b)

which is read as: "l occurs in b," therefore the relation A is established. Such relation is called "occurrence relation."

The second step, in which S is the *saṃjñā* and s is the *saṃkhyā*, is:

$$A\ (l, b)\ [(b = S) \wedge (S\ (:\,=)\ s)]$$

which may be read as: "if the relation A occurs, then b is equal to S and S stands for s."

By means of the relations A, a certain "object" (*bhūta*) can be established as a "technical term" (*saṃjñā*) standing for the number, its "quality" is in relation with, and therefore recognized as, a sign of the codified language *bhūtasaṃkhyā*.

Of course, the negation of the occurrence relation A, which represents here the premise, implies the negation of the other two identity relations.

The logical relations between the variables b, l, and s can be also expressed by the following syllogism consisting of two premises of the form R (x, y), "x is in relation to y," from which one conclusion of the same form is derived.[61] Here, *lakṣaṇa* clearly appears to be the middle term linking the two extremities *bhūta* and *saṃkhyā:*

R (b, l)
R (l, s)
R (b, s)

which can be read as: "if b is in relation to l, and l is in relation to s, then b is in relation to s." In other words, if a given "object" (*bhūta*) is in relation to a certain "quality" (*lakṣaṇa*), and this is in relation to a "number" (*saṃkhyā*), then the given object is in relation to that number.

Another important feature that can be noted concerns the fact that in the *bhūtasaṃkhyā* a certain number can be represented by more than one technical term. This condition can be expressed with:

$$R\ (n\ (s_b x, s_b y) \Leftrightarrow R\ (n\ (l_b x, l_b y)$$

which is read as: "the relation of n with $s_b x$ and with $s_b y$ occurs only and if only the relation of n with $l_b x$ and with $l_b y$ occurs." In this formulation, n denotes a certain number, $s_b x$ is the "technical term" of a certain "object" x and $s_b y$ the "technical term" of a certain "object" y, while $l_b x$ is the "quality" of the "object" x and $l_b y$ is the "quality" of the "object" y. In other words, a certain "number" can be represented by two different "technical terms" only and if only the "qualities" of the two respective "objects" are informed exactly by the same "number."

The *Bhūtasaṃkhyā* as Literary Practice, Mathematical Language, and Cultural Representation

After having attempted to outline the structure of the *bhūtasaṃkhyā* by means of symbols and mathematical models of modern logic, I would like to come back to the relation between "number," "object," and the (culturally established) "quality" of the object in the sociocultural context of Indian thought, which affected the development of this peculiar system of notation. At this point, my question is: Can we assert that numbers embody worldviews? While this supposition cannot be developed here, due to limitations of space, if we characterize scientific knowledge as a material and social construction, in which ideas and logical concepts are products of and supported by collective practices, we must recognize that mathematical activities also are an echo of social representations.

I would suggest that we consider the *bhūtasaṃkhyā* as a conceptual map used by those (the "codifiers") who share the interpretative process of the relationship between the four logical terms introduced above, "number," "object," "quality," and "technical term." It thus becomes a means of communication only for certain specialists within the Sanskrit learned tradition. As a literary practice, it developed from the needs of adopting Sanskrit for formal scientific expression and further elaborated it in a mechanism that reflects cultural identities. This connotes the *bhūtasaṃkhyā* as a "constitutively social form" of language, since what I defined as the "quality" (*lakṣaṇa*) of an "object" embodies the customs and traditions of Indian culture (Hindu, Buddhist, and Jain).

The list given by Mahāvīra in GSS 1.53–63 (see above) shows clearly that the technical terms used in the *bhūtasaṃkhyā* system are derived from different cultural and social areas. Each sign of this language becomes an "object of reality," a "sense-making" insofar as it is rooted in the semantic field "Indian culture," because it is not meaningful in itself. What I mean is that each sign is a "linguistic act" that cannot be extracted from its specific cultural background, and which cannot be valid without an effective process of interpretation that only the "codifiers" can put into practice. In other words, each sign of the *bhūtasaṃkhyā* is mathematically effective in universal terms. It acquires its own history and connotation that are familiar only to members of the sign-users' culture, who are able to interpret "the code" that governs the relationship between words and numbers by means of established, shared cultural values.

There are many ways in which cultures contribute to the design and shape of their texts. Sanskrit and mathematical texts took shape in working communities that developed conventions for reading and working with them. I do not want to risk imposing the conceptual framework of Western logic, but let me adopt Sara Mills' famous example of traffic lights.[62] According to the constructionist approach, of which Mills is an exponent, colors and the language of traffic lights work as a signifying or representational system. In the language of traffic lights it is the sequence and position of the colors, as well as the colors themselves, that enable them to carry meaning and thus function as effective signs. It is the code that fixes the meaning, not the color itself. So, as with the language of traffic lights, the meanings carried by the word-numerals are relational.

Meanings are produced within history and culture, as Jonathan D. Culler underlines,

> because it is arbitrary, the sign is totally subject to history and the combination at the particular moment of a given signifier and signified is a contingent result of the historical process.[63]

In this regard, Roland Barthes describes two levels of meaning: "denotation," which is the definitional, literal meaning of a sign (for instance, what the dictionary provides), while "connotation" is used to refer to the sociocultural (and personal) associations of the sign.[64] The "denotative" meaning of a sign is broadly agreed upon by members of the same culture. "Connotations" are determined by the codes to which the interpreter has access; cultural codes provide a connotative framework. Applying these categories to the *bhūtasaṃkhyā* language, we can say that the definitive meaning of *agni,* "fire," is linked to its denotative meaning as "three sacrificial fires," so that the association with the number 3 can be established.

In concluding this section, I would like to mention another perspective in relation to my analysis of the *bhūtasaṃkhyā* as a literary practice, a mathematical language, and a cultural representation, given in the so-called "Descriptivism," an approach to modern semantics generally attributed to Gottlob Frege and Bertrand Russell. In this regard, Genoveva Martí[65] provides an account of the mechanism of reference according to the theory of names elaborated by Descriptivists. Of course, while this line of inquiry is interesting this is not the place to investigate such a detailed approach;

what I want to bring forward here is the assumption that if names are semantically associated with descriptions, then by themselves and because of what they mean they find their referents. Descriptivists argue that speakers attach to names not only descriptive information, they also associate images, memories, and all sorts of connotations. All these associations undeniably play a very important role in cognition.

In a similar way, "objects" of everyday life become "technical terms" in the *bhūtasaṃkhyā* language because of the descriptive information, images, memories, and other associated connotations (what I previously defined as *lakṣaṇa*) attached to them by speakers of the network comprised of the Sanskrit branches of learning, and more broadly in Indian culture.

Conclusion

What are the implications of all of this for our understanding of textual practices in the Sanskrit mathematical tradition? As Pierre-Sylvain Filliozat writes, "[T]he Sanskrit mathematical text is a literary text; it imitates the form and spirit of the poetic text. . . . Sanskrit poetry is always situated in the structure of orality."[66] The mathematical text remains an "oral text," which can be transmitted through memory, used mentally, and is thus well adapted to such functions: propensity to orality, concision, emphasis on the essential point, links from formula to formula, and metaphorical expressions are some of the structural features of Indian mathematical texts. Moreover, I would argue that the shape of a specialized and well-defined lexicon conveys economy and recognizability to the elucidation of mathematical ideas, at the same time serving oral-mnemonic expository techniques as well as the formal structure of textuality.

At this point, my concern can be summarized in the following question: Can one define the *bhūtasaṃkhyā* system as an "artificial language"? In his article on artificial languages, Staal distinguishes between artificial and scientific Sanskrit.[67] In his definition, artificial Sanskrit is "any kind of artificial language intentionally created to deal with scientific problems, but deviating in some important respect or respects from ordinary, natural Sanskrit," while scientific Sanskrit is "any Sanskrit used for the expression of scientific statements or truths." He argues that although a wide range of technical terms are used, the Sanskrit language applied in mathematical texts is ordinary, "natural" language; there is a specialized lexicon and a technical terminology but this does not make the language an "artificial Sanskrit." Staal points out that during the first millennium

Indian mathematicians employed abbreviations and artificial notations,[68] but their Sanskrit was not artificial Sanskrit and they did not use other artificial language.

What I have attempted in this paper is to analyze the logic that characterizes the *bhūtasaṃkhyā* system as a linguistic practice and as a mathematical language. Having explored the interplay of cultural and cognitive aspects that may have influenced the peculiar development of this system, I suggest that the *bhūtasaṃkhyā* is the result of a process by which the flexibility of Sanskrit language has been used as an active tool functional to poetic structure and to the method of the oral transmission of Sanskrit texts. Moreover, as was rightly highlighted by Frits Staal,[69] it clearly shows that mathematical Sanskrit continues to be Sanskrit.

Notes

1 My thanks to Dr. Hugo David, Dr. Vincenzo Vergiani, Aleesandro Passi, and Marco Franceschini for their helpful comments on this paper.

2 Frits Staal, *Universals: Studies in Indian Logic and Linguistics* (Chicago and London: University of Chicago Press, 1988), p. 158.

3 Staal, *Universals: Studies in Indian Logic and Linguistics,* p. 31.

4 See Alessandra Petrocchi, *The Gaṇita Sāra Saṃgraḥa: A Linguistic Approach to a Sanskrit Mathematical Treatise* (MPhil Thesis in Sanskrit, Cambridge University, 2012).

5 These considerations concern the variety of systems for numerical expressions used by Mahāvīrācārya, his extensive use of the *bhūtasaṃkhyā,* and questions emerging from details given in this text that are found nowhere else.

6 In the modern historiography of mathematics, Bhibhutibhisan Datta and Avadesh Narayan Singh, in their 1935 work *History of Hindu Mathematics: A Source Book* (Bombay: Asia Publishing House, 1962, reprint), pp. 53–69, coined the term "word-numerals," which is generally used to denote the *bhūtasaṃkhyā.*

7 Stephen Chrisomalis, *Numerical Notation: A Comparative History* (Cambridge: Cambridge University Press, 2010), p. 3.

8 See Kim Plofker, *Mathematics in India* (Princeton, NJ: Princeton University Press, 2009); Sreeramula Rajeswara Sarma, "On the Rationale of the Maxim Aṅkānāṃ Vāmato Gatiḥ," *Gaṇita Bhāratī* 31/1–2 (2009): 65–86; Datta and Singh, *History of Hindu Mathematics.*

9 According to Sarma, "On the Rationale of the Maxim Aṅkānāṃ Vāmato Gatiḥ," p. 67, Sundararāja was the first to use the term *bhūtasaṃkhyā,* at the end of the fifteenth century.

10 Datta and Singh, *History of Hindu Mathematics,* pp. 16–88, investigate the history of place value notation in India.

11 See David Pingree, *The Yavanajātaka of Sphujidhvaja,* 2 vols. (Cambridge, MA: Harvard University Press, 1978).

[12] Christopher Z. Minkowsky, "Astronomers and Their Reasons: Working Paper on Jyotiḥśāstra," *Journal of Indian Philosophy* 30/5 (2002): 495–514.

[13] In 1503, Jñānarāja of Pārthapura composed the *Siddhāntasundara*. Plofker, *Mathematics in India*, p. 289, points out that he uses the number system with a literary and mathematical double meaning: if his sample problems are read with the standard numerical interpretations, the numbers provide quantities for solving the problem; but if read with their literal verbal meanings, they transform the problem into little anecdotes with no mathematical values. See the recent translation of Jñanarāja's work in Toke Lindegaard Knudsen, *The Siddhāntasundara of Jñānarāja: An English Translation with Commentary* (Baltimore: Johns Hopkins University Press, 2014).

[14] The term *jyotiṣa* includes the disciplines of mathematics, astronomy, and divination. See Pingree, *The Yavanajātaka of Sphujidhvaja*, vol. 1, p. 198; Plofker, *Mathematics in India*, p. 61.

[15] Sarma, "On the Rationale of the Maxim Aṅkānāṃ Vāmato Gatiḥ," pp. 73–84, investigates the reasoning behind the right-to-left direction in reading the *bhūtasaṃkhyā*.

[16] Sarma, "On the Rationale of the Maxim Aṅkānāṃ Vāmato Gatiḥ," p. 65.

[17] Datta and Singh, *History of Hindu Mathematics*, p. 71.

[18] Chrisomalis, *Numerical Notation: A Comparative History*, p. 209.

[19] Plofker, Mathematics in India, p. 75.

[20] Annette Wilke and Oliver Moebius, *Sound and Communication: An Aesthetic Cultural History of Sanskrit Hinduism* (Berlin and New York: De Gruyter, 2011), p. 492. In relation to the tradition of Indian alphasyllabic numeration, Chrisomalis, *Numerical Notation: A Comparative History*, pp. 211–212, also mentions the *akṣarapallī* system used with great frequency in Jain manuscripts until the sixteenth century.

[21] The has been critically edited and translated in M. Raṅgācārya, ed., *The Ganita Sāra Saṃgraha of Mahāvīrācārya, with English Translation and Notes* (Madras: Government Press, 1912).

[22] See GSS 1.3–8.

[23] See Petrocchi, *The Gaṇita Sāra Saṃgraha*.

[24] See, for instance, the *Gaṇitatilaka* by Śrīpati (eleventh century C.E.).

[25] It is possible that this heading was added by an editor or scribe.

[26] See Raṅgācārya, *The Ganita Sāra Saṃgraha of Mahāvīrācārya*, p. 7.

[27] The printed edition reads *madri* here, instead of *mahīdra;* see Raṅgācārya, *The Ganita Sāra Saṃgraha of Mahāvīrācārya*, p. 7.

[28] The printed edition reads *pannagā* here, instead of *pannaga;* see Raṅgācārya, *The Ganita Sāra Saṃgraha of Mahāvīrācārya*, p. 7.

[29] Most of the last verses are unmetrical.

[30] The first part of this paper is partly the result of research I conducted for my 2012 MPhil thesis, *The Gaṇita Sāra Saṃgraha*. All the translations given here are my own, unless otherwise noted.

31 The correct reading should perhaps be *khecara* instead of *keśava,* which in no way is related to the number 9. On the other side, *khecara* means "planet," of which there are said to be nine in Hindu astrology and astronomy.

32 *Navaratna* and *navanidhi* are common expressions in Sanskrit literature. It is difficult to track the origin of the association of the number 9 to the term "jewel." However, I am inclined to think that this usage may be related to the number of the (nine) planets.

33 *Ṛgveda* 3.9.9 reads *trīṇi śatāni trisahasrāṇi triṃśa ca nava ca,* "three hundred and three thousand and thirty and nine."

34 See Petrocchi, *The Gaṇita Sāra Saṃgraḥa.*

35 Plofker, *Mathematics in India,* pp. 212–214, explains the role of the Sanskrit commentarial tradition of mathematics.

36 See Petrocchi, *The Gaṇita Sāra Saṃgraḥa.*

37 The term *udāharaṇa* is also found to denote "sample problem" in Sanskrit texts.

38 Plofker, *Mathematics in India,* pp. 173–178.38

39 I have unfortunately not been able to examine the manuscripts of the GSS. For his edition Raṅgācārya used five manuscripts, all of which are in Sanskrit. One is written in Grantha characters and contains the first five chapters of the work with a running commentary in Sanskrit. Two are palm-leaf manuscripts in Kannada characters, one of which contains the first five chapters and the other contains the seventh chapter on geometry. Another manuscript is a transcription on paper in Kannada characters of an original palm-leaf manuscript belonging to a Jaina pandit, which contains the whole of the work with a short commentary in Kannada. A fifth manuscript is a transcription on paper in Kannada characters of a palm-leaf manuscript found in a Jaina monastery in South Karnataka. It also contains the entire work and gives a brief statement of the problems and their answers in Kannada.

40 I find Raṅgācārya's translation, *The Ganita Sāra Saṃgraha of Mahāvīrācārya,* p. 8, of this verse imprecise:

> By means of the [following] eight qualities, viz., quick method in working, forethought as to whether a desirable result may arrived at, or as to whether an undesirable result will be produced, freedom from dullness, correct comprehension, power of retention, and the devising of new means in working, along with getting at those numbers which make (unknown) quantities known [by means of these quantities] as [an] arithmetician is to be known as such.

A similar translation is found in Plofker, *Mathematics in India,* p. 164, who translates *laghukaraṇa* with "swift work" and strangely renders *vyaktikarāṅka-viśiṣṭair* as "having the answers."

41 See for instance, *badhirīkṛ* ("to deafen"), *śuklīkṛ* ("whiten"), and *vājīkṛ* ("to strengthen").

42 It is interesting to notice that traditionally gaṇita, "mathematics, computation" was distinguished in vyaktagaṇita (lit., "manifest computation" or computation with known quantities) and avyaktagaṇita (lit., "unmanifest computation" or computation with unknown quantities).

[43] The verb *vyaktīkṛ* literally means "to make manifest, clear."

[44] In Sanskrit mathematical texts, *karaṇa* means "calculation, procedure."

[45] *Ūha,* together with *tarka,* is a term belonging to the classical Indian tradition of logic and disputation. Both are linked to the relation between perception, logical reasoning, and means of knowledge.

[46] *Apoha* is another terms belonging to classical Indian tradition of logic. The *apoha* theory was expounded in Dignāna and Dharmakirti's school, for instance.

[47] *Arthaśāstra* 6.1.4 has "the qualities of the intellect" (*prajñāguṇāḥ*) of a king are *śuśrūṣāśravaṇagrahaṇadhāraṇavijñānohāpohatattvābhiniveśāḥ prajñāguṇāḥ.*

[48] See Vettam Mani, *Purāṇic Encyclopaedia: A Comprehensive Dictionary with Special Reference to the Epic and Purāṇic Literature* (Delhi: Motilal Banarsidass, 1975, reprint), p. 62.

[49] In *Jñānasiddhānta* 11.5, 11.11, and 11.18 eight supernatural faculties are mentioned. These parallel those found in *Paśupatasūtra* 1.23–26, 21–22, and 28–37. See Andrea Acri, Helen M. Creese, and Arlo Griffiths, eds., *From Laṅkā Eastwards: The Rāmayāṇa in the Literature and Visual Arts of Indonesia* (Leiden: KITLV Press, 2011), p. 80.

[50] *Vargaṇa* refers to a sort of karmic molecules formed by a number of *varga*s, or karmic atoms.

[51] See Raj Pruthi, *Jainism and Indian Civilization* (New Delhi: Discovery Publishing House, 2004), p. 45.

[52] In his 1916 work *Course in General Linguistics* Ferdinand de Saussure details his views on the nature and structure of language. In his paradigm, a sign is the basic unit of communication and a mental construct. Signifier and signified are the two labels used to denote what constitute a sign. A signifier is the form that the sign takes, while the signified is the concept it represents.

[53] See the list found in GSS 1.53–62, for which I provided a words-numbers correspondence above.

[54] Donald Davidson, *Inquiries into Truth and Interpretation* (Oxford: Clarendon, 1984), p. xiii.

[55] Sara Mills, *Discourse* (London: Routledge, 1997), p. 15.

[56] I refer here to the practitioners of the *jyotiḥśāstra* branch of knowledge.

[57] Staal, *Universals: Studies in Indian Logic and Linguistics,* p. 17.

[58] Staal, *Universals: Studies in Indian Logic and Linguistics,* pp. 17, 130.

[59] These four terms can be also defined as *lakṣya, bhūta, hetu,* and *lakṣaṇa.* I mean that a given number (*saṃkhyā*) is the *lakṣya,* i.e., it is the thing "to be defined"; an object is the *bhūta; hetu* is the "condition, reason"; and *lakṣaṇa* is the definendum, thus the technical term (*saṃjñā*). If a certain *bhūta* meets a certain condition (*hetu*), then it becomes a *lakṣaṇa* able to define a certain corresponding *lakṣya.* For instance, again in the case of *agni:* the *lakṣya* is the number 3, *bhūta* is the object "fire," *hetu* is the "three sacrificial fires," and the *lakṣaṇa* is the word *agni,* which has become a technical term standing for the number 3.

However, I prefer the formulation *saṃkhyā, bhūta, lakṣaṇa,* and *saṃjñā* because, in my opinion, it better clarifies the logic correspondence between the four elements.

60 Staal, *Universals: Studies in Indian Logic and Linguistics,* pp. 130–131, uses this formula in investigating the concept of pakṣa in Indian thought.

61 Staal, *Universals: Studies in Indian Logic and Linguistics,* p. 130, uses this kind of formula to analyze the notions of *pakṣa, hetu,* and *sādhya* in Indian traditional logic.

62 Mills, *Discourse,* p. 26.

63 Jonathan D. Culler, *Structuralist Poetics: Structuralism, Linguistics, and the Study of Literature* (London: Routledge and Kegan Paul, 1975), p. 36.

64 See Roland Barthes, *Mythologies* (Paris: Éditions du Seuil, 1957).

65 Genoveva Martí, "Reference," in Manuel García-Carpintero and Max Kölbel, eds., *The Continuum Companion to the Philosophy of Language* (London and New York: Continuum International Publishing Group, 2012), pp. 106–124.

66 Pierre-Sylvain Filliozat, "Ancient Sanskrit Mathematics: An Oral Tradition and a Written Literature," in Karine Chemla, ed., *History of Science, History of Text* (Dordrecht, The Netherlands: Springer, 2004), pp. 137–157.

67 Frits Staal, "Artificial Languages across Sciences and Civilizations," *Journal of Indian Philosophy* 34 (2006): 102.

68 Staal, in "Artificial Languages across Sciences and Civilizations," gives the example of the mathematical notation used in the *Bakshālī Manuscript* (third to ninth centuries C.E.?).

69 Staal, "Artificial Languages across Sciences and Civilizations," pp. 89–141.

References

Acri, Andrea, Helen M. Creese, and Arlo Griffiths, eds. *From Laṅkā Eastwards: The Rāmayāṇa in the Literature and Visual Arts of Indonesia.* Leiden: KITLV Press, 2011.

Barthes, Roland. *Mythologies.* Paris: Éditions du Seuil, 1957.

Bose, D. M, S. N. Sen, and B. V. Suppraybba. *A Concise History of Science in India.* New Delhi: Indian National Science Academy, 2009.

Chemla, Karine, ed. *History of Science, History of Text.* Studies in the Philosophy of Science vol. 238. Dordrecht, the Netherlands: Springer, 2004.

Chrisomalis, Stephen. *Numerical Notation: A Comparative History.* Cambridge: Cambridge University Press, 2010.

Culler, Jonathan D. *Structuralist Poetics: Structuralism, Linguistics, and the Study of Literature.* London: Routledge and Kegan Paul, 1975.

Datta, Bhibhutibhisan, and Avadesh Narayan Singh. *History of Hindu Mathematics: A Source Book* (1935). Bombay: Asia Publishing House, 1962, reprint.

Davidson, Donald. *Inquiries into Truth and Interpretation.* Oxford: Clarendon, 1984.

Filliozat, Pierre-Sylvain. "Ancient Sanskrit Mathematics: An Oral Tradition and a Written Literature," in Karine Chemla, ed., *History of Science, History of Text*, pp. 137–157. Dordrecht, The Netherlands, Springer, 2004.

García-Carpintero, Manuel, and Max Kölbel, eds. *The Continuum Companion to the Philosophy of Language.* London and New York: Continuum International Publishing Group, 2012.

Kāpadiā, H. R., ed. *Gaṇitatilaka, with the Commentary of Siṃhatilaka Sūri.* Baroda: Oriental Institute, 1937.

Knudsen, Toke Lindegaard. *The Siddhāntasundara of Jñānarāja: An English Translation with Commentary.* Baltimore: Johns Hopkins University Press, 2014.

Mani, Vettam. *Purāṇic Encyclopaedia: A Comprehensive Dictionary with Special Reference to the Epic and Purāṇic Literature.* Delhi: Motilal Banarsidass, 1975.

Martí, Genoveva. "Reference," in Manuel García-Carpintero and Max Kölbel, eds., *The Continuum Companion to the Philosophy of Language*, pp. 106–124. London and New York: Continuum International Publishing Group, 2012.

Mills, Sara. *Discourse.* London: Routledge, 1997.

Minkowsky, Christopher Z. "Astronomers and Their Reasons: Working Paper on Jyotiḥśāstra," *Journal of Indian Philosophy* 30/5 (2002): 495–514.

Pingree, David. *Jyotiḥśāstra: Astral and Mathematical Literature.* Wiesbaden: O. Harrassowitz, 1981.

—. *The Yavanajātaka of Sphujidhvaja*, 2 vols. Cambridge, MA: Harvard University Press, 1978.

Plofker, Kim. *Mathematics in India.* Princeton, NJ: Princeton University Press, 2009.

Pruthi, Raj. *Jainism and Indian Civilization.* New Delhi: Discovery Publishing House, 2004.

Rangācārya, M., ed. *The Ganita Sāra Saṃgraha of Mahāvīrācārya, with English Translation and Notes.* Madras: Government Press, 1912.

Sarma, Sreeramula Rajeswara. "On the Rationale of the Maxim Aṅkānāṃ Vāmato Gatiḥ," *Gaṇita Bhāratī* 31/1–2 (2009): 65–86.

Saussure, Ferdinand de. *Course in General Linguistics* (1916). Wade Baskin, trans.; Perry Meisel and Haun Saussy, eds. New York: Columbia University Press, 2011.

Srinivasiengar, C. N. *The History of Indian Mathematics.* Calcutta: World Press, 1967.

Staal, Frits. "Artificial Languages across Sciences and Civilizations," *Journal of Indian Philosophy* 34 (2006): 89–141.

—. *Universals: Studies in Indian Logic and Linguistics.* Chicago and London: University of Chicago Press, 1988.

Wilke, Annette, and Oliver Moebius. *Sound and Communication: An Aesthetic Cultural History of Sanskrit Hinduism.* Berlin and New York: De Gruyter, 2011.

Five Jewels in the University of Pennsylvania's Rare Book and Manuscript Library

Peter M. Scharf

A 2009–2012 pilot project funded by the National Endowment for the Humanities (NEH) undertook to catalog and digitize manuscripts of the *Mahābhārata* and *Bhāgavata Purāṇa* in the collections at Brown University and the University of Pennsylvania. Interestingly, most of the manuscripts listed in H. I. Poleman's *Census of Indic Manuscripts in the United States and Canada* under one or another parvan of the *Mahābhārata* do not contain substantial portions of the epic. Instead they contain self-contained treatises, some with tenuous connection to the *Mahābhārata*. Most of the manuscripts contain what apparently comprised a well-recognized set of five jewels (*pañcaratna*). The transmission of these minor treatises independent of the epic or of any major purāṇa reaffirms the generally accepted view of modern scholarship concerning the composition of purāṇas, which Ludo Rocher aptly summarizes, "[E]veryone agrees that, to a large extent, purāṇas are made up of originally independent pieces."[1] Indeed the *Gajendramokṣana*, the fifth jewel, epitomizes what Rocher there calls "mini-purāṇas." Yet in contrast to the consistency of opinion regarding purāṇas, opinion is divided concerning the composition of epics, where much contemporary scholarship, including several prominent European and American scholars, resists applying a similar view to the *Mahābhārata*. The transmission of the other four jewels in a manner similar to the fifth, however, corroborates just such a view: the *Anusmṛti*, the *Bhīṣmastavarāja*, the *Viṣṇu-sahasranāman*, and even the *Bhagavadgītā* constitute independent treatises incorporated into the great epic.

Introduction

The transmission of texts is an important criterion for determining their original constitution. The history of the transmission of particular texts contributes to determining whether those texts constitute originally independent works or are parts that belong to one work or another. Transmission together is evidence for the unity of a work. If a text is transmitted only as part of a certain work, there is no question that it belongs to that work and does not have independent status. If a text is transmitted independently and also as part of a work, the question arises as to whether it belongs to the work or is fundamentally independent. If one text is included in two or more different works, it is possible that it belongs to one work and that the other is an anthology that incorporates parts of other works as well as the work in question. If a text is included in different locations in different manuscripts of a work and is also included in another work, it is highly doubtful that it belongs fundamentally to the first work.

In a 2009–2012 project funded by the NEH, "Enhancing Access to Primary Cultural Heritage Materials of India: Integrating images of literary sources with machine-readable texts, lexical resources, linguistic software, and the web (PW50408)," project personnel digitized and catalogued 162 manuscripts of the *Mahābhārata* and the *Bhāgavata Purāṇa* in the collections at Brown University and the University of Pennsylvania: 13 palm-leaf manuscripts in Telugu script at Brown, and 169 paper manuscripts in Devānagarī script at U. Penn. Interestingly, only a small portion of the manuscripts listed in Poleman's Census under one or another parvan of the *Mahābhārata* contain substantial portions of the epic. While seven of the nine Telugu-script palm-leaf manuscripts contain one or more complete parvans of the *Mahābhārata* in Sanskrit, only five of the 81 paper manuscripts at the University of Pennsylvania do. (The other Telugu manuscripts contain Nannaya's (eleventh century) Telugu-language translation of the *Ādiparvan* and Tikkanasomayāji's (thirteenth century) translation of the *Karṇaparvan* and *Śalyaparvan*. Several of the Devānagarī manuscripts contain other short pieces, such as two extracts from the *Bhagavadgītā:* the *Aṣṭādaśaślokīgītā* (2) and the *Saptaślokīgītā* (3); the *Durgastotra* (2); the *Oṅkāramāhātmyagītā* (2), etc. The overwhelming majority, however—62 of the 81 paper manuscripts at the University of Pennsylvania, to be exact, more than two-thirds of the entire group of *Mahābhārata* manuscripts in the project—contain one of five self-contained works devoted to Viṣṇu. These include the well-known *Bhagavadgītā* and the *Viṣṇusahasranāmastotra,* and three less famous texts: the *Bhīṣmastavarāja,* the *Anusmṛti,* and the *Gajendramokṣaṇa.* These five works apparently comprised a well-recognized set collectively called the five jewels (*pañcaratna*). The status of these texts has significant bearing on the integrity of the constitution of the great epic.

Five Jewels

The five jewels (*pañcaratna*) constitute a thematically related set of texts that were often transmitted together as a unit, the most famous of which were usually transmitted independently. They all have a tenuous connection with the *Mahābhārata*. The *New Catalogus Catalogorum*,[2] under one of the 13 entries with the title *Pañcaratna*, lists more than a dozen manuscripts that contain the five works discussed in this paper. Other entries with the title *Pañcaratna* include one or more of these five works in a manuscript that includes different texts as well. For example, one includes the *Gajendramokṣaṇa* together with a number of stotras.[3]

The *Bhagavadgītā*

The *Bhagavadgītā*, narrating Kṛṣṇa's instructions to Arjuna on the battlefield, is included in the text of the *Mahābhārata* established in the Pune critical edition in chapters 23–40 of the *Bhīṣmaparvan* (MBh 6.23.1–6.40.78). Although our collection includes two lengthy manuscripts of the *Bhīṣmaparvan*, one in Telugu script at Brown and one with Nīlakaṇṭha's commentary in Devanāgarī script at U. Penn, the collection includes 19 manuscripts of the *Bhagavadgītā* as an independent treatise in which form it is celebrated as the most famous text of India. Six of these manuscripts include a commentary, 12 include a preface, and one consists solely of the tenth adhyāya. Two of the manuscripts contain the commentary by Śaṅkara (eighth century), one of which has Ānandagiri's subcommentary. One manuscript contains a commentary by a Hanumat (date unknown), and three contain the commentary by Śrīdhara (c. 1400). All of these commentators, as is well known, comment on the *Bhagavadgītā* as an independent treatise. Popular editions of the *Bhagavadgītā*, such as the Gītā Press edition,[4] typically include a preface consisting of a *Nyāsa* and *Dhyāna* not included in the text of the *Mahābhārata* established in the Pune critical edition,[5] and most of which is not included in the critical apparatus either. In the 12 manuscripts that include it in our collection, this preface is fairly uniform and also agrees with the popular editions.

The final rubrics of the *Bhagavadgītā* usually place the text in the context of the Upaniṣads, and the sciences of Vedānta and Yoga rather than in the text of the *Mahābhārata*. Only two of our collection's 19 manuscripts of the *Bhagavadgītā* as an independent text place the work in the *Bhīṣmaparvan* of the *Mahābhārata* (for example, UPenn 2366):

(1) *iti śrīmahābhārate bhīṣmaparvaṇi bha(ga)vadgītāsūpaniṣatsu brahmavidyāyāṃ yogaśāstre śrīkṛṣṇārjunasaṃvāde mokṣasaṃnyāsayogo nāma aṣṭādaśo* <'> *dhyāyaḥ* ..18..

The other 17 manuscripts make no mention of the *Mahābhārata,* but instead count the text as an independent philosophical work in final rubrics, such as that of UPenn 2241.

(2) *iti śrīmadbhagavadgītāsūpaniṣatsu brahmavidyāyāṃ yogaśāstre śrīkṛṣṇārjunasaṃvāde mokṣasaṃnyāsayogo nāma aṣṭādaśo* <'>*dhyāyaḥ* 18 (UPenn 2241, f. 78v)

Although the critical edition of the *Mahābhārata* includes the *Bhagavadgītā,* the evidence of its manuscripts is not universally supportive that the *Bhīṣmaparvan* included it. Two of the five manuscripts of the commentaries on the *Bhīṣmaparvan* do not include it.[6] The only manuscript available of Devabodha's commentary is missing the relevant portion, and the manuscripts of Arjunamiśra's commentary, though they include the complete text of the *Bhagavadgītā,* have the commentary of Śrīdhara instead. The editor writes:

Of the commentators drawn upon in the critical apparatus for the *Bhīṣmaparvan,* Arjunamiśra has no proper commentary on the *Bhagavadgītā,* i.e. adhyāyas 6.23–40, but in its place the Ca manuscripts write Śrīdhara's commentary, which is not used in the critical apparatus. Devabodha probably wrote a commentary on the *Gītā* portion of the parvan, but it has not so far come to light.[7]

Nor are manuscripts consistent in exactly where the *Bhagavadgītā* occurs. The southern recension manuscripts generally read the *Bhagavadgītā* after chapter 41 while the northern recension manuscripts read it before chapter 41.[8]

The *Viṣṇusahasranāman*

Just as the inclusion of the *Bhagavadgītā* is not universally supported by the manuscripts of the critical edition of the *Bhīṣmaparvan,* likewise the evidence of the manuscripts used to constitute the critical editions of the *Śāntiparvan* and of the *Anuśāsanaparvan* do not universally support the inclusion of the *Bhīṣmastavarāja* and the *Viṣṇusahasranāman.*

The *Viṣṇusahasranāman,* "the thousand names of Viṣṇu," is extant in two forms, a verse form called the *Viṣṇusahasranāmastotra,* and a prose form listing mantras paying obeisance to Viṣṇu called the *Viṣṇusahasranāmāvali.* The verse form is included in the text of the *Mahābhārata* established in the Pune critical edition as the 135th adhyāya of the *Anuśāsanaparvan* (MBh 13.135.1–142). Yet the text as an independent treatise typically appends a *phalaśruti* not included in the critical text and most of which is also absent from the critical apparatus.

Our collection includes twenty-two manuscripts of the *Viṣṇusahasranāmastotra* and two of the *Viṣṇusahasranāmāvali.* Most of the final rubrics of these manuscripts claim that the thousand names of Viṣṇu is part of the *Mahābhārata.* However, they disagree about where in the epic to locate the work. Only a third agree with the editors of the Pune critical edition; the final rubric of one manuscript of the prose version and the final rubrics of only seven manuscripts of the verse version place the work in the *Anuśāsanaparvan,*

> (3) *iti śrīmanmahābhārate śatasāhasryāṃ saṃhitāyāṃ !va!<vai>yyāsikyām anuśāsanike parvaṇi bhīṣmayudhiṣṭhirasa<ṃ>vāde śrīviṣṇor divyasahasranāmastotraṃ sa<ṃ>pūrṇaṃ* (UPenn 0390)

while the overwhelming majority, i.e. 13 of the verse version, place the work in the *Śāntiparvan,*

> (4) *iti śrīmanmahābhārate śatasahasrasaṃhitāyāṃ vaiyyāsikyāṃ śāṃtiparvaṇi uttamānuśāsane [dha] dānadharmopadeśe mokṣadharme bhīṣmayudhiṣthirasaṃvāde śrīviṣṇor divyasahasranāmastotraṃ saṃpūrṇaṃ* (UPenn 0388)

and one places it in the *Bhīṣmaparvan:*

> (5) . . . *iti śrī mahābhārate śatasāha!sryaṃ!<sryāṃ> saṃhitāyāṃ vaiyāsikyāṃ dānadharme bhīṣma!varpa!<parva>ṇi viṣṇor divyasahasranāmastotraṃ saṃpūrṇaṃ* (UPenn 0426)

The final rubrics of one prose and one verse manuscript claim that the work is included in the *Mahābhārata* but do not specify in which parvan.

None of our MBh manuscripts actually include the *Anuśāsanaparvan.* Of the nine that claim to be of the *Anuśāsanaparvan* in the final rubric, seven are *Viṣṇusahasranāmastotra,* one is *Anusmṛti,* and one is *Viṣṇusahasranāmāvali.*

Of the 29 manuscripts in our collection that claim to contain the *Śāntiparvan,* only the Telugu manuscript Brown Indic 37 (br37) actually includes the *parvan.* One of the Devanāgarī manuscripts at the University of Pennsylvania (UPenn 2408) includes adhyāya 338 in the *Mokṣadharma*parvan. Thirteen (as just mentioned) are manuscripts of the *Viṣṇusahasranāmastotra.* Two are similar recitations of the names of Śiva, one of the *Dakṣaprokta Śivasahasranāmastotra* included by the Pune critical edition in the appendices (MBh 16, Appendix I, No. 28, lines 155–435) and one of a different *Śivasahasranāmastotra* included in the text as established in the critical edition in the *Anuśāsanaparvan* (MBh 13.17.1–13.17.171). The remaining twelve are the works to be discussed presently: five are the *Bhīṣmastavarāja*, two the *Anusmṛti*, and five the *Gajendramokṣaṇa*.

Recensions differ on the status of the *Anuśāsanaparvan*. While the southern manuscripts used to constitute the critical edition treat the parvan as independent, there is a tradition according to which the *Anuśāsanaparvan* constitutes a part of the *Śāntiparvan*.[9] Only one of the five commentators on the text, Nīlakaṇṭha, regards it as a separate parvan. Neither Vimalabodha nor Arjunamiśra mentions the name *Anuśāsanaparvan*, and Vādirāja and the unknown author of the fifth commentary regard the *Anuśāsanaparvan* as a part of the *Śāntiparvan*. It is not surprising, therefore, that the independent versions of the *Viṣṇusahasranāman* disagree on whether the recitation of names belongs in the *Anuśāsanaparvan* or in the *Śāntiparvan*. The absence of the *Viṣṇusahasranāman* from one of the manuscripts used to constitute the text of the critical edition of the *Anuśāsanaparvan*, however, attests to its late insertion into the text.

The *Bhīṣmastavarāja*

The *Bhīṣmastavarāja*, in which Bhīṣma sings the praise of Viṣṇu prior to abandoning his arrow-filled body, is included in the text of the critical edition of the *Śāntiparvan* of the *Mahābhārata* at MBh 12.47.1–72. There it ends with a verse in Rucirā meter describing Kṛṣṇa rejoicing at hearing the voices of brāhmaṇas on the road repeating Bhīṣma's hymn of praise and seeing other people with hands cupped in devotion.

> *tato giraḥ puruṣavarastavānvitā*
> *dvijeritāḥ pathi sumanāḥ sa śuśruve.*
> *kṛtāñjaliṃ praṇatam athāparaṃ janaṃ*
> *sa keśihā muditamanābhyanandata. . . .*
> (*rucirā:* 13 syllables/foot)
> (double *sandhi* contraction of *muditamanā abhyanandata*)
> (MBh 12.47.72)

Yet, like the independent manuscripts of the *Viṣṇusahasranāman*, the text as an independent treatise typically extends to a length as much as twice that of the text as in the critical edition and appends a phalaśruti not included in the critical text and much of which is also absent from the critical apparatus.[10]

The transmission of the *Śāntiparvan* suggests that it in particular is a compilation of independent material. Even the transmission of each of the three subsections of the *Śāntiparvan* (*Rājadharma*, *Āpaddharma*, and *Mokṣaparvan*) is largely independent. Only four of the six commentaries on the *Śāntiparvan* comment on the *Rājadharma* section; the other two comment exclusively on the *Mokṣadharma* section. Only fifteen of more than a hundred manuscripts included in the critical apparatus include all three subsections.[11] Notably, one such complete manuscript (Sarasvathi Mahal Library no. 11819) does not include the *bhīṣmastavarāja*, hinting at its original absence.

Our collection includes six manuscripts containing the *Bhīṣmastavarāja*, the final rubrics of all of which place the text where found in the critical edition in the *Śāntiparvan* of the *Mahābhārata*. For example,

> (6) *iti śrīmahābhārate !sa!<śa>tasahasryāṃ saṃhitāyāṃ śāṃtiparvaṇi rājadharme bhīṣmoktaṃ stavarājastotraṃ saṃpūrṇam..* (UPenn 0490)
>
> Finished is the regal hymn of praise uttered by Bhīṣma in the *Rājadharma* section in the *Śāntiparvan* in the *Mahābhārata* of a hundred thousand verses (UPenn 0490, f. 17v).

But, like several manuscripts as reported in the critical apparatus (MBh 12*98, lines 3–4; 12*99, lines 9–10), five of our six manuscripts include a closing verse which refers to the hymn as having been sung in the past in the context of the *Mahābhārata* narrative:

> (7) *stavarājaḥ samāpto 'yaṃ viṣṇor adbhutakarmaṇaḥ gāṅgeyena purā gītaḥ mahāpātakanāśanaḥ..* (MBh 12.47.65*98, lines 3–4)
>
> Finished is this sin-destroying regal praise of Viṣṇu of wonderful deeds previously sung by the son of the Ganges (Bhīṣma).

By referring to the hymn as having been sung in the past by Bhīṣma, the verse, as part of the hymn, removes the work from the very context in which the final rubric places it and confirms the status of the hymn as an independent treatise. The verse thereby reduces the final rubric's placement of the hymn to a status claim. The final rubric of UPenn 2462 designates the hymn by the term *ratna* 3.

> (8) *iti śrīmahābhārate śatasahasrasaṃhitāyāṃ śāṃtiparvaṇi rājadharmeṣu bhīṣmastavarājaḥ saṃpūrṇaḥ .. ratna ..3..* (UPenn 2462, f. 22r–22v)

The term confirms the status of the hymn as a work independent of the *Mahābhārata* that belongs to a set of works called "jewels."

The *Anusmṛti*

Our collection includes seven manuscripts that contain a text called the *Anusmṛti.* The core of the work is a mantra to Kṛṣṇa given by Nārāyaṇa in answer to Nārada's question of what one ought to recite at the moment of death in order to obtain liberation, but the main substance of the work is a hundred verses in praise of Viṣṇu sung by Nārada. The manuscripts in our collection agree in framing the dialogue between Nārada and Viṣṇu within a dialogue in which Śatānīka first poses the question to Śaunaka, and in placing the text within the *Mahābhārata.* Yet the final rubric of only one mentions its context simply as the *Mahābhārata.* The final rubrics of three manuscripts place the *Anusmṛti* in the *Viṣṇudharmottara* as well as in the *Mahābhārata,* for example Ms. Indic 5.

> (9) *iti śrīmahābhārate śatasahasrasaṃhitā!yaṃ!<yāṃ> vaiyāsikyāṃ viṣṇudharmottareṣu anusmrti!ṃ ..!<ḥ> samā!ptaḥ!<ptā>* .. (Ms. Indic 5, f. 205v)

The final rubric of one other manuscript places the text in the *Anuśāsanaparvan* and also in the *Viṣṇudharmottara,*

> (10) *iti śrīmahābhārate śatasahasrasaṃhitāyāṃ vaiyā!śa!<si>kyāṃ anu!sā!<śā> sanike dāna!dhamau!<dharme> vi!ṣṇu!<ṣṇo>r anusmrtistotra<ṃ> saṃpūrṇa!ṃ!m* (UPenn 2666)

and the final rubrics of the two remaining manuscripts place it in the *Śāntiparvan* and also in the *Viṣṇudharmottara.*

> (11) *iti śrīmahābhārate śāṃtiparvaṇi śatasahasrasaṃhitāyāṃ viṣṇudharmot<t>are anusmṛti<ḥ> saṃpū!rṇa!<rṇā>* (UPenn 2496)

Yet this work is not included in the text of the Pune critical edition of the *Mahābhārata,* nor in the *Viṣṇudharmottara Purāṇa.*[12] A similar passage, though with significant differences, which likewise calls itself the *Anusmṛti,* is included.[13] There the dialogue between Nārada and Nārāyaṇa is framed within a dialogue in which Yudhiṣṭhira first poses the question to Bhīṣma. The Kumbhakonam edition of the *Mahābhārata* and Vādirāja's commentary include the dialogue, but it is not supported by the manuscripts.

There is little doubt that the *Anusmṛti* was originally an independent composition later inserted into the *Śāntiparvan.* The fact that the editors of the Pune critical edition of the *Mahābhārata* relegate the *Anusmṛti* to an appendix and do not include it in the established text indicates that they considered it to be an independent work. The placing of a dialogue within a different locutionary frame is a characteristic sign of oral transmission and a sign that the text was orally transmitted independently. The placing of a text in different parvans in the *Mahābhārata* is a signal that it does not properly belong in either but was an independent text inserted in both. Yet not only is there evidence that the *Anusmṛti* has status as a work independent of the *Mahābhārata;* the final rubric of UPenn 2388 designates the work by the term *ratna* 4.

> (12) . . . *iti śrīmahābhārate śa<ta>sahasrasaṃhitāyāṃ vaiyyāsikyāṃ śāṃtiparvaṇi viṣṇudharmottare śauna!kā!kaśatā!ni!<nī>kasaṃvāde viṣṇunoktā vedānusmṛtiḥ saṃpū!rṇaṃ!<rṇā>* .. .. *ratna* ..4.. (UPenn 2388)

The term affirms that the text belongs to a set of works called jewels.

The *Gajendramokṣaṇa*

Our collection includes seven manuscripts that contain a text called the *Gajendramokṣaṇa*. The *Gajendramokṣaṇa* is a narrative that tells of an elephant herd leader whose leg has been caught in the jaws of a crocodile. After struggling to free himself in vain, he recognizes that his fate is due to bad karma, and composes verses in praise of Viṣṇu to change the balance. Viṣṇu descends, slays the crocodile, and frees the elephant. The crocodile, it turns out, is an incarnation of the Gandharva Hūhū cursed by the divine sage Devala for insulting his acuity in musical judgment. In some versions, such as UPenn 2491, the elephant is an incarnation of the Gandharva Hāhā. The narrative is framed by a dialogue in which Śatānīka asks Śaunaka how to destroy bad dreams since they instigate corresponding karmic results. Śaunaka responds in verse 5,

> (13) *idam eva mahābhāga pṛṣṭavāṃś ca pitāmahaṃ bhīṣmaṃ dharmabhṛtāṃ reṣṭhaṃ dharmaputro yudhiṣṭhiraḥ* ..5.. (UPenn 0488, v. 5, f. 2r)
>
> Yudhiṣṭhira, O fortunate one, asked his grandfather Bhīṣma, the best of those supporting dharma, the very same question.

Verse five claims that the text narrates what Bhīṣma told Yudhiṣṭhira, and the final rubrics of all five complete manuscripts (UPenn 0488 and Ms. Indic 5 are missing the end) agree in placing the text in the *Śāntiparvan* of the *Mahābhārata*. For example,

> (14) *iti śrīmanmahābhārate śatasahasrasaṃhitāyāṃ vaiyyāsikyāṃ śāṃtiparvaṇi śaunakaśatānīkasaṃvāde gajeṃdramokṣaṇastavaḥ saṃpūrṇaḥ* .. *ratne* ..5.. *samāpto yaṃ paṃcaratnaḥ* .. (UPenn 2487, f. 29r)

The claim of verse five itself, however, intimates exactly the opposite, namely, that the work is not part of the *Śāntiparvan.* If it were, Bhīṣma would simply narrate; the frame removes the story to an independent context. There are several other indications that the story is an independent work: (1) Verse 22 (UPenn Indic 5, v. 22, f. 212v–213r) introduces the narrative proper as an ancient *itihāsa* (*itihāsaṃ purātanaṃ*). (2) The text is not included either in the text established in the Pune edition or in its critical apparatus. (3) A variant of the episode narrated by Bādarāyaṇi to Parikṣit is told in *Bhāgavatapurāṇa* 8.2–4 and summarized by Vettam Mani.[14] (4) The episode was published as an independent treatise in 1914.[15]

It is clear that the *Gajendramokṣaṇa* is not part of the *Mahābhārata* but is an independent composition which itself makes the claim to have a prior narration in the great epic. The final rubric of UPenn 2487 (14 end) calls the *Gajendramokṣaṇa* the fifth *ratna,* indicating the inclusion of the work as an independent treatise in a set of so-called jewels.

The Five Jewels (*Pañcaratna*)

Correlation of the hands by which the manuscripts of the five works discussed were copied likewise testifies to the fact that they belonged together in a set. Sections 5–7 have shown that the final rubrics of UPenn 2462, 2388, and 2487 (8, 12, 14) designate the three works *Bhīṣmastavarāja, Anusmṛti,* and *Gajendramokṣaṇa* by the terms *ratna* 3, *ratna* 4, and *ratna* 5, respectively. These three manuscripts were copied by the same scribe (15). Several other manuscripts containing these works were similarly written by the same scribe. Hence UPenn 490, 489, and 488, containing the *Bhīṣmastavarāja,* the *Anusmṛti,* and the *Gajendramokṣaṇa* respectively, were written by a single hand, as were UPenn 2445 and 2491 containing the *Anusmṛti* and *Gajendramokṣaṇa,* and UPenn 2334, 2476, and 2475 containing the *Viṣṇusahasranāmastotra,* the *Bhīṣmastavarāja,* and the *Anusmṛti,* respectively. Likewise, UPenn 773, 2639, and 2563 contain two copies of the *Bhagavadgītā* and one of the *Bhīṣmastavarāja,* respectively, written in beautiful calligraphy by the same hand. Finally, the same scribe is responsible for the production of U. Penn. Ms. Indic 5, which contains all five works in beautiful calligraphy with appropriate illustrations.

(15) Manuscripts Grouped by Scribe

UPenn 0490 *Bhīṣmastavarāja*
UPenn 0489 *Anusmṛti*
UPenn 0488 *Gajendramokṣaṇa*

UPenn 2462 *Bhīṣmastavarāja*
UPenn 2388 *Anusmṛti*
UPenn 2487 *Gajendramokṣaṇa*

UPenn 2445 *Anusmṛti*
UPenn 2491 *Gajendramokṣaṇa*

UPenn 2334 *Viṣṇusahasranāmastotra*
UPenn 2476 *Bhīṣmastavarāja*
UPenn 2475 *Anusmṛti*

UPenn 0773 *Bhagavadgītā* (same hand as Ms. Indic 5)
UPenn 2639 *Bhagavadgītā* (same hand as Ms. Indic 5)
UPenn 2563 *Bhīṣmastavarāja* (same hand as Ms. Indic 5)

Ms. Indic 5 *Bhagavadgītā*
Ms. Indic 5 *Viṣṇusahasranāmastotra*
Ms. Indic 5 *Bhīṣmastavarāja*
Ms. Indic 5 *Anusmṛti*
Ms. Indic 5 *Gajendramokṣaṇa*

The final verses that are slight variants of each other in four manuscripts of the *Gajendramokṣaṇa* (UPenn 2486, v. 162, f. 21r–21v; UPenn 2487, v. 159, f. 29r; UPenn 2654, v. 161, f. 14v; UPenn 2664, v. 160, f. 15r) explicitly call these five works the "five jewels" (*pañcaratna*). The most correct, verse 160 in UPenn 2664, states:

(16) *gītā sahasranāmaiva stavarājo hy anusmrtiḥ ..*
gajeṃdramokṣaṇaṃ caiva paṃca ratnāni bhārate ..60.. (UPenn 2664, v. 160, f. 15r)

The *Bhagavadgītā*, *Viṣṇusahasranāman*, *Bhīṣmastavarāja*, *Anusmṛti*, and *Gajendramokṣaṇa* are the five jewels (*pañca ratna*) in the *Mahābhārata*.

Conclusion

Contrary to the fact that the verse that refers to the five works discussed above as the "five jewels" places them "in the *Mahābhārata*" (*bhārate*), these five works do not belong in the great epic. They are independent works, separate from the epic, that were transmitted together in a thematic anthology called the five jewels (*pañcaratna*). The editors of the critical edition of the *Mahābhārata* have taken different views toward the inclusion of these five works in the edition, no doubt justified by the presence and absence of each in the long manuscripts of complete parvans used to establish the text of the edition. The first three works are included in the established text, the fourth is included in Appendix I, and the last is not included at all. While the inclusion of all five in the devotional *pañcaratna* anthology does not contradict the results of manuscript correlation that established the text of the critical edition, it certainly establishes that these works have a history independent of the epic. Because manuscripts date back at most several hundred years, the critical edition based upon them can testify to the composition of the epic only so far back. The evidence of the status of the five jewels as separate from the epic, presented in this paper, raises suspicion that the sort of blatantly false claim of their inclusion in the epic made by the *Gajendramokṣaṇa* is quite widespread.

The transmission of these minor treatises independent of the epic, and independent of any major purāṇa, reaffirms the generally accepted view of modern scholarship concerning the composition of purāṇas, which Ludo Rocher aptly summarizes: "[E]veryone agrees that, to a large extent, purāṇas are made up of originally independent pieces."[16] Indeed the *Gajendramokṣaṇa,* the fifth jewel, epitomizes what Rocher calls "mini-purāṇas." Yet in contrast to the consistency of opinion regarding the purāṇas, opinion is divided concerning the composition of the epics, where much contemporary scholarship, including that of several prominent European and American scholars, resists applying a similar view to the *Mahābhārata.* The transmission of the other four jewels in a manner similar to the fifth, however, corroborates just such a view: it is very likely that the *Anusmṛti,* the *Bhīṣmastavarāja,* the *Viṣṇusahasranāman,* and even the *Bhagavadgītā* constitute independent treatises that have been incorporated into the great epic.

Notes

1 Ludo Rocher, *The Purāṇaṣ,* in Jan Gonda, ed., *A History of Indian Literature, Epics and Sanskrit Religious Literature* (Wiesbaden: O. Harrassowitz, 1986), vol. II, fasc. 3, p. 95.

2 V. Raghavan, K. Kunjunni Raja, N. Veezhinathan, E. R. Ramabai, and Siniruddha Dash, eds., *New Catalogus Catalogorum: An Alphabetical Register of Sanskrit and Allied Works and Authors* (Madras: University of Madras, 1949, 2014), pp. 46–48.

3 V. Raghavan, et al., eds., *New Catalogus Catalogorum,* p. 47b, Bhandarkar Oriental Research Insititue (BORI) 192(v) of 1887–1891; BORI. D. XIII.iii, 964.

4 *The Bhagavad Gītā, or, The Song Divine* (Gorakhpur: Gītā Press, 2004).

5 Vishnu S. Sukthankar, et al., eds., *The Mahābhārata,* 19 vols. (Pune: Bhandarkar Oriental Research Institute, 1933–1959).

6 Sukthankar, et al., eds., *The Mahābhārata,* vol. 7, pp. lxii–lxiii, lxxxv.

[7] Sukthankar, et al., eds., *The Mahābhārata,* vol. 7, p. 114.

[8] Sukthankar, et al., eds., *The Mahābhārata,* vol. 7, p. lxvii.

[9] Sukthankar, et al., eds., *The Mahābhārata,* vol. 17, Part I, p. xliii.

[10] Sukthankar, et al., eds., *The Mahābhārata,* vol. 18, p. clxxxvi.

[11] Sukthankar, et al., eds., *The Mahābhārata,* vol. 18, p. iii.

[12] Nag Sharan Singh, *Śrīviṣṇudarmottarapurāṇam* (*The Viṣṇudharmottarapurāṇam*) (Delhi: Nag Publishers, 1998).

[13] Sukthankar, et al., eds., *The Mahābhārata,* vol. 12, Appendix I, No. 17B, lines 1–171.

[14] Vettam Mani, *Purāṇic Encyclopedia* (Delhi: Motilal Banarsidass, 1975): pp. 328–329.

[15] *Gajendramokṣa,* 20-page booklet. (Bombay: Nirṇayasāgara Press, 1914).

[16] Rocher, *The Purāṇaṣ,* p. 95.

References

Bhagavad Gītā, or, The Song Divine, The. Gorakhpur: Gītā Press, 2004.

Gajendramokṣa, 20-page booklet. Bombay: Nirṇayasāgara Press, 1914.

Mani, Vettam. *Purāṇic Encyclopedia.* Delhi: Motilal Banarsidass, 1975.

Poleman, H. I. *Census of Indic Manuscripts in the United States and Canada.* New Haven, CT: American Oriental Society, 1938.

Raghavan, V., K. Kunjunni Raja, N. Veezhinathan, E. R. Ramabai, and Siniruddha Dash, eds. *New Catalogus Catalogorum: An Alphabetical Register of Sanskrit and Allied Works and Authors.* Madras University Sanskrit Series no. 18, 26, 28–35, 37–62. Madras: University of Madras, 1949, 2014.

Rocher, Ludo. *The Purāṇaṣ,* in Jan Gonda, ed., *A History of Indian Literature, Epics and Sanskrit Religious Literature,* vol. II, fasc. 3. Wiesbaden: O. Harrassowitz, 1986.

Singh, Nag Sharan. *Śrīviṣṇudarmottarapurāṇam* (*The Viṣṇudharmottarapurāṇam*). Delhi: Nag Publishers, 1998.

Sukthankar, Vishnu S., et al., eds. *The Mahābhārata,* 19 vols, Pune: Bhandarkar Oriental Research Institute, 1933–1959.

What Did Arjuna Want to Know?

Arvind Sharma
McGill University

I

The *Bhagavadgītā* is written in the form of a dialogue between Kṛṣṇa and Arjuna. Our point of entry into this dialogue is represented by the question: Why are the two engaged in conversation? In other words, what are the interlocutors talking about, and what, if anything, are they trying to talk each other into doing?

Their respective reasons for engaging in and then continuing a dialogue, which virtually lasts for two hours of (mundane) time, soon become apparent. Kṛṣṇa's interest in the dialogue consists of overcoming Arjuna's disinclination to engage in combat. Arjuna's interest also becomes apparent from his questions that fuel the dialogue: How can he be saved from the sin of killing, which will ensue should he continue the fight? The dialogue continues until the two parties' interests are resolved to their mutual satisfaction.

Simple as it seems, this setting has an important bearing on our understanding of the text. Kṛṣṇa's goal is to persuade Arjuna to fight and Arjuna's goal is to be saved—which, it turns out, is precisely what Kṛṣṇa finally promises, whereupon Arjuna is persuaded to resume the fight. If these respective dialogical goals are kept in mind, I argue that our understanding of the *Bhagavadgītā* becomes clearer. Before we look at the *Bhagavadgītā* from our own or anyone else's point of view, let us first look at it from the point of view of its protagonists, Kṛṣṇa and Arjuna. I begin by looking at it from Arjuna's point of view.

It is usually the case that one ends a presentation by offering the conclusion. In this case, however, I will depart from this convention and begin by placing the conclusion first, and then follow up with a discussion of the considerations that led me to it. There is, of course, the danger of placing the cart before the horse here. I draw comfort from the fact that on uphill climbs the train is sometimes placed before the engine.

II

What does Arjuna want to know? In the context of the *Bhagavadgītā*, gaining two kinds of knowledge seem to make particular sense, and these two kinds of knowledge may be formulated as answers to two kinds of putative questions: (1) What is truth? and (2) Will I be saved? In other words, from a philosophical standpoint, I distinguish between ontological truth and soteriological truth; between veridical knowledge and salvific knowledge. There is a difference between the two. Knowing that water is comprised of the molecules H_20 is one kind of knowledge; knowing that potable water can be found in yonder oasis in a burning and trackless desert is another kind of knowledge. If we may call the first kind of knowledge the knowledge of truth (for its own sake) and the second kind of knowledge is the knowledge of salvation, then I conclude that the kind of knowledge Arjuna seeks is not that of truth but of salvation. Kṛṣṇa, meanwhile, is working on the assumption that the "truth shall set you free." If Kṛṣṇa tells Arjuna the truth, he will be freed from sin. But Arjuna is suspicious of the intervening variable of truth. He is looking for certainty, not truth; he seeks the certainty, rather than the truth, of being saved.

III

My discussion in this paper hinges on this point, that what Arjuna seeks is not truth but salvation. The evidence that may be adduced in support of this seems to me to be fairly clear-cut. As the *Bhagavadgītā* begins, Arjuna casts down his bow and arrow, overcome with grief and fear of the sin he would incur by slaying his kinsmen. Nevertheless, he is ready to wage war as soon as Kṛṣṇa assures him, "I shall free you from all sins, do not grieve" (XVIII.66). Thereupon the *Bhagavadgītā* ends.

There is a difference between a seeker of salvation and a seeker of truth. The difference may seem slight at first glance, but closer inspection reveals a world of difference. As a seeker of salvation one must be free from sin, either because he or she is a paragon of virtue and is thus intrinsically free from sin; or, if a devotee, he or she has been freed from it. In this sense, a seeker of salvation must be free of sin, while a seeker of truth must be free of ignorance, not necessarily of sin. He or she must be free from any trace of ignorance about himself, the universe, and the

Real, and of the true relationship obtaining among them. He or she must be free of deception, either self-deception or of being deceived by the world, or in it, or into it. The truth can save, of course, but it can also damn, as happened famously in the case of Adam and Eve. We do not, of course, know whether there is some reality out there or in here, but we do know that the search for it is real enough. Arjuna is not searching for freedom from ignorance, however, but for freedom from sin.

The role of Kṛṣṇa, in relation to Arjuna, must be reassessed in light of this distinction. Kṛṣṇa has to rouse Arjuna to fight. Even when Kṛṣṇa claims to reveal the truth about himself, as in chapter XI, when he puts the universe in fast-forward and shows himself on the screen, as it were, he never loses sight of this fact. In the midst of that theophany—sometimes manifesting a martial cacophony, sometimes a celestial symphony—his calm didactic voice never wavers: "Stand up and dispatch your enemies whom I have already accounted for" (XI.33). The message is again clear. As Kṛṣṇa has already accounted for them, the act of killing his enemies cannot taint Arjuna. Arjuna, however, is still not persuaded. Maybe he had the same problem with divine grace experienced by all of us mortals—that it fluctuates. Not for another seven chapters is the problem of the alternating current generated by God's electrifying self-disclosure resolved.

The fact that Arjuna's concern is salvation but Kṛṣṇa's concern is to persuade him to fight has pivotal significance for understanding the text. It means that we cannot quite take Kṛṣṇa at his word, not in the sense that he may not be telling the truth but in another sense: that the fact that he expresses some opinions does not necessarily mean that he holds or endorses them. What is crucial is not that Kṛṣṇa holds these opinions but that they gain a hold on Arjuna's mind. For instance, when Kṛṣṇa says that even a little Dharma goes a long way, this may be in the same spirit as the modern idea of "Do what you like, and money will follow." What we are not told, and what we may not hear from the person who tells "to do as we like" and stay on that course, is that "If you do what you like money follows—but not in large amounts!"

I do not want to put Kṛṣṇa in the dock here. He has already been accused of being a warmonger by superficial readers of the *Bhagavadgītā;* with this, I fear he might be branded as a liar to boot. The point is that if we keep in mind the purpose for which a statement is made, it may be false in a technical sense and yet potent in a soteriological way. Would anyone be accused of lying if he were to see a child wandering off into the path of an oncoming car and, in order to save the child's life, makes the child rush toward him with the promise of offering him a chocolate he claims to have his closed fist, when in fact there is no chocolate? It is a helpful insight to share at this point, though perhaps only tangentially relevant, that the goal of both factual and fictional writing is to present truth in some form. The fact that fiction can be a source of truth may serve to prevent a glib dismissal of the point I am making here: that a statement may not be "true" and yet still be "right."

When Arjuna does not heed Kṛṣṇa's call to shake off his despair and rise up and fight like a man, Kṛṣṇa's discourse takes another trajectory in the second chapter of the Gītā. The paradox is that while truth may or may not be convincing, what we find convincing we naturally also assume to be true. It is to this shade of truth that Arjuna is led by Kṛṣṇa, not the truth for which truthseekers will sacrifice their lives. In any case, the problem faced by Arjuna is not one of giving up one's life (he has already expressed willingness to give up his own life) but that of taking others' lives. Ironically, everyone has his or her own agenda in life, and all will invariably die—as Kṛṣṇa reminds Arjuna, while everyone is on death's agenda, death is not on anybody's. It can also be pointed out that while no one might wish to kill, everyone is actually killing all the time, for in the very process of living (eating and consuming), many forms of life are unavoidably destroyed. Life feeds on life, as the saying goes. In view of this fact, it is indeed surprising that this argument is never adduced by Kṛṣṇa to induce Arjuna to fight on.

For a long time nothing from Kṛṣṇa's arsenal quite seems to hit the target. Nothing seems to work. Arjuna remains immobile and Kṛṣṇa's efforts seem like an exercise in navel-gazing. He tells Arjuna that temptation poses a greater threat to the accomplishment of a goal than opposition. In this case, the "temptation" to which he refers is Arjuna's temptation to throw in the towel. Even the glorious descriptions of the "accomplished person" (*sthitaprajña*) elicit further questions from Arjuna rather than his immediate emulation of the archetype. Kṛṣṇa's attempt at positive pop psychology, that what we say about who we are is invariably tinged with the hue of what we would rather be—in Arjuna's case, a *kṣatriya*—does not click. Arjuna is not stirred by Kṛṣṇa's appeal that as a born warrior he should resume the struggle. Kṛṣṇa's appeal, neither to the god in us nor to the god among us—nor the god in between us—ultimately works. Arjuna is still, as it were, looking for the god between him and Kṛṣṇa. Kṛṣṇa even attempts reverse psychology in his description of the poised person who treats success and failure, the "two impostors," as just the same. But this also does not work, even when Arjuna is told that success creates the temporary illusion that we are not like other people, only then to discover that we are!

From another perspective, in modern terminology, the task the *Bhagavadgītā* sets up for itself is to "deconstruct" our everyday notion of action and to try to demonstrate that no matter how one deconstructs it—theistically, nontheistically, transtheistically, naturally, immanently, transcendentally, and so on—our normal way of acting in life causes such actions to become overlaid with ego, and it is this egocentricity that converts ordinary action into karma, thereby insinuating us into the process of samsara.

Some consider it scandalous that Kṛṣṇa does not address the question of violent action that Arjuna finds so unsettling; what Kṛṣṇa finds troubling and has difficulty getting Arjuna to see is that the problem that Arjuna specifies with one form of action is generic to all action. Inasmuch as philosophy consists of seeing any single issue as a specific example of a more general problem, it may be said that Kṛṣṇa attempts a philosophical resolution of Arjuna's personal dilemma. The sense that when my personal mortality—the fact that I die—is transformed into a larger issue the moment I realize that "all human beings are mortal," my fear of personal mortality then releases its hold on me. I see my life as a wave on the surface of an ocean and am thereby released from the clutches of my individual terror.

This philosophical approach also founders. Taken to its extreme, it is like telling a person who is suffering in the world and in need of salvation that the world is merely *māyā,* illusion (and thus, one's suffering is also illusory), or going a step further, saying that even this apparently suffering world is after all grounded in Brahman. This is tantamount to telling a drowning person that the water contains oxygen within it, in fact, it is a constituent element of water (H_2O) itself. The point is that the drowning person is in no position to access the oxygen, to benefit from it, when floundering in the water. Or we could go a step further and say that to be told in such a situation that the world, and therefore all one's worldly suffering, is an illusion is like being told by a quantum physicist, while one is being tortured on the rack, that the iron of the rack is at a subatomic level not a solid substance at all but full of holes and empty spaces. That vision of reality, while not incorrect, is not relevant to the person's present condition.

When we return to Arjuna's present condition we realize that he is in need not of truth but insight—the insight that the spiritual quest, however sublime, cannot be a substitute for performing one's martial duty once war has commenced. The performance of one's duty (dharma) might appear ridiculous to Arjuna, due to its inherent contradictions, which he so clearly identifies in the course of the first chapter—but is not life itself riddled with such contradictions?

To sum up: Arjuna's search is the search for salvation; what he wants to know is: Will I be saved? He declines to fight as soon as his awareness of the sin associated with it (and, for him, association is causation) arises, and he resumes fighting as soon as he is assured of being delivered from the karmic results of that sinful action. By the same token, if Arjuna's search is a search for salvation, then Kṛṣṇa's message is one of action. Kṛṣṇa imparts that message as soon as Arjuna decides to desist from action, and he continues to instruct Arjuna through every convolution of his questioning until the moment Arjuna declares that he is ready to fight. As soon as Arjuna vows to resume fighting, Kṛṣṇa is ready to stop talking—but not until then.

These two points lead to a third and slightly different point. Kṛṣṇa offers to free Arjuna of sin, presumably because he is God and/or Arjuna believes him to be so. But you and I may not believe in God or in a god beyond God. In other words, we may find neither *bhaktiyoga* nor *jñanayoga* compelling. While *bhaktiyoga* sufficed for Arjuna, it may not suffice for us. However, we may or may not know God—personal or impersonal—but we do and can perform actions. In other words, Kṛṣṇa's message of action is more universal in scope that Arjuna's concern for salvation. We can all heed Kṛṣṇa's message without necessarily sharing Arjuna's need.

Why Perform Vedic Sacrifice in the Twenty-first Century? Notes on Recent Vedic Ephemera

Frederick M. Smith
University of Iowa

Introduction[1]

It is easy to repeat the observation that the dwindling numbers of Vedic ritualists who perform *śrauta* sacrifices do so out of a sense of cultural preservation or maintenance (or revival) of family and community tradition, while clinging to the notion that through an invisible force (*apūrva,* or, more presently, *adṛṣṭa*) their performances enhance or positively influence their lives and the lives of their communities. To whatever extent this is socially, politically, or ontologically true (or believed to be true), I would like to add a few further observations, based on notes and queries that have grown out of more than thirty-five years of "Vedic fieldwork," during which I have had extensive contact with *śrauta* ritualists in Maharashtra, Gujarat, Madhya Pradesh, Karnataka, Andhra Pradesh, and Kerala. Some of the viewpoints of these ritualists are predictable, and predictably "traditional" in ways that I will elaborate. But their reflections on topics critical to their lives and practices are unexpectedly broad and perhaps surprisingly modern, ranging from issues of authenticity and self-actualization to notions of cosmogonic reality, divine inspiration, worldly rectification, science real and imagined, social responsibility, and the enactment of *vidhi* or injunction inspired by an esoteric, and therefore empowering, understanding of the Vedas.

A cursory glance at the history of Indology reveals that Western and Western-trained scholars have been deeply suspicious, and often hastily dismissive, of modern Vedic education and ritualism. While it has received serious attention in the last few decades, most of this attention has been in the spirit of investigating an antiquarian enterprise (even though it has morphed into something decidedly and incomprehensibly modern). The early Indological suspicion resulting from religious and cultural bias, clothed as intellectual bias, has been replaced with positivist presuppositions that leave little room for serious consideration of the viewpoints and logic of classical exegetical and ritual texts, which up to the present have continued to influence śrauta ritualists more strongly than Western positivism. For this reason, the motivations of modern ritualists—and the contemporary local literature, ephemeral though it is, through which these are often presented—have barely entered the realm of scholarly analysis.[2] The issue, however, is not so simple as extracting a few standard ideas from Vedic or Purāṇic textuality and ascribing them to modern ritualists. It is more complex than this, to a great extent because the present era of multicultural and crosscultural influence leaves no area of "traditional" Indic activity and thought isolated or unaffected. Jason Fuller describes the indistinct boundaries between the traditional and the modern in Hinduism:

> When we identify rationalism, reform, social engagement, and the politicisation of religion as constitutively modern, we threaten to relegate other forms of Hinduism that emphasize non-rationalism, revival, social withdrawal, and political apathy to the realms of something variously referred to as "traditional" or the "pre-modern," The problem with any such categorisation of religious phenomena in the modern period is that it overlooks the fact that both traditional and modernist thinkers ("reformers" and "revivalists" alike) developed their ideas within a shared discursive and socioeconomic context.[3]

With this caveat, then, we must take seriously the claims and rationale of contemporary Vedic "traditionalism" in theorizing about the socioreligious praxis of modern ritualists, which is almost never as "traditional" as they might assert (or advertise). In doing so, we must distinguish this traditionalism within (and from) its political trappings, and try to determine what may be of lasting value for it (as well as for us).

We may ask a number of questions in addition to raising the issues noted above, aware that in the brief space of this essay I will be unable to do more than point toward a few answers. How, for example, do modern ritualists, including the comparatively passive (and by no means exclusively elitist) corps of patrons who perform or have the sacrifices performed for them, view their religious objectives and responsibilities? How do they view their social objectives and responsibilities? What forms of social responsibility and caste relations do they objectivize? How has the authority accorded to brahmans stood the tests of modernity? Have the various pressures of modernity that have induced them to behave in a more socially inclusive manner dented this traditional stance? There may be as many answers to all these questions as there are Vedic ritualists and patrons.

Have the rituals become unrecognizably compromised as a result of this modernity, or have the adaptations and accommodations to modern social and political realities, and a decidedly middle-class Hindu ethos[4] allowed the rituals to survive in a manner that reflects approximately the same quality and quanta of change that may be found in other historical periods? Do today's Vedic ritual forms follow, consciously or otherwise, the creative impulse of the Arya Samaj and other reformist groups in the late nineteenth century to both simplify the rituals and esotericize them? Finally, and most important for our present purposes, how are these questions addressed in ephemeral, disposable literature produced by these ritualists for public consumption at the time of the performance of *śrauta* sacrifices?

These are only some of the questions that may be asked of the modern performances of Vedic ritual. Following in the footsteps of Nārada in the *Sabhāparvan* of the *Mahābhārata,* who asks at least a hundred questions to Vaiśaṃpāyana on the responsibilities of kingship, very few of which are directly answered (MBh 2.5.8–114), it is not my intention to answer all of these questions here, only to suggest that they might be relevant to the central concerns of this essay.

I will deal here—again, all too briefly—with two models of Vedic ritualism in the late twentieth and early twenty-first centuries. First, I will look at some of the cultural practices of three śrautins of modern Maharashtra who have performed a large number of complicated soma sacrifices, as well as at the ephemera produced by them. Second, I will look at three śrautins of the Puṣṭimārga, a sect of Kṛṣṇa devotion primarily found in western India (Gujarat, Rajasthan, Mumbai), the rationale they resort to for their performances, and the literary ephemera they have produced. For the latter, it will be helpful to examine a revealing precedent from the sixteenth century in the form of a fragment of a Vedic commentary. What will be seen here are examples of how this literary ephemera augments performance, how even the most seemingly innocuous material is qualitatively interpretative and commentarial, and how the pressures of modernization have influenced modern ritual thinking. As several of the articles in the second volume of Frits Staal's *Agni: The Vedic Ritual of the Fire Altar*[5] demonstrated more than thirty years ago, many of the innovations and reinterpretations found today may be labeled modern, but are not at all abnormal or in any way ritually disfiguring in a tradition that has been stable for millennia because of its dynamism.[6]

The Contemporary Culture of *Śrauta* Ritual in Maharashtra

In an earlier paper[7] I dealt with the topic of *śrauta* ritual in Maharashtra, discussing current trends and the performance histories of recent *śrautins*. Here I would like to add to what I wrote in that article, addressing my concerns to the issues cited above. The most prominent *āhitāgnis* of the last thirty-five years in Maharashtra were Nārāyaṇ Govind (Nānā) Kāḷe of Barsi (Solapur Dist., b. 1932), Raṅganāth Kṛṣṇa Selūkar of Gangakhed (Parbhani Dist., d. 2002), and Mahādev Viṣṇu (Nānā) Atre of Solapur (1911–1994). These three *āhitāgnis* have performed a large number of *soma* sacrifices, of which many, perhaps even most, could be characterized as exotic even by the standards of *śrauta* ritual. For the performance of these rituals, these men of relatively modest means required large endowments.

Among them, the wealthiest and most independent is Śrī Kāḷe, the owner of a fairly large tract of productive farmland a few kilometers from Barsi. Although all three were thorough and methodical in their dedication to the performance of śrauta ritual, Śrī Kāḷe was the only one with his own Vedic memory school (*pāṭhaśālā*), in which he also instructed his students in all aspects of Vedic ritual.[8] He has thus been able to draw increasingly on his own students for officiating duties, including three his sons, who have studied different Vedic texts, one the *Ṛgveda,* one the Taittirīya texts of the *Yajurveda,* and the third the Rāṇāyaṇīya branch of the *Sāmaveda.* By keeping the performances very much under his control, and with less need to appeal to outside sources for funding, Śrī Kāḷe has been able to perform his *somayāgas* with *pratyakṣapaśu,* or offerings of "actual animal" parts rather than ghee substitutes, as was the practice of Śrī Selūkar and Śrī Atre.[9]

These three *āhitāgnis* produced items of ritual ephemera with every major sacrifice they performed. In addition to performance manuals (*prayogas*) produced by the late *paṇḍit* Viśvanāth Śrauti of Nellore for Śrī Atre and Śrī Selūkar, including, for example, *prayogas* for an *ātreya-catūrātra* for Śrī Atre[10] and a *gavāmayana* for Śrī Selūkar.[11] I will here present two *nimantraṇa-patras*, letters of invitation, to different *somayāgas*. The first is an invitation distributed by Śrī Atre in 1985 to attend a *mahāvrata,* a complicated sacrifice containing much of interest, including music, lewd dialogue, and sexuality; the lewd dialogue was toned down and the sexuality was thoroughly ritualized, which means it was not enacted at all—a young married couple sat on a bench brought into the ritual arena and repeated the Sanskrit dialogue, which they did not understand, at the prompting of the *adhvaryu*, or chief priest.

The *mahāvrata* probably originated as a seasonal festival that was integrated with a *soma* sacrifice.[12] It was performed in Bhopal in May 1985 as a purificatory ritual in the wake of the lethal Union Carbide gas leak on December 4, 1984, which killed thousands of local residents and injured probably tens of thousands of others. The ideological frame for this was drawn from Śrī Atre's guru, Gajanan Maharaj of Akkalkot (about 35 kilometers from Śrī Atre's home in Solapur), who was responsible for promulgating an abbreviated *"laukika"* performance of the Vedic *agnihotra* to ordinary, noninitiated, nonbrahman householders, untrained in Sanskrit, of any ethnic or class background, in part because he alleged that it eliminated toxins and pollutants from the atmosphere.[13] The *nimantraṇa-patra*, which has pages in Hindi, Marathi, and English, reads:

> *kṣetre 'smin pālite bhoje janādaivāt kilādhunā /*
> *pīḍitā viṣavātena dhyāyo hy atra sadāśivaḥ /*
> *taṃ devaṃ ca mahādevaṃ mahāvratena toṣaye /*
> *yajñena tārkṣyarūpena svasti me 'stu sadā bhuvi //*

> "Mahavrata Maha Somayaga" in Bhopal.
> This region, the kingdom of great king Bhoja, had the misfortune of facing a serious calamity. Today the people are troubled and are suffering because of the air which is polluted by poisonous gases. Now, as a redress, we shall perform here a great yajnya. This yajnya is an antidote to the poisonous gases. This great Somayaga will heal the atmosphere. Let this Somayaga do good to all of us wherever we are on the face of this planet.
>
> This "Mahavrata Maha Somayaga" is being performed on the Supreme Command of Parama Sadguru by Yajamana Shri Mahadev Vishnu Atre Somayajee for the welfare of the gas stricken people and also for the benefit of the whole world.
>
> It is decided to perform the Yajnya at the Madhav Ashram, Sehore Road, Bairagarh, Bhopal, in the immediate and distinguished presence of Parama Sadguru Shri Gajanan Maharaj (Shivapuri, Akkalkot, Maharashtra) from May 15 to May 20, 1985—Vaisakha Krishna Ekadasi Wednesday to Pratipada Monday, Uttara Praushtpada Nakshatra in the Jyeshta month of Shri Krodhanam year.
>
> The Maha Yajnya will be held according to Srouta method for the welfare of the world and for the removal of the sufferings of the people.

> We request all devotees to extend their cooperation by timely participation and deserve to receive the blessings of Yajnya Narayana.

The invitation does not mention the Bhopal gas leak except in the Sanskrit verse at the beginning, which states that Śiva should be propitiated by this *mahāvrata* sacrifice because poison gas has afflicted the city that, because of the good fortune of its people, has earned the protection of King Bhoja. Both the invitation and the sacrifice were thus embedded in the local political and religious context in several ways: (1) They offered a uniquely "Indian" solution to a catastrophe inflicted by the excesses of Westernization (though, to be fair, the *yajña* as a political countermeasure was underplayed in favor of the message of *yajña* as a spiritual and environmental corrective to these excesses).[14] (2) The blessings of the *yajamāna*'s guru, Gajanan Maharaj of Akkalkot, were declared paramount in bringing about the goals of the sacrifice. (3) The deities Śiva and Yajñanārāyaṇa were invoked. This conferred on the sacrifice a link with local religious culture. In all likelihood no one in Bhopal had ever witnessed a Vedic *soma* sacrifice. (4) The invitation appealed to Hindu ethical sensibilities in declaring that *śrauta* ritual was effective in "the removal of the sufferings of the peoples." (5) Identifying the sacrifice's commencement on an auspicious day (*tithi*) and under an auspicious lunar asterism (*nakṣatra*) further contextualized it in the realm of Hindu ritual. Thus, the *mahāvrata* could be identified as an auspicious and special ritual performance that should be supported.

The next example is an invitation by Śrī Selūkar in April 1983, in mixed Sanskrit and Marathi, to an "Aptoryāma Somayāga Mahāyajña" performed in Beed, a midsize industrial town in Parbhani district. The sacrifice was a *dvisāhasracayana* with *sarvastoma,* meaning that it was a double *agnicayana,* with ten layers of bricks rather than five, featuring the chanting of a large number of *sāman*s. First, Śrī Selūkar, the putative author of the invitation, announces that due to the grace of the supreme Lord (*parameśvarasya paramayā kṛpayā*) he has decided to perform an *aptoryāma yāga.* He supplies the date or commencement (*caitra śukla dvitīyā śake* 1905 *śukravār*) and the location. He continues:

> [T]he supreme Lord, the enjoyer of sacrifices (*yajñabhoktā*), having become satisfied by our sacrificial performance (*yajñānuṣṭhānena*), will bestow on us wealth and enlightenment (*abhyudaya-niḥśreyasaḥ*), as well as the grace that allows us to realize the highest goals of life (*paramapuruṣārthasiddhiḥ*).

Śrī Selūkar explains that according to the correct Vedic viewpoint (*iti vaidikadharmasya siddhāntaḥ*) *yajña* is a *pūjā* to Agni and Sūrya, the two great deities who consist of brilliance (*tejas*). The mantras and invocation of Agni reach Sūrya, and through him are relayed to Sūryanārāyaṇa or Viṣṇu in the form of the sun. From Sūryanārāyaṇa, the mantras and invocations reach all the gods. Finally, the highest deity internal to all, the deity responsible for *sat-chid-ānanda* (being-consciousness-bliss) is satisfied. This is verified by a "well-known Smṛti," which says that an offering properly made to Agni will approach Sūrya, who then gives birth to rain, after which rain becomes food and food becomes offspring (*agnau prāstāhūtiḥ samyag ādityam upatiṣṭhate / adityāj jāyate vṛṣṭiḥ vṛṣṭer annaṃ tataḥ prajā //*).

Śrī Selūkar explains that the gods themselves obtain their character (*devatvam*) and divinity (*divyatvam*) through the sacrifices. He states that Lord Rāmacandra demonstrated through his protection of Viśvāmitra's sacrifice that the institution of Vedic ritual should be supported by *dakṣiṇā,* fees paid by the patron to the ritualists. Furthermore, Bhagavān Gopālakṛṣṇa performed his sacred duty by removing the dirty vessels of the *brāhmaṇa*s at the time of the Rājasūya of the Pāṇḍavas.

The institution of sacrifice, says Śrī Selūkar, has been propagated by the Veda for the complete development of man. But today this has been forgotten. Everyone should agree that man once enjoyed the happiness of divinity through the observance of these Vedic rituals. He goes on to say that life today can definitely be nourished and protected by the performance of these great sacrifices. Just as only one's own cherishing mother can protect her children and wish them greatness and prosperity, similarly only "Vedamātā" has the ability to confer on all people the capacity for divinity. On the greatness of the Veda, Jñāneśvara sings the following:

> *pai ahitā pāsonī kāḍhitī / hit deūnī vādhavītī /*
> *nāhī śrutīparautī / māūlī yā jagī /* (*Jñāneśvarī* 16.459)
>
> There is no mother like the Vedas who takes away the bad and lets the good flourish.[15]

It then announces that Śrī Raṅganāth Kṛṣṇa Selūkar will perform the Aptoryāma Somayāga in Beed from 4/4/1983 to 15/4/1983 with this religious ideal in mind.

The leaflet continues, explaining that the principal offering to Agni in this *yāga* is the juice of the plant called *soma.* Thus, we have the well-known name "Somayāga." The leaflet then notes that

> great authorities on the *yajñakarmakāṇḍa* from all over India and the West, including America, Germany, and other Western countries (*pāścātyadeśāt*)

> will be coming. Also coming will be great priests, brahmans, Vedic scholars, experts in *Mīmāṃsāśāstra,* lecturers, *kīrtankārs*, devotees, observers of dharma, and others with great spiritual experience (*mahānubhāvāḥ*). They will come from major pilgrim centers, including Kashi, Gokarna, Kurukshetra, Madras, Prayag, Pandharpur, Nasik, and Tryambakeshvar. They will all be gathering according to Vedic injunction in order to contribute and share their knowledge as well as to perform the sacrifice, lecture, and sing religious songs.

The leaflet then states, "this Mahāyajña is undertaken with the cooperation of the great dharma abiding people of India," and that "the following great *vidvān*s will be coming:

(1) *adhvaryu*—Vedamūrti Viśvanāth Śrautī and his learned co-workers from Nellore.

(2) *hotā*—Vedamūrti Keśavaśāstrī Jogḷekar and other officiants from Gokarṇa.

(3) *sāmagāna*—Vedamūrti Naṭarāj Ghanapāṭhī and his learned co-workers from Madras.

(4) Vedamūrti Nārāyaṇa Śāstrī Bhānose and a few other officiants from Nasik.

(5) Pradhānavacanakāra (featured lecturer)—Vedamūrti Paṇḍita Yudhiṣṭhira Mīmāṃsaka from Bahālgaḍh, Sonīpat (Haryāṇā).

(6) Pradhānapravacanakāra—Svāmī Satyaprakāśa Sarasvatī from Allahabad.

(7) Pravacanakāra—Vedamūrti Narendra Brahmacārī of the Ārya Sāmaj.

The leaflet concludes formally: "You are hereby invited to assist in serving and awakening Dharma by gathering for this *yajña.*"[16]

This attractive announcement conveys the same messages to the target audience of prospective donors that we saw in Śrī Atre's *mahāvrata* invitation.[17] Invoking the statement from the "well-known Smṛti," Śrī Selūkar assents to the message that Vedic ritual is of benefit to the environment. This message is not Gajanan Maharaj's alone but is often found elsewhere India as well.[18] The addition of the names of some of the best-known Vedic families in the area was also undoubtedly attractive to a few potential donors. The name of the elderly Yudhiṣṭhira Mīmāṃsaka, perhaps the best-known Vedic scholar of his time within the Arya Samaj, might have also contributed to the cachét of the performance.[19] What is missing from these announcements, and which would have been less appealing, are explanations of the mechanics of *śrauta* ritual, although many of the dozens of announcements I have collected over the years do in fact have daily schedules of ritual events.[20]

Puṣṭimārgī *Śrauta* Ritual

Three Puṣṭimārga *ācārya*s who have taken up the *śrauta* fires in the last thirty-five years have produced some of the most extensive ritual ephemera I have encountered. These *āhitāgni*s include the following: Gosvāmī Raṇchoḍācārya Mahāhāj of Kota (1930–1989), otherwise known as Prathameśjī, because he was the lineage holder of the first (*prathama*) house of the seven Puṣṭimārga houses or lineages, making him one of the most important and influential members of the Vallabh *sampradāya*. He was the first member of this sect of Kṛṣṇa devotion to set the Vedic fires (he performed his *agnyādhāna* in 1979) in more than two centuries, reviving the practice of *śrauta* ritual in the *sampradāya*. Indeed, Vallabhācārya himself (1479–1531?) descended from a family of Tailāṅga *somayājins*, and the first few generations of his descendants were *āhitāgnis*. The second modern Puṣṭimārgī *ācārya* to set the Vedic fires was Gosvāmī Vallabharāyjī of Surat (a lineage holder in the sixth house, headquartered in Surat), who performed his *agnyādhāna* in 1984 on the inspiration of Prathameśjī. The third was Gosvāmī Gokulotsavajī Mahārāj of Indore (a lineage holder of the second house), who performed his *agnyādhāna* in 1991. All three have performed the *vājapeya,* and both Prathameśjī and Gokulotsavajī have performed the *agnicayana.*

All of their ritual performances were, until the early 2000s, under the direction of Agnihotram Ramanuja Tatachariar (1907–2009)[21] of Chennai, primarily because he is a Vaiṣṇava (though he is known to have offered *pratyakṣapaśu* himself), but also because he followed the ritual of the Āpastamba *śākhā* of the Taittirīya rescension of the *Kṛṣṇayajurveda,* the same *śākhā* followed by Vallabhācārya and his descendants. Vaiṣṇava theology, rather than reflection on the mechanics of Vedic ritual, is most vividly profiled in the Vedic writings—and indeed in the Vedic performances—of these Puṣṭimārgī *āhitāgnis*.[22] This is not, however, as modern an innovation as might be thought, as we shall see.

While the ephemera examined above do not address the issue of nonviolence and animal sacrifice, this was always a major issue, as mentioned, and it has certainly been crucial for the *śrautins* of Maharashtra.[23] Indeed, for more than 800 years, since Rāmānuja (twelfth century C.E.) and Madhvācārya (1238–1317 C.E.), it has been the single issue that has sequestered Vaiṣṇava *śrautins* from others. More recently, however, Śrī Selūkar and Śrī Atre, both non-Vaiṣṇavas, vehemently opposed it, under the influence of Gajanan Maharaj, who asserted that it was never a part of "original" Vedic sacrifice,[24] while Śrī Kaḷe, who was initially inspired by Śrī Selūkar, has strongly advocated it since 1994.[25] Some of the more extensive ephemeral literature addresses this issue, though it is not usually present in leaflets or letters of invitation.

The *śrautin*s of the Puṣṭimārga, *ācārya*s in the highest positions of authority in their sect, are Vaiṣṇavas with a long history of adherence to the strictest rules of personal purity, vegetarian cooking, and opposition to animal sacrifice.[26] This is not neglected by the three late–twentieth-century Puṣṭimārgī *śrautin*s, who have often supported their religious lifestyles as Vaiṣṇava *śrautin*s with devotional explications of Vedic statements such as "Viṣṇu is the sacrifice" (cf. *Śatapatha Br.* 5.2.3.6, *yo vai viṣṇuḥ sa yajñaḥ;* 5.4.5.1, *eṣa viṣṇur yajñaḥ*).

This position will be best illustrated if we reach back to the sixteenth century for an important precedent to this element of Puṣṭimārga sacrificial ideology. This precedent is drawn from the early literature of the Vallabha tradition.[27] In his commentary on Vallabhācārya's brief treatise called *Siddhāntamuktāvalī,* verses 17–19, Viṭṭhalnāthjī, the second son of Vallabhācārya, who is accorded virtually equal status in the Puṣṭimārga with his father, interprets at length *Ṛgveda* 1.156.3, a verse from a hymn to Viṣṇu by Dīrghatamas Aucathya:

> *tám u stotāraḥ pūrvyáṃ yáthā vidá ṛtásya gárbhaṃ janúṣā pipartana //*
> *asya janánto nāma cid vivaktana mahás te viṣṇo sumatiṃ bhajāmahe //*
>
> O singers, from your very birth you have satisfied him, the ancient source of cosmic order, to the best of your knowledge. You, understanding merely his name, have spoken it out. May we, O Viṣṇu, the mighty one, share in your benevolence.

Viṭṭhalnāthjī interprets this verse as demonstrating the superiority of the path of *bhakti* over the path of knowledge. His gloss on the first half of the verse (occasionally paraphrased) is as follows: "O singers, you speak of Him in the true sense of the term, which puts you on an equal footing with Him." He then puts the following in the mouth of the lord himself:

> You are dedicated to describing the greatness of me, the highest lord who is well known in the world and the Vedas, whose original form was the cause of everything (as the Lord who brought the *akṣarabrahman* into being), of me, the womb which has within it the Veda as the manifestation of true speech.

Viṭṭhalnāthjī changes registers here and adds his own thoughts: "You are describing this greatness right from your birth, O singers; it is your full time occupation. By always praising his glories you have satisfied him."

The subcommentator on this work, Puruṣottama (1657 or 1668 to 1725), the greatest and most learned commentator on Vallabha's work, explains that when the Lord is in a state of *ātmarati,* an undistracted condition of enjoyment prior to manifestation and prior to time and space, the Veda remains within him. Indeed, during the period of cosmic dissolution the Veda remained within Kṛṣṇa's belly. His authority for this statement is the *Bhāgavata Purāṇa* (11.14.3; also 11.21.42–3).

Viṭṭhalnāthjī now interjects his own thoughts on this *śruti.* The singers referred to here are called *yathā vida* bcause they know Puruṣottama, the Supreme Lord, in his true form, which is to say they are complete knowers of the Veda. The *śruti* is telling these sages of pure knowledge that because they are born for this purpose they should understand that their bodies, external sense organs, breath, internal sensory organ (*antaḥkaraṇa*), and their very lives must be dedicated to worshiping and satisfying the lord alone. The *śruti* itself thus enjoins these sages to enter the path of *bhakti.* In this way, the fruitfulness of knowledge is in devotion to the lord. Keeping this in one's heart, says Viṭṭhalnāthjī, one should understand that in the second part of this śruti the lord in the form of the Veda addresses those who are incapable of offering their bodies, senses, etc., to the Lord.

Viṭṭhalnāthjī continues:

> Fully comprehending that divine speech (*śabdabrahman*) is name, know that the Lord exists in two aspects: name and embodied form (*mūrtisvarūpa*). Though you may merely understand the name, and not yet have realization of the form of the Lord, you should at least recite the names of the lord, which are the very form of divine speech. You should thus speak those names that are alone relevant. *Śruti* is requesting that even if one does not know much about the lord's greatness and other supreme qualities of beauty, omniscience, etc., one should at least recite His name. In this way, knowledge of the supreme qualities of the lord's form will arise. The name thus develops into the form. The name, which embodies *saccidānanda,* indicates this. Beyond this, if knowing the complete body of divine speech is impossible, then simply utter the names of the lord without singing entire vedic hymns. If one cannot even master this, then the śruti instructs one to find a guru and at least gain a nodding familiarity with the idea and form of brahman. We should know that the form of the guru is free of shortcomings and full of great attributes. Let us know, O Viṣṇu, that the guru is your own form and allow us to enter the service of the guru knowing him as your own form. By his divine aura (*svatejasā*), the guru destroys the ignorance of others.

In this way, Viṭṭhalnathjī has intellectually valorized and made ritually relevant the Vedic utterance of Dīrghatamas Aucathya by conferring on it a sectarian reading.[28]

Now, let us turn back to the late twentieth century. As elucidated by Gokulotsavajī, following one of the other Puṣṭimārgī *āhitāgnis*, Gosvāmī Vallabharāyjī, the understanding of Vedic ritual is first derived from the *Pūrvamīmāṃsā*, because it is from there that the doctrines of heaven (*svarga*) as the goal of the rituals and the eternality and *apauruṣeyatva* of the Veda are systematized. Then, extrapolating from Vallabhācārya's *Śuddhādvaita*, *svarga* is recognized as a Vedic expression of divine bliss (*ātmasukha*) and the Veda and Vedic ritual are identified as the *akṣarabrahman*, the eternal body of Kṛṣṇa.[29] Thus, through this progression of theological resonances, the performance of Vedic ritual is reclaimed as *sevā*, divine service, to the supreme Lord.

I should mention here another sixteenth-century interpretation. K. Kunjunni Raja notes in his article "Sanskrit and Malayalam References from Kerala"[30] that Melputtūr Nārāyaṇa Bhaṭṭa, the early sixteenth-century author of the well-known *Malayalam Nārāyaṇīyam*, states in his *Rājasūyaprabandha* that the bricks called *yaśodā*, "fame-giver," in the *agnicayana* are symbolic of Yaśodā, the foster mother of Kṛṣṇa.

I have in my possession a forty-four page pamphlet (unpaginated) in Hindi entitled *Somayajña Mahotsava*, which is an excellent example of Indian religious literary ephemera.[31] It was issued on the occasion of an *agnicayana* performed by Prathameśjī and contains a six-page spirited defense (unsigned, but apparently by him) of the performance of *somayāgas*. This is preceded by twenty pages containing hymns by Vallabhācārya and Viṭṭhalnāthjī that are well known in the Puṣṭimārga. The intent of the booklet appears to have been to provide casual viewers of the *agnicayana* with new copies of these well-known hymns, along with Prathameśjī's brief tract on Vedic ritual, as bonus reading.

I also have in my collection a fifty-page commemorative magazine in Gujarati and Hindi (with a large number of advertisements in English), entitled *Śrī Virāṭ Somayajña Mahotsav Smaraṇikā*,[32] released on the occasion of a *vājapeya* performed by Gokulotsavajī Mahārāj in New York City in July 2000.[33] The magazine contains a number of short articles, including a brief biography of Gokulotsavajī (who, besides being a *śrautin* and a descendant of Vallabhācārya, is one of India's best-known *dhrūpad* vocalists, with many CDs to his credit) and an article on the history of *soma* sacrifice ("Somayajñano Itihās" by Bhāratī Rājeś Śāh), which argues for its consistency with recitation of sacred texts, that it is an ancient expression of well-known and commonly practiced dharma, and is the revelation of Yajñanārāyaṇa. The magazine also includes a brief article by Gosvāmī Śrī Śyām Manoharjī from Mumbai ("Kumbhparv evaṃ Somyāg"), currently the best-known Sanskrit pandit in the Puṣṭimārga, arguing that Vallabhācārya himself has accepted Vedic ritual as a legitimate practice with a history in the *sampradāya;* two relatively lengthy unsigned articles giving general points of Vallabhācārya's teachings drawn from verses in his *Ṣoḍaśagranthāḥ;*[34] and an unsigned article entitled "Why Perform *Soma* Sacrifice?" ("Somayajña kyā hai").

A few points argued in this last article are: (1) that *somayajña* is the highest form of Indian culture; (2) that Śrī Kṛṣṇa in the *Gītā* states that *soma* is the essence of all mood (*rasa*); (3) that the statement from the *Taittirīya Upaniṣad* (2.7), *raso vai saḥ, rasaṃ hy evāyaṃ labdhvānandī bhavati* ("this is indeed rasa; having obtained that *rasa,* one becomes filled with bliss") must be interpreted as a Vedic argument for identifying Kṛṣṇa with both the essence of sacrifice and the highest state of *bhakti,* which the commentators on Vallabhācārya's work recognize as a *rasa;* (4) that in the *Sarvottamastotra,* an oft-recited Puṣṭimārga hymn listing the names of Vallabhācārya, he is given the designations *yajñabhoktā* ("enjoyer of sacrifice") and *yajñakartā* ("performer of sacrifice"). Thus, Gokulotsavajī Mahārāj is depicted as an exemplar in the Puṣṭimārga: he manifests the highest realms of Indian culture and realizes the highest states of *bhakti* through the same Vedic means that Vallabhācārya himself practiced 500 years ago. The *somayajña,* then, should be supported by good *bhakta*s, who are directed to revere other good *bhakta*s whenever possible.[35]

The Art of Sacrifice

Let us look briefly at the artwork that adorns the covers of three examples of ritual ephemera: the invitation to Śrī Selūkar's *aptoryāma* in Beed in 1983 (Fig. 1); the invitation to Śrī Selūkar's *trisāhasracayana* (construction of a fifteen-layered *agnicayana* consisting of 3,000 bricks, 200 for each layer), also performed in Beed, April–May 1986 (Fig. 2); and the cover of the souvenir magazine for Gokulotsavajī Mahārāj's New York City *vājapeya,* performed in July 2000 (Fig. 3). The full-color cover of the latter is strikingly different from that of the former, expressing differences in the ritual outlooks of the Puṣṭimārgi and the Maharashtrian *śrautin*s. The front of the *aptoryāma* invitation is replete with Vedic images, including the five fires and *vedi* employed by *śrautin*s of the Kātyāyana *śākhā* to

Fig. 1. Invitation to the *aptoryāma soma* sacrifice in Beed, Maharashtra, 1983.

which Śrī Selūkar belonged, a banner reminiscent of a renunciant's staff, and a sunburst with the syllable *oṃ* inscribed on them; Sanskrit mantras border these images on all sides, in a similar manner to that found on *yantra*s. The souvenir magazine issued on the occasion of Gokulotsavajī Mahārāj's New York *vājapeya* has a small picture of Gokulotsavajī in the upper left, next to the Gujarati title, while the greatest amount of space depicts the baby Kṛṣṇa on the right, flute in hand, looking up, and on the left Vallabhācārya emerging translucently from a three-tiered sacrificial fire, surrounded by leaping flames. This harks back to his birth and death narratives, both celebrations of fire that hold great mythic power in the Puṣṭimārga.

Vallabhācārya's birth, the story goes, was prophesied by Viṣṇu himself, who emerged from the fire altar of Vallabha's distant ancestor, Yajñanārāyaṇa Dīkṣita, a Tailāṅga brahman from Andhra Pradesh. Viṣṇu informed Yajñanārāyaṇa Dīkṣita that he, Viṣṇu himself, would take birth in his family once he and his descendants had performed a hundred *soma* sacrifices. Eventually Lakṣmaṇa Bhaṭṭa, five generations later and well settled in Varanasi, performed the hundredth *soma* sacrifice. Shortly thereafter, Lakṣmaṇa Bhaṭṭa and his pregnant wife Illamagāru were forced to flee Kāśī in the wake of rumors of invading Muslims. In the weariness of their flight back to their ancestral home in Andhra Pradesh, Illamagāru, in the Champa forest in Raipur district of present-day Madhya Pradesh, gave birth prematurely to a son, apparently stillborn,

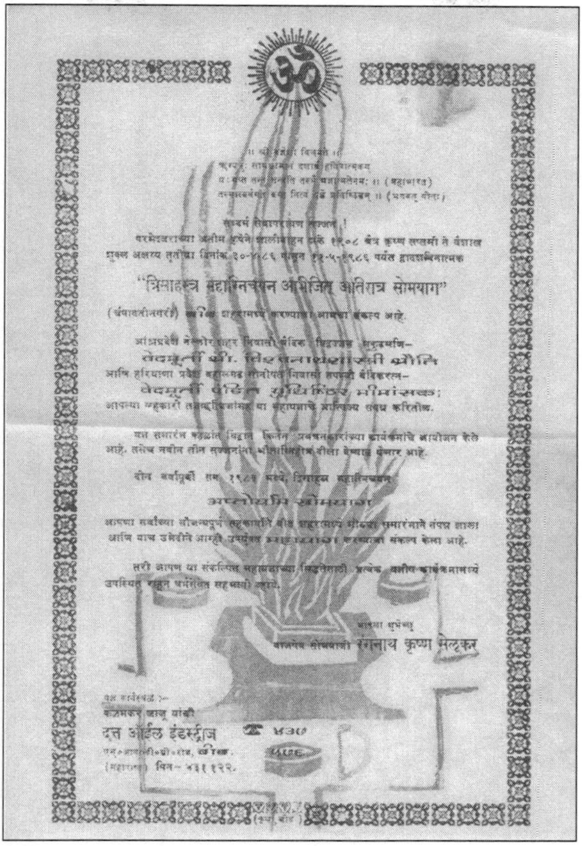

Fig. 2. Invitation to the *trisāhasracayana* in Beed, 1986.

on the eleventh day of the dark half of the month of Vaiśākha. The couple wrapped the child in cloth and left him in the hollow of a *śami* tree before continuing on their journey. The next morning, however, in response to a dream, Illamagāru led her husband back to the site of the delivery and there discovered a newborn babe cheerfully playing, encircled by flames, with a halo around his head.

The tale of Vallabhācārya's death was equally important to the significance of ritual fire. Soon after his *saṃnyāsa* initiation, probably in the year 1531, Vallabhācārya set out for Varanasi, and after an eighteen-day journey he arrived and settled into a hut on Hanumān Ghāṭ, where he sat in undistracted contemplation for a week. His family and followers knew that his days were numbered, that he clearly intended to leave this world; nevertheless, they respected his desire for solitude. After a final written exhortation to his disciples to maintain their devotion to Kṛṣṇa, Vallabhācārya rose from his seat and entered the Ganges, singing to himself the *Gopīgīta* (*Bhāgavata Pur.* 10.21) and the *Yugalagīta* (*Bhāgavata Pur.* 10.35), which express separation and union with the lord, respectively. Then, as he gazed transfixed as if beholding the lord, a flame arose from the waters in the form of the lord and swept Vallabhācārya away forever. The miraculous event was witnessed by several thousand people.[36]

Fig. 3. Cover of the booklet introducing the *vājapeya* performed in New York, 2000.

Conclusions and Comments

The central concerns of the nearly extinct *śrauta* communities are, first, the survival of *śrauta* ritual, and second, the authenticity of the ritual, which, we have seen, varies according to the religious ideologies of the ritualists. I have dealt with this question of authenticity and its tryst with romanticization in an earlier essay[37] and cannot deal further with that issue here. In general, however, I can reassert that whether or not compromise, adaptation, or innovation undermines and eventually destroys the fabric or "authenticity" of the Vedic traditions or merely distributes their legitimacy differently is very much a matter of debate.

The knowledge of these ritualists is so vast, precise, contextualized, and difficult to sustain that almost no one outside the *vaidika* communities would want to undertake their mastery, or would be able to do so even if they desired. In most cases, the textual and performative knowledge of śrauta ritual, including context-sensitive knowledge that is transmitted along with it, such as gestures, preservation practices, strategies of textual organization, and so on, can be comprehended only by a few highly trained members of these communities. Thus, these traditions can, in the end, only be directed toward a few individuals within these communities. This renders the practice of this traditional knowledge incomprehensible or meaningless outside of these small groups.[38]

The production and practice of this knowledge is not just religious but social as well. In this way, Vedic ritual is multivalent: it is the repository of a number of levels of meaning. Thus, introducing it to the outside world is fraught with danger, from promises of intercaste or extra-community inclusion that are practically impossible to fulfill, to fears of dissipation of the knowledge, to guardedness against destruction of personal purity. Increasingly, I find that the ritualists are not opposed to the idea of brahmanical power breaking down, though family and community loyalty require that most of them maintain to some extent both the ritual and the business of ritual. The few cases we have briefly examined here bear out the range of options and choices open to modern-day Vedic ritualists, and the dangers inherent in them.

Śrauta ritual has always possessed a certain quanta of cultural cachét. This is already clear in the early and middle Vedic literature. Both the Vedic literature and the late first-millennium B.C.E. or early first-millennium C.E. Sanskrit epics demonstrate handily that *śrauta* ritualists, whether brahman or *kṣatriya,* were widely revered. Brahmans in the epics are almost always depicted as performing sacrifices, and the sacrifice provided an array of tropes on which the epics were constructed. It is likely, however, that even in the first millennium B.C.E., *śrauta* ritualists were a tiny, if visible and recognizable, segment of a general population that was itself unimaginably small by today's standards. In the *Brāhmaṇa* texts, the epics, and elsewhere in Indic literature, the *śrauta* rituals were romanticized disproportionately to the actuality and possibility of their performance. This legacy of romanticizing, of manipulating the cachét of *śrauta* ritual, continues up to the present, as we have seen.

This is not to say that *śrautin*s of two or three past millennia were not sincere in their beliefs and practices, just as today's *śrautin*s are sincere—indeed, they are disarmingly sincere in their view that these rituals are beneficial not only to the sacrificer as a means of bringing about material prosperity and spiritual fulfillment (see above: *abhyudaya-niḥśreyasaḥ*) but are also "a powerful means of promoting social solidarity and progress."[39] It is clear from the materials examined above that this same sentiment exists today.

The study of Vedic ritual has advanced considerably in the last thirty-five years. Among the themes that emerge from these studies is the intimate link between performance and preservation: in spite of a stable initial level of textuality, the ritual was constantly modified, albeit subtly, due to both external pressures and internal reinterpretations. Among the external factors were geographical relocation or redistribution of the ritual communities, climactic and environmental change that forced substitutions in the materials of sacrifice, and accretions of sectarian ritual that emerged from the Purāṇic or Āgamic religion. Internally, modifications were due to the influence of other Vedic *śākhā*s, vague or elliptical *śruti* and *Śrautasūtra* passages that lent themselves to scholastic reinterpretation within a *śākhā,* and a growing reliance on epiphenomenal interpretation, such as that offered by the *Pūrvamīmāṃsā* or the *Bhāgavata Purāṇa.* A further item of significance is the loss in the consciousness of *yājñika*s throughout India of a sense of an "original meaning" of the sacrifice, which paved the way for epiphenomenal interpretations such as those of Viṭṭhalnāthjī on ṚV 1.156.3.

These, then, were the dynamic elements that effected subtle but important shifts in the astonishingly stable and durable institution of Vedic sacrifice. As anthropologists and ritual theorists Caroline Humphrey and James Laidlaw write: "Revisions always take the form of new theories about what the 'real' (original, ordained, authentic, divinely decreed, or 'reborn') nature of the act is."[40]

It is also important to recognize that the Vedic traditions shifted away from *śrauta* performance, as only a select few *vaidika*s who had memorized the *saṃhitā* texts actually performed the *śrauta* rituals. The great majority served as temple priests or performed domestic ritual, while a few others became *paṇḍita*s or Sanskrit teachers. Whereas the performance of rituals and the memorization of primary texts appear to have operated largely in tandem until approximately the fifth century B.C.E., after that date the production of Vedic knowledge became much more diffuse, inclusive of not only the preservation of primary texts and ritual performance but of ancillary matter such as *vedāṅga*s and systematic philosophy, which were increasingly turned over to specialists with schools of their own.

Before the twentieth century, modifications within the Vedic ritual traditions occurred inside the boundaries set by the traditions themselves. Few outside the elite circles of *śrauta* ritualists, not even other Sanskrit *paṇḍita*s, would have read *śrauta prayoga*s and *paddhati*s (though many other ritual *prayoga*s were read by others, including those describing various *pūjā*s and tantric rituals). Finally, when the old patronage systems consisting of local kings and brahman *agrahāram*s dried up, *śrautin*s were forced into a kind of commodification that ran counter to their history. This loss of historical status meant, essentially, opening up their knowledge, or at least some credible version of it, to the public. With the decline of the British Empire and the rise of India as an independent, modern, democratic country, cultural elites functioned almost entirely outside governmental (read: royal) agencies for the first time. Thus, patronage was for the first time sought largely from mercantile classes, which increasingly cut across caste boundaries. This shift in patronage of brahmanical Hinduism to the middle classes is addressed by Jason Fuller, John Stratton Hawley, and many others.[41] This pecuniary requirement is what has led to the ephemera that I have collected here.

I do not claim to have a complete, or perhaps even major, collection of this ephemera. My collection consists mostly of leaflets, posters, and small- to medium-sized booklets or magazines, such as the souvenir booklet put out at the time of the New York City *vājapeya*. Most of this material is too ephemeral or transient to warrant putting forth much effort to collect it in large quantities; indeed, most of it is designed to be disposable. Although such ephemera constitute valuable archival materials, they are not generated with a sense of posterity or permanence, as part of any religious or ritual canon. They are rather like advertisements for openings at art galleries; no one except the owner of the gallery, his or her mother, or an occasional art historian would be interested. That these materials were written in English and a number of regional languages, including Hindi, Gujarati, Marathi, Tamil, Telugu, and Malayalam, but rarely in Sanskrit (I have one example of an explanatory manual written in Marathi by Nānā Kāḷe that was then translated into Sanskrit), testifies to the fact that these materials were relegated to a position lower, which is to say, more distant from the Vedas, on the scale of sacred literature than performance manuals such as prayogas and *paddhati*s.

Nevertheless, as I hope to have shown here, a great deal can be learned from such ephemera about the ideologies of contemporary Vedic ritual performance, and much more still can be read into the performance of Vedic ritual historically if we can prudently connect this ephemera with earlier genres of ritual literature. In sum, the answers to the many questions asked at the beginning of this essay may be sought in a combined sociocultural and textual analysis of the Vedic ritual traditions—and there are important clues to this in some of the literature that is not usually studied, such as the ephemera addressed here.

Notes

1 A seed form of this essay was first presented in the Veda section of the World Sanskrit Conference in Helsinki in 2003. It is relevant to add now that my first encounter with a living performance of large-scale Vedic sacrificial ritual was in 1975, when, as an M.A. student at the Centre for Advanced Study

in Sanskrit at Poona University, I accompanied my eventual mentor, Dr. C. G. Kashikar, to Panjal, Kerala, to observe an *agnicayana* that had been largely organized by Frits Staal. Frits was magnanimous, charming, good-humored, urbane, fair, and genuinely inquisitive, even toward a young student whom he had never met. These *sadguṇa*s conferred on me a respect and admiration for Frits, and for his prodigious knowledge and far-reaching scholarship, that was foundational for a friendship that endured until his passing in 2012.

2 See, however, Frederick M. Smith, "Indra Goes West: Report on a Vedic Soma Sacrifice in London in July 1996," *History of Religions* 40/3 (2000): 247–267.

3 Jason Fuller, "Modern Hinduism and the Middle Class: Beyond Reform and Revival in the Historiography of Colonial India," *Journal of Hindu Studies* 2 (2009): 161.

4 Cf. Fuller, "Modern Hinduism and the Middle Class"; Timothy Lubin, "Science, Patriotism, and Mother Veda: Ritual Activism in Maharashtra," *International Journal of Hindu Studies* 5/3 (2001): 85–101; John Stratton Hawley, "Modern India and the Question of Middle-class Religion," *International Journal of Hindu Studies* 5/3 (2001): 217–225.

5 Frits Staal, ed., *Agni: The Vedic Ritual of the Fire Altar,* 2 vols. (Berkeley: Asian Humanities Press, 1983).

6 K. Balasubrahmanya Sastri, "Agnicayana in the Mīmāṃsā," in Frits Staal, ed., *Agni: The Vedic Ritual of the Fire Altar* (Berkeley: Asian Humanities Press, 1983), vol. 2, pp. 178–198; M. R. Raghava Varier, "The Nambudiri Ritual Tradition with Special Reference to the Kollengode Tradition," in Staal, ed., *Agni,* vol. 2, pp. 279–299; and J. C. Heesterman, "Other Folk's Fire," in Staal, ed., *Agni,* vol. 2, pp. 76–95, among many others, reveal a tradition in development and transformation.

7 Frederick M. Smith, "The Recent History of Vedic Ritual in Maharashtra," in Klaus Karttunen and Petteri Koskikallio, eds., *Vidyārṇavavadanam: Essays in Honour of Asko Parpola, Studia Orientalia* 94 (2001): 443–463.

8 Lubin mentions Selukar's attempts "to establish some durable institutions in Gangakhed that may continue after his death" ("Science, Patriotism, and Mother Veda," p. 97), but, except for a single disciple, Sudhākar Digaṃbar Kuḷkarṇī, who became an *āhitāghi* in Pune, no durable institutions have survived to the present date.

9 This is one of the most contentious issues among the ritualists of Maharashtra (and elsewhere in India); see Jan E. M Houben, "To Kill or Not to Kill the Sacrificial Animal (yajña-paśu)? Arguments and Perspectives in Brahmanical Ethical Philosophy," in Jan E. M. Houben and Karel R. van Kooij, eds., *Violence Denied: Violence, Non-Violence and the Rationalization of Violence in South Asian Cultural History* (Leiden, Boston, Köln: Brill, 1999), pp. 105–183; Jayashree Gune, "Paśu-sacrifice in the Sūtras," *Annals of the Bhandarkar Oriental Research Institute* 74 (1994): 153–167; Lubin, "Science, Patriotism, and Mother Veda."

10 Probably a modified *gosava,* cf. *Āpastamba Śrautasūtra* (ĀpŚS) 22.12.17, 13.1–3; for the *goṣṭoma,* see ĀpŚS 22.13.22.

[11] *Prayogas* for Śrī Selūkar were always problematic because he was a Mādhyandina Śuklayajurvedin following the Kātyāyana *śākhā* of ritual praxis, while the entire *ādhvaryava*, including Viśvanāth Śrautī, were Taittirīya Kṛṣṇayajurvedins belonging to the Āpastamba *śākhā*. Reconciling these in performance created nearly intractable problems that I cannot address here (but see my article "The Recent History of Vedic Ritual in Maharashtra"). For the *gavāmayana*, see Alfred Hillebrandt, *Ritual-Literatur. Vedische Opfer und Zauber* (Graz: Akademische Druck-u. Verlagsanstalt, 1981), p. 157.

[12] Cf., e.g., Alfred Hillebandt, *Vedic Mythology* (Delhi: Motilal Banarsidass, 1981), vol. II, p. 128.

[13] In this way he drew on the history of perpetuation of abbreviated Vedic ritual of Dayānanda Sarasvatī and the Arya Samaj. An organization set up by disciples of Gajanan Mararaj, Fivefold Path, has sponsored a good deal of meteorological research to prove this; http://www.agnihotra.org/content/what-fivefold-path, http://www.agnihotra.org/content/scientific-experiments-agnihotra. Like all science done in the service of Indian religion, however, this research was conducted by insiders whose scientific inquiry was prompted by their esoteric convictions. While this does not automatically invalidate the research, it, at least in part, predetermines the results. This calls for renewed and impartial research. Such scientific research has been questioned even within the larger community of Vedic ritualists, although not entirely on scientific grounds; see Lubin, "Science, Patriotism, and Mother Veda," p. 95. For an intelligent statement on scientific method, its presuppositions, and what kind of scientific research should and should not be profitably applied to Vedic studies, see Dominik Wujastyk, "Science and Vedic Studies," *Journal of Indian Philosophy* 26/4 (1998): 335–345.

[14] Neither Atre, the *yajamāna*, nor Gajanan Maharaj were involved in Hindutva politics.

[15] From Jñāneśvar's commentary on *Bhagavadgītā* 16.24 (*Jñāneśvarī* 16.462). See also the "rendering" by Swami Kripananda: "The Vedas protect us from evil and give us what is good. There is no mother in the world who is better than they are"; *Jnaneshwar's Gita* (Albany: State University of New York Press, 1989), p. 272.

[16] It should be mentioned here that no matter how well reasoned her suppositions might be, Meera Nanda's speculations in *The God Market: How Globalization is Making India More Hindu* (New York: Random House, 2009), pp. 82–86, regarding Selūkar's right-wing political involvement are incorrect. Selūkar was not interested in Hindutva but in his personal status as a spiritual teacher. His first large-scale sacrificial rituals were held in Nanded, in the early 1980s, in the shadow of the largest Sikh *gurudvāra* south of Delhi. Sikh leaders were present, and he honored them. He maintained decidedly amicable relations with other communities, including Muslims (although see Lubin, "Science, Patriotism, and Mother Veda," for ideologies that somewhat countered these).

[17] Both Atre and Selūkar occasionally experienced financial difficulties, going into substantial debt due to the expenses incurred in conducting the sacrifices.

I was present at one of Atre's *somayāgas* when he was unable to pay the proper *dakṣiṇā* at the *dakṣiṇādāna* rite during the afternoon before the *sūtya* day. The *ṛtviks*, led by Viśvanāth Śrautī, went on strike, in the form of a siesta, in the middle of the *yāgaśālā* until Atre could secure the promise of a bank loan from a friendly banker in Solapur a few hours later.

18 Note the following, from an invitation to an *agniṣṭoma* in Kerala in April 2003. P. Vinod Bhattathiripad, "Jt. Convenor & International Correspondant, Somayaagam 2003 Committee," writes:

> The word "Yaagam" in Kerala-context is the same as "Yajna" in other states. The attractions of the Somayaagam in Kerala is that all Rithwiks learn all manthras by heart and chanted in the traditional style, with Vedic accents like Udaatha, Anudaatha and Svarita as well as the special hand gestures ("Mudra") that accompany special features of Vedam recitation. This method of Vedic recitation is believed to release maximum positive energy for purifying the environment. It is well known that large quantity of fumes arising out of burnt ghee, seeds and vast quantity of appropriate herbals, cleanse the environment. . . . The goal of all Yaagams is the prosperity of the people at large by energizing and protecting the environment. The Sun is considered as the main source of energy supply, and fire is considered as a representation of the Sun's energy. According to the ancient texts on Yaagam, any offer to Fire as a god, is actually an offer to Sun. Any such offer is either to enrich energy in the environment or to destroy the undesirable elements in the environment, and thus, in both ways, environment is protected.

19 See Lubin, "Science, Patriotism, and Mother Veda," p. 89 ff.

20 These will appear in a future publication on Vedic ritual in the twentieth century that will bring together the tangible results of my fieldwork and field notes.

21 See Srilata Raman, "Tamil, Vaiṣṇava, Vaidika: Kiruṣṇacuvami Aiyaṅkār, Irāmānuja Tātācāriyār and Modern Tamil Literary History," *Journal of Indian Philosophy* 39 (2011): 647–676.

22 See Smith, "Indra Goes West."

23 Smith, "The Recent History of Vedic Ritual in Maharashtra"; Timothy Lubin, "Veda on Parade: Revivalist Ritual as Civic Spectacle," *Journal of the American Academy of Religion* 69/2 (2001): 377–408, and "Science, Patriotism, and Mother Veda."

24 Gune, "Paśu-sacrifice in the Sūtras"; Houben, "To Kill of Not to Kill the Sacrificial Animal (yajña-paśu)?"

25 Lubin, "Science, Patriotism, and Mother Veda."

26 Cf. Peter Bennett, *The Path of Grace: Social Organization and Temple Worship in a Vaishnava Sect* (Delhi: Hindustan Publishing Corporation, 1993), pp. 88 ff., 124–136.

27 Much of the following on this is adapted from Frederick M. Smith, "Dark Matter in Vārtāland: On the Enterprise of History in Early Puṣṭimārga Discourse," *Journal of Hindu Studies* 2/1 (2009): 30–31; see also Christopher Z. Minkowski, "Nīlakantha Caturdhara's Mantrakāśīkhaṇḍa," *Journal of the American Oriental Society* 122/2 (2002): 329–344, and "Nīlakaṇṭha Caturdhara and the Genre of Mantrarahasyaprakāśikā," in Y. Ikari, ed., *Proceedings of the Second International*

Vedic Workshop (Kyoto); accessed online at http://dsal.uchicago.edu/sanskrit/papers/index.htm.

28 Viṭṭhalnāthjī is not alone in this. Nīlakaṇṭha Caturdhara, in his *Mantrakāśīkhaṇḍa,* analyzes ṚV 1.122.14 along similar lines; see Minkowski, "Nīlakantha Caturdhara's Mantrakāśīkhaṇḍa" and "Nīlakaṇṭha Caturdhara and the Genre of Mantrarahasyaprakāśikā."

29 Cf. Go. Śrī Vallabharāyjī, *Vaiṣṇavbhāvpracūr vājapeya yāga (svarūp aur mahattva)* (Surat: Ṣaṣṭhī Pīṭh, 1989); *Somayāgkā śāstrīya paricay* (Surat: Ṣaṣṭhī Pīṭh,1983), esp. pp. 30 ff.

30 Cf. K. Kunjunni Raja, "Sanskrit and Malayalam References from Kerala," in Frits Staal, ed., *Agni: The Vedic Ritual of the Fire Altar* (Berkeley: Asian Humanities Press, 1983), vol. 2, p. 309.

31 *Somayajña Mahotsava* (Calcutta: Antarrāṣṭrīya Puṣṭimārgīya Vaiṣṇava Pariṣad, 1998).

32 *Śrī Virāṭ Somayajña Mahotsav Smaraṇikā* (New York: Shri Nidhi Universal, Inc., 2000).

33 For my remarks on Gokulotsavajī Mahārāj's *agniṣṭoma* performed in London in July 1996, see "Indra Goes West: Report on a Vedic Soma Sacrifice in London in July1996."

34 See, e.g., James D. Redington, *The Grace of Lord Krishna: The Sixteen Verse-Treatise (Ṣoḍaśagranthāḥ) of Vallabhacharya* (Delhi: Sri Satguru Publications, 2000); Frederick M. Smith, "Nirodha and the Nirodhalakṣaṇa of Vallabhācārya," *Journal of Indian Philosophy* 26/6 (1998): 589–651, and "The Hierarchy of Philosophical Systems according to Vallabhācārya," *Journal of Indian Philosophy* 33/4 (2005): 421–453.

35 That the *vājapeya* itself was riddled with insuperable problems is not the point here; I shall address this in a future publication. To the best of my knowledge no *śrauta* sacrifices have been attempted outside of India since then.

36 No single early account of Vallabhācārya's life is available from within the tradition. The usual sources are the comparatively recent Gujarati *Vallabhākhyān* by Gopāldas; the *Śrīvallabhadigvijaya,* a Sanskrit work by Yadunāthjī, one of Vallabhācārya's grandsons; and several works in Brajbhāṣā by various descendents of Vallabhācārya. These include the *Śrī Ācāryajī Mahāprabhun kī Nijvārtā Gharū Vārtā* by Harirāyjī, one of Vallabhācārya's great-grandsons, and the *Caurāsi Baiṭhak Caritra* by Gokulnāthjī, one of Vallabhācāya's grandsons.

37 Smith, "The Recent History of Vedic Ritual in Maharashtra"; see also Lubin, "Science, Patriotism, and Mother Veda," p. 98.

38 On how this specialization affects present-day audiences when provided with ritual choices, see Frederick M. Smith, "A Brief History of Indian Religious Ritual and Resource Consumption: Was there an Environmental Ethic?", *Asian Ethnology* 70/2 (2011): 163–180; Lubin, "Veda on Parade: Revivalist Ritual as Civic Spectacle."

39 R. N. Dandekar, *Śrautakoṣa,* Volume 1; English section, Part 1 (Poona: Vaidika Saṁśodhana Maṇḍala, 1958), p. 6.

40 Caroline Humphrey and James Laidlaw, *The Archetypal Actions of Ritual: A Theory of Ritual Illustrated by the Jain Rite of Worship* (Oxford: Clarendon Press, 1994), p. 157. More often than we would like to see, however, revisionism moves very far afield from the facts on the ground, not to speak of in the texts. See, for example, Kireet Joshi, *The Veda and Indian Culture* (New Delhi: Rashtriya Veda Vidya Pratishthan, 1991), which is no more than an introductory book that relies heavily on Aurobindo—indeed, it outright proselytizes for Aurobindo. Joshi favors the earliest conceivable or inconceivable dates for the Vedas, suggests the Age of Intuition as identifying the Vedic period, ending with the Age of Reason with the advent of the Buddha, etc. It is defensive and nationalistic, repeating the familiar claims of politically motivated neo-Hindus. It is not unimportant to note that for a few years in the 1990s Joshi was head of the Rashtriya Veda Vidya Pratishthan in New Delhi, a branch of the Ministry of Education.

41 Jason Fuller, "Modern Hinduism and the Middle Class"; Hawley, "Modern India and the Question of Middle-class Religion."

References

Bennett, Peter. *The Path of Grace: Social Organization and Temple Worship in a Vaishnava Sect.* Delhi: Hindustan Publishing Corporation, 1993.

Dandekar, R. N. *Śrautakoṣa,* Volume 1; English section, Part 1. Poona: Vaidika Saṁśodhana Maṇḍala, 1958.

Fuller, Jason. "Modern Hinduism and the Middle Class: Beyond Reform and Revival in the Historiography of Colonial India," *Journal of Hindu Studies* 2 (2009): 160–178.

Gune, Jayashree. "Paśu-sacrifice in the Sūtras," *Annals of the Bhandarkar Oriental Research Institute* 74 (1994): 153–167.

Hawley, John Stratton. "Modern India and the Question of Middle-class Religion," *International Journal of Hindu Studies* 5/3 (2001): 217–225.

Heesterman, J. C. "Other Folk's Fire," in Frits Staal, ed., *Agni: The Vedic Ritual of the Fire Altar* (Berkeley: Asian Humanities Press, 1983), vol. 2, pp. 76–95.

Hillebrandt, Alfred. Ritual-Literatur. *Vedische Opfer und Zauber.* Strassburg: Trübner, 1897; Graz: Akademische Druck-u. Verlagsanstalt, 1981, reprint.

—. *Vedic Mythology,* vol. II. S. Rajeswara Sarma, trans. Delhi: Motilal Banarsidass, 1981. Originally published in German, *Vedische Mythologie,* vol. II, second revised edition. Breslau: M. & H. Marcus, 1929.

Houben, Jan E. M. "To Kill of Not to Kill the Sacrificial Animal (yajña-paśu)? Arguments and Perspectives in Brahmanical Ethical Philosophy," in Jan E. M. Houben and Karel R. van Kooij, eds., *Violence Denied: Violence, Non-Violence and the Rationalization of Violence in South Asian Cultural History,* pp. 105–183. Leiden, Boston, Köln: Brill, 1999.

Humphrey, Caroline, and James Laidlaw. *The Archetypal Actions of Ritual: A Theory of Ritual Illustrated by the Jain Rite of Worship.* Oxford: Clarendon Press, 1994.

Joshi, Kireet. *The Veda and Indian Culture.* New Delhi: Rashtriya Veda Vidya Pratishthan, 1991.

Lubin, Timothy. "Science, Patriotism, and Mother Veda: Ritual Activism in Maharashtra," *International Journal of Hindu Studies* 5/3 (2001): 85–101.

—."Veda on Parade: Revivalist Ritual as Civic Spectacle," *Journal of the American Academy of Religion* 69/2 (2001): 377–408.

Kripananda, Swami. *Jnaneshwar's Gita.* Albany: State University of New York Press, 1989.

Minkowski, Christopher Z. "Nīlakaṇṭha Caturdhara and the Genre of Mantra-rahasyaprakāśikā," in Y. Ikari, ed., *Proceedings of the Second International Vedic Workshop* (Kyoto). Accessed online at http://dsal.uchicago.edu/sanskrit/papers/index.htm.

—."Nīlakantha Caturdhara's Mantrakāśīkhaṇḍa," *Journal of the American Oriental Society* 122/2 (2002): 329–44.

Nanda, Meera. *The God Market: How Globalization is Making India More Hindu.* New York: Random House, 2009.

Raja, K. Kunjunni. "Sanskrit and Malayalam References from Kerala," in Frits Staal, ed., *Agni: The Vedic Ritual of the Fire Altar,* vol. 2, pp. 300–310. Berkeley: Asian Humanities Press, 1983.

Raman, Srilata. "Tamil, Vaiṣṇava, Vaidika: Kiruṣṇacuvami Aiyaṅkār, Irāmānuja Tātācāriyār and Modern Tamil Literary History," *Journal of Indian Philosophy* 39 (2011): 647–676.

Redington, James D. *The Grace of Lord Krishna: The Sixteen Verse-Treatise (Ṣoḍaśagranthāḥ) of Vallabhacharya.* Delhi: Sri Satguru Publications, 2000.

Sastri, K. Balasubrahmanya. "Agnicayana in the Mīmāṃsā," in Frits Staal, ed., *Agni: The Vedic Ritual of the Fire Altar,* vol. 2, pp. 178–198. Berkeley: Asian Humanities Press, 1983.

Smith, Frederick M. "A Brief History of Indian Religious Ritual and Resource Consumption: Was there an Environmental Ethic?", *Asian Ethnology* 70/2 (2011): 163–180. Reprinted in Will Sweetman, ed., *Hinduism: Critical Concepts in Religious Studies,* vol. 3. New York: Routledge, 2014.

—."Dark Matter in Vārtāland: On the Enterprise of History in Early Puṣṭimārga Discourse," *Journal of Hindu Studies* 2/1 (2009): 27–47.

—."Indra Goes West: Report on a Vedic Soma Sacrifice in London in July1996," *History of Religions* 40/3 (2000): 247–267.

—."Nirodha and the Nirodhalakṣaṇa of Vallabhācārya," *Journal of Indian Philosophy* 26/6 (1998): 589–651.

—."The Hierarchy of Philosophical Systems according to Vallabhācārya," *Journal of Indian Philosophy* 33/4 (2005): 421–453.

—."The Recent History of Vedic Ritual in Maharashtra," in Klaus Karttunen and Petteri Koskikallio, eds., *Vidyārṇavavadanam. Essays in Honour of Asko Parpola, Studia Orientalia* 94 (2001): 443–463.

—.*The Vedic Sacrifice in Transition: A Translation and Study of the Trikāṇḍamaṇḍana of Bhāskara Miśra.* Poona: Bhandarkar Oriental Research Institute, 1987.

Somayajña Mahotsava. Calcutta: Antarrāṣṭrīya Puṣṭimārgīya Vaiṣṇava Pariṣad, 1998.

Śrī Virāṭ Somayajña Mahotsav Smaraṇikā. New York: Shri Nidhi Universal, Inc., 2000.

Staal, Frits, ed. *Agni: The Vedic Ritual of the Fire Altar*, 2 vols. Berkeley: Asian Humanities Press, 1983.

Vallabharāyjī, Go. *Śrī. Somayāgkā śāstrīya paricay*. Surat: Ṣaṣṭhī Pīṭh, 1983.

—. *Vaiṣṇavbhāvpracūr vājapeya yāga (svarūp aur mahattva)*. Surat: Ṣaṣṭhī Pīṭh, 1989.

Varier, M. R. Raghava. "The Nambudiri Ritual Tradition with Special Reference to the Kollengode Tradition," in Frits Staal, ed., *Agni: The Vedic Ritual of the Fire Altar*, vol. 2, pp. 279–299. Berkeley: Asian Humanities Press, 1983.

Wujastyk, Dominik. "Science and Vedic Studies," *Journal of Indian Philosophy* 26/4 (1998): 335–345.

Remembering Frits Staal

Romila Thapar
Jawaharlal Nehru University, New Delhi

I first met Frits Staal in the late 1950s at the School of Oriental and African Studies in London, where he was a Lecturer in Sanskrit. I was working on my Ph.D. and was in the Junior Common Room, where students took coffee breaks and caught up with gossip. We heard that Frits was planning to race around Kerala on a motorcycle making recordings of Vedic recitations by various families of Nambudiri brahmans, which in fact he did a couple of years later. Some thought that this was an unconventional way of conducting research, while others argued that it was innovative and, in any case, that the recitations needed to be recorded.

I next saw Frits fifteen years later, when he was teaching at the University of California, Berkeley. He was one of many impressive scholars who were gathered at Berkeley at that time to teach various aspects of Indian studies, and I got to know him as a friend. In 1974 I had spent a semester as a Visiting Fellow at Cornell University, and was finishing up the academic year with a brief month in Berkeley at the invitation of George Dales. I was then teaching at the Centre for Historical Studies at Jawaharlal Nehru University in New Delhi.

I spent my first weekend in California going to Cannery Row in Monterey, as a background for reading John Steinbeck. But the second weekend made a deeper impression on me. Someone suggested that I visit Yosemite to experience the splendor of the Sierra Nevada mountains and forests. One of the historians had a cabin in Yosemite, and Frits and his wife, Sarasvati, and their children decided to take me along with them for the weekend. During that sojourn I got to know Frits and his family and developed a close affection for them. We also spent many hours in discussion of Vedic texts, between long walks in the forest with the children. I had ventured into the highly complicated field of the history of what was called the Vedic period, and was attempting to correlate texts with archaeological excavations, a topic I had discussed with Dales. Frits' interpretation of some of the ritual texts was a revelation. Talking with him made me realize the centrality of understanding ritual, a subject that I had tended to set aside as unimportant to historical investigation.

Frits had mentioned during conversations at Berkeley that ideally he would like to witness an actual performance of one of the major sacrificial rituals, and that he and Asko Parpola, who was keen on the same idea, were trying to persuade some friends among the Nambudiris to arrange for this. Frits' mentors, of whom he often spoke, C. V. Somayajajipad and M. Itti Ravi Nambudiri, were the co-editors of his well-known study[1] of one of the major rituals that was eventually performed. So I was not altogether surprised when a year later I received a letter from Frits, saying that there was to be a performance of an *agnicayana* ritual in Kerala, to which he was inviting a few scholars to witness—and would I like to join them? It was a rare chance to be present at a Samavedic *homa* of *atirātram.* So I set out for Panjal, near Trissur in Kerala, where not far from the village a site had been selected for the ritual.

It was an incredible experience to see the ritual site being prepared from scratch. We stayed in the village and it was convenient for walking down to the site. The sacred enclosure of the *mahāvedi* was marked off and the bricks of particular measurements to form the eagle-shaped altar had been prepared and were placed with appropriate rituals. To the west was the smaller space of the *prācīnavaṃśa* for associated rituals. Adjoining the *mahāvedi* on one side was a small area where the visiting scholars Frits had invited could sit, as we were not permitted into the sacred enclosure. We had a ringside view of the entire sequence of rituals for two weeks.

There were inevitably altercations and arguments. When the ritual event was announced in the press there was agitation from some that no animals would be sacrificed, as is called for in the texts. Various organizations threatened to disallow the performance of the ritual. Frits was in any case not eager to sacrifice animals, and agreed that the required sacrifical animals would be substituted by clay figures, a practice that is permitted in some texts, such as the *Dharmasūtra* of Baudhāyana. The degree of personal conflict among the ritual participants on this issue was palpable, in terms of observing the exact requirements of the texts. There were some objections to the ritual being recorded and filmed, but these too became marginal, and the main purpose to make such a record was achieved.

During the course of the performance the small enclosure for the visiting scholars was often filled with heated arguments about the pronunciation of the Vedic texts by the Nambudiri brahmans. The visitors hailed from Tirupati, Varanasi, Pune, and other places in India and the pronunciation of Vedic Sanskrit, as everywhere, was tinged with the flavor of the modern regional languages. Frits repeatedly reminded the visitors that it was not a performance of the ritual precisely as it would have occurred in the Vedic period but was a modern performance by the local Nambudiri brahmans. The various categories of priests from Nambudiri families involved in the ritual had spent quite a few months training in the correct recitation of the text. Some had ceased practicing the recitation after their teenage years, having sought employment in a variety of secular and mundane jobs. One priest, for example, was working in the office of a rubber production company.

It was a source of some amusement when occasionally, during a pause in the recitation, the *adhvaryu* would step out for a quick smoke. Frits argued that as long as he did not light his cigarette from the ritual fire (which he did not) it was acceptable, since smoking a cigarette was outside the function of the ritual. The lengthy nonstop *soma* recitation left the reciters exhausted, and one felt that if *soma* had in fact been a hallucinogen it was understandable why it was required for the performance of the rite.

The most dramatic moment was the finale. As required, the site, the wooden posts and thatch, and all the instruments and vessels had to be burned. When the ritual structure and implements were set on fire in the open space the flames leaped from one point to the next. We sat at a distance and watched. Suddenly an eagle soared into the sky and flew away. A shout went up from the crowd gathered to see the finale that the eagle was the soul of the altar. Soon after there was a heavy downpour of rain. The timely occurrence of these natural events was viewed as an indication of the success of the *atirātra.* Frits seemed a bit skeptical about this claim, but nevertheless he was very pleased with the performance.

The texts, the recitations, and the record of the ritual were published in two substantial volumes, to which I contributed a chapter on the possible archaeological correlations of the ritual with the texts.[2] This was the first time that I had attempted to make such a correlation and I learned a lot in the process of formulating my argument. Experiencing the ritual itself had made me very aware that its origins and articulation are rooted in an agricultural-pastoral context, in a society that is not wealthy, and that the prayers for wealth in such rites are genuine requests. Except for the impressive pouring of ghee in the *vasordhārā* ceremony, the ritual materials are that of a simple rural culture and the complexities of the rite emanate from the way language and imagery intertwine in the form of the recitations.

It has often been asked what was it in the *soma* ritual that became such a significant part of Frits' life. Some said that he was especially drawn to the mysticism of the ritual, a subject he wrote about in his book on mysticism.[3] Others thought it was the language and sound of the recitation that he found so compelling, or that he was intrigued by the fact that such a rite is a quintessential part of a continuous heritage, or because such rites reveal a reverence for that which we do not fully understand. In addition to carrying out an Indological study, Frits addressed the question of the meaning of ritual and brought to it an intellectually stimulating analysis. His discussion of "the meaninglessness of ritual"[4] made many of us rethink the role of ritual in society and consider what he meant by the rules of ritual.

The opportunity to participate in a close observation of the *agnicayana* ritual and hear the commentary of the visiting scholars entailed a two-week period of focusing intently on just the ritual and the texts. The conversations, conducted sotto voce on site, continued and became quite animated and even argumentative in the evening when we returned to the village. There was no question that there was immense admiration for Frits having organized such a complicated intellectual "happening."

After this event I began to see Frits more often when he visited Delhi, either on stopovers on his way to Kerala or some other place he had been invited, or increasingly because of invitations to conferences in Delhi. The Indira Gandhi National Centre for the Arts had been established and was actively building its library and making itself known to scholars. Two conferences in particular in which Frits participated were on "Space" (*kham*) and on "Time" (*kāla*). These tended to be rather laid-back occasions in which many ideas floated around, some intriguing and worth pursuing and others of little consequence.

I hosted Frits in my home when he wanted a change from official hospitality in an arid government-run hotel. On one occasion he arrived at my doorstep early one morning, obviously very ill. I took him to the hospital, and while he complained bitterly about being treated like a child, he was obviously relieved to receive medical attention. He sheepishly admitted that the day before he had drunk a glass of fruit juice from a roadside juice stall in Bangalore.

On another visit, quite spontaneously in the course of conversation, we started reading some of the Rgvedic hymns together. We each selected hymns that we thought were important and went through them verse by verse, giving our individual explanations. For me this was a remarkable experience: Frits' comments ranged over his wide span of knowledge about Vedic texts and various aspects of their contents. His interpretations were naturally much more on the philological and ritual aspects, whereas I was seeing clan societies and bardic forms. Yet I was surprised when after I had sent him a chapter from a book I was then writing,[5] focusing on the *dāna-stuti* hymns of the *Ṛgveda,* he replied that he had not paid much attention to them, and that analyzing them as possible nuggets of historical information embedded in the hymns was a new perspective he had not thought about before.

Needless to say, our conversations went well beyond the *Ṛgveda* to the other Vedas and related subjects. I particularly remember his lively interpretations that some of the practices are parallel to shamanistic forms. I brought up the reference made by D. D. Kosambi to *dāsyaḥ-putraḥ brāhmaṇa*s[6] and this led the conversation down many byways in which Frits discussed what the *brāhmaṇa varṇa* may have meant at that time, drawing upon a range of priestly functions.

Some years later, when Frits was visiting Delhi, I mentioned that I was going to Chamba in Himachal Pradesh, along with Michael Meister and some of his research students. Michael was in India on a field trip with his students and they were going to examine the temples at Brahmaur and in Chamba and the adjoining valleys. I was then working on the Chamba *vaṃśāvalī* and was trying to gather information on it from various sources. Frits decided to join us, since he had not been to Chamba and he loved being in the mountains. We would each do our own research at various places during the day and then meet for a drink and a chat in the evenings.

One evening in Chamba, both Frits and I expressed our dismay about the fact that although the Vedas are held by many in India as the foundation of Indian civilization, very few people have actually read the texts, even when they are translated into a familiar language, or, for that matter, even know of their contents. And yet so many people rush to pronounce on what they think the texts say. I suggested to Frits then that he should do a book on the Vedas, which should discuss when and why the Vedas were written, what they contain, how they are organized, and what their varied meanings might be. Such a book should be written in an accessible style for the general reader, since the more reliable books in print were written for scholars.

Predictably, Frits' first reaction was that this would be too big a task—it would require much time and thought and there would be few readers. Michael and I assured him that he would enjoy writing such a book, if only for the challenge, and that if a publisher such as Penguin published it reaching a wide readership would be no problem. By the time we left Chamba a few days later, Frits had agreed to give it a try. Penguin India agreed to publish a paperback right away, so that more or less clinched the idea. Frits began work on the book and we exchanged many emails during its writing. Choosing a title became something of a game between us all, until finally Frits put a stop to it and settled on *Discovering the Vedas.*[7] Unfortunately, the handling of the book and its distribution left much to be desired, and it barely reached its intended audience.

I regret not having kept some of the e-mails we exchanged during Frits' writing of the book. I recall that there were some themes that were troubling both of us for different reasons. At that point DNA evidence was beginning to enter the debate on the origin of the Aryans, but the reading of the data was controversial and he wisely omitted it from the book. I was intrigued that in the *purūsasūkta* hymn, in which the first three categories are body parts but the fourth, the *sudra*s, come out of the feet. I reverted back to the social affiliations of the *Kakṣīvant* in the context of *ārya-dāsa* marriages, but these were not of central interest to Frits.

Discovering the Vedas is dedicated to Frits' wife, Sarasvati, and his two children. Soon after its publication, Frits moved with a friend to Thailand. He found a retreat near Chiang Mai where he built himself a most attractive and spacious home that could accommodate all of his books and the objects that had been a part of his life, including an enormous artistic construction that went up from the ground floor to the second level. In 2011 I was invited to Chulalongkorn University in Bangkok to give some lectures. I wrote to Frits that I was arriving in Thailand a few days early and would like to visit him in Chiang Mai. It was somewhat difficult to find his home after I arrived in Chiang Mai, as he refused to have a telephone installed and he himself rode on the back of a friend's motorcycle if he had to go into town.

I drove out to his retreat and spent the day with Frits. He showed me around the area, introduced me to his neighbors, and we caught up on news. Despite his claim that his books and the Internet allowed him to be in touch with the world of scholarship, and indeed he did participate from time to time in various online debates, nevertheless I had the sense that he felt somewhat cut off and lonely. I asked him why he had not thought to find a retreat somewhere in Kerala, where he would be surrounded by friends and the Nambudiri families who specially welcomed him. His answer was characteristic: he did not wish to lose his independence by going anywhere where he might become dependent on others.

Frits had also been invited to Chulalongkorn University during the week I was in Bangkok. He gave a talk on the theme that was foremost in his mind at the time: the mountains and rivers of Asia and their role in structuring Asian civilizations. We dined together the night before I left and Frits was in great form, holding forth on landscape and ritual. That was the last time I saw him.

I recently re-read Frits' Preface to *Agni: The Vedic Ritual of the Fire Altar,* where he reflects on his involvement with ritual. While there is a touch of romanticism and mysticism in his reflection, it also reveals his interest in logic and rules, which was a substantial part of his thinking. I would like to quote from Frits' concluding sentences:

> I have long stood in awe of this unique survival, so archaic and so sophisticated. . . . [The continuity of the Vedas] verges on immortality, though not of any individual person. And so I found myself involved not merely in the past but in the present and the future as well.[8]

Notes

1 Frits Staal, in collaboration with C. V. Somayajajipad and M. Itti Ravi Nambudiri, *Agni: The Vedic Ritual of the Fire Altar,* 2 vols. (Berkeley: Asian Humanities Press, 1983).

2 Romila Thapar, "The Archaeological Background to the *Agnicayana* Ritual," in Frits Staal, *Agni: The Vedic Ritual of the Fire Altar* (Berkeley: Asian Humanities Press, 1983), vol. 2, pp. 19–26.

3 Frits Staal, *Exploring Mysticism: A Methodological Essay* (Berkeley: University of California Press, 1975).

4 Frits Staal, "The Meaninglessness of Ritual," *Numen* 26 (1979) 2–22.

5 Romila Thapar, *The Past Before Us: Historical Traditions of Early North India* (Delhi: Permanent Black, 2013).

6 See Damodar Dharmananda Kosambi on the Dasyah-putra brahmanas in *An Introduction to the Study of Indian History* (Delhi: Popular Prakashan Ltd., 2009, second ed.), p. 97.

7 Frits Staal, *Discovering the Vedas: Origins, Mantras, Rituals, Insights* (New Delhi: Penguin Books India, 2008).

8 Staal, *Agni: The Vedic Ritual of the Fire Altar,* vol. 1, p. xxxiii.

References

Kosambi, Damodar Dharmananda. *An Introduction to the Study of Indian History* Delhi: Popular Prakashan Ltd., 2009, second ed.

Staal, Frits, ed., in collaboration with C. V. Somayajajipad and M. Itti Ravi Nambudiri. *Agni: The Vedic Ritual of the Fire Altar,* 2 vols. Berkeley: Asian Humanities Press, 1983.

—. *Discovering the Vedas: Origins, Mantras, Rituals, Insights.* New Delhi: Penguin Books India, 2008.

—. *Exploring Mysticism: A Methodological Essay.* Berkeley: University of California Press, 1975.

—. "The Meaninglessness of Ritual," *Numen* 26 (1979) 2–22.

Thapar, Romila. "The Archaeological Background to the *Agnicayana* Ritual," in Frits Staal, ed., *Agni: The Vedic Ritual of the Fire Altar,* vol. 2, pp. 19–26. Berkeley: Asian Humanities Press, 1983.

—. *The Past Before Us: Historical Traditions of Early North India.* Delhi: Permanent Black, 2013.

A Brief Anthology of Hymns in the *Ṛgveda* Having to Do with *Soma* (and Shamanism)

George Thompson
Montserrat College of Art,
Beverly, Massachusetts

About ten years ago I decided to produce an anthology of poetic, literary translations from the *Ṛgveda* (RV). Wendy Doniger O'Flaherty's popular 1981 anthology[1] had already attempted this, but while her translations were readable and more or less accurate (for the time period), they were not, in my view, entirely successful as literary or poetic translations. O'Flaherty's translations are in very plain prose, with no attempt to indicate line breaks or mark the length of the lines of a stanza, and there is little attempt to signal that a given passage from the RV actually exhibits clear poetic patterns, such as assonance or other emphatic sound repetitions, which are very common. This is not a criticism only of O'Flaherty. In fact, I am not aware of any translation in any language that successfully attempts to mark these poetic features of the RV's highly poetic style. The first stage in good philology is to get the literal meanings right. The second stage is to attempt to capture a text's fundamental metaphors, similes, and allusions. The third stage is to attempt to capture a text's *enthousiasmos*, its rhythmic energy, its physicality. In my view, no one has succeeded in reaching this third stage.

I now understand why such attempts to convey the rich complexity of the poetry of the RV have not appeared in print to date. Over the years I have learned that it is very, very difficult to convey the brilliance of the language of the RV into English, or perhaps into any language. Nevertheless, I attempt to do so here, in the very small sample of hymns translated below. My hope and ambition is to eventually produce an anthology of roughly 100 hymns that I have already worked on extensively. What I have not yet been able to do is to make a translation for each hymn that also succeeds as genuine poetry in English.

As for the difficulties in the interpretation of the RV, I refer to the complaints about this in a recent, monumental translation of the RV by Stephanie W. Jamison and Joel P. Brereton.[2] Examining their commentary on the few hymns that I translate here makes clear how difficult it is to produce good RV exegesis. In their acknowledgements, Jamison and Brereton recall that, having been encouraged to do a "quick" translation of the RV for a general audience by Patrick Olivelle at the annual meeting of the American Oriental Society 1998, it took them 16 years to publish it. Jamison and Brereton have also created a website where further commentary on the RV can be continued collectively by members of the Vedic studies community. When it comes to the RV, there is no such thing as a "quick" translation that will also be good.

I focus on a handful of hymns in order to make a minor point about *soma*—the god, the plant, and the juice that is extracted from it—as well as evidence of shamanism in the RV. For the most part Vedicists have expressed little interest in (or perhaps rather a certain uneasiness about) the question of identifying the plant or characterizing the effect of the extracted juice on those who drink it. For example, Jamison and Brereton feel obliged to mention the long debate among Vedicists concerning whether *soma* juice was a hallucinogen or a stimulant, because the interpretation of at least some of the *soma* hymns in the RV require consideration of what the texts of these hymns say about the effects of drinking *soma.* A key question, acknowledged by Jamison and Brereton, is the meaning of the verbal root *mad-* and variants derived from it—no small task, since there are more than 700 attestations of all of these variants in the RV and the semantic range of the root *mad-* is rather wide. Nevertheless, they claim to find more textual evidence to interpret the RV *soma* extract as a stimulant rather than a hallucinogen:

> Neither the imagery of the poems nor the vision of the poets requires a hallucinogen to explain them. Our view of the hymns is that they are careful, often intricate compositions that attest to the skill and imagination of the poets. There is no need to assume that the poets experienced the effects of a hallucinogen. . . .[3]

I disagree with these two excellent scholars, whom I also consider to be my friends. It may well be that there is no requirement to embrace the view that *soma* juice was hallucinogenic, but I think there is indeed a requirement to at least consider the possibility. I have looked for good evidence that the juice, the *soma* extract, must have been an extract from an ephedra, a stimulant, but I have found only a few dozen passages that may be read as suggestive of this. In order to defend their bold claim Jamison and Brereton would need to present good exegesis of more than half of the 700 or so attestations of *mad-* in the RV, but they have not done so. Of course, it is also true that I too have not produced convincing exegesis of the majority of attestations of all of the RV attestations of *mad-* here.[4] Until a thorough discussion of all of these attestations can be had, claims on both sides of the question seem to be insubstantial surmises, driven perhaps by little more than preconceptions.

About 15 years ago, during a tour of the United States giving talks on Vedic topics, Frits Staal visited Harvard University to give a lecture, of course mostly concerning ritual. He invited me to attend his Harvard lecture and as I hadn't seen Frits in a few years I was eager to attend. The lecture was a great success and afterward Michael Witzel invited Frits and me to his office to talk about all things Vedic. Eventually the subject of *soma* came up: was it a stimulant or a hallucinogen? Michael was inclined to accept the most popular view at the time, that the *soma* plant was an ephedra.[5] Frits and I both demurred. We spent some time talking about R. Gordon Wasson's book *Soma: Divine Mushroom of Immortality,*[6] published in the psychedelic Sixties. Neither Frits nor I were confident that the original *soma* plant was a mushroom, but we both felt that whatever kind of plant *soma* was, the substance drawn from it was hallucinogenic in nature. Michael turned to me and said something along the lines of "You should explore this. Someone has to," and Frits agreed. At the time I declined to take up the challenge, knowing that the task would require a lot of time that I did not then have.

The question nagged at me, however, and it seems that it nagged at Frits too. Separately, without either of us knowing what the other was doing, Frits wrote a little-known paper published in 2001, "How a Psychoactive Substance Becomes a Ritual: The Case of Soma,"[7] in which he argues that indeed the original *soma* plant (also known in Old Avestan as *haoma*) must have produced a psychoactive substance. He also suggests that as the Vedic clans migrated deeper into the Indian subcontinent they could no longer find good specimens of the *soma* plant, which was known to grow best in the high mountains, and he claims that as a result they resorted to substitutes that lacked psychoactive properties. Thus, in the absence of pyschoactive drugs, the Vedic clans resorted to ritual. Just a couple of years later, I published a paper on "Soma and Ecstasy in the Ṛgveda,"[8] in which I support the view that the *soma* drink was hallucinogenic.

The only other recent major Vedicists who may agree with the view shared by Frits and myself (at least in print) are, as far as I know, Rainer Stuhrmann, in "Ṛgvedische Lichtaufnahmen: Soma botanisch, pharmokolisch, in den augen der Kavis,"[9] a work that is not much cited in recent literature, though it should be; and Frederick M. Smith, in *The Self Possessed: Deity and Spirit Possession in South Asian Literature and Civilization,* which talks usefully about *soma* as well as shamanism (though he does not explicitly link these two topics).[10] Jamison and Brereton acknowledge Stuhrmann's 2006 paper in their translation; they also cite my 2003 paper, "Soma and Ecstasy in the Ṛgveda." This debate may go on forever without final resolution, or perhaps it will simply be ignored. After all, when confronted with something that we don't know much about, such as the subject of hallucinogens vs. stimulants, it is probably better (and certainly easier) to simply ignore it. In my view, this is what Vedicists generally have done. Nonetheless I here propose a short argument that the *soma* drink was indeed a hallucinogen.

Jamison and Brereton seem to suggest that because the RV hymns "are careful, often intricate compositions that attest to the skill and imagination of the poets," they could not have been composed by people under the influence of hallucinogenic substances. Similar suggestions have already been dismissed long ago, and correctly, by Staal.[11] John Brough had already suggested the same thing in his 1971 review of Wasson's book on *soma.*[12] The intricate poetry of the RV, in Brough's view, could not have been composed by someone under the influence of a hallucinogen. Let me point out, however, that neither Frits or I have ever said that the RV poets were actually under the influence of a hallucinogen *while* composing the hymns! We simply suggest that they were familiar with hallucinogens. Even so, examples can be found of great intellectual work being done while under various altered states.[13]

The first piece of evidence I offer here is RV 10.119.[14] Frits considered this hymn to be our best evidence that the *soma* drink was hallucinogenic. Note that Jamison and Brereton also embrace my interpretation of this hymn, although they are not convinced that the ecstasy or intoxication reflected in it is evidence of a hallucinogenic state.[15] While it is gratifying that they accept my interpretation, I don't think that they actually entirely understood it. In the essay I assert clearly my belief that the *soma* drink was hallucinogenic. Jamison and Brereton do not confront my claim; they simply ignore it.

Another reason to quote this translation is that Philo Bregstein, one of Frits' oldest friends, also cites it in his contribution to this memorial to

Frits.[16] Frits and Philo became good friends as schoolboys and stayed in touch over their long, successful careers in very different fields. In his essay Philo compares my translation of RV 10.119 to Molly Bloom's lovely final soliloquy in James Joyce's Ulysses. Without the inclusion of my translation of the hymn here, many readers would likely find his reference to Molly Bloom's ecstatic "yes, yes" rather inscrutable. This emphatic "yes, yes" is also found in RV 10.119. Both texts clearly refer to some sort of ecstatic experience (in the case of Joyce's Ulysses, Molly's ecstasy is clearly erotic in nature; in the case of the RV poets, it is visionary).

The chief importance of this hymn is that it shows clearly that drinking the *soma* extract produced ecstasy in the RV poets. This was an experience of flight, of inspiration; an "experience of multitudes" not unlike that described by Walt Whitman in his epic poem *Song of Myself.* It is also an experience of greatness, unimaginable greatness. In their discussion of RV 10.119, Jamison and Brereton also refer to my paper "Ahamkāra and ātmastuti: Self-assertion and Impersonation in the Ṛgveda,"[17] in which I characterize the Vedic *ātmastuti* as a poet's impersonation of a god. They do not point out my conclusion, however:

> The implication of this study is that the RV poet in performing an *ātmastuti* is adopting the persona of a god, and thereby he can legitimately be said to be a human god, as the Brahmin is said to be at SB 2.2.2.6.18

This is just a brief step away from saying that the RV poet was channeling a god; therefore, he was acting as a shaman.

Around the same time this article appeared I presented a paper, "Shamanism in the Ṛgveda and Its Central Asian Antecedents," at one of Michael Witzel's Vedic "round tables" at Harvard University,[19] in which I argue that the Indra of the RV is often a god that the Vedic poets channel in their *ātmastuti*s, and that Indra's roots are not Indo-European but more specifically Indo-Iranian. The translations of RV 10.48 and 10.49 presented in this paper suggest, in my view, that Indra was originally a shamanic shape-shifting figure. I recall that the essay was well received by Witzel and others in attendance. I have since had many conversations with Michael about traces of shamanism not only in Vedic materials but also in the Bactria-Margiana Archaeological Complex (BMAC).[20] This is a culture with which the Vedic clans are likely to have been in contact before arriving in the Punjab roughly around 1400 B.C.E. Witzel has in fact expressed a great deal of interest in shamanism in his landmark book, *The Origins of the World's Mythologies.*[21]

A growing literature in Vedic studies argues that the evidence for shamanism in the RV is significant.[22] Traces of shamanism are evident in other places in Vedic, for example, tree climbing.[23] See also Indra's shamanic role in the later *śunaḥśepha* story in the *Aitareya Brāhmana* (7.13–18). Given the existing evidence of contact between the reindeer peoples of northern Central Asia and the horse peoples of southern Central Asia, including Indo-Europeans, there is good reason to seek additional evidence, both linguistic and archaeological, of contact between these cultures. Wasson's book should not be dismissed out of hand: the northern reindeer peoples certainly used mushrooms to induce visions and ecstasy (and his ethnographic sources are also valuable). As I argue, the RV preserves memory in their Vedic horse cult of the reindeer cult of their northern neighbors, and the evidence is both archaeological and textual. If the RV poets did remember reindeer antlers (suggested by the fact that they placed reindeer masks on their horses), perhaps they also remembered the psychotropic mushrooms of the reindeer people!

Consider RV 1.163, one of only two hymns in the *Ṛgveda* that are dedicated to the sacrificial horse (*aśvastuti*s). Where RV 1.162 is focused on the ritual dismemberment of the horse and on the ritual handling of its body, RV 1.163 is much more metaphysical and metaphorical. This horse sings and flies. He has the wings of an eagle and the leaping forelegs of an antelope. He has a soul or spirit (*ātmán*) that flies. He has a mind (*cittá*) that races like the wind and he himself is described as being as swift as the mind (*mánojavas*). Most importantly, in stanzas 9 and 11 he has antlers. As Victor Mair has pointed out to me, this Vedic horse with his "horns" is a clear sign of an earlier reindeer cult that is found all over Eurasia.[24] In excavations at sites that are about 2,500 years old, such as Pazyryk in the western regions of Western Siberia among the Altai Mountains, horse skulls wearing reindeer masks with antlers have been found.[25] While all previous translations of this hymn of which I am aware assume that the phrase "horns of the sacrificial horse" is a metaphorical reference to a horse's flaring mane that resembles the rays of the sun, the simple truth seems to be that the horns referred to were actually antlers. In stanza 11 the "horns" are said to "branch in many directions" (*viṣṭhitā purutrā'*). Clearly, they are antlers there.

Asko Parpola also points to loan words in Finnish that derive from Indo-European and Indo-Iranian) languages.[26] The cumulative evidence for contact between these peoples is strong.

For years I have been studying these reindeer peoples, searching for evidence of possible influences of their culture on the later culture of the horse peoples, such as the early Indo-Europeans. In RV 1.163 the behavior of the sacrificial horse is strikingly reminiscent of the behavior of the Siberian reindeer. This suggests earlier contact between these peoples and there is further linguistic evidence of this contact, as Alexander Lubotsky,[27] Witzel, and Parpola have offered.

My son Akira, whose fiancée is a genealogist, recently took a DNA test to discover his genetic heritage. The results suggest that he is 25 percent Siberian, and that I, his father, am 50 percent Siberian. My wife and I have two sons: Akira has a Japanese name, my other son has a Russian name, Nikolai. What were we thinking when we gave them these names more than 30 years ago? Most friends and neighbors (and, no doubt, strangers) who look at me do not see a Scot or a German (my mother's roots); they see an Asian,[28] and in fact everyone concedes that I look quite Asian. I lived for almost 20 years in the San Francisco Bay Area, a place I loved and where I was easily recognized as one of its own, an Asian. In Chinatown people assumed I was Chinese. At San Francisco's Japantown it was assumed I was Japanese. In Korean markets I was assumed to be Korean. The point is that while I was quite sure that I was at least partly Asian, I didn't know the details. Now I know some of the details. While I know nothing else about him, it appears that my father was a Siberian, perhaps a Yakut or an Eveni.

Another significant feature of RV discourse is animal vocalization. I have done extensive (as yet unpublished) research into the verbal roots that express animal vocalization in the RV.[29] Reference to animal vocalization in the RV is surprisingly extensive yet it has rarely been discussed seriously, as far as I know. This calls for an explanation. In my view, it is a reflection of a distinct shamanizing substrate in the cosmology of the RV.

I am convinced that we cannot approach the RV only as philologists. We must also be anthropologists and archaeologists and students of comparative mythology and religion. Does anyone believe that, as Vedicists, we could easily step into the world of the RV poet and arch-riddler Dīrghatamas and have a readily intelligible conversation with him? We do not share a common conceptual universe with the poets of the RV, just as we do not share a common conceptual universe with anyone who lived three, four, or more millennia ago. Of course, we share a common core of humanity with them, but in my view it is simply not possible that we would all think alike even now. This is not to say that we Vedicists are modern and rational while the Vedic clans we study are archaic and irrational. This is certainly not the case: Vedicists may be modern but we are not always rational. And while the Vedic clans were archaic, in the sense that they were pre-literate and pre-urban for the most part, certainly they were not always irrational. In fact, when it comes to the science of language, Vedic culture was ahead of the Greeks by a thousand years. For me, the RV poets were prehistoric Dadaists.[30] In other words (admittedly jocular ones), they were prehistoric post-modernists, and they certainly considered themselves to be the smartest members of their Vedic clans, just as I imagine that Marcel Duchamp was among his clan.

Returning to RV 10.119, Frits also embraced my translation of it because he found it to be very poetic. At a Vedic conference in Leiden in 2002, he and the French Vedicist Charles Malamoud urged me over dinner to translate the RV into some kind of poetic equivalence in English. I have been working on this for years, and for both of them.

I include my translation of another often-quoted hymn, RV 8.48, here as well, of course and for obvious reasons. It confirms the view—both Frits' and my own, but also that of Stuhrmann and Smith, as well as of Jamison and Brereton (in spite of themselves)—that the extract of *soma* produced visions, hallucinations, enthusiasm (in the etymological sense of this word in Greek, mentioned in the first paragraph), the experience of flight, of becoming godlike, etc. Ephedra extractions do not evoke these qualities and feelings; instead, they generate hyperstimulation and sleeplessness and serve to fuel battle rage, and indeed there is some of this in the RV. By my count, however, there are a mere few dozen passages that suggest that *soma* might have been a stimulant (the extent of Harry Falk's evidence, in my view; see note 5). What about the other hundreds of attestations of the root *mad-*? Falk does not cite them. Jamison and Brereton do not cite them. And, unfortunately, I cannot cite them here either—but I have at least looked at them all. I don't assume that my view is to be trusted on this: look for yourselves!

I have also included a translation of another well-known hymn, RV 10.136. Jamison and Brereton note (as have others before them) that this hymn describes the experience of drinking some unnamed poison (*viṣá*), in which emphasis is placed on the experience of flight, of the smallness of heaven and earth, compared to the greatness of the *mu'ni,* the overwhelming power of the poet. This language is very similar to that of RV 10.119. Significantly, the hymn tells us "you mere mortals, you are able to look only upon our [human] bodies." What the "Long-haired one" drinks in this hymn is called "poison" only in this hymn, and nowhere else (unspecified drugs are mentioned in the RV occasionally, but not in reference to *soma*). The question raised by this hymn is whether or not it refers to some other drug, or to the soma drink as a drug. My view, which does not differ significantly from that of Jamison and Brereton, is that, given the fact that this hymn uses the highly formulaic language of the *soma* hymns, this suggests that it may refer to *soma* as a potent drug, quite possibly a hallucinogen. There is a lot that we do not know, however, about this hymn. Who is Kunamnamā, for example? We have no idea.

Did the RV poets consider ephedra a drug? We also can't answer this, because we don't know what their word for ephedra was. An interesting, much-discussed Indo-Iranian term in the RV, *aṃśú* (*ąsu* in Avestan), may well be the original name of the Indo-Iranian *soma* plant.[31] This word is not attested in other Indo-European languages; it can be reconstructed only as Indo-Iranian. It may well be the name of the original *soma* plant, the original name of the pre-Vedic, non–Indo-European *soma* plant. Lubotsky suggests that it is a loan word from an Indo-Iranian substrate language, possibly the language of the BMAC.

There is no doubt in my view that these very few passages establish, by themselves, a strong link between prehistoric Siberian and prehistoric Indo-Iranian cultures. We can now assert with confidence that the RV poets preserved a strong memory of their ancestors' contact with the reindeer peoples of Siberia. It is time for Vedicists to resume the debate about the identity of the *soma* plant and the qualities of the intoxicant that was extracted from it.

Let us return to the topic of animal vocalization. There are dozens of roots that express one sort of animal vocalization or another in the RV. Here I will focus on only one root: *mā*-2, *mímāti*, bellows, roars, bleats.[32] This root is clearly onomatopoeic: thus more accurately it means to make the "*m*-sound," i.e., nasalization. This root is rare in the RV, occurring only 16 times there, of which seven instances belong to the Dīrghatamas cycle. However, most of the non-Dīrghatamas cycle RV citations seem to have clear formulaic links with the Dīrghatamas cycle, so that it is possible to argue that there is a coherent use of this verbal root in the RV, which revolves around the crucial late Rgvedic cycle of hymns attributed to the riddling poet Dīrghatamas. After the RV this verbal root seems to have disappeared from common use. See also the related noun *māyú* at 1.164.28, 29; also 7.103, the frog hymn (notice *gómāyu* and *ajámāyu* at 7.103.6, 10, discussed below). At 10.95.3 the sound of thunder is compared to the bleating, or rather the nasalization, of sheep.

The root is most frequently applied to cows. But it is also applied to goats, horses, and sheep, as well as frogs and thunder (Parjanya). If we acknowledge that the clearly metaphorical uses of the term refer to the flow of speech, then we can say that it refers also to humans (see AV 6.38.4). This results in the curious fact that, besides other creatures, all five of the canonical Vedic sacrificial victims are attested as "nasalizing."

Given the preponderance of reference to cows, it is often glossed as "to moo." On the other hand, since it frequently refers to the vocalization of other animals, it is often glossed in such a way as to reflect the conventional transcription of animal vocalization in Western languages: when a cow does a *māyúm* it is glossed as a "moo." When a horse does it, it is a "neigh." When a goat or a sheep does it, it is transcribed as a "bleat." When the thunder does it, it is a "roar." These glosses are facile and wrong. The feature that is expressed by this root is nasalization, or extended nasalization, as in *mmmmm,* otherwise *ommmmm* if preceded by that vowel. The common feature is *mmmmm* preceded by a vowel.

Other verbs that characterize animal vocalization capture other features of animal vocalization: resonance is expressed by the roots *ru-, nu-;* other roots, such as *nad-, krand-,* and *rap-/lap-,* capture other features as well, for example, stop features. Others, like *śvas-, svan-,* and *svar-,* mark the hissing sound of sibilants. Generally these roots do not accurately capture animal vocalizations in general, however. They are just as inaccurate as our English versions: moo, meow, bow-wow, ribbit, neigh, oink, etc.

In any case, we learned long ago from Mircea Eliade that shamans have long cultivated "a language of the animals"[33] known by them alone, a language that not only mimics the sounds of their familiar animals, as in the case of the Vedic clans, but which these Vedic poets have also turned into sacred mantras.

To illustrate my remarks on the root *mā-,* I also offer my translation of RV 7.103, the famous "frog hymn." Briefly, this hymn cannot possibly be only about literal frogs.[34] The hymn explicitly refers to frogs who *"mā"* like a cow (*gómāyu*) or like a goat (*ajámāyu*) in stanzas 6 and 10. Frogs don't do this sort of thing—that is, they don't mimic the sounds other creatures make—but Vedic priests do. In my view, animals in general are not very much interested in the topic of "animal vocalization," whereas Vedic priests emphatically are.

This material clearly shows that human vocalizations are not significantly different in the RV than the vocalizations of a large number of other animals. What is going on here? Well, what is going on here is a conversation between Vedic clans and the animals that they knew intimately: humans, horses, cows, sheep, goats, frogs, etc. The Vedic clans had a rich vocabulary that mimicked the sounds of their animal neighbors. Is this evidence of their shamanism? I believe that it is.

In Vedic these animal vocalizations also led to the sacred syllable OM. Very briefly, here's how. The late-RV poet Dīrghatamas, author of RV 1.163 as well as the *brahmodya* hymn RV 1.164, was not only familiar with horses that wore antlered reindeer masks; he was also familiar with the sacred syllable OM,[35] which he alludes to famously in RV 1.164.39:

> That syllable of the *Ṛg*[*veda*], that highest space
> Where all the gods have taken their places,
> What will he do with the *Ṛg*[*veda*], who does not know this [syllable]?
> Only those who know that sit together here with me!

This long, enigmatic, and riddling hymn is deliberately obscure, as is indicated by the poet's very name, Dīrghatamas, "he who dwells long in darkness." He also is clearly interested in Sāmavedic song traditions,[36] as well as poetic meters, numerical symbolism, poems as weavings (or texts), etc. In the final line of stanza 5, he chants *ví tatnire kaváya ótavā́ u*. In the second line of stanza 28, he chants *mūrdhā'naṃ hínn kṛnom mā́tavā́ u*. In my view these two line-final infinitives, *ótavā́* (from *vā-*, to weave) and *mā́tavā́* (from *mā-*, to nasalize), both followed by the emphatic particle *u*, are esoteric allusions to OM, as well as to esoteric Sāmavedic traditions.

Let us ponder, then, and debate, these issues.

The Translations

1.163

1. When you were first born, you sang.
Then you arose from the sea and/or the earth.
You had the wings of an eagle, the arms of an antelope.[37]
O quick one, your birth was magnificent and worthy of song!

2. He was given to us by Yama, and then Trita yoked him.
Indra was the first one ever to mount and ride him.
The Gandharva seized the reins that guide him.
And you Vasus, you fashioned this horse from the sun!

3. O quick one, you are Yama and you are Āditya,
And through esoteric rule you are also Trita.
When mixed with Soma you are almost like him.
They say that you have three magical ties with heaven.

4. Yes, they say you have three magical ties with heaven,
And three ties within the waters, and three within the deep sea.

And, O quick one, you also seem like Varuṇa to me,
And that is where they say your greatest birth is!

5. O prize-winner, these are the waters that wash you down.
These are the hoof-prints left behind by a victorious horse,
And in them I have seen your auspicious reins
Which the defenders of truth (*Ṛta*) defend!

6. In my mind I saw your spirit (*ātmânam*) there in the distance.
It was a bird flying down here beneath the sky.
I saw your head, with its wings. You were breathing
Heavily, crossing over easy dust-free paths.

7. It was there that I saw your highest form
As it sought its food in the footprint of the cow.
When a mortal man gets to enjoy this food like you,
That great hunger for grain awakens in him.

8. O quick one, the chariot pursues you, the young man too.
The cows also pursue you, as does the pleasure
Of young girls! Young warriors also seek your company.
Even the gods themselves have mimicked your manliness!

9. The antlers of this horse were golden! His feet were made of bronze.
He is as fast as a thought is. Even Indra was not as fast as he was!
The gods have come to taste the sacrifice of Indra's horse,
He who was the first one to mount that swift horse.

10. These heavenly horses with their flaring nostrils,
Their hind-legs stand still while their midsection flies open.
When the horses reached the race course in the sky
They hold together in formation like wild geese!

11. Your body is in full flight now, quick one,
And your mind is racing like the wind!
Your antlers branch out in many directions.
They go careening through the forests!

12. The quick prize-winning horse has come to the slaughter,
Meditating, with his mind stretched out to the gods.
The goat his kinsman is led forward.
Behind them come the poets and the singers.

13. The swift one has now approached the highest seat,
There, to his father and to his mother.
May he go there now, a most pleasing gift to the gods, who
Promises the sacrificer that his wishes will now be granted!

RV 7.103

1. After lying silent for a year,
The Brahmins are now performing their vows.
The [clan of the] Frogs has sung
The song that Parjanya has released like rain.

2. When the divine waters have approached this one,
Lying in a pond like a dried out sack,
Then the call and response of the Frogs arises,
Like the calling of the cows to their calves.

3. And at the coming of the monsoon, when the rains have
Poured down upon these eager, thirsty Brahmins,
Then, as a son, singing the *akhkhala,* repeats after his father,
So one Brahmin of the Frog clan repeats after the other.

4. One of the two greets the other from behind,
When they rejoice at the downpour of the monsoon.
And when this Brahmin of the Frog clan leaps excitedly in the rain,
The spotted one mixes his song with the song of the green one.[38]

5. And when, among them all, one recites the song of the other,
As a student recites his teacher's song,
It's as if every part of their song is in harmony,
When you good singers sing them over the waters.

6. One does the cow chant; another does the goat chant.
The spotted one chants; the green one chants.
Their songs all have the same name, but each has a different form.
When they utter a song they embellish it in many ways (i.e., with
different melodies).

7. Like Brahmins at the overnight soma sacrifice,
Like ones singing around a full lake of soma
You celebrate in a circle that first day of the year,
Frogs, now that the monsoon has finally come!

8. Brahmins who possess soma have performed their song.
They are performing their annual hymn (*bráhman*).
The ritual priests sweating with their pots of boiling milk
Show themselves. They are not hidden.

9. These men (i.e., the Brahmins, not the frogs) have observed the order of
The twelve-month year set by the gods. They don't ignore the season.
When after a year the monsoon comes again,
The heated *soma* pots also achieve their release.

10. He who recites the cow chant has given. He who recites the goat chant has given.
The spotted one has given. The green one also has given us wealth.
The members of the Frog clan have given hundreds of cows.
They have thereby extended our lives by a thousand *soma* pressings!

8.48

1. I have shared in the potency of this sweet drink
That arouses good insight and best finds the open spaces—
And so I have become wise. All the gods and mortals too
Gather together to seek this drink. And they call it honey.

2. Now that you have entered me, you will become Aditi—
She without boundaries—who turns away the wrath of the gods.
O juice of Soma, O Indu, you who enjoy Indra's friendship,
Be like a mare attentive to the yoke, and yield your wealth to us.

3. We have drunk the *soma!* We have become immortals!
We have gone to the light! We have found the gods!
O immortal one, what can the malice and deceit
Of a mere mortal man do to us now?

4. O juice of Soma, O Indu, now that we have drunk you,
Be very gentle to our heart, as a father is gentle to a son.
O far-famed one, be mindful of us, as a friend is of a friend.
Prolong these days of our lives, O Soma, so that we may thrive!

5. These are the famous liberating juices that I have just now drunk!
You have sewn me together in my joints, as leather straps hold together
My chariot! May these juices protect me from the breaking of a leg;
May they keep lameness as well far away from me.

6. Like fire ignited by kindling sticks, may you burn me.
Make us able to see far (i.e., into darkness?). Make us more blessed.
For now I am in an ecstasy of you, Soma, and I think that I
Am like a rich man now! Come now and bring me prosperity!

7. May we now, with reverent minds, have a share in you, as we
Would a share in the wealth of our fathers, now that we have pressed you.
O king Soma, prolong these days of our lives,
Just as Sūrya, the sun, prolongs these days of spring!

8. O king Soma, show us mercy and give us good health.
For we are your devotees, and you should know this.

O Soma drink, a burning rises up, a wrath rises up in me!
Please do not give us over to the pleasure of our rivals.

9. For you are the guardian of our bodies, O Soma.
You are our eyewitness. As such you have settled into all our limbs.
Whenever we offend your laws, O god, you should be merciful to us.
You should be a dear friend to us, for the sake of our well-being!

10. I would be a friend to a kindhearted friend, to Soma,
Who, now that I have drunk him, surely will not harm me. Indra,
Lord of the bay stallions, this is the Soma that is placed in us.
For Soma I now go to Indra, to prolong the days of our lives.

11. These hungers, these diseases, have departed from us.
These demons of darkness have trembled. They are frightened.
Soma has risen up in us, becoming enormous now.
We have gone to where they go who prolong the days of their lives.

12. O fathers, this soma potion which we have just now drunk
Has seized our hearts. An immortal has possessed us mortals.
So we will give our oblations to this god Soma.
Because of him we will always be rich men now!

13. O Soma, you who keeps company with the fathers,
You have stretched out the expanse of heaven and earth.
O Indu, with this oblation let us pay homage to you!
May we ourselves remain lords of great riches!

14. O gods, advocate for us as our protectors.
Let neither sleep nor thoughtless speech overcome us!
May we always be the precious friends of Soma.
May we, with our fine sons, address him well at the sacrifice!

15. It is you, O Soma, everywhere our source of strength!
It is you, the finder of the sunlight, man's witness. Enter us!
It is you, O Indu, sharing your pleasure with us, your helpers!
Please protect us from the past, as well as the future![39]

10.119

1. Yes, yes, this is my intention.
I will win the cow, the horse. Yes!
Have I drunk of the *soma?* Yes!

2. Forth like raging winds
The drinks have lifted me up.
Have I drunk of the *soma?* Yes!

3. The drinks have lifted me up,
As swift horses lift up the chariot.
Have I drunk of the *soma?* Yes!

4. Inspiration has come to me
Like a bellowing cow to her precious son.
Have I drunk of the *soma?* Yes!

5. I, as a craftsman the chariot seat,
I bend around in my heart this inspiration.
Have I drunk of the *soma?* Yes!

6. Not even a blink of the eye to me
Have seemed the five tribes.
Have I drunk of the *soma?* Yes!

7. Neither of these two worlds to me
Seems equal to one of my two wings.
Have I drunk of the *soma?* Yes!

8. I have overwhelmed heaven with my greatness,
I have overwhelmed this great earth.
Have I drunk of the *soma?* Yes!

9. I myself, I myself will set down this
Earth, perhaps here, perhaps there.
Have I drunk of the *soma?* Yes!

10. Heatedly will I smash the earth,
I will; smash it, perhaps here, perhaps there.
Have I drunk of the *soma?* Yes!

11. In heaven is the one of my two wings.
The other I have dragged down here below.
Have I drunk of the *soma?* Yes!

12. I myself, I am become great, great,
Impelled upward to the clouds.
Have I drunk of the *soma?* Yes!

13. I go forth a home that is well made,
A vehicle of oblations to the gods!
Have I drunk of the *soma?* Yes!

10.136

1. Long-hair takes the fire, Long-hair takes the poison.
Long-hair takes the two wide worlds.

Long-hair is said to be this light, yes—
Long-hair—so that all may see the sun!

2. Silent sages shrouded by the winds,
They are dressed in soiled yellow robes.
And when the gods possess them, they
Follow the wide path of the winds!

3. Exhilarated by our silent vows,
We have ridden upon the winds!
You mere mortals, you are able
To look only upon our bodies!

4. The silent sage flies high upon
The middle region of the sky,
Looking down upon all things, a friend
Of the gods, in search of great power!

5. He is the horse of the Wind, Vāyu's friend,
And thus a silent sage driven by the gods.
He is the one who dwells in both seas,
Both the eastern one and the western!

6. Long-hair, an interpreter of signs,
A sweet, most exhilarating friend,
He pursues the path of the water-spirits,
Of celestial boys, and wild untamed beasts!

7. Vāyu has stirred it up, and Kunannamā
It is who grinds it down for him,
When Long-hair drank with Rudra
From this cup of Rudra's poison!

Notes

1 Wendy Doniger O'Flaherty, *The Rig Veda: An Anthology. One Hundred and Eight Hymns, Selected, Translated, and Annotated* (London: Penguin Books, 1981).

2 Stephanie W. Jamison and Joel P. Brereton, *The Rigveda: The Earliest Religious Poetry of India*, 3 vols. (New York: Oxford University Press, 2014).

3 Jamison and Brereton, *The Rigveda: The Earliest Religious Poetry of India*, vol. I, p. 32.

4 I have compiled a folder of handwritten notes on all of these passages, and perhaps at some point I will find the time to contribute them to Jamison and Brereton's website, http://rigvedacommentary.alc.ucla.edu/.

5 The view that the *soma* plant was an ephedra was held by Harry Falk, "Soma

I and II," *Bulletin of the School of Oriental and African Studies* 52 (1989): 77–90, and this remains the view of Jamison and Brereton even now.

6 R. Gordon Wasson, *Soma: Divine Mushroom of Immortality* (New York: Harcourt, Brace & World, 1968).

7 Frits Staal, "How a Psychoactive Substance Becomes a Ritual: The Case of Soma," *Social Research* 68/3 (Fall 2001): 745–778.

8 George Thompson, "Soma and Ecstasy in the Ṛgveda" *Electronic Journal of Vedic Studies* 9/1 (May 2003).

9 Rainer Stuhrmann, "Ṛgvedische Lichtaufnahmen: Soma botanisch, pharmokolisch, in den Augen der Kavis," *Electronic Journal of Vedic Studies* 13 (2006): 1–93.

10 Frederick M. Smith, *The Self Possessed: Deity and Spirit Possession in South Asian Literature and Civilization* (New York: Columbia University Press, 2006).

11 See Staal's discussion, for example, in *Discovering the Vedas: Origins, Mantras, Rituals, Insights* (New Delhi: Penguin Books, 2008), p. 99f.

12 John Brough, "Soma and Amanita Muscaria," *Bulletin of the School of Oriental and African Studies* 34/5 (1971): 331–362.

13 Frits once mentioned to me that he knew of a physicist at UC Berkeley who composed careful papers, filled with intricate mathematical formulae, while completely drunk. We both also talked a lot about the German poet Friedrich Hölderlin, who, as is well known, would sit silently inarticulate in a room when receiving visitors. After the visitors left, he would return to his desk and compose careful, extraordinarily intricate compositions, still in silence. The great Russian linguist Roman Jakobson, to whom Wasson dedicates his book on *soma,* has written about the linguistics of Hölderlin's situation: he was utterly incapable of oral discourse, yet utterly brilliant in silent, written poetic discourse. His was a kind of unusual autism.

14 I translated RV 10.119.14 in my 2003 article "Soma and Ecstasy in the Ṛgveda" This has been a very popular translation that has been reprinted many times, including in Staal's *Discovering the Vedas,* p. 96ff.

15 Jamison and Brereton, *The Rigveda: The Earliest Religious Poetry of India,* vol. 3, p. 1589.

16 Philo Bregstein, "Discovering Frits Staal," pp. 59–78.

17 George Thompson, "Ahamkāra and Ātmastuti: Self-assertion and Impersonation in the Ṛgveda," *History of Religions* 37 (1997): 141–171.

18 Thompson, "Ahamkāra and Ātmastuti," p. 171.

19 My essay "Shamanism in the Ṛgveda and Its Central Asian Antecedents" is not well known. After I presented it at Harvard in 2003 it was posted to Witzel's website, https://www.academia.edu/5584897/Shamanism_in_the_RV_2_.

20 In particular, the cover of Fredrik Hiebert's *Origins of the Bronze Age Oasis Civilization in Central Asia* (Cambridge, MA: Peabody Museum of Archaeology and Ethnography, Harvard University, 1994) reproduces an image of a cylindrical

seal clearly depicting a shamanic scene with drummers, pole-vaulting, and dancers wearing animal masks, as well as flying animals.

21 E. J. Michael Witzel, *The Origins of the World's Mythologies* (New York: Oxford University Press, 2012).

22 See, e.g., Romano Mastromattei and Antonio Rigopoulos, eds., *Shamanic Cosmos: From India to the North Pole Star* (Venice: Venetian Academy of Indian Studies, 1999).

23 See Mircea Eliade, Shamanism: *Archaic Techniques of Ecstasy* (Princeton, NJ: Princeton University Press, 1964), p. 269 et passim.

24 Victor Mair, "Horse Sacrifices and Sacred Groves among the North[western] Peoples of East Asia," *Eurasian Studies* 6 (2007): 22–52.

25 Sergei Rudenko, *Frozen Tombs of Siberia: The Pazyryk Burials of Iron-Age Horsemen* (Berkeley: University of California Press, 1970). Piers Vitebsky, *The Reindeer People: Living with Animals and Spirits in Siberia* (New York: Houghton Mifflin, 2005), p. 8, reproduces a photograph of the horse's reindeer mask found at Pazyryk.

26 Asko Parpola, *The Roots of Hinduism: The Early Aryans and the Indus Civilization* (New York: Oxford University Press, 2015).

27 Alexander Lubotsky, "The Indo-Iranian Substratum," in Christian Carpelian, Asko Parpola, and Petteri Koskikallio, eds., *Early Contacts between Uralic and Indo-European: Linguistic and Archaeological Considerations, Papers Presented at an International Symposium Held at the Tvärminne Research Station of the University of Helsinki 8–10 January 1999* (Helsinki: Suomalais-Ugrilaisen Seuran, 2001), pp. 301–317.

28 For the curious, see the author photograph in my translation, *The Bhagavad Gita: A New Translation* (New York: North Point Press, 2008).

29 However, there is public record of my work on animal vocalization on the Indology email list; a search for "animal vocalization" will yield some discussions there.

30 See Barend Faddegon, "Ritualistic Dadaism," *Acta Orientalia* 5 (1926–1927): 177–195.

31 Lubotsky, "The Indo-Iranian Substratum," p. 310.

32 Manfred Mayrhofer, *Etymologisches Woerterbuch des Altindoarischen* (Heidelberg: Carl Winter, 1986–1996), **vol. X, p. X. [GIVE VOL/PAGE CITE]**

33 Eliade, *Shamanism: Archaic Techniques of Ecstasy,* p. 98.

34 *Pace* Stephanie Jamison, "Natural History Notes in the Rigvedic 'Frog' Hymn," *Annals of the Bhandarkar Oriental Research Insititute* 72/73 (Amṛtamahotsava Volume) (1991–1992): 137–144, and Jamison and Brereton, *The Rigveda: The Earliest Religious Poetry of India.*

35 *Pace* F. M. M. Gerety, *This Whole World is OM: Song, Soteriology, and the Emergence of the Sacred Syllable,* doctoral dissertation, Harvard University, Graduate School of Arts and Sciences, 2015.

36 On which see Gerety's valuable dissertation, *This Whole World is OM.*

[37] Two arms = two forelegs.

[38] Perhaps this last line has a double sense, referring not just to the coloring of the frogs; it may refer as well to priestly clan colors. The point I wish to emphasize is that this hymn is more about priests, Brahmins, than it is about frogs; *pace* Jamison, "Natural History Notes in the Rigvedic 'Frog' Hymn."

[39] Literally, from behind (the past), as well as in front (the future).

References

Eliade, Mircea. *Shamanism: Archaic Techniques of Ecstasy.* Bollingen Series 77. Princeton, NJ: Princeton University Press, 1964.

Faddegon, Barend. "Ritualistic Dadaism," *Acta Orientalia* 5 (1926–1927): 177–195.

Gerety, Finian McKean Moore. *This Whole World is OM: Song, Soteriology, and the Emergence of the Sacred Syllable.* Doctoral dissertation, Harvard University, Graduate School of Arts and Sciences, 2015.

Hiebert, Fredrik. *Origins of the Bronze Age Oasis Civilization in Central Asia.* American School of Prehistoric Research Bulletin 42. Cambridge, MA: Peabody Museum of Archaeology and Ethnography, Harvard University, 1994.

Jamison, Stephanie. "Natural History Notes in the Rigvedic 'Frog' Hymn," *Annals of the Bhandarkar Oriental Research Insititute* 72/73 (Amṛtamahotsava Volume) (1991–1992): 137–144.

Jamison, Stephanie W., and Joel P. Brereton. Rigveda Translation: Commentary website, http://rigvedacommentary.alc.ucla.edu/.

—. *The Rigveda: The Earliest Religious Poetry of India,* 3 vols. New York: Oxford University Press, 2014.

Lubotsky, Alexander. "The Indo-Iranian Substratum" in Christian Carpelian, Asko Parpola, and Petteri Koskikallio, eds., *Early Contacts between Uralic and Indo-European: Linguistic and Archaeological Considerations, Papers Presented at an International Symposium Held at the Tvärminne Research Station of the University of Helsinki 8–10 January 1999,* pp. 301–317. Mémoires de la Société Finno-ougrienne 242. Helsinki: Suomalais-Ugrilaisen Seuran, 2001.

Mair, Victor. "Horse Sacrifices and Sacred Groves among the North[western] Peoples of East Asia," *Eurasian Studies* 6 (2007): 22–52.

Mastromattei, Romano, and Antonio Rigopoulos, eds. *Shamanic Cosmos: From India to the North Pole Star.* Venice: Venetian Academy of Indian Studies, 1999.

Mayrhofer, Manfred. *Etymologisches Woerterbuch des Altindoarischen,* 3 vols. Heidelberg: Carl Winter, 1986–1996.

Meisig, M. "Eine schamanistische Se'ance im Rgveda (RV 10.108)," *Mitteilungen fuer Anthropologie und Religionsgeschichte* 10: 119-142. 1995;

O'Flaherty, Wendy Doniger. *The Rig Veda: An Anthology. One Hundred and Eight Hymns, Seleceted, Translated, and Annotated.* London: Penguin Books, 1981.

Parpola, Asko. *The Roots of Hinduism: The Early Aryans and the Indus Civilization.* New York: Oxford University Press, 2015.

Rudenko, Sergei. *Frozen Tombs of Siberia: The Pazyryk Burials of Iron-Age Horsemen.* M. W. Thompson, trans. Berkeley: University of California Press, 1970.

Stuhrmann, Rainer. "Ṛgvedische Lichtaufnahmen: Soma botanisch, pharmokolisch, in den Augen der Kavis," *Electronic Journal of Vedic Studies* 13 (2006): 1–93.

Thompson, George. "Ahamkāra and Ātmastuti: Self-assertion and Impersonation in the Ṛgveda," *History of Religions* 37 (1997): 141–171.

—. "Shamanism in the Ṛgveda and Its Central Asian Antecedents," https://www.academia.edu/5584897/Shamanism_in_the_RV_2_.

—. "Soma and Ecstasy in the Ṛgveda," *Electronic Journal of Vedic Studies* 9/1 (May 2003).

—. *The Bhagavad Gita: A New Translation.* New York: North Point Press, 2008.

Vitebsky, Piers. Shamanism. Norman, OK: University of Oklahoma Press, 1995.

—. The Reindeer People: Living with Animals and Spirits in Siberia. New York: Houghton Mifflin, 2005.

Wasson, R. Gordon *Soma: Divine Mushroom of Immortality.* New York: Harcourt, Brace & World, 1968.

Witzel, E. J. Michael. *The Origins of the World's Mythologies.* New York: Oxford University Press, 2012.

An Adventurous Mountaineer in the Lowlands: Frits Staal's Uncommon Presence in The Netherlands

Laurens van Krevelen

Introduction

Frits Staal, born in Amsterdam in 1930, spent most of his professional life in the United States, but he stayed in contact with his Dutch friends and took an active part in the intellectual debate of his native country until the end of his life. Most of his Dutch publications were intended for the general reader, unlike the books and papers he wrote as an American scholar. This article reviews the Dutch presence of Staal and his decisive role to safeguard Asian studies in The Netherlands.

> "Baby Krishna was playing outside, Mother, and he ate dirt."
> "Is that true, Krishna?"
> "No! Who has said this?"
> "Your brother Balarama."
> "No, it is not true, Mother, just look inside my mouth."
> "Open your mouth!"
> He opened his mouth, and she was struck dumb. Inside his mouth, she saw the universe.

Frits Staal chose this funny and profound Krishna legend as a motto for his very successful publication, *Baby Krishna,*[1] an official report to the Dutch Minister of National Education on the preservation of Asian studies at Dutch universities. The report was signed collectively by a commission of experts chaired by Staal (known as "the Staal Commission"), but Frits' hand and wit mark every page of the report, so on this occasion it may be considered "his" publication. It was an important news item; major news magazines and radio reporters interviewed Staal, and made him famous to the general public in the Netherlands. Before this impressive report he had been known and admired only by progressive intellectuals, but outside of this small group of admirers he was not taken very seriously by his fellow scholars, even though he held a professorship at the University of California, Berkeley.

Mysticism, Logic, and Sanskrit Grammar

Staal's friends and teachers at the University of Amsterdam, where he studied mathematics and logic along with Arabic, immediately considered him to be an unusually brilliant student. In 1953, he read a rather ambitious paper on the cyclic and the linear concepts of time for a closed group of kindred spirits in the students' union. The paper discussed some themes that were to become the core of Staal's later work as a scholar, including ritual, the absence of the idea of religion in Asian thought, and the similarity between pre-Christian Greek philosophy and ancient Asian scientific thought and in particular their common interest in logic. The text of that lecture was published two years later in a very marginal literary journal,[2] but despite its initial obscurity it became a celebrated text within a small but influent group of intellectuals. Others found it to be a rather esoteric text. Quite a few of the students who had attended his speech became friends for life.

In 1954, Staal published three very different essays on Arabic mysticism in another marginal literary journal[3] about the Sufi poet Mansur al-Hallaj and the Andalusian philosopher Ibn al-Arabi, who had been sources of inspiration for the great Dutch symbolist poet J. H. Leopold. These essays became highlights for a small circle of philologists, though only a few effectively understood what he had written. Mysticism was to remain one of Staal's primary fields of research. Who could have foreseen this for a student of mathematics and logic?

After eight years of adventurous peregrinations in India (where he studied Sanskrit grammar and discovered ancient Veda rituals), England (where he taught Sanskrit), and the United States (where he taught Indian philosophy and logic and became acquainted with Noam Chomsky and his new model in linguistics), Staal was appointed a professor in general and comparative philosophy at the University of Amsterdam in 1962. The appointment was proposed by the famous logician Evert Beth, who had not forgotten his bright pupil. Beth wanted to strengthen the international scope of the Department of Philosophy. Staal's inaugural lecture, in which he compared the philosophical relevance of the ancient Greek mathematician Euclid with that of the old-Indian grammarian Pāṇini, was published by a new literary publishing initiative begun by a friend from his student years.[4]

Several other friends from the university were at that moment among the upcoming new leaders. Staal felt the growing discontent of the younger generation with the conservative social structures in Holland and with the imperialistic international politics of the United States, and he was of the same mind. He met promising young writers, artists, and musicians in Amsterdam, joined them in the cafés, and took part in their debates. Among this intellectual milieu were Harry Mulisch, the leading novelist of his generation; Sybren de Groot, a highly esteemed young scholar in theoretical physics; the rising composer Peter Schat, a gifted pupil of Pierre Boulez and Bruno Maderna;[5] the writer and filmmaker Philo Bregstein; and the sociologist Abram de Swaan, whose focus of research was power structures, and who had been a foremost pupil of Norbert Elias. Staal felt at home among these critical and creative minds.

He saw the rise of the Provo movement in Amsterdam,[6] and assisted at the "revolution" in music in reaction to the conservative music establishment brought about by young composers like Peter Schat, Louis Andriessen, and Jan van Vlijmen.

Meaningless and Meaningful Philosophy

During the five years of Staal's tenure as professor in Amsterdam, he became gradually more involved in the organization of the Department of Philosophy and the Humanities faculty. He said of it, "After having had a more or less peripheral existence as a specialized scholar, I became suddenly a center of interest, even of veneration." This did not prevent him from publishing intensively in his scholarly specializations in international professional journals.

However, among the faculty, opposition to the mathematicological orientation of the philosophy department began to manifest a short while after the untimely death of Evert Beth. Opponents wanted to shift the focus to phenomenology and existentialism which Staal called examples of meaningless philosophy, "a mythology and metaphysics of backwardness." Ideological and scientific struggles ensued.

Staal decided to speak about the fundamental debates in contemporary philosophy in a detailed essay for the general reader. This polemical essay, "Meaningless and Meaningful philosophy," did not appear in a scholarly journal but in the influential literary journal *De Gids*,[7] the Netherlands' oldest cultural journal (founded in 1837). Staal's friends Harry Mulisch and Sybren de Groot had recently been elected editors.

De Gids was at the time the most progressive and cosmopolitan journal in Holland, constantly on the front line of public debates that were shaking up the introverted and provincial mentality of those years. Anti-authoritarian movements by students and youth, Vietnam War protests, the human rights movement, and other such political subjects were discussed in detail in the journal.

Frits Staal's essay made a big impression on the readers of *De Gids,* but it also added to the bitter differences within the faculty. Staal was interviewed on the problems in the faculty by a national newsmagazine, which turned a quarrel between philosophers in Amsterdam into a national scandal. He later said about this time, "The conflict dragged on and it began to cost me a lot of time." At that same time Staal received an invitation from Noam Chomsky, with whom he had been in contact since 1960 on the similarities between Pāṇini's Sanskrit grammar and the generative linguistics developed by Chomsky, to become a temporary professor of Sanskrit grammar at the Massachusetts Institute of Technology (MIT) in Cambridge for one year.

Expat in Philosophy and Sanskritist Studies

Staal, longing for the possibility to devote himself again to his research, and to be freed from his organizational duties in the faculty, readily accepted Chomsky's invitation and left for Boston. He continued to have frequent contacts with his Dutch friends and became a regular collaborator with *De Gids,* to which he contributed a long interview with Chomsky in 1968. The historic May 1968 students' revolt in Paris had his intense interest, as did the 1969 occupation of the administrative building of the University of Amsterdam by students demanding more democratic management.

Staal was not a political activist like Noam Chomsky, yet he shared many of the same opinions. He once said, "I am against American imperialism and colonialism, as much as I am against all sorts of imperialism and colonialism." In 1970, in an article in the *New York Review of Books* about the destruction of ancient civilizations in Vietnam and Cambodia by U.S. military bombing, he wrote:

> In the present Era of Destruction, destructions are not carried out to exploit other people or countries, but mainly because of political paranoia without the slightest notion of what is being destroyed.[8]

Staal was a very sociable man; he maintained contact with his many friends and he was a dedicated correspondent because he loved to receive letters. He was also a frequent guest of various friends in Holland since he always tried to include time for private visits when traveling to Europe to participate in academic congresses and symposia.

I first met Frits Staal on June 5, 1984, at the well-known Amsterdam music hall Concertgebouw for a presentation of the book *De toonklok* (*The Tone Clock*)[9] by the brilliant composer Peter Schat, which I had published. Schat had arranged for the book's presentation to the press and public at a concert during which the inaugural performance of his "Serenade for Strings" would be given. Peter wanted something special in addition to this: a speech on his book by his learned friend, Frits Staal.

Schat was undoubtedly the most gifted Dutch composer of his generation. He called himself an anarchist musician, and he shared the attitude of protest against all authoritarian behavior with the Provos (the cellar of his Amsterdam canal house had been used by the Provos for a time as their headquarters). His music was equally a revolt against rigid musical traditions, and even against modern so-called serial music. He was an unrivaled creator of marvelous sounds on the basis of both the classical heritage and the possibilities that serialism had opened. Schat felt himself to be a kindred spirit with Staal, and the feeling was apparently mutual. *De toonklok* is about the new tone system and the "third keyboard" Schat had invented in order to accommodate the traditional harmonic tonality with atonical serialism introduced by such composers as as Arnold Schoenberg.

Staal happened to be in Berlin as a visiting professor when the concert was to be held, and he let me know that he would be willing to speak on the condition that a car and driver would be provided to transport him to and from Berlin. I have never discovered the true reason for this rather unusual request. Did he hope that the request would not be met, because he had other things to do? Or was he interested in experiencing traveling on the 170-kilometer non-stop road on the narrow corridor that passed through communist German Democratic Republic between West Berlin and Helmstedt-Marienborn at the border of the German Federal Republic? Fortunately, I was able to find a student who was willing to drive the long round-trip from Amsterdam to Berlin and all went well.

Staal arrived in the concert hall bearing a charming smile, radiant and pleased, without a trace of fatigue. After the excellent performance of Schat's beautiful "Serenade," he spoke extempore on the composer's theories and inventions in a profound and witty way. His talk, transcribed from an audio recording, was later published in *De Gids.*[10] Staal discussed the philosophical and logical aspects of Schat's essays and his musical intentions with the "tone clock." The composer had made two important discoveries, Staal remarked: first, in music, the relationship between tones is more important than their substance, and second, music can be made three-dimensional by adding a third keyboard of a super-diatonic scale alongside the two usual keyboards of diatonic and pentatonic scales. Staal referred to the legend about the Greek philosopher Pythagoras, who coined the concept of the "music of the spheres" and who healed illnesses by pronouncing magical incantations and making music. Staal urged Peter Schat to continue doing the same.

Sense and Nonsense in Philosophy, Religion, and Science

After the festive event at the Concertgebouw, Peter Schat invited some friends to have a drink at his home. His ancient canal house had a lush tropical courtyard garden covered by a movable Plexiglas roof and offered ample space for the party. I had the opportunity to get to know Staal better when I asked him if he would let me publish a volume of his essays for the Dutch general reader. He was immediately pleased with the idea, and promised to make a proposal for the contents. There was one problem, however: he had already promised a book to his old friend Johan Polak some years before, though Polak had not insisted on it since. I told Frits that I knew Johan quite well and that I could propose to him to copublish the book. Frits thought that this was a brilliant idea and we agreed that I would contact Polak. Thinking more about the new project, Frits proposed that the book should have a preface by Harry Mulisch, who was present at the gathering, and who straightaway was asked if he could do the preface. Mulisch usually declined all such requests, but he found irresistible the disarming way that Frits urged him to write it.

Staal kept his promise and made a provisional list of 12 essays, four written in Dutch, while the remaining more recent texts would have to be translated from English. He wrote an introductory essay on the evolution of his scientific orientation, adding to each essay a personal comment on the circumstances in which it was conceived. The book was to be a kind of "reader" of Staal's work. The first essay in the book was the now-famous 1958 student lecture on the concept of time, followed by his 1962 speech on Euclides and Pāṇini. Then came his polemical essay about meaningless and meaningful philosophy, which became his farewell speech to Amsterdam University. The texts chosen from his work in Berkeley up until 1985 included essays about language, Sanskrit, ritual, and the specific nature of Asian philosophy. The text of a successful speech he had given to a literary audience in Amsterdam on "Eastern wisdom" for export completed the book. Staal supervised the translation of the English essays.

Mulisch was equally punctual and delivered his preface in September 1985, so the manuscript could be prepared for the printers. At that time, Staal's friend Johan Polak told me that it would be best if the book were published by me alone, as his own list of forthcoming titles had unfortunately overloaded his work schedule. In his preface Mulisch called Staal a "conquistador," a conqueror of the vast unknown areas of human thought,

> who belongs to the true international academy: the stronghold where the members do not deal with classifying and re-classifying of the known things, but from which they make since many centuries thrusts at the unknown in order to map it.

In a slightly chauvinistic tone, Mulisch ends his preface with the appeal:

> The moment has come that The Netherlands should call [Frits Staal] back from the diaspora. That is an obligation independent from the question [of] if he is willing to come or not.[11]

A Wise Man in East and West

In 1987, Frits Staal combined a private research project into surviving Hindu rituals in Java and Kalimantan (the Indonesian part of the island of Borneo) with a lengthy travel report commissioned by a Dutch weekly newsmagazine. The report, printed over several issues, was a great success. Frits proposed that I publish the report as a book; he wanted to expand the text with more information about what he had experienced.

Within a year we brought out the magnificent small book *Een wijsgeer in het Oosten* (*A Wise Philosopher in the East;* the Dutch word *wijsgeer,* "philosopher," plays on the biblical words "wise men from the East"). It combines lively impressions of Staal's travels with his thoughts about the remains of Hindu heritage in a country dominated by Islam. Staal writes:

> The power of Indonesia is expressed by the national motto *Bhinneka Tunggal Iku:* "Many are One." That great power could also be its great weakness;

> Indonesian Islam has both sides. It will depend on whether Indonesia will follow its own tradition of tolerance or the monotheist tradition of intolerance.[12]

Much to my discontent, I was not successful in my efforts to convince colleague publishers in the English-, French-, Scandinavian-, and German-language areas to translate this pearl of travelogue literature. It compares with the best works of Ryszard Kapuscinski, Paul Theroux, and Jan Morris, to mention a few well-known authors in this field. My fellow publishers were right in saying that because Frits Staal was a completely unknown name on the trade market, the commercial prospects for his book were too small. Still, it is a pity that this fantastic book cannot be read by non–Dutch-speaking readers. What Staal writes about surviving Hindu rituals in Indonesia would certainly be of great interest to his fellow scholars as well.

My professional relationship with Frits Staal soon became a real friendship. Frits kept me informed on the texts he was going to contribute to journals so that I could evaluate whether any of them would be suitable for publication in Holland. He also sent me new manuscripts of books he wanted to publish and asked my opinion, though he was well aware that I am a complete layman in those particular fields. He told me that the subject matter of his books did often not fit into most academic publishing programs, because he never wrote on just one disciplinary field, but rather explored the connections between several fields. This made the academic reviewers uncertain, since they could judge only from their own fields, and they rejected the more complex manuscripts. I recall at least two large manuscripts were never published, one called "The Cloud of Knowing" and the other "The Language Animal." These titles have since reappeared as the titles of shorter articles. Staal was never disturbed by the rejections, saying that it had often happened to him. He would then split rejected book manuscripts into parts and rework them into independent articles.

Baby Krishna's Victory Over Destruction

The "Era of Destruction," to use Staal's colorful term, was also responsible for the systematic dismantling of specialist sections at universities that, due to small attendance numbers, were considered "uneconomic" by university administrators in most Western countries. This followed the so-called neoliberal ideology and the so-called "free market" propagated by U.S. President Ronald Reagan, U.K. Prime Minister Margaret Thatcher, and their followers. After the drastic reduction in public financing for universities in the Netherlands in that period, many small specialist sections were closed down even as the total number of students was on the increase. Because of this dramatic trend, practically all the Asiatic studies sections were at risk of extinction, alongside many European language sections.

The academic world sounded the alarm and the Dutch Minister of National Education reacted in early 1990, announcing the installation on short notice of an advisory commission to investigate the specific problem of the threatened destruction and loss of scientific knowledge and experience of many well-known research and educational centers of international standing. In the search for an authoritative chairperson for this committee, Staal's name was immediately mentioned. He had an unquestioned international reputation in the field of Asiatic studies, he knew the Dutch scientific structures very well, he was independent and unbiased, and it was expected that he would be accepted by all the players in the rather divided field of Dutch academia. Staal was also known to have created the very successful Department of South and Southeast Asian Studies at UC Berkeley, so he would be able to oversee the scientific quality of the Dutch specialist sections from an international perspective.

The minister nominated Frits Staal and, after consultation with him, three members of the commission were nominated: Eugene Smith, director of the Field Office of South East Asia at the U.S. Library of Congress; Henk Verkuyl, professor of linguistics in Utrecht; and the eminent scholar of Arabic Seeger Bonebakker, at Columbia University in New York. The commission became generally known as the "Commission-Staal."

In the year during which the report of the Commission was in preparation, Frits Staal lived for some months on the ground flour of our large canal house in Amsterdam, practically next door to Peter Schat's place, in the medieval center of Amsterdam. My wife, Frida, and I came to know him even better as an exceptional and generous friend. We enjoyed his company very much; we never saw him in a bad mood—he was full of good humor and always had fascinating stories to share. Frits was fond of inviting his friends to relaxed parties in his apartment, and he had made his rooms into a very personal, homey place.

Gene Smith, a member of the commission, also stayed in Staal's rooms for a couple of weeks. Once, when Frits was expecting a visit from his beloved Thai friend Wichai Kampusan, he placed a large Thai golden buddha figure in one corner of the front room on a wooden pedestal he had designed himself. Wichai was very pleased with this special welcome, and felt immediately at home walking around in the old part of the city with its many Chinese and Thai restaurants and Asian supermarkets. One day Wichai said that the Buddha would be much more beautiful with a nice cloth to cover the bare wooden pedestal, and he asked us if he could use the antique treadle sewing machine in the entry hall of our house to sew some cloth he had found in a Chinese shop for a pedestal cover. We had no objection but had to tell him that the machine was not functional. Wichai had a knack for machines and made it operable again in less than an hour. He then sewed the cloth with ease and pleasure. The Buddha was grateful, as was Frits.

On January 15, 1991, the "Staal Commission" presented its report, entitled Baby Krishna, to the Minister of National Education.[13] Although it was written and signed collectively, Staal's noticeable hand throughout the text was apparent not only in the copious statistical data but also the very relevant proverbs from many Asian languages, in the original followed by a Dutch translation.

The report made clear the disastrous situation of the "small language sections" in a surprisingly convincing manner. The report reduced the problem of funding these small sections to a simple question: "What are The Netherlands prepared to invest (and how much) in fundamental knowledge on languages, cultures, and societies that will be increasingly of importance for Europe, especially those in Asia?" It also commented dryly on the remark frequently heard from civil servants that Chinese studies would be better carried out by the Chinese themselves instead of by a small institute that fully depends on funding from a tiny, faraway country like The Netherlands:

> It is a very unscientific idea to study just what is nearby. . . . If, in science, "the skin is nearer than the shirt," our zoologists should study nothing but apes, no lions, birds, or fishes, and certainly no insects, microbes, or viruses.

The Commission-Staal suggested to the Minister an easy solution to the financial problems:

> If there is a political will, the problems of the small sections of languages and literature can immediately be solved by moving 1 percent of the public funding of the universities in favor of the faculties of the humanities, and a comparable shift of 1 percent of the total budget earmarked for scientific research projects.

This proposal made clear that the cost of investment to preserve the smaller humanities departments was relatively very low, while the loss of scholarly capital and international prestige would be immense.

The Commission also addressed some advice to scholars in specialist sections in the humanities: they should bridge their many mutual differences and start a joint lobby in order to protect their field. Considering lobbying as too vulgar or below their standing as scholars was an outdated attitude.

The report ends with a weighty appeal to the Minister to leave Asian studies in place for at least 10 years, so there would be a chance to conduct long-term scientific projects.

Baby Krishna was so eloquent and convincing that the Minister of National Education made available the needed extra annual funds for the small sections during the next ten years. This was an unbelievable success for Staal and the Commission—no one had dared hope for such a result. Because of the report's success, Staal gained the immediate admiration and respect of all the specialist scholars. In 1992 the Minister of Education, the Royal Dutch Academy of Sciences, the Netherlands Institute for Scientific Research (NWO), and the involved universities signed a covenant on the supplementary funding of the small specialist sections in the Humanities; this extra funding was called "the Staal funds." In August 1995 the first evaluative assessment issued by the Academy of Sciences on the effects of the extra funds stated that all partners had followed up the covenant, not without problems in some cases, but

> in spite of this, the covenant has offered a noticeable protection. Without the covenant, the situation would have been much worse for the facilities available for the small sections in languages and literatures.[14]

Frits could well be pleased at the results of his efforts, but ten years of protection is a brief period, and history tends to repeat itself. Had he lived long enough to hear of the heated protests of students and professors of the faculty of the Humanities in Amsterdam in early 2015, against the decision of the central administration of the university to phase out a series of small specialist sections (this time for a number of European languages studies and medieval Dutch studies), he would likely have been especially pleased that the scholars now stand up for their specialist fields of research and training. The protests escalated; the faculty building was occupied, and after it was cleared by the police the students occupied the central administrative building, under the slogan: "Away with the output criterion!" The occupation of the central building lasted for six weeks. The chairperson of the board resigned and the decision to close the small sections in the Humanities was revoked. In a letter to the parliament the Minister of National Education endorsed the importance of a nuanced judgment on the different sections in the Humanities. Clearly, Baby Krishna's struggle is not over.

New Roads and Transgression of Demarcations

Thanks to Staal's further initiatives, Leiden University and the University of Amsterdam co-founded the International Institute of Asian Studies (IIAS) in 1993. The institute proved to be a very successful combination of activities in the field of specialist studies, and an extremely effective platform for international cooperation. Staal had hoped initially that IIAS would be a European organization, offering a much larger cross-border combination of scholarship, but the time was not yet ripe for such a venture. The European Union is, first of all, an economic union, hardly one of science and culture. Inter-European differences in national science policies proved to be an impediment, but future developments will compel European scholars to unite, as Staal had hoped. In 1997 the IIAS board and concerned international scholars presented him a large volume of essays called *India and Beyond,* written and published in his honor.[15] His *collega proximus* and friend George Thompson wrote that the book was an homage to "his freedom of thought, his willingness to speculate, his risk-taking."

In 1995, Staal was invited to become a foreign correspondent of the Royal Dutch Academy of Sciences, and accepted the role with enthusiasm. The rather late invitation (Staal had retired from Berkeley in 1991) no doubt had to do with the success of *Baby Krishna* and, sad to say, not primarily with his very original pioneering research and publications. On June 12, 1995 he presented his first communication to the Academy, *Mantras between Fire and Water: Reflections on a Balinese Rite,* a brilliant text that appeared with many illustrations in the monograph series of the Academy.[16] In the last paragraph, Staal defined "the inspiration of mantras" as "breaths of fresh air," and this aptly describes the effect of his stimulating intellect in the Dutch academic world.

Staal did not rest on his laurels and worked to establish a strong Dutch Center for Islam Studies in a joint effort with several colleagues, as a sort of complement to the IIAS. Unfortunately, there was little willingness among the different existing institutions in this particular field to join forces, and the technical problems seemed insurmountable. As a result, Leiden University decided to host the Netherlands Interuniversity School for Islamic Studies (NISIS), a national network of Islam studies at nine Dutch universities, administered by the Humanities Faculty of Leiden University. Staal has been proven right in his assessment that much more reliable knowledge about the Islamic world and culture is very much needed in Europe.

Staal never felt the need, apparently, to design new pathways for the Dutch university institutes of philosophy, despite his academic foundation in logic and philosophy. He had been clear enough about his opinion on meaningless and meaningful philosophy and he was confident that logic was being taught in the best possible way at Amsterdam University by his friend Johan van Benthem. Staal preferred to continue sailing under his own flag as a philosopher without a label. His motto was "I never attached much importance to demarcations of scientific disciplines."

In 2002 Staal initiated an exceptional academic ritual in Amsterdam to highlight an unusual book that challenged the discipline of philosophy by an all-embracing theory on humankind and the universe. The famous Dutch novelist Harry Mulisch, Frits' close friend, had published this theory in a rather esoteric and lengthy essay, *De compositie van de wereld* (*The Composition of the World*).[17] This book could have been written by Goethe had he lived in the twentieth century. Mulisch comments on the origins of the universe and of life on earth, and also discusses the unity of human beings. A fundamental key to the universe and to human life, according to the author, is the "octavity" of all phenomena in the universe, like octavity in music where tones and their octaves sound both similar and different at the same time. Mulisch further demonstrates that rationality and irrationality complement each other in human thought, and that both are indispensable for a proper understanding. He had worked on the book for over six years. Frits once elegantly commented that Mulisch had found in his experience of music an enrichment of logic. The general critical opinion of the book, however, was that it was a forgivable diversion by an otherwise brilliant author, and it was simply ignored.

Frits thought that Mulisch's theory deserved serious discussion all the same, so why not treat it as a philosophical thesis? He proposed the idea to Mulisch and a number of colleagues of organizing an academic promotion ritual at a virtual university. Mulisch wholeheartedly agreed, and the Minister of National Education and seven professors of six Dutch universities accepted the invitation to join the game.

On June 11, 2002, the special academic session of the "University Felix and Sophia" was established by the Minister of Education at an old building in Keizersgracht, called Felix Meritis, that had been the eighteenth-century seat of the Enlightenment academy of Amsterdam. Staal acted as Mulisch's supervisor, and seven professors of the academic commission questioned Mulisch on his book. The famous doctoral student made a short presentation of his thesis before a large audience, followed by a ceremonial procession of the cortege of robed professors. The questions to Mulisch were polite and sometimes critical; his replies were a proof of eloquence and cogency. After the *hora est* call and the closed deliberation of the academic commission, supervisor Staal was pleased to congratulate the young doctor on his graduation from University Felix and Sophia, and in his eulogy he praised Mulisch for his consistent freedom of thought and his refusal to adhere to conventional behavior. The unusual philosophical doctor of "octavity" received lengthy applause as a reward. After this, the minister formally closed the university.

The graduation ritual was impeccable, neither a satire nor a student joke. It represented something else, perhaps a transgression of the demarcations between science and fiction and a manifestation of Mulisch's "octavity."

Understanding *Maya*

The year 2002 and the following years were an exceptionally creative period for Frits. He prepared a major IIAS workshop in Leiden on "The Emergence of Artificial Languages," a theme that had been coming to his attention more and more. His point of view was clear:

> The history of ancient and medieval science can only be studied properly if the Eurasian continent is treated as an undivided unit rather than a collection of impermeable cognitive worlds.

He called the translation of Newton's Latin into the language of algebra by Euler and others "a greater revolution perhaps than the so-called European scientific revolution. The roots of that revolution in language lie in Asia."[18] Staal devoted one of his most important papers to this topic, "Artificial Languages across Sciences and Civilizations."[19]

Staal also composed a book in Dutch based on his work since 1986, when *Over zin en onzin* had appeared. He chose the title *Drie bergen en zeven rivieren* (*Three Mountains and Seven Rivers*)[20] to indicate the geographical area of his studies: Central Asia from the east shore of the Aral Sea to the Indus valley. This work, published in 2004, includes a revealing essay about homosexuality in Asia and an autobiographical sketch of his development as a young scholar, with affectionate notes about his six "gurus": Evert Beth, T. R. V. Murti, John Brough, Noam Chomsky, C. V. Somayajipad, and M. Itti Nambudiri. Most of the book deals with the genesis of ritual and language and on the early evolution of science (including the humanities), all this against the background of the prehistoric migrations between the Eastern part of Central Asia and the Indus valley. The traces of those migrations tell a lot about the development of rituals and the ancient Veda histories and Sanskrit.

Unfortunately, Dutch philosophers responded to this rich and fascinating new book by Staal, composed largely of essays that had not previously been published, with a shrug. One reviewer wrote that in contrast with Staal's previous publications there was little new in the book. Staal was quite indignant about this comment, since his book presented many new insights on fundamental issues, and he was frustrated by the lack of response. He wrote to me, "I wish someone would say something about my work. Most people in The Netherlands continue to look upon my work as if I died in 1968."[21]

In 2003, he started writing the synthesis of his discoveries concerning mantras, rituals, and the Vedas that would become the masterpiece of his life's study, *Discovering the Vedas*,[22] published in 2005, a year after he had settled in Thailand. The book was immediately successful in India (where it had been published) and went through several reprints, but even though it is very readable and appeals to all kinds of audiences, not just scholars, it did not receive wide distribution outside of India.

I read *Discovering the Vedas* with great pleasure and admiration, and asked Frits if he would allow me to try to find a Dutch publisher for it. As he had not granted the translation rights he was very pleased with my offer. I did my best to raise interest with three serious nonfiction houses I trusted, but they were all of the opinion that there would not be a big enough audience for such a specialized subject. Frits Staal was considered to be a great name but only for a small group of intellectuals. I was shocked by the lack of interest in a major author and by these publishers' lack of courage to publish the translation of one of the great books of those years. I realized then that the general Dutch book market had shifted to more trendy and entertaining subjects by authors who could be promoted in television talk shows. Frits lived far away in Thailand and could not be expected to help promote his book in Holland.

Not a single review of the book appeared in the mainstream press in The Netherlands. Annette van Hoek wrote a review in the Spring 2010 issue of the *IIAS Newsletter,* and it was mentioned in an essay on Staal's work published in a small literary journal by Philo Bregstein. Staal's masterpiece *Discovering the Vedas* is available in only one Dutch library, at Leiden University where the IIAS, Frits' brainchild, is established. Interested students and scholars elsewhere have applied for it in vain from the National Dutch Library (KB) in The Hague, the University Library of Amsterdam, and other academic libraries. Is the fact that this work is not widely available a sign of provincialism, or of incompetence? Perhaps the old wisdom, *scripta manent,* is useful here: someday someone will say of Frits Staal what he once said about a great Sanskritist who worked a century before him: "He would certainly have been awarded the Nobel Prize, if that prize had existed in his field of study."[23]

In 2006, immediately after publishing *Discovering the Vedas,* Staal conducted another seminar at IIAS in Leiden on "Artificial Languages in an Asian Perspective," together with Wim Stokhof, Martin Stokhof, Johan van Benthem, and Robbert Dijkgraaf. He lectured in several countries and gave an impressive speech on the Indian fire ritual at the Royal Dutch Academy in 2009. During those years he also wrote two books he had long wanted to do, a detailed essay on the origin of science and the concept of truth, as well as an autobiography. Frits was not aware that he suffered from a fatal disease, despite his incessant cough. He came to know the gravity of the situation toward the end of 2011, but the medical prognosis had given him hope that he would have time to finish these two last projects. He wrote to me on December 14, 2011:

> I wish to work on the autobiography, but I have to tell you that my health is not really good—not too bad either. You see that I am able to write and I am fairly quick in writing (if I wish!). On the other hand, the doctors are not very optimistic. They have their reasons to think so, and I will explain why.
>
> Approximately a month ago, I got the invitation from Adelaide de Menil[24] to come and see her in New York. Plane ticket and hotel voucher were enclosed. I could not and did not want to decline the invitation, and I traveled business class. However, it was really tiresome.
>
> Apparently, Adelaide de Menil is the last person in my autobiography! She had organized a meeting to celebrate her late husband Edward Carpenter, who had died unexpectedly. Carpenter was an archeologist and anthropologist; she had worked with him in the most unattractive places, such as North Siberia, to excavate ancient civilizations of twenty thousand years ago or more. His son was there as well as a few filmmakers, economic advisors, former assistants of Carpenter, etc. Part of her invitation (planned at the spot) was to bring me to a good physician, who did an immense number of tests

> on me. Those tests indicated a serious angina and all kinds of unattractive complications of the lungs and the respiratory system. The prognosis was no longer than two years.
>
> I have accepted this and am rather optimistic because it is very pleasant to live here in my home; I don't leave often, as I have no car.[25]

We continued our regular e-mail exchange. He had already sent me the draft of the initial scheme for the book on science and truth, titled "May These Bricks be Cows for Me," consisting of 75 pages plus 25 pages of notes, which he planned to expand. He had already shown the draft to several editors of scholarly presses in the United States, soliciting their advice on what should be worked out further.

I had received from him in early autumn 2011 a short outline, consisting of 10 pages, of the planned structure of his autobiography, to which Frits had given the provisional title "From Architecture to Trotting the Globe." On October 15, 2011, he sent me a moving passage in which he describes his wartime experiences:

> It happened in the fall of 1943, shortly after my foster parents had put me in the room that was immediately to the right after entering their apartment. The window was open, though it must have been cold. I was suffering from tuberculosis and the treatment of the time was to lie in bed in the cold air.
>
> I heard that someone was downstairs on the street, got up, and looked out of the window. It was my brother Arthur who was bringing me something—probably some books to read or something to eat. By that time many people in Amsterdam had nothing to eat. He would not have shouted; everything was dangerous during the German occupation and he was a young man, not much older than I was myself. The Germans would have put him in prison or in a camp, as they did later to my foster father.
>
> The obvious solution was to drop the key of the apartment so that he could come upstairs, and that is what I did.
>
> And then it happened: I heard that it had fallen on the ground. So I looked out of the window again and I saw that he had picked up the key. The next moment, he was in my room and left carefully soon thereafter.
>
> I recall every part of this brief episode and how he was struck by the functioning of my ears. I has been engraved in my memory from where it emerged just now.[26]

On January, 13, 2012, he wrote, "I have corrected some passages, and will send you a selection [of the manuscript] so we will be able to correspond on it." A couple of weeks later, on February 3, he wrote, "I have worked hard on my autobiography. In the next week, Karin and Daan

(Frits' niece and her husband) will return to Amsterdam from Chiang Mai. I will ask them to take a copy with them and send it to you." Karin and Daan had stayed for awhile at Frits's place, and just a few minutes after they had left for the airport they were called back. Frits had fainted and fallen, and was now in coma. He died shortly thereafter.

Frits's son Nanoo arrived the next day. He, Karin, and Daan arranged for the funeral and took care of all the other formal and material things there were to do. The digital file of the manuscript of his autobiography was handed over by Karin to Nanoo. No copy was made. I do not know whether the file of the draft version of Frits' autobiography is still in Nanoo Staal's possession. It would be of great interest to examine it, even if it did not prove fit for publication, because Frits had the intention to write more personal details about his "gurus" in science.

Like many of Staal's writings, the draft outline of the autobiography opens with a anecdotic myth. In this case, he chose the rather cruel myth on the illusion of time:

> The substance of an autobiography—any biography in fact—is time. Time is a fiction as everyone knows. We have known it at least since Einstein, but the Indians regarded it as *maya,* which is generally translated as "illusion."
>
> The Indian sage Narada asked the god Vishnu to explain *maya.* Here is Vishnu's answer: "You will not be able to understand it, but why don't you go to the village that is in front of us, tell the people who live there that we are thirsty and ask them to give us some water?"
>
> Narada does so and knocks at the door of the first house. It is opened by a girl, so beautiful as he has never before seen. Her eyes remind him of the eyes of Vishnu. She simply invites him inside where he is treated by the family as a welcome guest.
>
> When he asks the girl whether she would marry him, everyone thinks it is a good idea and after three years the couple has three children.
>
> In the same year there is a thundershower and everything is covered by water. Narada is unable to save his wife and children; they disappear in the mud.
>
> It is then that he hears a familiar voice. It is Vishnu, who asks him: "Do you now understand *maya*?"[27]

Could Frits have meant by quoting this mythic tale that his own life had been a fiction or an illusion? He would rather have considered that the truth to which he had always aspired is more important than accidental facts, whether happy or unhappy. Certainly Frits lived as a happy person, enjoying the adventures he sought and that he was lucky to live out.

Notes

1 *Baby Krishna,* Rapport van de Advies-Commissie Kleine Letteren (The Hague, 1991).

2 "Over het cyclische en het rechtlijnige tijdsbegrip." An edited version is included in Frits Staal, *Over zin en onzin in filosofie, religie en wetenschap* (Amsterdam: Meulenhoff, 1986), pp. 116–168.

3 *Amsterdams Tijdschrift voor Letterkunde,* 1954, first volume.

4 The text of this speech is included in Frits Staal, *Over zin en onzin in filosofie, religie en wetenschap* (Amsterdam: Meulenhoff, 1986), pp. 77–115.

5 Staal assisted at the sensational first performance of Peter Schat's ballet-opera, *Labyrinth,* in 1966.

6 The Provo movement was an anti-authoritarian and anti-establishment Dutch countercultural movement in the mid-1960s.

7 Frits Staal, "Zinloze en zinvolle filosofie," *De Gids* 1/2 (1967): 49–75. This essay is also included in Staal, *Over zin en onzin in filosofie, religie en wetenschap* (Amsterdam: Meulenhoff, 1986), pp. 116–168.

8 "Cambodia: Sanskrit Inscriptions," *The New York Review of Books,* July 2, 1970.

9 Peter Schat, *De Toonklok* (Amsterdam: Meulenhoff, 1984).

10 Frits Staal, "Schat onderschat Schat," *De Gids* (1984): 503–508.

11 Harry Mulisch, "Voorwoord," in Frits Staal, *Over zin en onzin in filosofie, religie en wetenschap* (Amsterdam: Meulenhoff, 1986), p. 10.

12 Frits Staal, *Een wijsgeer in het Oosten* (Amsterdam: Meulenhoff, 1988), p. 97.

13 See note 1.

14 *Evaluatie van de uitvoering van het convenant ter consolidatie van de kleine letteren* (Amsterdam: KNAW [Royal Dutch Academy of Sciences], 1995).

15 Dick van der Meij, ed., *India and Beyond: Aspects of Literature, Meaning, Ritual, and Thought. Essays in Honour of Frits Staal* (Leiden and London: International Institute of Asian Studies and Kegan Paul, 1997).

16 Frits Staal, *Mantras between Fire and Water: Reflections on a Balinese Rite* (Amsterdam: Koninklijke Nederlandse Akademie van Wetenschappen, North Holland, 1995).

17 Harry Mulisch, *De compositie van de wereld* (Amsterdam: De Bezige Bij, 1980).

18 *IIAS Newsletter* no. 27, March 2002.

19 Frits Staal, "Artificial Languages across Sciences and Civilizations," *Journal of Indian Philosophy* 34 (2006): 89–141.

20 Frits Staal, *Drie bergen en zeven rivieren* (Amsterdam: Meulenhoff, 2004).

21 Personal email from Frits Staal, October 3, 2005.

22 Frits Staal, *Discovering the Vedas: Origins, Mantras, Rituals, Insights* (New Delhi: Penguin Books India, 2008).

23 Staal said this about the Dutch Sanskritist Willem Caland (1895–1932), in his

essay "Waarom is ritueel nog geen taal?", in *Drie bergen en zeven rivieren*, section 9, p. 256.

[24] Adalaide de Menil is an American photographer and philanthropist. She worked with Staal on his *Agni* project. Her photographs of the fire ritual are included in Staal's two-volume *Agni: The Vedic Ritual of the Fire Altar* (Berkeley: Asian Humanities Press, 1983).

[25] Email from Frits Staal, December 14, 2011.

[26] Email from Frits Staal, October 15, 2011.

[27] This legend is also mentioned in Staal's essay "Varen onder eigen vlag" and another version of it appears in *Drie bergen en zeven rivieren*, section 1, pp. 12–13.

References

Mulisch, Harry. *De compositie van de wereld*. Amsterdam: De Bezige Bij, 1980.

—. "Voorwoord," in Frits Staal, *Over zin en onzin in filosofie, religie en wetenschap*. Amsterdam: Meulenhoff, 1986.

Royal Dutch Academy of Sciences. *Evaluatie van de uitvoering van het convenant ter consolidatie van de kleine letteren*. Amsterdam: KNAW (Royal Dutch Academy of Sciences), 1995.

Schat, Peter. *De Toonklok*. Amsterdam: Meulenhoff, 1984.

Staal, Frits. *Agni: The Vedic Ritual of the Fire Altar*, 2 vols. Berkeley: Asian Humanities Press, 1983.

—. "Artificial Languages across Sciences and Civilizations," *Journal of Indian Philosophy* 34 (2006): 89–141.

—, et al. *Baby Krishna*. Rapport van de Advies-Commissie Kleine Letteren. The Hague, 1991.

—. "Cambodia: Sanskrit Inscriptions," *The New York Review of Books*, July 2, 1970.

—. *Discovering the Vedas: Origins, Mantras, Rituals, Insights*. New Delhi: Penguin Books India, 2008.

—. *Drie bergen en zeven rivieren*. Amsterdam: Meulenhoff, 2004.

—. *Een wijsgeer in het Oosten*. Amsterdam: Meulenhoff, 1988.

—. *Mantras between Fire and Water: Reflections on a Balinese Rite*. Amsterdam: Koninklijke Nederlandse Akademie van Wetenschappen, North Holland, 1995.

—. "Over het cyclische en het rechtlijnige tijdsbegrip," in Frits Staal, *Over zin en onzin in filosofie, religie en wetenschap*, pp. 116–168. Amsterdam: Meulenhoff, 1986.

—. *Over zin en onzin in filosofie, religie en wetenschap*. Amsterdam: Meulenhoff, 1986.

—. "Schat onderschat Schat," *De Gids* (1984): 503–508.

—. "Waarom is ritueel nog geen taal?", in Frits Staal, *Drie bergen en zeven rivieren*, section 9. Amsterdam: Meulenhoff, 2004.

—. "Zinloze en zinvolle filosofie," *De Gids* 1/2 (1967): 49–75. Reprinted in Frits Staal, *Over zin en onzin in filosofie, religie en wetenschap*, pp. 116–168. Amsterdam: Meulenhoff, 1986.

van der Meij, Dick, ed. *India and Beyond: Aspects of Literature, Meaning, Ritual and Thought, Essays in Honour of Frits Staal.* London and New York: Kegan Paul International, 1997.

Reminiscences of Frits Staal and the *Agnicayana*

Michael Witzel
Harvard University

In this paper I wish to honor Frits Staal with a few recollections of our friendship and of the last time we met, at the great 2011 *agnicayana* ritual in Kerala, some features of which I will address below. I will concentrate on the ritual, leaving for others to discuss the many-sided aspects of Frits' voluminous, seminal work in grammar, philosophy, ritual, geometry, the history of science, and so on.

As a graduate student I had read Frits' *Nambudiri Veda Recitation*[1] and carried a copy with me to Nepal, to take up my post as local director in Kathmandu (1972–1978) of the Nepal-German Manuscript Preservation Project, run by the German Oriental Society (DMG) at the National Archives of Nepal, 1970–2014. (We filmed and described the important Sanskrit, Newari, and Tibetan manuscripts preserved in Nepal, some 150,000 altogether.[2] I intended an eventual visit to Kerala to search for rare Vedic manuscripts, but while I made many other trips to India, from Kashmir to Madras, the trip to Kerala did not materialize. Instead, Frits and I first met when he suddenly turned up at the gate of my compound in Kimdol, Svayambhu, Kathmandu, in summer 1974.

Frits had come to Nepal with a group of some forty students, including Michael Aris, his wife Suu Kyi, and their infant son, Alexander. Frits' aim was to explore the Himalayan pilgrimage routes from India to Tibet, and also any connections with South India.[3] He had contacted the Tribhuvan Viśvavidyālaya in Kirtipur, Kathmandu, then the only university in Nepal, for the necessary trekking permits.

That turned out to be a mistake. Purna Harsha Bajracharya, the deputy director of the Department of Archeology, told me, "If he had come this way (that is, straight to the department) . . . but he came that way (the university)," so the project was not granted the necessary permits. In addition, at that time there was greater suspicion of Western foreigners operating in the mountains. The Royal Nepalese Army, under covert Chinese pressure, had launched a campaign against the Khampa insurgents who had been financed by the CIA to fight in Tibet against the Beijing government. After the rapprochement between the United State and China in 1972, the Khampas had retreated into Nepalese territory, operating from the small northern, semi-autonomous Tibetan kingdom of Mustang.[4]

Frits and I met again in 1978, after I had moved to Leiden University. Frits often visited his homeland, the Netherlands, to attend various functions and publish in the local press. He loved to talk about Vedic ritual with his "sparring partner," as he used to refer to the late J. C. Heesterman. Heesterman called this exercise *dikke planken zagen* ("to saw thick wooden boards").

Frits was later invited by the government of the Netherlands to write a report on the "restructuring" of "small humanities subjects" (*kleine letteren*) that had begun with the decimation of Dutch Indology in 1983–1986. He published his "Baby Krishna" report in 1991[5] in response to the plan of Wim Deetman, then the minister of education, to cut down substantially on university positions. In the end, two entire Faculties of Letters among the 14 Dutch universities and some 40 institutes were eliminated.[6]

Of course, Frits and I had some scholarly disagreements, notably about his "no meaning" theory with regard to ritual,[7] but that did not hinder our exchanges and friendship. After I moved to America in late 1986, we met again at an American Oriental Society's meeting in Berkeley. Frits invited some of us to his beautiful house in the Oakland hills, with a perfect view of the Bay from behind a cherry tree. Clad in a leather jacket, he drove a red sports car. In 1991 Frits was profiled in a long interview published in a local (student) newspaper, in which he gave a retrospective account of his work and his views on Asian studies—with the additional benefit, he emphasized, of having an Asian (Japanese) boyfriend.

Around that time Frits was induced to retire, along with many other UC California professors, with a generous retirement package. After he accepted this golden handshake he moved to Thailand, to the northern town of Chiang Mai, where he built a beautiful house on the outskirts of town[8] and lived there with his Thai boyfriend. An elaborate housewarming, more like an inauguration (*gṛhapraveśana*), was attended by local colleagues, and graced by the presence of Princess Sirindhorn, with whom Frits frequently met to talk about Sanskrit and read the Vedas together. He later sent me a video and CD of the event, expressing his regret that I could not attend. Indeed, unlike in the 1970s, when I traveled to Thailand several times to meet with the royal priest (*rajkru*) and his successor in Bangkok, I unfortunately never had an opportunity to visit Thailand in those years, and now it is too late to go see Frits at his home in Chiang Mai. However, Frits and I met a few more times over the years in America and India.

In 2007 Frits stopped over at Harvard and some other locations on the east coast as well as attending the Vedic Workshop in Austin, Texas.[9] After some trips to Europe (Paris and Holland) he gave a talk at Harvard in 2009 on one of his favorite topics, "The Himalayas and the Rivers of Southern Asia."

A few years earlier Frits and I had tried to start a trilateral comparative project on Brahmins in "borderland" areas of the Hindu tradition, such as those in Thailand (the *rajkru* and his colleagues), in Bali (though Frits doubted that the Balinese were "real Brahmins"), and in the Kathmandu Valley (the near-indigenous Newar Rājopādhyāyas).[10] We intended to gather materials and offer interpretation about the spread of Hinduism to these areas around the beginning of the first millennium C.E.[11] Unfortunately, this project did not come to fruition due to our inability to garner sufficient funding.

However, another project we undertook was successful, due to the timely intervention of my colleague Peri Bhaskararao (now a retired professor, Institute of Languages and Cultures of Asia and Africa, Tokyo University of Foreign Studies, where I spent a year in 2004–2005). We were able to have all the sound recordings of his 1975 *agnicayana* performance digitized,[12] and they are now preserved in the sound archives at UC Berkeley. Frits also gave digital copies of his films and recordings to the traditional Olappamana Mana,[13] near Palghat, Kerala.

This brings us to one of Frits' greatest projects, the performance by the Kerala Nambudiri Brahmins at Paññal in 1975 of the *atirātra agnicayana,* of which he gave a detailed description and analysis in *Agni: The Vedic Ritual of the Fire Altar.*[14] This performance was important not only because it was filmed and preserved for future generations, but also because the event led to a subsequent revival of the ritual.

At the time Frits and many colleagues thought that the Nambudiri Brahmins' tradition of performing this elaborate twelve-day ritual (which is no longer performed anywhere else) would soon come to an end, due to "modernization," lack of funds, the changing interests of young Nambudiris, and the like. As he reported in *Agni,*[15] combined local and an international efforts secured the necessary funding, $40,000 at that time.[16]

Elaborate preparations, included training the officiating priests, were completed and the twelve-day ritual was carried out successfully. The entire ritual performance filmed (in black and white) on videotape,[17] and selected portions of it were captured on much more expensive color film. A sixty-minute color film produced from these materials[18] has been used in many classes dealing with Hinduism all over the world. The audiotapes of the performance were recently digitized, as noted above.

The subsequent revitalization, if not revival, of the *atirātra agnicayana* after these documentaries were produced by Frits and others is an example of a cultural phenomenon that has been called the "pizza effect."[19] This is when a local, indigenous practice becomes more highly regarded locally after it has been appreciated abroad (by "foreign savants"), preferably in a culturally important center.[20]

Frits later on went to study some of the revivals of the *soma* and *agnicayana* rituals in Kerala, such as at Kundur in 1990, and published a short report on it.[21] In 2011 he attended the *agnicayana* that was again held at Paññal near Cheruthuruthy, Thrissur District, in central Kerala, from April 4–15—as usual, in the hot season (*gharma, grīṣma*).

On this occasion Frits arrived from Thailand (via Chennai) to Calicut early on, and we all met at the house (Polpaya Mana) of Dr. Vinod Bhattathiripad[22] for discussion and lunch. The well-know historian M. G. S. Narayanan told us about the Nambudiri tradition. Frits, suffering from bronchitis, was a bit irritable, often insisting in the discussion, "I want to help you."[23] I was accompanied by three of my graduate students who were interested in the Veda, Caley Smith, Finnian Gerety, and Nataliya Yanchevskaya, and by my former student, Prof. Carlos Lopez.[24]

On our way south to the *agnicayana* site at Paññal (near Cheruthuruthy) we stopped over at the Naras Mana (near Edappal), where the *Ṛgveda* has traditionally been taught, such as by Naras Ravindran Nambudiri. We had an outdoor meeting with some members of the *mana,* with recitation of the *Ṛgveda* and discussion, and, as always, Frits was in the center. I took the opportunity to ask Ravindran about a possible recitation of a few stanzas that had doubtful readings. Later, at Paññal, he volunteered to do so and readily recited the desired stanzas (see below).

From Naras we headed toward Paññal. We lodged at the River Retreat Hotel,[25] a renovated former summer palace of the Maharajas of Cochin, above the Nīla Nadī (Bharathapuzha) River, with a nice view. Frits also stayed there, still weak from the severe throat infection he had brought with him from Chiang Mai, and accordingly was quite unwell and irritable.[26] He then bequeathed his infection to all of us.

From the hotel it was only a ten-minute (sometimes adventurous) rickshaw ride to the offering ground at Paññal, where the 1975 *agnicayana* (as well as the earlier rites in 1901 and 1956) had been held. I looked to the performance with much anticipation, though I had seen more simple Vedic rituals, notably in Nepal. Unfortunately, even though I was then living relatively nearby, in Nepal, I had not been able to attend the 1975 performance. At that time I needed to stay in Kathmandu to attend to my family, especially my then one-year-old son.[27] I was therefore very glad to be able to observe this new performance, along with our graduate students. For them, as for me, it was a unique chance to observe and record a complex ritual that has been performed in its ancient form since about 1,000 B.C.E.

My students and I had prepared for the 2011 performance by reading the relevant texts that were available in print, mostly the *Baudhāyana Śrauta Sūtra* (BŚS), which records all the steps to be undertaken in the performance of the ritual. In addition, there were helpful books on *soma,* including Caland-Henry's *Agniṣṭoma,* Dandekar-Kashikar's *Śrautakośa,* and Caland-Henry's lengthy Āpastamba translation.[28] There also exists a detailed account on the Nambudiri website.[29] Our main guide, of course, was Frits' 1983 work, *Agni: The Vedic Ritual of the Fire Altar,* which minutely records (nearly) all the actions undertaken in the ritual performance, and which we had all had properly digitized and available in our computers. We also looked at the scanty advance information that had come out of Kerala.

The 2011 ritual was organized by some wealthy merchants from Kerala, who have their business in the United Arab Emirates and "reinvested" their money in the tradition of paying for ritual performances—enhancing their social status through the well-known process of Sanskritization (about which Frits has also written).[30] Thus, a huge amount of money was spent for the ritual, its management, and feeding all the visitors; food was made available several times per day. To our surprise there was also free wifi connection, accessible right next to the offering ground. In contrast, during the 1975 *agnicayana* ritual the nearest phone was in Cheruthuruty, and there was no bus or rickshaw service then.

I was amused by the fact that, due to my being of similar age, I was mistaken to be Frits by many visitors to the *agnicayana.* Many people approached me to ask, "Are you Staal?" I eventually began responding, "Can't you see the tag on my chest that says 'I am not Frits Staal'?" Many people also tried to engage Frits, who brusquely dismissed them unless they had a serious question.

As in 1975, the ritual was professionally filmed, this time with several cameras filming from various angles, including a camera mounted on a giant beam that was moved around the offering ground to get close-up shots of the major ritual activities.[31] Ordinary people were not allowed inside the offering ground, a restriction that Frits was soon to experience.

Filming the rituals was not always easy, because of the crush of thousands of visitors surrounding and circumambulating the sacred ground. However, the spectators were very friendly and there was no theft; we could freely leave our cameras and other equipment on our reserved seats (in the "research wing") under the canopy next to the offering ground, when proceeding to the railing for viewing and filming.

People in the crowd, including the local Nambudiri Brahmins, were straightforward, open, and friendly. Unlike in some other areas of India we did not have any difficulty in talking to Brahmins or requesting them to recite certain RV, YV, or SV texts for us; indeed some volunteered to do so. This openness is perhaps best expressed in Frits' words:

> Over the decades, while I penetrated the riches of their Vedic heritage, I made many Namboodiri friends. . . . I have found them sincere, straightforward and disciplined. After initial reluctance, they are eager to explain the intricacies of their recitations, chants and ceremonies. They never claim knowledge that they do not possess. They will not preach or become pompous. . . . Though no longer averse to modernisation, they remain attached to their simple habits.[32]

I was able do a little fieldwork during our stay, for example recording several recited versions of our *Ṛgveda* text, where there are editorial problems. A few days into the *agnicayana,* Naras Ravindran told me to come to the house of a local Paññal SV Brahmin, and asked me what I wanted to know about his RV recitation. He took my list of questions (in Roman script), took a brief look at the first passage, and then readily recited the stanza, and continued reciting for the next ten stanzas or so.[33]

I regret now that I did not carry out my research in Kerala, as Frits had done since 1959. We have since organized the Sixth International Vedic Workshop at Calicut, in January 2014, and this event allowed us to witness and record many facets of Kerala Veda recitation and some rituals, many of them *in loco,* in the remote villages of the practitioners of the three Vedas.

Frits had planned to participate in this performance of the *agnicayana.* He wanted to sit between the two major ritual halls, well inside the offering ground, as he had been allowed to do in 1975. This time, however, he (and we other *mleccha*s) were not allowed to enter the actual offering ground, which was cordoned off by a sturdy bamboo fence. (Despite this, an obviously non-Brahmin carpenter was let in to construct the offering pole, the *yūpa,* and worked at the edge of the cordoned-off ground.) Having had to watch from the outside, like everybody else, Frits left in frustration after a few days, finding all of this a little too exhausting. In any case, his health was not good and he was fatigued by so many people approaching him with trivial questions.

Another deviation from the 1975 performance was that Brahmin women were allowed to enter the sacrificial ground and talk to the priests, and many women visited the hall of the sacrificer's (*yajamāna*) wife and chatted with her. No doubt her twelve-day ritual isolation would have otherwise been an ordeal.

After the *agnicayana* Frits and I still corresponded about various mutually interesting topics and he discussed with me his book *Nambudiri Veda Recitation,* which he felt had not been read much by colleagues and about which he wrote a short paper (not yet published). I assured him that we had done so since I had been a graduate student. In 2010 he was thinking of putting out a reprint or a new edition of this book. In his last years he also set up a website documenting his work, probably intended as his legacy.[34]

Frits suddenly passed away less than a year later, on February 19, 2012. Thankfully his niece, Karin Staal, was then visiting him, her "favorite uncle," as she later wrote to me. His son, Nanoo (Frederik) Staal, also contacted me later and kindly sent me some manuscripts that Frits had left me.

The local paper, *Malayala Manorama,* reported his passing, and his Nambudiri friends conducted a memorial[35] and performed the traditional immersion of his ashes, which had been brought from Thailand by his friend, T. P. Mahadevan (as reported by Express News Service and in *Mathrubhumi*), in the Bharatapuzha River, at Thirunavaya. This was a fitting burial in the land that he loved.[36]

Frits' visit to Paññal was my last chance to see him.[37] I will always remember him like that, in his favorite place that he first visited in 1959.

Notes on the 2011 *Agnicayana* Ritual

Performance

As is well known, the *agnicayana* ritual involves 17 priests, who have undergone special training for this long ritual, even though they know the recitation of the Vedic texts (RV, YV, SV), including the very intricate way of singing a large number of *sāman* melodies,[38] learned since childhood in family-based schools or in institutions such as the Brahmasva Madhom in Thrissur.

Ground

When we arrived at Paññal just before the *atirātra agnicayana* began, the offering ground had been well prepared in a large rice field. The sacrificial sheds and tents and awnings for the visitors, kitchen, etc., had all been erected. The preparation of the ritual ground closely followed the instructions in the sūtra texts (and their descendants, the medieval handbooks *Pakazhiya*). There were the required sheds, open on (nearly) all sides, with thatched roofs that protected the main actors from the hot sun during the ritual. Everything was ready for the start of the actual performance of the ritual.

As previously mentioned, the ritual ground was cordoned off from visitors by bamboo barriers. We could observe the rituals and film them from behind the barriers. Outside the fenced-off area it was possible to move around freely and observe the events from various angles.

The actual recitation was broadcast well outside the offering ground by a large bank of speakers situated right where visitors entered the ground. Most of us did not know Malayalam, the local language. Because Malayalam is full of Sanskrit words, however, I could make out a lot of what was announced over the loudspeaker, such as occasional summaries of what was going to happen next. As for as the actual ritual texts, recited or sung, we were able to follow them, as during the ritual the voices of the texts' reciters were amplified by microphone and loudspeaker, and the pronunciation in this part of India is very clear. A microphone was present at all times, held by a Brahmin inside the offering ground. There was also a live video feed of whatever was being filmed by the several cameras in one of the halls.

We also made use of technical innovations (there were numerous personal cell phones and cameras all over the place) and occasionally we asked Brahmin friends to film video for us inside the sacred ground, which we could not enter to closely observe what was performed. T. P. Mahadevan, from Howard University, who also actively participated in the ritual (as the *soma* merchant), made video recordings for us.

Publicity

The *agnicayana* was widely reported in the press.[39] Every day there were quarter- to half-page reports on the proceedings, mostly in the

Malayalam-language papers, but also in some English-language newspapers, such as *The Hindu*. Kerala Television was present as well, at least for the major part of the ritual.[40] Several of the visiting Western and Japanese scholars were interviewed about our interests, what the ritual meant to us, and what the "scientific" effects of the ritual might be (discussed further below).

The 1975 and 2011 Performances: Some Highlights

The 2011 performance closely followed that of 1975, and since the earlier ritual was thoroughly (though not 100 percent completely) documented in *Agni: The Vedic Ritual of the Fire Altar*, they can be compared in detail. As noted above, Staal and his associates had taken some 30 videotapes, a color film, and many dozens of photographs and audio recordings of the 1975 ritual. The sound recordings had recently become available to me on CD, and we had printouts of parts of Frits' book *Agni* with us as reference materials. We therefore were in a very good position to compare the two performances of the ritual.

Basically, both performances were close repetitions of each other, and all the major features of the 1975 ritual were repeated in 2011. Continuity of local tradition was clearly visible. One of the participants in the 1975 ritual was present, the *akkithiripad* Kapra Ankara Narayanan,[41] who sat in the middle of the offering ground, incongruously on a red plastic chair, and followed much of the performance.

Implements

The implements of the ritual had been prepared beforehand, as there would not have been enough time during the twelve-day performance to bake a thousand bricks and fashion the various clay vessels and wooden implements, such as a large number of offering ladles. However, as mentioned previously, the *yūpa* was constructed *in situ* on one the first few days, just inside the offering ground, by a low-caste carpenter.

Pravargya

One of the initial parts of the *soma* ritual, the *pravargya*, was of great interest for me; it had been the subject of my Ph.D thesis some forty years before.[42] Having seen the ritual only on one of Staal's videotapes in Holland in the early 1980s, I now had the opportunity to witness and follow this ritual step-by-step in live performance.

Even though the *pravargya* clay implements had already been prepared, the priests proceeded "as if" they were fashioning them during the ritual. They had to first collect the clay, load it onto a donkey, and bring it to the offering ground. Then they made three rough lumps of clay and fashioned them by hand into the form of small cylinders. These were then stacked on top of each other and hand-formed into a rough clay vessel, which was then baked in the fire. In this archaic ritual[43] a potter's wheel cannot be used. In any case, a potter (of low caste) cannot be called upon to prepare the ritual vessels.[44]

In this manner the *pravargya* vessel was "prepared" on the offering ground. It was used later on for the *aśvin,* the milk offerings to the twin deities. This is perhaps the most spectacular part of the actual ritual and people thronged to see it. The clay *pravargya* vessel is heated until it is glowing red, then milk is poured into it. On contact with the dangerously overheated vessel, the liquid virtually explodes, shooting up several yards high into the air. (The scientists present took special interest in this part of the ritual, as discussed below).

Sacrificial Animals

A major innovation in the 1975 ritual was the substitution of 11 sacrificial goats by vegetarian offerings (*piṣṭapaśu*).[45] The sūtra (BŚS) speaks of actual strangulation of the goats and offering their omentum. In 1975 there had been a serious dispute about sacrificing animals, not because of current vegetarianism and principles of *ahiṃsā,* but due to political interference. The Communist Party of Kerala had used the staging of the large ritual, in part financed by foreigners, to drum up controversy and emotions ran high. One of the local Brahmins, Itti Ravi (as captured in the film *Agni*) put it ironically, "Some people opined that the goats should not be offered; we discussed it and decided against it." In 2011, however, there was no discussion over the use of animal sacrifice, as the new tradition of substituting non-animal offerings had become a regular part of the performance, and thus the substitute vegetable rolls were tied to the offering pole.

Substitutions of this type are not something new; the use of *piṣṭapaśu* is already allowed in late Vedic texts. However, some Vedic Brahmins in various parts of the country still follow the old custom, sometimes very strictly. A colleague who had traveled throughout South India in search of rituals, some twenty years ago, told me that he was in a village where the Brahmins were preparing to sacrifice a goat during a *soma* ritual, but the villagers, vegetarian Hindus, opposed the killing. The Brahmins then took it upon themselves to carry out the sacrifice and strangled the goat somewhere outside the village. Its entrails were then offered during the *soma* ritual.

Consecration of the *Yajamāna*'s Wife

There were other small deviations from the ritual handbooks. The wife of the *yajamāna* is supposed to undergo a special ritual in the *patnīśālā,* her hut on the western side of the space, but this apparently did not take place. There was concern about the actual state of the *yajamāna* and his wife, because if she had not been consecrated properly the ritual would not be successful.

The situation was complicated by the fact (as mentioned above) that uninvolved Brahmin women were allowed access to the *patnīśālā* to visit with the *yajamāna*'s wife during her sequestration. This unorthodox permissiveness was behind one of the many rumors, which were circulating in the local tea stalls, that something would go wrong with the ritual. In fact something did go wrong: the rainshower, customarily expected after the offering sheds are burned down at the conclusion of the ritual, arrived about fifteen minutes too early, and the rest of the ceremonies took place in ankle-deep mud. (There had already been a heavy rainstorm in the middle of the twelve-day period, which had turned the ritual ground into a giant mud puddle that only gradually dried up).

The Role of the "Supervisor"

Conspicuous during the ritual performance was a particular Brahmin, Pantal Vaidikan Damodaran Nambudiri, whom we called the "supervisor," though this role is not mentioned in any text.[46] He knew the entire ritual performance by heart and, pointing stick in hand, he rushed around from one spot to the other, directing both major and minor participants in what to do and when to do it, throughout the twelve-day period. We learned that Pantal Vaidikan Damodaran Nambudiri had studied the ritual early his adult life and had mastered it completely when he was about thirty-five years old.

He also supervised the recitations and *sāman* melodies, which he knows by heart. For instance, he might notice that a priest, beginning to recite or sing a verse or *sāman,* made a mistake; he would then intervene and direct the priest to repeat the sentence or the melody. The ancient underlying belief that the ritual must be performed 100 percent correctly, was evident during this event. If a mistake is made and not corrected, the ritual will have no effect.

Priests

The priests that took part in this ritual ranged from quite elderly men to a young boy (about ten years old) who had learned only the part of the texts that were necessary for the *agnicayana.* The preparation of the priests had taken over six months, as several of them had to be specially trained, including some of the young performers, such as the young Subrahmaniam priest. It was especially interesting and indeed amusing to hear this young priest giving instructions in old Malayalam and Sanskrit. In his high-pitched child's voice he told the middle-aged *yajamāna* how to behave, what to do, and what not to do during the ritual and during the year following the *agnicayana.*[47]

As may be expected with any Indian ritual, occasional comments by onlookers about the competence of the reciters and singers were heard; however, to judge the accuracy of the recitation we must compare the actual recordings with the texts.

The Relationship of the Modern Performance with the Ancient Texts

As mentioned, there were a number of minor or major deviations from the underlying text (BŚS, etc.), discussed below.

Burning Down the Offering Sheds

In the 1975 and 2011 performances the thatched offering halls (*śālā*) were burned down at the end of the ritual, though the sūtra text refers only to burning the *kuśa* grass that had been strewn around the major offering fires. Generally speaking, however, the actual performance depends not on the *Śrautasūtra* but on (unpublished) medieval handbooks (*Pakazhiya*) composed in older Malayalam. So the question whether burning down the halls is already mentioned in these handbooks, which are read by few foreign scholars, is still to be resolved.

This innovation constitutes a major local event. Thousands of people assembled, awaiting the event eagerly, as well as the predicted rain. It is believed that after burning down the sheds, rain "always" follows. Indeed, at every occasion of the ritual in living memory a rainshower has arrived promptly at the very end. In the 2011 performance there was a hitch, however; the priests were a bit tired and performed more slowly toward the end, on the twelfth day of daily and nightly performances, so the rain actually arrived fifteen minutes before the end. Consequently, a number of rumors circulated regarding the ritual performance, including that allowing women into the offering ground (to visit the *yajamāna*'s wife in her hut, as noted above) was the cause for several glitches, among other rumors.

At the 2011 rite there was a huge blast of wind, followed by a strong downpour, typical for the pre-monsoon season. Actually this was the second unseasonal rainstorm that the area had seen during the *atirātra*. Nevertheless, the sheds burned well, accompanied by the shouts of the thousands of assembled spectators. The observers had to retreat a hundred yards due to the great heat generated by the burning sheds. In the end, the prediction and the expectations of the people were again fulfilled.

Soma Merchant

A medieval and recent innovation concerns the "*soma* merchant." The plant from which the sacred *soma* drink is prepared, by pressing out the *soma* plant, was collected, as the Vedic tradition instructs, in the Pamir/Himalayan mountains and then brought to the offering ground. Since the Himalayas are some 2,000 miles away from the location of the rite, however, the plant now is brought from the Western Ghat mountains, which reach heights of some 6,000 feet. The *soma* plant (nowadays, a local vine) was collected by an aboriginal tribe and brought to the offering ground. There one of our Kerala friends, T. P. Mahadevan, acted as the part of the *soma* merchant. He had to sell the *soma,* which he carried in a bundle on his head, to the assembled Brahmins. Some haggling is to take place and he would receive a cow as payment. However, once the deal is done, the *soma* merchant is supposed to be beaten by the Brahmins and sent away.

This time, in 2011, the *soma* merchant was not actually beaten. Mahadevan stayed with us in the only local hotel available, some five miles away, from where we had to commute by motor rickshaw to the offering ground. I had been present quite early on the day of the *soma* pressing but he had not yet arrived, which made the other Brahmins quite nervous. A prominent *sāmavedin* asked me, "Mahādevan *kutra*?" ("Where is Mahadevan?"). In the end, our merchant arrived just in time, and the *soma* sale proceeded in due order.

Thus, in various ways tradition persists or undergoes slight innovation, sometimes with a recurrence to old Vedic traditions (such as with animal sacrifice vs. *piṣṭapaśu,* described above).

The Current Interpretation of the 2011 Performance

As mentioned previously, the local people came to visit the *agnicayana* in droves. They regard the *āhavanīya* fire as the main deity in some kind of *pūjā*. When it was installed on the main altar they not only circumambulated the offering ground clockwise, as they had done before, but also prostrated themselves, turning toward the fire. I have seen this practice in Indian temples as well, when the concealing curtain is opened and the deity is finally revealed.

In the first two days of the rite only a few visitors came and circumambulated the offering ground; however, by the last few days there was a constant stream of worshipers and we could hardly move among the throngs. In the crush of the crowd we had to grab onto to the supporting poles of the balustrade, as a sort of *dvārastambha,* in order to film. The local volunteers (both male and female) tried to move people along at a steady pace but nonetheless there were many delays.

During the final three days the crowd was so large that it was virtually impossible to do any work, and even our reserved "research wing" seats were increasingly occupied as soon as we left them. So we elected to come at night to escape the worst of the crowding, and also because during the last two nights the ritual continued without pause (*atirātra* means "overnight"). One thousand *Ṛgveda* mantras had to be recited, and similarly prolonged singing of *Sāmaveda* melodies took place. We arrived around midnight to 2:00 A.M., when as few as only three or four people were present, and stayed on until sunrise, when many people began to arrive. After dawn it became quite hot; on the last day some screening was taken down, in preparation for burning the offering sheds, and we were subject to the intense glare of the sun.

Garuḍa

Because the fire altar is built out of five layers of bricks in the shape of a falcon (*śyena*) or eagle, people eagerly scanned the skies hoping to spot an "eagle." They were not disappointed: a large bird (perhaps a vulture?) started circling high above the offering ground on the third day, later joined by others. There was a great commotion as people stopped, looked up, and pointed out the "mythical" bird, saying that Garuḍa had appeared. This happened a few more times over the next two days. The real appearance of Garuḍa was supposed to occur on the last day of the ritual.

The background of this belief is difficult to understand. Like so many others, it may be grounded in some ancient textual references, but in this particular case the association is not clear, apart from the bird shape of the altar. In the Vedic texts the falcon-shaped bird altar transports the sacrificer to heaven after his death. The disposal of the offering implements of the *pravargya* ritual in human form is a premonition of the laying out the dead body of the sacrificer and his subsequent transport to heaven.[48] The circling eagle may prophecy the success of the ritual. None of this is known to the local population, however, yet nevertheless they still regard the bird-shaped altar and its replica in the sky, the eagle, as very important. In this fashion, the old Vedic tradition continues in form, if not in meaning.

"Scientific Interpretation"

This brings us to another belief system, the so-called "scientific interpretation" of the ritual. Since at least 1975 the *agnicayana* has been interpreted "scientifically," with "measurable" effects of the sacrifice. In 1975 Frits told me that there was at least one person, a Dr. Raghavan, who believed in certain "scientific" effects. At the 2011 ritual there was a sizable contingent of scientists who went about measuring with various instruments whatever they thought was relevant in order to show the effects that the ritual had on the surroundings, nature, plants, and humans.

In the same vein, many of the local visitors often approached Frits and myself and asked many questions, usually about the "scientific effects" of the ritual. I tried to avoid the question by pointing to other more ritualistic and scholarly items. Similarly, Kerala TV took me aside for an interview and posed similar questions about the "scientifically measurable effects," which I again took pains to avoid answering directly.

The background of this situation is that since the 1870s the revisionist and fundamentalist factions of some Hindu sects (such as Arya Samaj, etc.) have tended to interpret Vedic texts and rituals in "modern" (i.e., quasi-scientific) fashion. Whatever the contemporary science of 1870, 1920, or 2011 had revealed about the nature of the universe, human beings, technology, and so on had now to be rediscovered in the ancient Vedic texts. It was therefore to be expected that from the late nineteenth century on these new interpretations have sought out quantifiable effects of the fire ritual on nature and human life. Beliefs that the performance of a fire ritual cleanses the air, kills bacteria, and establishes good relations between various groups of people became increasingly more widespread. These ideas have mushroomed and have become almost mainstream over the past 30 years, along with other "back to the future" Hindutva ideas.

Thus, at the ritual performances many aspects of the ritual were studied and measured, and some of this "research" was posted on a website dedicated to this particular ritual (in Telegu). During the 2011 *agnicayana* the spectacular *pravargya* ritual, which was carried out each morning and evening, attracted not only local visitors but also some rather serious scientists. A large spectrometer was put on a table, inside the offering ground, to measure the "explosion" of the milk. As could be expected, when the milk exploded this showed a major deviation from "normal" activity, to the pleasure of the scientist involved. Another scientist had planted some seeds and measured their growth rate with exposure to the ritual.[49]

Another Telugu-language website goes into great detail regarding the scientific measurements. It also mentions, for additional clout, the "Harvard group" that had visited the offering ground. Indeed, in general, many people automatically assumed that the academics present (including those of us from Harvard) had come to study the "scientific effects" of the ritual, and this led to our being asked about this aspect very often. When we responded that we were interested in the performance as such, as we had studied it, our interlocutors still insisted, "But what about the effects?"

It would be quite interesting to study the underlying belief system (though we did not at the time pursue it in great detail) and to follow up on the development of this now widely held belief, in order to examine how the intrusion of so-called scientific method in the margins of the ritual took place. Compared to 1975, in the last few decades "scientific" interest in the ancient rituals has exploded. One can observe this also in the performance and "interpretation" of similar, much smaller rituals, much of which is represented on the Internet, especially on YouTube. In the commentary accompanying such online presentations the various benefits resulting from the rituals on the surroundings and on those present in general are emphasized.

Some of our students had longer discussions with the scientists but, speaking for Frits and myself, and the other scholars who attended, our primary interest was in the ritual itself—the performance, the recitation, the singing. In the end, the experience was multidimensional, ranging from archaic recitation to current performance, contemporary belief, and "scientific interpretation."

We all have Frits to thank for having taken an interest in the *agnicayana* in 1975, thus laying the foundation for its preservation and its current resurgence.[50] As Frits wrote just a couple of weeks before his passing: "*Atiratram*s cannot be stopped now, so let us celebrate that as well."[51]

Notes

1 J. F. Staal, *Nambudiri Veda Recitation* ('s-Gravenhage: Mouton, 1961).

2 See: http://www.uni-hamburg.de/ngmcp/about_e.html.

3 See my note on such long-distance connections in "Textual Criticism in Indology and in European Philology during the 19th and 20th Centuries," *Electronic Journal of Vedic Studies* (2014): § 4.2, nn. 191–192; http://ejvs.laurasian-academy.com/witzel-philology.pdf.

4 The Summer School of Linguistics was another casualty of Chinese pressure. They had been operating throughout the country, recording the dozens of minority languages (obviously for missionary purposes) and they were now accused of spying and making flights without previous notification. This event was later fictionalized by Mani Dixit in his novel *The Red Temple* (Kathmandu: Sharda Prakashan Griha, 1977). I received my share of this habitual Nepalese fear of Western spies right from the start, when a taxi driver ("a well-known spy," as I later learned) observed me for a month before giving up, and again, much later, in the summer of 1977, I was about to sign an agreement for our microfilming project (NGMPP) and the Nepal Research Centre with the Nepalese Government and Tribhuvan University when I overheard a secret agent in the Home/Panchayat Ministry speaking in Nepali, referring to me and Dixit's book. I rushed to the embassy and we signed the same day.

5 Frits Staal, *Baby Krishna, rapport van de adviescommissie Kleine Letteren* (Amsterdam: KNAW, 1991).

6 These drastic measures were taken to save $150 million over three years. I accosted the Education Minister, Mr. Deetman, at an Indian Republic Day function, but he was of course evasive. My attempt may have helped my entomologist friend, Boštjan Kiauta, but that is a long story for another time. In 1986, Leiden's Indology program won out by a fluke, but all five other Indology institutes were closed; otherwise, only Groningen survived, with half of a position. Like some others, I preferred to leave for America.

7 See my pointedly titled paper, "Meaningful Ritual: Structure, Development, and Interpretation of the Tantric Agnihotra Ritual of Nepal," in A. W. van den Hoek, D. H. A. Kolff, and M. S. Oort, eds., *Ritual, State and History in South Asia: Essays in Honour of J. C. Heesterman* (Leiden: Brill, 1992), pp. 774–827.

8 Frits Staal's house is located at 67/1 Ban Pong, Hang Dong, Chiang Mai, Thailand 50230.

9 Vedic Workshop held at the University of Texas, Austin, May 2007. Material presented at this conference is collected in Joel Brereton, ed., *The Vedas in Indian Culture and History* (forthcoming).

10 See my paper, "Zur Geschichte der Rājopādhāyas von Bhaktapur," in H. Franke, et al., eds., *Folia Rara: Festschrift W. Voigt* (Wiesbaden: Verzeichnis der Orientalishen Handschriften in Deutschland Supplementband 19, 1976), pp. 155–175.

11 To which should be added its spread to Dravidian-speaking South India: the archaic *Baudhāyana Śrautasūtra* and even the *Baudhāyana Gṛhyasūtra* still advise

not to go to Kalinga, etc., while today all the Baudhāyanīya live in the Deccan and the deep South.

12 I have a complete copy, given to me by P. Bhaskararao.

13 http://www.olappamannamana.com. For a list of Frits' recordings made in Kerala in 1957, see his *Nambudiri Veda Recitation,* pp. 87–97.

14 Frits Staal, Agni: *The Vedic Ritual of the Fire Altar,* 2 vols. (Berkeley: Asian Humanities Press 1983).

15 The two-volume book also includes sound recordings. Frits previously published a recording that includes some Kerala recitation, *The Four Vedas,* Asch Mankind Series Album No. AHM 4126 (New York: Asch Records); http://lfs.alexanderstreet.com/liner/35d888e274854e00262a8fa74be311c9/FW04126.pdf.

16 See Itti Ravi Mamunne, "Agni and the Foreign Savants," Electronic Journal of Vedic Studies, Vol. 10, Issue 2 (2003); reprint of "Kerala Yajna with Foreign Participation" from the Illustrated Weekly of India, May 25, 1975, *Electronic Journal of Vedic Studies,* Vol. 10, Issue 3; http://ejvs.laurasianacademy.com/ejvs1003/cayana1.jpg sqq; http://ejvs.laurasianacademy.com/ejvs1002/1002.txt.

17 The approximately 30 Betamax videotapes (in black and white) were preserved at Berkeley and at the Instituut Kern, Leiden. I had two small sections copied to videotape in the 1980s, of the *pravargya* and interviews with Staal, Heesterman, and Sreekrishna Sarma. See https://www.youtube.com/watch?v=X5lfYRl3oqc.

18 Robert Gardner and J. F. Staal, *Altar of Fire* (color, 58 min.) (Film Study Center at Harvard University, 1976). The film is now available on CD/DVD: http://www.der.org/films/altar-of-fire.html. The original film cuts, some 25,000 feet, are in the collection of the Smithsonian Institute, Washington DC.

19 The "pizza effect" is so called after the fate of this originally low-class Italian food, which was exported to America, where it gained tremendous popularity, and was then reimported to Italy and is now also greatly appreciated there. The term goes back to the Hindu scholar Agehananda Bharati (L. Fischer); cf. http://en.wikipedia.org/wiki/Pizza_effect.

20 I too have experienced the "pizza effect," beginning in 1975. After I heard about an *agnihotra* being performed daily in Thambu, southern Patan, in the Kathmandu Valley, I arranged to have it filmed in February 1975, with the help of the Japanese broadcasting company NTV. Aiśvaryadhar Sharma, who belonged to the same *agnihotri* group of the Patan Rājopādhyaya Brahmins and who was then working in our Nepal-German Manuscript Preservation Project (NGMPP), became interested in the event and printed a small volume in Newari, *Agiṃ Maṭh,* which pointedly referred on the first page to "foreign intelligentsia" (the term was given in English!).

I later published two papers, "Agnihotra-Rituale in Nepal," in B. Kölver u. S. Lienhard, ed., *Formen kulturellen Wandels und andere Beiträge zur Erforschung des Himalaya* (St. Augustin: VGH Wissenschaftsverlag, 1986), pp. 157–187, and "Meaningful Ritual" (see note 7). The matter was taken up by some Dutch scholars who filmed more of the rituals in 1992, when the long-serving *agnihotri* died, and again in 2004; see https://www.academia.edu/648153/Filming_fire_rituals_in_Nepal.

By now the matter has come full circle again, as the local Patan community has picked up the case; see, for example, the recent illustrated book in Newari by Nijiros Srestha, *Yalayā agiṃmaṭha* (Lalitpur: Vijaya Prakāśana, 2013). The Patan community have also opened a Facebook page (mostly in Nepali): https://www.facebook.com/Agnishala.

21 Frits Staal, Agni 1990 (photocopy). This Agnicayana was held at Kundur, April 28–May 10, 1990. It was sponsored by Dr. T. I. Radhakrishnan of Thrissur. Frits describes (as discussed below for 2011) the many ritual criticisms and discussion among the priests and some onlookers. He prominently mentions the by-then pervasive study of the "scientific effects" of the ritual, as also was seen in 2011. For a modern "scientific" interpretation of a Soma Yajña, see https://www.youtube.com/watch?v=M4ZvxK7u7y0; https://www.youtube.com/watch?v=SgR9sdy6y8A. Note also, for Nepal: http://www.agnihotrausa.net/Nepal-Somayaag.html.

22 Dr. Vinod Bhattathiripad organizes the Nambudiri website, http://www.namboothiri.com/.

23 A few days later, in Thrissur, Frits gave a presentation on his favorite topic, the meaninglessness of ritual, in the Brahmasva Madhom, a traditional Veda school in Thrissur where the *Ṛgveda* (and now also other Vedas) are taught. He had written to me previously about his plan: "I want to show my PowerPoint presentation which is called 'Trichur—2011: A Theory of Ritual.' It is full of pictures of Nambudiris (as well as very different ones) but is basically informative—a university lecture but for a somewhat specialized audience of, say, 'Indologists.'" After he gave the presentation he later remarked to me, "I think it was a bit above their heads." Of course, hearing about the "meaninglessness" of their ritual was not welcome; as the *Mīmāṃsā* says, *svargakāmo [yajñena] yajeta, or agniṣṭomena sarvakāmo yajeta,* "The one who wishes to obtain heaven should offer [with a sacrifice]" or "The one wishing to obtain everything should offer with an *agniṣṭoma* (*soma* ritual)."

24 At Paññal we were later joined by some Japanese colleagues, Michio Yano, Makoto Fujii, Mieko Kajihara, and Hideki Teshima, but other than T. P. Mahadevan, no other Indologists attended, strangely enough.

25 http://www.ayurvedariverretreat.com.

26 Frits had written to me in 2010, long before the ritual event, that he had told the organizers: "I do NOT want to attend the *atiratra.* (I thought I was getting too old to stand in or more or less in the sun—excepting the real *atiratra* on the last night when all takes place during the relatively cool night)."

27 At that time Kathmandu had only three phone lines to Delhi, which were located in the central post office, and the telephones were constantly occupied by Indian (Agrawal) smugglers. So there was no way to be in contact with my family while in Kerala. Kathmandu got the first international shortwave radio/phone connection with Tokyo only later. Of course, Paññal then was without any communication infrastructure as well.

[28] Victor Henry W. Caland, *L'Agniṣṭoma: Description complète de la forme normale du sacrifice de Soma dans le cult védique* (Paris: Société Asiatique, 1906–1907) and *Das Śrautasūtra des Āpastamba* (Göttingen: Vandenhoeck & Ruprecht, 1921; Amsterdam: Koninklijke Akademie van Wetenschappen, 1924, 1928, reprints); R. N. Dandekar and C. G. Kashikar, *Śrautakośa (English and Sanskrit Sections)* (Poona: Vaidika Saṁśodhana Maṇḍaḷa, 1958).

[29] http://www.namboothiri.com/articles/programme-athiraathram.htm.

[30] Frits Staal, "Sanskrit and Sanskritization," *Journal of Asian Studies* 22 (1963): 261–275. The first, seminal investigation of this topic is M. N. Srinivas, *The Role of Sanskritization and Other Essays* (New York: Oxford University Press, 1988).

[31] We had hoped to get copies of the films, some 160 hours, but so far we have not succeeded in persuading the main donor to part with a copy. He posted only a few rather irrelevant small snippets on YouTube, which are no longer available. So we have had to rely on our own recordings, numerous photos, and footage from dozens of hours of filming.

[32] Quoted from his obituary in *The Hindu*, http://www.thehindu.com/news/national/kerala/frits-staal-an-influential-indologist-passes-away/article2913333.ece?ref=relatedNews. Due to constant demands for such rituals, some of these Brahmins have become relatively wealthy.

[33] I have audio and video recordings of this encounter. The Brahmin hesitated only briefly on a stanza in book 8, looked at it three times, then asked, "Is it from the *Vālakhilya*s?" When I said yes, he answered, "We don't study them. . . ." Basically, he confirmed what Max Müller, Theodor Aufrecht, C. G. Kashikar, etc., have published over the past 150 years.

[34] The original webpage, www.fritsstaalberkeley.com, so named in 2010, has since disappeared; the home page (but no other contents) is still visible at http://web.archive.org/web/20120111175216/http://www.fritsstaalberkeley.com/. His website at Berkeley, http://philosophy.berkeley.edu/staal, is also no longer available. See https://www.google.com/a/UniversalLogin?service=jotspot&passive=1209600&continue=http://sites.google.com/site/fritsstaal/&followup=http://sites.google.com/site/fritsstaal/. His obituary note can be found at http://sseas.berkeley.edu/news/johan-frederik-frits-staal-1930-2012.

[35] See http://www.ivw2014.org/images/Frits%20Memorial%20lecture.pdf.

[36] Present were Dr. P. Vinod Bhattathiripad, Chief Coordinator, and Mr. A. P. Namboothiri, Treasurer, of www.namboothiri.com; Mr. Thamarakkulam Vasudevan Namboothiri, Mr. Kakkad Parameswaran Namboothiri, Mr. Koithadi Parameswaran Namboothiri, and Mr. Kaippilli Neelakantan Namboothiri of the Yogakshema Sabha; Dr. Naaraas Ravindran Namboothiri, Representative of Thirunaavaaya Brahmaswam Madhom; and, of course, his old friend T. P. Mahadevan.

[37] See the photo in my blog: http://vedagya.blogspot.com/.

[38] However, there is no AV; it is well known from reports made by early Christian missionaries, that the AV was not found in South India (except, briefly under the Cola kings, around 1,000 C.E.).

39 Also in America, see: http://wapo.st/eyNt4R.

40 A TV crew began filming even before the ritual began, in Kannada; see http://wn.com/ tv9_athirathram_ancient_vedic_ritual_at_panjal_thrissur.

41 A photo of Frits greeting Kapra Ankara Narayanan was published along with Frits' obituary in *The Hindu;* see http://www.thehindu.com/news/national/kerala/frits-staal-an-influential-indologist-passes-away/article2913333.ece.

42 Michael Witzel, *Das Kaṭha Āraṇyaka: Textkritische Edition mit Übersetzung und Kommentur,* Diss. Phil. Erlangen-Nürnberg (Erlangen: Friedrich-Alexander-Universität, 1972).

43 Note, however, the artificial archaism in the incipient *Śrauta* ritual around 1,000 B.C.E.: the RV specifies a metal *pravargya* vessel.

44 Even the clothes worn by the ritualists during the sacrifice must be new, *ahata;* that is, unwashed by low-caste launderers.

45 See http://www.namboothiri.com/articles/yaagam-photos.htm, no. 18.

46 He can be seen on the left, assisting with the measuring the *yajamāna*'s height, at the beginning of this video: http://tinyurl.com/p8jaqrj.

47 A video (in Malayalam) by Varthathe, the foundation that sponsored the 2011 *agnicayana,* can be found online, under athirathram 2011.com. See http://tinyurl.com/l2gm38u; the fashioning of implements is at 5:30, excerpts from the ritual start at 9:30.

48 See Michael Witzel, ed., *Kaṭha Āraṇyaka: Critical Edition with a Translation into German and an Introduction* (Cambridge, MA: Harvard University Press, Department of Sanskrit and Indian Studies, 2004), pp. 68–71.

49 http://archive.indianexpress.com/news/ancient-ritual-has-positive-impact-on-environment-scientists/803474/.

50 Since 2011 there has been an *agnicayana* performance almost every year, in Kerala or elsewhere (with imported Nambudiris).

51 In an email to www.namboothiri.com; see http://www.ivw2014.org/images/Frits%20Memorial%20lecture.pdf, p. 4.

References

Caland, Victor Henry W. *Das Śrautasūtra des Āpastamba.* Göttingen: Vandenhoeck & Ruprecht, 1921; Amsterdam: Koninklijke Akademie van Wetenschappen, 1924, 1928, reprints.

—. *L'Agniṣṭoma: Description complète de la forme normale du sacrifice de Soma dans le cult védique.* Paris: Société Asiatique, 1906–1907.

Dandekar, R. N., and C. G. Kashikar. *Śrautakośa (English and Sanskrit Sections).* Poona: Vaidika Saṁśodhana Maṇḍaḷa, 1958.

Dixit, Mani. *The Red Temple.* Kathmandu: Sharda Prakashan Griha, 1977.

Gardner, Robert, and J. F. Staal. *Altar of Fire* (color, 58 min.). Cambridge, MA: Film Study Center at Harvard University, 1976.

Mamunne, Itti Ravi. "Agni and the Foreign Savants," *Electronic Journal of Vedic Studies,* Vol. 10, Issue 2 (2003).

—. "Kerala Yajna with Foreign Participation," reprint from the *Illustrated Weekly of India*, May 25, 1975, *Electronic Journal of Vedic Studies*, Vol. 10, Issue 3; http://ejvs.laurasianacademy.com/ejvs1003/cayana1.jpg sqq; http://ejvs.laurasian academy.com/ejvs1002/1002.txt.

Srestha, Nijiros. *Yalayā agiṃmaṭha* (in Newari). Lalitpur: Vijaya Prakāśana, 2013.

Srinivas, M. N. *The Role of Sanskritization and Other Essays*. New York: Oxford University Press, 1988.

Staal, Frits. *Agni 1990*. Photocopy.

—. *Agni: The Vedic Ritual of the Fire Altar*, 2 vols. Berkeley: Asian Humanities Press 1983.

—. *Baby Krishna, rapport van de adviescommissie Kleine Letteren*. Amsterdam: Koninklijke Akademie van WetenschappenKNAW, 1991.

—. *Nambudiri Veda Recitation*. 's-Gravenhage: Mouton, 1961.

—. "Sanskrit and Sanskritization," *Journal of Asian Studies* 22 (1963): 261–275.

—. *The Four Vedas*. Asch Mankind Series Album No. AHM 4126. New York: Asch Records; http://lfs.alexanderstreet.com/liner/35d888e274854e 00262a8fa 74be311c9/FW04126.pdf.

Witzel, Michael. "Agnihotra-Rituale in Nepal," in B. Kölver u. S. Lienhard, ed., *Formen kulturellen Wandels und andere Beiträge zur Erforschung des Himalaya*, pp. 157–187. St. Augustin: VGH Wissenschaftsverlag, 1986.

—. *Das Kaṭha Āraṇyaka: textkritische Edition mit Übersetzung und Kommentur*. Diss. Phil. Erlangen-Nürnberg. Erlangen: Friedrich-Alexander-Universität, 1972.

—, ed. *Kaṭha Āraṇyaka: Critical Edition with a Translation into German and an Introduction*. Harvard Oriental Series, vol. 65. Cambridge, MA: Harvard University Press, Department of Sanskrit and Indian Studies, 2004.

—. "Meaningful Ritual: Structure, Development, and Interpretation of the Tantric Agnihotra Ritual of Nepal," in A. W. van den Hoek, D. H. A. Kolff, and M. S. Oort, eds., *Ritual, State and History in South Asia: Essays in Honour of J. C. Heesterman*, pp. 774–827. Leiden: Brill, 1992.

—. "Textual Criticism in Indology and in European Philology during the 19th and 20th centuries," *Electronic Journal of Vedic Studies* (2014); http://ejvs.laurasian academy.com/witzel-philology.pdf.

—. "Zur Geschichte der Rājopādhāyas von Bhaktapur," in H. Franke, et al., eds., *Folia Rara: Festschrift W. Voigt*, pp. 155–175. Wiesbaden: Verzeichnis der Orientalischen Handschriften in Deutschland Supplementband 19, 1976.

King Sūryavarman II and the Power of Subjugation

Hiram Woodward
Walters Art Museum

A well-known scene among the bas-reliefs in the southern gallery of the temple known as Angkor Wat depicts King Sūryavarman II (r. 1113–after 1150) as commander of his troops. In his right hand he holds what appears to be a snake (Figs. 1, 2). This attribute is so strange that it is generally explained away or ignored. Eleanor Mannikka clearly describes what she saw:

> Quite inexplicably, King Sūryavarman is holding a dangling snake in his right hand; his left hand, extending toward the men in front of him, holds a small unidentified object apparently wrapped in cloth.[1]

More commonly the object has been turned into something else. Etienne Aymonier writes that the right hand

> holds an object in the form of a lizard with short paws, a sort of perfume sachet, one supposes, with which most of the blessed ones, kings and queens, in the succeeding reliefs are provided.[2]

George Cœdès, writing in 1911, quotes Aymonier and then asks, "Wouldn't it more likely be a purse, an attribute indicating wealth, akin to Kubera's mongoose?"[3] More recently Vittorio Roveda describes it as "a small elongated object, probably a piece of jewelry in the shape of a lotus."[4] In an extended interpretive analysis of the galleries with bas-reliefs, Thomas Maxwell ignores it altogether.[5] Sure enough, the object is not actually a snake, dead or alive. On the basis of texts and rituals preserved in Siam, with a high degree of confidence it can be identified as a *nāgapāśa,* a "serpent noose," a section of a lasso, doubtless gilded. If this object was like the later Thai manifestations, it was the emblem of a powerful mantra that served to pacify elephants. In light of a Sanskrit text from Bali, it was the embodiment of the magical power of subjugation, *vaśīkaraṇa.* The evidence is summarized in the following sections.

Figure 1 (above). Angkor Wat, southern gallery of bas-reliefs: King Sūryavarman II. (Photograph by Martin Polkinghorne.)

Figure 2 (left). Angkor Wat, southern gallery of bas-reliefs: the snake (*nāgapāśa*) in King Sūryavarman's right hand. (Photograph by Martin Polkinghorne.)

The Subjugation of Elephants in Siam

There are four sources of especial significance. One is a legend recorded in the nineteenth century. Another is a page opening, with both text and illustrations, in a class of manuscripts concerning the characteristics of elephants, here shown in an example in the Walters Art Museum, dating from the 1810s or 1820s (Fig. 3). The third source is a record of the capture of a white elephant, and the fourth a description of a royal ceremony, as found in the book "Royal Ceremonies of the Twelve Months" by King Chulalongkorn (r. 1868–1910).

The legend, or myth, is found in "The Incarnations of the Gods" (*Deva pāṅ*).[6] A group of wizards and hermits calls on Śiva on Mt. Kailāsa to lodge a complaint about an evil marauding elephant named Ekadanta, "one tusk." Śiva sends two of the group to Viṣṇu, then lying on the cosmic ocean. Viṣṇu ("Nārāyaṇa Devakarma," referred to as Nārāyaṇa subsequently in this paper) comes to earth in a six-armed form, with each hand holding a weapon, one of which is a lasso formed by the *nāga* king, Anantanāgarāja. The lasso is therefore a *nāgapāśa,* although this term is not used in "The Incarnations of the Gods." Nārāyaṇa encounters four farmers who are astonished at seeing a man with six arms, and when the god asks about the location of Ekadanta, the farmers tell him it is a long

Figure 3. Six-armed Viṣṇu (Nārāyaṇa Devakarma). "The Characteristics of Elephants," accordion-pleated manuscript, Bangkok, Siam, ca. 1810–1830, face 1, f. 5. The Walters Art Museum, Baltimore, W.893, gift of the Doris Duke Charitable Foundation's Southeast Asian Art Collection, 2002.

journey that includes a sea voyage. At last they meet Ekadanta. Nārāyaṇa uses his weapons and tells the four men to memorize a mantra called *bṛḍhipāśa.* (*Bṛḍhipāśa,* pronounced *phrütthibāt,* is the spelling in the modern printed texts, but there is evidence that the historically correct spelling is *bṛddhapāśa,* i.e., *vṛddhapāśa.* The meaning is "old brahmin priest specializing in the lasso.") Eventually Nārāyaṇa snares Ekadanta's right foot with his serpent lasso, and he returns to the cosmic ocean. The four farmers are now in possession of the *bṛddhapāśa* mantra, and they teach it to their sons, who become masters of *gajakarma,* "elephant affairs"—or, more narrowly, elephant ritual—and the same privileged ability is passed down for the benefit of future generations.[7] The suffix *karma* is common in texts having to do with elephants. *Karma* can be understood as meaning "business," "activities," or "affairs," and *gajakarma,* "elephant affairs," includes capturing and training elephants. It includes as well the mastery of mantras and of ritual activities, in line with karma understood in a narrower sense. It also refers to personifications.

At the beginning of the Elephant Characteristics manuscripts, there are three presiding deities, the first two elephant-headed, with an opening devoted to each. First is Śivaputrabighneśvara ("Lord of Obstacles, Son of Śiva"), who is the encompassing god. Then comes Koñcanāneśvaraśivaputra ("Lord Elephant Head, Son of Śiva"), who stands for knowledge, including knowledge of the different types of elephants, the subject of the bulk of the manuscript that follows. Both can be understood as manifestations of the elephant-headed god Gaṇeśa. The third god (Fig. 3) is Nārāyaṇa Devakarma, the very deity who made an appearance in "The Incarnations of the Gods."

On this opening the caption at the top center says, "This lord is called Debakarrma" (in Thai pronounced Thepphakam), that is, Nārāyaṇa Devakarma. He is not shown with all his weapons, only with two *nāgapāśa,* snake-headed nooses, green in color. Flanking him, identifiable on the basis of their headdresses, are two *ṛṣis,* whom we can imagine to be the ambassadors to Nārāyaṇa while he was reclining on the cosmic ocean. Captions state their names (they are nameless in "The Incarnation of the Gods").[8] Below Nārāyaṇa, two seated figures, their palms pressed together in adoration, are encircled by a long blue snake intertwined with six shorter red snakes. Each is labeled Debaputa, "Son of a God," but they don't specifically match any of the characters in "The Incarnations of the Gods." I understand them to be two of the four farmers, who have become semidivine because they are now in the possession of the *bṛddhapāśa* mantra, symbolized by the encircling snakes.

There are also three distinct texts on this opening. At lower left are five Sanskritic lines that probably would be called *wet* in Thai, i.e., the Veda. Their relationship to the mantra entrusted by Nārāyaṇa to the farmers is unclear.[9] The first two lines are apparently directed to Gaṇeśa, or to Śivaputrabighneśvara, the first of the three presiding deities in the manuscript. He is Mahodaro, "great-bellied one," and possesses a trunk that achieves victory by means of loud trumpeting. The third line invokes the lasso, which is called a *nāgapāśa.* The epithets in the fourth line appear to be directed to Ekadanta, the marauding elephant. The fifth line expresses hope for success.

On the right-hand side of the opening are two lines with this mantra:

Om he he tiṣa caḥ tiṣa ha na ya
Tejena asai svā hāya svā phat

And below this there are instructions in Thai, "After the mantra is read three times the coiled and subjugated lasso becomes loose." In other words, reciting the mantra is equivalent to using the noose to snare the mad elephant.

An account of the capture and transport of a white elephant in 1812 provides a significant detail that serves as a link to the use of the lasso in a Siamese royal ceremony:

> The lasso that had been used to snare the Lord White Elephant was lacquered and gilded and preserved as the premier lasso, for use in royal ceremonies.[10]

This means that a ceremonial *nāgapāśa,* which stands directly for Nārāyaṇa's gift to the farmers, has in addition acquired its sacred nature by an entirely different route, due to the fact that the divine character of the white elephant has rubbed off on it.

Three gilded lassos figure in the "casting off and pulling in the rope" ceremony of the fifth month (around April). It is described in *The Ceremonies of the Twelve Months* by King Chulalongkorn.[11] Ritual needs to be looked upon as an independent source of information, distinct from myth, from the content of an opening in a manuscript, and from mantras; quite possibly the ritual has sources older than any of these three. King Chulalongkorn's vivid and dramatic description offers a complementary perspective.

The ceremony takes place on the evening of the third day of the waning moon, fifth month. A temporary pavilion is set up on the Sanam Luang, the open area adjacent to the royal palace, and curtains are hung around it, because the ceremony must remain secret. On a set of tiered shelves inside, images of Iśvara, Nārāyaṇa, and Vighneśvara (Gaṇeśa) are placed on the top shelf, with ritual utensils below. In front are four low tables, three holding gilded nooses, the fourth a silver-plated noose, and food offerings stand in front of each. Further out there is a fifth table, for the elephant harness paraphernalia, rope for the *phatchā* dance.[12] Following the customary rites involving the images and ceremonial objects, the brahmins "read the Veda"—possibly the texts in the manuscript (Fig. 3)—and lustrate the lassos. There are established sequences of music. One of the *bṛddhapāśa* brahmins, the Director of the Elephant Department, and the Deputy Director kneel in front of the lassos and raise them up (how many lassos is not clear), either symbolically or by actually uncoiling them. An elephant driver whose position is at the elephant's rear crouches on the ground. A senior *bṛddhapāśa* brahmin places a coiled elephant harness on his back and then sticks an elephant goad into it, which the driver grasps. Two *bṛddhapāśa* brahmins recite an old poetical text, sections of an "Elephant Lullaby."[13] Meanwhile, conches are sounded, and people sprinkle *khao tok* (popped rice kernels) and flowers, which have been carried on two pairs of trays: golden trays for royalty and silver trays for government officials.

Then either the Director or the Deputy Director of the Elephant Department, whoever is the more skillful dancer, takes the role of Nārāyaṇa, at the time that Nārāyaṇa, writes King Chulalongkorn, changed his face into the face of an elephant, descended, and taught the knowledge of *gajakarma* to the four men at the time of the pacification of the elephant Ekadanta. (In the manuscript opening, Fig. 3, Nārāyaṇa retains his divine face.) Then the elaborate *phatchā* dance begins, accompanied by appropriate music and characterized by the assumption of various poses, including a rhythmic prostration, and the repetition of certain sequences. The performer takes the lasso rope—the section that had been placed on the fifth table—and dances with it, rhythmically extending it three times, executing other actions, and bringing the dance to a close with a prostration.

Perhaps it would be a mistake to attempt to analyze how the myth and the ceremony correspond. What does seem to be the case, nevertheless, is that the instruction on the bottom right-hand side of the manuscript opening (Fig. 3), "after the mantra is read three times the coiled and subjugated lasso becomes loose," is the equivalent of the performer's dance with the rope, and that a kind of mystic identity between Nārāyaṇa, the four farmers, and the officials of the Elephant Department has been achieved.

The Context of the Angkor Wat Relief

The inscription over Sūryavarman's head reads *"Saṃtac Vraḥ pāda kamrateṅ añ Paramaviṣṇuloka nā stac nau vnaṃ Çivapāda pi pañcuḥ vala,"* according to the transcription made by George Cœdès in 1911.[14] He translates it as "S. M. le roi Paramaviṣṇuloka, au moment où reside sur le mont Çivapāda pour faire descendre l'armée."[15] Thomas S. Maxwell translates, "His Supreme Majesty, Lord Paramavishnuloka, staying on Mount Sivapada and commanding the army to descend."[16] The words are susceptible to a fairly narrow range of interpretations: *nā* (a locative participle, referring to time or space) *stac* (to stand, of elevated beings; sacred beings, especially princes) *nau* (to remain) *vnaṃ* (mountain or temple) *pi* (and then) *pañcuḥ* (to cause to go down; to subdue; to receive homage) *vala* (forces).[17] For reasons that will become apparent, I would like to find in the inscription a temporal sequence, as in "the king has been staying at Mount Śivapāda and then he has his army descend."

There are two proper names. "Paramaviṣṇuloka," writes Cœdès, can only be interpreted in a single way, to mean "the king who has gone to Paramaviṣṇuloka," that is, the "world of the supreme Viṣṇu," because there are inscriptions that spell this out, using the word *tau,* "to go."[18] Although these inscriptions all involve other monarchs, and the name Paramaviṣṇuloka is nowhere else attested, it can only refer to Sūryavarman II. The form of the name indicates that the inscription was carved after the king's death. Proposing any other interpretation of the name would be a losing battle. Śivapāda, "Śiva's footprint," appears elsewhere in Khmer epigraphy as the name of a temple, almost always with the words "East" or "West" attached. These two temples have been identified, respectively, as Prasat Neak Buos, 30 kilometers southwest of Preah Vihear, and Prasat Preah Net Preah in far western Cambodia.[19] The heading *vnaṃ,* the tree canopy in the scene, and the fact that a little further on soldiers are actually shown descending a hill all suggest that it may not be a temple or a temple site that is here referred to but rather an unidentified and undeveloped mountain location actually thought to have been the site of a Śiva footprint.

In order to provide a context for this scene, there are reasons for wanting to invoke the mythological depictions in the bas-reliefs of the southwest corner pavilion, the reliefs that immediately precede in a circumambulation of the temple. One is the way Sūryavarman is depicted. As George Cœdès writes:

> [W]hat can and should be noted is the divine appearance of the king enthroned on the mountain, dressed similarly to the gods in the mythological scenes, almost identical to Viṣṇu, whose name is part of his posthumous title.[20]

The Thai myth also prompts a backward glance; if the king's *pāśa* has been presented to him through divine intervention, perhaps such a scene is actually depicted.

For the most part the scenes in the southwest corner pavilion consist of fairly well-known episodes from the mythology of Śiva, Rāma, and Kṛṣṇa, though questions remain about the character of any underlying structural rationale for their placement.[21] The scenes in the eastern wing, however, the wing opening directly into the southern gallery, remain puzzling. They are three in number: the scene directly above the doorway (Fig. 4), and the two scenes facing each other to the left (the north, Fig. 5) and right (the south, Fig. 6).

Figure 4. Angkor Wat, southwest corner pavilion, east wing, Viṣṇu over the entrance to the southern gallery. (CAM 05816_3, fonds Cambodge © EFEO.)

The scene above the doorway (Fig. 4) is the least complex. Cœdès, writing in 1911, sees

> two young men, accompanied by a bearded man wearing a sort of tiara and by servants carrying cakes or covered dishes, pay[ing] homage to a statue of Viṣṇu. Giving names to the participants in this scene is for the present impossible.[22]

Here is Mannikka's description:

> Opposite this scene, a four-armed Viṣṇu, majestic and hierarchical, is illustrated vertically and frontally, with offerings being made to him in a composition that is compositionally heraldic. The deity is now seen in full transformation: from Viṣṇu incarnate as a child (Kṛṣṇa) to Viṣṇu as a symbol of power. It is under this inspiring image of the four-armed standing Viṣṇu that the visitor passes to view the panel of King Sūryavarman. There could be no better introduction to the Vaiṣṇnava ruler—and no better balance to the emphasis on Śiva in this pavilion.[23]

In 1928 Jean Przyluski, seeking a textual source for the scene, proposed that it depicts an episode in the *Bhagavata Purāṇa,* in which Kṛṣṇa persuades the cowherds not to make offerings to the god Indra, resulting in their presenting them to Kṛṣṇa instead. This is a far-fetched interpretation that later scholars have repeated.[24]

The same need to find a textual source has arisen in the interpretation of the panels on the north and south. As for the northern one (Fig. 5), sometimes labeled the Dvāravatī Water Festival, Cœdès writes:

> It is otherwise impossible to determine the legend the scene refers to, these two galleys navigating in formation and carrying various people busy playing or watching various spectacles, including cockfighting.[25]

Figure 5. Angkor Wat, southwest corner pavilion, east wing, north side, section showing the boat in the upper part, with the game of chess. (CAM 05813_4, fonds Cambodge © EFEO.)

The Dvāravatī Water Festival is an episode in the life of Kṛṣṇa, described in the *Harivaṁśa Purāṇa:* "These ships carry large buildings with porticoes, verandas, and gardens with wild animals and birds, in an arrangement that simulates Mount Meru").[26] Roveda writes that if the textual source is truly the *Harivaṁśa,* then the lower boat would hold Kṛṣṇa and his wives, while the upper, smaller boat (Fig. 5) carries his brother Balarāma, playing chess.[27]

The poorly preserved last panel (Fig. 6) on the southern side of the wing also puzzled Cœdès. Within a broad panorama showing *ṛṣi* in a mountain setting and celestial beings, there is a central depiction where

> It is only possible to identify a figure of Śiva conversing with four men, the first of whom has a coiffure like that of Viṣṇu and Rāma. He appears to receive from the god, or to hand to him, various objects impossible to make out. This scene would doubtless be difficult to identify.[28]

Figure 6. Angkor Wat, southwest corner pavilion, east wing, south side, section showing the presentation of gifts to Śiva or to a *sādhaka.* (CAM 05818_1, fonds Cambodge © EFEO.)

Roveda speculates that the scene could have a connection with Śiva's request for the daughter of the king of the Himalayas as a bride, making the personage proffering (or receiving) a gift from Śiva this king. There is little in the way of supporting evidence for this proposal, but Roveda does make a pertinent and provocative observation about the object Śiva carries in his left hand: "[H]e holds a piece of fine jewelry with a tapering flexible stem (almost identical to the object that Suryavarman II is holding in the Historic Procession)"[29]—that is, the object that has been identified as a gilded *nāgapāśa* (Fig. 2).

The *Mahāmāyā*

The expectations of scholars that eventually a textual source would be uncovered have not been misplaced. In 1978, Teun Goudriaan published *Māyā Divine and Human,* an investigation of the textual sources for the belief that, as the *Matsya Purāṇa* put it, *indrajāla* or *māyā,* the practice of delusion and magic, both defensive and offensive, is a necessary component of *rājanīti,* the science of politics.[30] The centerpiece of the book is a brief text from Bali, in 21 stanzas, called *Mahāmāyā,* "The Great Delusive Manifestation," describing the powers of the god Viṣṇu. Here are the first nine stanzas (Goudriaan's translation):

1. One who will have heard of or meditated upon
   The nature of this Delusive Manifestation in pacified (*śāntaṃ*) form
   Which is a Purifier difficult to obtain,—
   He is released from all evil.

2. The God [of your meditation] be Viṣṇu,
   And He with two eyes, bearing
   Mace, conch, sword and disc; with four arms,
   Golden of colour, standing upon a lotus as pedestal.

3. He is to be honored by all the hosts of the Immortals,
   Adorned with all kinds of ornaments;
   In the case of a recitation in combination with the sound *Oṃ*
   This [mantra] averts all danger.
   Oṃ oṃ Viṣṇave namaḥ svāhā

4. If one needs an act of attraction (*ākarṣaṇa*),
   One should meditate on the God as white;
   With a white garment, and flowers (and other gifts) white;
   One utters the words *vaṣaṭ aṃ vaṣaṭ.*
   Oṃ vaṣaṭ Aṃ vaṣaṭ namaḥ svāhā

5. [Then] a king, even when he lives in another continent
   And when he has been driven away to a remote place,
   Will appear on the scene and humbly present
   His riches to the performer (*sādhaka*).

6. A river filled to the rim with water
   Which came from the swollen rain clouds,
   Quietly streams forth with her water pacified
   And is pulled into the opposite direction.

7. And in the case of an act of subjugation (*vaśīkaraṇa*),
   One should meditate on the god as red,
   With a red garment, and flowers and other [gifts] red;
   One utters the words *vaṣaṭ ghoṃ vaṣaṭ*.
   Oṃ vaṣaṭ Ghoṃ vaṣaṭ namaḥ svāhā

8. And [then] elephants in rut, excited and of a cruel mind,
   And also unconquerable enemies
   Are subjugated by the recitation [of this spell].

9. [Damsels] with the gait of rutting elephants,
   With breasts full and high,
   With faces shaped like the moon,
   Become his servants if a man recites [the spell].[31]

There are five magical powers in the text, each of which is assigned a color: white for attraction (*ākarṣaṇa*), red for subjugation (*vaśīkaraṇa*), yellow for immobilization (*stambhana*), dark blue for eradication (*uccāṭana*), and all four colors for pacification (*prāyaścitta*). Goudriaan's book is an investigation into the background and context of a text such as this, which he believes was composed in India, although he admits that he had not succeeded in tracing it to its origins.

The Angkor Wat sculptures cannot be understood as a translation into narrative relief of any of the texts or sources so far presented—not the *Mahāmāyā* or the Thai materials. It is, rather, yet another variation, with some of the same elements and some quite distinct ones. Let us take the four scenes, one by one, and see how they relate, first to the *Mahāmāyā*, and second to the various Thai sources.

The scene over the doorway (Fig. 4): stanza 3 of the *Mahāmāyā* says that "He is to be honored by all the hosts of the Immortals (*sarvāmaragaṇasevyaḥ*), adorned with all kinds of ornaments." This does not fit particularly well; the figures in the air could well be immortals, but they are only four in number, though the floral banners they hold could perhaps be conceived as ornaments. The men at Viṣṇu's feet do not appear to be immortals. The innermost ones, with their hands outstretched, bear an uncanny resemblance to the pair of *ṛṣi*s that flank Nārāyaṇa Devakarma in the manuscript opening (Fig. 3). This implies that this Viṣṇu has already manifested himself in the world. If so, then the cast of characters might resemble that in the Royal Ceremony. The figure on the right with the pointed headgear would be the senior *bṛddhapāśa* brahmin. We might expect four trays with rice cakes, but here there are only three. Still, this is not a bad fit.

The scene on the southern wall (Fig. 6), according to the *Mahāmāyā:*

> [Then] a king, even when he lives in another continent
> And when he has been driven away to a remote place,
> Will appear on the scene and humbly present
> His riches to the performer (*sādhaka,* "adept," "magician," "worshiper").

If this is the case, then the man to the immediate left of the enthroned figure is indeed a king and he really is presenting gifts. The two similarly attired men beside him would have to be identified as princes of some sort. Is it possible that the enthroned figure is not Śiva at all, but a ritual performer (*sādhaka*) in the guise of Śiva?

The Thai material suggests a different interpretation. The bearded man is Śiva, who is being approached by humans seeking his assistance in ridding the world of the evil Ekadanta. But none of the sources can tell us for sure if he is holding a *nāgapāśa,* or, if it is a *nāgapāśa,* whether it's the same one that ends up in the hand of Sūryavarman II or another one. Equally uncertain is whether this forest setting is also the Phnom Śivapāda mentioned in the inscription over Sūryavarman's head.

The northern wall (Fig. 5): "A river filled to the rim with water/which came from the swollen rain clouds, quietly streams forth with her water pacified/and is pulled into the opposite direction." Even the most imaginative scholar would have been unlikely to be able to conjure up an explanation of the relief based on the change of direction of the Tonle Sap River, toward the sea from November to May, into the Great Lake from June to October. Perhaps both boats are headed toward Angkor; perhaps one is departing. The magical power involved here, as in the relief on the southern wall, is attraction (*ākarṣaṇa*). It is the king's power of attraction that causes the waters and the boats upon it to flow toward him. There is no hint of rivers that change direction in the Thai sources. One possible connection, however, is calendrical. The noose ceremony was traditionally also performed six months later, in the eleventh month, conceivably distantly echoing the seasonal change.

Sūryavarman (Figs. 1, 2): "And in the case of an act of subjugation (*vaśīkaraṇa*),/one should meditate on the God as red/. . . And [then] elephants in rut, excited and of a cruel mind,/and also unconquerable enemies/are subjugated by the recitation [of this spell]." Goudriaan comments that stanza 8 is exceptional because two different objects, elephants and enemies, are dealt with rather than a single one. He goes on to say that elephants are also mentioned in an Old Javanese paraphrase of this text.[32] The presence of elephants is, of course, an essential element in the argument I am making in this paper, that the power of subjugation was divinely granted on the basis of the need to calm a cruel elephant and only subsequently extended to having power over one's enemies, and, in the following stanza, to women. In the relief, the power is made evident quite discretely, by the presence of the *nāgapāśa* in Sūryavarman's hand.

A significant difference between the reliefs and the Thai traditions must be acknowledged. In Siam possession of the mantra and the *nāgapāśa* was reserved for the *bṛddhapāśa* brahmins and officials of the Elephant Department. It may be that in an earlier period, when monarchs were masters of elephant-mounted combat, the situation was different. Nevertheless, the features of the Angkor Wat reliefs are sufficiently distinct that it must be asked whether a plausible narrative structure can be surmised. It seems to depend on the interpretation of the mountain scene (Fig. 6) and the identification of the enthroned figure, of the object he holds, which I am inclined to think really is a *nāgapāśa*, and of the gift-giver, whom I am prepared to call Sūryavarman.

If the enthroned figure is indeed Śiva, it could be said that he hands the *nāgapāśa* to Sūryavarman and that Viṣṇu, overhead at the entrance to the southern gallery (Fig. 4), is a statement that the king's reentry into the world of humans is like Viṣṇu returning to earth. In this narrative Sūryavarman would be playing the role of Nārāyaṇa Devakarma in the Thai myth (somewhat like the performer in the Royal Ceremony, except that this would be a lifetime commitment). A second line of interpretation, which I tend to favor, follows from the identification of the enthroned figure on the mountain (Fig. 6) as a *sādhaka* who has identified himself with Śiva. In this case, Viṣṇu has already appeared on earth (the Viṣṇu in the relief, Fig. 4) and entrusted the *nāgapāśa* to the *sādhaka* who dwells on Phnom Śivapāda. The *sādhaka* directly hands the *nāgapāśa* over to Sūryavarman. This second narrative has an advantage in that it makes the two scenes facing each other, north and south (Figs. 5, 6), both mundane, sea opposed to mountain. Both scenes would be manifestations of Viṣṇu's magic power (*māyā*). This need for interpretation suggests that there never was a master text that served as the basis for the reliefs, only a group of related texts (or images, mantras, or ceremonies) that were drawn from in various ways.

A Broader Setting

It seems at least possible that elephant subjugation was a realm in which rituals and magical sayings played a role prior to the advent of Indian influence on Southeast Asia. In one of two articles on elephant hunting in Siam by Francis Giles, he describes the lasso cult of a village of elephant hunters in northeastern Thailand:

> The lasso is housed in a building standing high and separated from the homes of the villagers, no woman is allowed to trespass within the precincts of this house. A fact stands forth with clear definition which is of importance and must be set down here, it is that the lasso is not protected by any particular spirit or possessed by one. It is the spirit itself, and it is for this reason that such honour is paid to it.[33]

The issue brings to mind Frits Staal's belief that

> Balinese rites seem to have been provided with Indian names without changing substantially. They probably incorporated other Indian elements, possibly mudras, but the chief respect in which they were Indianized was mantras.[34]

Staal challenged us to think about the relationship of myth, rituals, and mantras. He wrote that ritual "does *not*, or only rarely reflect myths" and that "the chief instruments of Indianization were mantras."[35] The material presented in this paper—myths, rituals, mantras, as well as images—all seem so interlocked that I can say only that it may support Staal's views. Or it may not. Still, it provides an opportunity for reflection, as does the fact that mantras and ritual, in this instance, seem to have arisen from the need to communicate with non-humans.[36]

Notes

1 Eleanor Mannikka, *Angkor Wat: Time, Space, and Kingship* (Honolulu: University of Hawai'i Press, 1996), p. 148.

2 Etienne Aymonier, *Le Cambodge* (Paris: Ernest Leroux, 1900–1904), vol. 3, pp. 241–252: "la main tenant un objet en forme de lézard à courtes pattes, sorte de sachet perfumé, peut-on supposer, dont sont munis la plupart des bienheureux, rois ou reines, de la galerie suivante."

[3] George Cœdès, "Les bas-reliefs d'Angkor Wat," *Bulletin de la Commission Archéologique de l'Indochine* 2 (1911): 201–202, n. 5: "Ne serait-ce pas plutôt une sorte de bourse, un attribut indiquant la richesse, analogue à la mangouste de Kubera?"

[4] Vittorio Roveda, *Sacred Angkor: The Carved Reliefs of Angkor Wat* (Trumbull, CT: Weatherhill, 2002), p. 29.

[5] Jaroslav Poncar and Thomas S. Maxwell, *Of Gods, Kings, and Men: The Reliefs of Angkor Wat* (Heidelberg: Edition Panorama, 2006), p. 133. It is also unmentioned in Albert le Bonheur, *Of Gods, Kings, and Men: Bas-reliefs of Angkor Wat and Bayon* (London: Serindia, 1995), p. 19.

[6] "Incarnations of the Gods": *Thewa Pāng* (Bangkok: Krom Sinlapakòn, 1970). The myth is related in Henry Ginsburg, *Thai Manuscript Painting* (Honolulu: University of Hawai'i Press, 1989), pp. 36–38. For additional references see Hiram Woodward, "'The Characteristics of Elephants': A Thai Manuscript and its Context," in Justin McDaniel and Lynn Ransom, eds., *From Mulberry Leaves to Silk Scrolls: New Approaches to the Study of Asian Manuscript Traditions*, pp. 15–41 (Philadelphia: University of Pennsylvania Libraries, 2015). The information in this section is based on this article.

[7] *Thewa Pāng*, pp. 8–11. For *karman* as ritual, opposed to knowledge (*vijñāna*), see Frits Staal, *Mantras between Fire and Water: Reflections on a Balinese Rite* (Amsterdam: North-Holland, 1995), p. 41.

[8] On the left, "Ṛṣī Darabhāṣa Debakarrma," and on the right, "Ṛṣī Siddhi Braḥ Karrma."

[9] For a transcription and a tentative translation (courtesy of Phillip Scott Ellis Green) see Woodward, "'The Characteristics of Elephants,'" pp. 37–38, n. 20.

[10] *Čhotmāi het rüang rap phrayā sawettakunchòn chāng phüak ræk dai nai ratchakān thī* 2 (Bangkok: Watchīrayān Library, 1927), p. 36.

[11] King Chulalongkorn of Siam, *Phra rātchaphitthī sipsòng düan* (Bangkok: Khlang Witthayā, 1964), pp. 249–254. This classic text, never translated into English, was the primary source for H. G. Quaritch Wales, *Siamese State Ceremonies: Their History and Their Function* (London: Bernard Quaritch, 1931). This particular ceremony was not discussed in Quaritch Wales, but a related fifth-month ceremony, *snāna*, the sprinkling of the elephants and horses, is briefly described on p. 297. In the account of this ceremony by Nang Nopphamat (first half of the nineteenth century), it is said to honor Braḥ Devakarrm, an image of whom is carried upon an elephant; *Nāng Nopphamāt* (Bangkok: Krom Sinlapakòn, 1960), pp. 71–72. I am grateful to Dr. Samerchai Poolsuwan for his assistance in the interpretation of King Chulalongkorn's description. Remaining errors are my own responsibility.

[12] The three named utensils are *klot*, *sang*, and *benchakhap* (King Chulalongkorn, *Phra rātchaphitthī*, pp. 251–252). *Klot* is either a one-tiered parasol or a *kalaśa*, "ewer" (misspelled). For ewer, see Wales, *Siamese State Ceremonies*, fig. 5 (opp. p. 248), no. 6. *Sang* is a conch. *Benchakhap* (= *pañcagarbha*) is either a set of five cups (Wales, *Siamese State Ceremonies*, fig. 5, no. 5) or the vessel described in G. E. Gerini, *Chūḷākantamaṅgala: The Tonsure Ceremony As Performed in Siam*

(Bangkok: Siam Society, 1976, reprint), pp. 129–130. The lasso is *chüak* (rope) *bāt* [*pāśa*], the elephant harness *chāng* (elephant) *chanak,* and the rope for the *phatchā* dance, *chüak rām,* transcribing the Thai words phonetically. The etymological meaning of *phatchā* is not known to me.

13 For references to this literature, see Woodward, "'The Characteristics of Elephants.'"

14 Cœdès, "Les bas-reliefs," p. 201.

15 Cœdès, "Les bas-reliefs," p. 202n. An earlier translation by Aymonier reads: "Sa Majesté, les Pieds sacrés, seigneur et maitre, Parama Viṣṇuloka, lorsque le roi est sur le mont S'ivapāda (donnant les orders) pour le rassemblement des troupes"; *Le Cambodge,* vol. 3, p. 251. Picking up on the semantic difference, Roveda suggests that the legend could mean either "receiving homage from his troops" or "who makes his troops descend Mount Shivapada"; *Sacred Angkor,* p. 29. Judging from Phillip N. Jenner and Saveros Pou, *A Lexicon of Khmer Morphology* (Manoa: University Press of Hawai'i, 1980–1981), p. 60, *pañcuḥ* should be taken here as a transitive verb, meaning to lower or to subdue, thereby excluding the sense of "to gather." In Le Bonheur, *Of Gods, Kings, and Men,* p. 19, the two suggested possibilities are "receiving homage from his troops" and (crediting Mr. Sunseng) "bestowing [Śiva's power] from above upon the troops," in the latter instance understanding *pañcuḥ* as a transitive verb and inserting an unstated object.

16 Poncar and Maxwell, *Of Gods, Kings, and Men,* p. 183; cf. p. 133.

17 Saveros Pou, *Dictionnaire vieux khmer–français–anglais* (Paris: L'Harmattan, 1992), pp. 279, 508, 287, 458, 312, 295, 434. According to Phillip N. Jenner, the core meaning of *nā* is "place" (personal letter, April 16, 1982). I thank Ashley Thompson for recommending taking *stac* as a noun ("sacred beings, especially princes") and as a reiteration of "the king" following his long title (personal email, February 11, 2015).

18 George Cœdès, "La destination funéraire des grands monuments khmèrs," *Bulletin de l'École française d'Extrême-Orient* 40 (1940): 339n.

19 For references to inscriptions naming these two temples, see George Cœdès, *Inscriptions du Cambodge* (Hanoi and Paris: École française d'Extrême-Orient, 1937–1966), vol. 8, p. 64. Aymonier, *Le Cambodge,* vol. 3, p. 251, wonders whether perhaps there was a Phnom Śivapāda in the Angkor region. He made the identification of Prasat Preah Net Preah in *Le Cambodge,* vol. 2, p. 322, on the basis of the inscription there (K. 216). In Claude Jacques and Philippe Lafond, *L'Empire khmer: cités et sanctuaries* (Paris: Fayard, 2004), p. 245, Jacques writes that an inscription at the site of Ta Muan (Surin province, Thailand, just north of the Cambodian border in Prasat district) identifies Ta Muan as Western Śivapāda (no reference provided). There are three different temples at Ta Muan.

20 Cœdès, "Les bas-reliefs," p. 201: "Mais, ce que l'on peut et ce que l'on doit noter, c'est l'aspect divin de ce roi trônant sur une montagne, semblable par le costume aux dieux des scènes mythologiques, presque identique à Viṣṇu dont le nom entre dans la composition de son titre posthume."

21 Mannikka, *Angkor Wat*, pp. 136–47, 179–191; Roveda, *Sacred Angkor*, pp. 91–173.

22 Cœdès, "Les bas-reliefs," p. 197: "Deux jeunes gens, accompagnés d'un homme barbu coiffé d'une sorte de tiare, et de serviteurs portant des gateaux ou plats couverts, rendent hommage à une statue de Viṣṇu. Donner un nom aux acteurs de cette scène est, pour le moment, chose impossible."

23 Mannikka, *Angkor Wat*, pp. 146–147.

24 Roveda's discussion in *Sacred Angkor*, p. 131, makes it clear that this is a far-fetched proposal. See Jean Przyluski, "La légende de Kṛṣṇa dans les bas-reliefs d'Angkor Vat," *Revue des Arts Asiatiques* 5/2 (1928): 91–97.

25 Cœdès, "Les bas-reliefs," p. 199: "Il est d'ailleurs impossible de décider à quelle légende se rapportent ces deux galères naviguant de concert et transportant divers personages occupés à jouer ou à regarder divers spectacles, entre autre un combat de coqs."

26 Roveda, *Sacred Angkor*, p. 125, evidently translating from the French translation by Simon A. Langlois, *Harivansa, ou Histoire de la famille de Hari: ouvrage formant un appendice du Mahabharata* (Paris: Printed for the Oriental Translation Fund of Great Britain and Ireland, 1834–1835).

27 Roveda, *Sacred Angkor*, p. 126.

28 Cœdès, "Les bas-reliefs," p. 198: "Bas-relief très ruiné où l'on distingue q'une figure de Çiva s'entretenant avec quatre personnages dont le premier a une coiffure analogue à celle de Viṣṇu et de Rāma. Celui-ci semble recevoir du dieux, ou lui remettre, divers objets impossibles à discerner. La scène sera sans doute assez difficile à reconnaître."

29 Roveda, *Sacred Angkor*, p. 126.

30 Teun Goudriaan, *Māyā Divine and Human* (Delhi: Motilal Banarsidass, 1978), p. 235, referring to *Matsya Purāṇa* 222, 2 f.

31 Goudriaan, *Māyā Divine and Human*, pp. 136–138.

32 Goudriaan, *Māyā Divine and Human*, p. 147.

33 Francis H. Giles, "Adversaria of Elephant Hunting (together with an account of all the rites, observances and acts of worship to be performed in connection therewith, as well as notes on vocabularies of spirit languages, fake or taboo language and elephant command words)," *Journal of the Siam Society* 23, pt. 2 (1929–1930): 76. In the same article Giles describes fires at the hunters' camps (left, right, and center) where the blessing of Agni was invoked (p. 85). There is a preliminary discussion of triadic structures in Woodward, "'The Characteristics of Elephants.'" The international connections have not been explored. See Richard K. Payne, "Ritual Studies in the Longue Durée: Comparing Shingon and Śaiva Siddhānta Homas," *Pacific World: Journal of the Institute of Buddhist Studies*, 3rd series, no. 13 (Fall 2011): 223–262.

34 Staal, *Mantras between Fire and Water*, p. 39.

35 Staal, *Mantras between Fire and Water*, pp. 30, 47.

36 Staal writes, "Ritual, after all is much older than language. Unlike language, it can originate on all fours. It is common among animals"; *Rules Without*

Meaning: Ritual, Mantras, and the Human Sciences (New York, Bern, Frankfurt, Paris: Peter Lang, 1989), p. 111. Frits Staal visited me in Baltimore while I was working on my review article, "Practice and Belief in Ancient Cambodia: Claude Jacques' Angkor and the Devarāja Question," *Journal of Southeast Asian Studies* 32/2 (June 2001): 249–261, and I remain grateful for his aid and encouragement.

References

Aymonier, Etienne. *Le Cambodge,* 3 vols. Paris: Ernest Leroux, 1900–1904.

Čhotmāi het rüang rap phrayā sawettakunchòn chāng phüak ræk dai nai ratchakān thī 2 ("The document concerning the reception of the lord Śvetakuñjara, the first white elephant in the Second Reign," in Thai). Bangkok: Watchīrayān Library, 1927.

Chulalongkorn, King. *Phra rātchaphitthī sipsòng düan* ("Royal ceremonies of the twelve months," in Thai). Bangkok: Khlang Witthayā, 1964.

Cœdès, George. *Inscriptions du Cambodge.* 8 vols. Hanoi and Paris: École française d'Extrême-Orient, 1937–1966.

—. "La destination funéraire des grands monuments khmèrs," *Bulletin de l'École française d'Extrême-Orient* 40 (1940): 315–343.

—. "Les bas-reliefs d'Angkor Vat," *Bulletin de la Commission Archéologique de l'Indochine* 2 (1911): 170–220.

Gerini G. E. *Chūḷākantamaṅgala: The Tonsure Ceremony As Performed in Siam* (1893). Bangkok: Siam Society, 1976, reprint.

Giles, Francis H. "Adversaria of Elephant Hunting (together with an account of all the rites, observances and acts of worship to be performed in connection therewith, as well as notes on vocabularies of spirit languages, fake or taboo language and elephant command words)," *Journal of the Siam Society* 23, pt. 2 (1929–1930): 61–96.

Ginsburg, Henry. *Thai Manuscript Painting.* Honolulu: University of Hawai'i Press, 1989.

Goudriaan, Teun. *Māyā Divine and Human.* Delhi: Motilal Banarsidass, 1978.

Goudriaan, Teun, and Christiaan Hooykaas. *Stuti and Stava (Bauddha, Śaiva and Vaiṣṇava) of Balinese Brahman Priests.* Amsterdam: North-Holland Publishing, 1971.

Le Bonheur, Albert. *Of Gods, Kings, and Men: Bas-reliefs of Angkor Wat and Bayon.* London: Serindia, 1995.

Jacques, Claude, and Philippe Lafond. *L'Empire khmer: cités et sanctuaries.* Paris: Fayard, 2004.

Jenner, Phillip N., and Saveros Pou. *A Lexicon of Khmer Morphology.* Mon-Khmer Studies IX–X. Manoa: University Press of Hawai'i, 1980–1981.

Langlois, Simon A. *Harivansa, ou Histoire de la famille de Hari: ouvrage formant un appendice du Mahabharata.* Paris: Printed for the Oriental Translation Fund of Great Britain and Ireland, 1834–1835.

Mannikka, Eleanor. *Angkor Wat: Time, Space, and Kingship*. Honolulu: University of Hawai'i Press, 1996.

Nāng Nopphamāt ("The Account of Lady Nopphamat," in Thai). Bangkok: Krom Sinlapakòn, 1960.

Payne, Richard K. "Ritual Studies in the Longue Durée: Comparing Shingon and Śaiva Siddhānta Homas," *Pacific World: Journal of the Institute of Buddhist Studies*, 3rd series, no. 13 (Fall 2011): 223–262.

Poncar, Jaroslav, and Thomas S. Maxwell. *Of Gods, Kings, and Men: The Reliefs of Angkor Wat*. Heidelberg: Edition Panorama, 2006

Pou, Saveros. *Dictionnaire vieux khmer–français–anglais*. Paris: L'Harmattan, 1992.

Przyluski, Jean. "La légende de Kṛṣṇa dans les bas-reliefs d'Angkor Vat," *Revue des Arts Asiatiques* 5/2 (1928): 91–97.

Quaritch Wales, H. G. *Siamese State Ceremonies: Their History and Their Function*. London: Bernard Quaritch, 1931.

Roveda, Vittorio. *Sacred Angkor: The Carved Reliefs of Angkor Wat*. Trumbull, CT: Weatherhill, 2002.

Staal, Frits. *Mantras between Fire and Water: Reflections on a Balinese Rite*. Amsterdam: North-Holland, 1995.

—. *Rules Without Meaning: Ritual, Mantras, and the Human Sciences*. Toronto Studies in Religion, vol. 4. New York, Bern, Frankfurt, Paris: Peter Lang, 1989.

Thewa Pāng ("Incarnations of the Gods," in Thai). Bangkok: Krom Sinlapakòn, 1970.

Vasu, Srisa Chandra. *The Daily Practice of the Hindus, Containing the Morning and Midday Duties*. New York: AMS Press, 1974.

Woodward, Hiram. "Practice and Belief in Ancient Cambodia: Claude Jacques' *Angkor* and the *Devarāja* Question," *Journal of Southeast Asian Studies* 32/2 (June 2001): 249–261.

—. "'The Characteristics of Elephants': A Thai Manuscript and its Context," in Justin McDaniel and Lynn Ransom, eds., *From Mulberry Leaves to Silk Scrolls: New Approaches to the Study of Asian Manuscript Traditions*, pp. 15–41. Philadelphia: University of Pennsylvania Libraries, 2015,